LESBIAN CULTURE

An Anthology

The Lives, Work, Ideas,
Art and Visions
of Lesbians
Past and Present

Edited by Julia Penelope
and Susan J. Wolfe

The Crossing Press, Freedom, California

Book design by Sheryl Karas
Cover design by Carolyn Saso and Sheryl Karas
Cover photo by Joan E. Biren (JEB)

Printed in the U.S.A.

Library of Congress Cataloguing-in-Publication Data

Lesbian Culture: an anthology / edited by Julia Penelope and Susan J. Wolfe.
    p. cm.
    Includes bibliographical references.
    ISBN 0-89594-592-4 — ISBN 0-89594-591-6 (pbk.)
    1. Lesbians—United States—Literary Collections.
2. American literature—Women authors. 3.
American literature—20th century. 4. Lesbians'
writings, American. 5. Lesbians. I. Penelope,
Julia, 1941- . II. Wolfe, Susan J., 1946- .
    PS509.L47L47 1993
    810.8'09206643--dc20   93-25552
                              CIP

Our thanks to the following authors, artists, journals, and publishers for permission to reprint their work in this anthology (unless otherwise noted, copyrights for all works published in this anthology belong to the author or artist, and cannot be reprinted or excerpted without their express consent; in general, journals and publishers are cited here as first place of publication):

The *Advocate* for vegetarian/leather jacket cartoon © by Kris Kovick;

Ainjee Graphics for "Women's Community Design," © 1974, Phyllis Birkby;

Alberta Status of Women Committee (ASWAC) newsletter for "Lesbian Invisibility" cartoon © Leslie Stewart;

Alyson Publishers for excerpt from *The Wanderground,* © 1979, Sally Miller Gearhart (originally published by Persephone Press);

The Estate of June Arnold for the excerpt from her novel *Sister Gin,* 1975, © June Arnold, originally published by Daughters, Inc.;

Aunt Lute Book Co. for excerpts from *Are We There Yet?: A Continuing History of* Lavender Woman, © 1985, Michal Brody; "Letter to the Editor," © 1972, Vernita Gray; "Lavender Consciousness," © 1972, Susan Edwards; "Documenting the Dyke Conference," © 1973, Joan E. Nixon; cover of first issue of *Lavender Woman;*

Beacon Press (Boston) for: excerpts from "The Fourth Daughter's Four Hundred Questions," © 1982, Elana Dykewomon, from *Nice Jewish Girls,* Evelyn Torton Beck, ed.; excerpt from *The Female Man,* © 1975, Joanna Russ;

Celeste West of Booklegger Publishing (555 29th Street, San Francisco, CA 94131): excerpts from *Elsa: I Come With My Songs,* © 1956 by Una Lady Troubridge;

Clothespin Fever Press for "Looking for Lesbians" and "Homophobia and Death in the Closet," from *Are You Girls Traveling Alone?,* © 1991, Marilyn Murphy (these essays originally appeared in *Lesbian News,* POB 1430, Twentynine Palms, CA 92277);

Common Lives/Lesbian Lives for: "Remembering As A Way of Life," © 1986, Tee Corinne; "Lesbian Confidentiality Problems," © 1988, Diane F. Germain; "Annie: 1958" © 1989 and Cass, 1959: First Day of a Courtship," © 1982, Merril Mushroom; "Whole Cloth," © 1986, Susan Stinson, and "Lifting Belly Again," © 1988, Susan Stinson;

© 1980, Tee Corinne for the following photographs: Labrys (which was the cover of the first edition of *The Lesbian Path,* edited by Margaret Cruikshank); photograph, "Dykes Kissing, with wheelchair"; cover of issue #3 of *Sinister Wisdom,* © 1979; photograph, "Three Fat Dykes";

© 1974, 1975, Liza Cowan for "What the Well-Dressed Dyke Will Wear" from *DYKE;*

© 1975, Nancy Crooks for Amazon woodcut from *DYKE;*

The Crossing Press for: "Me and Ahnie Silver," © 1982, Sandy Boucher, from *The Notebooks of Leni Clare, and Other Short Stories;* "I'm Not a girl," "in the place where," "IV: Carol, in the park, chewing on straws," "A History of Lesbianism," "I am the wall at the lip of the water" from *Work of a Common Woman,* 1978, Judy Grahn (originally published by Diana Press); excerpt from *Zami: A New Spelling of My Name,* © 1982, Audre Lorde (originally published by Persephone Press); "Trespassing," © 1989, Valerie Miner, from *Trespassing and Other Stories;* excerpt from *All Good Women,* © 1987, Valerie Miner;

Alix Dobkin for the lyrics to "Gay Head," © 1973, "New Ground," © 1985, "Talking Lesbian," © 1973, "Amazon ABC," © 1973.

Eighth Mountain Press (Portland, OR) for "Fortieth Birthday Song" from *History and Geography* © 1989,

Judith Barrington; "Car Spray" from *Incidents Involving Mirth* © 1990, Anna Livia;

Elana Dykewomon for "New England Cemetery" from *They Will Know Me By My Teeth,* © 1976 (Megaera Press) and "diving, i kiss" from *fragments from lesbos,* © 1981 (diaspora press);

© 1991, Elliott, for "Six Pomegranate Seeds and One Lesson in Manners: A Piece about Straight Folks Who Don't Mind Gays, But...," "Poem of Affirmation," and "This Summer I'm Going to Learn to Eat Tofu" from *The Separatist Revolution;*

The Feminist Press for excerpt from *I Dwell in Possibility: A Memoir,* © 1992, Toni McNaron;

© 1976, Sue Fink and Joelynn Grippo for lyrics of "Leaping Lesbians";

Firebrand Books (Ithaca, NY): "Angst in Right Field," "Butch and Femme," and Saturday Night, Part I" from *More Dykes To Watch Out For,* © 1988, Alison Bechdel; "The Cure" and "You Are What You Eat" from *New, Improved! Dykes To Watch Out For,* © 1990, Alison Bechdel; "ii" and "iii" from *Living as a Lesbian,* © 1986, Cheryl Clarke; "Butch-Femme Relationships: Sexual Courage in the 1950s" from *A Restricted Country,* © 1987, Joan Nestle (originally published in *Heresies*); "Boots are being polished. . ." and "For the white person who wants to know how to be my friend," from *Movement in Black,* © 1978, Pat Parker; "Growing Avocados" from *Eye of a Hurricane,* © 1989, Ruthann Robson; Chapter Four of *Diamonds Are a Dyke's Best Friend,* © 1988, Yvonne Zipter;

Hag Rag Books for photograph of Mabel Hampton and cover photograph of JEB (Joan E. Biren) from *Eye to Eye: Portraits of Lesbians* (© 1979, JEB) and photographs of Colevia Carter, J. Casselberry and Jaqué DuPreé, Elana Dykewomon, Amie Laird and J. Finch, and Del Martin and Phyllis Lyon from *Making a Way: Lesbians Out Front* (© 1987, JEB);

HOT WIRE: The Journal of Women's Music & Culture and Toni Armstrong Jr. for: cover of May, 1991 issue; Kay Gardner, "Early East Coast Women's Music and The Squirrel," © 1986; Diane F. Germain, "Lesbian Movies I'd Like To See," © 1992; Pam Hall, "I Am Pam Hall, Fifth Generation Dyke," © 1992; Jorjet Harper, "Sappho: Rediscovering Lesbian Space"; Toni Armstrong Jr. for "Women's Music for the '90s: Jamie Anderson, © 1992; "True to Life Adventure in Women's Music: Sue Fink," © 1991; "The Great White Folk Music Myth," © 1988; Ellen Meyers and Toni Armstrong Jr. for "A Visionary Woman Creating Visions: Barbara Hammer," © 1991; Cheryl Miller for "In the Life: New Works by Black Lesbian Filmmakers," © 1992; Toni Armstrong Jr. for photographs of Jamie Anderson with Bonnie Morris, Sue Fink with microphone, Sue Fink with Camp Nowannaweenee T-shirt, Kay Gardner, Pam Hall, and Myriam Fougére;

IKON for "Words" from *Women Poems Love Poems* © 1975, Susan Sherman;

Indiana University Press for "Crooked and Straight in Academia" by Susan J. Wolfe and Julia Penelope, from *Pulling Our Own Strings,* © 1980;

Institute for Lesbian Studies for excerpt from *Lesbian Ethics,* © 1988, Sarah Lucia Hoagland;

Laura Kaye for drawing of Gorgon, © 1976;

Lace Publications for Lynn Yamaguchi Fletcher's "Turtlehawk dreams an ocean breathing," from *Bushfire: Stories of Lesbian Desire,* ed. Karen Barber, © 1991, Alyson Publications;

Lesbian Ethics for "The Warexx," © 1986, Ruth Byrn; "The Spread of Consumerism: Good Buy Community," © 1989, Lee Evans; "Women, Lesbians and Prostitution: A Workingclass Dyke speaks Out Against Women for Sex," © 1987, Toby Summer;

Lesbian News for "Don't Worry Honey," cartoon, © 1991, Diane F. Germain; "Rings, Zippo Light Up the Past," © 1991, Lee Lynch;

Lesbian Outlook (c/o Lesbians For Lesbians, POB 1062, Greenfield, MA 01302) for cover of issue #7, "dicks of america," © 1993, Diane F. Germain, and "Why is This Festival Different from Any Other?: The East Coast Lesbians' Festival," © 1992, Lin Daniels;

The Ellen Levine Literary Agency and The Crossing Press for "Postscribbles," © Joanna Russ, 1980, 1989, from "Not for Years But for Decades" in *The Original Coming Out Stories,* eds. Julia Penelope and Susan J. Wolfe (1989);

Audre Lorde for "Love Poem" from *New York Head Shop and Museum,* © 1974, "Woman" and "Walking Our Boundaries" from *Black Unicorn,* © 1978, "The Master's Tools Will Never Dismantle the Master's House," from *This Bridge Called My Back: Writings by Radical Women of Color,* eds. Cherríe Moraga and Gloria Anzaldúa (Kitchen Table: Women of Color Press, 1983 [originally published by Persephone Press, 1981]);

excerpt from *Patience and Sarah,* © 1969, Isabel Miller (McGraw-Hill, 1972, originally self-published with the title *A Place for Us*);

The Naiad Press for: excerpt from *Beebo Brinker,* © 1962, 1986, Ann Bannon; excerpt from *Riverfinger Women,* © 1975, 1992, Elana Dykewomon (originally published by Daughters, Inc.); "Lesbian Stew," from *Amazon Trail* © 1988, Lee Lynch; "Prolong the Night" and "The Touch" © 1977, The Naiad Press, from *The Muse of the Violets* by Renée Vivien; permission to quote from the Naiad edition of *Lifting Belly* by Gertrude Stein,

(continued on last page of book)

Acknowledgments

The existence of a Lesbian culture, something unthinkable, or, at least, undoable, prior to the twentieth century, illustrates the ways individuals actively combine their efforts to construct what a more removed viewer might perceive as more abstract social, political, and historical processes. Like any culture, Lesbian culture belongs to its consumers as well as its creators for it is a participatory, collective endeavor.

Attempting to name every Lesbian who has made her contribution to our culture is not only impractical but impossible. Yet, this collection owes its existence to the Lesbians who have worked to create and sustain places where our culture could grow and thrive: the editors of journals such as *Amazon Quarterly, Common Lives/Lesbian Lives, HOT WIRE, Lesbian Connection,* and *Sinister Wisdom;* publishers, among them Spinsters Ink, Firebrand Books, Naiad Press, and the Seal Press; the producers of gathering places, including Campfest, East Coast Lesbians' Festival, Gulf Coast Women's Music Festival, Michigan Womyn's Music Festival, New England Women's Music Retreat, Southern Women's Music Festival, Rhythmfest, and West Coast Women's Music Festival; concert producers; coffeehouse collectives (such as the Mountain Moving Coffeehouse in Chicago); conference coordinators and workshop leaders; Lesbians living on and creating Lesbian land; booksellers (such as Amazon Bookstore in Minneapolis, Crones' Harvest in Jamaica Plain, Massachusetts, Dreams and Swords in Indianapolis, Judith's Room in New York City, Mama Bear's in San Francisco, and Women and Children First in Chicago); and distributors of crafts, music, and books (such as Ladyslipper and Goldenrod).

Lesbian culture is a multi-faceted, diverse creation that a collection such as this can barely begin to represent. Our acknowledgments here will be spare; we intend them to recognize those who have worked directly with us in the years it has taken us to compile this book. First, we want to thank all the Lesbians whose work does not appear in these pages as well as the contributors to this anthology. Second, to our Lesbian correspondents who shared their ideas about what Lesbian culture is or might be, spread the "word" to their friends, and suggested specific names and works that should be included in this anthology—Isabel Andrews, Sheila Anne, Claudia Card, Tee Corinne, Emma Joy Crone, Diane G. Crowder, Alix Dobkin, Elana Dykewomon, Bett Farber, Martha Ficklen, Barbara Gerber, Barbara Grier, Lee Lynch, Lepa Mladjenovic, Kate Moran, Bonnie Morris, Marilyn Murphy, Nancy Osborne, Minnie Bruce Pratt, Jessica Robbins, Marthe Rosenfeld, Joanna Russ, Joyce Trebilcot, and zana—thank you!

Third, there were Lesbians who, from the beginning of the project, helped us to track down individual Lesbians and/or their works so that we could contact them. Toni Armstrong Jr. of *HOT WIRE,* Alison Bechdel (who created "Dykes to Watch Out For"), Elana Dykewomon of *Sinister Wisdom,* and Barbara Grier of Naiad Press are among the Lesbians who provided us with names, addresses, and other kinds of information, sometimes without much notice, so that we could complete this collection.

The existence of Lesbian culture owes much to the political vision and creative activism of both June Arnold and Parke Bowman, the founders of Daughters, Inc. In particular, we want to thank June Arnold for her contributions as a publisher and novelist to Lesbian culture, and her daughters, Kate and Roberta, for allowing us to reprint an excerpt from one of her novels, *Sister Gin.*

We also want to acknowledge the importance of the Schlesinger Library at Radcliffe College and the helpfulness of its librarians. We were able to fill crucial gaps in this collection because of the Lesbian work preserved in the Schlesinger's collections.

Finally, we wish to thank our publishers, Elaine and John Gill of The Crossing Press, for their enthusiasm and support for this project. ■

We dedicate this volume to all Lesbians, past and present, who have helped create and who go on creating our culture, and to those Lesbians of the future who will continue to create it.

More particularly, we dedicate it to
Sarah Valentine and Catherine Flum,
whose love and support are central in our lives.

Table of Contents

Part 3: New Ground

Preface

by Sarah Dreher

For those of us who came of age as Lesbians in the mid-decades of the 20th Century, the world was a lonely and frightening place. If we knew—or guiltily guessed—that we loved women more than men, we stood alone. If we looked around for someone to tell us what that meant, what kind of people we were, what kind of life we could expect to live, there was no one there. We turned to the media, and saw ourselves depicted as sick, desperate, dangerous, ugly, predatory, sleazy and doomed to desperate lives that would end badly. Lesbians were all alike, we were told, and these man-imitating women who hung around drunk in filthy bars waiting to prey on innocent young women were who *we* were. No wonder so many of us fled into dishonest marriages, or accepted the stereotypes and tried to live them. No wonder some chose to accept and repeat the heterosexual, patriarchal image with which they were presented. No wonder some of us looked at the future and, seeing only the same loneliness, the same despair, killed ourselves.

There was a term in frequent use among my colleagues in psychology: homosexual panic. It meant, simply, that a woman (or man), suspecting that she had loving impulses toward members of the same sex, would be overwhelmed with agonizing, devastating anxiety. The usual way of dealing with the problem was to give the sufferer enough tranquilizers to "get her through" until she could discover (or you could convince her) that she really was "normal." If, along the way, she found some nice boy to marry and live with happily ever after, so much the better.

The Women's Movement changed all that, of course. "Homosexuality" became psychiatrically legal, and we were no longer isolated and ashamed of who we were. Those early years of freedom were heady ones, as our energies and creativity burst forth, gasping for breath and screaming to be born. Suddenly we were taking ourselves seriously, as individuals and as a people. We insisted on defining our own politics. After decades of trying to shape ourselves to a hostile world, we set out to express our visions for a world that was shaped by us. We generated mountains of writing and art—some brilliant, some terrible, some idealistic, some angry, some joyful, some tragic. But it was all Lesbian.

We discovered some important things along the way. We found that we had a great deal in common with one another merely because we were Lesbian, no matter where we came from or how we got here. We had a way of looking at the world that was simply and uniquely Lesbian. We had a Lesbian culture.

This book is about that culture. Many voices with many visions, a tapestry of many colors, but all identifiable to us as Lesbian. We can find passages which are familiar, and passages which are new and exciting. Penelope and Wolfe have given us a book that tells us who we are and who we can be. A book that shows us in all our variety and all our similarities. A book that gives us pride in our herstory, and strength to face our futures. A book that says, "Be proud of who you are. We are all your sisters. We are behind you. You're not alone."

If we had had a book like this in my youth, perhaps we wouldn't have had to fight so hard to accept ourselves. Perhaps more of us would have succeeded. Perhaps more of us would have survived.

Preface

by Elana Dykewomon

Lesbian Culture is both artifact and quest: it's a collection of treasure maps. Most lesbians will find clues in this book, reflections of our lives. Julia Penelope and Susan J. Wolfe show the shapes of our culture; their creation is at once part of that culture as well as its herstory. That is, *Lesbian Culture* is past, present and future in one volume. A thick text, full of connections and hidden meanings, with specific, affirming information for the initiated and layers of reverberating sources for the newcomer. For those lesbians who've been involved in lesbian communities for years, many of the names and pieces will be familiar; what's new will be a source of delight and deepening appreciation. For those coming into "the life," *Lesbian Culture* will be compelling, exciting, mysterious, a series of revelations. For those who exoticize or objectify lesbians it will simply be incomprehensible. In this it reminds me of the mystical writings of other cultures—The Kabalah, The Egyptian Book of the Dead. As a text, it opens in widening, fantastic circles to those who participate in the creation of its meaning as they read.

In the early '70s I came across a column by Adrienne Rich, who was just then in the process of coming out. She was writing about *Amazon Quarterly* and, if I have this right in memory, she wrote something to the effect of: "the answer to the question: 'what do lesbians do in bed?' may well be: they talk to each other." *Lesbian Culture* is the product of years of talking to each other—as well as howling, moaning, crying, laughing, struggling, debating, accusing—everything that goes into sharing a life, making a community.

How *does* a culture form? By accretion: the building up, over time, of new forms from an existing base. The way a shore line is formed, filled in by silt trickling down from mountain rivers, mixing with sand. The way shelled creatures build fantastic geometrical homes from their own substance, molded and licked into place. Lesbian culture is silt and a lick. A natural building up in the midst of sometimes violent upheaval.

The first book I read about lesbians was written by a man. I bought it in a porno store in Baltimore in 1965 when I was fifteen and I kept it under my bed. When no one was around I'd pull it out and read about the strange, sick deviates who lived in seamy subcultures. The prose was at once lurid and clinical. Freaks of nature, the book implied, glands gone wrong. Freaks, queers, dykes, tortilleras, lesbians! How I longed to find and know them. What, who, where were the lesbians?

Thirty years have brought me answers (and *Lesbian Culture!*). Lesbians are everywhere and from everywhere—for that reason no simple "we" includes us all—we are constantly making new anthologies which illuminate the lives of dykes who had been invisible even among lesbians. But as universal a statement as I can make about us is: lesbians are women who have discovered we can make choices. Among those choices we choose to create our primary emotional, material and sexual partnerships with other women.

Straight women who come out testify to the enormity of difference—everything changes. The way you *can* wear your clothes, the way you *can* eat, the way you *can* walk or wheel down the street, the things you *can* talk about, the ways you *do* "do it," the ability to choose other than what has been prechosen for you, your active involvement in making choices; that's the source of lesbian culture, isn't it? That we can argue and still recognize each other. That we can be disappointed and celebrate how far we've come at the same instant.

Lesbian culture is the manifestation of appetite let loose in womyn. Of the desire to make, change, put our hands to, put our minds together, turn our hearts inside out, to tell the truth, to tell the most fantastic lie we can think of. Outrageous. Lesbian culture is the act of making the outrageous. It's a place of the strictest indignation, the most righteous anger, where, having seen the answer, we are impatient for everyone to know how right we are. What a wonderful arrogance for those "born to be women"!

Lesbian culture is my life. It is the place where I live. It's my bookshelves and my friends and the way I celebrate chanukah and birthdays. It's the way I have learned about other cultures and lives: the lives of dykes of color, of working class and poor dykes, of old and young dykes. It is the place where I have learned to live *with* others, every kind of "other," as the beneficiary of many forms of dyke love and challenge. It is the place where I have been able to develop the self-respect that enables me to respect and admire lesbians, to give (at least in my best moments) with love.

My friend Lina had a vision in one of those all-night solstice circles certain groups of dykes still hold. In her vision there was a secret calendar which had all the dyke holidays on it—every month

was full of dykedays, we just couldn't see them on our regular calendars. I live there, in that calendar. Where lesbians tell each other stories about wandering lesberados who still travel between dyke land groups in beat-up vans. Where lesbians in high-tech jobs develop secret dyke computer networks, periodically programming $500 checks to be sent to every single womon on their corporate computer lists. Where lesbians who hardly know each other hold scheduling meetings to get a mutual friend through an operation or a fatal disease. Where there are emergency funds beginning to distribute the economic resources of our communities to working class and poor dykes.

Lesbian communities are amazing, vital, complicated places. They are occasionally confusing, overwhelming. Books like *Lesbian Culture* bring us back to ourselves, speaking our many names, saying: inside you is the treasure of thousands of dyke lives. Here's a way in…Here's a way in…

Introduction

Lesbian Identity/Lesbian Communities/Lesbian Culture: Creating Our Survival

When we (Susan Wolfe and Julia Penelope) first began to think about bringing together a collection of what we and, hopefully, other Lesbians might call Lesbian culture, we had only the most general idea of what we were going after and what we would do when and if we found whatever we found. Given the quantity of cultural material produced by Lesbians, particularly over the past twenty years, the idea of producing an anthology was somewhat daunting. However large the volume, we would be forced to omit selections worthy of inclusion. Finally, however, we had to choose. The result of our choices is before you.

This is **an** anthology of Lesbian culture, one of a myriad of possible collections exemplifying Lesbian work, Lesbian ideas, Lesbian relationships. It is, as far as we know, a first attempt to bring together between two covers a collection of Lesbian creation focused on our Lesbian lives and to provide a sampling of Lesbian culture representing the diverse media Lesbians have used to create our culture. Compiling material representing all that Lesbians have done in the past and present would require an encyclopedia, not a single volume. At times, we could envision what such an encyclopedia would look like: how many volumes our culture would require and how many library shelves it would fill. We would have liked to compile that encyclopedia, but such a large undertaking must await a political, financial, and publishing climate more congenial to Lesbian concerns.

Defining Lesbian Culture

We were aware that creating an anthology even imperfectly representative of Lesbian culture presupposed a definition, however fuzzy, of what we consider Lesbian culture to be. But it would be presumptuous to attempt an all-encompassing definition for our culture, when we can't agree on a definition of *Lesbian*. The purpose of a collection such as this—and of the culture generally—can be seen as expressing the values of the Lesbian community, or, at least, of values shared across Lesbian communities.

Being only two Lesbians out of millions, in an effort to involve as many Lesbians as possible, we asked for definitions of Lesbian culture from over 300 Lesbians in the U.S. and Canada, asking which works they thought exemplified Lesbian culture, aware that such a procedure involves a kind of selection process. Their thoughtful suggestions helped us both to remember materials we might otherwise have forgotten and to weigh others in light of a broader Lesbian perspective. (For the names of the Lesbians who contributed in this way, see our Acknowledgments.)

When we wrote to Lesbians seeking their ideas about what Lesbian culture might be, we tentatively defined it as the collected practices and artifacts which Lesbians recognize as Lesbian, and which therefore both arise from and help to define our commonalities, and thereby to create our community. We listed several categories into which we thought these artifacts might be grouped: dress, food and eating, music, literature, spirituality, sports, dwellings, relationships, sensuality/sexuality, and theory. We also made the arbitrary decision to create an anthology selecting from our artifacts, including our art works, rather than one focusing on theoretical essays *about* Lesbian culture. We wanted to show, not tell, what Lesbian culture is.

Using the lists sent to us by our correspondent Lesbians as our starting point, we set about collecting examples of Lesbian culture—drawings, cartoons, poems, photographs, short stories, whatever we might include in a book—that represent it in its variety but also illustrate what Julia has called the "Lesbian Perspective" (1990; 1992). The work collected here represents some facets of the Lesbian gaze as it peruses the world Lesbians live in: for example, Diane DiMassa's cartoon about the world being run by "straight white guy[s]" (she's the creator of the comic book series *Hothead Paisan*)[1]; Marilyn Frye's essay, "Lesbian 'Sex,'" in which she analyzes how heterosexual assumptions about what sex "is" obscure and distort what Lesbian "sex" is or might be when they are unquestioningly accepted as appropriate for Lesbian sexuality.

While there were differences among the definitions Lesbians sent us, four general ideas emerged. First, many wished to define Lesbian culture broadly, to include everything Lesbians do. Second, others narrowed the scope of the term "Lesbian culture" so that only activities informed by a Lesbian sensibility, one reflecting Lesbian priorities, would "count" as Lesbian culture. Third, some focused on the fact that Lesbian culture is a culture under siege, one in which we set ourselves apart from males and from heteropatriarchal culture and one which is, as a consequence, continually threatened by them. Finally, many emphasized the importance of maintaining a uniquely Lesbian perspective, grounded in Lesbian identity, within whatever we might identify as a Lesbian culture.

I. Lesbian Culture Is Whatever Lesbians Do

Several of our Lesbian correspondents suggested that Lesbian culture "is anything that Lesbians do—theorizing physics, raising children, making love, throwing tires on an assembly line." But there are problems with equating Lesbian culture with the mere presence of Lesbians doing anything at all. Such activities and roles certainly occur in a social context, but they are not uniquely Lesbian. Lesbians aren't identified by what we do because the things we do are pretty much the same things that non-Lesbians do, and this includes the sexual activities we engage in with other Lesbians. What is uniquely Lesbian is the way in which we do them and who we choose to act with and for. What identifies us is the focus of our lives: other Lesbians, other queers, other women, depending on our self-identification and the politics that enacts our identification. Virtually no Lesbians (except those who still live as though they were heterosexual) live in ways that require us to place het men at the center of our lives. In her letter to us, Diane Griffin Crowder, noting that "there are so many different lesbian cultures," went on to remark:

> The one thing that *most* lesbians seem to have in common is the more or less conscious rejection of the societal imperative that women must define ourselves in relation to men. In fact, it is the indifference to men that society finds so threatening. The act of women defining ourselves without respect to men is so subversive that it alone is sufficient to account for all the backlash lesbians experience. Monique Wittig's image of lesbians as "runaway slaves" (in *Virgile, non* [Paris: Minuit, 1985]; translated as *Across the Acheron* [London: Peter Owen, 1987]) is pertinent here, because in a

slave society even the runaway or freed slave is still always defined as a once-or-future slave. She must, in order to create a new self-definition, find a way to break out of the slave/master, female/male dichotomy. Thus, at this juncture in our efforts to develop a culture, we still find ourselves faced with both rejecting heterosexist definitions and simultaneously trying to envision what lies beyond those dualisms. Whether one looks at fiction, at art, at music, or at such manifestations as dress, etc., we constantly find these tensions between destroying the old and building the new. Unfortunately, all too often we have not got beyond simple rejection or reversal of heterosexual values and concepts. But despite all the difficulties, lesbian culture at least rejects the notion that women can exist only in a dialectal relation with men, and that is the beginning of a new exploration.

The one sphere of our lives in which many Lesbians cannot avoid having to deal with heterosexuals—men in particular—is work. Whatever kind of work Lesbians do, whether it's in a factory or in academia, we do it because we know we must support ourselves; our work is not a supplement to a man's earnings, and we enter our workplaces with the consciousness that we are Lesbians working for a living. Although most Lesbians work at the same kinds of jobs as heterosexuals and in heterosexual contexts, we go home to our Lesbian dwellings and Lesbian contexts, to the lives we have constructed around our Lesbian identities. We draw our strength from and establish our identities through interaction with other Lesbians, both with individual Lesbians and within our communities of Lesbians.

II. Lesbian Culture Reflects our Motives and Values

Unwilling to accept an all-inclusive definition of Lesbian culture—one which allows for the existence of Lesbian culture wherever and whenever one or more of us is engaging in any activity at all—some of our correspondents said that Lesbian culture was distinguished from our cultures of origin and the dominant heteropatriarchal culture by how and why we do things. Our activities and interactions can be said to be part of Lesbian culture when they reflect our Lesbian sensibility, a set of assumptions and priorities uniquely Lesbian. We assume the responsibility for learning to treat each other as we wish to be treated, for acting in ways that reflect and develop our awareness of self and community. There is, then, an implicit valuing of ourselves and other Lesbians informing what has been called "lesbian sensibility." Although Lesbians have only begun to articulate values, it is nonetheless true, as Alix Dobkin has asserted, that this method is the basis of our interactions—we agree to "attend" to each other (Hoagland, *Lesbian Ethics* [1988]) and therefore, according to Dobkin, "to learn how to properly treat each other":

Like all cultures, Lesbian culture must exhibit universal and general sets of shared values and assumptions. In our Culture these spring entirely from our need for a Lesbian environment which means that we need each other's presence. How we manage to be together and what then occurs varies as much as we do.

Determining, even establishing guidelines for social interactions is characteristic of other societies, but what is important to us is discovering the ways Lesbians believe we should interact among ourselves. And so this process of identifying how we want to be among other Lesbians isn't clear or predetermined or linear; it's constantly being debated/discussed/argued, evolving, moving now in one direction then in another, and, because we are not always who we aspire to become, the process is also visionary.

III. Lesbian Culture: A Culture Apart, A Culture Under Siege

Several writers noted that Lesbian culture was a culture under siege. Like individual Lesbians, Lesbian culture is threatened by males and by the power they wield. Male-dominated media and the social, economic, and political institutions whose assumptions they promulgate are constant threats to Lesbian existence and Lesbian culture. Lesbian culture exists in opposition to this dominant culture, and reflects Lesbian resistance to its values.

There are, of course, those Lesbians who say they're very happy with the *status quo*, who say they have no reason for wanting social change. Still, there are many other Lesbians who are not happy with the dominant culture, who work hard to promote a wide range of changes in the structures and attitudes of U.S. society, who want nothing less than a full-scale revolution that will sweep white men from power and keep them from regaining power in the future. These are the Lesbians responsible for creating and maintaining Lesbian culture. It is such Lesbians who require Lesbian culture for their/our very survival.

While Lesbian culture is grounded in our sense of Lesbian identity, what we think it means to be a Lesbian and how we perceive our Lesbian identity affecting the ways we think and behave, it is also true that Lesbian culture is established against the background of heteropatriarchal culture and created from within it, both at the same time. Thus, the third and fourth kinds of definition cannot be separated; the one informs the other. The Lesbian's sense of self draws upon a community and a culture set apart from the dominant, often hostile culture. Because the forms we produce and the activities in

which we engage will be those of our time and place, what constitutes Lesbian culture varies. Moreover, Lesbian culture may occasionally seem to resemble the heteropatriarchal culture which surrounds it as, for example, the numbers of Lesbians taking to two-stepping (a variety of western/country dancing popular in heterosexual bars) in the early 1990s.

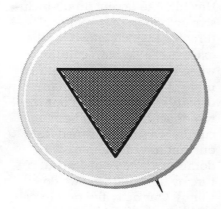

It is true that, in some ways, most Lesbians aren't very different from non-Lesbians: we want to be able to find others of our kind and to associate freely with them; we want to be secure in our lives, to have our own inviolable spaces; we want to be able to work without having to disguise ourselves and deny our Lesbian selves; in short, we want to live proudly and with dignity. But to want such things, as Lesbians, is complicated and difficult because we live in cultures which have forbidden our existence, and scapegoated and murdered those of us they identified as Lesbians (or "unnatural,"

"sick," or "mad"). What might appear to be perfectly simple and reasonable desires are perceived by those who hate us as "unreasonable"; once they've defined us as subhuman, we can be denied the most basic of rights. The right wing in the U.S. has, since the mid-1970s (when Anita Bryant launched her "Save the Children" campaign), insisted that our demands for equal protection under the law are attempts to gain "special rights" for ourselves. Recently, however, the christian right-wingers have become more aggressive in imposing their bigotry and, as we write, have succeeded in legalizing discrimination against Lesbians and gaymen in Colorado and are attempting to do so in Oregon. (On September 26, 1992, one of our contributors who lives in Portland, Oregon told us that someone had fired a bullet through her window the day before.)

Even finding other Lesbians is difficult and risky, although there have been some significant changes for the better in some places where Lesbians live. In order to set about consciously looking for other Lesbians, one must first identify herself as a Lesbian and then find places where other Lesbians are. The first step may, and the second almost certainly will, expose a Lesbian to heterosexual hostility and violence. Because we are badly represented in the mainstream media—when we are represented at all—endeavors some might imagine to be simple become lifelong searches: finding other Lesbians, finding spaces in which we can gather without threat or danger, finding our own identities. Because our lives are shaped and determined by our class and family of origin, the places we will look for Lesbians and the Lesbians we will find are largely a matter of chance and opportunity.

But chance and opportunity, like choice, are circumscribed by our racial, ethnic, and class identities. Because Lesbians are seeking the company of other Lesbians, we go to the places where we think we're likely to find each other: softball games, bars, festivals, concerts, bookstores, and other places/events known or rumored to be Lesbian gathering places. And in such places, Lesbians of different classes and ethnic backgrounds may mix. Nevertheless, our closest intimates are likely to end up being Lesbians much like ourselves. Lesbians who are working-class have access to information about working-class Lesbian bars (which is how Julia found out about Googie's in Miami in the 1950s). Middle-class Lesbians hear about middle-class Lesbian bars. In big cities, Black Lesbians often frequent one bar, while white Lesbians go to a different one. Because of the long history of racism in the U.S., many Black Lesbians don't trust white Lesbians. In addition, neither Black nor white Lesbians feel comfortable going into a bar where they know no one and are likely to be a mi-

nority of one. In fact, in cities like Chicago and New York, Black Lesbians have been refused entry to bars frequented by white Lesbians. (See Michal Brody's excerpt from her introduction to *Are We There Yet?* for a description of how racism affected attempts of Chicago Lesbians to organize themselves politically in the early 1970s.) Although discrimination against Lesbians of color has sometimes been successfully protested, it continues, and perpetuates distrust and hostility among us.

There are signs that Lesbians, especially those of us who are Lesbian activists, have been working to understand and revalue our differences. But we are likely to feel most welcome and at ease in those Lesbian networks which allow us to associate with Lesbians with whom we have more in common than we do with other Lesbians, whether it's dancing, bowling, playing softball or pool, socializing at potlucks, reading books as members of Lesbian study groups, or attending Lesbian caucuses at academic conferences. Poor, working-class and lower middle-class Lesbians tend to associate in small groups, mostly couples, to play cards, party, and share meals, or they go to Lesbian and gay bars to drink and dance. (Neither of us knows how upper-class Lesbians find each other and socialize; the few upper-class Lesbians we do know may not be characteristic of the class, and so we cannot generalize.) We gather in places and engage in activities

familiar to us from our class and ethnic backgrounds, and so our social circles tend to be made up of other Lesbians who go to the same places and do the same things.

Thus, although Lesbians have identities defined and shaped by the racism and classism of U.S. society, and although most Lesbians enjoy at least some activities popular among non-Lesbians, Lesbian culture, as the comments of our correspondents suggest, is practiced by Lesbians for Lesbians. Participating in and contributing to Lesbian culture helps to develop a Lesbian sensibility, reflects and reinforces Lesbian identity, and strengthens Lesbian communities. What matters, then, is not simply what we do, but how and why we do it. "The underlying priorities and attitudes [of Lesbians and non-Lesbians]," as Alix Dobkin has said, "differ sharply":

> The forms we choose are the forms of the time at hand in the culture at large. What's now popular with them will be current with us, and to the careless observer it may look the same. Closer examination, however, discloses a marked variance. They play baseball. They do it mainly for money and/or the thrill of competition (to determine who gains control). We play softball mainly to exercise and socialize. The game may look the same but the underlying priorities and attitudes differ sharply....

Whether we are two-stepping, bowling or playing

bridge, softball or pool, we are Lesbians seeking the company and community of other Lesbians at a music festival, a concert, or in a bar. Moreover, because a Lesbian culture expresses *Lesbian* realities, priorities, and perceptions, affirming our individual lives and the value of Lesbian community, we expect commonality among Lesbian cultures. Ruth Simkin, a Canadian, defines Lesbian culture as "anything that reflects and validates my life; where the pronouns in the music are meaningful, the images in art are familiar and meaningful; the language reflective and not oppressive," and notes that "you can plunk a lesbian down anywhere in the world with other lesbians and within a few minutes we will be discussing commonalities" such as when and how we knew we were Lesbians, how we met our first lover, how long that relationship lasted, how many relationships we've been in, whether or not we're "out" to our family of origin, heterosexual friends, at work, and so on.

Lesbians frequently point to our "invisibility" in the dominant culture as a significant factor in our lives, yet even conceiving of ourselves as "invisible" misses the specific ways our lives are constructed by a hostile, male-dominated society. We are not, strictly speaking, "invisible." Some of us are certainly visible during the times we live in. Men have institutionalized the punishment of Lesbians (and those sus-pected of being Lesbians) throughout recorded (patriarchal) history—a practice that continues as we write—whether the justification has been "unnatural acts," or "acts against god," or "bourgeois decadence" hardly matters. It doesn't matter that what many of us call ourselves today, *Lesbians*, wasn't used to refer to us until the late nineteenth century, or that many modern dictionaries continue to give the primary definition of the word as "an inhabitant of Lesbos." We know, and so do those who hate us. Outside our doors the christian right-wingers are calling (again, still) for our destruction.

We are, in fact, more and more *visible* in heteropatriarchal culture. What remains "invisible" to heterosexuals and to other Lesbians as well is our *human* nature, our realities, our daily struggles, and the consequences for us of the oppressive conditions under which we grow up and in which we still live. When we are portrayed in the media of the dominant culture, too often such "lesbian" characters turn out to be bisexual women, not Lesbians at all. Bisexuals are used to dilute Lesbian identity, to implicitly claim that there aren't any "real" Lesbians—women who are not sexually available to men—only bisexual women. Much of what is touted these days as Lesbian "visibility" erases us.

Lesbians are invisible to ourselves *as* Lesbians at crucial times in our lives, especially as teenagers, when we are inun-dated, and sometimes swept under, by this society's obsession with heterosexuality. Heterosexuals systematically suppress information about the existence of Lesbians, while coercing us to conform to and participate in heterosexual behaviors and rituals. We rightly fear, for example, that the same hatred of us that fuels white, christian political fanaticism will succeed in erasing us from the historical record of the twentieth century. Already we have lost unknown numbers of Lesbians, their lives, and their works. Important individuals, even those famous during their own lifetimes, may simply be absent in conventional historical documents— their names, the names of their partners, and references to their works omitted—because Lesbians and our lives aren't regarded as "significant" according to the narrow perspective of men's histories. Scanning such histories as Isaac Asimov's *Chronology of the World* (1991) reveals not a single Lesbian or her works. Many of us know the names of famous Lesbians, such as Sappho, Gertrude Stein and Alice B. Toklas, but how many Lesbians today know that Katharine Lee Bates (1859– 1929), a professor of English at Wellesley College, wrote "America the Beautiful," a song that almost became the U.S.'s national anthem, or that her partner and colleague of twenty-eight years was Katharine Coman?[2] How many of us know that two Lesbians, Molly Dewson and Polly Porter, were friends, colleagues, and political allies of Eleanor Roosevelt's throughout FDR's presidency?[3] These are two examples, both from the twentieth century; how many more are there we'll never discover?

For millennia, men have systematically suppressed any and all information about the existence of Lesbians, with only sporadic (and often bowdlerized) exceptions. Lesbian culture is a culture erased from history and therefore absent from non-Lesbian accounts of the present. Even though we have participated in events documented in male histories, our names and deeds are either discounted or ignored, or our identity as Lesbians is suppressed. We are a people unrecognized, unacknowledged, unchronicled in the world of men. There will be no national days declared to remember the lives of Jeannette Foster, Pat Parker, or June Arnold. (See Tee A. Corinne's essay in the anthology, "Remembering as a Way of Life," for her assessments of the importance of Jeannette Foster's and June Arnold's work on behalf of Lesbians.) Town councils won't call special meetings in order to be the first to name a boulevard or city park after Meg Christian, Judy Grahn, or Audre Lorde; costly gigantic, bronze statues of Edmonia Lewis or Karla Jay won't dominate parks or gardens, and we aren't likely to find portraits of Radclyffe Hall or Gloria Anzaldúa on postage stamps.

It is true, as Claudia Card has said, that the Lesbian history we have "tends to come from the lowest and the highest social classes" (1982: 21). The only Lesbians we know of are those who "make it" into patriarchal documents, either because they were privileged, like Sappho, Queen Christina, Natalie Barney and Renée Vivien, and Eleanor Butler and Sarah Ponsonby (the Ladies of Llangollen),[4] or they were poor, and so were apprehended as "criminals," such as Catherine Margaretha Linck[5] (executed in 1721 for dressing and living as a man), Marianne Woods and Jane Pirie (see Lillian Hellman's *The Children's Hour*, a play based on their early nineteenth-century trial in Scotland, and Lillian Faderman's *Scotch Verdict* [1983]), or, in the 1990s, Aileen Wuornos in Florida, who seems likely to go down in U.S. patriarchal history as the "first" female serial killer.

Cognizant of our need to establish and to recount our own lives and experiences for ourselves and each other, Bonnie Zimmerman has written of Lesbian culture:

> It is a culture so absent from the present and past media, in all the media's power to make public other "realities," that lesbians must serve as our own biographers, no non-lesbians being either qualified or willing to chart our herstory. It is a culture occurring in singular and plural and mass: one dyke-identified dyke, two dykes in love or in confrontation, hundreds of dykes in the woods or at a lake.

Perceived as a threat to male dominance and heteropatriarchal values, Lesbian culture is threatened *by* them. Lesbian culture therefore exists as a culture in opposition, and our existence, lived against and within a society which not only assumes but mandates that women's identities are "naturally" subsumed by those of men, is shaped by the knowledge that we are not as they would have us. Lesbian identity is an identity of resistance and survival in spite of the forces that would destroy us and often succeed in overwhelming and burying us.

IV. Lesbian Culture Is Informed by Lesbian Sensibility

Many of those who wrote offering their thoughts on Lesbian culture emphasized the visionary, transformative potential of identifying Lesbian values, of articulating how we want to interact with, how we want to be among, other Lesbians. They stressed that Lesbian culture was not simply established in opposition to hostile male culture, but in response to the new ways we perceive the world, and the new ways we therefore choose to act in it.

As a culture in opposition, Lesbian culture certainly draws upon our conscious absenting of ourselves from patriarchal culture and our rejection of its heterosexual "imperative." Perhaps more importantly, however, it simultaneously draws upon our presence as Lesbians to each other. Lesbian culture must at once repudiate the values of heteropatriarchal culture and establish distinct values, values which reflect a uniquely Lesbian sensibility.

Claudia Card has remarked that her interpretation of the term "Lesbian culture" as those forms, practices, and artifacts that cultivate or reflect the cultivation of lesbian sensibility, appreciation, or bonding led her "to detect some of it as long ago as 612 b.c.e. and to speculate about its existence during the second or third millennium b.c.e." There may indeed be evidence suggestive of Lesbians and Lesbian culture dating back three to five millennia. But because male-dominated cultures have so consistently suppressed, erased, and denied such evidence, we can only speculate, offering our interpretations for the data we find.

To establish the existence of Lesbian culture in earlier periods requires more (and less) than evidence of Lesbian sexual activity, under this definition. What is required is evidence of a Lesbian sensibility, of Lesbian values and sensitivities. To establish Lesbian culture(s) in the present and for the future, what will be required is a sense of Lesbian identity which goes beyond merely repudiating the heterosexual "imperative," however difficult and important that struggle may be. Lesbian culture, like any culture, requires more than a "setting apart"

from other cultures. It must have beliefs and values, as well as the traditions and objects capable of expressing them, and a community committed to their preservation.

Lesbian Identity and Lesbian Culture: An Attempt at Synthesis

If we claim that Lesbian culture is at once a turning away from males and patriarchal culture and a turning toward other Lesbians, we may seem to have defined it, to an extent. At least, we have suggested what its origins are, leaving to its artifacts, the creations of others, the burden of demonstrating how Lesbian culture manifests this dual focus. But many have argued that the issue of Lesbian identity itself—the question of who is and who isn't, or wasn't, a Lesbian—must be settled before we can talk about Lesbian culture or Lesbian community in any meaningful way. And debates about Lesbian identity are not trivial or abstract, for, as many individual Lesbians come to understand, it is possible to be aware that one is "different" without knowing exactly how one is different, possible to understand vaguely how one is different from others while remaining unaware that there are others like herself, possible to know that there are others like oneself—other Lesbians—without having a label or a precise sense of how she is like them. Although, as we shall argue, Les-

bian culture is an important source of Lesbian identity, Lesbian culture is also dependent upon it—a paradox which is more apparent than real.

Lesbian culture arises from a Lesbian sense of self. Compiling an anthology of works identified as "Lesbian culture" presupposes an idea of who is a Lesbian. As Jorjet Harper pointed out in "Towards a Lesbian Aesthetic" (1990):

> There is something that resonates in us when we feel a lesbian sensibility emanating from art. Lesbians—even lesbians who aren't out to themselves yet—often gravitate toward works by lesbians that have no explicit content and which they do not realize were created by lesbians. For example, lesbians have been quick to recognize the lesbian focus of Sappho despite many absurd arguments by academics and homophobes that she was not 'really' a lesbian.

If some of us spend some amount of time "not being out" to ourselves; if some of us are lifelong Lesbians while others are, in Marilyn Murphy's words, Lesbians-come-lately; if some women live all their lives loving women without calling themselves Lesbians while others who are heterosexual or bisexual insist upon labeling themselves as "Lesbians" (and, they claim, thereby "broadening" the definition of *Lesbian*), how can we establish a definition of Lesbian that most Lesbians (we aren't so optimistic as to hope for agreement by all) will agree with?

We concede that Lesbian identity, like other identities, arises within a social and communal context. Like other marginal and outcast identities, our first inkling of difference begins with the realization that "we" are not like "them"—heterosexuals—and so our initial sense of who we are is largely negative, based on what we are not or who we are told we ought to be. Our positive sense of our Lesbian identity is thoroughly communal in that it depends upon our ability to find other Lesbians and then to establish a niche for ourselves among them.

Though we agree that Lesbian identity arises within a communal context, we wish to contest the arguments which might be advanced by those who believe that a clear, indisputable sense of Lesbian identity must be shared by a large community of Lesbians, each of whom arrived at her identity in isolation from other Lesbians, before Lesbian culture can be said to exist. This anthology is premature, they might say, because Lesbian culture does not yet exist. Lesbian culture can't exist for two reasons: first, Lesbian communities exist within larger communities many of whose interests they share, rather than in comparative isolation, with a set of specific and clearly defined behaviors and interests; and second, we haven't yet established what Lesbian identity is, how it can be defined, or how it is formed.

In our (Julia's and Susan's) discussion of Lesbian culture, we may seem to have taken a shared definition of *Lesbian* for granted, presuming that we all "know" what we mean when we refer to "Lesbians" or to a "Lesbian sense of self." But, as we've just suggested, there has been a great deal of contemporary controversy surrounding the issue of Lesbian identity. Academics and other intellectuals have debated the meaning of the word

Lesbian, noting that there are problems with its use. There is no universal agreement upon how it should be defined, they argue. Can we, for instance, assign the term to those women in history for whom no sexual activity can be proven? Can we use it to refer to women who lived and loved women when the term *Lesbian* identified only dwellers of Lesbos? Even those who would call ourselves "Lesbians" seem unable to arrive at a consensus.

As in the past, there are, of course, many women who are afraid to identify themselves as Lesbians (and often with good reason); in recent years, we have heard and read women whose primary sexual and emotional relationship is with a man insist that they are Lesbians. We have even heard *men* insist that they are Lesbians!

Why, Lesbians might ask, would men and non-Lesbian women wish to claim Lesbian identities for themselves in the face of the persecution endured by Lesbians? And why would they expect us to believe such claims? What does it mean, according to them, to call oneself a "Lesbian," and what does it mean to us, when we do so? Because the second of these two questions concerns the very definition of the word "identity," not to mention that of the word *Lesbian*, we'll address it first.

For most of us (speakers), what a word means is connected intimately with the circumstances under which we would use it. So we expect to be able to list, or at least hint at, those characteristics an individual or a group needs to have before we'd use a certain word to describe it. As our discussion of Lesbian culture suggests, both we and our contributors use *Lesbian* to refer to a woman whose emotional and sexual energies are directed toward other women, and not toward men. We also extend its meaning to refer to ways of thinking and behaving that draw upon this primary identification, particularly when a Lesbian has become self-aware and consciously seeks out others like herself.

Fifteen years ago, these uses of the word *Lesbian* might

have seemed logical and obvious. Recently, though, many theorists have decided that common sense, like identity, is merely the product of social consensus...that both are really "constructed" by social and cultural forces. In that case, since there are no "real" Lesbians, but only those constructed in and by a hostile heteropatriarchal culture, the term *Lesbian* can be appropriated by anyone, used willy-nilly to label anyone and any form of behavior.

Such theories are undoubtedly clever, and many seem to have found them liberating. But, given the very real threats confronting real Lesbians, the arrogation of the word *Lesbian* by men and non-Lesbian women strikes us as one more threat—the threat, once again, of erasure and invisibility, of the denial that there are, in fact, women who choose to love other women. We exist, physically and materially, as well as emotionally.

When a woman has identified herself as a Lesbian in this way, she asserts that she *is* a Lesbian. Those of us who have done so, at whatever personal cost, resent intensely the efforts of others to appropriate the word and assume (when they find it convenient or politically expedient) what they believe to be Lesbian identity. To the extent that a (conscious) sense of self arises within a communal context, from the awareness of what one is in relation to others, we can establish a positive Lesbian identity only in a Lesbian communal context—the only one within which a positive Lesbian identity *can* be "constructed."

Our claim, then, is that the relationships among Lesbian identity, Lesbian community, and Lesbian culture are not linear and unidirectional. Lesbian identity is a turning toward other women—emotionally, physically, sexually—and a turning away from males, from heterosexual feelings and acts, and finally from male-dominated culture. Lesbian identity expresses itself through seeking out not only individual women to love, but communities in which we find ourselves lovingly reflected, and a culture which expresses those reflections.

However, it is also within those communities, and in the context of that culture, that each woman, coming to a sense of her identity as a Lesbian, can best find herself. Among other Lesbians, contemplating and enjoying Lesbian art, seeing images of Lesbian selves, turning over the pages of a book with Lesbian characters and historical figures, resonating with the self-loving lyrics of Lesbian music, laughing at Lesbian humor, each Lesbian can come to a proud sense of self, assured and reassured that yes, there are Lesbians, and she is one of them. There is wonder in the moment when any of us comes to that sense of awareness, in a Lesbian community, surrounded by the artifacts of Lesbian culture.

Unfortunately, many Lesbians must live (at least for a portion of their lives) in places where other Lesbians, living openly as Lesbians, are few and hard to find. The discovery of a copy of *Lesbian Connection* or *Sinister Wisdom*, of a Lesbian novel in a bookstore or library, or of a recording with Lesbian lyrics in a store may be the first affirmation of identity for a Lesbian living in apparent isolation. Her first brush with Lesbian culture becomes her first assurance that other individual Lesbians, and a wider community of Lesbians, exist. Even more significantly, the book or compact disc she holds in her hand may be her first clue as to who *she* is, and why she feels "different" from those around her.

For such a Lesbian, the value of Lesbian culture is incalculable, the existence of its artifacts crucial to her very existence. Without them—the concrete evidence of Lesbian existence and Lesbian culture—we must continually reinvent ourselves and our individual sense of identity out of nothing. Miraculously, we have often done so despite the pain we have suffered and because of repeated attempts to suppress us, individually and collectively. This anthology, then, is both another assertion of our continued existence and a collection of such assertions, celebrating the achievements of individual Lesbians and of the culture we are creating together.

We also believe that the unique value of Lesbian culture lies in its profound connections with ourselves, and with those selves who have existed in other societies and who have existed throughout time, however much their identity as Lesbians may have been denied or suppressed. We share Toni McNaron's conviction, expressed in her 1977 article "Finding and Studying Lesbian Culture," that "our deepest notions of culture begin and center on our selves," selves shaped by the process of becoming a lesbian, regardless of time, place or situation (14–16). Regardless of where, when, or how we come/came out, came to the realization that we were Lesbians, there is a sense of commonality to the struggles we have had, and these inform the creations of Lesbian culture: the coming out process itself, the loss of our birth families when we did so, the need or desire to establish new "families" among our Lesbian friends and those non-Lesbians who could and would support us, the difficulties of moving in and out of Lesbian relationships (McNaron, 17). The knowledge that we are not alone, a knowledge which we can gain within a community or from the artifacts of a Lesbian culture, contributes to our individual and collective survival as well as to our individual and shared sense of Lesbian identity.

In what is certainly one of the first efforts to attempt an analytical exposition of Lesbian culture, Toni McNaron and eleven other Lesbians spent six weeks exploring and sharing their ideas about what Lesbian culture is. As Toni McNaron described it, "Out of a personal conviction that our deepest notions of culture begin and center on our selves, our behavior and values, I [Toni McNaron] brought to the opening session a design within which we might operate." Starting with that circular design, McNaron and her friends framed our connectedness and sense of self within a series of concentric circles radiating out from that containing the self ("me"), to one circumscribing our close Lesbian connections ("you's"), to one containing the "live others" of more distant acquaintance, with whom we rarely come into contact, and, finally, ending the circles with a ring of "dead others," Lesbians from former times. As McNaron notes, our knowledge of them has been partial and distorted, filtered through male, heteropatriarchal perceptions (15):

Our group agreed that contemporary and future lesbian scholars must redo much that history has overlooked or misinterpreted. The prospect for at least several decades—of gently brushing away the dust of neglect and crud of denial—made us feel that special breath-holding which must accompany any archeological dig. And the civilization we will uncover will be our own. (15)

Our desire to see that the work of Lesbians of our generation isn't "lost," buried, or destroyed, that the knowledge we have accumulated of Lesbians past and present is not, once again, swept away or hidden, contributes to the sense of urgency with which we (Susan and Julia) undertook to collect the items in this volume of Lesbian culture. The forms of Lesbian culture, as Toni has pointed out, connect us in a way which defies the geographic and temporal barriers which separate us.

To establish a culture, to articulate it, express it, and give it form is part of the crucial task Lesbians are engaged in today. To ensure that its forms are maintained and our shared experiences clarified through them requires an ongoing commitment to ourselves, to other Lesbians, and to the culture which we are bringing into being. As Toni McNaron has put it:

This generation of dykes could leave to our culture posterity a way to organize our chaotic, often painful experience into some body of data...which would let lesbians fifty or five years from now build new layers on an already articulated base. Such a system would offer lesbians and the (homophobic) society at large much needed information about our history, our artifacts, and our day-to-day lives. (17)

For most of us, such information was lacking, although some of us have in the recent past been fortunate enough to come to a Lesbian sense of self-awareness within the context of Lesbian community and Lesbian culture. This anthology expresses our deep wish that other Lesbians will have the opportunity to come joyfully to Lesbian identity as an identity shared, within a Lesbian culture. Yet, as some of us are discovering, many of the younger Lesbians now finding their way to our communities, have never heard of some of the Lesbians we older Lesbians regard as central contributors to Lesbian culture. In the background information Michal Brody has provided for the herstory events held at Mountain Moving Coffeehouse in Chicago, she describes how the idea for storytelling events arose:

> A kitchen-table conversation with a friend in her twenties touched on younger lesbians, and how little they knew, generally, about lesbian life and struggle in times past. That conversation led us to conceive a storytelling event where ordinary, schlep-a-day lesbians would tell stories and experiences of their lives.

Such projects as storytelling events and anthologies like this one work against the heteropatriarchal tides that continually wash our lives away like so much historical flotsam. If we can start now to preserve every shred of evidence about our lives, as the Lesbian Herstory Archives is doing, we will have begun to weave together the strands of culture and memory into a patterned history. Tee A. Corinne, in a paper delivered in 1990, opened her talk by describing how art and culture feed and enhance memory:

> Art is culture made manifest. Images are culture made visible. Repetition lodges images in memory.

Against the general historical background of Lesbian invisibility, and in spite of the possibility that this collection might also eventually be "lost" to future Lesbians, we assemble some of the documents and artifacts of Canadian and U.S. Lesbian cultures. Along with them we include some works from the past which have informed contemporary Lesbian culture and provided evidence for the continuity of Lesbian culture. We come to the task of compiling this anthology both with a sense of urgency—growing out of our commitment to Lesbian culture and community in the face of continued challenges to them—and with a sense of delight, reveling in the richness of the culture Lesbians have already produced. In producing this anthology, we acknowledge the countless contributions to Lesbian culture in all its diversity, while including material representing only a few of them.

The Contents of this Anthology

We Lesbians now have on our shelves numerous anthologies of personal narratives about our lives, our experiences, our oppressions: *The Coming Out Stories* (Persephone Press, 1980) and then *The Original Coming Out Stories* (Crossing Press, 1989); *This Bridge Called My Back: Writings By Radical Women of Color*, edited by Cherríe Moraga and Gloria Anzaldúa (Persephone Press, 1981; Kitchen Table:

Women of Color Press, 1983); *Nice Jewish Girls: A Lesbian Anthology* (Persephone Press, 1982; Beacon Press); *A Gathering of Spirit: A Collection by North American Indian Women*, edited by Beth Brant (originally published by Sinister Wisdom Books, 1984; Firebrand Books, 1988); *True to Life Adventure Stories*, edited by Judy Grahn (Diana Press, 1978). There is *Lesbian Connection*, the Lesbian publication with the longest consistent publishing record, eighteen years (at this writing), and journals like *Sinister Wisdom* (publishing sixteen years) and *Lesbian Ethics* (now published for eight years), which have produced special issues on subjects like racism, class, and Italian Lesbians. We have anthologies of Lesbian poetry and prose, such as *Lesbian Poetry*, edited by Elly Bulkin and Joan Larkin (Persephone Press, 1981), and *Lesbian Fiction*, edited by Elly Bulkin (Persephone Press, 1981), collections of poetry by individual authors, including Audre Lorde, Adrienne Rich, Marilyn Hacker, Jan Hardy, Joy Harjo, Melanie Kaye-Kantrowitz, H.D., Pat Parker, Minnie Bruce Pratt, Cheryl Clarke, and Becky Birtha, and novels by Sarah Aldridge, Maureen Brady, Katherine V. Forrest, Claire Morgan, Patricia A. Murphy, Joanna Russ, and Barbara Wilson. We have a few collections by Lesbian photographers, such as JEB's (Joan E. Biren) *Eye to Eye: Portraits of Lesbians* and *Making A Way: Lesbians Out Front*. We even have published collections by Lesbian cartoonists, Alison Bechdel's several collections of *Dykes to Watch Out For* (published by Firebrand) and N. Leigh Dunlap's *Morgan Calabresé: The Movie* (New Victoria Publishers, 1987). We have calendars, T-shirts, bumper stickers, buttons, stained glass labryses to hang in our windows and silver ones by Lesbian silversmiths to wear around our necks. We have fine pottery that satisfies both our aesthetic and practical needs, made by Lesbian hands from Lunar Works, Amazon Earthworks, and numerous other potters, and in 1991, a Chicago group, the Queens Rule Poker Club, gave us the Queens Rule deck of cards with all-female cards (Queens, Ladies, and Maidens).

For more than twenty years we have had Lesbian recording artists and concerts. The first openly Lesbian music was recorded on 45 records by Lisa Ben (an anagram for *Lesbian*) and advertised for sale in *The Ladder* through the DOB (Daughters of Bilitis) Book Service in 1963 as "The Gayest Songs on Wax" (but see Kay Gardner's essay in "The Early Years of East Coast Women's Music and the Squirrel" in this anthology, in which she identifies Maxine Feldman's recording of "Angry Atthis" as the first Lesbian record). Alix Dobkin's and Kay Gardner's *Lavender Jane Loves Women* (1973) preceded Meg Christian's *I Know You Know* by only a few months as the first openly Lesbian album to be internationally distributed. As

well as acknowledging firsts, seconds and thirds, however, we also wanted to bring together Lesbian works that bespoke Lesbian voices across time, voices too often silenced by histories. Thus, although songs by Ma Rainey and Bessie Smith contained lyrics which all but sang the L-word out loud, we elected to represent the Lesbians who sang the blues in two poems by

Cheryl Clarke, to record how their voices have spoken to her. In this way, we, like other Lesbians, honor those who have gone before us.

We have Lesbian writers' conferences, Lesbian philosophers (among them Claudia Card, Jackie Anderson, Jeffner Allen, Joyce Trebilcot, and Jacqueline Zita), and gatherings of Lesbians in business. There is also a growing body of work by Lesbian filmmakers, a medium pioneered by Barbara Hammer and Michelle Parkerson. We have created the artifacts of a culture with which we surround ourselves and from which we draw comfort and inspiration

and the strength to persevere in a hostile environment.

There was no way we could hope to represent adequately every facet of the culture that many Lesbians spend some portion of their lives immersed in. We cannot transport you to the Michigan Womyn's Music Festival or the East Coast Lesbians' Festival or recreate in this medium the experience of spending a week among thousands of Lesbians. It isn't possible in a book like this to hear the rhythms, sounds, chords, or voices of the music Lesbian musicians have created (although the magazine *HOT WIRE*, edited by Tony Armstrong Jr., includes a 45 record inside the back cover of each issue), but we have included photographs of Kay Gardner, Jamie Anderson, Sue Fink, Pam Hall, and Casselberry and Dupreé, and song lyrics by Alix Dobkin, Sue Fink and Joelyn Grippo, and Karen Eskovitz (aka Otter) and Elliott. We cannot reproduce here the texture and color of paintings by Lesbian artists, but we have included drawings by Rainbow and Sudie Rakusin and photographs of posters made by Diane F. Germain. Furthermore, the print medium is altogether inadequate for conveying specific arts. It could not, for example, do justice to the wit and delivery of Lesbian comics like Kate Clinton, Karen Williams, Suzanne Westenhoefer, and Marga Gomez. In short, given the limitations of a single, printed volume, we have tried to bring together examples of Lesbian culture that represent some of its diverse aspects and, at the same time, by their juxtaposition, to illustrate how the culture Lesbians are creating resonates with our awareness of Lesbians who have preceded us and those who are contemporaneous with us. Like any culture, Lesbians produce and create art in the context of what we know, and "what we know" is drawn both from our own experience and the experiences of other Lesbians as they report them.

We narrowed our scope by including only work produced by Lesbians living in Canada and the U.S., those born here or those who lived a large portion of their lives here. We include, for example, two love poems from *The Muse of the Violets* by Renée Vivien who, like Natalie Barney, was a member of the American expatriate culture in Paris early in this century. There are two photographs by Myriam Fougére, a Québécoise Lesbian. (In addition to her work as a sculptor, Myriam also works in video, and, with Lin Daniels, a U.S. Jewish Lesbian, produces the East Coast Lesbians' Festival, until 1992 the only Lesbian festival in the U.S.)

Our Lesbian foresisters are underrepresented here. We decided early on to devote most of the anthology to Lesbian works produced in the second half of the twentieth century because they reflect a new Lesbian self-consciousness and were created in order to develop a Lesbian culture. Although we have not included any of Sappho's poems or Gertrude Stein's prose, one of Jorjet Harper's essays discusses Sappho and the importance of Lesbian space and Susan Stinson's "Lifting Belly Again" incorporates excerpts from the original poem by Stein. (Naiad has republished the entire poem, with an excellent introduction by Rebecca Mark, ed., 1989.) We have reprinted the last few pages of Radclyffe Hall's ground-breaking Lesbian novel *The Well of Loneliness* (1927) because that book was, for many Lesbians forty and older, the first Lesbian-identified novel we read. Here, too, are excerpts from one of the novels by Ann Bannon that older Lesbians smuggled past watchful parental eyes when we were teenagers, the notorious *Beebo Brinker*, and descriptions of Elsa Gidlow's relationship with "Tommy," excerpted from her autobiography, *Elsa: I Come With My Songs*.

We also want our readers to know that, while our own likes have been a factor in our decisions about what to include in this collection, other factors have also determined the exclusion of other artifacts of Lesbian culture. Some writers, for example, refused us permission to reprint their work because they were quarreling with their publisher or didn't want their work excerpted. (Excerpting is a difficult task, forcing us to constantly weigh the benefits of including portions of longer works so that their authors were represented and the often destructive potential of doing in-justice to an author's work in the process.) We took the problem seriously: for example, Jane Rule's *Desert of the Heart* isn't included here because we couldn't identify an excerpt that did justice to the novel. Some artists, like Kady Van Deurs (Axmaker to the Queen), "just said no." Others didn't respond, perhaps because they didn't receive any of our letters or maybe they aren't speaking to one of us. (Susan hasn't offended anyone that we know of.) Then there are the "hasbeans," women who've decided, for one reason or another, that they're not Lesbians anymore. We didn't ask for their work.

We have divided the anthology into three sections, organizing the materials on the basis of our discussion of Lesbian culture and Lesbian identity rather than by genre or topic, because we wanted to illustrate the ongoing discussions, debates, arguments among Lesbians and the interconnections and influences among their works that make of our individual and collective efforts a culture. These back-and-forth, reciprocating ideas in motion demonstrate, in a visible way, that Lesbians are no longer merely a subculture of either the larger heterosexual or gay male cultures.

The first section, "Women Who Did Stand Alone," documents only a few of those Lesbian lives from the past which have touched our own and which remain important to us as we attempt to forge the Lesbian culture(s) of the present and future. The second, "We Are Not as They Say," contains selections which express the rage and grief of Lesbians living within a male-dominated society, striving to live as Lesbians and to be among other Lesbians, fighting those who would condemn us as "sick," who accuse us of "flaunting our lifestyle," who would imprison us in heterosexual marriages, psychiatric hospitals, jails, or failing any of those methods, kill us. Here, too, are expressions of pain for the other heteropatriarchal oppressions we bring with us into our Lesbian communities, and which therefore continue to divide us: racism, anti-Semitism, ableism, fat oppression. The third, "New Ground," is a selection of artifacts from the rich culture we are creating out of a positive sense of Lesbian identity, expressing our strength, affirming ourselves.

Part I: Women Who Did Stand Alone

The title of this section is taken from Joan Nestle's "Butch-Femme Relationships: Sexual Courage in the 1950s" (in *A Restricted Country*, Firebrand Books, 1987), but it echoes the sentiments expressed by other Lesbian writers who came out in the 1950s and whose work is reprinted here. Audre Lorde, for example, discussing how lonely it was being young and black

and gay in New York City's Greenwich Village during the 1950s, states, "We had to do it alone" (*Zami: A New Spelling of My Name*, originally published by Persephone Press, 1982; now published by The Crossing Press).

The section opens with a map of Llangollen, a location in Wales where Eleanor Butler and Sarah Ponsonby, the "Ladies of Llangollen," loved each other devotedly for years during the eighteenth century. Their relationship became a famous and respected one during their own time, and remains an inspiration to Lesbians two hundred years later. As Tee Corinne reminds us, in "Remembering as a Way of Life," we need images of women like these as part of our Lesbian heritage, demonstrating to us that it is possible not only to survive, but to change the world as we find it.

Here, then, are bits and pieces of our Lesbian heritage: words from Deborah Edel of the Lesbian Herstory Archives, founded in the 1970s to preserve the records of that heritage, on the importance of saving every scrap of paper, every photograph, that will convey the realities of our lives to Lesbians who come after us.[6] Here are a few photographs, and biographical and autobiographical accounts of those of us who lived and loved as Lesbians from the 1920s through the 1950s. Included are photographs of Julia Penelope (aka "Penny Stanley") and Merril Mushroom, of Mabel Hampton, and an excerpt from Elsa

Gidlow's memoir describing her "Tommy." And here are photographs of unknown Lesbians embracing, Lesbians about whose lives we can only conjecture because the documents that would clarify the truths of their lives have been lost to us.

This section also contains samples of the works which enabled us to define ourselves, one by one, in a hostile world which concealed us from each other: excerpts from Radclyffe Hall's *The Well of Loneliness* (1928), the only novel available to many Lesbians who came out before 1970, and from Ann Bannon's *Beebo Brinker*, one of the classic Lesbian novels which provided images of contemporary Lesbians for us in the 1950s and 1960s; Lesbian poems by Renée Vivien, writer and lover of Natalie Clifford Barney.[7]

Finally, we have included works which, although fictional or fictionalized accounts, offer us some insight into what our lives may have been like before the 1950s: Elana Dykewomon's poem "New England Cemetery," in which she imagines that death freed the women of early New England to lie at last together; an excerpt from Isabel Miller's *Patience and Sarah*, a novel inspired by the life of early nineteenth-century painter Mary Ann Wilson, who settled on a farm in New York with her "devoted companion"; Sarah Dreher's play *Hollandia '45*, depicting Lesbians in the U.S. Women's Army Corps during World War II, fighting simultaneously for themselves; and an excerpt from Valerie Miner's *All Good Women*, in which Lesbians during the same period fight the same battle, stateside.

Much of what we (Susan and Julia) would have liked to include is not here, of course, and our omissions are not simply due to the fact that this anthology represents the tastes and experiences of only a few Lesbians, or that some pieces were too difficult to excerpt from or to gain permission to reprint. Some things are missing because of the losses we have sustained, of the suppression of individual Lesbians and our culture(s), of the violence we have suffered. Time and time again, invaluable lives and materials have been lost to us as a hostile male world swept away Lesbians and everything belonging to our world.

Part II: We Are Not as They Say

The works and excerpts of works in Part II were created from the 1970s to the present. Many of them focus on the fact that Lesbian culture exists amidst another culture, one determined to ignore and eradicate it, and that we, as Lesbians within that larger culture, are at best misunderstood and at worst the targets of hatred and violence.

Although the dominant tones of the section are anguish, grief, and rage, and the dominant theme one of defiance and resistance, the works included here look out upon the non-Les-

bian world with humor as well as anger. Some of these drawings, cartoons, poems, and essays, while seeming to make light of the hatred and violence we endure, address the very real pain we suffer as we are misunderstood by neighbors and by our families of origin. Noreen Stevens' cartoons portray a mother protesting that she doesn't have pictures of naked

PLUS JE VOIS DES HOMMES, PLUS J'AIME MON CHIEN

men all over her house, implying that having images of naked women in their homes makes Lesbians not only perverse but also limited in our desires, and a sister on "Lesbian overload" from a three-day exposure to Lesbian culture that has left her defensive. Jorjet Harper's "Lesbomania" column on being called an "Elizabeth" (a mispronunciation of *Lesbian*) by the boy-child of a "normal" (read "dysfunctional") family calls to mind all the strange ways *Lesbian* can be heard by heterosexuals who seem unable to process the phonetic shape of the word.

There is no humor veiling the fear of the characters in Valerie Miner's "Trespassing," whose home in the woods is threatened by an intruding male hunter, and whose violent presence is an ominous reflection of the world beyond the woods. Nor is humor appropriate in Pat Parker's poem from *Movement in Black*, which warns us that "Boots are being polished" as righteous right-wing citizens prepare to attack us, not as an unruly mob, but in the "orderly" fashion made possible by patriarchy. In the face of such attacks, Pat warns, every act of silence or denial is "a perversion." Like her, Marilyn Murphy reminds us that remaining in the closet is "death"; we do our families as well as ourselves a disservice in failing to come out. Michal Brody's interview with Adrienne J. Smith (part of one of the storytelling events in Chicago), a gentler reminiscence, suggests that Marilyn is right: having waited fifteen years to tell her mother of her Lesbianism, Adrienne discovered that her mother knew all along.

"The common woman," says Judy Grahn in "Carol, in the park, chewing on straws," "is as common as a thunderstorm." Though male domination and male violence against Lesbians (and all women) are central themes in Joanna Russ's *The Female Man*, another is that of female resistance, even violent resistance, as the narrator speaks of "firing these…murderers…off the face of the earth"

(173). The women in June Arnold's *Sister Gin*, less violently if equally effectively, move like a thunderstorm across the Southern landscape they inhabit to avenge an old woman's rape by tying the rapist to a board, naked, to face public humiliation, and the narrator reminds us that this is not the first time they carried out the vengeance of the Furies. Like Chrystos, the contributors to this section find that their tormentors can still "touch [their] last raw tired nerve" ("On My Way") and tap their rage. With Janet Aalfs, they declare "This is war/ and I have been branded" ("Branded"), affirming with her: "when I am taken/I will not go face down."

Whether or not we fight back through acts of vengeance, many of these pieces seem to say we must fight for survival. We may, like Abby and Inez in Elana Dykewomon's *Riverfinger Women*, learn to protect ourselves through concealment, "by never touching or looking at each other in public" (9). But there is no real safety to be had among those who "say we are crazy" (Chaia Zblocki Heller, "to the women who weep") or brand us "dyke, bitch, manhater,/diseased" (Janet Aalfs, "Branded"). We can only declare that "we are not as they say" and hold to each other against the pain.

Even in the midst of the Lesbian culture we seek to create, our contributors remind us, we often recreate the negative divisions of male-dominated so-ciety within our own communities and reinforce their existence outside of it. To avoid contributing further to the racist oppression suffered by American Indians, two Native women in Chrystos's poem, "Ya Don Wanna Eat Pussy," keep silent when a Chippewa man makes offensive remarks about eating "pussy" because they are all in the presence of a white man. Amy Edgington's essay, "A Medal for Not Drowning," describes her ambivalence when she received a "special award for trying hard," and asks, "whose sense of inadequacy was being soothed by that fake medal?" Susan Stinson asks us to be like the right "whole cloth," making room for "so much wild fatness" that it makes "a song in largeness." As Lesbians, we risk much in failing to see each other as figures of power, welcoming and cherishing our differences. As Audre Lorde reminds us, "The master's tools will never dismantle the master's house." Perpetuating the hatred and distrust of our differences can still divide and destroy the culture we are trying to build.

Part III: New Ground

In this section are artifacts of the new culture we are beginning to create, a culture planted firmly in Lesbian identity. Since the Lesbian sense of self is grounded in our love for other women, it is natural that much of our literature and art depicts our love for each other and its sexual expression. Here, then, are examples of the expression of Lesbian sexuality: photos by Tee Corinne and a sculpture by Myriam Fougére of women embracing; beautiful lyric poems by Chrystos, Audre Lorde, Judy Grahn, Olga Broumas and Elana Dyke-womon, celebrating our passion for each other; an exciting short story by Lynne Yamaguchi Fletcher, "Turtle-hawk dreams an ocean breathing," in which lovemaking lifts the lover like waves until all is water.

We have called this section "New Ground," after a song by Alix Dobkin of the same name, and, indeed, many of our contributors describe Lesbian sexuality as a new "place." The reliance on metaphors which draw their power from the Earth and Her oceans echoes the sense expressed by Toni McNaron's group that our connections with each other transcend geographic and temporal boundaries, and emphasizes our feeling that, when we have declared ourselves Lesbians, we are immigrants, coming upon a landscape still undescribed on the maps of the world from which we've escaped. Chrystos, for example, in "Song for a Lakota Woman," states that "We came to a place where we knew/our mouths would meet," and Audre Lorde, in "Woman," declares "I dream of a place between your breasts." In Lynne Yamaguchi Fletcher's story, "Turtlehawk dreams an ocean breathing," Elana Dykewomon's "diving, I kiss," and Judy

Grahn's "in the place were," the sea becomes a metaphor for Lesbian sexuality. In her "Love Poem," Audre Lorde invokes the power and beauty of the earth, and both lovers become a part of it, with their lovemaking the richest part.

Here are affirmations of the Lesbian body, in all its beauty. There is Tee Corinne's photo of three fat dykes, and Susan Stinson's "Lifting Belly Again," as she declares with Gertrude Stein "Lifting belly is so satisfying…Large quantities of it."

Because being Lesbians together is often as difficult as it is wonderful, we have included pieces which examine the ways we are learning to be together in relationships: the ways in which we connect, and do not connect, in the cartoons of Alison Bechdel and Diane F. Germain and in Lee Lynch's short story, "Jacky and the Psychic"; the miracle of the ordinariness of our lives, when uninvaded moments are possible, in Chaia Zblocki Heller's poems, "gardening" and "yentas"; the horror of Lesbian battering in Ruthann Robson's story, "Growing Avocados." And, in "This Is Not a Poem for Wimmin Drinking Diet Colas Just to Save Those Few Extra Calories," Elliott describes how we sometimes do not fit each other, physically or emotionally, and warns us against denying our differences.

Holding you
is not easy.
Regardless of what we don't say

With the explosion of Lesbian publishing that began in the early 1970s, numerous newspapers, journals, and presses were established, and some, like Diana Press and Daughters, Inc., did not survive beyond 1977; Persephone Press, which published many books still considered classics, declared bankruptcy in 1984. Journals and newspapers that have disappeared include *Lavender Woman, Amazon Quarterly, Big Mama Rag,* and *Ain't I a Woman* (named by a line in a famous speech by Sojourner Truth). We have reprinted excerpts from books originally published by some of these, and included, when possible, logos, title pages, and covers of premiere issues of *Sinister Wisdom* and *Lavender Woman*, believing that they attest to the energy and vitality of Lesbian publishing. Even though Diana Press expired by an act of sabotage, other presses have been founded to keep our dreams alive and available to us.

We intended, as we created this anthology, to represent as many of the media as possible that Lesbians have used to create our culture. So, in this section we have included *HOT WIRE* articles on Black Lesbian filmmakers (among them Michelle Parkerson, a producer and director working on *The Audre Lorde Project*, thus documenting as well as creating Lesbian culture) and on Barbara Hammer, an experimental filmmaker who asserts that "being a lesbian and being an artist is always creating and always defining." With

them is "Tortilleras," by Terri de la Peña, a fictional account of a film made by a dynamic Latina Lesbian filmmaker.

We have also included lyrics by Alix Dobkin, a force in Lesbian music for two decades, as well as the lyrics of two songs by Karen Eskovitz and Elliott. We've supplemented these with the following: an article by composer-musician Kay Gardner on the "early days" of Lesbian ("women's") music on the East Coast; an essay by Toni Armstrong Jr., editor of *HOT WIRE*, exploding the myth that "women's music" is and has always been a "white-girl-with-a-guitar" (often shortened to the WGWG syndrome) circuit, confined to creating and promoting folk music, and a quiz to test your knowledge of women's and Lesbian music; a Toni Armstrong Jr. interview with Jamie Anderson, who has been performing at Lesbian festivals and concerts throughout the 1980s; Armstrong's interview with Sue Fink, whose "Leaping Lesbians" has been a favorite with Lesbian audiences for more than fifteen years; and an article by Pam Hall, a singer who composes and performs her music out of "my love of womyn, and my deep respect for Southern womyn," and who begins her sets with a song "called 'L-E-S-B-I-A-N' to let everybody know where I'm coming from" (48–49).

This section also contains photos of Lesbian musicians in performance: Kay Gardner, Casselberry and DuPreé, Sue Fink, and Alix Dobkin. But nothing can convey the sense of excitement and connectedness, the sense of community, from attending a Lesbian concert or a festival on Lesbian land, listening to music by Lesbians that affirms the fact of our lives. No book can capture music in performance, or the response of the audience to performer and music, echoed and returned by the performer. We have nonetheless included a photo of the Michigan Womyn's Music Festival (courtesy of Lisa Vogel), a copy of the brochure for the Fourth Annual East Coast Lesbians' Festival (1992), lyrics to "The Waiting for the Festival Lesbian Jam," and Jorjet Harper's column "Michiguilt," along with an article by Therese Edell (with Teresa Boykin) on Michigan. If we cannot convey directly the emotional impact and the energizing forces these gatherings have within the Lesbian community, we can at least demonstrate indirectly their significance to it.

This section also contains a chapter from *Diamonds Are a Dyke's Best Friend*, one which outlines the importance of softball games as a place to meet other Lesbians as well as a place to play the game, and an Alison Bechdel cartoon as well as a humorous description of the rites due the "found goddess" Umpira/Tempura (from *Found Goddesses*, by Morgan Grey and Julia Penelope).

Here we have included articles, song lyrics, and cartoons on food: on its consumption as a means of Lesbian celebration,

on vegetarian cuisine as an expression of oneness with the Earth, or at least of political correctness, and in its centrality as an intimate activity—two lovers, for example, share a first dinner and a fifteenth-anniversary dinner in the same French restaurant in Jess Wells's "A Favorite Haunt." We have also included photos by JEB, an essay by Liza Cowan, cartoons by

Noreen Stevens, Alison Bechdel, and Kris Kovick, and drawings by Sudie Rakusin, pieces displaying and explaining Dyke finery and poking fun, both at heterosexuals who wonder why we choose clothing that makes us "look like Lesbians," and at ourselves, struggling to find just the "right look."

Ultimately, however, if Lesbian culture is to endure, we must have more than books and music, more than potlucks and festivals, more than distinctive ways of dressing. We must break new ground, finding ways for Lesbians to live together in Lesbian communities. We must

develop a Lesbian consciousness, and that consciousness must inform our interactions.

We must begin by finding other Lesbians, and move toward creating Lesbian space in which we can form communities both temporary and permanent. In this section, then, we have included Marilyn Murphy's "Looking for Lesbians," which, more than merely describing characteristic Lesbian looks and walks, speaks to our continuing need to find each other and identify ourselves to each other. We have included Phyllis Birkby's design for a women's community; a copy of the flyer for the Pagoda, a "Lesbian Spiritual and Cultural Community," a residential cottage community offering a place for "wimmin for rest, retreat, recuperation and healing"; Jorjet Harper's article on Sappho's Lesbos as women-only space.

We decided early on that the selections we finally included had to be self-critical, that collecting only positive, celebratory artifacts of Lesbian culture would be dishonest. Our communities are often the sites of vigorous, angry disputes. Within various communities some of these arguments are called "Lesbian Wars" because we do indeed suffer wounds and losses from which some do not recover. Yet, without these disputes, our communities could not change. Within our communities, we must debate and must decide what constitutes a Lesbian sensibility, and how we can ensure that our interactions sustain that sensibility. How we speak to each other, the words we use and those we do not, are important; our speaking can become, as it does in Julia Penelope's fable, "A Cursory and Precursory History of Language, and the Telling of It," "a language of acting in the world," "our meaning in the life of the world." Part of that process is self-examination and a constant dialogue about which elements are truly of and for our Lesbian sensibilities. We must decide which rituals we will perform in these communities— whether none at all, or those modeled on Lesbian consciousness, like Judith Barrington's "a mid-life ritual," in which we try to find ways to recognize and celebrate the significant phases and periods of our lives. We must learn which behaviors *cannot* be "redeemed" simply by transferring the power for them from males to Lesbians: Lee Evans, for example, suggests in her essay that consumerism is destructive of Lesbian community and to the Lesbian sense of community, and Juana Maria Gonzalez Paz speaks of the need to balance many concerns against easy ideological solutions to problems arising within Lesbian communities.

In this section are the articles on what might constitute specifically Lesbian humor, which sacrifices we must be prepared to make and which struggles to undertake to create a Lesbian present and the potential for a Lesbian future. Sudie Rakusin's drawings sug-

gest what Lesbian spirituality might look like as it is manifested in our movements and gestures, and Anna Livia's essay on the impromptu nature of much of Lesbian humor explores some of the ways Lesbian humor differs from that of non-Lesbians. Poems by Audre Lorde and Chaia Zblocki Heller honor and celebrate the simple acts of matching our footsteps to one another's, holding hands, spading a garden for planting, breaking bread together.

Here are portraits of real Lesbians of strength, and of those in Lesbian-created fantasies. And here is an excerpt from Sarah Lucia Hoagland's *Lesbian Ethics*, enjoining us to move in the direction of intimacy, of power which enables each other, of moral agency which enables integrity and choices.

What we have compiled, in short, is an anthology of beginnings, one among many possible collections of Lesbian work and works, representing our lives, our ideas, our dreams for the future. Don't expect, though, to find here only the well-known, the celebrated, the already acknowledged Lesbian artists and thinkers, although many of them have been included. Many of our contributors, such as Karen Eskovitz, Elliott, Amy Edgington, Debbie Alicen, Deborah Edel, and Janice Gould, are either recent newcomers to the perpetuation of Lesbian culture or longtime cultural workers who are rarely visible to Lesbians beyond their

immediate communities. We have included in this anthology new work, published here for the first time, as well as recognized classics treasured by many Lesbians. The material ranges over the ages, from Sappho to the eighteenth century to the 1950s, even if its publication date is 1969, 1990, or 1992. In fact, the "new" material, regardless of when it was published, is included because of the insights it provides into the values and struggles of our lives. The excerpts from Elsa Gidlow's and Toni McNaron's autobiographies and Michal Brody's interview with Adrienne Smith all describe significant changes, transitions, and transformations in Lesbian lives by those who lived them. Our culture is made of the very substance of our lives and how we understand our changes.

The viability of a culture, any culture, depends on its ability to carry itself forward over and through time, a feat rarely managed by Lesbians who lived prior to the twentieth century, so we believe that it's significant that there is already a new wave of Lesbian artists and writers who are committed to the task of carrying Lesbian culture forward for the lives of future generations of Lesbians. This collection is a beginning among many beginnings, and, we hope, only the first of many anthologies that enable us to contemplate how the things we create for ourselves and each other are integral to our survival and well-being. To those Lesbians who have come before us and those who are continuing to create our Lesbian culture even as we conclude work on this anthology, we offer our gratitude. To them and to the Lesbians who will continue the work of building Lesbian culture in the future, we dedicate this volume.

Endnotes

1 *Hothead Paisan* is published four times a year. For more information or to order copies, write to: giant ass publishing, POB 214, New Haven, CT 06502; also on sale at Lesbian bookstores.

2 An excellent article on the relationship of Katharine Lee Bates and Katharine Coman is Judith Schwarz's "Yellow Clover: Katharine Lee Bates and Katharine Coman" (1979)

3 Susan Ware has written an excellent, detailed book on the lives and relationship of Molly Dewson and Polly Porter, *Partner and I: Molly Dewson, Feminism, and New Deal Politics* (1987). They are also mentioned briefly at several points in the first volume of Blanche Wiesen Cook's biography of *Eleanor Roosevelt, vol. 7* (1992).

4 Several books have been written about the Ladies of Llangollen, Sarah Ponsonby and Eleanor Butler, among them: *The Ladies of Llangollen* (1971) and *A Year with the Ladies of Llangollen* (1984), both by Elizabeth Mavor, and *The Ladies* (1984) by Doris Grumbach.

5 Information about the life and execution of Catherine Margaretha Linck can be found in *Does Khaki Become You?* by Cynthia Enloe (1983), *The Women's History of the World* by Rosalind Miles (1988), and "Tribades on Trial: Female Same-Sex Offenders in Late Eigh-

teenth-Century Amsterdam" by Theo van der Meer (1991).

6 To contact the Lesbian Herstory Archives, write to: POB 1258, New York, NY 10116.

7 In *A Perilous Advantage* (1992), Anna Livia has translated and edited writings authored by Natalie Barney that are available for the first time in English, including Barney's portraits of figures such as Colette and Gertrude Stein.

References*

Asimov, Isaac. *Asimov's Chronology of the World: The History of the World from the Big Bang to Modern Times*, New York: Harper Collins, 1991.

Beck, Evelyn Torton, ed. *Nice Jewish Girls: A Lesbian Anthology*, Watertown, MA, Persephone Press; now published by Beacon Press in Boston, 1982.

Biren, Joan E. (JEB), *Eye to Eye: Portraits of Lesbians*. Washington, D.C., Glad Hag Books, 1979.

Biren, Joan E., *Making a Way: Lesbians Out Front*, Washington, D.C., Glad Hag Books, 1987.

Brant, Beth, ed., *A Gathering of Spirit: A Collection by North American Indian Women*, Plainfield, VT, Sinister Wisdom Books, 1984; now published by Firebrand Books, 1988.

Bulkin, Elly, *Lesbian Fiction*, Watertown, MA, Persephone Press, 1981.

Bulkin, Elly, and Larkin, Joan, *Lesbian Poetry*, Watertown, MA, Persephone Press, 1981.

Card, Claudia, "Lesbian Culture before 1940: Search and Re/Search," *Feminist Collections: Women's Studies Library Resources in Wisconsin 3*, 3 (Spring) 1982, 18–24.

Cook, Blanche Wiesen, *Eleanor Roosevelt*, vol. 1, 1884–1933, New York, Viking, 1992.

Corinne, Tee A., "Lesbian Art and Artists," Introduction to the panel Lesbian Artists: Reclaiming the Past, Defining the Present, at the national conference of the Women's Caucus for Art of the College Art Association, New York, 1990.

Dunlap, N. Leigh, *Morgan Calabresé: The Movie*. Norwich, VT, New Victoria Publishers, 1987.

Enloe, Cynthia, *Does Khaki Become You?* Boston, South End Press, 1983.

Faderman, Lillian, *Scotch Verdict*, New York, William Morrow, 1983.

Grahn, Judy, *True to Life Adventure Stories*, Oakland, CA, Diana Press, 1978.

Harper, Jorjet, "Towards a Lesbian Aesthetic," *HOT WIRE* (January) 1990, 14–15; 59.

Hellman, Lillian, *The Children's Hour*, New York, Knopf, [1932] 1934.

Hoagland, Sarah Lucia, *Lesbian Ethics: Toward New Value*. Palo Alto, CA, Institute of Lesbian Studies, 1988.

Livia, Anna, *A Perilous Advantage: The Best of Natalie Clifford Barney*. Norwich, VT, New Victoria Publishers, 1992.

Mavor, Elizabeth, *The Ladies of Llangollen*. Harmondsworth, Middlesex, Penguin, 1971.

Mavor, Elizabeth, *A Year with the Ladies of Llangollen*. Harmondsworth, Middlesex, Penguin, [1984] 1986.

McNaron, Toni, "Finding and Studying Lesbian Culture," *Radical Teacher 6* (December) 1977, 14–20.

Miles, Rosalind, *The Women's History of the World*. London, Michael Joseph, 1988.

Moraga, Cherríe, and Anzaldúa, Gloria, eds. *This Bridge Called My Back: Writings by Radical Women of Color*. Watertown, MA, Persephone Press 1981; now

published by Kitchen Table:
Women of Color Press.

Penelope, Julia, "The Lesbian
Perspective." In Jeffner Allen, ed.
Lesbian Philosophies and Cultures.
Albany, SUNY Press, 1990, 89–
108. Reprinted in Julia Penelope's
collected essays, *Call Me Lesbian:
Lesbian Lives, Lesbian Theory.*
Freedom, CA, Crossing Press.

Penelope, Julia [Stanley], and Wolfe,
Susan J., eds. *The Coming Out
Stories.* Watertown, MA,
Persephone Press, 1980. Published
in a revised and expanded second
edition in 1989 by Crossing Press.

Schwarz, Judith, "Yellow Clover:
Katharine Lee Bates and
Katharine Coman," *Frontiers 4*, 1:
59–67, 1979.

Stein, Gertrude, *Lifting Belly,* ed. by
Rebecca Mark. Tallahassee, FL,
Naiad Press, [1953] 1989.

van der Meer, Theo, "Tribades on
Trial: Female Same-Sex Offenders
in Late Eighteenth-Century
Amsterdam," *Journal of the History
of Sexuality* 1, 3 (January) 1991,
424–45.

Ware, Susan, *Partner and I: Molly
Dewson, Feminism, and New Deal
Politics.* New Haven, CT, Yale UP,
1987.

*Some works mentioned in this in-
troduction do not appear in this list
of references because they are cited
in the credits on the copyright page.
                    —Julia Penelope and
                    Susan J. Wolfe,
                    September, 1992

Part I

Women Who Did Stand Alone

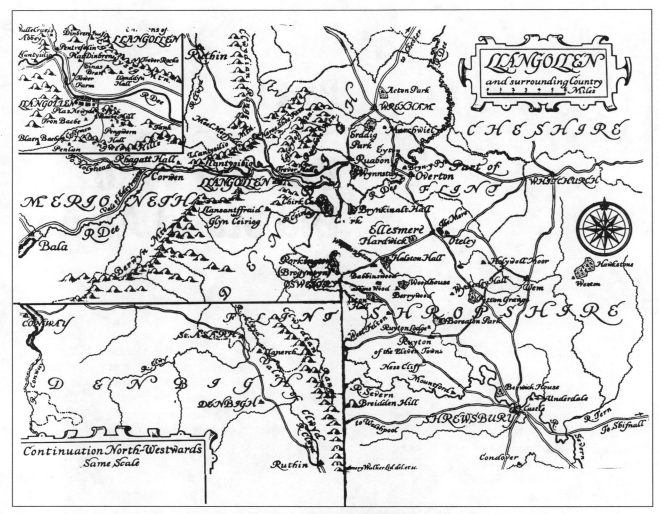

Map of Llangollen

This map of Llangollen, home of Eleanor Butler and Sarah Ponsonby, the Ladies of Llangollen, appeared in *The Hamwood Papers of the Ladies of Llangollen and Caroline Hamilton* by Mrs. G. H. Bell and published by Macmillan and Co., London, in 1930. Thanks to Claudia Card for sending it to us.

Lesbian Herstory Storytelling

by Michal Brody

"A kitchen-table conversation with a friend in her twenties touched on younger lesbians, and how little they knew, generally, about lesbian life and struggle in times past. That conversation led us to conceive a storytelling event where ordinary, schlep-a-day lesbians would tell stories and experiences of their lives. We thought this would be a great format for an event because it would honor and validate the experiences of the women who lived them, and give applause and acclaim to the women who may not be in the lesbian limelight through writing or sports or music. In addition, we would be documenting (through memory and the magic of videotape) important parts of our herstory, and creating a pleasant lesbian cultural event for the present. We also decided to make the event a benefit for the Lesbian Herstory Archives in New York.

Photo from a Mountain Moving Coffeehouse flyer. The flyer invited women to come to the coffeehouse where "real live Chicago lesbians will tell tales of the past 35 or so years. There will be photos, *(BRING YOURS!)*, displays, and many other interesting things…so that our own stories won't be left to luck."

In our ads that solicited storytellers, we suggested that women could tell their own stories from the stage, write them up ahead of time for someone else to read, or be interviewed on tape, and that I would transcribe and edit the tape for someone to read. Adrienne's story was one of two that were edited from interviews.

The event was a great success; in addition to the stories, we had exhibits of various types from Lesbian Herstory Archives, Gerber-Hart Library—a local lesbian/gay archives, and personal photo collections.

My partner, Martha Gass, and I produced another Lesbian Herstory Night in 1992. The theme was *Beyond Coupledom— what (besides lover relationships) sustained us as lesbians?* We are calling ourselves *Tell Us A Story Productions*, and we plan to continue with similar projects in the future." ■

Remembering as a Way of Life

by Tee A. Corinne

When death comes into our lives it is important not to become victims in our own grief, for in the passivity pain may induce, we suffer not only personal losses but the loss of our own history, our culture. Somehow we must take the time, summon the energy to write obituaries, to insure the survival of work, to honor the dead in ways that will be visible and available to succeeding generations.

Recently I attended a *Women in Print* conference, the third national conference of its kind in the last ten years. The first conference was held in 1976 outside Omaha, Nebraska, literally in the center of the continent. June Arnold, author and publisher, was a prime mover in conceiving and creating that initial conference. Now, in 1985, three years after her death, many women attending the third *Women in Print*

In: *Common Lives/Lesbian Lives 19* (Spring, 1986)

conference in Berkeley, California, had never heard of June Arnold. Her books are out of print. Daughters, Inc., the publishing house which she cofounded along with her lover Parke Bowman, has ceased to exist. No one, to my knowledge, is working on a biography. This is common within our movement, and it is a disaster.

If only you had known June Arnold, understood what she accomplished: the novel without gender-specific pronouns, published anonymously (*The Cook and the Carpenter*), the novel of older lesbians causing trouble, making love, oral sex when you can finally take your false teeth out, "...no more beautiful word...than withered" (*Sister Gin*).

What is radical anyway? What expands our understanding of that which is possible? June Arnold certainly expanded the vision for many of us, lesbians and other women, who loved the written word, the published work, dreams in print.

Jeannette Foster, who died the year before June Arnold, fed a different range of lesbian dreams with her literate and witty *Sex Variant Women in Literature*, first published in 1956. Jeannette Foster, finally self-published her 40 years worth of research because no established publisher would touch it. Diana Press brought out an edition of this unique and extraordinary work in 1975. Naiad Press published an edition of it in 1986.

I wanted to meet Jeannette Foster because I admired her work, because we shared the same birthday, and because I have a passion for old and older ladies...yes, *Ladies*, those women for whom gentility and grace are not flotsam to be discarded but rather ways of moving through the world. The year was 1977. I was living in San Francisco, preparing to drive across country with Honey Lee Cottrell. Surely a swing through rural Arkansas could be incorporated into our trip.

Barbara Grier, Jeannette

Foster's friend and confidante for something over twenty years at the time, arranged the meeting and gave me detailed instructions, including an admonition not to tire Jeannette. Barbara and her lover Donna McBride would join us at the nursing home where Jeannette lived five days each week. We would all go to lunch, then proceed to the home Jeannette shared with two other women her own age.

I wanted to bring her yellow roses. As we searched for a florist in successively smaller towns, I realized that the undertaker's parlor might be my last resource. Although I had grown up in the South, I had forgotten how isolated large areas of it could be. We located a flower shop just south of Pocahontas, the town where Jeannette lived, but the only roses they had were long stemmed red ones.

"Oh, yes!" Jeannette said when she saw them. "Richmond roses. My favorite kind."

I fell in love with her as soon as I saw her, standing, neatly dressed and combed, holding on to the metal bar at the foot of her bed. I fell in love with her again as she watched, appreciatively, the retreating form of a nurse, commenting favorably on the shape of her legs. I fell in love with her a third time when, on another visit, I realized she was looking me over the way a lover or potential lover might. I felt, as they used to say in my family, warmed to my bones.

I took pictures of Jeannette because I need images of women like her to be part of my heritage as a lesbian. I need models of intelligent, determined women who survived, who made their ways in the world, who left an impression, a dent in whatever realities they passed through.

Jeannette Foster died in 1981 at the age of eighty-five. She died quietly and with little notice taken in the women's press and none at all in the larger world. Many people are alive who still remember her but, again, no biography is in progress. Who is going to write about Jeannette Foster's life, her dedication, her passion?

It seems important to me that we conserve and nourish our lesbian "National Treasures" while they are still alive. Author Valerie Taylor, for example, is a veteran of the Lesbian Pulp '50s and '60s with paperback titles like *Whisper Their Love, Unlike Others, Stranger on Lesbos, The Girls in #3-B.* Later in that 1977 trip Barbara Grier introduced Honey Lee and me to Valerie Taylor who lived near Albany, New York. Valerie fed us soup and filled our minds with stories of her travels, her struggles to make a living as a writer, life in Chicago and the origins of that city's Lesbian Writers conference, her retirement and move to this small and lovely town. She was involved in organizing meals for the elderly, quietly counseling local kids.

Valerie Taylor currently lives and writes in Tucson where she gives talks as a Gay Grey Panther and wraps her heart around women needing a lesbian grandmother. She keeps trying to find ways of helping a straying world to find saner paths toward world peace.

Valerie, in her seventies, is having eye surgery this summer. Noticing that I haven't heard from her in several months, I find I want reassurances that she is well, that her next book will come out soon, that someone will start writing about her life: as an activist, a writer, a mother, a lover of women.*

Among the living lesbian seniors is Anita Cornwell, that dignified matriarch of Philadelphia whose *Ladder* essays and other writings were published in 1983 as *Black Lesbian in White America* (Naiad). I remember first seeing Anita on a panel with Audre Lorde, discussing butch/femme relationships and the women who fell outside of those perimeters. I remember also watching Anita encourage Becky Birtha, hearing Becky talk about Anita cheering her on as a writer. Who's going to write about Anita's clarity, her hon-

* Update: Valerie Taylor now requires our financial help to pay for medical care. You can mail contributions to:

Valerie Taylor Fund
c/o Antigone Books
600 N. 4th Avenue
Tucson, AZ 85705

If you can't afford to donate money, write and tell Valerie what her books have meant to you.

esty, her tenaciousness, her willingness still to take on community issues and write about them with eloquence?

Whoever writes about Audre Lorde will have a good foundation in the biographical material to be found in Anita's 1975 interview with Audre, an interview that encompasses the nature of inspiration as well as the details of personal history. Anita, with her fine conserving of the past of others and her own biography in process, needs also to be the subject of serious academic studies like the one SDiane Bogus has undertaken of Ann Allen Shockley.

And then there's Sarah Aldridge who began writing novels after retiring from a demanding professional career. Sarah Aldridge whose *All True Lovers* is one of the most charming evocations of young love that I've ever read. With six or seven novels now to her credit, Sarah has a large and devoted following but remains a thoughtful, private person. How can we honor her in her lifetime? What kinds of attention are appropriate and not intrusive? Will anyone think to make notes on her life while she's still living it?

When, in the 1940s, Natalie Barney learned that her friend and lover Dolly Wilde had died, she asked people to write about Dolly. Natalie then gathered these memories and published a small book to be shared among Dolly Wilde's friends. Remembering needs to become a way of life for all of us. Modern technology makes publishing easy. It's the writing, the remembering, the gathering that's hard.

At this year's *Women in Print* conference, I learned that Sonny Wainwright had recently died of the cancer she wrote about so movingly in *Stage V: A Journal Through Illness*. Sonny Wainwright, so thoughtful and strong, so incredibly vibrant. Sonny spent years learning to live with and around her illness, empowered others with her insights and sharing. Who is going to write Sonny Wainwright's biography, keep her book in print, gather our memories of her life and work?

And where can we have city parks named after openly lesbian women? Formal gardens framing statues of our foremothers, of our cultural heras? Where are the cast bronze plaques announcing the houses we've lived and died in, the public monuments and cemetery markers, the written guides with quaint encapsulated histories, noting where we are buried, what we did, how long we lived? ■

A History of Lesbianism

by Judy Grahn

How they came into the world,
the women-loving-women
came in three by three
and four by four
the women-loving-women
came in ten by ten
and ten by ten again
until there were more
than you could count

      they took care of each other
      the best they knew how
      and of each other's children
      if they had any.

How they lived in the world,
the women-loving-women
learned as much as they were allowed
and walked and wore their clothes
the way they liked
whenever they could. They did whatever
they knew to be happy or free
and worked and worked and worked.
The women-loving-women
in America were called dykes
and some liked it
and some did not.

they made love to each other
the best they knew how
and for the best reasons

How they went out of the world
the women-loving-women
went out one by one
having withstood greater and lesser
trials, and much hatred
from other people, they went out
one by one, each having tried
in her own way to overthrow
the rule of men over women,
they tried it one by one
and hundred by hundred,
until each came in her own way
to the end of her life
and died.

> The subject of lesbianism
> is very ordinary; it's the question
> of male domination that makes everybody
> angry.

In *Work of a Common Woman* (The Crossing Press
[1978])

The Archives is filled with voices announcing our autonomy and self-possession.
The roots of the Archives lie in the silenced voices, the love letters destroyed,
the pronouns changed, the diaries carefully edited, the pictures never taken,
the euphemized distortions that patriarchy would let pass.

—Joan Nestle, *Lesbian Herstory Archives Newsletter*, Spring 1979

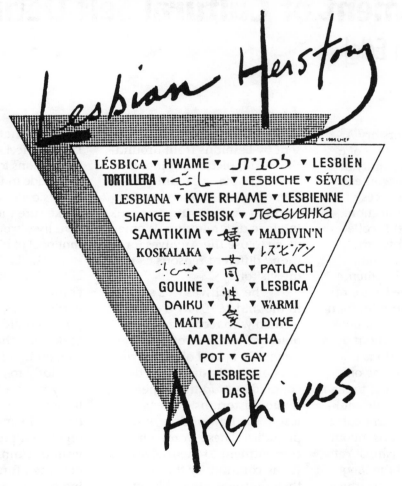

The Lesbian Herstory Archives
Lesbian Herstory Educational Foundation, Inc.
P.O. Box 1258, New York, NY 10116
(212) 874-7232

The Lesbian Herstory Archives:
A Statement of Cultural Self-Definition
by Deborah Edel

The Lesbian Herstory Archives is a mixture of a library and a family album, a place where women come to use the resources of a vast and growing collection. Some women visit this collection of Lesbian documents, art, literature, and memorabilia, searching for a book remembered, a journal needed for an article, reference material for a term paper, sources for a book or film, information about organizations, or connections in other cities. Others come on more personal searches, to read about coming out, about making love, about Lesbian health problems and solutions, about work, about relationships. Yet others come to read the biographies of our foremothers, the paperbacks of the 1950s and 1960s, the collections of unpublished poetry and stories, the novels of today, difficult to find in local bookstores and libraries.

Still others come to look—at the work of Lesbian artists and photographs on the walls and in the files, the snapshots sent by Lesbians from around the world, pictures of individuals, of couples, of teams, of friends, of children, of women working and playing and making love and relaxing. Women come to use the Archives for as many different reasons as there are visitors.

The Archives was started in the mid-1970s by a group of women who recognized how quickly the stories of their foremothers and of their own lives and activities, often discounted by traditional heterosexual historians, were being lost in the flow of time and prejudice. These women made a commitment to themselves and to the community that from then on there would always be a place to gather and preserve the herstory of Lesbian lives and activities. It was to be a place that would reflect the diversity of the Lesbian experience and work towards building intergenerational understanding.

It was to be a grassroots program that would make all Lesbians feel welcomed, a place for Lesbians to visit, not only to take pride in their diverse history as it is collected, but also to make sure the meaning of their own lives would become part of that pool of history.

The Lesbian Herstory Archives has always been staffed entirely by volunteers. In the earliest days, the co-founders put in endless time and money to develop the Archives. Now, a core group of volunteers meets regularly to keep up with the daily needs of archiving the collection, answering the mail, updating the mailing list, working on special projects, attending to visitors, running benefits and activities, fundraising, and going out on speaking engagements. The commitment to making the early dream an ongoing reality has never faltered. Funding for the Archives has always come from within the Lesbian and Gay community and from small grants from radical funding sources. There seems to be always just enough to pay for the things that need to be done, and never anything extra.

Letters come from all over the globe requesting both general and specific information about Lesbian lives and culture. Each letter is answered individually, and research requests are addressed as completely and fully as possible. In addition, the Archives publishes a newsletter which is available to all who request it. The newsletter serves an important function, as this is the way information about the collection and Archives activities can be shared with women who cannot visit the Archives in person.

In the late fall of 1992 the Archives raised funds sufficient for a downpayment on its own home. A limestone row house in Park Slope, Brooklyn, New York now houses the permanent collection. When the mortgage is paid off our permanence as a visible presence in history is assured. Though the move represented a transformation in location and form from the original apartment where the collection was located, the initial spirit and vision remains constant at the core of all our work. ■

Deborah Edel is a co-founder of the Lesbian Herstory Archives and is actively involved in the ongoing process of keeping the Archives running as smoothly as possible.

The pieces accompanying this article are excerpts from Archives newsletters. We hope that readers will want to write for more information about the work of the Lesbian Herstory Archives.

Lesbian Herstory Educational Foundation, Inc. (LHEF, Inc.) can be reached at P.O. Box 1258, New York, NY 10116. Telephone: 718/768-DYKE (718/768-3953).

Excerpts from *The Lesbian Archives Newsletter*

"The Gutter Letter," Newsletter #7, December 1981:

This letter was found by a Gay friend among a stack of papers and boxes lying outside a Greenwich Village apartment house. Attracted by the file folders, he did not realize what they contained until he had lugged the many boxes home. What he found, among other personal documents, were love letters and photographs portraying the Lesbian relationships of a labor activist and educator. She had just died and these letters had been thrown out as trash. The discovery became symbolic to us and we refer to the following letter as the gutter letter. The documents testifying to our love are too often considered garbage, and are destroyed by dismissing or frightened families.

(circa 1920)
Thursday night

Best Beloved,

I'm writing by the light of the two tall candles on my desk, with the flaming chrysanthemums you arranged, before me. It's such a lovely soft glow and I'm glad because this is a "candle-light" letter. I wish you could know what a wonderful person you are, Eleanor darling, and what joy your letter written last night gave me. Not the part about me—that is pitifully wrong and only a standard for me to measure up to—but you make it all so wonderful and are clear about it. You know I feel terribly much the way you do about it all, but I never could say so, even in incoherent fashion, and so many times back of my nobler resolves I am just plain selfish about wanting you to "look at and talk to" especially in the future when I know you won't be there. And that's why you are so wonderful, darling, because now I never can be but I shall have to strive oh so ardently to ever measure up and be worthy at all of you....The candles are burning low, dear heart and the world is very still and beautiful outside. And I am so, oh so happy that I know you and love you. And may God bless you through all time.

—Alice

"Mabel Hampton's Coming Out Story," Newsletter #7, December, 1981:

This piece is from our tape collection, taped at The Coming Out Stories Panel, Lesbian Feminist Liberation, June 21, 1981.

"I'm Mabel Hampton and I'm seventy-nine years old....I had one special girlfriend and then I meets a woman....I mean she was a real woman. She lived in the life for seven or eleven years. So I falls hook, line and sinkin for this woman. I didn't know what it was all about but I fell for her anyhow.... Her and I was in the show in Coney Island.... So this woman, I never will forget, I was sitting in the middle of the table and she was sitting at the end, all of a sudden it struck me that I loved this woman. And I know now, I got it down pat, I just loved her. And she looked at me and I looked at her....I'll tell you the truth I was so crazy over the woman why I couldn't even speak. I'd look at her and she was just like candy, you know. She was a Lesbian. And I mean she was one because—she knew all the answers and everything else. So that night, I spent the night with her. Then she tells me all the story. She says that she loved me....She came back a week later and I asked her did she want to stay with me. We got along nice. I won't tell you what happened... everything fitted to a tee....She came to live with me....[In October, 1932, Mabel met Lillian Foster, and] we stayed together until four years ago when she passed away. So you can count how many years we lived together....I must have come out when I was eight years old. To tell the truth I never was in so I must have been out."

"The Old Moody Gardens Gang, 1950," Newsletter #8, Winter, 1984:

In Newsletter #7 we documented the old Moody Gardens Gang, a Lesbian community from Lowell, Massachusetts that began in the 1950s. The following letter was written by Jean, who was part of the original all-women's band which played at the Moody Gardens bar.

"Are you 'Gay'?"

I must have had a very stupid look on my face when Emma asked me that. If she had said "queer" or "lesbian" I would have known what she was talking about but the word "gay" didn't mean anything to me. When I realized what she meant I clung to the word, feeling at last a name I could swallow "gay"....

When I was asked to play at the "Silver Star Cafe" in the '50s there wasn't a place around for the gay people and the few friends you had found, would get together but always felt that fear of being asked to leave a bar or physically being hurt when you left the bar at night. But here was a chance to be myself and be accepted for what I was. We started playing Friday, Saturday and Sundays all day and within a short time you had to be there early to get a seat. The "kids" poured in and even though it was still a straight bar, we outnumbered the "straights" four to one and sometimes more than that. They came from all around, some travelling for two or three hours just for an evening with us. It was our "Mecca"; we were family and we had found a home.... ■

New England Cemetery

by Elana Dykewomon

Carved into branches some rocks shine.
Jade shines, and purple quartz.
Newspapers shine full of headlines,
these skulls shine beneath the corpse.

It's luxury the dead indulge in—
                              Narcissa and Polly,
                              the deacon's wife.

        Keeping it hushed
        with the handmade lace:
        what their lives where like.

                November air   sweet moss   old stone
                exact the price
                of married silence.

What luxury now
to lie stopped in the country by crooked rows.
No longer shrews or virgins,
their chipped names
                        rise and fall in relief
                        as the breath of women left alone.

Daughters free
for the first time
to caress their mother's bones,
three generations wide and deep.
No immigrant secrets left,
their bibles shut
& all children tucked in:

        Narcissa and Polly
        lie back with a laugh

        reflecting the elements.

Elana Dykewomon, *They Will Know Me By My Teeth*
(Northampton, MA: Magaera Press, 1976)

Patience and Sarah

by Isabel Miller

You come to me through the dark, when you need rest, when the snow is deep and blowing, when no sister is gracious about accompanying you, when your mother protests and your father threatens, you come to me. And now you known as well as I, that you cannot resist me. We both need the proof.

You are so much finer than I, noble, generous, devoted to freedom, unwilling to bully. But it is I, and the traits in which I differ from you, who will save us.

I love to alarm you by making my lips into a kiss when our chaperone is intent on her book. She could look up at any time, of course, and it makes the fun, watching you try to shake your head without shaking it, try to indicate her without moving. I stay reckless and imperious, not pitying your blush and your puffed-up throat, leaving it up to you whether to get us caught by leaving me there unanswered. You can always be made to answer, and then I bow my head and smile.

We even make some progress in reading. Your sisters, too, learn easily, I am fond of them, but I begin to be sorry that they are so fond of

Editor's Note: Patience and Sarah was originally self-published by Isabel Miller in 1969, and she distributed it out of a shopping bag she carried with her, until McGraw-Hill published it in 1972. This is an excerpt.

me. Now they will be as sorry to part from me as from you.

Sometimes I wonder how much of your love for me is gratitude for the ways I have made their lives more interesting. I have made them small gifts, such as cards and jack-straws, and of course the reading, if they are able to go on with it, can give them the world. You dream, I think, of the number of times your mother may be moved to smile. I suspect you of wanting to spend not only your own life but mine in adding to their pleasures. If I would let you, you would be happy to consider our love the weekly refreshment we need for going on with this main task.

As a teacher I groan for your wasted family, but as a woman I must choose only one of you to be devoted to.

Perhaps you are too young. At twenty-two, would I have left everything for love, as I ask you to? Even last year, at twenty-seven (to remember what I would rather forget), I couldn't go with you. But you are better than I. Everything depends on your being better than I. You have nothing to learn. You need only to be guided to recover what you always knew.

We are lying together on my winter bed in the kitchen, in a sweet afterwards.

"Stay by me. Live here," I say.

"You said to think on it, so I did. I think you

don't need me here and my folks do."

"Not need you! I need your warm body in bed and your—I *need* you."

"Not my work. You don't need that. And the folks do. Here I'd just be your pet, and get in your brother's hair."

I say, "Do you want another winter like this one?"

"Yes!"

"Exactly like this one?"

You bite your lip and pretend to think. "I'd settle," you say.

"Do you want ten more exactly like this one?"

"I'd settle."

"How about twenty-five? Fifty? We can live to be eighty. Who's to say we won't? Old maids often do."

"I hope we do."

"You hope to be tottering across the ice on your rickety brittle old bones every night of your seventy-fourth winter? Which will be my eightieth winter?"

Your eyes are so bright, laughing and unimpressed. You get up and creak around the room, to show me age seventy-four as it is usually experienced, and then leap to show the form it will take in you. I am rebuked that I believe in death. It is our whole difference, I see now. Believing in death has made me brave. It could do the same for you, but maybe there's no hurry. You charm me so, just as you are. Leap, leap you go, holding your skirt up to show me your legs. In lax and heathen York State, surely we can dance? You land so lightly in your soft blue stockings, washed and darned a thousand times. I love you.

In an old cracked voice you say, "Patience? Pate? Patty?" and peer for me everywhere and see me and become young and bound towards me. I curl up laughing, for I suspect that you intend to tickle me. You pry my body straight and lie on it and kiss me. "*Just like this, I'll settle*," you say.

It may take years. It may take age twenty-eight, to believe in death. I decide to enjoy the six years. I reach up and hold your face, luring you into a kiss. You are in no hurry. You like it up there, looking at me, making me wait. Before it can go to your head I pull you down and we join

our mouths together in a seal I am willing to make permanent and then someone says, "*What are you doing?*" not gentle or in sympathy or in any way that belongs in the same room with love, and I consider who might be capable of such an offense.

Who but Martha?

You pull up from me and stand, oh greatly agitated. I almost think you may run out without your shoes or wraps. I sit up and take your hand. "Settle down, darling," I say.

You look at me wildly. I smile. "It's nothing," I say. And then you're not afraid either. You are not a coward. You are not afraid that I am. I am so relieved that I am not, just as I hoped not to be.

Martha stares a while. I don't suppose she wants an answer. I don't suppose there can be any need to ask of two people with disarrayed hair and opened bodies who are lying in bed and kissing so deeply they can't hear someone come in, what are you doing? I stand beside you, holding your hand, and wait for her to go away. She doesn't, and then I neaten your clothes and hair, and mine, and neaten the bed, and tug the rope that lifts it back to the ceiling. Edward will be along.

He pounds the door vigorously and waits until I call, "Come in." His wife should take up the custom. Perhaps she will in the future. He never has before. It is not the country way. My poor brother. He would like very much to see our embrace, and so he concludes he mustn't.

But I don't despise his decency and honor. I rely on them.

You are on the bench, looking into the fire. I am at the wheel. He goes to the window and looks at it. It is too frosty to look through. We say nothing. I will not be forward and unwomanly and set him against us. I meekly wait. He clears his throat, and then clears it again.

"I hoped all this was done with," he says.

I say nothing, and of course you don't.

He says, "Have you prayed to be free of it?"

I say, "I meant to. Last summer I got as far as my knees." (You turn and stare at me. Well, darling, of course there are some things about me you don't know.)

"But didn't pray?" he asks.

"I found I didn't wish to be freed of it."

Gravely he says, "The Devil wouldn't let you pray."

"I prayed. But not for that. I prayed to be fulfilled in it."

He thinks it over. It is impressive that God didn't strike me with lightning for such a prayer. There is a chance that God is not offended.

I must leave everything for Edward to think of. I wait.

"Martha's upset," he says.

I say, "I'm sorry."

"She says she hoo-hooed pretty loud and you didn't hear."

I bow my head.

"She says it could've been anybody. One of the children. A neighbor. It's God's blessing she was the one."

"Yes."

"She feels you must be made to stop. Can you tell me you will try?"

I am silent.

He says, "She wasn't told about the other time."

"Thank you."

"So she thinks it's still a bud that can be nipped."

Now there is a long silence.

He says, "I won't be rushed. I need time to think this through. Martha can't make up my mind for me. I have to meditate and pray."

"I'll do the same," I say.

"Good day, Miss Dowling," he says, looking at you for the first time. He is taking your measure. Your worth is clear to see. I trust he sees it. In any case, he likes you.

"Mr. White," you say shyly, and nod.

He goes. I sit beside you on the bench. You put your arm around me. I lean against your side.

"What do you think he'll do?" you ask.

"I think he'll ask me to leave. I needn't, though. I am protected by my father's will. We needn't go until you want to."

"If we don't go, then he'll do something else. Like keep me away. Should I come tomorrow?"

"Of course. We won't stop anything we can still do."

"Patty?" you say, "Patty, did you know Martha was going to come in?"

"No. But I knew someday somebody would."

Martha and I meet in the barn. It is early morning. She sits at her cow and I at mine. The milk hisses into our pails. She wants to remark but can't decide how to begin. I won't help her.

"I always knew there was something wrong with you," she says. That needn't have taken so much thought. She could have blurted that out first thing. "Many times I've tried to make Edward see it, but no."

"He wouldn't see?" I ask, pleased.

"Oh, no! Not *his* sister! Nothing could be wrong with *his* sister! How many times I said it, 'Edward, she means to make you keep her all her life. She means not to marry and do her part,' and he'd just say, 'Oh, she's young yet.' Young!"

"Good Edward," I say.

"Well, now he's got to see. Spoiled and indulged like a princess! And see what comes of it. If I had my way you'd soon be glad to marry like any other woman, and not too fussy who, and do your part. Nothing but spoiled. What made you think you needn't marry except pure spoiled? And think you could do things man and wife don't do?"

"Kiss? Don't you kiss?" I am very curious. I have had no such confidences before. To skirt so close to someone else's secret life! Yes. I am curious.

"I won't say," she says. With stool and pail she flounces to her next cow. "Not like that we don't. I wouldn't care to. Not like that."

I say, "Well, of course, if you wouldn't care to—"

"I wasn't brought up that way."

(But I wasn't either.)

She says, "Wait till I tell Edward how you've been this morning. Cool as a pirate, not an ounce of decent shame in you. It's a *sin*, you know. I don't expect Edward remembered to mention that to you. Saint Paul forbids it."

"He does?"

"With all your Bible reading and Bible pictures, you don't know that? And your fronts all open like no-good Jezebels, and not caring who might walk in and find you, and *her not even in the family!*"

I am astonished. "Martha—Sister—" I begin, but I am too astonished to go on. And perhaps she doesn't realize what she has said.

It is afternoon. I am at my table, painting Saul on the road to Damascus. There's a tap at my door and then I hear it open. That will be Martha with her Bible.

She sits down half across the table from me. "I had some trouble finding the passage," she says. "It's not one I expected to have a need for."

I say, "You see, you put my mind on Paul. Here comes Saul, the raging wolf with all his attendants, who will all be wolfish too—perhaps you can't tell at this stage. But, see, the road bends, and we can see, although Saul can't, that in just about one minute he will be knocked flat by love and rise up Saint Paul."

"I expect you want to claim that's what happened to you."

"No."

"Well, don't because here's what he says," and Martha reads in her false flat reading voice: "'Wherefore God also gave them up to uncleanness through the lusts of their own hearts, to dishonor their own bodies between themselves: who changed the truth of God into a lie, and worshipped and served the creature more than the Creator, who is blessed forever. Amen. For this cause God gave them up unto vile affections: for even their women did change the natural use into that which is against nature: And likewise also the men, leaving the natural use of the women, burned in their lust toward one another; men with men working that which is unseemly, and receiving in themselves that recompence of their error which was meet. And even as they did not like to retain God in their knowledge, God gave them over to a reprobate mind, to do those things which are not convenient; being filled with all unrighteousness, covetousness, maliciousness; fully of envy, murder, debate, deceit, proud, boasters, inventors of evil things, disobedient to

parents, without understanding, covenantbreakers, without natural affection, implacable, unmerciful: who knowing the judgment of God, that they which commit such things are worthy of death, not only do the same, but have pleasure in them that do them. Therefore thou art inexcusable, O man, whosoever thou art that judgest; for wherein thou judgest another, thou condemnest thyself; for thou that judgest doest the same things.'"

Martha doesn't like the drift of the last part, so she stops there.

The condemnation is powerful indeed. I cannot answer it. I must bear it. May God save my heart for love, despite Saint Paul.

"I see you thought you could argue it away, but you can't," Martha says.

"No. He says it. He says I am worthy of death. So be it."

I continue to paint. She watches against her will. Everybody likes to see a painter at work. She needn't be ashamed.

Since I cannot dispute Saint Paul, we sit in silence. My house smells good, from a cake I am baking for you. It is snug here and pretty and quiet and fragrant. Martha is bothered by the seductions of my house. She starts to go, but doesn't. Close by my side, alarmingly close, she lingers and says, "It could've been so sweet, working and helping each other here. It was what I thought about. It was what I thought would be. Edward and you and me together. And then you didn't like me anymore, and I forgot I liked you, and I just lately remembered. Do you remember we used to like each other?"

Keeping such distance as I can, I say, "Yes."

"I get so lonesome with just Edward. We don't kiss. There's something he does to me, but we don't kiss. We're not sweet together. And the children. And the girl. She's no better than you were, Patience. She's sullen too. So many times I wish I could sit by you of an evening, but I expect you wouldn't want that."

How cruel and cold to leave her there, unhugged, unreceived. But she's too late. I am yours now, and my hugs are only yours.

She says, "No, you wouldn't." (Her voice hard again.) "You've got those Dowlings trooping in here every night, and them not even in the family."

She and her Bible go. I am uneasy. What would Saul have done if love had flung him down and then decided not to keep him after all?

♀♀

Edward has finished two days of meditation and prayer. He is here to tell me my fate. I sit with my hands folded, meekly ready to accept it, in case it is a fate I am willing to accept.

"You have made a great mistake," he begins. "These are the passions marriage is meant to discourage and then extinguish. At first we imagine and hope, but in marriage we learn we are not wanted. But we find solace in work and in making the world go. I speak of men. I have no idea what women feel or want. Have you?"

"No. Not in general."

"Most people manage well enough with marriage and work, but what's to become of you? You have wakened feelings marriage can't help you with. You let them wake, and you let them grow, and you took pleasure in thinking of them, and here we are. As to work, I honestly don't see how a woman's work uses her mind enough to help her this way. She can't fight these feelings by work. The only hope is not to let them wake."

"But here we are," I say, quite timidly. I do, in fact, feel timid. I have taken a terrible risk. His power is very real. I am grateful to Martha for telling me that he cares more for me than he ever seemed to. Except for knowing this, I might not be able to bear the frights of this confrontation.

"Have you decided?"

"I considered all the things I might do," he says. "First was the possibility of turning my back on it all and letting it go on. But Martha found you, and someday the children could, or a neighbor, and then the family is disgraced and the children unmarriageable. I confess I couldn't be quite blind. I turned my back all this while, I confess, and here we are."

"Yes."

"Next was asking the girl's father to keep her away, as he did before. It would mean brute force, considering the feelings you've encouraged in each other. It would be difficult, but duty often is. It's what Martha wants."

Oh praise God for Martha! Except that she wants this, it is what he would do.

He says, "I think the end of such a course would be that I had to declare you mad and build you a cage in the loft."

I am shocked. I haven't thought of this at all.

"But I'm not mad," I say.

"No. But you soon would be."

"Yes."

"And there's grounds to question that it would be best to drive you mad. It's a blot on a family, madness. I think it's not my duty to bring it on."

"I hope not," I choke.

"You spoke last year of wanting to go to Genesee."

To hide my relief and pleasure—because I don't want him to think that he is shirking the duty of punishing me—I say, "That has come to seem unreasonable."

"I thought so at the time."

"Yes, I know you did."

"It's the only solution I see now. It needn't be to Genesee, of course. But I can't let you stay here."

"Our father's will—" I say, knowing Edward must have thought of it. I don't want to think of an objection he hasn't anticipated and dismissed.

"I am prepared to make a money settlement for your property here."

"But then my subsistence. Who can say how much it might be worth over the years?"

"Woman! Are you trying to drive a hard bargain? You are in no position to." He frowns magnificently. We are a handsome family. I hope that God will someday give Edward, too, the great task he longs for. "You can trust me to be fair."

"I know I can, Edward. When must I go?"

"You are not helpless. You are in good health, and you know how to do all the female things, and how to keep school."

"Yes. When must I go?"

"And she'll be with you, I assume. At least there can be no children. The two of you alone can manage, if you'll go where land is cheap and the arts you know are wanted."

"How soon?" I say.

"The sin is for your own soul to bear. I've done what I can if I protect my family."

What can I say to reassure him that he is being harsh enough?

I try. "To leave the home my father built me! The protection of my brother! His children! My friends!" To say it is to see some truth in it. My tears are quite unexpected and unforced, almost guileless.

"You might have thought of that before," he says, feeling better.

"Couldn't Sarah just live here with me?" He can tell Martha that I begged for that, but that he was strong and cruel.

"I'm not obliged to keep her in food and shoes, to let her be an example to my daughters."

I submit and say no more, but think sad true thoughts to bring the tears along.

He says, "There's a parcel of land I can turn into money. I'll have it soon."

"It's winter!" I say.

"If you want to make a crop this year, you should be starting. It won't be long. Can you be-have yourself, knowing it won't be long? There can be no more in this house."

I nod.

"Tell me there will be no more in this house. I know your nods."

"There will be no more in this house." I'm afraid it will be easy to keep this promise. I pray that my feeling can flow again when we have built our private place.

He says, "I'll draw up the papers. You can't squander your birthright and then come back. Don't expect to."

"No."

"You'll need a map. I can spare you one."

"Thank you."

He pushes back his chair and gets up. At the door he turns and says, "Would you really rather go than give her up?"

I risk the truth. "Yes, Edward."

He shakes his head. "So be it," he says, and opens the door to go. Again he turns. "But what do you *do*?" he asks.

My maidenly blush calls forth in him a manly blush. He does not stay for answer.

I must see you. There is no time to lose. I am flinging on my cloak to go to you, when I notice that it is almost evening already. You will soon be here, perhaps before I can get my milking done.

No matter who comes with you, I will speak.

⚢

You bring the one I would have chosen, your mother. She is not awkward now, knowing my affection for her. I take her hand and lead her to the fireside. You must make your own way.

"I have news," I say.

Your mother says, "I hope good."

"I'll tell you, and let you decide which. I'm going to the west." I feel you start and tighten.

She says, "Oh! When?" and although she must have had some idea she has to stop and blow her nose and look away.

"It could be as little as a week. Whenever my brother gets my money for me."

"Oh. In such weather?"

"It's none too early. I have a long way to go and I want to buy land and get a start this year."

"It's a chancy step," she says.

"Yes, it is. But I've wanted it for a long time. Last summer when I kept school, I made up sto-ries for the children about the frontier, when I was supposed to be reading them the Bible."

She smiles weakly. "I'll miss you. We all will."

"I want to take Sarah with me."

"I figured."

"I knew you did."

I turn to you. "Will you?"

You stride around my kitchen. "Going's a different thing to making up stories," you say. "You got no more idea than a jaybird," you say. "Just when I can be some good here," you say.

You keep on pacing. Your mother and I wait.

You say, "I want to. But is that any reason? When I can be some good here finally?"

You mean, is it right to choose pleasure over duty? Can you yield to a longing for kisses, when other people's necessities are at stake? Nothing you ever heard of tells you you have a right to choose me. I hoped you'd thought this through before. I may have to go without you. There may not be time, before, for you to face and learn to endure your own necessities. When I am gone you will, and then I will send for you.

"I'll be going anyway," I say, to let you know that I am being compelled to go. "First will you do something for me?"

"Anything!"

"Stand still and let me measure you. I have a length of goods I can't look at without thinking of your hair."

"Oh, no!"

"You said, 'Anything.'"

You press your lips together, a stubborn child, but I will not let you off. What are you to travel in if I do? I bring my measure and make you stand. Your mother keeps the notes. She draws numerals very nicely now. I suppose she's been practicing in the hearth dust.

(You see, sweetheart, it's not so bad to be measured when I do it.)

"What'll Pa say about me living off of him all winter and then leaving again as spring comes on?"

Your mother says, "He'll say nothing."

I see a new Mrs. Dowling. Women are not so very powerless after all. He will say nothing. She should make up her mind more often. ▪

Prolong the Night

by Renée Vivien

...If it was permitted to Sappho to ask in her prayers
"that the night be doubled for her," why should I not
dare, on my turn, implore a similar favor...

                  —Libanios.

Prolong the night, Goddess who set us aflame!
Hold back from us the golden-sandalled dawn!
Already on the sea the first faint gleam
      Of day is coming on.

Sleeping under your veils, protect us yet,
Having forgotten the cruelty day may give!
The wine of darkness, wine of the stars let
      Overwhelm us with love!

Since no one knows what dawn will come,
Bearing the dismal future with its sorrows
In its hands, we tremble at full day, our dream
      Fears all tomorrows.

Oh! keeping our hands on our still-closed eyes,
Let us vainly recall the joys that take flight!
Goddess who delights in the ruin of the rose,
      Prolong the night!

From *The Muse of the Violets* [1923/24] (1977), trans. from the French by Margaret Porter and Catharine Kroger. Tallahassee: Naiad Press.

The Touch

by Renée Vivien

The trees have kept some lingering sun in their branches.
Veiled like a woman, evoking another time,
The twilight passes, weeping. My fingers climb,
Trembling, provocative, the line of your haunches.

My ingenious fingers wait when they have found
The petal flesh beneath the robe they part.
How curious, complex, the touch, this subtle art—
As the dream of fragrance, the miracle of sound.

I follow slowly the graceful contours of your hips,
The curves of your shoulders, your neck, your unappeased
      breasts.
In your white voluptuousness my desire rests,
Swooning, refusing itself the kisses of your lips.

From *The Muse of the Violets* (1923/24) 1977, trans. from the French by Margaret Porter and Catharine Kroger. Tallahassee: Naiad Press.

The Well of Loneliness

by Radclyffe Hall

The first faint breath of spring was in the air, bringing daffodils to the flower-stalls of Paris. Once again Mary's young cherry tree in the garden was pushing out leaves and tiny pink buds along the whole length of its childish branches.

Then Martin wrote; 'Stephen, where can I see you? It must be alone. Better not at your house, I think, if you don't mind, because of Mary.'

She appointed the place. They would meet at the Auberge du Vieux Logis in the Rue Lepic. They two would meet there on the following evening. When she left the house without saying a word, Mary thought she was going to Valérie Seymour.

Stephen sat down at a table in the corner to await Martin's coming—she herself was early. The table was gay with a new check cloth—red, and white, white and red, she counted the squares, tracing them carefully out with her finger. The woman behind the bar nudged her companion: 'En violà une originale—et quelle cicatrice, bon Dieu!' The scar across Stephen's pale face stood out livid.

Martin came and sat quietly down at her side, ordering some coffee for appearances' sake. For appearances' sake, until it was brought, they smiled at each other and made conversation. But

This is an excerpt from the novel, originally published in 1928.

when the waiter had turned away, Martin said: 'It's all over—you've beaten me, Stephen…The bond was too strong.'

Their unhappy eyes met as she answered: 'I tried to strengthen that bond.'

He nodded: 'I know…Well, my dear, you succeeded.' Then he said: 'I'm leaving Paris next week'; and in spite of his effort to be calm his voice broke, 'Stephen…do what you can to take care of Mary…'

She found that she was holding his hand. Or was it someone else who sat there beside him, who looked into his sensitive, troubled face, who spoke such queer words?

'No, don't go—not yet.'

'But I don't understand…'

'You must trust me, Martin.' And now she heard herself speaking very gravely: 'Would you trust me enough to do anything I asked, even although it seemed rather strange? Would you trust me if I said that I asked it for Mary, for her happiness?'

His finger tightened: 'Before God, yes. You know that I'd trust you!'

'Very well then, don't leave Paris—not now.'

'You really want me to stay on, Stephen?'

'Yes, I can't explain.'

He hesitated, then he suddenly seemed to come to a decision: 'All right…I'll do whatever you ask me.'

They paid for their coffee and got up to

leave: 'Let me come as far as the house,' he pleaded.

But she shook her head: 'No, no, not now. I'll write to you...very soon...Good-bye, Martin.'

She watched him hurrying down the street, and when he was finally lost in its shadows, she turned slowly and made her own way up the hill, past the garish lights of the Moulin de la Galette. Its pitiful sails revolved in the wind, eternally grinding out petty sins—dry chaff blown in from the gutters of Paris. And after a while, having breasted the hill, she must climb a dusty flight of stone steps, and push open a heavy, slow-moving door; the door of the mighty temple of faith that keeps its anxious but tireless vigil.

She had no idea why she was doing this thing, or what she would say to the silver Christ with one hand on His heart and the other held out in a patient gesture of supplication. The sound of praying, monotonous, low, insistent, rose up from those who prayed with extended arms, with crucified arms—like the tides of an ocean it swelled and receded and swelled again, bathing the shores of heaven.

They were calling upon the Mother of God: 'Sainte Marie, Mère de Dieu, priez pour nous, pauvres pécheurs, maintenant et à l'heure de notre mort.'

'Et à l'heure de notre mort,' Stephen heard herself repeating.

He looked terribly weary, the silver Christ: 'But then He always looks tired,' she thought vaguely; and she stood there without finding anything to say, embarrassed as one so frequently is in the presence of somebody else's sorrow. For herself she felt nothing, neither pity nor regret; she was curiously empty of all sensation, and after a little she left the church, to walk on through the windswept streets of Montmartre.

Chapter Fifty-Six

1

Valérie stared at Stephen in amazement: 'But...it's such an extraordinary thing you're asking! Are you sure you're right to take such a step?

For myself I care nothing; why should I care? If you want to pretend that you're my lover, well, my dear, to be quite frank, I wish it were true—I feel certain you'd make a most charming lover. All the same,' and now her voice sounded anxious, 'this is not a thing to be done lightly, Stephen. Aren't you being absurdly self-sacrificing? You can give the girl a very great deal.'

Stephen shook her head: 'I can't give her protection or happiness, and yet she won't leave me. There's only one way...'

Then Valérie Seymour, who had always shunned tragedy like the plague, flared out in something very like temper: 'Protection! Protection! I'm sick of the word. Let her do without it; aren't you enough for her? Good heavens, you're worth twenty Mary Llewellyns! Stephen, think it over before you decide—it seems mad to me. For God's sake keep the girl, and get what happiness you can out of life.'

'No, I can't do that,' said Stephen dully.

Valérie got up: 'Being what you are, I suppose you can't—you were made for a martyr! Very well, I agree'; she finished abruptly, 'though of all the curious situations that I've ever been in, this one beats the lot!'

That night Stephen wrote to Martin Hallam.

2

Two days later as she crossed the street to her house, Stephen saw Martin in the shadow of the archway. He stepped out and they faced each other on the pavement. He had kept his word; it was just ten o'clock.

He said: 'I've come. Why did you send for me, Stephen?'

She answered heavily: 'Because of Mary.'

And something in her face made him catch his breath, so that the questions died on his lips: 'I'll do whatever you want,' he murmured.

'It's so simple,' she told him, 'it's all perfectly simple. I want you to wait just under this arch—just here where you can't be seen from the house. I want you to wait until Mary needs you, as I think she will...it may not be long...Can I count on your being here if she needs you?'

He nodded: 'Yes—yes!' He was utterly bewildered, scared too by the curious look in her eyes; but he allowed her to pass him and enter the courtyard.

3

She let herself into the house with her latchkey. The place seemed full of an articulate silence that leapt out shouting from every corner—a jibing, grimacing, vindictive silence. She brushed it aside with a sweep of her hand, as though it were some sort of physical presence.

But who was it who brushed that silence aside? Not Stephen Gordon...oh, no, surely not...Stephen Gordon was dead; she had died last night: 'A` l'heure de notre mort....' Many people had spoken those prophetic words quite a short time ago—perhaps they had been thinking of Stephen Gordon.

Yet now someone was slowly climbing the stairs, then pausing upon the landing to listen, then opening the doors of Mary's bedroom, then standing quite still and staring at Mary. It was someone whom David knew and loved well; he sprang forward with a sharp little bark of welcome. But Mary shrank back as though she had been struck—Mary pale and red-eyed from sleeplessness—or was it because of excessive weeping?

When she spoke her voice sounded unfamiliar: 'Where were you last night?'

'With Valérie Seymour. I thought you'd know somehow...It's better to be frank...we both hate lies...'

Came that queer voice again: 'Good God— and I've tried so hard not to believe it! Tell me you're lying to me now; say it, Stephen!'

Stephen—then she wasn't dead after all; or was she? But now Mary was clinging—clinging.

'Stephen, I can't believe this thing—Valérie! Is that why you always repulse me...why you never want to come near me these days. Stephen, answer me; are you her lover? Say something, for Christ's sake! Don't stand there dumb...'

A mist closing down, a thick black mist. Someone pushing the girl away, without speaking. Mary's queer voice coming out of the gloom, muffled by the folds of that thick black mist, only a word here and there getting through: 'All my life I've given...you've killed...I loved you...Cruel, oh, cruel! You're unspeakably cruel...' Then the sound of rough and pitiful sobbing.

No, assuredly this was not Stephen Gordon who stood there unmoved by such pitiful sobbing. But what was the figure doing in the mist? It was moving about, distractedly, wildly. All the while it sobbed it was moving about: 'I'm going...'

Going? But where could it go? Somewhere out of the mist, somewhere into the light? Who was it that had said...wait, what were the words? 'To give light to them that sit in darkness...'

No one was moving about any more—there was only a dog, a dog called David. Something had to be done. Go into the bedroom, Stephen Gordon's bedroom that faced on the courtyard...just a few short steps and then the window. A girl, hatless, with the sun falling full on her hair...she was almost running...she stumbled a little. But now there were two people down in the courtyard—a man had his hands on the girl's bowed shoulders. He questioned her, yes, that was it, he questioned; and the girl was telling him why she was there, why she had fled from that thick, awful darkness. He was looking at the house, incredulous, amazed; hesitating as though he were coming in; but the girl went on and the man turned to follow...They were side by side, he was gripping her arm...They were gone; they had passed out under the archway.

Then all in a moment the stillness was shattered: 'Mary, come back! Come back to me, Mary!'

David crouched and trembled. He had crawled to the bed, and he lay there watching with his eyes of amber; trembling because such an anguish as this struck across him like the lash of a whip, and what could he do, the poor beast, in his dumbness?

She turned and saw him, but only for a moment, for now the room seemed to be thronging with people. Who were they, these strangers with the miserable eyes? And yet, were they all strangers? Surely that was Wanda? And someone with a neat little hole in her side—Jamie clasping Barbara by the hand; Barbara with the white flowers of death on her bosom. Oh, but they were many, these unbidden guests, and they called very softly at first and then louder. Aye, and those lost and terrible brothers from Alec's, they were here, and they also were calling: 'Stephen, Stephen, speak with your God and ask Him why He has left us forsaken!' She could see their marred and reproachful faces with the haunted, melancholy eyes of the invert—eyes that had looked too long on a world that lacked all pity and all understanding: 'Stephen, Stephen, speak with your God and ask Him why he has left us forsaken!' And these terrible ones started pointing at her with their shaking, white-skinned, effeminate fingers: 'You and your kind have stolen our birthright; you have taken our strength and have given us your weakness!' They were pointing at her with white, shaking fingers.

Rockets of pain, burning rockets of pain—their pain, her pain, all welded together into one great consuming agony. Rockets of pain that shot up and burst, dropping scorching tears of fire on the spirit—her pain, their pain...all the misery at Alec's. And the press and the clamour of those countless others—they fought, they trampled, they were getting her under. In their madness to become articulate through her, they were tearing her to pieces, getting her under. They were everywhere now, cutting off her retreat; neither bolts nor bars would avail to save her. The walls fell down and crumbled before them; at the cry of their suffering the walls fell and crumbled: 'We are coming, Stephen—we are still coming on, and our name is legion—you dare not disown us!' She raised her arms, trying to ward them off, but they closed in and in: 'You dare not disown us!'

They possessed her. Her barren womb became fruitful—it ached with its fearful and sterile burden. It ached with the fierce yet helpless children who would clamour in vain for their right to salvation. They would turn first to God, and then to the world, and then to her. They would cry out accusing: 'We have asked for bread; will you give us a stone? Answer us: will you give us a stone? You, God, in Whom we, the outcast, believe; you, world, into which we are pitilessly born; you, Stephen, who have drained our cup to the dregs—we have asked for bread; will you give us a stone?'

And now there was only one voice, one demand; her own voice into which those millions had entered. A voice like the awful, deep rolling of thunder; a demand like the gathering together of great waters. A terrifying voice that made her ears throb, that made her brain throb, that shook her very entrails, until she must stagger and all but fall beneath this appalling burden of sound that strangled her in its will to be uttered.

'God,' she gasped, 'we believe; we have told You we believe...We have not denied You, then rise up and defend us. Acknowledge us, oh God, before the whole world. Give us also the right to our existence!' ▪

Elsa: I Come With My Songs
The Autobiography of Elsa Gidlow
by Elsa Gidlow

Then, in the year 1924, on a soft, rainy weekend, I got married. Quite unintentionally. Tommy said, "Marry me for tonight." The ring was slipped on my finger without witness or benefit of clergy. Who could imagine we would be together for thirteen years—"till death did us part."

Tommy—Violet Winifred Leslie Henry-Anderson—was for years an almost mythical character I used to hear spoken of by my Montreal friends Estelle, Roswell, and Harcourt. Actually, it was "Tommy and Mona." They came into conversation paired, like salt and pepper. But Tommy, in the comments and gossip, seemed to call forth more admiration than her companion. I had never heard anyone refer to her with other than pleasure and respect. I used to think: Why can't I meet a woman like that? I never thought I should meet her. She had moved far across Canada to British Columbia, and was in an apparently indissoluble bond with the younger woman, Mona.

Both had lived in Montreal for a short time, when Tommy left Edinburgh after the breakup of her home due to some unfortunate defection of her barrister father and subsequent loss of fortune. Her elder sister, Joan, moved to London, her two elder brothers migrated to different parts of

Canada. Tommy chose Montreal at the start because her money would take her no further. She had never expected to work. She was born to ease, had devoted herself to sports and books, was a golfer, and had played in women's amateur championships. When disaster struck the family, she was world runner-up and aiming at top honors.

Instead, she had to consider how to earn her living. She knitted ties of a kind that were worn by upper class men and women. British women wore tweedy and tailored suits until it was time to "dress for dinner." The knitting earned her enough, along with what her family could contribute, to put her through secretarial school. Recommended by her father's associates, she found work in law offices as a legal secretary. In a few years she became expert and felt confident enough to dare the new world. She was as knowledgeable in law as many of the lawyers for whom she worked. In our day she would have become a lawyer. At the beginning of the century, such a step was unheard of.

Tommy and Mona Shelley met in Montreal. Mona wanted to go on the stage. She was a protégé of Harcourt Farmer, and had acted in some of his productions surviving somehow in the Bohemian circles. Then Tommy fell in love with her, and they left together for Vancouver seven or eight years before my time. They were a legend by then, lingering in my thoughts wistfully as the only living lesbians anyone I knew had known.

Excerpts from the autobiography, originally published in 1986 by Booklegger Press and Druid Heights Books, San Francisco.

Later, in New York City, Harcourt had written that Mona would be arriving any day. Still stage-struck, she intended to remain there and try to break into acting. The inference was that Tommy might follow, but I learned later that had been Mona's hope, not Tommy's. Roswell had brought Mona to meet me one evening. She was a cuddly, puppy-like young woman, maybe a few years older than me, outgoing and physically energetic. Except for her good voice, I could not see her as an actress. She was convinced there were parts she could take and was haunting managers, producers, and casting agents. Roswell and Mona went to plays together, and she was frequently at the studio. I was surprised when she made advances to me. This was shortly after my breakup with Muriel. Roswell may have told her about it.

I asked her about Tommy. "Oh, she wouldn't mind if we made love. She never wanted to bind me."

"Is Tommy coming to join you?" I had no wish to cut in to their relationship, which had always been referred to as ideal.

"She might if she could get work."

Mona and I did kiss and cuddle and make superficial love a few times. I was very lonely. Mona never meant much to me. I liked her as one would a kitten that purrs her way into your affections. Mona was living with a teacher named Miss Jonas. I never heard a first name. Miss Jonas was "in love" with Mona but adamantly refused to make love. This was all becoming very complicated. Once more I asked, "But what about Tommy?" Tommy, she said, knew about Miss Jonas.

I was in my last months with *The New Pearson's* when we needed a secretary to help me with my many new duties. Mona asked eagerly: "May I tell Tommy? Would you—they—consider her?"

I certainly would. *Pearson's* management left it to me. Violet Winifred Leslie Henry-Anderson arrived with excellent credentials and joined the staff. During the months before the magazine's move to Chicago, she was "Miss Anderson" to me, one who "belonged" to Mona. She found a place to live. Mona was with her when she was not with Miss Jonas. I did not know what was transpiring or if Miss Anderson would remain in New York. Our association in the office was strictly business.

In a sense I was immune to a new relationship by my continuing pain over Muriel's defection. The abysmal depression I have described was gathering and efforts to "save" the magazine were absorbing my remaining energies. When it became certain that *The New Pearson's* would move to Chicago, I felt very badly about telling Miss Anderson. She was so efficient, had such good recommendations, I was sure she would have no trouble finding a new job if she decided to remain in New York. She said, quietly, she thought she would—until Mona "made up her mind."

The best I could do to help her was to introduce her to the editor of *The Forum*, who later gave me freelance work. It turned out that his secretary was leaving, and he immediately engaged Miss Anderson. Ultimately, Mona refused to go back to Vancouver. She was sure of at least two acting prospects. And she was in love with Miss Jonas. She seemed to have the idea that she could keep Tommy as her physical lover and Miss Jonas as her "pure beloved." Neither Tommy nor Miss Jonas would have any of it. Tommy was being very quiet, but I knew felt deeply betrayed at being enticed to New York, which she immediately disliked. She loved and needed outdoor life, where she could play her beloved game of golf. She was living in an expensive, cramped little room. She had not decided whether, with or without Mona, she would return to Vancouver. She had friends of many years there and was a member of a club. At the moment, she wished to find a better place to live.

Roswell was by now established with Khagen in Brooklyn. I had the studio to myself. I asked Tommy if she would care to share it, taking over Roswell's half. She immediately agreed. At the time we came to live together and become friends, I was working with Gough in the bookstore. There is no doubt that from our first meeting I had felt a strong attraction for Tommy, but as I said, I regarded her as committed to Mona. Now that was ended. Tommy, it turned out, had been equally drawn to me. But, with English reserve and quixotic propriety, we both behaved as though we had no interest in one another beyond what the business of the day required. Until that rainy weekend.

We had been sharing the studio for a few days, bringing in Tommy's possessions, mainly clothing, golf clubs, a suitcase of books. I had made dinner one evening. She couldn't cook, it turned out, and disliked doing it. The next evening she invited me out. We found a place where we could order bootleg wine served in demitasse cups. For the first time we talked frankly about ourselves, our lesbianism, our commitment to women. She told me about her life in Scotland, mourning for the beauty of the Highlands. She discussed a little of her early love life there: a disastrous love for a woman she had never ceased to love, who was committed to men, although as girls they had been lovers. She said little of her disappointment over Mona, enough for me to know that it cut deep, more for the way the break had been handled, than for the loss itself. Suddenly she looked straight at me, an altered expression in her grey-green eyes:

"But if she had not deceived me about her intentions in bringing me here, I should have not met you."

"Is—that important?"

She put out her cigarette in silence, reached across the table and took my hand. "It could be." That was all. Then we both became silent and shy. I do not know if her heart was beating as mine was. The waiter came and took away the dishes, poured more wine into the coffee cups from a disguised container and asked if we would like dessert. Soon we went home, that night each to our own beds.

It was the next evening, Friday, that she took from her finger one of three gold rings she wore, and placed it on the traditional "engagement" finger of my left hand, saying, "Marry me for tonight." Her two remaining rings were on the little finger of her left hand.

The woman whose eyes I looked into as she held my hand with her ring seemed to have been long known: that I knew so little about her was of no significance. She *felt* familiar when her arms went round me and we held one another close. I responded to the gentle strength of her athletic body. When I opened my eyes, I liked the honesty

of her fine-featured face, the wide clear forehead from which the light-brown, wavy hair was drawn back to a knot at the back of her head.

I do not remember our first kiss: there were so many as we lay together on my couch that they merged as if into one continuous kiss I had waited for a long time. And the love-making was different from what had transpired with Muriel. More *real* is the only way I can put it, than the almost disabling excitement of that brief romantic affair. I was not only transported as then, but satisfied.

Is there any better way to become deeply familiar with a new lover and friend-to-be than to spend two rainy days and nights alone? We were body to body in bed exploring passion and satiety, now held close in sleep or half sleep, now in dressing gown or pajamas beside the fire laughing over an impoverished meal, or enjoying toasted English muffins with Dundee ginger marmalade. Tommy had brought a gift of the Scotch marmalade.

Whether we lay touching or caressing one another, or quietly talking, she was equally easy to be with. I liked her matter-of-fact self-acceptance. It reinforced or corroborated my own deep conviction that I had a right to be, to love, according to my nature.

Tommy was able to tell me more than I had ever suspected of women's passionate, romantic involvement with one another. In the Edinburgh upper classes and among her golfing associates, there were many such liaisons, she said.

"Did they make love?"

"Of course—those who did not get married, and even those who did for economic or family reasons. An heir was needed. Or they did not like being 'old maids.' Once married they were freer anyway. The men went off to posts in India, Africa, or the Colonies."

"And when they were left alone?"

"Some quietly turned back to one another."

"No one criticized or condemned?"

"People may not have thought, or known, there could be anything to condemn. Some people imagine women have no bodies below the navel."

We drew closer to one another—"below the navel," laughing. She asked me if I had heard the story about Queen Victoria's response to women's relationships. As we lay beside one another listening to the gentle rain, she told the following story. A proposed law concerning sexual practices between men, then called buggery or sodomy, was set before Queen Victoria for approval. Then someone asked if women should not also be included in the legal strictures. "Women!" she is reported to have laughed, "what could the poor things do?"

Little did she know. Throughout the European continent and in England, even among Victoria's own court ladies, women were finding and loving each other, some in lifelong relationships.

"In talking with Frank Harris I had learned a little about that," I told her.

"You discussed that with him!"

"He guessed about me, probably from reading my poetry to women, and from what he considered my 'boyishness.' He sometimes called me *androgyne*. He thought I should write about it frankly, in prose as well as poetry."

Tommy wasn't sure that would be advisable. "You probably wouldn't get it published." Tommy's general feeling was, then and later, what the average person did not know wouldn't hurt them.

"Remember the Oscar Wilde-Alfred Douglas affair? They were welcome in all the best homes in London until Queensbury precipitated the scandal. Most people were aware in those sophisticated circles what was going on. You know the British attitude: keep the small conventions, maintain the proprieties, and you can break the large ones. If you tell people, and they are forced to recognize what we are doing, or even thinking about, they imagine we are obliging them to accept what they may consider, or believe others may consider, unconventional—or worse. If superficial decorum is kept, they can be spared that responsibility, and we'll not be bothered.

"You mean we are the beneficiaries of a tacit innocence or ignorance, but not real good will or tolerance?" She wasn't sure, but felt it was unwise to test the average person too far.

Tommy had no trouble as a lesbian, even in western Canada. Friends in Vancouver all knew that she and Mona were together and had lived so for years. The couple did not conceal their affection or commitment. If Tommy arrived alone at a gathering or sports event, one friend, Sir George Bury, an executive on the Canadian Pacific Railway, would unfailingly ask in railroad language, "Where's the second section?" Everyone would laugh. It was all done in a friendly, jocular way like one referring to a member of a married couple.

However, a story appeared in the Vancouver newspaper about an individual presumed to be a man, but who was found to be a woman working at a man's job, and with a "wife." Discovery had come when she had a heart attack and died in the hospital. Vancouver was scandalized and indignant. Tommy remarked, "If she hadn't died I suppose she could have been put in prison. According to the news report, many people knew she was a woman masquerading as a man, but as long as there was no publicity they didn't care."

It was from Tommy I first heard the term "Boston marriage," as applied to households where two women lived together in life affinity. I was most curious about her experiences in Edinburgh and in London, and about women's love alliances other than her own. Did they conceal their attachments? "Not at all," she said, "they were quite affectionate with one another. None of us thought it was anybody's business."

I realize now that a certain arrogance of class pervaded European society with respect to individual behavior rights. The King can do no wrong, and the aristocracy, taking their cues from royalty, evidently found a wide range of amatory and sexual mores acceptable. The permissiveness stopped at the middle class, at least so far as open behavior went. The bourgeoisie seemed to need the bulwark of respectability for status.

Where did artists fit in? Tommy remarked that many of these were "pets" of the court or of other patrons with power and full purses. This was corroborated in my reading of the flowery and toadying dedications in some of the old books I was working with at Gough's. But it was also true that artists were usually able to transcend class, even as "pets" of privilege or as entertainers. Prevailing authority was often indulgent toward artistic sensibility, idiosyncrasy, and morality.

Perhaps, I suggested to Tommy, partly to tease her but also somewhat seriously, Frank Harris had therefore been correct that I as a poet might be able to write frankly about women loving women. In fact, I had already done it—and often. "The *average* person does not read poetry," she responded.

By dusk of our first weekend together, the falling rain had ceased. We decided to go out and find a restaurant where we could have a good meal. But we did not do so immediately. It was hard to break the spell of our new-found delight in one another. Presently we did wash and dress, then walk into the mild, moist dark in search of a place to eat.

Looking at her in the bright restaurant as we waited for our orders, I thought what a lovely woman she was and of my good fortune in finding her. Our coming together struck me as miraculous. I said something of the sort to her. She said:

"I'll be forty in December."

"What of that?"

"You told me you were twenty-five."

"Why should that matter?"

"It doesn't matter to me. If it doesn't to you—"

"I've always liked friends older than myself. They know more, have had more experience. I can learn much from them besides..."

"Besides?"

"Loving."

She noticed my eyes resting on the ring she had slipped on my finger. She told me it was made for her and placed on her finger by her first love who had left her for marriage and whose loss had caused an abiding pain.

"Take it off—"she began.

"You mean the night it was to marry us is over?" I was sure she did not mean that; but smiling, half playful, held the ring out to her across the table.

"No, no, you are to keep it—as long as you wish to stay with me. But—" with a searching look into my eyes she said, "Love is not only joy and happiness. There are hard times. We may have them. Look inside, at the inscription."

It was hard to read but I made out the engraved words: *Vincit qui patitur.* She translated: "She conquers who endures."

I remarked on the beauty of the ring's design: three braided strands. She told me it represented the indissoluble bond of body, mind, and spirit and then placed the ring back on my finger.

When we were back in the studio she took me in her arms. "There is something I should like you to know as long as we are together..."

"I hope it will be a long time."

"You are free. I shall not bind you. If you should ever desire to make love with anyone else, or wish our relationship to end, all I ask is that you be honest about it. Tell me. Dishonesty is the most destructive thing in love and friendship. Do you agree?"

I said I did, wholeheartedly.

Within myself, I prayed that I might be worthy of the affirmation.

I was going to be more alone because Marie was returning to San Francisco. We had grown closer since seeing so much of one another, mainly at her mother's apartment talking far into midnight, drinking the *fine* she provided. Curiously, the growing affection I felt for her was without erotic excitement, what might be felt between sympathetic sisters.

She loaned me a book that was causing scandal and sensation, *The Well of Loneliness* by Radclyffe Hall. The author was involved in court suits over the lesbian novel. I was stirred by the story, though found it not very well done. In my journal I wrote: "It is a remarkable book, but I am sad because it might have been so much stronger. It was self-pitying...pathos on the verge of bathos. The heroine, Stephen, takes herself with terrible solemnity, yet there are scenes in the book, many of them so real that I got cold shivers down my back." I added: "If the dramatic situations had been used for what they were worth, regardless of bourgeois morality, the book might have been great," rather than propaganda.

I knew nothing about the author, imagining she might be a struggling writer like myself; I resolved to write to her, expressing appreciation for the courage it must have taken to so expose herself. With the letter, sent in care of her publisher, I enclosed several of my love poems to women. I had a hope that if she responded, I might meet women who would be my friends.

It was not until the first week in January that I heard from Radclyffe Hall. She wrote from London saying she expected to be in Paris in February, would like to see me and talk about my work. It greatly excited me to personally meet another lesbian besides myself writing about our passions and tribulations. Alone on the literary island of heterosexuality, it was like sighting a friendly ship on the horizon.

Several months passed before we met, due to illnesses and her legal and other struggles with authorities over *The Well*. Finally in March a letter came from a Miss Una Troubridge on behalf of Radclyffe Hall. Hall was convalescing from the influenza, but inquired if I would meet them for tea. I wondered about the "them." Was Miss T. her friend or secretary?

I met them both at the fine hotel where they were staying. A painful attack of shyness overtook me in the presence of their opulence, which I had not anticipated. I did my best to conceal it, but imagined I must be making a bad impression. Radclyffe Hall was older than I had expected; stocky of figure where I thought she would be tall, slim, athletic. The strong scent of violet perfume or toilet water preceded her as she welcomed me into the hotel sitting room and introduced me to Lady Troubridge. They led me upstairs to their rooms and ordered tea.

There I was surprised to see two birds in cages—Radclyffe Hall with caged birds! She wore a finely tailored brown suit with mannish shirt and tie. Her pale blond hair was cut as short as possible with inch-long sections combed down over each cheek. She had pearl earrings about the size of filberts, wore bracelets and half a dozen rings. So much feminine jewelry with an aspect otherwise masculine struck me as incongruous. My values then were more austere than now. I expected artists to be simpler, unconcerned with show.

Lady Troubridge also wore tailored clothes, but of a more feminine cut and even more jewelry than Radclyffe Hall. She was slim and handsome. Her iron-grey hair was cut page boy fashion about a face still young. Her eyes, unlike Radclyffe Hall's which, although kind in their expression and giving a message of deep suffering, were dark and smiling. Both had good legs and nice hands.

The birds twittered in their cages. The women, in their cages of class and privilege, questioned me politely about my writing. We sipped tea and nibbled the little cakes. I felt their graciousness conferred as from above. This inequality, unfounded on intrinsic worth, where I hoped to find possibility of friendship, disappointed and saddened me. I was too proud to seek patronage, which I recognized was being offered as they asked to see more of my poetry, suggesting that they might be able to interest a London publisher in bringing out a book collection. I told them that I did not feel I had enough good work yet, that I was not writing poetry just then but prose. But I agreed to send them a copy of my book, *On a Grey Thread*.

We talked about Hall's work, the translations of *The Well*. She told me her own favorite of her work was an earlier novel, *The Unlit Lamp*. They spoke of perhaps visiting California, asked me about Los Angeles and prices there. They seemed very conscious of money. The more of it people have, the more they seem to worry about it.

⚢

Since my stay in Paris was during the now legendary period of the Natalie Barney salon, the feverish fame of Renée Vivien and her poetry, and all the *epater les bourgeois* behaviors of the lesbian and other bohemian expatriots, I am frequently asked if I participated. I must say that I did not even know they existed until years later when I read about that colorful scene in the pages of *The Ladder*. It occurs to me that if I had been in Hall and Troubridge's position, encountering a young, and as they evidently thought, talented poet, obviously lonely, I would introduce her where she might find a compatible social environment. Was it snobbism that they did not even mention that such a group existed in Paris, and did they feel that my shoe-string existence would prove mutually embarrassing? Or, protectively, that my unsophistication might be corrupted? It probably is just as well. I was adventuresome enough to have got into emotionally difficult situations.

Hands hold a lot of history, but I was skeptical about doing this sort of thing for money. At eighteen, after reading a few books on the subject, I had played at palm reading as a social game to overcome shyness; it was an easy way to be popular. It bothered me when what I was doing as entertainment began to be taken seriously. Word spread that what I was telling was "true." For example, a woman about whom I knew little except that she was divorced (unusual then in Roman Catholic Montreal) and had two children came up to me at a party and asked if I would read her hand. After some superficialities, I said: "You have had four children…I see two marriages…" She seemed startled, grew flustered, said, "Two children, the others…well, they were—miscarriages"—as if accused of something. I know now that "miscarriage" was often a euphemism for abortion. She added, "One marriage, so far. Do you see another?" Eagerly, "Jacques and I…we've talked of marriage. Will he really marry me?" I did not want the responsibility involved in such incidents, which became frequent, and discontinued the game.

The psychic compared my hands for a long time in silence. I wondered if he was waiting for me to ask questions. I said nothing. He began to speak. Most of what he said could have been told to anyone. "Many troubles…hardships…work…artistic talents…a serious illness, but you will live a long time, to sixty-nine at least…late success." He paused, lowered his voice, "I see death in your hand…someone close…more troubles, you overcome them—." I looked at his expressionless pale face, eyes that seemed not to see the people in front of him. His "I see death in your hand, someone close," stayed in my mind as I rejoined our

party who were discussing whether to visit a nearby antique shop and browse.

"I See Death in Your Hand." The psychic's words from Canada lingered at the back of my mind, then receded entirely from consciousness as I began setting up my own business. The one person I thought of was my little sister, Phyllis. Not long after, I received word of her death from Mother. I thought no more about the oracle until a sad letter came from Roswell saying that our old Montreal friend, Lucien, had died suddenly of brain tumor. Not long after there was the shock of Eric's suicide in the mental hospital. My native skepticism was confounded. Who next? Seriously, I did not believe there would be a next. Everyone else I cared for, friends, family, were in good health.

If death were craving mere fodder, it never once crossed my mind that there could be any threat to the woman most entwined with my life. It was unthinkable that Tommy might cease to be sharing it. When in midsummer of 1935 she died of lung cancer at fifty-one, it was like an amputation of part of myself. It is said that a person who loses a limb continues to feel it as still there. The loss of my lover and friend whose life had been interwoven with mine throughout thirteen years left that sensation. Her presence was everywhere, almost tangible. My emptiness was as full of echoes as a deserted house.

Taking the cable car to our Joice Street flat after appointments; pausing at a Chinatown restaurant to pick up the special fried rice or *tao fu* she liked, thinking as I started the walk up Sacramento Street: "Is she home yet?" Then sudden bleakness. She is not home. Will not be. Not ever again.

There were no tears at the numbing verdict of cancer. "It's in every part of her body." There was nothing to be done but spare her the worst suffering. The cough that had become more persistent and troublesome never was, by her, attributed to lifelong smoking. In those early days there were no warnings. She was never told the truth about terminal cancer. It was not medical practice. I knew her courage, her honesty. I believed she would prefer to know. The medical people were adamant: "It's too much to take." Near the end, before morphine shut off communication, I was in her hospital room. A friend of hers, a physician who was often her golfing partner, came to visit. Hesitantly, Tommy asked her what I believe she had been afraid to ask her own doctor: "How long before I shall be able to play golf again?" Her friend, "It takes time." Could Tommy feel the lie?

Sitting with her in the midsummer dusk after somehow getting through a meaningless work day, I suffered the burden of my duplicity in pretending that today she looked better. Flesh was melting from her thin body, a few months ago so seemingly robust. My awareness (and hers) that we were not sharing this most important transition of her life which should have had its easing rituals, froze me to numbness. Kneeling hour after hour massaging her swollen feet and legs at least gave me some illusion of contact, morphine-dimmed that it was.

With relief, tears finally came, melting dry-eyed weeks of endurance. I was in the dark concert hall at the symphony to which we had season tickets. Fingering my half, having given away hers, I sat alone. I was unable to let Bach's joy enter me. Frozen, the fingers of my right hand moved of their own accord to the ring she had placed on my finger just before our first night of love with the half playful words: "Marry me for tonight." What was engraved inside struck me with new force: *Vincit qui patitur*. She conquers who endures. A long endurance stretched ahead.

There was no one to share it. None of my loyal heterosexual friends could be expected to have any awareness of what this love, this friendship, had meant to me. Helen Westlake and Mary Meisinger, who had made their lives together for years, were the only lesbian couple we were acquainted with. We had known them for only a short time. They shared their understanding by inviting me to their place in the Santa Cruz Mountains. Tommy and I had been there once with these new librarian friends. The depth of their understanding was mainly unspoken, though we became friends for the rest of our lives. Their care was felt like the quiet benediction of the mountains. ■

All Good Women

by Valerie Miner

Chapter Twenty-Two

Late Fall 1944, San Francisco

ROOSEVELT PREPARES FOR FOURTH TERM

US COST OF LIVING RISES 30 PER CENT

STRASBOURG LIBERATED

'Concentrate,' Teddy told herself as she sat tall at her desk outside Mr. Whitney's office. She inserted a familiar form into the typewriter, placed her fingers on the keys and was suddenly overwhelmed with a rush of Moira's soft pink skin. She closed her eyes and there was Moira lying next to her breathing evenly. She cleared her throat to conjure Miss Fargo. She tried to smell the teacher's carbolic soap and hear the tart instructions. 'Back straight; head to the side; fingers moving as lightly as if you were whipping a soufflé.' Nothing seemed to help. She was in a fog of happiness. Every time she thought of the new Moira in her life she had to stop herself from breaking into a grin.

'In the life,' was what Dawn called it. 'It ain't all roses,' Dawn had warned her yesterday. And for the first time in their friendship, Teddy was cross with Dawn, who wouldn't permit her to enjoy this love, who seemed to bear some kind of grudge against Moira, herself. 'Just watch out. You gotta be careful *inside* and *out* when you're in the life.' Teddy shook herself. Well, she did have to be careful, to pay more attention with the typing. Mr Whitney had brought back three forms this morning. That had never happened before. Never had Teddy received one complaint about her work at the Emporium. The strangest thing was she didn't know if she cared.

Moira was happier too, more relaxed, slower somehow. She had recovered quickly from the last phone conversation with Mrs Finlayson. Teddy had heard only half the exchange. But she could imagine Mrs Finlayson's sure, crisp voice when she insisted Moira surrender the baby for adoption.

'I will *not* sacrifice my child for your sense of propriety.' Moira had gripped the phone, staring at her tea.

'Selfish? How is it selfish to want to be a mother to your child?' Moira took a sip of tea and closed her eyes.

'Mother,' her voice grew higher, 'this is my life. And my baby's life.'

After a long silence, Moira said, 'Mother? Are you still there, Mother? Oh, damn.' She slammed down the phone. 'She hung up. That woman, Teddy, if she calls again, just tell her I'm not here.'

Excerpt from the novel, The Crossing Press, 1987.

♀♀

Teddy had thought Moira was kidding until several days later when Moira did, indeed, refuse to come to the phone. It had been weeks since mother and daughter talked. Teddy found this an unnatural state so close to the birth. Still, what could she do? And being so happy, she found it hard to worry, even about her father, who had been in the hospital last week.

♀♀

Startled by the sound of her buzzer, Teddy noticed her hand trembling as she pressed the button.

'Yes, Mr Whitney?'

'Time, Teddy. Have you noticed the time?'

Teddy checked the impassive moonface of the old wall clock. The black hands seemed like skis set at cross purposes over the lunar craters. '3.30,' she read with distraction. 'Oh, no, your tea. Sorry sir. I'll be right there.'

Concentrate, she told herself, concentrate. Yet even as she served Mr Whitney's tea, she was in a state of oblivion. She forced herself to check the number of sugars and to stir in just the right amount of milk. Grateful that her boss was too busy to talk, she returned to her desk and breathed deeply. The strange thing was that this happiness was much more distracting than trouble. She felt so excited all the time, as if she might spin off into the universe. As if she might throw up. She couldn't believe the fullness she felt with Moira, the joy and satisfaction of making love and the contentment of sleeping with her arms around the girl. She couldn't believe it. Yes, that was the problem. She couldn't believe she was so happy.

The phone startled her as if Teddy were in a deep sleep. She had to let it ring again while she caught her breath. Her stomach knotted suddenly. If she didn't get a hold on herself she would lose this job and a fine thing that would be now that Moira was on leave from the shipyard.

'Mr Whitney's office,' Teddy answered in her most polished secretary voice.

'Miss Fielding, please.'

Teddy couldn't quite place the woman's voice.

'This is Teddy Fielding.' What was it, bad news about Pop? Or Moira, had she already gone to the hospital?

'Teddy, this is Moira's mother.'

'Oh, Mrs Finlayson, how are you?' Teddy tried to restrain the panic in her voice. Instantly, she understood something about Moira. Just the sound of her mother's voice put you on alert.

'Fine, thank you. I am sorry to disturb you at work. I need to inquire about my daughter, about Moira. Is she all right? Has she, has she had the baby yet?'

'No, Mam. I mean she's fine and, no, the baby hasn't come yet.'

Mrs. Finlayson sighed and spoke more slowly. 'Then I wonder if I might ask you a favor?'

'Yes, Mam?' Teddy said tentatively. She felt that familiar sensation of standing between Jolene and Pop.

'Please call me when Moira goes into hospital. I'd like to come up.'

'I, I don't know, Mrs Finlayson. That's something between you and Moira and I don't want to but....'

'Yes, dear, I understand. I wouldn't bring you into this if it weren't absolutely necessary. But you must know that my daughter refuses to speak to me at the moment. This is the only way. I do regret involving a stranger.'

Stung by the 'stranger', Teddy could only say, 'I don't know.'

'Of course, I appreciate your position.' Mrs Finlayson's voice was so tight Teddy thought it might snap. 'But please think about it. For Moira's sake.'

'Yes, Mam.' Teddy sometimes regretted her endless fund of deference. The truth was Moira needed her mother at a time like this.

'Thank you, Teddy. I must let you get back to work now.'

Back to work. Teddy stared at the moon and watched the skis sliding past the minutes. Yet another thing to think about. Would she be betraying Moira if she called? Or would Moira be grateful to be saved from her own pride? No, it didn't seem right. But there were at least two weeks to worry about it. She stared at the form in her type-writer, drawing it into focus.

'Watch it. Be careful. Don't slip. Can't you see I just washed it?'

Teddy stared at the kitchen floor and then at Moira scrubbing her way out of the back door. A tilting, hennaed buddha banishing ancient stains.

'Yes,' Teddy said finally. 'I can see you. But I'm not sure I believe you. Didn't the doctor say that the point of leaving the shipyard was to rest, to avoid strain, to prepare....'

'Oh, Teddy, I feel like a pressure cooker. If I don't do something I'm going to explode. Besides, I'm not due for two weeks.'

'But you push yourself too much and you might have the baby right here, while I'm at work.' Teddy leaned on the doorframe.

'Dear, that could happen anyway. The baby isn't punched into your time clock, smart as any child of mine might be. Besides, Mrs Bertoli said she'd take me to the hospital any time. And Mr Minelli offered. He came around this afternoon with more eggs from his sister in Petaluma.'

'Well, a man with a heart condition isn't the best....' Teddy stopped herself. Mrs Bertoli was reliable; she was always around the shop. Moira had it all under control. It was such a funny feeling—to see Moira cool at the helm.

'You're the one who needs to relax. Just go into the living room and read your mystery. Supper will be ready in half an hour. And,' she rubbed her back, 'so will I.'

After supper, they snuggled on the couch, listening to 'People Are Funny' on the radio. Teddy didn't follow the program at all, waking from her daze only when the audience laughed or when Moira shifted to a more comfortable position. 'Inside and outside,' Dawn's words kept coming back to her. She understood the outside problems—that this new life could cost the Emporium job and this house. Although Mr Minelli was remarkably tolerant of Moira's pregnancy, he would hardly accept homosexuality. But inside? No, Dawn just didn't like Moira, that was all there was to it. She—they—were perfectly safe in each other's arms.

'Oh, oh, ohhhhh,' Moira gasped and sat forward.

'What is it?' Teddy demanded.

'You mean who is it?' Moira smiled, her upper lip beaded with sweat.

'Now? Already? Now?'

'Calm down,' Moira said, amazed at her own composure. 'Could be false labour pains, remember. We have to time them if they—oh, ohhh—yes, time this—ohhh—one, Teddy.'

Two hours later when the contractions were close enough, they borrowed Mr Minelli's car and drove to the hospital. Teddy had planned the trip a hundred times and proceeded automatically. She had planned where she would park, how long it would take to walk from the car to the hospital. Yes, she told herself, it was going to be fine. Concentrate, Teddy, concentrate.

Moira could not believe the pain. She had to control herself. She couldn't break down here in the car. Teddy would crash. She was an adult. Millions of women had done this. Her own mother at nineteen. Ohhhhhh, she couldn't believe the pain; she just couldn't. 'Teddy?' she heard herself ask.

'You all right?' Teddy maneuvered around a double parked car. 'Moira.' She turned quickly. 'You're not having it now. Not yet, not here, I mean if you have to....'

'Teddy.' Moira's voice was steady now that the contraction had passed. 'I'm fine. But could you do me a favor? Would you call Mother for me? Tell her where I am and say if she wants to....'

'Oh, that's a girl.' Teddy patted Moira's thigh. 'That's a good thing to do.'

Teddy held Moira's hand as they checked into the hospital. She was distressed by the chaos: rolling stretchers, bustling nurses, ringing phones. Ten o'clock at night. Finally the nurse turned to Moira.

'Yes, your doctor called.'

'But where is he?' Teddy persisted. 'She needs the doctor to have the baby.'

The nurse studied Teddy and then turned to

Moira. 'Your first, isn't it? Well, that'll take a while. Dr. Emerson will be here. Hasn't missed a launch yet.'

Teddy carried the bag and followed Moira and the nurse down the hall.

Overcome with pain, Moira leaned against the wall. Teddy took her elbow, soothing her. Inside and outside, Teddy thought, holding on to Moira despite the nurse's stare. How much was she imagining?

The nurse cleared her throat. 'I think we should be moving on.' She took the satchel from Teddy and smiled kindly. 'The waiting room is over there. If that's what you want. It's likely to take quite some time.'

'Oh, yes, of course,' Teddy blushed. 'Yes, I will wait. Thank you.' Would Moira be all right? The girl was exhausted. If only she could stay and hold her hand.

Moira glanced back forlornly, her face suddenly overtaken by pain.

'I'll be right here,' Teddy called, using her will to restrain herself from hugging her friend good-bye. Oh, this was horrible. If only she could have the baby for Moira. She was so much better at handling pain. She stood in the hallway until Moira and the nurse had turned the corner, then rushed to the telephone.

Moira lay on the stiff bed feeling impossibly alone. Which was longer—the time between the contractions or the pain itself? Why had they left her here? What if the baby decided to come right now? No, she reminded herself, it took time. They had plenty of other people to care for. She tried not to hear the screams from the next room. Mother would be horrified if she behaved like that. Oh, why hadn't she broken down and asked for Mother? Still, they wouldn't let Mother in here. Yes, she would have to wait outside with...oh, dear, what had she done to poor Teddy...of course, it would take her hours to arrive. The baby would be born by then. The little girl or boy....Oh, no, Moira tried to hold her breath against the pain, but still it came in waves of sharp determination. 'Owwwww,' she heard another scream

from the other...no, not from the other room, but from this room, from her own mouth. Then she felt a damp cloth on her forehead.

'Relax honey and breathe.' She looked up to the face of a new nurse and thought she heard a trace of South in her accent. Why had they given her another nurse? Had they discovered she wasn't married? Is that why she was in this room alone? Was this the unmarried nurse? The anxiety and pain disappeared as quickly as it had come. And so did the nurse.

This was so unfair; she hadn't asked for a baby. They had been careful. She was too young. She had been inducted involuntarily. Why did she think she was so special? Because Sister Lawrence had said so. A sin is a knowing offense against...she hadn't meant to get pregnant, so why was she having a baby? Sin, sin sin. Pregnancy was punishment for sex. No, that didn't make sense; it hadn't felt evil. It had felt right. She thought of Randy holding her tight, whispering—no, she mustn't think about him. Sex was a mortal sin, a very fleshy, very mortal sin. Oh, she would be punished doubly for this blasphemy. Her baby would be born deformed. Owww, the pain. Breathe, the disappearing nurse had said, breathe against the pain. Oh, the pain.

Anger coursed through her now. She did not deserve this. She had tried to do everything right, but there were no more reliable models like Susie Fitzpatrick and Cindy Patton. Whatever happened to them? Had they wound up here too? Were they, perhaps, the ones screaming in the next room? The married room, for no doubt they had done it right. You can't have models your whole life. At some point you just have to fly, to trust your instinct and your conscience. But every time she did that, she seemed to lose. She lost Randy after she gave him all she had. If you couldn't trust your judgment and there were no models, what did you have? A code of behavior, a sense of morality. She heard Mother's voice. Oh, the pain, the pains were getting closer.

Teddy leaned back and stretched her legs. On the couch opposite snored a young, expectant father. Teddy had learned he was waiting for twins. Might as well rest while he could.

Teddy picked up her cup of cold tea and set it down again. 4 a.m. She read her watch and shook her head. It was 5 a.m. in Arizona. Wanda would be asleep. Teddy felt overwhelmed with sadness, thinking about Wanda still stuck in that place. She was paralyzed with remorse that she had never made her visit. Of course Wanda wrote to say she understood that Teddy didn't want to leave Moira in her condition. Wanda understood. Wanda was called upon to understand a great deal these last few years.

Teddy stared down the empty hall. At midnight, the nurse had said it might be five hours yet, had told her to go home, but if Teddy knew anything about Moira it was that she was unpredictable. Well, maybe the child wanted to come at dawn. This was going to be some day. New baby. Reconciliation between Moira and her mother. Mrs Finlayson should be getting to town this evening. Good timing—allowing Moira to recover and freshen up and get to know her daughter. Why did she keep picturing a girl? She tried to think of a little boy. She had practiced saying Moira's favorite names: Tim, Bruce. This just didn't work. It would be a girl.

Teddy closed her eyes and imagined the three of them, Moira and the baby and herself, sitting out in the garden together. She loved children, hated to see her youngest brother and sister growing up. And now she was going to be a parent. Never had she featured herself as a parent. That was OK, wasn't it? True, she wasn't a mother, but maybe a kind of auxiliary mother or a step-mother. That's how Moira thought of it, wasn't it? After all, she talked about 'raising our baby'. Well, names weren't so important. It was the feeling they all had, the bond that counted.

Bonds. They had been through a lot together since July, she and Moira. First that horrible night with Moira lying at the top of the stairs. The frantic race to the hospital—this very hospital—and the agonizing wait while they ran tests. Then the coming-to-terms with her pregnancy. Then that

wonderful night of Moira's birthday. The glorious days of loving since then. And now tonight, another birthday, any minute now.

Moira could not believe the wild, searing pain. The intensity. The endurance. How could it go on this long? There didn't seem to be any pauses between the contractions. But how could she survive if there wasn't some relief, some space for herself? She began to hate this thing inside her. Then she felt intense sympathy, because if this hurt her how did it feel to a tiny child? She knew she could not survive the pain much longer.

The nurse shook Teddy's shoulder. Startled, she almost knocked the woman getting to her feet. 'Is she born? Is Moira all right?'

The woman smiled and sighed. 'Progress, but not product. I'm going off shift now. And I've told Hazel,' she nodded toward the thin, young woman behind the counter, 'to keep tabs for you.'

Teddy blinked and yawned. 'Why thank you very much. Thank you for your help.'

Stretching, she noticed that the father of twins had gone, replaced by a younger man, smoking furiously. Teddy checked her watch and rushed to the phone to tell Mr Whitney that she was very sorry, but she had come down with a terrible case of stomach flu.

This is it, thought Moira, I'm going to die in childbirth. They had wheeled her into a different room. Dr Emerson had given her something for the pain, but she needed to remain awake to push. Push? She was already almost over the edge. Had they called a priest? She should have told Teddy to call a priest instead of Mother. Well, if anyone could get her into Heaven, it was Mother. Maybe they would say the rosary in the same church where they prayed for Uncle Willie. This time sweet, wee Jenny would hang on to competent Aunt Evie.

'Push.' The nurse was shouting in her ear.

Poor woman didn't understand. Would the baby survive if she....

'Push. Push. Puuuuush. Push. Pu....'

Moira could hear the wails. High pitched and angry. So different from the deep howls of terror she, herself, had made a moment before. The child cried again. Her child. She raised her head and stared at the squalling, red baby. Girl. They told her it was a girl.

Teddy brought Mrs Finlayson a fresh cup of tea. 'It sure takes a long time.' She shook her head.

'Yes.' Moira's mother faltered. 'It's completely unpredictable. You must be exhausted, Teddy.'

'Yes, Mam. No more than you. Or Moira. Or....' She saw the thin, young nurse approaching them. The man with the cigarette looked up nervously.

The nurse seemed to be trying to remember something.

'How is my daughter, Moira?' Mrs Finlayson stood tall.

'Well, Mam, it's a girl. The mother is fine.'

'Thank God.'

Teddy reached over and squeezed Mrs Finlayson's shoulder. She felt the older woman try to relax.

A girl, thought Teddy. And she was OK. Everybody was OK.

'When may I see my grandchild?'

Teddy looked on expectantly.

The nurse frowned as if she were still trying to remember something and said, 'Since you're the grandmother, I'm sure it will be all right. Just follow me.'

Teddy remained standing, confused and then disappointed. Well, she would get to see them soon enough. They were all right. Everything was going to be all right. ■

Del Martin and Phyllis Lyon

Founders of the Daughters of Bilitis, the first national Lesbian organization in the U.S., and authors of *Lesbian/Woman* (1972). Photo by JEB.

Hollandia '45

by Sarah Dreher

Author's Introduction

When I was a child, my grandmother had a good friend named Beatrice Bowman. "Auntie Bea," as I called her, was a retired Navy nurse and lived in a winterized cottage at Brown's Dam alo.·ɔ the Conewago Creek a few miles from my home in Pennsylvania. She had a dog named Judy, had never been married, and shared my love of woods and camping and the outdoors. I never thought of her as "old," and she never treated me as "young." I loved her, as much as I loved anyone in my family, maybe more. Later, years after she had died, it occurred to me in one of those flashes of brilliant hindsight in which we see things that have been under our noses for decades, that Auntie Bea had probably been a lesbian. She had served for a while in the South Pacific, on a hospital ship, before the start of World War I, and liked to tell me stories and show me artifacts and pictures of those days.

I was thinking about Reality, a greatly overrated concept, which some people are fond of foisting upon persons who are powerless to resist, and which none of us is going to survive anyway. In particular, I was thinking about the current Mental Health fad called "Normalization." Normalization involves taking very elderly patients away from institutions and placing them in community homes, from which they are forced to attend jazz concerts, shopping malls, supermarkets, and other piquant tortures of everyday life. They are deprived of all objects of harmless fantasy and forced to live in the Real World—a great place to visit, if you could get any two people to agree on what it looks like.

WACs, Auntie Bea, and fantasy, three seemingly unrelated threads. Until they spiralled down together in my head and became *Hollandia '45*.

One night after a performance of *Hollandia '45*, a woman approached me to say she had actually been a WAC in Hollandia in 1945, and that she was leaving the next week for a reunion with other women who had been there. She said what she had seen on stage was "exactly what it was like"—the greatest compliment an author can receive.

While I was in Washington for the 1987 Gay Rights March, I took time to go to Arlington Cemetery, where Auntie Bea is buried. She is in the Nurses' Section, on a sloping hillside dotted with falling leaves, surrounded by the graves of women. It seemed right.

Hollandia '45 by Sarah Dreher was originally published in *Lesbian Stages* (Norwich, Vt: New Victoria Publishers, 1988).

Characters

KIT FORTESCUE, a woman in her early 70s. She is retired from the Army Nurse Corps. During the course of the play, her age shifts between 35 and 70.

MARY CLEVELAND, Kit's lover, a WAC in the Signal Corps, WWII.

HAZEL BAINBRIDGE, an Army nurse, WWII.

EDITH RUSKIN, a WAC typist, WWII.

(Kit, Mary, Hazel, and Edith were stationed together in Hollandia, New Guinea, during the closing days of World War II.)

MARIAN JOHNSON, Kit's niece, in her 50s.

Set

There is one set, with the stage divided into two discrete sections: the tent, representing the Hollandia memories; and the porch of Kit's home.

The TENT is standard WWII Army issue, with two cots, footlockers, and a table made from orange crates. A kerosene lamp hangs from the ridge pole. On the table is a handmade chess set, with painted rocks for chessmen. Outside the tent, a handlettered sign reads "Hollandia, Jewel of the Pacific."

The PORCH belongs to a winterized summer cottage, furnished with well-worn chairs, a rocking chair, and a table. A hurricane lamp and fishing tackle are in evidence. All incidental objects and *bric-a-brac* are vintage pre-1945. There is an air of comfortable clutter about the place. Entrances lead to the yard and to the interior of the house.

PLACE: Along a stream in the hills of Maryland.

TIME: The present, a Saturday in June.

Act One

SCENE 1: A Saturday morning in June.

SCENE 2: A few minutes later.

Act Two

SCENE 1: That night.

SCENE 2: Early the next morning.

Program Note

Between January 1944 and the end of World War II, 5500 members of the Women's Army Corps served in the South Pacific. They were billeted in compounds surrounded by barbed wire, and marched to and from work under armed guard. They were not permitted to ride in jeeps or public transportation, or to attend recreational activities except in groups. The official explanation for these "protective" measures was that they were "in danger of being raped by Negro soldiers." The real reason was that their presence was resented by the men.

Each WAC arrived on New Guinea with one pair of woolen slacks and a light cotton shirt, even though the temperature was normally above 100 degrees, rain fell constantly, the humidity was unbearable, and the island was infested with malaria-carrying mosquitoes. They were refused men's uniforms because they were considered "unsightly for women." They were not provided with pajamas, bras, or sanitary napkins—because the men didn't use them—and were not allowed into R and R areas where they might purchase them. Eventually, most managed to scrounge some of the men's cast-off clothing.

A typical work day ran from 7 a.m. to 10 p.m., with time off in the heat of the day, seven days a week. When a woman was moved forward to Manila, the others were expected to pick up her work. They often worked double shifts, three days in a row. There were no replacements.

Malaria, jungle rot, skin rashes, and respiratory diseases were rampant. Many of the women doing censorship work developed headaches and anxiety attacks from reading obscene letters written by the soldiers. Their clothes never dried, and the heat kept them from sleeping. They were forced to submit to monthly pelvic examinations under primitive conditions. By the end of the war, the medical loss rate was 30%, due mostly to exhaustion, anxiety, and tropical diseases.

Very few WACs received promotions or commendations, as the Army feared the men would be jealous.

This play is dedicated to the memory of Josephine Beatrice Bowman, U.S. Navy Nurse Corps.

Act One

SCENE 1: Early on a Saturday morning in June. The gray dawn of a rainy day. There is a sound of rain on the porch roof, which fades over to the sound of rain on canvas.

Mary, Edith, and Hazel are in the tent. They are dressed in bits and snatches of worn Army uniforms and civilian clothes. Edith and Hazel are seated at a homemade chessboard, playing. The chess pieces are odd lumps of an unidentifiable substance resembling rocks, shells, etc. Kit stands on the darkened porch holding a cup of tea. She is dressed in slacks, old shirt, and ragged sneakers. When she is in the present, she walks with a cane and the stiffness of old age. When entering the tent, she leaves her cane behind and moves with the ease of a 30-year-old woman. For now, she is old, and stands watching the action in the tent like an actress awaiting an entrance cue. Mary extinguishes the lamp, bringing up the light in the tent. She watches the chess game.

EDITH: If they let us kill, would you?

MARY: No.

HAZEL: Sometimes I get mad enough to kill.

EDITH: I killed yesterday, in self-defense.

MARY: Who?

EDITH: I don't know, but it was in my soap dish. One of the girls in the typing pool is keeping a list of all the insects on New Guinea. She's found ten different kinds of mosquitoes.

MARY: I've met every one of them.

EDITH: Only the female bites, you know. It has something to do with sex.

HAZEL: Fabulous.

EDITH: She's already done the tropical diseases: beriberi, hookworm, malaria, dysentery, pellagra, dengue fever....

HAZEL: I've met every one of *them*.

EDITH: Dengue fever. Sounds like a popular song. What's it like?

HAZEL: Give me a break. I just got off duty.

EDITH: Do they have any dengue fever at the hospital?

HAZEL: Yes, they have dengue fever. And all the rest of them.

EDITH: There are four kinds of malaria: benign tertian, quartan, ovale tertian, and malignant.

HAZEL: *Edith.*

EDITH: When she finishes insects, she's going to do fungus.

HAZEL: Oh, good Lord.

MARY: Is that all you do over there?

EDITH: Yes, it gets pretty dull.

MARY: Want to trade jobs?

EDITH: I can't work a radio.

MARY: That's okay, I can't type.

Mary and Edith laugh.

HAZEL: Five thousand WACs in the South Pacific, and I get stuck with Laurel and Hardy.

MARY: Come on, Hazel, you wouldn't part with us for the world.

HAZEL: Make me an offer.

EDITH: The symptoms of malaria are....

HAZEL: KNOCK IT OFF!

MARY: Gosh, Edith, maybe you should transfer to the Nursing Corps.

HAZEL: Keep her out of my hospital!

EDITH: Want to have some fun tonight? Let's blow up the U.S.O.

MARY: Can't. I have to work.

HAZEL: You just finished a shift.

MARY: We're short-handed.

HAZEL: You've been short-handed for seven months.

MARY: Yeah. You should have heard the pep talk we got from the new Sergeant this morning. "This is a war, ladies. Not afternoon tea. So let's cut the griping and get this job done." I'm twice his age, and been in this man's Army twice as long. I've suffered, kids, *suffered* for the War Effort, and here comes a little twerp fresh from the States....You can still smell the dye on his olive drabs. and he *outranks* me.

EDITH: (*Sniffing her own shirt*) Nobody outranks me.

MARY: Maybe I'll radio MacArthur's headquarters and tell them Japan surrendered.

EDITH: Tell them Truman surrendered.

HAZEL: Tell them I surrendered.

EDITH: Let's stow away on a plane to Australia.

HAZEL: Australia's off limits to women.

MARY: Everything's off limits to women.

EDITH: Do you remember when we came through Australia?

MARY: Not very well.

EDITH: Neither do I. (*Sighs*) This war is taking too long.

MARY: The Army grinds exceeding slow. And exceeding small.

HAZEL: I thought that was God.

MARY: The Army is God. If you don't believe me, ask Sergeant What's-His-Name.

EDITH: I think I have jungle rot.

HAZEL: *Edith....*

EDITH: Can you get jungle rot from boredom?

HAZEL: Probably.

MARY: I want to go home.

HAZEL: Through six thousand miles of sharks, submarines, and deranged *kamikazes*?

EDITH: I can name every kind of fighter plane. Both sides.

HAZEL: Don't.

MARY: (*Looking out the tent door*) Darn it, hasn't the Medical Service ever heard of *schedules*?

HAZEL: Relax, she'll be here.

MARY: This war needs unions. Refuse to maim or kill except between nine and five.

HAZEL: Bolshevik.

MARY: Do you know they have *rules* about wars? They all sit down and decide on the *rules*. If they can agree on the *rules*, why can't they agree not to *fight* the darn war. Does that make any sense? I mean, who's crazy here? Us or them?

HAZEL: Watch it, kid. You can get thrown out for thinking.

EDITH: Know what gets me? Back home they have a War College. A *War College*. They go to school to learn how to kill.

HAZEL: Some do. Some come by it naturally.

EDITH: Well, at least they get uniforms. Ours look like something out of a rag bag.

HAZEL: Killing doesn't get you a uniform. You need that extra little appendage.

EDITH: Hazel! I haven't played wife in so long I've forgotten what they use it for. Ask your Major, will you?

HAZEL: Ask him yourself. (*Quickly*) I take that back.

EDITH: Come on, I wouldn't bird-dog a pal. Not at my age. Back home they give a girl nylons when they want to make a pass. Hold out for that gold band, buddy.

HAZEL: What would I do with nylons out here?

EDITH: I don't know, but I sure know what I'd do with a bra. (*Looks down at her breasts*) By the time I get home, I'll have to tote these around in a bushel basket.

HAZEL: Oh, stop griping.

EDITH: They *hurt*.

HAZEL: I'm sorry.

MARY: Darn, I wish I could put a cap on my nerves.

HAZEL: Read a magazine.

MARY: I've read *the* magazine.

HAZEL: There's the Signal Corps for you. Make a girl a specialist, and she wants new magazines every month.

MARY: I bought that *Modern Screen* in San Francisco. It's probably a collectors' item now.

HAZEL: Well, light somewhere, will you?

MARY: You may outrank me, Hazel, but that doesn't mean you can order me around.

HAZEL: (*With a laugh*) I think it does.

EDITH: Want me to name all the movie stars in the U.S.O.?

HAZEL: Oh, dear God, transfer me to Okinawa.

EDITH: They're invading Okinawa.

HAZEL: I *know* they're invading Okinawa. They've been invading Okinawa for six weeks.

MARY: They won't let you near the front. Remember, all WACs are whores and sluts.

HAZEL: Not the Nursing Corps.

MARY: The Angels of Mercy.

EDITH: Yeah? How come they live in the mud with us?

HAZEL: To set a higher moral tone.

MARY: Now I know why Kit's giving me a hard time. It's her high moral tone.

EDITH: Is she still holding out on you?

MARY: I think she's saving herself for something better to come along.

HAZEL: Not a chance.

MARY: Sometimes I wonder.

HAZEL: She's afraid it'll get out. She doesn't want me to walk into the latrine and have the other girls run out screaming.

EDITH: Hey, if it'll buy me a little privacy in the privvy, start a rumor about *me*.

Kit enters.

KIT: Morning, soldiers.

HAZEL: How goes the war, Kit?

KIT: Great. Head wounds are up, tonsillectomies are down, and we're losing the battle against jungle rot. (*To Mary*) Hi, Sparks. Any news from the front?

MARY: We're invading Okinawa.

HAZEL: Do they need me at the hospital?

KIT: Not that I know of.

HAZEL: You're late. I thought they might have brought in a new shipment of parts.

KIT: I stopped off to feed the chickens.

HAZEL: Why don't you just turn them loose? They haven't laid in months.

EDITH: Who has?

KIT: Why, Edith, you're a married woman!

EDITH: For all the good *that* does me. Hazel, old buddy, if you ever land that surgeon of yours, stay out of wars.

HAZEL: I wouldn't be in this one if I hadn't gotten carried away. The recruitment posters promised romance and adventure. (*They all laugh*) There wasn't much to see in Wilkes-Barre but coal and slag.

EDITH: They promised us we'd win the war together, side by side, fighting to make the world safe for Democracy. Six weeks later he was in France and I was on my way here. He'd better be wearing that darned wedding ring.

KIT: I thought I saw you down on the beach last night. With a Marine.

EDITH: Must have been some other girl. All clerk-typists look alike. Especially without brassieres.

HAZEL: Can't you think of anything but your foundation garments?

EDITH: I suppose you like your khaki drawers.

HAZEL: Love 'em. They make me feel so G.D. Army.

KIT: I'm in the *Army*? I thought I joined the Girl Scouts. And all this time I've been slaving on my Homemaker's badge.

MARY: From the looks of this tent, you'll never make it.

KIT: That's all Hazel's stuff.

HAZEL: It is *not*. I keep my half *by the book*.

KIT: When Hazel dies, they're going to bury her with Emily Post in one hand, and an Army Training Manual in the other. (*Pulls a lemon from her pocket*) Anyone want a lemon?

HAZEL: I had a lemon back in Pennsy. It was a Ford.

EDITH: Lemons are good for scurvy.

HAZEL: Edith, if you don't shut up about disease....

MARY: Where'd you get it?

KIT: I happened to be strolling by the Officers' Mess....

MARY: You've lost your morals. War's turned you into a crook.

KIT: We live in desperate times.

MARY: (*Sighs*) I know.

EDITH: Mary wants to go home.

KIT: *Home*? They're *suffering* back there. Gas rationing, sugar rationing, coffee rationing, meatless Tuesdays....

HAZEL: That's the charm of this place. We don't have anything to give up.

KIT: Army life. Luxury and self-indulgence from sun-up to sun-down, and all points in between.

HAZEL: How can any human being work all night and be so cheerful?

KIT: I'm not human.

MARY: I've been trying to make time with a robot.

KIT: Mary.

EDITH: I'm hungry.

HAZEL: Don't worry, it's a sign of life. (*To Kit*) The U.S.O.'s in town.

KIT: (*Rubbing her hands gleefully*) Hot split!

MARY: What do you care? You never go to the shows.

HAZEL: Not since Vera Lynn refused to dance with you.

KIT: I *love* the U.S.O.

EDITH: You rob them blind.

KIT: They have, we need. That's the Democracy we're making the world safe for.

HAZEL: That isn't Democracy, it's Communism.

EDITH: I'm *hungry*.

HAZEL: I thought you swore off Army food.

EDITH: I can't live on your cookies from home. The last batch was oatmeal raisin.

HAZEL: You told me you liked oatmeal raisin.

EDITH: The raisins were moving. (*Innocently*) Gee, didn't you notice?

HAZEL: One of these days, Edith Ruskin, I'm going to strangle you in your sleep.

EDITH: Coming? Gosh, I hope it's Spam and canned peaches. I haven't had Spam and canned peaches since yesterday. Hey, Mary, what's Morse code for Spam?

Hazel grabs Edith by the scruff of the neck and drags her out. Kit collapses on a cot.

MARY: Rough night?

KIT: Rough enough.

MARY: Why the big act?

KIT: Trying to keep up morale. Mine.

MARY: Want me to rub your back?

KIT: (*Jumping up*) No, thanks.

MARY: Kit.

KIT: (*Quickly*) Got your mail. (*Pulls out a post card*) Boise.

MARY: My mother-in-law?

KIT: Yep.

MARY: You read it. Tell me if there's anything new.

KIT: (*Scanning the card*) She wants you to come home and "resume your rightful place in the community."

MARY: Whatever that is. Bill joined the Army to get away from me, and I joined to get away from his mother. Running was all we had in common.

KIT: You're not a runner.

MARY: You do enough running for both of us.

KIT: (*Nervously changing the subject*) Why'd you marry him, anyway?

MARY: We were too young to know the difference between love and a quick grope in the back of a Studebaker.

KIT: Why didn't you have children?

MARY: Because, contrary to what your mother might have told you, you can't get pregnant from a toilet seat.

KIT: She didn't tell me. She wouldn't say the word.

MARY: Pregnant? Or toilet seat?

KIT: Neither. Mother was a proper lady. I come from a long line of proper ladies.

MARY: I can tell.

KIT: Didn't you ever...you know...with him?

MARY: Not after we sold the Studebaker. You're full of questions today.

KIT: I guess so.

MARY: I wonder what they'd say back in Boise if they knew I'd fallen head over heals for an Army nurse.

KIT: Probably wonder where you met a male nurse. What will you do after the war?

MARY: That depends on you, Kit. (*Pause, gently*) This gives you the creeps, doesn't it?

KIT: Sometimes, a little.

MARY: Well, maybe the next war will make the world safe for love. We have to *take* what we want, Kit. Nobody's giving us any handouts.

KIT: I know.

MARY: One of these nights I'm going to hide out behind the latrine, and when you come out of the shower...BANG! Right in front of God and the entire Women's Army Corps.

KIT: You wouldn't!

MARY: If you don't loosen up, I won't be responsible for my actions

KIT: I'm sorry, Mary. It's just...I've never....

MARY: Good God, woman. Back home even the *cows* do it.

KIT: Not in Maryland.

MARY: Sure, they do. You're so well-bred you probably look the other way.

KIT: I do not. (*Sheepishly*) Yeah, I do. Anyway, what makes you so sure I want....

MARY: You talk in your sleep. Hazel told me.

KIT: (*Embarrassed*) Mind stepping outside for a minute while I slit my wrists?

MARY: Oh, sit down. And take your hands out of your pockets.

KIT: What for?

MARY: I'm not going to compromise you. I'm going to rub your shoulders.

> *Apprehensively, Kit obeys. Mary rubs her shoulders for a moment. Kit stiffens.*

What's wrong?

KIT: World War III just erupted in my stomach.

> *Kit reaches up and touches Mary's hand. Mary turns her around to face her. They start to kiss.*

MARY: (*Pulling back*) Look out!

KIT: What did I do?

MARY: (*Brushes at Kit's back*) Bug!

KIT: What kind of bug?

MARY: (*Chasing the bug*) Tyrannosaurus Rex! Got it.

KIT: Mary.

MARY: What?

KIT: Do you always kiss with your eyes open?

> *Mary hits her playfully. Kit grabs Mary, they tussle a little, ending up on the cot. They are about to kiss when Marian's voice is heard offstage.*

MARIAN: Kit. Yoo-hoo, Kit!

> *Marian enters. She is in her mid-fifties, dressed in a garish, flowered dress and slingback pumps, plastic raincoat and rain bonnet. She carries a handbag and a large paper sack.*

Kit!

> *Notices she is dripping on the floor, takes off her coat and bonnet, shakes them out, rummages in her handbag, finds a Kleenex, and tries to wipe the water from the floor. Shakes her head over the tracked mud (not her own) on the porch.*

Darn.

> *Giving up trying to clean up, she takes a small table lamp from the paper bag, sets the kerosene lamp aside with a gesture of distaste, replaces it with the table lamp, and looks around for a light socket.*

> *Kit enters.*

KIT: Well, Marian. As usual your timing is flawless.

MARIAN: Oh, were you in the bathroom?

KIT: No.

MARIAN: I've made a terrible mess here. But it's always something, isn't it? We no sooner finish coping with slush, and the mud is upon us. Where's your sponge mop?

KIT: Why didn't you call first?

MARIAN: It's impossible to get you on the phone. You're always out fishing.

KIT: Not at night.

MARIAN: Well, I wouldn't want to wake you.

KIT: I never go to bed before midnight.

MARIAN: Oh, dear. Insomnia?

KIT: Antiquity.

MARIAN: Just like Mother, poor thing. Her light was on at all hours. It must run in the family.

KIT: It must. (*Marian wipes furiously at the floor with her Kleenex*) Leave it alone, Marian. It'll dry.

MARIAN: Then you'll never get it up.

KIT: I can plant tomatoes.

MARIAN: You should have a cleaning lady.

KIT: I don't need a cleaning lady.

MARIAN: Nonsense, your windows look like an abandoned warehouse.

KIT: They're old, not dirty.

MARIAN: Then you should have them replaced.

KIT: I like them the way they are.

MARIAN: Of course you don't. I'll call around and find someone to do it first thing Monday morning.

KIT: Marian....

MARIAN: You're worried about money, aren't you? They can bill me. It won't cost you a thing. (*As Kit starts to protest*) Now don't be silly and proud. I know how hard it is to manage on a pension. I watch television.

KIT: And vote Republican.

MARIAN: I won't have my favorite Aunt....

KIT: Your *only* Aunt.

MARIAN: ...living in shabby surroundings. Not as long as there's breath in my body. Where's your mop?

KIT: Leave my dirt alone.

MARIAN: Oh, Kit, don't be childish.

KIT: Cleanliness reminds me of death.

MARIAN: Dirt causes death. Disease and death.

KIT: Marian, what are you doing here?

MARIAN: I haven't seen you in ages.

KIT: It's been a week.

MARIAN: And since you're too stubborn to call...Well, how am I supposed to know if you need anything?

KIT: You don't give me *time* to need anything. Marian, I really don't like these spot inspections.

MARIAN: You don't mean that, you're in a bad mood. Did you have an uncomfortable night?

KIT: I'm having an uncomfortable morning.

MARIAN: Poor thing, it must be the dampness. This house positively *exhales* dampness. I don't know how you stand it. (*Pause*) Would you like me to leave?

KIT: No, but I do wish you'd learn to mind your own business.

MARIAN: I'm awful, aren't I?

KIT: Not awful, but pretty bad.

MARIAN: I don't know what gets into me. Some mornings I wake up so frightened...do you suppose it's menopause?

KIT: I think you have too much time on your hands.

MARIAN: I haven't been right since Mother died.

KIT: It'll pass. Give yourself a while. If I know my sister, you never had to think about how to spend your spare time while *she* was alive.

MARIAN: (*Sighs*) She needed so much care at the end.

KIT: She demanded so much attention from the beginning.

MARIAN: You never got along with her, did you?

KIT: We didn't have much in common.

MARIAN: She always said you'd never come back here.

KIT: Well, she was wrong, wasn't she?

MARIAN: She said you wouldn't dare.

KIT: Why?

MARIAN: Because of...how you spent your life.

KIT: Really?

MARIAN: She said a woman only worked for a living if she couldn't snag a husband.

KIT: (*Laughs*) Helen certainly saw things from her own point of view. It never occurred to her that I might simply like the way I lived.

MARIAN: Well, you must admit it's a little hard to understand.

KIT: I've never had trouble understanding it. Though, to be perfectly fair, I didn't make much of an effort to understand her, either.

MARIAN: You worried her.

KIT: Oh, I doubt that. But I will admit I annoyed her. It was one of the few things that made visiting worthwhile.

MARIAN: I always wanted a sister.

KIT: You could have had mine.

MARIAN: I did. Kit, why didn't they have other children? Was there some problem?

KIT: Helen couldn't stand the competition. When you were a baby and people made a fuss over you, she bristled like a hairbrush.

MARIAN: I have terrible dreams about her. I should have done more.

KIT: Helen didn't die of neglect, she died of old age. All the doing in the world wouldn't have changed that.

MARIAN: You're not going to die, are you, Kit? I couldn't bear it.

KIT: Not in the foreseeable future.

MARIAN: You know what they say. When people retire…

KIT: I survived three wars. I think I can handle retirement.

MARIAN: I've always envied your moral fiber.

KIT: You make me sound like whole wheat bread.

MARIAN: You were the strong one. Mother always said so.

KIT: Don't try to put a nice face on it. "Pig-headed" was the expression she used.

MARIAN: Well, it's the same thing. (*Gets the lamp*) What do you think of this?

KIT: Charming, in a boudoir sort of way.

MARIAN: It's perfect for this table. (*Looks around for the outlet*)

KIT: Marian….

MARIAN: There it is! (*Tries to plug in the lamp. The cord is too short.*) Honestly, I don't know what people use for brains nowadays. They charge an arm and a leg for a lamp, and put a cord on it that barely reaches the floor. Where do you keep your extensions?

KIT: I know you mean well, Marian, but….

MARIAN: (*Looking at her lamp*) I wonder if this was intended for a motel.

KIT: You keep the lamp.

MARIAN: Have they shut off your electricity? The public utilities have no compassion for the elderly. I'll have Chet give them a call. A man can get things done.

KIT: The electricity is in perfect health. I prefer the kerosene lamp.

MARIAN: And before you know it you'll go stumbling around in the dark and smash your other hip. When old people smash a hip, it's all downhill from there.

KIT: Good God.

MARIAN: The last time I was here, the minute I got home I said to Chet, "Kit has those smelly kerosene lamps all over the house. She's going to poison herself." If you don't believe me, ask him.

KIT: I believe you. And what did he say to that?

MARIAN: Oh, he mumbled something or other, you know him. (*Holds up the lamp*) Well, if you won't have it on the porch, where should I put it?

KIT: Don't tempt me.

MARIAN: What? (*Gets the joke, laughs*) You dirty old lady.

KIT: Can I get you something? Coffee?

MARIAN: Let's visit for a while first. (*Fans herself*) It's delightfully cool here. I don't know when we've had such a hot spring. If this is any indication, the summer will be an abortion. I envy you.

KIT: It's the breeze of the stream, and the trees.

MARIAN: I'm not too crazy about trees, myself. They're always dropping things. Leaves, twigs....

KIT: Bird plop.

MARIAN: That, too. Do you know what you should do?

KIT: Tell me.

MARIAN: Have the Fourth of July picnic here, the way you used to.

KIT: Oh, Marian.

MARIAN: Why not?

KIT: For one thing, there isn't much family left.

MARIAN: (*Sighs*) I suppose not.

KIT: We have a tendency to die off. It's probably hereditary.

MARIAN: I have such fond memories of those picnics. It broke my heart when you closed the place. The Fourth of July isn't the same any more.

KIT: I hope not. You spent the entire day under the kitchen table.

MARIAN: I never.

KIT: You did. You were afraid of the Baptist Aunties from upstate New York.

MARIAN: (*With a laugh*) Weren't they terrible?

KIT: They went after sin faster than a coon hound on a fresh scent. I'll bet they knew more about sin than God Himself. They'd sit out there under that Norway maple, eating peppermint drops and watching for the rest of us to transgress, while the men sneaked behind the outhouse for a drink.

MARIAN: My father never sneaked.

KIT: John was the worst of the lot. He'd parade around here giving orders like Captain Bligh on the bridge of the Bounty, and the minute the old ladies' Model A pulled up, it was all "Yes, Ma'am" and "No, Ma'am."

MARIAN: He was only being polite.

KIT: The whole family was afraid of Baptists, even the in-laws. I don't know why we kept inviting them.

MARIAN: Of course you had to invite them.

KIT: They'd have come, anyway. At least the War did one thing for me. It cured me of my fear of Baptists. And everyone else. I went out to New Guinea timid, and came back mad. Love and death do that, I suppose.

MARIAN: Really, Kit, I wish you wouldn't talk like that.

KIT: What offends you? Love? Or death?

MARIAN: War.

KIT: It offends me, too.

MARIAN: Then put it out of your mind. It's over and done with.

KIT: What were Korea and Vietnam? Echoes?

MARIAN: You're obsessive on the subject. You plunk that rotten old tent right down in the middle of your lovely yard—God only knows why. Army blankets on your beds, old pictures ripped out of *Life* magazine on the walls, every available space littered with dime store rubbish. Your house looks like a garage sale.

KIT: You know, Marian, you can be very rude.

MARIAN: How can I be rude to you? You're family.

KIT: There's a subtlety here that eludes me.

MARIAN: Families can speak their minds. Niceness is for strangers, and guests.

KIT: I see. Excuse me.

MARIAN: Well, it isn't your fault. You've been away so long you probably don't know any better.

KIT: I probably don't. Thank you for clearing that up.

MARIAN: You're welcome. (*It occurs to her something's not right*) Kit, are you laughing at me?

KIT: I suppose I am. I apologize.

MARIAN: You think I'm stupid.

KIT: No.

MARIAN: Everyone else does.

KIT: Marian, it would take an Einstein to follow your twists and turns.

MARIAN: Why, thank you.

KIT: You're welcome.

MARIAN: Now, as long as I'm here, why don't I help you clear this place out?

KIT: Marian!

MARIAN: We'll get some nice chintz curtains for the windows. And chenille bedspreads. They're quaint and old-fashioned.

KIT: Quaint and old-fashioned?

MARIAN: I'm not calling *you* old-fashioned. But you like old-fashioned things, and they might as well be in good taste.

KIT: Chenille bedspreads are in good taste? They have them in rundown motels in small towns in Ohio.

MARIAN: When were you ever in Ohio. (*With an edge*) Excuse me, I forgot. You've been everywhere with your beloved Army.

KIT: There's nothing beloved about the Army.

MARIAN: You could have fooled me.

KIT: Marian, I...oh, never mind. You wouldn't understand.

MARIAN: I suppose not, given my limited intelligence.

KIT: (*Frustrated*) I'm not criticizing you! Honest to God, if someone breaks wind, you think they're criticizing you!

MARIAN: Well, I'm delighted to hear I'm not being criticized.

KIT: The Army wasn't a nice place. As corporations go, its products left something to be desired. (*Marian looks bewildered*) War isn't culturally enriching. I've always felt guilty for being part of that.

MARIAN: No one forced you to stay.

KIT: I did try to leave, several times. But there were things we had been through, those of us who had served in the wars, that people on the outside could never understand. Things they didn't want to hear about. We shared a language, an experience. I was lonely without it.

MARIAN: Well, you're out now.

KIT: With some regrets.

MARIAN: If you're going to retire, retire. There's nothing worse than someone who hangs on.

KIT: I can't erase my whole life, Marian. I don't

have the time, or the strength, to start a new one. So I surround myself with memories. And, as the shadows creep toward me, those memories take on a special glow.

MARIAN: I think that's morbid and peculiar.

KIT: It's a harmless pastime. People expect the elderly to be morbid and peculiar. It's probably the first normal thing I've ever done.

MARIAN: It must be terrible to be old.

KIT: Not so terrible. It didn't happen overnight.

MARIAN: Mother hated being old.

KIT: Well, you see, it cramped her style.

MARIAN: I worry about you.

KIT: There's no need.

MARIAN: This ramshackle place....

KIT: I'll be gone long before the roof caves in.

MARIAN: But it's stood empty for years. A house that stands empty for years is never the same.

KIT: Twenty-four hours of your presence, Marian, makes up for centuries of disuse.

MARIAN: Are you insulting me?

KIT: How can I insult you? You're family.

MARIAN: The only family you have.

KIT: That's a fact.

MARIAN: (*Firmly*) Kit, I think you should move into town.

KIT: Me?

MARIAN: We have plenty of space. We'll fix up Mother's old room for you.

KIT: I never knew you had a sense of humor.

MARIAN: You don't have anyone here.

KIT: I have neighbors.

MARIAN: Hillbillies.

KIT: Marian, have you heard a single word I've said?

MARIAN: You have memories. Memories are portable. Bring them along.

KIT: (*Tired of arguing*) Go make coffee.

> *Marian exits to kitchen, carrying on the ensuing conversation as she bangs cupboard doors offstage.*

MARIAN: If you came to live with us, you wouldn't have to be afraid.

KIT: I'm not afraid now.

MARIAN: You should be.

KIT: Thank you, dear niece, for that comforting thought.

MARIAN: I can't find the coffee.

KIT: Over the stove.

MARIAN: I've got it. This can't be it. (*Enters with a nearly empty jar of instant coffee.*) Is this it?

KIT: That's it.

MARIAN: It's nearly empty.

KIT: It'll do for now.

MARIAN: I'll borrow some from the neighbors.

KIT: They don't drink coffee. It's a caffeine-free, salt-free, sugar-free, chemical-free vegetarian hillbilly household.

MARIAN: How in the world do they *live*?

KIT: Moonshine and acorns.

MARIAN: I suppose I'll have to drive down to the store, then.

KIT: You take the coffee. I'll be fine with tea.

MARIAN: We still need coffee for the morning. (*Kit looks at her*) Oh. Well, I thought I'd stay the night, if you don't mind. Chet's out of town.

KIT: Afraid to be alone?

MARIAN: It's such a big house. With the children gone, and now Mother…It…makes funny noises. No, not really noises. Silences. The silences that come at the end of noises. Isn't that silly?

KIT: You're welcome to stay.

MARIAN: Well, I'd better get going. We could have torrential rains later. (*Hurries into her raincoat and bonnet, talking nonstop.*) I might as well pick up a few things for dinner. I barged right in, it's not as though you have to feed me, too. Suppose I make us some nice popovers for breakfast. And for tonight…a cute little roast with browned new potatoes and tiny peas. You must have peas in your garden. Or is it too late for peas?

KIT: I have peas. Not tiny peas, monstrous, mind-boggling peas. And the store doesn't have cute little roasts. Or darling little steaks. They have an ingenuous little pork chop from time to time, but rarely.

MARIAN: What kind of a grocery store is that?

KIT: The kind that's never open when you need it, and never has what you want. A convenience store.

MARIAN: What in the world do you *eat*?

KIT: Adorable little tuna fish, mostly. I had a precious little omelet last week.

MARIAN: Well, there's precious little in your refrigerator now. You're making fun of me again.

KIT: I'm sorry, Marian. But sometimes I can't resist.

MARIAN: Oh, go ahead. Chet and the boys do it all the time.

KIT: Then I'm doubly sorry. Do you ever stop to realize you married a man exactly like your father?

MARIAN: I did, didn't I? Think what a heyday a psychoanalyst would have with that?

KIT: John treated his hunting dogs better than he treated you.

MARIAN: Well, Chet doesn't keep dogs, thank God. But he does hunt pheasant. I swear, Kit, every time he comes striding in the kitchen door, reeking of bourbon, and tosses those dear, beautiful, dead birds in the sink, I could…break down and cry. (*Turns to leave*)

KIT: Marian? (*Marian turns back*) This is a very nice lamp. Thank you for your kindness.

MARIAN: Do you really like it? It was Mother's, you know.

KIT: No, I didn't know.

MARIAN: She kept it on that little table beside her bed. The last thing I'd do every night was give her a kiss and turn it out. Every night.

KIT: Then I'll put it beside my bed, and think of you.

Marian exists.

BLACKOUT

SCENE 2: A few minutes later. Lights up in the tent.

> *Hazel and Edith are playing chess. Mary is reading an old magazine.*

> *Kit enters carrying four Cokes.*

KIT: Who's winning?

EDITH: Three guesses.

KIT: (*Looks at the board*) Take her coral with your lava.

HAZEL: (*As Edith moves*) That isn't fair, Kit. (*Moves*)

KIT: (*To Edith*) Now block her shale with your…(*Picks up a piece*) What is this thing?

EDITH: Petrified brownie.

KIT: Looks more like fruitcake.

HAZEL: Kit….

EDITH: Really? (*Studies it*) I've been playing it as a brownie.

KIT: What's that green stuff?

HAZEL: Will you put it *down*?

EDITH: (*Still studying the piece*) I don't know. Mold?

KIT: Hazel got those brownies in January. They should be past mold.

EDITH: Yeah, you're right.

HAZEL: For crying out loud.

EDITH: It *is* fruitcake. (*To Hazel*) Cheater!

HAZEL: We've been playing it as brownie, so it's brownie.

EDITH: Let me see your sand dollar. (*Grabs it*) Congo square!

HAZEL: Congo squares are square.

EDITH: You filed off the corners.

HAZEL *With what*???

EDITH: Yeah, with what? Hazel, do you have a nail file?

HAZEL: Of course I don't have a nail file. There isn't a nail file in Hollandia.

MARY: Will you two please knock it off?

KIT: Anyone want to run up to Iwo Jima and watch the moon rise over Mount Suribachi?

MARY: I'm *trying* to read.

KIT: *Photoplay*? They going to quiz you on it?

MARY: By the time I get home I won't remember *how* to read. I'll have to communicate in Morse code. Dit-dit-dit, dit-dit-dit-dit, dit-dit, dah.

HAZEL: What was that?

KIT: I don't know, but I think it was obscene.

EDITH: I had an IQ of 120 when I left the States. It's probably about 72 now.

HAZEL: I thought that was your bust size.

EDITH: How would I know? I haven't seen the inside of a bra in eight months.

MARY: Seven months.

EDITH: That was last month.

MARY: It was?

EDITH: We've been here eight months.

MARY: I'm losing track of time.

HAZEL: Doesn't surprise me. How can we tell one day from another?

EDITH: I hate this place.

KIT: Have a Coke.

HAZEL: Who'd you rob this time?

KIT: U.S.O.

HAZEL: Again?

KIT: If they're going to leave this stuff hanging around…(*Passes out the Cokes*) A sailor told me if you put aspirin in Coke it'll make you high.

HAZEL: Sailors are crazy.

MARY: What do we have to lose? Where's your aspirin?

KIT: I don't know. Around somewhere.

Mary paws through Kit's things looking for the aspirin.

HAZEL: (*To Kit*) What are you going to do when they ship out? Go into withdrawal?

KIT: Back to Spam and canned peaches, I guess.

MARY: (*Tossing things out of Kit's footlocker*) I thought nurses were supposed to be compulsive.

KIT: Go easy on that stuff. It has to last me the duration. (*Opening her Coke*) Anybody going to the show?

MARY: Not me. I'm not in the mood for Bob "Ain't Dying Fun?" Hope.

HAZEL: I'm on duty.

EDITH: Tough break.

KIT: Not really. So is Clark Guidry.

HAZEL: Coincidence.

KIT: Yeah, *he* makes up the duty roster.

EDITH: I think I'll pass it up. All I do at those shows is covet. I covet their make-up. I covet their clothes. I even covet their nail polish.

HAZEL: I have nail polish.

EDITH: Where?

HAZEL: A tiny speck, right there.

KIT: (*Peering at Hazel's nail*) That isn't nail polish, it's blood.

HAZEL: Oh, must be from that leg amputation.

MARY: (*Flinging something to the floor*) Will you cut it out? If I have to hear one more word about gore, I'll lose my mind.

KIT: Something bothering you, Mary?

MARY: There's a war on.

HAZEL: Didn't your mother ever tell you not to listen to rumors?

MARY: I didn't have a mother. We couldn't afford it.

HAZEL I think we have a small morale problem here.

MARY: (*Flaring up*) Morale problem! We sit here on this garbage scow of an island with nothing to do but count the dead and observe the life cycle of mildew, and you say we have "a small morale problem!" (*A shocked silence*) I'm sorry. It's the noise and static in my head, day after day. And now the guns all night....

KIT: What guns?

MARY: Artillery practice, I guess. (*Finds the aspirin*) Do you always keep aspirin in your socks?

KIT: Those are Hazel's socks. Mary, I haven't heard any...

HAZEL: What are *my* socks doing in *your* foot-locker?

KIT: I thought they were mine.

HAZEL: My socks don't fit you.

KIT: They don't fit you, either. Mary....

HAZEL: They don't fit me better than they don't fit you.

MARY: (*Drops aspirin into her Coke*) Here goes nothing. (*Drinks*) Nothing.

HAZEL: I told you sailors were crazy.

KIT: Mary, what guns?

MARY: I don't know what guns. Guns.

HAZEL: They wouldn't invade Hollandia again, would they?

EDITH: What for? There's nothing left on New Guinea that's worth anything.

HAZEL: Now we know where *we* stand.

MARY: I'd have heard about it. I haven't missed a single golden moment of this war. Where's Tinian?

EDITH: Tinian? Sounds like something you get between your toes.

KIT: North. What about it?

MARY: It's all very hush-hush, but it sure has the Air Force aroused.

KIT: It's too far away for us to hear it.

HAZEL: Maybe you heard Edith blowing up the U.S.O.

EDITH: (*Fighting with the bottle opener*) I'd *like* to blow up the U.S.O. It's a walking drug store, and we can't even get soap.

KIT: I'll see what I can do while they're performing their little dimples off.

EDITH: It isn't fair.

KIT: It's for the press. You don't want the folks back home to think this is an ugly war.

EDITH: (*The bottle opener slips, breaking a nail. She throws it across the tent*) This *is* an ugly war.

HAZEL: For Heaven's sake, it'll grow back.

EDITH: I'm tired of being dirty. I'm afraid to look in the mirror.

HAZEL: Well, we don't have mirrors.

MARY: Don't, Hazel.

KIT: It's getting us all down, Edith.

EDITH: Aren't we ever going home?

KIT: Sure, kid. As soon as the world's safe for Democracy.

EDITH: I don't care about Democracy. I want to wash my hair. I want to look nice. I want to smell good. I'm nothing but a *lump*.

HAZEL: Oh, grow up.

MARY: Hazel, lay off.

KIT: Terrific! Let's pick on each other.

HAZEL: At least *you* know who you're going home to.

EDITH: Aw, Hazel, honey, I'm sorry. You've got it bad, huh?

HAZEL: Yeah, I've got it bad.

EDITH: If he doesn't want you, he's a horse's behind. Who wants to go through life hitched to a horse's behind?

KIT: Not me. I certainly don't want to do that.

HAZEL: It gets the spring plowing done.

EDITH: Trouble is, once you've got a man, how do you keep him? When you're getting uglier by the week and he's lying in a hospital in Belgium surrounded by cute young nurses like Kit?

HAZEL: If they're all like Kit, I don't think they'll be looking his way.

MARY: Men! Who needs them!

EDITH: Middle-aged women with grandchildren, stretch marks, no money, and only a high school education, that's who needs them.

KIT: I'll bet he's not too pretty himself right now.

EDITH: Men don't have to be. Besides, I love the old stallion.

HAZEL: Judging from his letters, you don't have much to worry about. Torrid stuff.

EDITH: He wrote those letters to a photograph.

KIT: You have letters? *Dirty* letters?

HAZEL: I don't know how they got past the censors.

KIT: Can I see one? Just one?

EDITH: You sure have changed *your* tune.

HAZEL: Ah, young love. Ain't it wonderful?

EDITH: Unless my memory deceives me, it was awful. Does he, doesn't he? Will he, won't he? I guess there are advantages to middle age. All *I* have to worry about is...does he, doesn't he?

HAZEL: Will he, won't he?

EDITH: *Can* he?

KIT: I thought you lost interest when you got older.

EDITH: Who told you that?

HAZEL: Why Edith, I believe you're horny.

EDITH: I *know* I'm horny. I'm so horny I'd be climbing the walls, if we had any walls.

HAZEL: Me, too. Do you think it's the climate?

EDITH: It sure isn't the Spam.

HAZEL: We'd better knock it off. We're embarrassing the children. (*Looks at the Coke*) This stuff really *does* make you high.

MARY: There! Did you hear it?

KIT: What?

MARY: Guns.

KIT: There aren't any guns, Mary.

MARY: I *heard* them.

HAZEL: You're tired.

MARY: We're all tired.

HAZEL: Well, be careful. Half the WACs on this island are walking around with malaria.

MARY: (*Irritable*) Why not? They work us sixteen hours a day in hundred-degree heat. Keep us on short rations of food I wouldn't give to a pig. Dress us in clothes the men can't wear. The mosquitoes breed on our toothbrushes, and my shoes haven't been dry since I left Idaho.

EDITH: She doesn't sleep, either. (*Mary glares at her*) Well, you don't.

HAZEL: Are you taking your atabrine?

MARY: I've swallowed so much atabrine I could hide in the jungle and pass for moss. Leave me alone.

HAZEL: I'm ranking medical officer in this crowd. It's my job to make sure you take care of yourself.

MARY: (*Bitter*) Good girl, Hazel. Protect the Army's investment.

KIT: You know Hazel's not like that.

MARY: I'm sorry. I'm not myself.

HAZEL: It's okay, Sparks. Who is? Go take a nap. Now.

MARY: I'm on duty in ten minutes.

KIT: You just got *off* duty.

MARY: Double shifts.

KIT: They can't do that.

MARY: Tell it to the Marines.

> *Mary strides out of the tent. Kit follows.*

KIT: Mary....

MARY: Don't start in on me, Kit.

KIT: Hey. (*Embraces her*) Take it easy, will you?

MARY: I'm all nerves, Kit. What's happening to me?

KIT: Too much sun and rich food?

MARY: Please don't joke. I'm frightened.

KIT: So am I. You feel a little feverish.

MARY: I can't be. I'm cold. (*They look at each other*) It's lack of sleep, that's all.

KIT: Sure.

MARY: I'm adjusting to jungle living. Turning into a reptile.

KIT: Sure.

MARY: I have to go. See you tonight?

KIT: I'm on the night shift.

MARY: This is an inhuman war.

> *Mary exits. Kit returns to the tent.*

EDITH: I don't like it.

HAZEL: Neither do I.

EDITH: Do you think she's sick?

HAZEL: Maybe.

KIT: She's sick.

HAZEL: Don't jump to conclusions.

KIT: Why not? It's the only approved form of exercise around here.

HAZEL: She's working too hard, that's for sure.

KIT: Those replacements better show up before the whole thing falls apart.

EDITH: There aren't any replacements.

KIT: What?

EDITH: The request went out months ago. It was denied.

KIT: You mean we're it? For the duration?

EDITH: I'm afraid so.

KIT: Christ!

HAZEL: Easy, Kit.

KIT: What the hell are we doing in this mess?

HAZEL: You wanted to comfort the afflicted.

KIT: Next time I'll stay home and afflict the comfortable.

EDITH: Maybe there won't be a next time.

KIT: There'll be a next time.

EDITH: I don't think she looks so bad.

KIT: She looks terrible.

EDITH: No worse than your chickens.

KIT: The chickens are dying.

A stunned silence.

EDITH: Listen, some of the girls are being transferred to Manila. They say things are better there.

KIT: Manila's a hell hole.

EDITH: They sleep in real buildings. They work real hours. The sun even comes out once in a while.

KIT: Are they sending Signal Corps?

EDITH: It can be arranged.

HAZEL: How?

EDITH: I'll forge the papers. What do you say?

HAZEL: Forget it! You may think you're only one termite in the woodpile, but step out of line and you'll find yourself in a very bright spotlight.

EDITH: I don't care.

HAZEL: It's not just you. If they come sniffing around, and find out what Kit and Mary are up to…We're Court Martial material, kid.

EDITH: Then we're stuck.

HAZEL: Like rats in a trap.

Kit starts out.

Where are you going?

KIT: For a walk. What is it we're making the world safe for?

EDITH: Life, liberty, and the pursuit of happiness.

KIT: Somebody lied.

Kit exits.

BLACKOUT

END OF ACT I

Act Two

SCENE 1: That night. Marian's lamp is lit on the porch table. There is a little moonlight, and the night sound of insects.

Marian is setting up a game of scrabble.

In the tent, Hazel and Edith are playing their endless game of chess. Mary is asleep under a blanket.

Kit enters from the kitchen, a dish towel over her shoulder.

MARIAN: Finished?

KIT: Finished.

MARIAN: I wish you'd let me do it.

KIT: What's a little more KP in my life?

MARIAN: I don't want you to injure yourself.

KIT: Injure myself?

MARIAN: You might slip on the wet floor.

KIT: I only washed the dishes. I didn't climb in with them.

MARIAN: Well, you can't be too careful. (*Continues setting up the game board, blithering along neurotically*) I never know what to expect when I come here. I have a terrible apprehension that one day I'll find you curled in a corner drooling.

KIT: One more crack like that and I'll toss you to the Gray Panthers.

MARIAN: Do you want to play, or not?

KIT: Yes, I want to play, unless you'd rather sit here and watch me deteriorate.

MARIAN: Don't be silly. You draw first.

HAZEL: Check.

EDITH: Rats. (*Moves a piece as Hazel reaches over and adjusts Mary's blanket*) Is she asleep?

HAZEL: I think so.

EDITH: How can she even look at a blanket in this heat?

MARY: (*Looks up*) Kit?

HAZEL: (*Gently*) Go back to sleep.

MARY: Where is she?

HAZEL: She'll be along.

MARY: Are you sure?

HAZEL: I'm sure.

MARY: Wake me when she comes?

HAZEL: Since when did Kit enter quietly?

MARIAN: (*Making a word*) How do you like *them* apples?

KIT: I'm impressed.

MARIAN: (*As she counts up her score*) Chet won't play Scrabble with me. He says it's no challenge.

KIT: Let's give him a lobotomy.

MARIAN: Let's. Mother was crazy about Chet.

KIT: Of course she was. He's male.

MARIAN: And a gentleman.

KIT: Except when he's killing birds, and making fun of his wife.

MARIAN: Well, nobody's perfect.

KIT: I hope Helen never heard you say that. She thought she was.

MARIAN: She *was* very beautiful.

KIT: I'll grant you that.

MARIAN: That was why she hated it so, I guess.

KIT: Being beautiful?

MARIAN: Growing old. She said it was a nightmare.

KIT: I think it's unfair to say things like that. It frightens the young and gives a false impression.

MARIAN: It isn't a nightmare?

KIT: Heavens, no. It *is* a surprise. We spend so much of our lives young, old is always what we aren't yet. Of course, there are a lot of things I can't do anymore. But, by and large, I'm horrified I ever did them. The worst of it is the way people treat you. They speak very simply, as if you've lost the capacity for abstract thought.

MARIAN: Don't you worry about dying?

KIT: Not as much as you do.

MARIAN: What about afterward?

KIT: I think we go on living as long as we're remembered with affection.

MARIAN: Then my immortality will be brief.

KIT: Why, Marian, are you fishing?

MARIAN: Mother didn't believe in life after death.

KIT: Your mother hardly believed in life *before* death. It was something she had to put up with between cocktail parties.

MARIAN: The last few years, she seemed to be waiting to die.

KIT: Marian, aren't you well?

MARIAN: I have high blood pressure.

KIT: You always had high blood pressure. Probably had it *in utero*.

MARIAN: The doctor says I have to stop worrying.

KIT: Wonderful. Now if you run out of things to worry about, you can worry about worrying. It won't kill you, if you quit smoking and watch your diet.

MARIAN: It's impossible to watch your diet in a house full of men. Maybe I should take my meals with your neighbors.

KIT: I don't recommend it. They have small children. Small children and Granola are a vile combination.

MARIAN: You don't like children, do you?

KIT: Only for brief, meaningful, and mutually rewarding encounters.

MARIAN: That must be why you never married. Mother loved children.

KIT: She did not.

MARIAN: Did you like my boys?

KIT: Your boys were horrors.

MARIAN: They still are.

HAZEL: (*Looks over at Mary sleeping*) I never noticed how young she is.

EDITH: Twenty-five.

HAZEL: Too young for this. We're all too young for this.

EDITH: Hazel, do you think we'll ever feel safe again?

KIT: (*As Marian is pondering her next play*) Poor Hazel. All the way home, she planned her wedding. The first thing Clark Guidry did when we docked was introduce her to his wife.

MARIAN: She died, didn't she?

KIT: They all did.

MARIAN: So you're the last of the bunch.

KIT: Someone had to be, I guess.

MARIAN: You could have had a mass suicide.

KIT: Now, why didn't I think of that?

MARIAN: (*As she counts up her score*) I'm not too crazy about all that closeness. It feels sticky. Women aren't dependable.

KIT: Who told you *that* one?

MARIAN: Mother.

KIT: I don't know why I asked.

MARIAN: With men, you always know where you stand.

KIT: If that's where you want to stand.

MARIAN: Women are so messy.

KIT: Not Hazel. She was compulsive.

MARIAN: *Emotionally* messy.

KIT: Marian, if you don't like women, how can you like yourself?

MARIAN: I never said I did. "Family," she used to say. "The only people you can really count on are your family. Blood is thicker than water." (*Looks at the word Kit has made*) Kit! A triple word! And you used the X. Whatever made you think of noxious?

KIT: I can't imagine.

MARIAN: Well, that wipes out my lead. Now, don't talk to me. I have to be clever.

EDITH: Do you ever want to walk away from all this?

HAZEL: Right into a dishonorable discharge? No, thanks. It's going to be hard enough to find work.

EDITH: We might as well be in prison.

HAZEL: Food's probably better in prison.

EDITH: I could stand it if I knew when it'd be over.

HAZEL: You'll drive yourself nuts with that kind of thinking. Try to look at this as...home.

EDITH: You're demented.

MARY: (*Half asleep*) No...don't....

HAZEL: Mary?

MARY: *Don't....*

HAZEL: (*Goes to her*) Wake up, Mary. (*Pulls her to a sitting position*) Mary. Mary Cleveland. Look at me. (*Mary looks around in a daze*) Look at me, Mary. Come on, come on, focus. Focus, damn it!

MARY: (*In a panic*) Can't...get...back....

HAZEL: Touch your arms. Feel. Stay with me. Feel your hands, your face. Now get up, move around. (*Mary does*) Better?

MARY: I thought I was dying.

HAZEL: It'll pass.

MARY: I couldn't get back. What'll happen if I can't get....

HAZEL: You can bring yourself back. Walk it off. (*Mary still looks distraught*) It'll be okay, Sparks. I promise.

> Mary exits.

Edith, when Kit gets here, let Mary tell her.

EDITH: Sure.

HAZEL: (*Edith is looking after Mary*) Your move.

MARIAN: You're not paying attention.

KIT: Sorry.

MARIAN: How do you bear this silence? I know I won't sleep a wink. I'll lie there and listen to the roaches cantering across the kitchen floor.

KIT: There are no roaches in my kitchen.

MARIAN: How do you know? They don't come out in the daytime. This place should have been torn down ages ago.

KIT: Because you're afraid of silence?

MARIAN: It reeks of decay.

KIT: (*A little irritated*) You're having an olfactory hallucination. Probably a brain tumor.

MARIAN: Mother had hallucinations. They say crazy people get worse during the full moon. Of course, it isn't very scientific.

KIT: Well, science hasn't done much for me lately.

MARIAN: They put men on the moon.

KIT: And they hit golf balls. Your turn.

MARIAN: You're too quick for me.

KIT: Millions of years of evolution, for what? To hit golf balls on the moon. We should have stayed in the primordial muck.

MARIAN: I'm not going to worry about it.

EDITH: Mary didn't eat lunch.

HAZEL: Did you?

EDITH: Of course not. It was disgusting.

MARIAN: Let's see you beat *that*.

KIT: Very nice.

MARIAN: (*As she counts her score*) Kit, does life ever frighten you?

KIT: Constantly.

MARIAN: But are you ever...down deep, in the marrow of your bones, frightened?

KIT: I have been. What do you say we call it a night?

MARIAN: I'll never get to sleep. I'm afraid I won't wake up.

KIT: (*Exasperated*) You're afraid to live, you're afraid to die. There isn't any middle ground, you know.

MARIAN: Some people are in comas for years.

KIT: Well, try that.

MARIAN: I can't imagine anything worse.

KIT: Marian, did anyone ever tell you you're a little neurotic?

MARIAN: It's my claim to fame.

KIT: Life is long, and fame is fleeting.

MARIAN: Now you're impatient with me.

KIT: My dear niece, you are exhausting.

MARIAN: (*Pouting*) We might as well go to bed, then.

KIT: (*As Marian starts to clean up*) Leave that. We can do it in the morning.

MARIAN: It won't take a minute.

KIT: *Leave it.* I have the roaches trained.

MARIAN: Do you want to use the bathroom first?

KIT: You go ahead. I'll take a walk.

MARIAN: You shouldn't stumble about in the dark with that bad hip.

KIT: I won't stumble.

MARIAN: You might.

KIT: I do it every night.

MARIAN: Well, all right, then. I'll lock up.

KIT: I never lock up.

MARIAN: You should.

KIT: (*Wearily*) Then lock up.

MARIAN: Popovers for breakfast?

KIT: That would be fine.

MARIAN: I forgot to get eggs. I'll go to the store first thing.

KIT: Don't bother.

MARIAN: It's no bother. Don't prowl all night.

KIT: Marian, if I wanted a dog, I'd *get* a dog. Good *night.*

MARIAN: There's a little something for you in that bag. Don't forget a flashlight.

> *Marian gives Kit a quick kiss on the cheek, which Kit tolerates.*

> *Marian exits.*

> *Kit peers into the bag, draws out a dress, very dull and old ladyish. Holds it up against herself, looks down, and laughs.*

KIT: God love you, Helen, no *wonder* you died.

> *She returns the dress to the bag and goes to the tent.*

Pack up your troubles, kids. The invasion of Japan has begun.

HAZEL: Glory be! We're invading a place I've heard of.

KIT: It's finally winding down.

EDITH: The country won't be the same without the war.

HAZEL: Don't break out the champagne. It took them twelve weeks to take Okinawa.

KIT: Where's Mary?

EDITH: Out for a stroll.

KIT: Anything new with her?

HAZEL: Not that we've heard.

KIT: (*Pulls a bra from her pocket*) Can anyone give this a good home?

EDITH: A brassiere? A *real* brassiere?

KIT: Looks about your size. Not that I've been peeking.

HAZEL: All right, who was it this time?

KIT: WAC Officers' laundry.

HAZEL: Those are *our* people.

EDITH: If a guy gives you nylons, he gets to make a pass. What's a brassiere worth?

KIT: (*Embarrassed*) For crying out loud.

EDITH: Name it, I'm yours.

KIT: Just try it on, will you?

HAZEL: Let's see what you've been bragging about.

EDITH: Hold onto your hats!

Edith exits.

HAZEL: That was a very nice thing to do, Kit. You look bushed.

KIT: Yeah. I thought Mary'd be here.

HAZEL: She will be.

KIT: Hazel, is she all right?

HAZEL: Sure.

KIT: Something's wrong.

HAZEL: Relax.

KIT: Tell me!

HAZEL: It won't help for you to carry on.

> *Mary enters with her laundry bag. Seeing Kit, she forces a light tone.*

MARY: I was going to wash out a few unmentionables, but the line's a mile deep at the washtubs.

HAZEL: Hang it on a bush. The rain'll wash it.

MARY: Well, at least I don't have to wrestle with a soggy girdle. That's one advantage to wartime.

KIT: Hello, Mary.

MARY: Oh, hi, Kit. Rough day?

KIT: The usual.

MARY: I'm sorry to hear that.

KIT: How are you?

MARY: Not bad. How about you?

KIT: Fine.

HAZEL: I Don't believe you've met. Kit, this is Corporal Mary Cleveland. Mary, Lieutenant Kit Fortescue. Kit's from Maryland—where the crabs come from.

KIT: All right, Hazel.

HAZEL: Kit says they're hitting Japan.

MARY: I know. I heard it on the squawk box.

KIT: How does it look?

MARY: With luck, we'll be out of here by the time we're ninety.

KIT: Home for Christmas.

MARY: They didn't say which Christmas.

> *Edith enters, strikes a pose.*

KIT: Hubba-hubba.

HAZEL: That's what I call standing at attention.

MARY: Step aside, Jane Russell.

EDITH: (*Hugs Kit*) Kit, I love you.

MARY: (*Teasing*) Now, just a darn minute....

HAZEL: Come on, kid, let's show you off to the other girls. They're going to be green with envy.

MARY: They're already green with atabrine.

> *Hazel and Edith leave. An uncomfortable silence. Mary doesn't know how to start. Kit suspects what's coming, doesn't want to hear it.*

I was over at the hospital today.

KIT: Hope Clark Guidry didn't make a pass at you.

MARY: I didn't see Clark....

KIT: (*Quickly, picking up a chess piece*) How can they tell who wins with these things?

MARY: I didn't see Clark Guidry.

KIT: It's a real Garden of Eden, isn't it? No matter how much creosote they use, it smells of blood. *I* smell of blood. For the rest of my life, I'll smell of blood.

MARY: Kit....

KIT: You'd think they'd be through with war. You'd think they'd have had enough of fear and pain. I'd had enough after four days.

MARY: Kit....

KIT: As soon as they put that uniform back on, a little light comes into their eyes, and the muscles at the corners of their mouths start to work. And you know they're hungry for it.

MARY: Kit, listen to me.

KIT: When it's over they'll go home and sit in bars and show their scars like medals.

MARY: You have to hear this!

KIT: Please don't....

MARY: Yes! Saying it won't make it real, Kit. It's already real. I have malaria. (*Silence. Kit looks at the floor*) It's an ugly word, isn't it?

KIT: How...bad?

MARY: Bad enough.

KIT: Will they send you home?

MARY: Not a prayer. I'm needed for the war effort.

> *Helpless, Kit takes her hand, still staring at the floor.*

It explains a lot, but it doesn't explain the guns.

KIT: Doesn't it?

MARY: Yes, it does.

> *Marian enters the porch.*

MARIAN: Kit, are you out there?

> *Kit doesn't hear her. Marian lights a cigarette, sits down.*

MARY: Please say something, Kit.

KIT: (*Explodes*) I HATE THIS GODDAMN WAR!!

MARIAN: (*Hearing*) Oh, dear God in Heaven.

BLACKOUT

SCENE 2: The next morning, early.

> *Marian creeps out into the yard, goes to the tent and removes blankets, chessboard,*

lantern, and Mary's laundry bag. She places them at the edge of the porch, and creeps back into the house.

> *Kit enters, takes a few wake-up breaths.*

> *Marian enters.*

KIT: You're up early.

MARIAN: I couldn't sleep. Rustlings and patterings overhead all night. When I finally drifted off for a few minutes, there was the most horrible screaming. I *know* someone was being murdered.

KIT: You checked, of course.

MARIAN: I took a peek out the window. You don't think I'd go out in the dark with some maniac running loose.

KIT: Your maniac was a pair of screech owls.

MARIAN: It was hideous. I don't know how you stand it.

KIT: They're usually the picture of decorum. I set them off when I walked too near the tree.

MARIAN: God only knows who might be lurking out there.

KIT: Owls are very effective against lurkers.

MARIAN: I suppose. (*Briskly*) Well, what would you like to do today?

KIT: Whatever pleases you. (*Quickly*) I take that back. Who knows what you might come up with.

MARIAN: I could drive you to church.

KIT: I haven't been to church in so long, I wouldn't know how to behave.

MARIAN: You should have told me. You'd think the least those hillbillies could do is give an old lady a lift to church.

KIT: We all meet in the clearing and perform obscene rituals.

MARIAN: I wish you wouldn't talk like that.

KIT: God and I had a falling out some years ago. I'm not going down on my knees to a deity that sits around picking his nose while the rest of us claw each other to death.

MARIAN: Nobody kneels in church anymore, only the Catholics.

KIT: That's a relief!

MARIAN: You don't go to town, you don't go to church, you don't go anywhere.

KIT: I moved twenty-seven times in my life. I think I'll stay home today.

MARIAN: I might as well make breakfast.

KIT: Aren't we out of eggs?

MARIAN: I've been to the store. They open at six.

KIT: (*As Marian exits*) Give me a shout when you're ready. I'm going to tackle the weeds.

MARIAN: (*Offstage*) Before breakfast?

KIT: It's a jungle out there. (*Starts to leave—notices the things piled on the porch*) Marian, what is this?

MARIAN: (*Entering*) What? Just some old junk. I cleaned out the tent for you.

KIT: You did *what*?

MARIAN: I'll drop it off at the dump on my way to town.

KIT: (*Explodes*) Damn it, Marian, keep your nose out of my business!

> *Kit tries to carry the things back to the tent, but can't handle them all in one trip. Frustrated, she tosses the laundry bag down and hobbles to the tent with the blankets.*

MARIAN: I don't know what you want those disgusting old things for. Those blankets are riddled with holes, God knows what's living in them. You could get a horrible disease. (*As Kit picks up the lantern*) What if that tipped over? You'd be burned to a crisp. (*Picks up the laundry bag*) And what in the name of all that's Holy is this?

KIT: (*Grabs it*) Take your hand off that.

MARIAN: It's packed with dirty clothes.

KIT: It belongs to Mary. (*Trying to keep her balance, she carries the laundry bag and chessboard back to the tent*)

MARIAN: Do you mean to tell me you've been carting that pile of rags around all these years?

KIT: I made it.

MARIAN: Oh, Kit, that's insane.

KIT: It's all I have. (*Starts trying to make the beds*)

MARIAN: I heard you out here last night, talking to shadows. Do you know what happens to people who talk to shadows? Pretty soon they don't know what's real and what isn't. And when that happens, they come and put you away. Do you hear me, Kit? They come and put you away.

KIT: (*Faces her*) Get out of my house, Marian.

MARIAN: Is that what you want, to be put away?

KIT: GET OUT!

> *Marian exits. Kit turns back to the tent, trying frantically to make up the cots. Frustrated at her clumsiness, she angrily kicks the laundry bag.*

Damn it!

> *Shocked, she retrieves the bag, sits on a cot, and wraps her arms around it.*

I'm sorry, Mary. I'm so sorry.

> *Puts her head down on the laundry bag and cries.*

> *Hazel enters.*

HAZEL: Who ransacked the tent?

KIT: I threw a fit.

HAZEL: I wish you'd thrown it on *your* side.

KIT: I can't take much more, Hazel.

HAZEL: I know. (*Teasing gently*) Developing a laundry fetish?

KIT: I see more of her laundry than I see of her.

HAZEL: It's going to get worse. They lost another girl today. Back to 24-hour shifts.

KIT: She can't handle that.

HAZEL: The Army says she can.

KIT: We have to *do* something.

HAZEL: Kit, you've done everything you can. Mary's done everything she can. I've tried, Clark's tried. We all get the same answer...as long as she can work, they won't make an exception. The only thing we can do is pray.

KIT: To what? For what?

HAZEL: (*Trying to reassure her*) Malaria isn't always fatal.

KIT: Not unless you're stuck on a rain-soaked island in the South Pacific. Not unless you work 24 hours a day and never rest. Not unless you hear guns that aren't there.

HAZEL: Don't, Kit.

KIT: There's no way to stop this war. It has its own life now. It feeds on beauty. It seeks out gentleness and crushes it, and picks its teeth with broken bones. And now it's coming for Mary. It's coming for Mary, and I love her.

Kit breaks down. Hazel holds her.

HAZEL: They move another bunch up every day. Her orders could come through tomorrow. When she gets to Manila, they'll take care of her. Look, buddy, I'm not much good at speeches, and I'm not the world's warmest gal. But I do love the two of you. So if you ever need me...well, send up a flare, will you?

KIT: Hazel, why do I have to love so hard?

HAZEL: I guess it's your nature.

Mary enters.

MARY: The way this place is clearing out, Hollandia's going to be a ghost town.

HAZEL: Everybody's headed north.

MARY: Kinda gives you the creeps. (*To Kit*) You look like the Wrath of God.

HAZEL: Morale problem.

MARY: Cheer up. It can't last forever.

KIT: It already has.

HAZEL: I hear they upped your quinine.

MARY: Yeah. Malaria has its bright side. Quinine kills the taste of Spam. Wish it killed the texture.

HAZEL: I thought you were working a double shift today.

MARY: Lunch break. I get to spend a whole half hour with my girl.

HAZEL: I think I hear my mother calling.

Hazel exits.

KIT: Hazel's a good woman.

MARY: Am I doing this to you?

KIT: No, I'm on my morbid break.

MARY: I'm really sorry, Kit.

KIT: For God's sake, it isn't your fault. When this is over, I'm going to dedicate my life to removing every mosquito from the face of the earth.

MARY: Kit, have you thought much about what's going to happen when we get home?

KIT: Every chance I get.

MARY: It won't be easy. New Guinea's more than an island. It's outside of time, outside of the order of things. They won't welcome what we've become.

KIT: I don't care.

MARY: Listen to me. I've known other women like us.

KIT: We'll have a lifetime together.

MARY: A lifetime of fear.

KIT: Christmas together. Vacations together.

MARY: We'll have to hide the way we feel. We'll always be a little afraid of someone finding out.

KIT: We'll hold hands in the movies, and spend hours lost in the five and dime.

MARY: We won't know who to trust. Even with our closest friends, we'll have to be careful.

KIT: You'll put your arms around me while I'm cooking, and I'll pretend to be annoyed.

MARY: We can't touch in public.

KIT: We'll have arguments, and make up.

MARY: When we travel, we'll have to ask for a room with twin beds.

KIT: If you wake in the night, I'll be there.

MARY: You have to know what you're getting into.

KIT: Mary, I'm *in* it. I'll do what has to be done.

MARY: There will be times when you hate it.

KIT: I *love* you.

MARY: Maybe you'll even hate that. Maybe you'll hate me. Maybe you'll hate yourself. I couldn't bear that, Kit.

KIT: Are you telling me to get lost?

MARY: No. God, no. But if the time ever comes that you want to leave…well, no hard feelings.

KIT: I'm no dewy-eyed bobby-soxer who believes life is what you see on the silver screen. I know life is what happens after the lights go on and the audience files out. My dear, ridiculous Mary.

Edith enters, depressed.

Morbidity's reaching epidemic proportions around here today.

EDITH: We're shipping out.

KIT: Home?

EDITH: Manila.

KIT: All of us?

EDITH: No.

KIT: (*Fearfully*) Who stays?

EDITH: (*Pause*) Mary.

They look at Mary. Mary turns away.

KIT: They can't toss you on the damn fire like a stick of wood.

MARY: That's where you're wrong, Kit. They can do anything they like.

Mary rushes off. Kit walks wearily to the porch, sits on steps, head in hands. Marian enters, approaches Kit tentatively.

MARIAN: Kit?

KIT: I told you to get out.

MARIAN: (*Holding out a pack of cupcakes*) I want to apologize.

KIT: What's that?

MARIAN: Peace offering.

KIT: You put a crack in our friendship the size of the Grand Canyon. You can't mend it with junk food.

MARIAN: Please take it.

KIT: Why do you have to look so pathetic? (*Takes it*)

MARIAN: Forgive me?

KIT It'll take time.

MARIAN: I did what I thought was best for you.

KIT: What you think is best for me is seldom what I want.

MARIAN: People don't always know what's best for them.

KIT: I'm not going to argue with you. You can mind your manners, or you can leave. The decision is yours. If you want to be on good terms with me, don't come here and rearrange my life. I know you mean well...you *do* mean well, don't you?

MARIAN: Of course I do.

KIT: Then understand one thing. My memories are very dear to me. They're all I have left.

MARIAN: You have your family.

KIT: "Family" has never been the center of my world.

MARIAN: It could be a great comfort to you.

KIT: Marian, for fifty years I've been surrounded by violence and death. I've loved, and been loved, and had that love taken from me. I've served in three wars....

MARIAN: No one forced you.

KIT: I wanted to help in the way I knew best. Ultimately, I believe it made very little difference, but it was what I wanted to do.

MARIAN: Put all that out of your mind.

KIT: That would be an act of unspeakable immorality. But I think I've earned the right to be left in peace.

MARIAN: To talk to shadows.

KIT: To talk to shadows, or weave baskets, or cut out paper dolls. Whatever gives me pleasure.

MARIAN: What I heard last night didn't sound like pleasure.

KIT: I don't expect you to understand that.

MARIAN: Of course not. I haven't been lucky enough to be in a *war*.

KIT: Marian, you are a very foolish woman.

MARIAN: (*Gesturing toward the tent*) *That* gives you pleasure, and you call *me* foolish.

KIT: My life...my life has been one of light and shadow, so intricately entwined that, if I were

to try to separate one from the other, the whole fabric would fall apart in my hands.

MARIAN: Those people are dead.

KIT: They're very alive to me.

MARIAN: You talk to *dead* people!

KIT: Sometimes it's easier than talking to the living.

MARIAN: I've always suspected you don't like me.

KIT: (*Wearily*) Oh, Marian, I've hardly known you.

MARIAN: You never took the time.

KIT: I've met many people over the years, people with whom I could have shared moments of great delight. There wasn't time to know them all.

MARIAN: There's time now.

KIT: But no more room in my heart.

MARIAN: That's cruel.

KIT: I'm sorry.

MARIAN: You only have room for dead people.

KIT: Are you jealous of my poor phantoms?

MARIAN: Your "poor phantoms" mean more to you than your living family. You've been back here three years, and all you've done in that time is deteriorate.

KIT: Well, that's what I came home for, to deteriorate.

MARIAN: Like an old dog dragging itself off into the woods to die.

KIT: What would you have me do?

MARIAN: Involve yourself with your family.

KIT: I did as much of that as the traffic would bear. Any more involvement with me would have shortened Helen's life.

MARIAN: What am *I*, invisible?

KIT: Marian, what do you want from me?

MARIAN: I want us to be a family.

KIT: Chet and the children are your family.

MARIAN: That isn't enough. I want *us* to be close, and loving. I want us to be a...safe harbor.

KIT: (*With a laugh*) How many families do you know like that?

MARIAN: We could have been, if you hadn't gone away.

KIT: I don't think so.

MARIAN: In the old days, when we drove up you'd be standing on the back porch. As soon as you saw me, you'd throw out your arms and shout, "There's my girl! There's my Marooch!"

KIT: Marian....

MARIAN: We'd sit on the swing and you'd make up stories for me. You'd let me help you cook, and set the table. You always put my chair next to yours.

KIT: I did those things because you were the only child among all those adults. Because your father was too busy talking about his Irish setters to notice you, and your mother couldn't stop flirting with the second cousins from North Carolina long enough to wipe your nose. I felt sorry for you.

MARIAN: You loved me.

KIT: I suppose I loved you, in a way. Please, don't make me say these things.

MARIAN: I *need* you. I'm lonely. I lie in bed at night, as close to the edge as I can get, trying not to touch that stranger I married.

KIT: There's nothing left inside me, Marian. I have nothing left to give you.

MARIAN: Some days I'm afraid to leave the house. I sit in my living room for hours, watching the cars go by on the street, waiting, waiting for it all to fall apart.

KIT: Marian, don't.

MARIAN: It's been like this since Mother died. I had someone to care for, and now she's gone. I reach out for her, like a blind person groping for a wall, but there's...no one there.

> *Moved, Kit reaches out to touch her. Mary appears at the entrance to the tent. Hazel and Edith enter, carrying duffel bags.*

HAZEL: Kit, it's time. The plane's leaving.

> *Kit looks toward them, hesitates, looks back at Marian.*

KIT: Marian, I can't.

MARIAN: Do you want me to get down on my knees and beg? All right, I'm begging. Love me, Kit. Please love me.

MARY: Don't go.

EDITH: *Come on.*

MARIAN: Love me, Kit.

KIT: Marian, I'm not Helen. I can't take her place.

MARIAN: (*Angry*) You're *exactly* like her. The world revolves around you. The moon and stars rise in your personal Heaven.

HAZEL: *Kit.*

MARY: Don't leave me. I'm afraid.

MARIAN: When I was a child I'd come to her, asking her to read me a story, wanting to tell her my day. And she'd say, "Run along, darling. Play with your little friends." She never even noticed I didn't *have* any "little friends."

MARY: Kit.

MARIAN: When I was sick she shut me away and let the housekeeper take care of me. Because sickness depressed her. She never touched my babies. Babies are messy. On my wedding day she didn't help me dress.

EDITH: They're loading.

MARIAN: She was too busy entertaining her guests.

MARY: Five minutes. Give us five minutes to say good-bye.

EDITH: You have to come *now*, Kit.

MARIAN: *She* was the center of attention. *She* got all the applause. When she came to live with us she brought all her old party dresses. Trunks of party dresses for an old woman.

KIT: I don't want to leave you, Mary.

MARIAN: Every day she dragged them out and made me look at them. "I wore this little organdy to my first tea dance. Isn't it pretty, Marian? See how perfectly the China blue sash matches my eyes?"

HAZEL: *Kit!*

MARIAN: "I was the Belle of the Ball. Everyone said so. 'Why, Helen, you're the Belle of the Ball.'"

MARY: Let me hold you one more time. Just one more time, Kit.

MARIAN: One day, as I was putting away one of those dresses, my foot caught the hem and tore it. She sat on the edge of her bed and cried. My mother, who never shed a tear for me, sat on the edge of her bed and cried over a torn dress.

KIT: Mary, forgive me.

MARIAN: The doctor said it was her age, her mind was going. He gave her something to calm her nerves. Then I knew what to do.

KIT: (*To Mary*) I thought we had a lifetime.

MARIAN: Every so often I'd take out one of those dresses and rip it to shreds. Right in front of her. I told them she did it. She was a senile old woman. She tried to say it was me, and we gave her more drugs.

EDITH: Kit, we have to go.

KIT: Mary!

MARIAN: Every night, when I bent down to kiss her, I'd whisper in her ear, "Which one will it be tomorrow, Mama?"

KIT: We'll be together, Mary. I promise. All of us.

MARIAN: I destroyed them all. The organdy, the wine satin, the dusty rose lace.

MARY: I'm afraid.

MARIAN: While she sat there, trembling, tears leaking from the corners of her China blue eyes.

HAZEL: Kit! Come with us now!

MARIAN: It took a very long time. A very long time.

KIT: All right, I'm coming.

> *Kit starts off. Marian grabs her.*

MARIAN: I tore up her memories, Kit. I'm very good at tearing up memories.

MARY: You had left Manila by the time they took me there. The moon was full that night I died. If I turned my head, I could see Corregidor, dark and silent, reflected in a pool of moonlight. I was too tired to cry. The only thing I wanted, the only thing I ever wanted was you.

MARIAN: Are you listening to me? I'll rip your memories to pieces.

KIT: Goddamn you, Marian, GET OFF MY PROPERTY!

MARIAN: I'll be back.

KIT: Not without a court order.

MARIAN: It's on the way.

KIT: I'll fight you, Marian.

MARIAN: Ah, but who'll speak for you, Kit? All your friends are *dead*.

KIT: I'll fight your courts and your doctors. I'll fight your love and your need. And when I can't fight anymore, I'll die. But I won't lose her again. Do you hear me, Marian? (*Goes to Mary, embraces her*) I won't lose her again.

BLACK OUT

THE END

CHICAGO AREA WOMEN!

BEYOND COUPLEDOM

Perhaps our lover relationships *are* at the center of what makes us lesbians, but lesbian life, lesbian culture is much more than simply what we do with our lovers. Our herstory is rich with connections and resources. Sometimes we've had lesbian ballgames, bars, discussion groups, community centers, C-R groups, newspapers, social networks, musical groups, card clubs, dances, circles of friends, work crews, some or all or none of the above. Sometimes our lovers were all we had.

MY COWBOY BOOTS

WHAT GOT YOU THROUGH?

The next evening of **Lesbian Herstory Storytelling** at **Mountain Moving Coffeehouse** is coming up, and we are looking for women to tell brief (5-8 minute) stories about some aspect of their lesbian lives before 1980- something that gave joy, meaning, or perhaps simply survival. It could be a friend, a club, a sports team, a bar, a book, an event - you name it!

TELL US A STORY

You can *tell your own story from the stage *write your story for someone else to read *tell your story on tape ahead of time and we will edit and transcribe it for someone else to read. Please call—

Tell Us A Story Productions

MARTHA	MICHAL
708/584-1255	312/252-3154

THE EVENT WILL BE A BENEFIT FOR SINISTER WISDOM

September 12
MOUNTAIN MOVING COFFEEHOUSE
See Nightlines for details, or call *Tell Us A Story Productions*

1992

Beebo Brinker

by Ann Bannon

Mona was not at the Colophon that night, nor for many nights afterward. In a way, Beebo was relieved. She wanted to meet her, but she wanted time to meet other people too, to see other places, and cruise around the Village without any pressure on her to prove things to herself. Or to a worldly girl like Mona Petry. Beebo was still a stranger in a strange town, unsure, and grateful for a chance to learn unobserved.

She would sit and gaze for hours at the girls in the bars or passing in the streets. She wanted to talk to them, see what they were like. She was often drawn to one enough to daydream about her, but she never mentioned it to Jack. Still, she was eagerly curious about the Lesbian mores and social codes. The gay girls seemed so smooth and easy with each other; talking about shared experiences in a special slang, like members of an exclusive sorority.

Beebo, watching them as the days and weeks passed, became slowly aware how much she envied them. She wanted to join the in-group. And she would watch them longingly and wonder if their talk was ever about her.

A few of Jack's friends, who had met her in his company, would come up and talk with her, and knowing for certain that they were Lesbians gave Beebo a violent pleasure, whether or not the girls themselves were exciting. Looking at one she would think, *She knows how it feels to want what I want. I could make her happy. I know it.* Even the word "Lesbian," that had offended her before, began to sound wonderful in her ears.

She shocked herself with such candid thoughts, but that was only at first. Little by little, it began to seem beautiful to her that two women could come together with passion and intelligence and make a life with and for each other; make a marriage. She dreamed of lovely, sophisticated women at her feet, aware even as she dreamed that she hadn't yet the *savoir faire* to win such a woman. But she was afire with ambition to acquire it.

She would walk into a bar, order a beer, and sit alone and silent through an evening. In her solitude, she seemed mysterious to the laughing chattering people around her. They began to point her out when she came in.

At first, ignorance and inexperience kept Beebo aloof. But she quickly understood that her refusal to be sociable made her the target of a lot of smiling speculation. When she got over being afraid of the situation, it amused her. The fact that she attracted girls, even ones she knew she would never pursue, was almost supernaturally strange and exciting to her. She submitted to their teasing questions with an enigmatic smile until she realized that one or two had worked themselves up to infatuation pitch over her.

Excerpts from the novel, originally published in 1962; reprinted in 1986 by Naiad Press.

There followed a period of elation when she walked into Julian's or the Cellar and saw the eyes she knew had waited all night to look into hers turn and flash in her direction. She always passed them by and went to a seat at the bar. But each time she came closer to stopping and answering a smile or asking someone to join her in a beer. And still, she couldn't find Mona.

⚲

Beebo and Jack were watching a TV show one evening when he asked her, during the commercial, why she wasn't going out that night. "Don't tell me you gave up on Mona," he teased.

Instead of answering she told him about the boy who was in love with her. "His name is Pat," she said. "The bartender told me. He looks hungry, as if he needed to be cared for." She laughed. "I was never much for maternal instincts—but he seems to bring them out."

"I'd like to meet him. He might bring mine out, too," Jack said.

"Why don't you come with me Friday? He's always at Julian's."

Jack looked away. "I've been trying to give you a free rein," he said. "You don't want me along. I'll find him myself."

"I do want you along," she said. "I like your company."

"More than the girls?" he grinned.

She felt herself tense all over. There had been so many chances lately to talk to him, and she had run away from them all. Now, she felt a surge of defiance, a will to have it out. He had a right to know at least as much about her as she knew about herself. He had earned it through his generosity and affection.

"I read a book once," she said clumsily. "Under my covers at night—when I was fifteen. It was about two girls who loved each other. One of them committed suicide. It hit me so hard I wanted to die, too. That's about as close as I've come to reality in my life, Jack. Until now."

He leaned over and switched off the television. The room was so quiet they could hear themselves breathing.

"I was kicked out of school," she went on

hesitantly, "because I looked so much like a boy, they thought I must be acting like one. Chasing girls. Molesting them. Everything I ever did to a girl, or wanted to do or dreamed of doing, happened in my imagination. The trouble was, everybody else in Juniper Hill had an imagination, too. And they had me doing all these things for real." She shut her eyes and tried to force her heart to slow down, just by thinking about it.

"And you never did?" he said. "You never tried? There must have been girls, Beebo—"

"There were, but all I had to do was talk to one and her name was mud. I wouldn't do that to anybody I cared for."

Jack stared at her, wondering what geyser of emotion must be waiting to erupt in someone so intense, so yearning, and so rigidly denied all her life.

"My father tried to teach me not to hate myself because I looked like hell in gingham frills," she said. "But when you see people turn away and laugh behind their hands....It makes you wonder what you really are." She looked at him anxiously, and then she said it. "I've never touched a girl I liked. Never made a pass or spoken a word of love to a single living girl. Does that make me normal, Jack?...And yet I know I could, and I think now I will, and God knows I want to desperately. Does that make me gay?" She spoke rapidly, stopping abruptly as if her voice had gone dead in her throat at the word "gay."

"Well, first," he said kindly, "you're Beebo Brinker, human being. If you are *gay*, that's second. Some girls like you are gay, some aren't. Your body is boyish, but there's nothing *wrong* with it." His voice was reassuring.

"Nothing, except there's a boy inside it," she said. "And he has to live without all the masculine trimmings other boys take for granted. Jack, long before I knew anything about sex, I knew I wanted to be tall and strong and wear pants and ride horses and have a career...and never marry a man or learn to cook or raise babies. Never."

"That's still no proof you're gay," he said, going slowly, letting her convince herself.

"I'm not even built like a girl. Girls are knock-elbowed and big-hipped. They can't throw or run or—look at my arm, Jack. I was the best pitcher on the team whenever they let me play." She rolled her sleeve back and showed him a well-muscled arm, browned and veined and straight as a boy's.

"I see," he murmured.

"It was the parents who gave me the worst of it," she said. "The kids weren't too bad till I got to high school. But you know what happens then. You get hairy and you get pimples and you have to start using a deodorant."

Jack laughed silently behind his cigarette.

"And the boys get big and hot and anxious, like a stallion servicing a mare."

Jack swallowed, feeling himself move. "And the girls?"

"The girls," she sighed, "get round and soft and snippy."

"And instead of round and soft, you got hot and anxious?"

"All of a sudden, I was Poison Ivy Brinker," she confirmed. "Nobody wanted whatever it was I had. My brother Jim said I wasn't a boy and I wasn't a girl, and I had damn well better be one or the other or he'd hound me out of school himself."

"What did you do?"

"I tried to be like the rest. But not to please *that* horse's ass." Her farmer's profanity tickled him. "I did it for Dad. He thought I was adjusting pretty well, and that was his consolation. I never told him how bad it was."

"So now you want to find Mona Petry," Jack said, after a small pause, "and ask her if you're gay."

"Not *ask* her. Just get to know her and see if it could happen. She makes me wonder so...Jack, what makes a feminine girl like that gay? Why does she love girls, when she's just as womanly and perfumed as the girl who goes for men? I used to think that all homosexual girls were three-quarters boy." She hung her head "Like me, I guess. And that they were all doomed to love feminine girls who could never love them back. It seems like a miracle that a girl like Mona could love a—" she stopped, embarrassed.

"Could love a girl like you," he finished for her. "Take it on faith, honey. She doesn't have to look like a Ram tackle to know that her happiness lies with other women. The girls you see around

town aren't all boyish, are they?"

"They're not all gay, either."

He ground out his cigarette. "Tell me why they ran you out of Juniper Hill. The whole story. Was it really just a nasty rumor about you and the Jones girl?"

Beebo lay down, stretched out on the sofa, and answered without looking at him. "They'd been hoping for an excuse for years," she said. "It was in April, last spring. I went to the livestock exhibition in Chicago with Dad and Jim. I was in the stalls with them most of the time, handling some of the steers from our county. Sweaty and gritty, and not thinking about much but the job. And then one night—I'll never know why—I took it into my head to wear Jim's good clothes.

"I knew it was dangerous, but suddenly it was so irresistible. Maybe I just wanted to get away with it. Maybe it was the feel of a man's clothes on my back, or a simple case of jealousy. Anyway, I played sick at dinnertime, and stayed in the hotel till they left.

"Jack, it was as though I had a fever. The minute I was alone I put Jim's things on. I slung Dad's German camera over my shoulder and took his Farm Journal press pass. On the way over, I stopped for a real man's haircut. The barber never said a word. Just took my money and stared.

"I looked older than Jim. I felt wonderful." She stopped, her chin trembling. "A blonde usher showed me to the press section. She was small and pretty and she asked me if I was from the 'working press.' I said yes because it sounded important. She gave me a seat in the front row with a typewriter. It was screwed down to a stand. God, imagine!" She almost laughed.

"I really blitzed them," she said, remembering the good part with a throb of regret. "Everybody else was writing on their machines to beat hell, but I didn't even put a piece of paper in mine. After a while I took out the camera and made some pictures. The girl came back and said I could work in the arena if I wanted to, and I did. It was hotter than hades but I wouldn't have taken that tweed jacket off for a fortune.

"I guess I took pictures for almost three hours...just wandered around, kidding the girls on horseback and keeping clear of the Wisconsin people." She hesitated and Jack said, "What happened then?"

"I got sick," she whispered. "My stomach. I thought it was bad food. Or that damn heat. Awful stomach cramps. In half an hour I was so miserable I could hardly stand up and I was scared to death I might faint. If I'd had any sense I'd have gone back to my seat and rested. But not Beebo. I didn't want to waste a moment of my glory. It would go away—it *had* to.

"Well, I was right about one thing—I fainted, right there in the arena. The next thing I knew, I was strangling on smelling salts and trying to sit up on a cot in the Red Cross station. The doctor asked how I felt and I said it was indigestion. He wanted to have a look.

"I was terrified. I tried to laugh it off. I said I was tired, I said it was the heat, I said it was something I ate. But that bastard had to look. He thought it might be appendicitis. There was nothing I could do but cover my face and curse, and cry," she said harshly. Jack handed her a newly lighted cigarette, and she took it, still talking.

"The doctor saw the tears, and that was the tip-off. He opened my shirt so fast the buttons flew. And when he saw my chest, he opened the pants without a word. Just big bug eyes." She gave Jack a look of sad disgust. "I had the curse," she muttered. "First time."

After a moment she went on, "I never meant to hurt anybody or cause a scene. But I hurt my father too much. He suffered over it. I had to wait till my hair grew out before I could go back to school, but I could have saved myself the bother. They let me know as soon as I got back I wasn't wanted. Before Chicago, they thought I was just a queer kid. But afterwards, I was really queer. There's a big difference."

Jack listened, bound to her by the story with an empathy born of his own emotional aberration.

"The principal of the high school said he hoped he could count on me to understand his position. *His* position. I wanted to ask him if he understood *mine*." There was hopeless bitterness in her voice.

"They never do," Jack said quietly. "Still,

that's not the only high school in the world. You could finish up somewhere else and go on to premed, Beebo."

"You didn't," she reminded him. "You got fed up and quit. But me—I've been expelled. I'm not wanted anywhere."

"Do you think a job as a truck driver is worth sacking a medical career for?"

"What did you sack yours for?" He was making her defensive.

"My story's all over," he said. "But there's still time for you. Beebo, do you know what you're trying to do? Get *even* with the world. You're so mad at it, and everybody in it for the bum deal you got, you're going to deny it a good doctor some day."

"I'd be a rotten doctor, Jack. I'd be scared. I'd be running and hiding every day of my life."

"Hell, plenty of doctors are gay. They manage." He was surprised at the importance it was assuming in his own mind. He really cared about it. It depressed him to think of what she might be and what she was in a fair way now of becoming. "You're thinking that if people are going to reject you, by God you're going to reject them first. If they make it hard for you to be a doctor, you'll make damn sure they never *get* that doctor. You've been keeping score and now you're avenging yourself on the world because most of the people in it are straight. You keep it up and you'll turn into a joyless old dyke without a shred of love in her heart for anyone."

Beebo sat up and frowned at him, surprised but not riled. "Are you telling me to go to hell because I—I think I'm gay?" she asked.

"I'm telling you to go to college," he said seriously.

"Jack, you goofed your chance for an M.D. for reasons a lot flimsier than mine. What are you trying to do? Push me into school so you can make peace with your conscience? You're the one who wants to give that good doctor to humanity. If it can't be yourself, better it should be Beebo than nobody. And Jack Mann will have made a gift to his fellow men. Jack, the Great Humanitarian. And you won't even have to crack a book." She spoke wryly, but without rancor.

Jack was stunned into silence by her flash of insight.

"I hit it, didn't I?" she said. "Jack, you don't know what you're asking me to do: wear a skirt for the rest of my life. Forget about love till my heart dries up. Go back and face the father I destroyed and the brother who hates me…well, I can't. I'm no martyr. I'm not brave enough to try to be a doctor now, just because you tried and failed. And feel bad about it."

He took her hands and rubbed them. "You hit it dead on, little pal, but only part of it," he said. "Sure, I'd like to see you with a medical degree and know I'd had something to do with it. But forget me. Be selfish about it. A degree would protect you, not expose you to more trouble. Knowledge, success, the respect of other doctors—that would be your defense against the world."

"There's no protection against myself. My feelings. I didn't tell you about the girls back home, Jack, walking down country lanes after school with their arms around the boys, kissing and laughing. The girls I couldn't touch or talk to or even smile at. The girls I'd grown up with, suddenly filling out their sweaters and their nylons, smooth and sweet with scented hair and pink mouths. I didn't tell you how I ached for them."

He got up and crossed the room, looking out his front windows. "I don't want you to end up an old bulldyke in faded denims, letting some blowsy little fem take care of you," he said acidly. "You're not a bum."

"I don't want that, either. But Jack, I can't spend the rest of my life wondering!" She went to his side, speaking urgently, wanting him to root for her, not against her. "They call this life gay," she said softly, following his gaze out the windows. "I need a little gaiety."

"They call it gay out of a perverted sense of humor," he said.

Across the street two young women were walking slowly in the mild evening air, arms around each other's waists. "There," Beebo said, nodding at them. "That's what I want. I've wanted it ever since I knew girls did such things."

"You mean Mona?" he said.

Beebo shoved her hands into her pockets, self-conscious as always when that name came up. "You have to start somewhere," she said.

"You have quite a thing about her, don't you?" he said.

Beebo's cheeks flushed and she looked at the floor. "I never dared to admit that I wanted a girl before, Jack. Maybe I picked the wrong time. Or the wrong audience."

"Pal, just picked the wrong girl."

"I don't want you to pity me. That's why I held out so long. I need you, Jack. You're the first friend—the first brother—I ever had."

Jack was touched and embarrassed. "I feel no pity for you, Beebo," he said. "You don't need pity. I feel friendship and…anxiety. If you've made up your mind to stay here, I'll do anything to help you, teach you, take you around. But, honey—not Mona. She doesn't believe in anything but kicks. She'll charm the pants off you and then leave you standing naked in front of your enemies."

"Are you trying to say you disapprove of Mona, but not of the fact that I'm—I *must* be—gay?" she said.

"Why would I disapprove of that?" he said and then he laughed. "I swear to God, Beebo, you can be thicker than bean soup. I've done everything but sing it for you in C sharp."

"I know you've tried to be tolerant and all, introducing me to your friends. I thought it was because you suspected about me and you wanted to be a good sport."

"I'm trying to explain about *me*, not you," he said, throwing out his hands and still chuckling.

Beebo smiled back, mystified. "Let me in on the joke, will you?"

"The joke's on me this time," he said.

She studied him a moment, her smile yielding to perplexity. And then she said, "Oh!" suddenly and lifted a hand to her face. She went back to the sofa and sat down with her head in her hands.

"Well, you don't need to feel badly about it, pal," he said, joining her. "I don't. There are even days when I feel sorry for the straight people."

"Jesus, I should have seen it," she murmured.

"No, you shouldn't. I'm a genius at hiding it."

"Jack, I'm sure a fool. I've been up to my eyes in my own troubles."

He shook his head. "I couldn't believe you wouldn't figure it out. It's hard to realize the kind of life you've been leading up to now. How little you've been allowed to see or understand."

She looked up at him. "Thanks for being patient," she said. "I mean it. Jack, how long have you been gay? How did you find out about yourself?"

"I didn't. I was told. In the Navy, by a hairy little gob who kept climbing into my bunk at night and telling me fairy stories. When he got a rise out of me, he made the diagnosis. I told him to go to hell, but the next night, I was climbing into *his* bunk."

It made her smile. "Can you forgive me?" she said.

"Nothing to forgive. and I'll let you back into my good graces on one condition. Do you think your friend Pat will be in bloom tonight?"

"Probably," she said, seeing him through her new understanding as through a rainbow curtain. He was a new shape, a new color, a new man. She was vastly relieved, and just a little awed. And ashamed of her bean-soup intuition.

"Let's go look at him," Jack said.

♀♀

Venus was waiting for them outside the elevator door in the service entrance, one early evening in the first week of September. Strangely, Beebo wasn't surprised. It had been coming for weeks, and now she had to face it.

Toby grimaced at his mother, and Beebo handed her the carton of home-cooked food. "Here's your dinner," she said. "Mrs. Pasquini appreciates all the orders."

"You might as well keep it, she never eats it," Toby revealed. "She just orders it to keep you coming over."

"Sh!" Venus exclaimed at him. She was wearing a bright-blue knit dress, into which her famous frame was smoothly slipped; a glowing target for the eyes.

"Toby says you're a good driver," Venus said. "Now I suppose he'll pester Leo to teach him when we get home."

"You know I can't drive, Mom," he said wearily. "They don't give licenses to epileptics."

"Well, we'll talk to the governor, darling," she said.

"Besides, what do you mean 'home?' California?" He looked at her suddenly, brightening. "I thought we were going to be here all winter."

Beebo felt almost dizzy at the thought of losing Venus before she had won her. It was too much to bear. Everything went wrong in bunches. "Home?" she repeated, frowning at Venus.

"Well, you both look as if I had dropped a bomb," Venus declared. "I just thought, with Toby's friends in California, and all those miserable horses and sunshine and ocean...I guess I can put up with the smog."

"Mom, that's great," he said, surprise all over his face. "Are you doing a new picture?"

"No, darling. I'm turning over a new leaf," she said.

They looked at each other and Beebo sensed an awkward rapport between them. After a decent pause she said, "Well—have a good trip, you two. I guess I won't be seeing you again, Toby."

He turned to her in consternation, and Venus said, "Don't be silly, darling. I have some lovely martinis all ready upstairs and a perfectly irresistible business proposition for you."

"Business?" Beebo said.

Toby made a face. "Monkey business," he said. "Can you walk on your hands, Beebo?"

"Hush, darling," Venus said, pulling them both into the elevator. "Not until she's had her martini."

Toby had a distant look on his face on the way up. "I'll have to write to everybody," he said. "So they'll know I'm coming."

♀♀

Beebo let herself be led into the living room, full of sharp doubts that made her jumpy. Venus watched Toby go with a smile. "He'll be busy for hours," she told Beebo. "He rewrites all his letters two or three times. You'd think he was going to publish them someday."

Beebo sat down on a long white sofa and accepted a martini with an unsteady hand. The trembling had started already, and it seemed impossible to talk or act like a normal human being.

But Venus, who was more of a sorceress than a goddess, talked softly to her for half an hour, letting the drinks and her own silvery charm relax her guest. Even then, Beebo looked so gloomy that Venus began to chuckle at her. She refilled their glasses and asked her, "Do you hate yourself for coming up tonight?"

"Not as much as I hate you for asking me," Beebo said.

"Be fair now, darling," Venus chided. "I'm not responsible for your weakness, am I?"

"You know damn well you are," Beebo said. And in the pause that followed she felt that if she didn't escape now, she never would. "I'm sorry, it's not your fault," she said, trying to sound matter-of-fact. "I guess you were born with—all that." She couldn't look at "all that" while she spoke of it.

"No, I had to grow it, darling. Took me fifteen years, and it was a hell of a wait."

Beebo moved to the edge of the sofa when Venus joined her. "Were you a poor proud orphan till some movie scout discovered you?"

"Oh, God, no!" Venus laughed. "My family was solid apple pie. The trouble was, I was always so damn beautiful I never had a chance to be normal." She spoke dispassionately, as if she were analyzing a friend. It wasn't snobbish. "I was supposed to be fast and loose because I looked it. At first the attention spoiled me. I was cocky. A candy-box valentine brat with corkscrew curls— my mother's pride and joy. Until I drove her frantic, and my friends out of my life. Nobody could stand me. *Honestly.* You laugh, but I cried when it happened. I couldn't understand why I was alone all of a sudden.

"I got shy and scared. Went my own way and told the world to go to hell. After a while, when my figure caught up with my face, I made some new friends: boys. It was so easy to give in. So hard to be anything but what people thought you were," she said, and Beebo responded with a startled swell of sympathy. "Well, in a phrase, they made me what I am today: a conniving bitch." Venus spoke defiantly…and regretfully.

"I'm not proud of it, but I want to be truthful with you. You're a sweetheart, Beebo. And very young, and maybe not too experienced. Tell me why you've made Toby come up alone with the food all these weeks. Did you think I'd throw spaghetti at you?"

Beebo took a swallow of her drink. "I don't want to crawl, Venus. I don't want to be hurt," she said harshly, defending herself with painful honesty in lieu of a worldly white lie.

"Nobody does," Venus said. "Were you expecting to be?"

"Isn't that what you want?" Beebo said, looking deep into her ice cubes. "To play games?"

Venus touched a finger to Beebo's cheek. "You're not crawling," she said. "You're being difficult. That's new for me."

"Is playing around with girls new for you, too?" Beebo asked, afraid to know the answer.

"Depends on how you mean it," Venus said. "You don't trust me, do you?" She smiled.

Beebo caught Venus's hand as it caressed her cheek and kissed it warmly. And remembered with sudden sadness the way Paula had done that to her when they met. She put Venus's hand down gingerly on the sofa.

Venus let her sit and stew for a minute and then slipped across the cushion toward her. Their faces were very near and Venus put her rejected hand on Beebo's leg. "I'm trying to give myself to you and you won't have me," she said. "Now who's crawling?" She let her other hand, cool and questing, touch Beebo's neck and slip over her shoulder, drawing fire with it.

"You're putting me on," Beebo said, determinedly suspicious as only the young and uncertain can be. She took a deep breath. "But I don't care," she cried suddenly. "I don't care. I'll have you any way I can." She put her head down and kissed Venus's throat, putting her arms around her and grasping her firmly. Venus leaned against her, warm and willow-supple.

"You want to know how it feels, don't you?" Beebo said, trying to hurt her feelings, so sure Venus would hurt Beebo first if she could. "You want to know what it's like for a girl to hold you instead of a man. Any time you get bored, let me know." She bent to kiss her again but Venus stopped her. She was dismayed, and Beebo was ashamed to see it.

"You really *do* hate me, don't you?" Venus said.

Beebo closed her eyes for a minute. "I'm sorry," she whispered. She felt Venus moving in her arms. "I thought you were bored and frigid. Taking me like a prescription, or something. The way you talked—"

"The way I talked was about *men*, not women. Beebo, do you know something. I was scared to death you'd take one look at this face of mine, panic, and run out." Her hands slid around Beebo's back and into her short dark hair.

Beebo's face turned hot while those hands trailed softly through her hair and over her eyes. "You're superb, Beebo," Venus said. "I think I'm the one who's afraid. I wouldn't be if I knew you better. And myself."

"You know more than I know," Beebo said. "Is this all a joke, Venus?"

Venus hushed her by pulling her down and kissing her mouth, and her tenderness was no pleasantry. Beebo kissed back: Venus's face, her ears, her pale throat, till Venus made her stop, shaking her curls to be let loose, and laughing.

"Who the hell am I," Beebo exclaimed, "that you should kiss me like this?"

Venus caught her breath. "You talk to me as if I were a woman, she said at last, gratefully. "Not a goddess, or a bitch. It hurts a little, but it feels good to hurt like that. Like when you're awfully young and you have a beautiful dreamy pain to cry over."

Beebo rubbed her head back and forth in the cradle of Venus's shoulder. "Did you cry over your dreams like other girls, Venus?"

"I cried, but not like other girls. I never did anything like other girls. I never even looked like them."

"Would you rather be plain?" Beebo asked.

Venus looked away and found the dignity to be honest. "No," she said. "It's a funny thing about women and me. Half the time I want to make them weep with despair over my beauty. And the other half I ache to be friends with them. Accepted. All the things I wasn't when I was growing up. My whole world is men. They're the only friends I have, and they aren't really friends at all. Not with a woman like me. The women close to me are either fat and old, like Mrs. Sack, or homely and heartless, like Miss Pinch."

"The cook? Is that her name?" Beebo gave in to laughter that relieved her tenseness a little.

"I know, it's too good to be true," Venus said. "Leo started calling her that, and it caught on. I fire her regularly but she comes back like a bad dream. She's devoted to Leo."

Beebo put her head down so she could talk without exposing her emotions to Venus's eyes. "Do you miss having a woman in your life?" she asked.

"Yes. The right kind. Somebody cultured and intelligent and well-educated. Somebody to teach me things. I'm so damned stupid."

Beebo gave a short wry laugh. "Venus? I think there's something you should know."

"What?"

"I didn't finish high school."

Venus laughed, a charming sound, full of pleasure. "I thought you meant, did I want a secretary, or something," she said.

"I'll bet you did." Beebo sat up and lowered herself to the floor, where she leaned back on the sofa, locking her fingers around her knees. She felt Venus's hand come down to play with her ear.

"Did I say something wrong, darling?" Venus said.

"Not a thing. Just that for a girl who likes girls, you did a damn queer thing marrying six men," Beebo said.

Venus answered pensively. "I kept thinking one of the six would set me straight somehow," she said.

Beebo felt those lovely hands in her hair, and she looked over at the kitchen door. It was about thirty feet away...thirty miles, it seemed.

"You've got such soft hair, Beebo," Venus said, and she leaned down and kissed the crown of Beebo's head, and then lifted her face and kissed everything upside-down from her perch on the couch. "You kiss me so gently," she said. "I never knew a lover so gentle before. There isn't a man who could come near you." And she kissed Beebo again till Beebo reached up from the floor and caught Venus's breasts in her hands, returning the kiss with a young warmth that struck sparks in Venus. Beebo held her hard and groaned, "Don't, don't, you don't know what it's doing to me. Oh, God...oh, please..."

"Do you still think I don't know?" Venus said. "Don't you understand by now I'm not doing this for kicks? Or to hurt you? Or God knows what other medieval torments you imagined? I think you're amazing. Exciting. Adorable. Did you think I'd never tried it before with a woman? I've tried everything, darling. Everything but corpses, anyway."

"Oh, Venus, Venus—"

"Hush, I'll explain. You see, it was always so rotten with men. It was as good as it ever got with a girl. But never this good." Her directness threw Beebo emotionally offstride. "I kept thinking it should be. If men were so bad there had to be something else worth living for. So I kept looking. But I have to be so damn careful. Whatever I do is news."

Beebo looked at her and saw tears on her cheeks. "My daydreams were always better than my life," Venus whispered, "and when you reach that point, you're in trouble. All the money in the world can't make those dreams real." She brushed lightly at the tears, embarrassed by them.

"I was wild when that dreadful Pasquini came up here," she said. "I'd been looking forward to seeing you all day. After he left, I began to think maybe his coming was a sign that I should give you up while I still could. An affair between us would seem like the world's worst cliché: the jaded vamp seducing the innocent girl for the sake of a few cheap kicks." She sat silent a moment and then she smiled at Beebo.

"Do you know what Miss Pinch said after you left? She came marching in and announced that you were a dyke and Pat was a queen."

"Miss *Pinch* said that?" Beebo said, and laughed at the incongruity of it.

"Well, she put it a little differently. She said, 'The dark young gentleman was a female and the blond young gentleman was a lady, if you know what I mean, ma'am.'"

They laughed together and Beebo felt suddenly close to Venus; her fear had vanished. "The only thing I worry about is, Miss Pinch might tell Leo," Venus said. "It makes him simply wild when I take up with a girl."

"Do you take up with them often?" Beebo asked, looking down.

Venus shook her head without answering. It was a wordless admission of her loneliness and frustration, as great, in its way, as Toby's. Beebo got up on her knees and encircled Venus's waist. "Venus, darling," she said softly, hesitantly. "I love you so much. I can't understand this thing. I thought you were—all glittery and cold. I thought we'd finally climb into bed, and you'd kill me with your laughter. And then to have you like this! God, I don't know what I'm doing. It's so crazy. Venus, Venus, I adore you." She began to kiss her again and Venus let herself be pulled off the sofa and into Beebo's arms, giving in a bit at a time, so that Beebo was trembling and wild-eyed one moment, and overwhelming Venus the next.

She had just enough sense to pick Venus up moments later and carry her to the bedroom, through the overstated boudoir, and out of the sight of Toby and the women. She laid Venus down on the blue silk coverlet of her bed, leaning over her with her fists planted in the mattress.

"This is where I do my dreaming," Venus told her. "I take off my clothes and lie down here and tell myself beautiful crazy stories. I've been doing it for years."

"Who do you dream about?" Beebo asked.

"Who do you think?" Venus smiled. "God, you're so tall for a girl. So tanned and strong. Like a boy."

"I hate to think of you all alone on that blue silk, wanting me," Beebo said. "And me out delivering salami."

"And talking to Toby," Venus said.

"That means a lot to you, doesn't it?"

"Everything," Venus admitted. "I can't tell you how much. I can talk to him now without screaming at him. I owe that to you, Beebo."

Instead of accepting the compliment gracefully, Beebo stared moodily out of the window. "Are you keeping me around so you won't lose Toby again? I don't want to find myself pounding on your locked door the day you learn you can talk to him without me."

"What does it take to make you trust a girl, Beebo?" Venus teased.

"I guess I never will trust you—quite," Beebo said truthfully. "You're too good to be true."

Venus pulled her head down on the pillow and asked seriously, "How many people know you have a crush on me? Don't fib, darling. I have a special reason for wanting to know."

Beebo gritted her teeth together a moment before she answered. "My roommate. His name is Jack Mann. He's gay, too. He's the best friend I ever had and I trust him more than I trust myself."

"Who else? Pasquini?"

"No," Beebo said, lying forcefully with the sudden knowledge that Venus was trying to decide how dangerous their affair could be. The safer it seemed to her, the better the chances she would keep Beebo with her...perhaps even take her to the West Coast.

"How about this girl who's in love with you?" Venus said.

"She's not in love with me. It's a crush," Beebo said, ashamed of the betrayal but unable to help herself. "She'll get over it."

"Do girls ever get over their crushes on you?" Venus said.

"Every day," Beebo protested. "Venus... would you ever lock me out...if people knew?"

Venus rolled away from her, sitting halfway up. Her face was dark. "I'd have to," she said. "For Toby, if for no other reason. And even without him, there's my career. It's my life, my anchor. I can't afford to jeopardize it, especially now that I'm thirty-eight." She glanced at Beebo. "Is that unforgivably selfish of me? Don't answer. It is, of course. I want you, and all the rest, too. And that means you're the one who'd have to sacrifice. It's just that...for some people a job is a job. For me, it's self-respect. Acting is about the only thing I've done in my life I'm not ashamed of. Is it too much to ask, Beebo—secrecy?"

"Is it possible?" Beebo said.

Venus nodded. "There are ways. I've had to learn them."

"With the other girls," Beebo said resentfully.

Venus stroked her shoulder. "You don't have to be jealous," she said. "I do."

"I'm jealous of all your husbands. All your lovers, male and female. Every slob who ever saw you in a movie."

Venus chuckled, letting her tripping voice twist her body back and forth on the blue silk, and Beebo suddenly forgot everything in her life that had preceded this moment. She lunged across the bed and caught Venus by the wrist, whirling her around just as Venus got to her feet.

For an instant they stayed as they were, breathless: Beebo stretched out the length of the bed, looking at Venus with her blue eyes shining like a cat's. Venus could feel the avalanche of passionate force trapped inside Beebo, ready to burst free at the flip of a finger. Already it was near exploding.

Venus stood there pulling against Beebo; warm, even hot to the point of perspiring. The light sweat excited Beebo far more than the perfume Venus usually wore. Her body was a soft pearly peach and between her breasts Beebo could see the quivering lift and fall of her sternum.

Beebo gave a swift tug on Venus's arm and brought her tumbling down on the bed, laughing. That laugh sprang the switch in Beebo. She stopped it with her mouth pressed on Venus's. And at last Venus submitted, all the twisting and teasing melting out of her. She let herself be kissed all over.

Beebo looked at her, stripped of the tinseled make-believe and the wisecracks; her lips parted and her eyes shut and her fine dark hair spilling pins over the pillow, coming down almost deliberately to work its witchery. Beebo kissed handfuls of it.

She fell asleep a long time later, still murmuring to Venus, still holding her possessively close, still wondering what she had done—or would have to do—to deserve it. ■

Butch-Femme Relationships: Sexual Courage In The 1950s

by Joan Nestle

For many years now, I have been trying to figure out how to explain the special nature of butch-femme relationships to Lesbian-feminists who consider butch-femme a reproduction of heterosexual models. My own roots lie deep in the earth of this Lesbian custom, and what follows is one Lesbian's understanding of her own experience.

In the late 1950s I walked the streets looking so butch that straight teenagers called me a bulldyke; however, when I went to the Sea Colony, a working-class Lesbian bar in Greenwich Village, looking for my friends and sometimes for a lover, I was a femme, a woman who loved and wanted to nurture the butch strength in other women. I am now forty years old (1981). Although I have been a Lesbian for over twenty years and I embrace feminism as a world view, I can spot a

From *A Restricted Country*. Ithaca, NY: Firebrand Books, 1987.

butch thirty feet away and still feel the thrill of her power. Contrary to belief, this power is not bought at the expense of the femme's identity. Butch-femme relationships, as I experienced them, were complex erotic statements, not phony heterosexual replicas. They were filled with a deeply Lesbian language of stance, dress, gesture, loving, courage, and autonomy. None of the butch women I was with, and this included a passing woman, ever presented themselves to me as men; they did announce themselves as tabooed women who were willing to identify their passion for other women by wearing clothes that symbolized the taking of responsibility. Part of this responsibility was sexual expertise. In the 1950s this courage to feel comfortable with arousing another woman became a political act.

Butch-femme was an erotic partnership serving both as a conspicuous flag of rebellion and as an intimate explo-

ration of women's sexuality. It was not an accident that butch-femme couples suffered the most street abuse and provoked more assimilated or closeted Lesbians to plead with them not to be so obvious. An excerpt from a letter by Lorraine Hansberry, published in the *Ladder*[1] in 1957, shows the political implications of the butch-femme statement. The letter is a plea for discretion because, I believe, of the erotic clarity of the butch-femme visual image.

> Someday I expect the "discrete" lesbian will not turn her head on the streets at the sight of the "butch" strolling hand in hand with her friend in their trousers and definitive haircuts. But for the moment it still disturbs. It creates an impossible area for discussion with one's most enlightened (to use a hopeful term) heterosexual friends.[2]

A critic of this essay has suggested that what was really the problem here was that "many other Lesbians at that time felt the adoption of culturally defined roles by the butch-femme was not a true picture of the majority of Lesbians. They found these socialized roles a limiting reality and therefore did not wish to have the butch-femme viewpoint applied or expressed as their own."[3]

My sense of the time says this was not the reason. The butch-femme couple embarrassed other Lesbians (and still does) because they made Lesbians culturally visible, a terrifying act for the 1950s. Hansberry's language—the words *discrete* and *definitive*—is the key, for it speaks of what some wanted to keep hidden: the clearly sexual implications of the two women together. The *Ladder* advocated a "mode of behavior and dress acceptable to society," and it was this policy Hansberry was praising. The desire for passing, combined with the radical work of survival that the *Ladder* was undertaking, was a paradox created by the America of the fifties. The writing in the *Ladder* was bringing to the surface years of pain, opening a door on an intensely private experience, giving a voice to an "obscene" population in a decade of McCarthy witch hunts. To survive meant to take a public stance of societal cleanliness. But in the pages of the journal itself, all dimensions of Lesbian life were explored including butch-femme relationships. The *Ladder* brought off a unique balancing act for the 1950s. It gave nourishment to a secret and

subversive life while it flew the flag of assimilation.

However, it was not the rejection by our own that taught the most powerful lesson about sex, gender, and class that butch-femme represented, but the anger we provoked on the streets. Since at times femmes dressed similarly to their butch lovers, the aping of heterosexual roles was not always visually apparent, yet the sight of us was enraging. My understanding of why we angered straight spectators so is not that they saw us modeling ourselves after them, but just the opposite: we were a symbol of women's erotic autonomy, a sexual accomplishment that did not include them. The physical attacks were a direct attempt to break into this self-sufficient erotic partnership. The most frequently shouted taunt was, "Which one of you is the man?" This was not a reflection of our Lesbian experience as much as it was a testimony to the lack of erotic categories in straight culture. In the fifties, when we walked in the Village holding hands, we knew we were courting violence, but we also knew the political implications of how we were courting each other and chose not to sacrifice our need to their anger.[4]

The irony of social change has made a radical, sexual political statement of the 1950s appear today as a reactionary, nonfeminist experience. This is one reason I feel I must write about the old times—not to romanticize butch-femme relationships but to salvage a period of Lesbian culture that I know to be important, a time that has been too easily dismissed as the decade of self-hatred.

Two summers ago in Kansas at the National Women's Studies Association Conference, a slide show was presented to the Lesbian caucus in which a series of myths about Lesbians was entertainingly debunked. The show was to be used in straight sex-education classrooms. One of the slides was a

If we deny the subject of butch-femme relationships, we deny the women who lived them, and still do.

comic representation of the "myth" of butch-femme relationships with voiceover something like: "In the past, Lesbians copied heterosexual styles, calling themselves butch and femme, but they no longer do so." I waited until the end to make my statement, but I sat there feeling that we were so anxious to clean up our lives for heterosexual acceptance that we were ready to force our own people into a denial of some deep parts of their lives. I knew what a butch or femme woman would feel seeing this slide show, and I realized that the price for social or superficial feminist acceptance was too high. If we deny the subject of butch-femme relationships, we deny the women who lived them, and still do.

Because of the complexity and authenticity of the butch-femme experience, I think we must take another look at the term *role-playing*, used primarily to summarize this way of loving. I do not think the term serves a purpose either as a label for or as a description of the experience. As a femme, I did what was natural for me, what I felt right. I did not learn a part; I perfected a way of loving. The artificial labels stood waiting for us as we discovered our sexualities.

We labeled ourselves as part of our cultural ritual, and the language reflected our time in history, but the words which seem so one-dimensional now stood for complex sexual and emotional exchanges. Women who were new to the life and

entered bars have reported they were asked: "Well, what are you—butch or femme?" Many fled rather than answer the question. The real questions behind this discourse were, "Are you sexual?" and "Are you safe?" When one moved beyond the opening gambits, a whole range of sexuality was possible. Butch and femme covered a wide variety of sexual responses. We joked about being a butchy femme or a femmy butch or feeling kiki (going both ways). We joked about a reversal of expectations: "Get a butch home and she turns over on her back." We had a code language for a courageous world for which many paid dearly. It is hard to re-create for the 1980s what Lesbian sexual play meant in the 1950s, but I think it is essential for Lesbian-feminists to understand, without shame, this part of their erotic heritage. I also think the erotic for us, as a colonized people, is part of our social struggle to survive and change the world.

A year ago some friends of mine were discussing their experiences in talking about butch-femme relationships to a women's studies class. Both had been gay since the 1950s and were active in the early gay liberation struggles. "I tried to explain the complex nature of butch sexuality, its balance of strength and delicacy," Madeline said. "The commitment to please each other was totally different from that in heterosexual relationships in which the woman existed to please the man."

As she spoke, I realized that

not only was there the erotic statement made by the two women together, but there was and still is a butch sexuality and a femme sexuality, not a woman-acting-like-a-man or a woman-acting-like-a-woman sexuality, but a developed Lesbian-specific sexuality that has a historical setting and a cultural function. For instance, as a femme I enjoyed strong, fierce love-making; deep, strong givings and takings; erotic play challenges; calculated teasings that called forth the butch-femme encounter. But the essential pleasure was that we were two women, not masqueraders. When a woman said, "Give it to me baby!" as I strained to take more of her hand inside of me, I never heard the voice of a man or of socially conditioned roles. I heard the call of a woman world-traveler, a brave woman, whose hands challenged every denial laid on a woman's life.

For me, the erotic essence of the butch-femme relationship was the external difference of women's textures and the bond of knowledgeable caring. I loved my lover for how she stood as well as for what she did. Dress was a part of it: the erotic signal of her hair at the nape of her neck, touching the shirt collar; how she held a cigarette; the symbolic pinky ring flashing as she waved her hand. I know this sounds superficial, but all these gestures were a style of self-presentation that made erotic competence a political statement in the 1950s. A deep partnership could be formed with as many shared tasks as there are now and with an encouragement of the style which made the woman I loved feel most comfortable. In bed, the erotic implications of the total relationship only became clearer. My hands and lips did what felt comfortable for me to do. I did not limit my sexual responses because I was a femme. I went down on my lovers to catch them in my mouth and to celebrate their strength, their caring for me. Deeper than the sexual positioning was the overwhelming love I felt for their courage, the bravery of their erotic independence.

As a way of ignoring what butch-femme meant and means, feminism is often viewed as the validating starting point of healthy Lesbian culture. I believe, however, that many pre-Stonewall Lesbians were feminists, but the primary way this feminism—this autonomy of sexual and social identities—was expressed, was precisely in the form of sexual adventuring that now appears so oppressive. If butch-femme represented an erotically autonomous world, it also symbolized many other forms of independence. Most of the women I knew in the Sea Colony were working women who either had never married or who had left their husbands and were thus responsible for their own economic survival. Family connections had been severed, or the families were poorer than the women themselves. These were women who knew they were going to work for the rest of their

Lesbian days to support themselves and the homes they chose to create. They were hairdressers, taxi drivers, telephone operators who were also butch-femme women. Their feminism was not an articulated theory; it was a lived set of options based on erotic choices.

We Lesbians from the fifties made a mistake in the early seventies: we allowed our lives to be trivialized and reinterpreted by feminists who did not share our culture. The slogan "Lesbianism is the practice and feminism is the theory" was a good rallying cry, but it cheated our history. The early writings need to be reexamined to see why so many of us dedicated ourselves to understanding the homophobia of straight feminists rather than the life realities of Lesbian women "who were not feminists" (an empty phrase which comes too easily to the lips). Why did we expect and need Lesbians of earlier generations and differing backgrounds to call their struggle by our name? I am afraid of the answer because I shared both worlds and know how respectable feminism made me feel, how less dirty, less ugly, less butch and femme. But the pain and anger at hearing so much of my past judged unacceptable have begun to surface. I believe that Lesbians are a people, that we live as all people do, affected by the economic and social forces of our times. As a people, we have struggled to preserve our people's ways, the culture of women loving women. In some

sense, Lesbians have always opposed the patriarchy; in the past, perhaps most when we looked most like men.

As you can tell by now, this essay is an attempt to shake up our prevailing judgments. We disowned the near-past too quickly, and since it was a quiet past—the women in the Sea Colony did not write books—it would be easy not to hear it. Many women have said to me, "I could never have come out when you did." But I am a Lesbian of the fifties, and that world created me. I sit bemused at Lesbian conferences, wondering at the academic course listings, and I know I would have been totally intimidated by the respectability of some parts of our current Lesbian world. When Monique Wittig said at the Modern Language Association Conference several years ago, "I am not a woman; I am a Lesbian," there was a gasp from the audience, but the statement made sense to me. Of course I am a woman, but I belong to another geography as well, and the two worlds are complicated and unique.

The more I think of the implications of the butch-femme world, the more I understand some of my discomfort with the customs of the late 1970s. Once, when the Lesbian Herstory Archives presented a slide show on pre-1970 Lesbian images, I asked the women how many would feel comfortable using the word *Lesbian* alone without the adjunct *feminism*. I was curious about the power of the hyphenated word when so few women have an understanding of the Lesbian 1950s. Several of the women could not accept the word *Lesbian* alone, and yet it stood for women who did stand alone.

I suggest that the term *Lesbian-feminist* is a butch-femme relationship, as it has been judged, not as it was, with *Lesbian* bearing the emotional weight the butch does in modern judgment and *feminist* becoming the emotional equivalent of the stereotyped femme, the image that can stand the light of day. Lesbianism was theory in a different historical setting. We sat in bars and talked about the challenge of knowing what we were not permitted to do and how to go beyond that; we took on police harassment and became families for each other. Many of us were active in political change struggles, fed by the energy of our hidden butch-femme lives which even our most liberal-left friends could not tolerate. Articulated feminism added another layer of analysis and understanding, a profound one, one that felt so good and made such wonderful allies that for me it was a gateway to another world—until I realized I was saying *radical feminist* when I could not say *Lesbian*.

My butch-femme days have gifted me with sensitivities I can never disown. They make me wonder why there is such a consuming interest in the butch-femme lives of upper-class women, usually the more removed literary figures, while real-

life, working butch and femme women are seen as imitative and culturally backward. Vita Sackville-West, Jane Heap, Missy, Gertrude Stein, and Radclyffe Hall are all figures who shine with audacious self-presentation, and yet the reality of passing women, usually a working-class Lesbian's method of survival, has provoked very little academic Lesbian-feminist interest.

Grassroots lesbian history research projects are beginning to change this, however. The San Francisco Lesbian and Gay Men's History Research Project has created a slide show called "…And She Also Chewed Tobacco," which discusses passing women in San Francisco at the turn of the century. The Buffalo Lesbian Oral History Project (Madeline Davis and Liz Kennedy) is focusing on the lives of pre-1970 working-class Lesbians.* The Lesbian Herstory Archives of New York has a slide show in progress called "Lesbian Courage, Pre-1970," and there are groups in Boston, Washington, D.C., and Philadelphia attempting to be more inclusive of the Lesbian experience.

Because I quickly got the message in my first Lesbian-feminist CR group that such topics as butch-femme relationships and the use of dildoes were lower class, I was forced to understand that sexual style is a rich mixture of class, history, and personal integrity. My butch-femme sensibility also in-

*To be published under the title, *Boots of Leather, Slippers of Gold.*

I am not a woman; I am a Lesbian.

corporated the wisdom of freaks. When we broke gender lines in the 1950s, we fell off the biologically charted maps. One day many years ago, as I was walking through Central Park, a group of cheerful straight people walked past me and said, "What shall we feed it?" The *it* has never left my consciousness. A butch woman in her fifties reminisced the other day about when she was stoned in Washington Square Park for wearing men's clothes. These searing experiences of marginality because of sexual style inform my feminism.

Butch-femme women made Lesbians visible in a terrifyingly clear way in a historical period when there was no Movement protection for them. Their appearance spoke of erotic independence, and they often provoked rage and censure both from their own community and straight society. Now it is time to stop judging and to begin asking questions, to begin listening. Listening not only to words which my be the wrong ones for the 1980s, but also to gestures, sadnesses in the eyes, gleams of victories, movements of hands, stories told with self-dismissal yet stubbornness. There is a silence among us, the voices of the 1950s, and this silence will continue until some of us are ready to listen. If we do, we may begin to understand how our Lesbian people survived and created an erotic heritage.

It took me forty years to write this essay. The following women helped make it possible: Frances Taylor, Naomi Holoch, Eleanor Batchelder, Paula Grant, and Judith Schwarz, as well as the *Heresies 12* collective, especially Paula Webster, who said "do it" for years. Most deeply I thank Deborah Edel, my butchy Lesbian feminist former lover who never thought I was a freak. ■

Notes

1 The *Ladder*, published from 1956 to 172, was the most sustaining Lesbian cultural creation of this period. As a street femme living on the Lower East Side, I desperately searched newspaper stands and drugstore racks for this small slim journal with a Lesbian on its cover. A complete set is now available in the Lesbian Herstory Archives in New York.

2 The *Ladder*, No. 1, May 1957, p. 28.

3 Letter from Sandy DeSando, August 1980.

4 An article in *Journal of Homosexuality* (Summer 1980), "Sexual Preference or Personal Styles? Why Lesbians are Disliked" by Mary Reige Laner and Roy H. Laner, documented the anger and rejection of 511 straight college students toward Lesbians who were clearly defined as butch-femme. These results led the Laners to celebrate the withering away of butch-femme styles and to advocate androgyny as the safest road to heterosexual acceptance, a new plea for passing. This is the liberal voice turned conservative, the frightened voice that warns Blacks not to be too Black, Jews not to be too Jewish, and Lesbians not to be too Lesbian. Ironically, this advice can become the basis for a truly destructive kind of role-playing, a self-denial of natural style so the oppressor will not wake up to the different one in his or her midst.

Mabel Hampton
Photo by JEB

Zami:
A New Spelling of My Name
by Audre Lorde

I remember how being young and Black and gay and lonely felt. A lot of it was fine, feeling I had the truth and the light and the key, but a lot of it was purely hell.

There were no mothers, no sisters, no heroes. We had to do it alone, like our sister Amazons, the riders on the loneliest outposts of the kingdom of Dahomey. We, young and Black and fine and gay, sweated out our first heartbreaks with no school nor office chums to share that confidence over lunch hour. Just as there were no rings to make tangible the reason for our happy secret smiles, there were no names nor reason given or shared for the tears that messed up the lab reports or the library bills.

We were good listeners, and never asked for double dates, *but didn't we know the rules?* Why did we always seems to think friendships between women were important enough to *care* about? Always we moved in a necessary remoteness that made "What did you do this weekend?" seem like an impertinent question. We discovered and explored our attention to women alone, sometimes in secret, sometimes in defiance, sometimes in little pockets that almost touched ("Why are those little Black girls always either whispering together or fighting?") but always alone, against a

greater aloneness. We did it cold turkey, and although it resulted in some pretty imaginative tough women when we survived, too many of us did not survive at all.

I remember Muff, who sat on the same seat in the same dark corner of the Pony Stable Bar drinking the same gin year after year. One day she slipped off onto the floor and died of a stroke right there between the stools. We found out later her real name was Josephine.

During the fifties in the Village, I didn't know the few other Black women who were visibly gay at all well. Too often we found ourselves sleeping with the same white women. We recognized ourselves as exotic sister-outsiders who might gain little from banding together. Perhaps our strength might lay in our fewness, our rarity. That was the way it was Downtown. And Uptown, meaning the land of the Black people, seemed very far away and hostile territory.

Diane was fat, and Black, and beautiful, and knew it long before it became fashionable to think so. Her cruel tongue was used to great advantage, spilling out her devastatingly uninhibited wit to demolish anyone who came too close to her; that is, when she wasn't busy deflowering the neighborhood's resident virgins. One day I noticed her enormous bosom which matched my own, and it felt quite comforting rather than

Excerpt from the novel, *Zami: A New Spelling of My Name* (1982, Persephone Press, later printings from The Crossing Press).

competitive. It was clothed in a CCNY sweatshirt, and I realized in profound shock that someone else besides me in the Village gay-girl scene was a closet student at one of the Uptown (meaning past 14th Street) colleges. We would rather have died than mention classes, or tests, or any books other than those everyone else was discussing. This was the fifties and the gulf between the Village gay scene and the college crowd was sharper and far more acrimonious than any town-gown war.

There were not enough of us. But we surely tried. I remember thinking for a while that I was the only Black lesbian living in the Village, until I met Felicia. Felicia, with the face of a spoiled nun, skinny and sharp-brown, sat on my sofa on Seventh Street, with her enormous eyelashes that curled back upon themselves twice. She was bringing me a pair of Siamese cats that had terrorized her junkie friends who were straight and lived on a houseboat with the two cats until they brought their new baby home from the hospital and both cats went bananas back and forth all over the boat, jumping over everything including the box that the baby screamed in, because Siamese cats are very jealous. So, instead of drowning the cats, they gave them to Felicia whom I ran into having a beer at the Bagatelle that night and when Muriel mentioned I liked cats, Flee insisted on bringing them over to my house right then and there. She sat on my sofa with her box of cats and her curly eyelashes and I thought to myself, "if she must wear false eyelashes you'd think she'd make them less obviously false."

We soon decided that we were really sisters, which was much more than friends or buddies, particularly when we discovered while reminiscing about the bad days that we had gone to the same catholic school for six months in the first grade.

I remembered her as the tough little kid in 1939 who came into class in the middle of winter, disturbing our neat tight boredom and fear, bringing her own. Sister Mary of Perpetual Help seated her beside me because I had a seat to myself in the front row, being both bad-behaved and nearsighted. I remembered this skinny little kid who made my life hell. She pinched me all day long, all the time, until she vanished sometime around St. Swithin's Day, a godsent reward I thought, for what, I couldn't imagine, but it almost turned me back to god and prayer again.

Felicia and I came to love each other very much, even though our physical relationship was confined to cuddling. We were both part of the "freaky" bunch of lesbians who weren't into role-playing, and who the butches and femmes, Black and white, disparaged with the term Ky-Ky, or AC/DC. Ky-Ky was the same name that was used for gay-girls who slept with johns for money. Prostitutes.

Flee loved to snuggle in bed, but sometimes she hurt my feelings by saying I had shaggy breasts. And too, besides, Flee and I were always finding ourselves in bed together with other people, usually white women.

Then I thought we were the only gay Black women in the world, or at least in the Village, which at the time was a state of mind extending all the way from river to river below 14th Street, and in pockets throughout the area still known as the Lower East Side.

I had heard tales from Flee and others about the proper Black ladies who came Downtown on Friday night after the last show at Small's Paradise to find a gay-girl to go muff-diving with, and bring her back up to Convent Avenue to sleep over while their husbands went hunting, fishing, golfing, or to an Alpha's weekend. But I only met one once, and her pressed hair and all too eagerly interested husband who had accompanied her this particular night to the Bagatelle, where I met her over a daiquiri and a pressed knee, turned me off completely. And this was pretty hard to do in those days because it seemed an eternity between warm beds in the cold mornings seven flights up on Seventh Street. So I told her that I never traveled above 23rd Street. I could have said 14th Street, but she had already found out that I went to college; therefore I thought 23rd was safe enough because CCNY Downtown was there. That was the last bastion of working-class academia allowed.

Downtown in the gay bars I was a closet

student and an invisible Black. Uptown at Hunter I was a closet dyke and a general intruder. Maybe four people altogether knew I wrote poetry, and I usually made it pretty easy for them to forget.

It was not that I didn't have friends, and good ones. There was a loose group of young lesbians, white except for Flee and I, who hung out together, apart from whatever piece of the straight world we each had a separate place in. We not only believed in the reality of sisterhood, that word which was to be so abused two decades later, but we also tried to put it into practice, with varying results. We all cared for and about each other, sometimes with more or less understanding, regardless of who was entangled with whom at any given time, and there was always a place to sleep and something to eat and a listening ear for anyone who wandered into the crew. And there was always somebody calling you on the telephone, to interrupt the fantasies of suicide. That is as good a working definition of friend as most.

However imperfectly, we tried to build a community of sorts where we could, at the very least, survive within a world we correctly perceived to be hostile to us; we talked endlessly about how best to create that mutual support which twenty years later was being discussed in the women's movement as a brand-new concept. Lesbians were probably the only Black and white women in New York City in the fifties who were making any real attempt to communicate with each other; we learned lessons from each other, the values of which were not lessened by what we did not learn.

For both Flee and me, it seemed that loving women was something that other Black women just didn't do. And if they did, then it was in some fashion and in some place that was totally inaccessible to us, because we could never find them. Except for Saturday nights in the Bagatelle, where neither Flee nor I was stylish enough to be noticed.

(My straight Black girlfriends, like Jean and Crystal, either ignored my love for women, considered it interestingly avant-garde, or tolerated it as just another example of my craziness. It was allowable as long as it wasn't too obvious and didn't reflect upon them in any way. At least my being gay kept me from being a competitor for whatever men happened to be upon their horizons. It also made me much more reliable as a confidante. I never asked for anything more.)

But only on the full moon or every other Wednesday was I ever convinced that I really wanted it different. A bunch of us—maybe Nicky and Joan and I—would all be standing around having a beer at the Bagatelle, trying to decide whether to inch onto the postage-stamp dance floor for a slow intimate fish, garrison belt to pubis and rump to rump (but did we really want to get that excited after a long weekend with work tomorrow?), when I'd say sorry but I was tired and would have to leave now, which in reality meant I had an already late paper for english due the next day and needed to work on it all that night.

That didn't happen too often because I didn't go to the Bag very much. It was the most popular gay-girl's bar in the Village, but I hated beer, and besides the bouncer was always asking me for my ID to prove I was twenty-one, even though I was older than the other women with me. Of course "you can never tell with Colored people." And we would all rather die than have to discuss the fact that it was because I was Black, since, of course, gay people weren't racists. After all, didn't they know what it was like to be oppressed?

Sometimes we'd pass Black women on Eighth Street—*the invisible but visible sisters*—or in the Bag or at Laurel's, and our glances might cross, but we never looked into each other's eyes. We acknowledged our kinship by passing in silence, looking the other way. Still, we were always on the lookout, Flee and I, for that telltale flick of the eye, that certain otherwise prohibited openness of expression, that definiteness of voice which would suggest, I think she's gay. *After all, doesn't it take one to know one?*

I was gay and Black. The latter fact was irrevocable: armor, mantle, and wall. Often, when I had the bad taste to bring that fact up in a conversation with other gay-girls who were not Black, I would get the feeling that I had in some way breached some sacred bond of gayness, a bond which I always knew was not sufficient for me.

This was not to deny the closeness of our group, nor the mutual aid of those insane, glorious, and contradictory years. It is only to say that I was acutely conscious—from the ID "problem" at the Bag on Friday nights to the summer days at Gay Head Beach where I was the only one who wouldn't worry about burning—that my relationship as a Black woman to our shared lives was different from theirs, and would be, gay or straight. The question of acceptance had a different weight for me.

In a paradoxical sense, once I accepted my position as different from the larger society as well as from any single sub-society—Black or gay—I felt I didn't have to try so hard. To be accepted. To look femme. To be straight. To look straight. To be proper. To look "nice." To be liked. To be loved. To be approved. What I didn't realize was how much harder I had to try merely to stay alive, or rather, to stay human. How much stronger a person I became in that trying.

But in this plastic, anti-human society in which we live, there have never been too many people buying fat Black girls born almost blind and ambidextrous, gay or straight. Unattractive, too, or so the ads in *Ebony* and *Jet* seemed to tell me. Yet I read them anyway, in the bathroom, on the newsstand, at my sister's house, whenever I got a chance. It was a furtive reading, but it was an affirmation of some part of me, however frustrating.

If nobody's going to dig you too tough anyway, it really doesn't matter so much what you dare to explore. I had already begun to learn that when I left my parents' house.

Like when your Black sisters on the job think you're crazy and collect money between themselves to buy you a hot comb and straightening iron on their lunch hour and stick it anonymously into your locker in the staff room, so that later when you come down for a coffee break and open your locker the damn things fall out on the floor with a clatter and all ninety-five

percent of your library co-workers who are very very white want to know what it's all about.

Like when your Black brother calls you a ball-buster and tricks you up into his apartment and tries to do it to you against the kitchen cabinets just, as he says, to take you down a peg or two, when all the time you'd only gone up there to begin with fully intending to get a little in the first place (because all the girls I knew who were possibilities were too damn complicating, and I was plain and simply horny as hell). I finally got out of being raped although not mauled by leaving behind a ring and a batch of lies and it was the first time in my life since I'd left my parents' house that I was in a physical situation which I couldn't handle physically—in other words, the bastard was stronger than I was. It was an instantaneous consciousness-raiser.

As I say, when the sisters think you're crazy and embarrassing; and the brothers want to break you open to see what makes you work inside; and the white girls look at you like some exotic morsel that has just crawled out of the walls onto their plate (but don't they love to rub their straight skirts up against the edge of your desk in the college literary magazine office after class); and the white boys all talk either money or revolution but can never quite get it up—then it doesn't really matter too much if you have an Afro long before the word even existed.

Pearl Primus, the African-American dancer, had come to my high school one day and talked about African women after class, and how beautiful and natural their hair looked curling out into the sun, and as I sat there listening (one of fourteen Black girls in Hunter High School) I thought, that's the way god's mother must have looked and I want to look like that too so help me god. In those days I called it a natural, and kept calling it natural when everybody else called it crazy. It was a strictly homemade job done by a Sufi Muslim on 125th Street, trimmed with the office scissors and looked pretty raggedy. When I came home from school that day my mother beat my behind and cried for a week.

Even for years afterward white people would stop me on the street or particularly in Central

Park and ask if I was Odetta, a Black folksinger whom I did not resemble at all except that we were both big Black beautiful women with natural heads.

♀♀

Besides my father, I am the darkest one in my family and I've worn my hair natural since I finished high school.

Once I moved to East Seventh Street, every morning that I had the fifteen cents I would stop into the Second Avenue Griddle on the corner of St. Mark's Place on my way to the subway and school and buy an english muffin and coffee. When I didn't have the money, I would just have coffee. It was a tiny little counter run by an old Jewish man named Sol who'd been a seaman (among other things) and Jimmy, who was Puerto Rican and washed dishes and who used to remind Sol to save me the hard englishes on Monday; I could have them for a dime. Toasted and dripping butter, those english muffins and coffee were frequently the high point of my day, and certainly enough to get me out of bed many mornings and into the street on that long walk to the Astor Place subway. Some days it was the only reason to get up, and lots of times I didn't have money for anything else. For over

eight years, we shot a lot of bull over that counter, and exchanged a lot of ideas and daily news, and most of my friends knew who I meant when I talked about Jimmy and Sol. Both guys saw my friends come and go and never said a word about my people, except once in a while to say, "your girlfriend was in here; she owes me a dime and tell her don't forget we close exactly at seven."

So on the last day before I finally moved away from the Lower East Side after I got my master's from library school, I went in for my last english muffin and coffee and to say goodbye to Sol and Jimmy in some unemotional and acceptable-to-me way. I told them both I'd miss them and the old neighborhood, and they said they were sorry and why did I have to go? I told them I had to work out of the city, because I had a fellowship for Negro students. Sol raised his eyebrows in utter amazement, and said, "Oh? I didn't know you was cullud!"

I went around telling that story for a while, although a lot of my friends couldn't see why I thought it was funny. But this is all about how very difficult it is at times for people to see who or what they are looking at, particularly when they don't want to.

Or maybe it does take one to know one. ■

Photo of Merril Mushroom, 1959

Annie: 1958
by Merril Mushroom

Annie Steiner was my first great love when I was a baby butch in Florida, sixteen years old, just coming out, and still too inexperienced to know how to make a proper pass. She lived down the dormitory hall from me in room 217, one of the two private rooms on the floor, and, actually, I had a crush on her room before I ever saw Annie Steiner in the flesh. The very air around her door carried a sense of mystery, felt loaded with something very special and intriguing. Sometimes, when I passed that door at night, I could see a blue light shining at the crack above the floor and could smell the perfume of incense burning.

The first time I ever saw Annie Steiner, the woman who lived in that mysterious room, she was striding hurriedly down the hallway toward me, head down, shoulders hunched, hands deep in the pockets of her trench coat which was belted and had the collar up all the way around. The blond curls on top of her head bobbed with her steps, and her brows were knit in a frown. I immediately guessed who she was. She was so beautiful that I was too stunned to say anything or even to smile. She never looked at me. She passed me, stopped in front of the door numbered 217, opened the lock, and let herself in.

I HAD to know who she was. I began to ask around the dorm if anyone knew the girl who

lived in room 217. The other girls just shrugged. No one seemed to know her or anything about her at all. My frustration mounted. Then, one evening, I brought up the subject among a group of girls who were visiting from a neighboring dorm, and I was rewarded. Kathy knew. Not only that, she was more than willing to discuss the subject. The mysterious girl was in Kathy's science lab, and Kathy sometimes had to work with her. Her name was Annie Steiner. She was older—almost 21. She was a beatnik. She had B.O. She was unfriendly. She didn't hang out with anyone. Kathy didn't care much for her. Since I didn't care much for Kathy, that was a point in Annie Steiner's favor.

I began to wander the hallway of my dorm, finding any excuse to go down to the other end of the corridor so that I could pass room 217 on the off chance of being able to bump into Annie Steiner either coming or going. Days went by, and I never saw her. But now that I knew her name, I'd whisper it under my breath, an incantation designed to woo her to me: "C'mon, Annie Steiner. C'mon, Annie, baby. Annie, come out of your room. Annie Steiner, come see me." It didn't work.

Then I had a real stroke of good fortune. I was talking with a group of people one day about having been to New York the summer before, and someone said, "Oh, there's a girl in your dorm who is from New York. Do you know her?"

Originally published in *Common Lives/Lesbian Lives 29* (Winter, 1989).

"No, I don't think so. Who is she?" I replied, interested.

"Her name's Annie. Annie Steiner. I think she's from New York. She's a little weird."

I got this tremendous rush. My head spun, and my heart started to beat fast. *Annie? Annie Steiner, the mysterious girl in room 217 was from New York?* Well, it made perfect sense, and it certainly explained her strangeness. I realized that this fact could be my pass to get to her, my excuse to connect with her. I began to rehearse in my mind what I would say and do, how I would approach her. I'd knock on the door to room 217. She'd open it, look at me questioningly. "Hi," I'd say, "I hear you're from New York. I've been there, too. Why don't we talk about New York for a while?" and she'd invite me in, and I'd go into that wonderful room, and...and just that idea alone was so overwhelmingly ecstatic for me that I could conceive no more, could not imagine what might happen next. I went over and over the scenario in my mind, preparing it, rehearsing and re-rehearsing it, savoring it. I decided to put it into action that very night.

I could hardly wait until after supper when most of the girls had come back to the dorm and evening classes were over. I showered, dressed carefully in my best casual ivy leagues, combed my butch haircut just so. My heart surging so that I was nearly breathless, I walked the long corridor to room 217, stood before the door, raised my clenched hand, and knocked. After a few seconds, I knocked again, harder this time; and after a few more seconds, I knocked quite loudly. There was no answer. Sighing with disappointment, I went back to my own room, sat at my desk, and tried to study. After a very unproductive half hour, I went back to knock at the door of room 217 again, and again there was no answer. Five more times that night I went to room 217 to knock at the door of the beautiful, fascinating older girl who was a beatnik and who was from New York where I had been, too. Finally I went to bed.

She was not in her room the next night, either, nor the next, and then my social life picked up for a while, and I did not think about Annie Steiner for a few days. One evening, I was returning from a visit to the dorm next door. I stopped into the bathroom nearest the stairwell, and there she was! Annie Steiner was standing at the sink brushing her teeth! The rush I got in my surprise rendered me speechless, but I was able to smile and nod, then raced into a cubicle before I peed down my leg. When I emerged, Annie Steiner was gone; but I knew that she was now in the dorm and, most likely, in her room.

I went back to my own room for a few moments and sat on my bed to give my racing heart a chance to be still and to go over The Approach scene in my mind one more time. Then, tucking a fresh pack of cigarettes into my shirt pocket, I stepped out of my room, closed the door behind me, and walked down the hallway to room 217. I stopped before the door. A faint blue light shone from the crack beneath the door, exuding mystery. I wiped sweaty palms together, raised a fist, and knocked. The door opened. She stood behind it, peered around the edge so that only the top of her head and face showed. "Yes?" God, she was beautiful!

"Um, uh. I hear you're from New York," I began The Approach right away, not even thinking about the niceties of introductions. "I've been there, too. I thought we could um, uh, talk about New York or something." There was no way to tell her that all I REALLY wanted was to get into her room and be close to her in that intimate space.

The top of the face frowned. "No, not tonight." The door closed.

This couldn't be happening, I thought. This definitely was not the way my fantasy had gone. I raised my fist, knocked again. The door opened, the top of the face frowning around the edge. "Yes?"

"Well," I couldn't stop myself. My desire to be near this woman had a life of its own, "when, then?"

"When what?"

"When can we get together to talk about New York?" I didn't say that this was intended to be a prelude for all sorts of potentially yummy possibilities.

The frown relaxed. "Tomorrow." The door closed.

But there was no answer at the door tomorrow. I knocked every half hour to no avail. Nor was there an answer at the door the next night, nor the next. Then, at 8:30 p.m. on the fourth night, the blue light was shining from under the door, and when I knocked, the door was opened. Annie Steiner stood halfway behind it. I was so relieved to see her that my head began to spin. "I came when you said to," I explained immediately, "and you weren't here. We were going to talk about New York, remember? You said 'tomorrow', and I came; but you weren't here."

She ignored my little speech. "Come on in," she replied, cool, distant.

Ah, those words, those magic words, the words I had so longed to hear for so long a time. I was nearly swooning, as I stepped into her room for the very first moment and looked around. The little space was almost filled by her bed, her desk, and a side table upon which rested her hi-fi and records. A blue light bulb burned in the lamp on her desk, and soft jazz music issued from the hi-fi. She closed the door, locked it, turned the music up just a little, and sank down onto her bed, stretching out on her back with her hands beneath her head. "Sit down," she said, nodding toward the chair by her desk. "People who keep standing make me nervous."

I practically fell into the chair. The naked eroticism of actually being in her room, being this close to her, was so overpowering that I felt weak from it. I could not look at her directly. I was afraid that she might notice how aroused I was by her nearness, by the flow of energy in this small space. I was in Annie Steiner's room! I was really here, listening to soft jazz, bathed in blue glow! I felt completely isolated from the rest of the world of the dormitory, encapsulated, enchanted.

"Well," Annie Steiner said impatiently, "I thought you wanted to talk about New York, and what's your name, anyhow?"

"Um, I'm Merril. I'm in room 204 at the other end of the hall. Uh, when did you live there?"

"I was born and raised there. I really miss it, too. There's nothing happening around this place," she said, a trace of bitterness in her voice. I caught a glimpse, then, of her great loneliness, her isolation here at school where everything was so different from where she had been and everyone was so different from herself.

"Why did you come here?" I asked. "Tell me about it. Why did you leave New York?"

And Annie Steiner began to talk, telling me about herself, about how her family moved from New York to a small Florida town while she went away to live for a year in Europe, then returned to finish school here, where her family was. And as she spoke, I began to fall in love.

After that night, I went to Annie Steiner's room as often as I could. Sometimes she was in, and sometimes she was not, sometimes I was welcome, and other times she would turn me away. "Not tonight," she would say, and a thrill would run through me even then, as I managed to find sexual meaning in those words. I wondered if she were gay, but I dared not approach her on the subject. I had done my best to send her signals, camping and cruising, holding my cigarette just so butch in the crotch between my first two fingers, sitting slumped on the chair at her desk, my legs carefully crossed horizontally, ankle over knee. I word-dropped into conversation gay innuendo—"what a camp!," "carry on, Mary," "mercy!"—but not too much. She was so "older," so sophisticated, so beat, I was afraid that she might think such behavior to be childish or offensive. She had such a very fine mind, and I wanted her to respect *my* mind, too.

We spoke occasionally of personal matters, but not very often. I did not tell her I was gay, nor did I refer in any way to my social life. I was completely intoxicated by being in her presence, and I dared not do anything to jeopardize our tenuous relationship. One of the sure things that could do that in 1958 was queerness on the part of one party found out about by the straight other. So even though I wondered about Annie, I dared not take the chance of asking her in order to find out.

"You have to develop your mind," she told me. "Read Kerouac. Read Sartre." And I did. "Read Ginsberg." I did. I read Camus and Goldman and Kierkegaard. I read Salinger and Golding and Gibran. I even read Tolkien before it was fashionable. I did not read anything by a woman at all.

She introduced me to jazz and blue lights,

Miles Davis, Mose Allison, Thelonious Monk, and Cannonball Adderly, funk and poetic intensity. We began to define our common interests. We both read, and we both wrote prose. We began to read our work to each other.

I never will forget the first time she ever read her written words to me—a short story she was working on. Now, the subject matter eludes my memory, but I do recall the intensity of the feelings I had, sitting across from her, watching her sweet mouth frame the pictures she created with the words she had written, her own personal, private words, her inner thoughts expressed for *me* to hear. As we commented, critiqued, edited each other's work, I felt an increasingly personal bond forming. Her words were so precious to me, and also precious to me was the giving of my own words to her. I gave them wholly, without reservation, as a gift to her, exposing my inner soul, trusting her to treat me gently and not endanger me, while I did the same for her.

Then, one day, I made the heartbreaking discovery that Annie Steiner had a boyfriend. I heard two of my dormmates talking about it in the bathroom, and I sat in the cubicle and eavesdropped with all my might. They were talking about how great it was that Annie Steiner and Ralph Beezak had found each other. Ralph Beezak, I learned by continuing to listen, was also a beatnik. He was older and had a beard. He and Annie Steiner had been seen together on campus. I sighed with dismay at this piece of news, but I was glad to at least have the mystery of her sexual orientation cleared up. At least now I knew. And we still had our relationship. And I was still in love with her.

One evening, I went to Annie Steiner's room to read her the latest revisions on a story she had critiqued for me. I knocked on the door lightly, then louder. "It's me," I called, knowing that she'd recognize my voice.

"Wait a minute!" Annie Steiner spoke from the other side of the door. I heard her slip the lock, then she said, "Wait just a minute. I was in bed. Give me time to get back into it and then come on in." *She was in bed! She must have been taking a nap when I knocked*, I thought. At one time in the the course of conversation, Annie Steiner had told me that she slept naked, and I had remembered that. Actually, I often had thought about it. I thought about it now, and my belly clenched all the way down into my cunt.

I opened the door, walked into the room, and closed the door behind me. Annie Steiner was in the bed with her head and shoulders propped against pillows and her arms outside the sheet that covered the top of her chest. "Come on in and sit down," she said. "Lock the door."

I locked the door and sat on the chair at the desk, manuscript on my lap. Annie rolled over to her side, looked at me. The sheet, I noticed, followed the contours of her body quite nicely. "Well," she said, "let's hear it."

"Really," I protested, "I don't want to bother you. I mean, if you were napping, I can always come back later."

"No," she stretched, and the sheet did the most wonderful thing over her curves, slipped down on top enough to reveal one of Annie Steiner's breasts all the way to the nipple. I started to sweat, fixed my gaze away from that breast, decided that I had better read my piece to give my eyes something else to look at. I felt dizzy. The room was hot, and I could smell the scent of Annie Steiner's body. My own breasts tingled, and my cunt began to throb.

I started reading, slowly, enunciating the words carefully, leaving plenty of time for Annie Steiner to think about my material, to formulate her comments. I finished the first section and waited for her to speak.

She stared at the ceiling for a while. Then she turned to me again. "That was much better," she said, "but I think you can involve the reader more in Jody's feelings about the river before he jumps over the precipice." I nodded. "Say," suddenly she raised up on her elbow, and I nearly fell out of my chair, as the sheet fell down to her waist, exposing ALL of the top of her body, breasts, nipples, ribs, waist, and back! Panic-stricken, I willed myself to breathe slowly, to retain my cool. But the worst was yet to come. "I'm hot as hell in here," Annie Steiner continued. "Do you mind if I get rid of this sheet?"

DID I MIND?!! DID I MIND?!! Lord have mercy, I minded, and I did not mind; it was like a dream come true! I felt feverish, and every organ in my gut was running at full speed about then, but I focused with all my energy on staying cool, concentrating on breathing slowly in and out, and managed to shake my head no, praying that Annie Steiner would never guess that I was incapable of speech at this point. She flung the sheet away from her body, and there it was! Annie Steiner's beautiful, lush, tantalizing, nakedness—breasts and nipples and shoulders and armpits and belly and waist and pelvis and cunt and thighs and knees and calves—and merciful Minerva I thought that I would die right then and there on the spot!

I couldn't believe it! I concentrated with all my might on not staring, forcing my eyes to focus on my manuscript, while really seeing only the peripheral image of the vision before me. I was aware that she was watching me, and I took all possible caution to remain cool, casual, as though this happened to me every day, as though nudity—particularly *her* nudity—was a perfectly natural thing and meant nothing to me at all.

Then I began to wonder if this were a come-on. Maybe she really knew that I was gay and wanted me to make a pass at her. But Annie Steiner was obviously straight, so why should she be coming on to me? After all, she had a boyfriend, and they were both beatniks; so he was obviously a real boyfriend and not like the gay boys my friends and I went out with for appearances only. Maybe she was curious. Or, worse than that, maybe she was a plant, a cop, someone to lure me into making a pass at her and then turn me in. Such things happened often enough in the gay life of the '50s—the woman one took to bed might turn out to be a plain-clothes detective or a straight woman who would then holler lesbian rape. She could even be an extortionist. But, no, I was gut-sure that this cool, beat chick from New York was not a cop, not a plant, not even an extortionist. So what could she want, then?

All these thoughts swirled around in my mind intensely within seconds. Meanwhile, what I really wanted to do was to roll over on top of Annie Steiner and grab her and kiss the hell out of her and then, slowly, make love to every millimeter of her wonderful body. But I was terrified. I could never do it! What if she was just waiting to see what I would do? What if I made a pass, and she really rejected me, got angry because I had dared to. Even at my tender age, I had experienced women like this, who teased a butch into making a pass at her, then became highly insulted and entirely straight and very, very hurtful. If Annie Steiner was, in fact, like this—and for all her beatness, she could be—then it was too great a risk for me to take. I would never jeopardize what we had developed in the way of a relationship.

All this went on in my head, while I stared at my manuscript, concentrating as hard as I could on the images sent to my brain by the peripheral vision, the one that caught delicious glimpses of Annie Steiner's body. Then I glanced at her face directly. She was staring at me, eyes riveted on my own face, staring as she often did while waiting for me to read, staring as though she was waiting for…waiting for something more? Did I dare?

Suddenly I felt clumsy like I never had felt before. Who was I to make a pass at Annie Steiner? She was worlds and worlds beyond me in so many ways. She was my teacher, my spiritual guide, my ideal. How could I even think about making a pass at her? How could I dare to be so presumptuous as to even consider the possibility that she might want this from me?

So I sat on the chair and I read my story; while Annie Steiner lay naked on the bed nearby, my heart's desire come to reality right there before me, and I could not take hold of it. I would not touch her. I read my story, hoping that Annie Steiner did not see the beads of perspiration that coated my forehead and upper lip, or, if she did, would assume that it was the heat of the room that brought them out and not any other kind of heat, like the one inside me. And I finished reading my story to Annie Steiner, and then I went back to my room. ▪

Rings, Zippo Light Up the Past

by Lee Lynch

Looking through the old jewelry box can sure stir up memories. Everything from the antique granny glasses of my long-hair radical days to my last and favorite Zippo lighter from the bars is piled hodge-podge in strange marriages.

First, in a great inextricable clump, come the necklaces. The dainty little girl atrocities that never succeeded in turning me into a dainty little girl are twisted with the worry beads from my hippie-dippy years. Some I bought at a wonderful bead shop down the block from Andy Warhol's Electric Circus: worry beads in the windows, worry beads on the walls, worry beads on the whirling racks. There was a style for every freak, head and lefty college kid in the metropolitan area. Each bead was a different color and, under the right chemical influence, had universes of significance.

One in a series of columns called "The Amazon Trail," published in the *Lesbian News*, December 1991.

My gym whistle, lying under the necklaces, is testimony to an earlier life. I bought it at the same time that I got my volleyball rule book in high school. I'd probably never felt prouder than the first time I walked across the volleyball court, Miss Birchielli watching, to referee. I wore the whistle like a badge. Finally I had a place, some status in the world.

Looking for Gym Teachers

After school I was haunting the lesbian bars, foolishly hoping for a glimpse of my gym teachers, learning lesbian ways. Dykes smoked. Some lit their cigarettes with wooden matches struck on the soles of their shoes, but the ones I emulated used Zippo lighters. My first Zippo was the same clunky silver device my father had—too butch. I switched to the slender style that's still stored in my jewelry box, engraved initials intact. I carried it in my right front pants pocket and was eager for opportunities to ignite it in front of the cigarettes of femmes.

When I gave up smoking seventeen years later it was more difficult to part with the lighter, and the style it gave me, than the cigarettes. Now I carry a pocket knife in its place. Lover does not smoke, but many's the time that I've gleefully rescued her from knotty strings and overzealous packaging.

I loved cufflinks. In the '60s, it wasn't unusual for women's shirts to be made with the french cuffs that required them. If it was possible to buy such items in women's jewelry departments, I never found any. That was fine with me. I grabbed any chance I could to cross-dress.

A Unique Fashion Sense

Aside from that tinge of transvestism in my make-up, I was very conservative. All jewelry had to be silver because gold was femmey. If there had to be a pattern, then I wanted the plainest I could find. My tie tacs or clips were subtle. That a woman wearing a tie wasn't anywhere near subtle didn't bother me at all. I had the fashion sense of a penniless, passing street urchin.

The rings in that magic jewelry box! Every relationship seemed to go through stages of rings. There are the first timid, silly rings, sometimes purchased from gum machines. The dollar rings, now $5, found in the shallow bins or display cases of import stores that sprang up in the hippie era. The import shops were generally next to the leather shop, down the street from the head shop. Who from that era hasn't had a collection of silver rings with tiny red or green or flat turquoise stones?

My homemade rings have disappeared. In the early 1970s, all the women in my living collective seemed to be stringing beads into bracelets, exchanging beaded rings, learning ever more complex patterns that evoked the feel of childhood summer projects.

In their own velour-covered boxes are the rings that have mates out there somewhere. Plain bands that promised so much at the time and now are sore reminders of ceremonies and certainties and ex-mates out there somewhere.

My pinky rings are happier tokens. The first one with the sapphire birthstone, a family gift. The second a signet ring with my dyke initials, L.L. Some

were lost, like the one with the red stone, purchased simply because the heroine of *The Swash-buckler* wore one. Today, I wear yet another ring. The stone is purple because it's the gay color. I chose a pinky ring because it's a gay tradition. I always wear it because there are still women out there who look for it, who use that signal along with dykey looks and manner to confirm sisterhood.

The Magic of Crystals?

Scrambling around the bottom of the box I come upon My First Crystal. A teeny thing, column-shaped with a pointed end. I bought it in the '80s when I was seeking self-healing and carried it briefly in my pocket, the pocket in which I once carried a lighter. Did it help me? Who knows? Did the rainbow crocheted bag of "rubies" hanging from my car mirror help? Or the bag of protective herbs? I haven't had a car accident (knock on wood) since I hung them.

My grandmother's pocket watch! It still works, but it's slow. What was she doing with a pocket watch? Well, this was the Grandma that made aprons by sewing together two red bandannas. The same kind of bandannas I carry, for equally practical purposes, in my back pocket today. This was the Grandma who wouldn't allow liquor in her house. The Grandma everyone thought was a little eccentric. Pocket watches are too butch even for me.

What other treasures are

in this box? Belt buckles from Provincetown. A mood ring like Mo's from *Dykes to Watch Out For* (would someone please tell her they're too, too '70s!). Key chains I keep without knowing why. A white braided rope bracelet like everyone had one summer at the Cape.

I may not wear these trinkets anymore, but my personal archeology reminds me who I've been.

I spent last weekend at a women's gathering high in the Oregon mountains. We pitched our tent alongside a raucously babbling creek. At the craft fair a woman sold "natural jewelry," the kind we dykes like so much. I fell for a handsome necklace of hematite, a silvery-black stone reputed to have a grounding effect on its wearer.

Later I ran into a lesbian real estate agent friend who'd bought one too. On the spot we declared it a butchstone. I'll wear it until it goes into my jewelry box. Like my gym whistle, my pinky rings, like the Zippo in my pocket. ■

Lee Lynch is a nationally known write and novelist who lives in Oregon.

Cass, 1959:
First Day of a Courtship
by Merril Mushroom

"Take each day, and gather the rosebuds in it..." sings Cass. I don't know her yet. She's a new woman on the beach. She is decorating the air around her with this wonderful music, her bulk a dark mountain in the middle of the blanket on the sand. She is surrounded by thin, pretty gay boys like flowers clustered about her, all adoring her, as she sings and plays her guitar.

She is beautiful. She sings like an angel. I listen to her, stare at her, feeling desire rise thick in my chest. Her hair is long and dark, hanging in ocean-wet twisted ropes over her shoulders and down her back. One strand sticks in the salt on the skin of her neck. Her eyes are large and brown, cheeks and nose sunburned red, and a roll of soft flesh rests beneath her chin, extending from ear to ear. She is wearing black bermuda shorts and a black short-sleeved blouse, tight on her huge body, fabric shining slick and wet from her swim. She strokes the strings of the guitar gracefully, expertly, with thick sausage fingers, and she moves her lips and tongue sensually around the words as she sings in a voice sweet as anything I've ever heard. She is lovely.

I am interested. I drift closer and closer to the blanket, listening to her, cruising her in the traditional 1950s style, watching her face and trying to catch her gaze. She looks back at me and smiles

Originally published in *Common Lives/Lesbian Lives 6* (Winter, 1982)

through her song, "...every day that comes comes one in a lifetime...," then looks down.

I carefully cover the lurch my stomach gives by drawing myself up very tall, extremely butch. I come closer to the blanket, cruise harder. Then I move in suddenly and sit on the edge of the blanket, relieved that the gay boys pull up their feet to make room for me. When she finishes her song and puts down the guitar, I speak: "That was wonderful. I really enjoyed listening." I am very cool, very butch.

"Thanks." She is casual. She leans back onto her hands, her upper arms rippling where they squeeze out of her sleeves. I try not to stare crassly at her body, but I do manage to get a panorama out of the corner of my eye of average-sized breasts, big belly with lots of rolls, and fat thighs.

"My name's Merril." I stick out my hand, look directly into her soft eyes, and want to throw myself in headfirst.

"I'm Cass." She sits up straight, takes my hand, firm-grips it, squeezes, then releases it. "New in town?" I don't want to let go of her hand.

"She's a singer," one of the boys breaks in, sibilant esses sounding in my ear like a horde of gnats. "She's trying to get a gig here. So am I." I am not particularly interested in what he is doing, except that then he stands up and pulls her by the arm. "C'MON, Cass," he whines possessively, "we have to GO, y'know. You SAID after this song..."

Cass heaves herself to her knees. "We have to practice for an audition," she sighs. She looks at me regretfully, dark eyes imploring, long eyelashes framing the plea: "We'll be rehearsing before hours in the lounge at the Sea Isle. It opens at four. Maybe you could meet me there at three."

I smile, butterflies threatening to riot in my belly. "I'll be there," I promise.

I go right home to shower and change from my swimsuit into white ducks and a madras shirt. I want to look nice for her, want to impress her as a "clean-cut butch"—one of my several images. I dab on a touch of Canoe, want to smell good in case we get close, want her to remember me by my scent.

Skin feeling tight from the sun, salt, and shower, I park my big old Buick in the back lot, then walk down the narrow steps behind the Sea Isle Hotel. I stride, swing my arms too vigorously, brush against the stucco walls which leave a smear of whitewash powdering the skin on my forearm and wrist. Impatiently I brush away the stuff, not wanting to appear clumsy and uncool with whitewash on me. Butterflies in my belly have grown huge, threaten to fly away and carry me with them. My mouth feels hot, dry, and I hold my hand up and blow against it to see if my breath smells bad. Just to be sure, I pop a peppermint lifesaver.

As I near the door to the lounge, I begin to anticipate the relief of air-conditioning, am ready for the aroma of beer and tobacco. I push the door. It swings open. I step through and in, and I am temporarily blinded by the dark. My pupils fight to dilate, win, and the shadows take on more definition. The little hairs on my arms press themselves partly erect against the movement of cool air over their surfaces, transmitting to the rest of my body the sensations of being inside any beer joint or cocktail lounge in every low-priced oceanfront hotel along the South Miami Beach shoreline.

"Hi." Cass comes through the door opposite where I am standing, and suddenly I am so excited that I can scarcely breathe. She is wearing a peasant-style dress and sandals. Her feet are fat. Her hair, dried and curled, falls heavily over her shoulders. Her chins lie in splendor down her neck and upon her chest. Her breasts press against the front of her dress, her belly swelling beneath, my memory of her thick legs in bermuda shorts filling in what I am not able to see beneath her long skirt. The blond boy is with her. I am not thrilled about that, pretend not to notice him.

The blond boy goes over to the piano, strikes a few chords, does a scale run. Cass looks at me. "I'm glad you came," she says.

The blond boy makes a sour face, begins a swing progression on the piano. Cass goes over to the microphone, speaks into it. It is on. Suddenly she begins to belt out a rendition of "St. James Infirmary," goes into "House of the Rising Sun," and continues with "Wild Women." She is fantastic!

"Let's try that one again," the blond boy lisps.

Cass moves her body in a slight rhythm as she sings, swinging her arms, snapping her fingers occasionally in time to the music. Every now and again she looks over at me, and when she does I am glad that the light is dim enough to hide the very un-butch flush which I feel creep into my face. I sit hunched over, elbows resting on my thighs, listening to her, watching her. I smoke one cigarette, after another, cruising her. She has full lips and white teeth. She has red lips and brown eyes with long lashes. She has big lips and a small mouth. She is soft and beautiful and sensual, and I want more than anything to kiss her.

The bartender arrives, steps behind the bar, drums fingers in time to the music. Cass comes away from the mike, and the blond boy leaves his seat at the piano. "Want a beer?" Cass asks me.

I look around. The time is four o'clock. The bar is open. I feel a sudden hot embarrassment close in on me. I am only seventeen years old. I live at home with my mother, father, sister, brothers. I am underage. Even though I carry phony proof of age so that I can get into the bars, I have to sneak around to do this so that my parents don't find out. My mother is strict. I have to answer to her. I have to be home for supper at five o'clock or I will get into trouble—in my house there is no excuse for being late to supper—and I wouldn't even dream of going home with beer on my breath.

"I have to go now," I mutter. I can't tell her why; not yet. Cass starts forward, disappointment showing on her face. The blond boy glares at her. I glare at him. I am mortified, do not want Cass to think I am a baby, a child; do not want her to suspect that I have to leave because my mother expects me home in time for supper. I cover up by being extra tough, super aloof. "I'd really like to see you again," I say to her. I am brusque, abrupt, very butch. "Here," I scrawl my telephone number on a soggy napkin I have found on the bar. I thrust it at her. "Call me tomorrow morning." Cass picks it up.

I slide off the stool and stride out of the bar, pushing the door hard so that it will swing back and forth behind me. I don't look back, but I want to. In my mind's eye, I see Cass snapping her fingers as she sings, her breasts moving beneath her dress, and I know that she will call me in the morning. ∎

Penny Stanley, 1959
(aka) Julia Penelope
Courtesy of Merril Mushroom.

for joan, in 1967
by Beth Karbe

I once had a friend who drove a schoolbus for a living,
a woman well into her 40s who wore her hair bleached a
brassy red and tied back in a curly tail.
she wore eye makeup thick and heavy and white lipstick and
talked tough like new yorkers can talk tough and she smiled to
rock and folk and peace music in a way that others in their 40s
just didn't back then.
i once had a friend who saved my life, who drove that schoolbus
to my front door, every day of the last two years I endured
high school, stopping on the street in front of my house and
risking her job every time she did.
and she kept *on* doing it, driving that schoolbus right up to my
house and honking, at 7 in the morning,
honking so anyone could hear and see that schoolbus she
drove right up to my house.
i once had a friend who saved my life, that schoolbus waiting
for me at 7 o'clock and the brassy redheaded
tough-talkin' woman who drove it, waiting for me to come out
of my house, clutching books tight to my chest and the burden
of the day ahead. it was 7 o'clock
and the brassy redheaded tough-talkin' woman
talked softly to me, sitting in that big leather seat,
smiling to the radio, to the rock and folk and peace music
in a way that others in their 40s just didn't back then.
i once had a friend who saved my life, drove that schoolbus
right up to my house so i wouldn't have to wait on the corner
two blocks up, so i wouldn't have to wait on the corner with
a dozen or so other kids my age, wait for the schoolbus

among taunts and jeers and words like "queer" and "lezzie,"
clutching books tight to my chest and the burden of the day
ahead. that brassy redheaded tough-talkin' woman
drove that schoolbus and let *me* on before anyone else,
smiled at the radio and talked softly to me as i rode in the seat
just behind her, that seat made for two that nobody else would
occupy even after the bus filled up with kids standing in the aisle.
i once had a friend who saved my life, smiled at the radio and
talked softly to me as i rode in the seat just behind her,
who never said the words
"queer" or "lezzie" or let anyone else say them either.
in that seat just behind her, that seat made for two that nobody
else would occupy even after the bus filled up
with kids standing in the aisle,
i once had a friend.

Originally published in *Sinister Wisdom* 40 (Spring 1990)

Two Willow Chairs

by Jess Wells

This is a lesbian portrait, I tell my friends, pointing at the photo in a silver frame on my desk, but they don't understand. To them, it's just a snapshot of two empty chairs, and they cock their heads at me, wondering why the photo has a place of honor and the chairs are the subject of such elaborate plans.

I took the picture when I was seventeen, which made the chairs brand new, my mother's sister Ruth and her lover Florence in their fifties, and their relationship in its fifteenth year. Flo's chair is made of willow branches, twisted into locking half moons, a rugged chair that somehow looks like filigree. Next to it on their lawn—a secluded, overgrown stretch of grass and overhanging vines—is Ruth's willow chair, a simpler one with a broad seat and armrests that circle like a hug. All around the chairs are flower beds, usually gone to seed, and grass that was "never properly cut," my stepfather would growl in the car on the way home from visits, grass thick like fur that Flo would wiggle her toes in, digging into the peat until her feet were black and she would hide them inside their slippers again.

The year of this snapshot, Aunt Florence was "struck with spring" as she used to say to me. We arrived on the Fourth of July to find blooming peonies and iris and marigold ("always marigold

against the snails," she would whisper to me, as if imparting the wisdom of womanhood). Florence and my mother wandered the garden, pointing at stalks and talking potting soil, promising cuttings to each other and examining the grapevines up the trellis, while Ruth and my stepfather faced each other silently, she slumped in the willow chair like a crest-fallen rag doll and he sitting rigid, twisted sideways on the plastic webbing of a broken chrome chair. After ten minutes of listening to the women's voices but not hearing anything, Ruth got up and slouched into the house to start bringing out the beers, calling in an overly-loud voice, "So, Dick (everyone else called him Richard), "how's business?"

Talking commerce was a great diversion for him, and my mother was already occupied with explaining her begonias, which left me to be the only one in the place grappling with the realization that this lesbian child was being deposited for the summer with the family's lesbian aunts because a new stepfather, two brothers and a male cat were more than I could possibly stand. It was the first of many such summers, visits that after a few years turned into summers with autumns and then special Christmases and soon all important holidays and all important matters of any kind. That first summer, nervously pacing the backyard, I knew it would develop into this and when my parents finally left, Ruth and Florence and I stared at each other with wonder-

Originally published in *Two Willow Chairs*. Chicago: Third Side Press, 1987.

ment. They'd never had a family before and all of a sudden they had a daughter, full-grown and up in their faces feeling awkward. Since my mother was straight, there was something I could dismiss about her, but here were these two, with the weight of maturity *and* the righteousness of twenty years of lesbian lifestyle behind them. Now *that's* what I considered authority.

Aunt Ruth breathed a sigh of relief after the car had pulled out of the drive. Florence let some of her gaiety drop but turned to me, ready to fulfill her last social obligation of the day.

"Beetle," as she had called me since the time I was a baby with big eyes, "Welcome." There was so much hesitancy in her voice, fear almost, as if this child, who did not really know about being a lesbian, were looking at a lesbian who did not really know about being in a family. I dropped the garden hose and wiped my hands on my pants, trying to smooth my carrot-red hair that was frizzy in six different directions. Florence strode over and gathered me in her arms.

"I don't know about these chairs," Ruth said, getting up and yanking one out of the grass. "Let's take them back by the trellis," she said to me, "Florence's favorite spot." And we all grabbed chairs, me taking my mother's chrome one since it was known to all but Richard that his was the only broken chair in the place. We settled into the afternoon, our conversation picking up pace while Florence shuttled lemonade and beers. That's when I got my first photo of the chairs.

Ruth was sitting sideways, her leg slung over the arm of the chair, head thrown back, her whole big body lit by a streak of afternoon sun. Florence was struck by spring only in selected places, and the back of the yard was not one of them: the grapevines behind Ruth's head dangled low and free, the grass crept up around her chair even though it was early in the season.

We had become very quiet for a moment and Ruth turned in her chair to talk privately to Florence. My camera caught her in mid-sentence, her mouth open, hand reaching for her lover's knee, her eyes still not aware that Aunt Flo was in the house and that she and I were alone. Her face showed all the tenderness, history, trust in her

femme as she turned to ask, "Wren, what was the name of that..."

Ruth looked back at me. "I wish you'd quit with that camera," she growled weakly as I laid the photo on the tops of the tall grass to develop, already sensing that I had exposed her. And in a way, she was right. Until then, I had used this camera as a form of self-defense, silently proving to my brothers that they looked stupid, threatening to catch them in the act, snapping photos of my mother as if to prove to myself that she wasn't just a phantom woman. But this day, this photo of Ruth and the empty willow chair was the first photo I had ever taken in an attempt to preserve something beautiful.

I handed the photo to Florence first as she returned with two beers and a lemonade. She stared at it a long time, seeing the look on Ruth's face.

"Oh God, Wren, get rid of that! I look like a jerk," Ruth protested, but Florence held the photo close to her.

"You look wonderful. Besides, I want a photo of my chairs. Here Beetle, take a picture of the chairs for me. Rudy, get up. God, I wish the garden looked better."

⚣

Florence kept the two photos in her jewelry box for years. The two willow chairs stayed in their places in the back of the yard and whenever I would visit (on leave from the Army, or home from another city) we would first convene at the chairs, even during the winter when we would huddle in big coats, and share important news like a ritual before rushing inside for the evening.

Years later, when Florence gave the photos to me, there was one taken of myself and Flo sitting on a porch step, our pant legs rolled up from gathering mussels in the tidepools. Florence is gesturing to me, her arms in the shape of a bowl.

"Now look, honey," she said that day, "don't give up. Love is just a matter of the right recipe: a cup and a half of infatuation, a pinch of matching class status, two tablespoons of compatible politics and three generous cups of good sex. Mix. Sprinkle liberally with the ability to communicate and fold into a well-greased and floured apartment. You bake it for at least six months without slamming the door and pray you have love in the morning. And it works—when you've got the right ingredients."

Of course their relationship was a serious one, so I have photos of times when the recipe wasn't quite right with the two of them, either. In the package with the other photos is a black and white from the '50s of Florence in a wool suit and a hat with a veil, standing at the rail of an ocean-liner. She and Ruth put all the money they had into a ticket for her to go to Europe and even though it was the best trip she'd ever taken, she looks miserable in the picture. The veil is down over her face, almost to her lips that are thick with lipstick, and she's wearing kidskin gloves but not waving. She looks very tight and cold to me in this picture, but Ruth liked how smart Flo looked. Aunt Florence would stand in front of it, holding my hand (even though I was home on leave for the third and last year) and say, "Beetle, I keep it because it reminds me of when I was less frightened of running and being alone than of staying and loving." She turned to me, one hand on her hip. "Now isn't that ridiculous, to think that it's less scary to have a lousy relationship than a good one? That intimacy is more terrifying than loneliness. God, the world is so crazy, Beetle. It's like saying garbage is more delectable than food." Well, I stood in front of that photo with her, looking up at her glowing face then back at the picture of that sunken young thing and it seemed her face now wasn't wrinkled by age, just stretched from being so open. I thought about my latest crush in the barracks and how good Florence's choice seems to have been (after all, here was home and warmth and Ruth loung-ing on the sofa throwing those cashews to the dog), but I looked back at that picture, those eyes big and scared and I knew that's where I was, a veil over *my* face. I turned from my aunt and thought, 'Oh Jesus, somebody send me a ticket and point me towards the ocean.'

Ruth kept the photo at her side of the bed, as if to remind herself of how far Florence had run and how close she now lived.

On Florence's side of the bed was a photo taken the summer after she returned. The two are in funny brown swimsuits with pointed bras, Ruth sleeping in Florence's arms. Flo is bending to kiss her on the neck and years later, she related to me that, lying in the sand with her lover in her arms, Florence could feel the years passing. She could feel Ruth getting older even though she was in her thirties, feel her getting heavier through middle age, belly growing across her hips, feel her shift in her sleep from an injury to her shoulder that she didn't have yet, see the scars she would have in the future, Ruth getting smaller and more frail as she aged, wrinkling into buttery skin. And all the time, holding Ruth encircled in her arms, Florence knew that this would be the progress of her world, that this was her future and her life, that this woman between her arms was her home.

Of course Flo had pictures of her mom and dad, who have been dead for nearly two decades now, and the family at picnics, Ruth playing horseshoes on her sixtieth birthday and pictures of me when I was a kid with teeth missing, though we won't go into that. There's another lesbian por-trait in this stack from Flo—it's a picture of a dog.

Clarise was the spaniel Florence had when she was lovers with the woman before Ruth (which is how she was always referred to, she never had a name) and Flo kept the photo on top of the televi-sion for years after she had left the woman and the dog. The little thing was sitting attentively on the beach, clumps of dirt hanging on its paws. It was the first dog Florence had ever learned to love, and every year, with a far-away look in her eyes, Flo would ramble on about how special and psychic and beautiful and protective it was. It was everything a dog should be. Just a few years ago, Ruth, sick and lying on the couch, threw off her afghan and snatched the photo off the t.v.

"For Godsake, Florence, it's over, and it's okay that it's over," she shouted, starting to cough. "The dog wasn't the only thing good and the woman wasn't the only thing bad. Now c'mon."

Florence went into the backyard and sat in her willow chair. It was her seventieth birthday and she should have a jacket on, I thought.

"Stay here, Beetle," Ruth said.

"I don't see why you're jealous of a dog,

Rudy. For Christsake, it was years ago."

"I'm not jealous. Florence doesn't know what to do with all those years she spent with that woman and so she puts them here," she said, tapping the glass frame. "When you're consumed with bitterness, where do you put all the good times? The dog. The only reason I'm even saying it is because she knows it herself. A couple of months ago, we went to Bolinas, remember the spot...?"

"Where we used to gather mussels?"

"Right. Well, Wren thought the air would make me feel better or something, but who should come trotting up but the spitting image of that dog. Splatters mud all over Wren's newspaper, knocks the damn iced tea into the potato chips and rolls over to stick up her tits, I mean it. Well, it finally dawns on Wren, 'Goddamn, maybe that Clarise was just a fucking dog, too.'"

Now I have the photo of Clarise. I keep it with a bunch of others Florence gave me in a white, unmarked envelope. These are the painful pictures, the ones that bring floods of heat to your face, pictures you look at and smell perfume.

There's a picture of Florence pointing at the flowerbeds with her cane, trying to get *me* to be struck with spring and do some planting while we waited for Ruth to get well. Then there's Ruth lying on the couch covered with the afghan, looking tiny and angry, and after Ruth died, a photo of Florence looking remarkably like her picture in the hat with the veil. Florence never went back to the chairs, never went into the back of the yard, only stared at it from the kitchen window, stricken now that Ruth, love, hope and future were dead and decaying, confused by the sight of the grass and the flowers blooming, as if life were threatening to overtake her when she knew it was death that was the encroacher. The grapevines grew lower, entwining with the bows of the willow chairs, as if threatening to scoop them into a cluster and throw them up to the sun to ripen, while the grass underneath fought to drown the chairs in green. I took a picture of the chairs last year in this condition but I conveniently lost it. I do have a snap of me, fifteen pounds thinner from not sleeping while Florence lay dying, and one of my mom at Flo's wake, crying like she couldn't at

Ruth's. Maybe someday I could frame them and hang them and still be able to walk through the room, but I doubt it. Right now all I can manage is that first snap of the two empty chairs. My friends don't understand it. Nor do they understand why I'm borrowing a truck and calling around for a hacksaw.

"I have to save the chairs," I tell them, slamming down the phone on my mother and dashing for my jacket. The house has been sold, finally, my mother tells me, and the new owners are sure to throw Wren and Rudy's chairs into the dump—if there's anything left of them. They were nearly part of the grapevine forest last year when Florence died. First thing in the morning I'll cut the chairs away from the underbrush and drive them to a field near Bolinas. They can sit together and watch the unruly grass grow up around them, again. ■

Part 2

We Are Not As They Say

Adrienne Smith

Interview by Michal Brody

I came out in 1959 when I was twenty-five years old. I saw this woman at a meeting who just intrigued me. It was a meeting of the UJA, the United Jewish Appeal. At the time I was living with a roommate, and she hosted a meeting at our house. I wasn't really involved in it; I was just hanging around, and I saw this woman. Her name was Darlene. And a few days later she called on the phone. There was something about a coffeepot; I think she had brought a coffeepot over for the meeting. So I decided to return the coffeepot to her. I don't think I left her apartment for days after that. And it was funny, because I think she was the first lesbian I met, and we spent fifteen years together.

She was two years older than I; she was twenty-seven. She'd had experience as a lesbian already, and she had been to New York! She told me all these wonderful stories; I was completely fascinated. I just sat there and I listened with my mouth open. I remember we were sitting in Morrie's (that was a delicatessen on Broadway), and I just sat there for hours, entranced, listening to her talk about this world that I never knew existed.

I think I was aware before that, that something was strange about me. I wasn't especially attracted to men; and I thought maybe I was just a failure as a social butterfly. It never occurred to me that I might be a lesbian.

So Darlene and I had known each other about a week before I moved in with her, and it lasted fifteen years.

For a long time, we knew only a handful of other lesbians and gay men. She worked at a bookstore, and there were several there. I started graduate school at the University of Chicago the following year, and I met a couple of people there.

There was this couple that Darlene worked for, and we socialized with them. We used to go out to their cottage often. It was clear that they were lesbians, but I don't think the word was ever used. They were in their sixties at the time, and they'd been together for twenty-five or thirty years. I'm not sure they ever used the word "lesbian," but it was obvious what they were, and we were, and we all knew.

Basically, the years before Stonewall were a time of great secrecy. I was even secretive with myself. I said, "Well, I'm not really a lesbian. I just happen to be living with this woman." It took me a long time to recognize myself as a lesbian.

I had a gut feeling that there was something very wrong with me and that I should get it fixed, so I made the rounds of several different therapists, none of whom helped. It was the Women's Movement that finally made the difference for me. Suddenly I was sane, and it was the rest of Them out there who weren't. The Women's Movement and the Gay Liberation Movement "cured" me.

I was working as a psychologist, and, as I became more active and involved in the movement, I became more and more out professionally. In 1974 I was invited to be a panelist on the David Susskind Show, one of the early television talk shows. It was going to be done in New York and shown nationally. This was going to be a show on homosexuality, and there were six of us on the panel, three lesbians, three gay men, all of us professionals in various fields. Susskind made a habit of doing one homosexual show a year—kind of a show and tell thing, so that people could see we didn't have horns and a tail.

The night before I was supposed to fly to New York, I knew something was wrong because I couldn't sleep. I kept pacing the floor. Suddenly I thought, "Good lord, I've got to tell my mother." I'm not certain exactly what I said to her. Something like, "I'm going to be on the David Susskind Show, and there's something I've got to tell you. It's about Darlene and me—you know—we're lesbians." And my mother said, "I know. What took you so long to tell me." I said, "You *knew*? Why didn't you ever say anything?" And Mother said, "It wasn't my place." And she was right.

Before the show aired, Darlene decided to tell *her* mother. She wanted me to come with her; she didn't want to do it by herself. So we took her mother out to dinner, and there was taking off of coats and the sitting down, and finally, there was no more putting it off.

Darlene said, "Adrienne just came back from New York." And her mother said, "What was Adrienne doing in New York?" And Darlene answered, "Well, she was on the David Susskind Show." And her mother turned to me and said, "What were you doing on the Susskind show?" And I said, "It was a show on homosexuality." And she said, "What were you doing on a show about homosexuality?" And Darlene said, "We're homosexuals." And her mother said, "No you're not; you're lesbians." She had known for years.

It was sad, and typical of the times, that we felt so scared and so untrusting. Especially with Darlene's mother, because she had known for about twenty years, and they had never talked about it.

In the years before the Movement, we didn't really talk to anyone about being lesbians, except each other.

I didn't talk about our relationship with anybody else. Ever. That's part of what was so difficult; there were no confidantes. It became very ingrown. If you were having trouble with a lover, the only one you could talk with about it was that same lover. So she and I were each other's only confidante, only best friend, only everything else.

With the coming of the Women's Movement, there were other options. And so the relationship, which had been *essential* until then, lost that quality of desperation. And I think at that point, there were enough differences between us that, without that, the relationship couldn't survive. To a great extent, relationships were held together then by the sense that there was nobody else out there; we couldn't go hunting or seeking.

The difference now is wonderful; and, in retrospect, I'm so glad to have been a part of that opening up generation. ■

The Female Man

by Joanna Russ

Part Eight

I

Who am I?

I know who I am, but what's my brand name?

Me with a new face, a puffy mask. Laid over the old one in strips of plastic that hurt when they come off, a blond Hallowe'en ghoul on top of the S.S. uniform. I was skinny as a beanpole underneath except for the hands, which were similarly treated, and that very impressive face. I did this once in my line of business, which I'll go into a little later, and scared the idealistic children who live downstairs. Their delicate skins red with offended horror. Their clear young voices raised in song (at three in the morning).

I don't do this often (say I, the ghoul) but it's great elevator technique, sticking your forefinger to the back of somebody's neck while passing the fourth floor, knowing that he'll never find out that you haven't a gun and that you're not all there.

(Sorry. But watch out.)

II

Whom did we meet in that matron blackness but The Woman Who Has No Brand Name.

"I suppose you are wondering," she said (and I enjoyed her enjoyment of my enjoyment of her enjoyment of that cliché) "why I have brought you here."

We did.

We wondered why we were in a white-walled penthouse living room overlooking the East River at night with furniture so sharp-edged and ultra-modern that you could cut yourself on it, with a wall-length bar, with a second wall hung entirely in black velvet like a stage, with a third wall all glass, outside which the city did not look quite as I remembered it.

Now J (as I shall call her) is really terrifying, for she's invisible. Against the black curtains her head and hands float in sinister disconnection, like puppets controlled by separate strings. There are baby spotlights in the ceiling, which illuminate in deep chiaroscuro her gray hair, her lined face, her rather macabre grin, for her teeth seemed to be one fused ribbon of steel. She stepped out against the white wall, a woman-shaped hole, a black cardboard cut-out; with a crooked, charming smile she clapped her hand to her mouth, either taking something out or putting something in—see? Real teeth. Those disbodied, almost crippled hands clasped themselves. She sat on her black leather couch and vanished again; she smiled and dropped fifteen years; she has silver hair, not gray, and I don't know how old she is. How she loves us! She leans forward and croons at us like Garbo. Jeannine has sunk down into a collection of glass plates that passes for a chair; her

Excerpt from the novel. Boston: Beacon Press, 1975.

cup and spoon make a tiny, spineless chattering. Janet is erect and ready for anything.

"I'm glad, so glad, so very glad," says J softly. She doesn't mind Jeannine's being a coward. She turns the warmth of her smile on Jeannine the way none of us has ever been smiled at before, a dwelling, loving look that would make Jeannine go through fire and water to get it again, the kind of mother-love whose lack gets into your very bones.

"I am called Alice Reasoner," says J, "christened Alice-Jael; I am an employee of the Bureau of Comparative Ethnology. My code name is Sweet Alice; can you believe it?" (with a soft, cultivated laugh) "Look around you and welcome yourselves; look at me and make me welcome; welcome myself, welcome me, welcome I," and leaning forward, a shape stamped by a cookie-cutter on to nothing, with pleasant art and sincere gestures, Alice-Jael Reasoner told us what you have no doubt guessed long, long ago.

III

(Her real laugh is the worst human sound I have ever heard: a hard, screeching yell that ends in gasps and rusty sobbing, as if some mechanical vulture on a gigantic garbage heap on the surface of the moon were giving one forced shriek for the death of all organic life. Yet J likes it. This is her *private* laugh. Alice is crippled, too; the ends of her fingers (she says) were once caught in a press and are growing cancerous—and to be sure, if you look at them closely you can see folds of loose, dead skin over the ends of her fingernails. She has hairpin-shaped scars under her ears, too.

IV

Her pointed fingernails painted silver to distract the eye, Alice-Jael plays with the window console: the East River clouds over to reveal (serially) a desert morning, a black lava beach, and the surface of the moon. She sat, watching the pictures change, tapping her silver nails on the couch, herself the very picture of boredom. Come up close and you'll see that her eyes are silver, most unnatural. It came to me that we had been watching this

woman perform for half an hour and had given not one thought to what might be happening around us or to us or behind us. The East River? "An artist's conception," she says.)

V

"I am," says Jael Reasoner, "an employee of the Bureau of Comparative Ethnology and a specialist in disguises. It came to me several months ago that I might find my other selves out there in the great, gray might-have-been, so I undertook—for reasons partly personal and partly political, of which more later—to get hold of the three of you. It was very hard work. I'm a field worker and not a theoretician, but you must know that the closer to home you travel, the more power it takes, both to discriminate between small degrees of difference and to transport objects from one universe of probability into another.

"If we admit among the universes of probability any in which the laws of physical reality are different from our own, we will have an infinite number of universes. If we restrict ourselves to the laws of physical reality as we know them, we will have a limited number. Our universe is quantized; therefore the differences between possible universes (although very small) must be similarly quantized, and the number of such universes must be finite (although very large). I take it that it must be possible to distinguish the very smallest differences—say, that of one quantum of light—for otherwise we could not find our way to the same universe time after time, nor could we return to our own. Current theory has it that one cannot return to one's own past, but only to other people's; similarly one cannot travel into one's own future, but only to other people's, and in no way can these motions be forced to result in straightforward travel—*from any baseline whatever*. The only possible motion is diagonal motion. So you see that the classical paradoxes of time-travel simply do not apply—we cannot kill our own grandmothers and thereby cease to exist, nor can we travel into our own future and affect it in advance, so to speak. Nor can I, once I have made contact with your present, travel into your past or your future.

The best I can do in finding out my own future is to study one very close to my own, but here the cost of power becomes prohibitive. My Department's researches are therefore conducted in regions far from home. Go too far and you find an Earth too close to the sun or too far away or nonexistent or barren of life; come too close and it costs too much. We operate in a pretty small optimal range. And of course I was doing this on my own, which means I must steal the whole damn operation anyway.

"You, Janet, were almost impossible to find. The universe in which your Earth exists does not even register on our instruments; neither do those for quite a probable spread on either side of you; we have been trying for years to find out why. Besides you are too close to us to be economically feasible. I had located Jeannine and not Joanna; you very obligingly stepped out of place and became as visible as a sore thumb; I'd had a fix on you ever since. The three of you got together and I pulled you all in. Look at yourselves.

"Genetic patterns sometimes repeat themselves from possible present universe to possible present universe; this is also one of the elements that can vary between universes. There is repetition of genotypes in the far future too, sometimes. Here is Janet from the far future, but not my future or yours; here are the two of you from almost the same moment of time (but not as you see it!), both of those moments only a little behind mine; yet I won't happen into the world of either of you. We are less alike than identical twins, to be sure, but much more alike than strangers have any right to be. Look at yourselves again.

"We're all white-skinned, eh? I bet two of you didn't think of that. We're all women. We are tall, within a few inches of each other. Given a reasonable variation, we are the same racial type, even the same physical type—no redheads or olive skins, hm? Don't go by me; I'm not natural! Look in each other's faces. What you see is essentially the same genotype, modified by age, by circumstances, by education, by edit, by learning, by God knows what. Here is Jeannine, the youngest of us all with her smooth face: tall, thin, sedentary, round-shouldered, a long-limbed body made of clay and putty; she's always tired and probably has trouble waking up in the morning. Hm? And there's Joanna, somewhat older, much more active, with a different gait, different mannerisms, quick and jerky, not depressed, sits with her spine like a ruler. Who'd think it was the same woman? There's Janet, hardier than the two of you put together, with her sun-bleached hair and her muscles; she's spent her life outdoors, a Swedish hiker and a farmhand. You begin to see? She's older and that masks a good deal. And of course she has had all the Whileawayan improvements—no rheumatism, no sinus trouble, no allergies, no appendix, good feet, good teeth, no double joints, and so forth and so forth, all the rest that we three must suffer. And I, who could throw you all across the room, though I don't look it. Yet we started the same. It's possible that in biological terms Jeannine is potentially the most intelligent of us all; try to prove that to a stranger! We ought to be equally long-lived but we won't be. We ought to be equally healthy but we're not. If you discount the wombs that bore us, our pre-natal nourishment, and our deliveries (none of which differ essentially) we ought to have started out with the same autonomic nervous system, the same adrenals, the same hair and teeth and eyes, the same circulatory system, and the same innocence. We ought to think alike and feel alike and act alike, but of course we don't. So plastic is humankind! Do you remember the old story of the Doppelgänger? This is the double you recognize instantly, with whom you feel a mysterious kinship. An instant sympathy, that informs you at once that the other is really your very own self. The truth is that people don't recognize themselves except in mirrors, and sometimes not even then. Between our dress, and our opinions, and our habits, and our beliefs, and our values, and our mannerisms, and our manners, and our expressions, and our ages, and our experience, even I can hardly believe that I am looking at three other myselves. No layman would entertain for a moment the notion that he beheld four versions of the same woman. Did I say a moment? Not for an age of moments, particularly if the layman were indeed a *man*.

"Janet, may I ask you why you and your neighbors do not show up on our instruments?

You must have discovered some theory of probability travel some time ago (in your terms), yet you are the first traveler. You wish to visit other universes of probability, yet you make it impossible for anyone to find you, let alone visit you.

"Why is that?"

"Aggressive and bellicose persons," said Janet with care, "always assume that unaggressive and pacific persons cannot protect themselves.

"Why is that?"

VI

Over trays of pre-cooked steak and chicken that would've disgraced an airline (that's where they came from, I found out later) Jael sat next to Jeannine and glued herself to Jeannine's ear, glancing round at the rest of us from time to time to see how we were taking it. Her eyes sparkled with the gaiety of corruption, the Devil in the fable tempting the young girl. Whisper, whisper, whisper. All I could hear were the sibilants, when her tongue came between her teeth. Jeannine stared soberly ahead and didn't eat much, the color leaving her little by little. Jael didn't eat at all. Like a vampire she fed on Jeannine's ear. Later she drank a sort of super-bouillon which nobody else could stand and talked a lot to all of us about the war. Finally, Janet said bluntly:

"What war?"

"Does it matter?" said Miss Reasoner ironically, raising her silver eyebrows. "This war, that war, isn't there always one?"

"No," said Janet.

"Well, hell," said Jael more genuinely, "*the* war. If there isn't one, there just was one, and if there wasn't one, there soon will be one. Eh? The war between Us and Them. We're playing it rather cool just now because it's hard to work up an enthusiasm for something forty years old."

I said, "Us and Them?"

"I'll tell you," said Sweet Alice, making a face. "After the plague—don't worry; everything you eat is stuffed with antitoxins and we'll decontaminate you before you go—besides, this all ended more than seventy years ago—after the bacteriological weapons were cleaned out of the biosphere (insofar as that was possible) and half the population buried (the dead half, I hope) people became rather conservative. They tend to do that, you know. Then after a while you get the reaction against the conservatism, I mean the radicalism. And after that the reaction against the radicalism. People had already begun gathering in like-minded communities before the war: Traditionalists, Neo-Feudalists, Patriarchalists, Matriarchalists, Separatists (all of us now), Fecundists, Sterilists, and what-have-you. They seemed to be happier that way. The War Between the Nations had really been a rather nice war, as wars go; it wiped the have-not nations off the face of the earth and made their resources available to us without the bother of their populations; all our machinery was left standing; we were getting wealthier and wealthier. So if you were not one of the fifty percent who had died, you were having a pretty good time of it. There was increasing separatism, increasing irritability, increasing radicalism; then came the Polarization; then came the Split. The middle drops out and you're left with the two ends, hein? So when people began shopping for a new war, which they also seem to do, don't they, there was only one war left. The only war that makes any sense if you except the relations between children and adults, which you must do because children grow up. But in the other war the Haves never stop being Haves and the Have-nots never stop being Have-nots. It's cooled off now, unfortunately, but no wonder; it's been going on for forty years—a stalemate, if you'll forgive the pun. But in my opinion, questions that are based on something real ought to be settled by something real without all this damned lazy miserable drifting. I'm a fanatic. I want to see this thing settled. I want to see it over and done with. Gone. Dead.

"Oh, don't worry!" she added. "Nothing spectacular is going to happen. All I will do in three days or so is ask you about the tourist trade in your lovely homes. What's wrong with that? Simple, eh?

"But it will get things moving. The long war will start up again. We will be in the middle of it and I—who have always been in the middle of it—will get some decent support from my people at last."

"Who?" said Jeannine crossly. "Who, who, for Heaven's sake! Who's Us, who's Them? Do you expect us to find out by telepathy!"

"I beg your pardon," said Alice Reasoner softly. "I thought you knew. I had no intention of puzzling you. You are my guests. When I say Them and Us I mean of course the Haves and the Have-nots, the two sides, there are always two sides, aren't there?

"I mean the men and the women."

Later I caught Jeannine by the door as we were all leaving; "What did she talk to you about?" I said. Something had gotten into Jeannine's clear, suffering gaze; something had muddied her timidity. What can render Miss Dadier self-possessed? What can make her so quietly stubborn? Jeannine said:

"She asked me if I had ever killed anybody."

VII

She took us topside in the branch elevator: The Young One, The Weak One, The Strong One, as she called us in her own mind. I'm the author and I know. *Miss Sweden* (she also called Janet this) ran her hands over the paneling and studied the controls while the other two gaped. Think of me in my usual portable form. Their underground cities are mazes of corridors like sunken hotels; we passed doors, barricades, store windows, branch corridors leading to arcades. What is this passion for living underground? At one barrier they put us in purdah, that is, some kind of asbestos-like fireman's suit that protects you against other people's germs and them against yours. But this time it was a fake, meant only to hide us. "Can't have them looking at you," said Jael. She went apart with the border guard and there was some low-voiced, aggressive by-play, some snarling and lifting of hackles which a third party resolved by a kind of rough joking. I didn't hear a word of it. She told us honestly that we couldn't be expected to believe anything we hadn't seen with our own eyes. There would be no films, no demonstrations, no statistics, unless we asked for them. We trundled out of the elevator into an armored car waiting in a barn, and across an unpaved, shell-

pocked plain, a sort of no-man's-land, in the middle of the night. *Is the grass growing? Is that a virus blight? Are the mutated strains taking over?* Nothing but gravel, boulders, space, and stars. Jael flashed her pass at a second set of guards and told them about us: unclean, unclean, unclean. No barriers, no barbed wire, no searchlights; only the women have these. Only the men make a sport of people-hunting across the desert. Bulkier than three pregnancies, we followed our creatrix into another car, from out that first one, through the rubble and ruin at the edges of an old city, left standing just as it had been during the plague. Teachers come out here on Sundays, with their classes. It looks as if it's been used for target practice, with holes in everything and new scars, like mortar scars, on the rubble.

"It has," says Jael Reasoner. Each of us wears a luminous, shocking-pink cross on chest and back to show how deadly we are. So the Manlanders (who all carry guns) won't take pot-shots at us. There are lights in the distance—don't think I know any of this by hearsay; I'm the spirit of the author and I know all things. I'll know it when we begin to pass the lit-up barracks at the edge of the city, when we see in the distance the homes of the very rich shining from the seven hilltops on which the city is built; I'll know it when we go through a tunnel of rubble, built fashionably to resemble a World War I trench, and emerge neither into a public nursery (they're either much further inside the city proper or out in the country) nor into a brothel, but into a recreation center called The Trench or The Prick or The Crotch or The Knife. I haven't decided on a name yet. The Manlanders keep their children with them only when they're very rich—but what posit I? Manlanders have no children. Manlanders buy infants from the Womanlanders and bring them up in batches, save for the rich few who can order children made from their very own semen: keep them in city nurseries until they're five, then out into the country training ground, with the gasping little misfits buried in baby cemeteries along the way. There, in ascetic and healthful settlements in the country, little boys are made into Men—though some don't quite make it; sex-change surgery begins at sixteen. One out of seven fails early and makes the full change; one out of seven fails later and (refusing surgery) makes only half a change: artists, illusionists, impressionists of femininity who keep their genitalia but who grow slim, grow languid, grow emotional and feminine, all this the effect of spirit only. Five out of seven Manlanders make it; these are "real-men." The others are "the changed" or "the half-changed." All real-men like the changed; some real-men like the half-changed; none of the real-men like real-men, for that would be abnormal. Nobody asks the changed or half-changed what *they* like. Jael flashed her civil pass at the uniformed real-man at the entrance to The Crotch and we trundled after. Our hands and feet look very small to me, our bodies odd and dumpy.

We went inside; "Jael!" I exclaimed, "there are—"

"Look again," she said.

Look at the necks, look at the wrists and ankles, penetrate the veils of false hair and false eyelashes to measure the relative size of eyes and bone structure. The half-changed starve themselves to be slim, but look at their calves and the straightness of their arms and knees. If most of the fully changed live in harims and whore-homes, and if popular slang is beginning to call them "cunts," what does this leave for us? What can we be called?

"*The enemy*," said Jael. "Sit here." We sat around a large table in the corner where the light was dim, snuggling up to the fake oak paneling. One of the guards, who had followed us inside, came up to Jael and put one giant arm round her, one huge paw crushing her bearishly to his side, his crimson epaulets, his gold boots, his shaved head, his sky-blue codpiece, his diamond-chequered-costumed attempt to beat up the whole world, to shove his prick up the world's ass. She looked so plain next to him. She was all swallowed up.

"Hey, hey," he said. "So you're back again!"

"Well, sure, why not?" (she said) "I have to meet someone. I have business to do."

"Business!" he said fetchingly. "Don't you want some of the real thing? Come on, fuck business!"

She smiled gracefully but remained modestly silent. This seemed to please him. He enveloped her further, to the point of vanishment, and said in a low voice with a sort of chuckle:

"Don't you dream about it? Don't all you girls dream about us?"

"You know that, Lenny," she said.

"Sure I do," he said enthusiastically. "Sure. I can see it in your face whenever you come here. You get excited just looking at it. Like the doctors say, we can do it with each other but you can't because you don't have nothing to do it with, do you? So you don't get any."

"Lenny—" she began (slipping under his arm) "you got us figured out just right. Scout's honor. I've got business to do."

"Come on!" he said (pleading, I think).

"Oh, you're a brick!" cried Jael, moving behind the table, "you surely are. Why, you're so strong, some day you're going to squash us to death." He laughed, basso-profundo. "We're friends," he said, and winked laboriously.

"Sure," said Jael dryly.

"Some day you're gonna walk right in here—"and this tiresome creature began all over again, but whether he noticed the rest of us or saw someone or smelt someone I don't know, for suddenly he lumbered off in a great hurry, rousting his billy-club out of his azure sash, next the gun holster. Bouncers don't use their guns at The Prick; too much chance of hitting the wrong people. Jael was talking to someone else, a shadowy, thin-lipped party in a green, engineer's suit.

"Of course we're friends," said Jael Reasoner patiently. "Of course we are. That's why I don't want to talk to you tonight. Hell, I don't want to get you in trouble. See those crosses? One jab, one little rip or tear, and those girls will start an epidemic you won't be able to stop for a month. Do you want to be mixed up in that? Now you know we women are into plague research; well, these are some of the experiments. I'm taking them across Manland to another part of our own place; it's a shortcut. I wouldn't take them through here except I have some business to do here tonight. We're developing a faster immunization process. I'd tell all your friends to stay away from this table, too, if I were you—not that we can't take care of ourselves and *I* don't worry; I'm immune to this particular strain—but I don't want to see you take the rap for it. You've done a lot for me in the past and I'm grateful. I'm very grateful. You'd get it in the neck, you know. And you might get plague, too, there's always that. Okay?"

Astonishing how each of them has to be reassured of my loyalty! says Jael Reasoner. *Even more astonishing that they believe me. They're not very bright, are they? But these are the little fish. Besides, they've been separated from real women so long that they don't know what to make of us; I doubt if even the sex surgeons know what a real woman looks like. The specifications we send them every year grow wilder and wilder and there isn't a murmur of protest. I think they like it. As moths to the flame, so men to the social patterns of the Army, that womanless world haunted by the ghosts of millions of dead women, that discarnate femininity that hovers over everybody and can turn the toughest real-man into one of Them, that dark force they always feel at the backs of their own minds! Would I, do you think, force slavishness and deformity on two-sevenths of my own kind? Of course not! I think these men are not human. No, no, that's wrong—I decided long ago that they weren't human. Work is power, but they farm out everything to us without the slightest protest—Hell, they get lazier and lazier. They let us do their thinking for them. They even let us do their feeling for them. They are riddled with duality and the fear of duality. And the fear of themselves. I think it's in their blood. What human being would—sweating with fear and rage—mark out two equally revolting paths and insist that her fellow-creatures tread one or the other?*

Ah, the rivalries of cosmic he-men and the worlds they must conquer and the terrors they must face and the rivals they must challenge and overcome!

"You are being a little obvious," says Janet pedantically from inside her suit, "and I doubt that the power of the blood—"

Hsst! Here comes my contact.

Our contact was a half-changed, for Manlanders believe that child care is woman's business; so they delegate to the changed and the half-changed the business of haggling for babies and taking care of children during those all-important, first five years—they want to fix their babies' sexual preference early. This means, practically speaking, that the children are raised in brothels. Now some Manlander real-men do not like the idea of the whole business being in the hands of the feminized and the effeminate but there's not much they can do about it (see Proposition One, about child care, above)—although the more masculine look forward to a time when no Manlander will fall away from the ranks of the he-men, and with an obstinacy I consider perverse, refuse to decide who will be the sexual objects when the changed and the half-changed are no more. Perhaps they think sex beneath them. Or above them? (Around the shrine of each gowned and sequined hostess in The Knife are at least three real-men; how many can a hostess take on in one night?) I suspect we real women still figure, however grotesquely, in Manland's deepest dreams; perhaps on that morning of Total Masculinity they will all invade Womanland, rape everyone in sight (if they can still remember how) and then kill them, and after that commit suicide upon a pyramid of their victims' panties. The official ideology has it that women are poor substitutes for the changed. I certainly hope so. (Little girls, crept out of their crèche at last, touching those heroic dead with curious, wee fingers. Nudging them with their patent leather Mary Janes. Bringing their baby brothers out to a party on the green, all flutes and oats and pastoral fun until the food gives out and the tiny heroines must decide: Whom shall we eat? The waving limbs of our starfish siblings, our dead mother, or those strange, huge, hairy bodies already beginning to swell in the sun?) I flashed that damned pass—again!—this time at a half-changed in a pink chiffon gown, with gloves up to his shoulder, a monument of irrelevancy on high heels, a pretty girl with too much of the right curves and a bobbing, springing, pink feather boa. Where oh where is the shop that makes those long rhinestone earrings, objects of fetishism and nostalgia, worn only by the half-changed (and usually not by them unless they're rich), handmade from museum copies, of no use or interest to fully six-sevenths of the adult human race? Somewhere stones are put together by antiquarians, somewhere petroleum is transformed into fabric that can't burn without polluting the air, and won't rot, and won't erode, so that strands of plastic have turned up in the bodies of diatoms at the bottom of the Pacific Trench—such a vision was he, so much he wore, such folds and frills and ribbons and buttons and feathers, trimmed like a Christmas tree. Like Garbo playing Anna Karenina, decorated all over. His green eyes shrewdly narrowed. This one has intelligence. Or is it only the weight of his false lashes? The burden of having always to be taken, of having to swoon, to fall, to endure, to hope, to suffer, to wait, to only be? There must be a secret feminine underground that teaches them how to behave; in the face of their comrades' derision and savage contempt, in the face of the prospect of gang rape if they're found alone on the streets after curfew, in the face of the legal necessity to belong—every one of them—to a real-man, somehow they still learn the classic shiver, the slow blink, the knuckle-to-lip pathos. These, too, I think, must be in the blood. But whose? My three friends and I pale beside such magnificence! Four lumpy parcels, of no interest to anyone at all, at all.

Anna, with a mechanical shiver of desire, says that we must go with him.

"Her?" says Jeannine, confused.

"Him!" says Anna in a strained contralto. The half-changed are very punctilious—sometimes about the changeds' superiority and sometimes about their own genitals. Either way it works out to *Him*. He's extraordinarily aware, for a man, of Jeannine's shrinking and he resents it—as who would not? I myself am respectful of ruined lives and forced choices. On the street once Anna did not fight hard enough against the fourteen-year-old toughs who wanted his twelve-year-old ass; he didn't go to the extremity of berserk rage, reckoning his life as nothing in defense of his virility; he forestalled—by surrender—the plucking out of an eye, the castration, the throat cut with a broken bottle, the being put out of his twelve-year-old action with a stone or a tire chain. I know a lot about Manlanders' history. Anna made a *modus vivendi*, he decided life was worth it on any terms. Everything follows from that.

"Oh, you're lovely," says Jeannine, heartfelt. Sisters in misfortune. This really pleases Anna. He shows us a letter of safe-conduct he has from his boss—a real-man, of course—and putting it back in his pink-brocaded evening bag, draws around him that fake-feather Thing which floats and wobbles in the least current of air. It's a warm evening. To protect his employé, the big boss (they are Men, even in the child-rearing business) has had to give Anna K a little two-way camera to wear in his ear; otherwise somebody would break his high heels and leave him dead or half-dead in an alley. Everybody knows that the half-changed are weak and can't protect themselves; what do you think femininity is all about? Even so Anna probably has a bodyguard waiting at the entrance to The Knife. I'm cynical enough to wonder sometimes if the Manlanders' mystique isn't just an excuse to feminize anybody with a pretty face—but look again, they believe it; look under the padding, the paint, the false hair, the corsetry, the skin rinses and the magnificent dresses and you'll see nothing exceptional; only faces and bodies like any other man's. Anna bats his eyes at us and wets his lips, taking the women inside the suits to be real-men, taking me to be a real-man (what else can I be if I'm not a changed?), taking the big wide world itself to be—what else?—a Real-Man intent on worshipping Anna's ass; the world exists to look at Anna; he—or she—is only a real-man turned inside out.

An eerie sisterliness, a smile at Jeannine. All that narcissism! Brains underneath, though.

Remember where their loyalties lie.

(Are they jealous of us? I don't think they believe we're women.)

He wets his lips again, the indescribable silliness of that insane mechanism, practiced anywhere and everywhere, on the right people, on the wrong people. But what else is there? It seems that Anna's boss wants to meet me. (I don't like that.) But we'll go; we maintain our outward obedience until the very end, until the beautiful, bloody moment that we fire these stranglers, these murderers, these unnatural and atavistic nature's bastards, off the face of the earth.

"Dearest sister," says Anna softly, sweetly, "come with me." ■

Femme at Heart

by Woodwoman

(To be sung to the tune of "Sweet Betsy from Pike")

I seem to have a problem,
I'm sure it's nothing new.
I've looked at it from every side, but I don't know what to do.
I call myself a heavy dyke and I try to play the part,
But way down deep inside of me I'm just a femme at heart.

CHORUS:

> I'm just a femme at heart, just a femme at heart.
> I need a brand-new image, but I'm stuck before I start.
> It doesn't make no difference if I cuss and spit and fart,
> 'Cause way down deep inside of me, I'm just a femme at heart.

My sweetie is a radical, she's full of lesbian pride.
We wear Jill Johnston buttons and read the *Lesbian Tide*.
But when she brings me flowers, I bake her a custard tart.
And lately I'm suspecting that I'm just a femme at heart.

(Chorus)

We go out to women's bars as often as we need.
And when we dance, we always fight over which one's going to lead.
But what's the use of hanging loose and wearing a 3-piece suit,
If I blush just like an April bride when she says I'm looking cute.

(Chorus)

Well, someone better help me before I lose my mind.
If this goes on much longer, God knows what else I'll find.
It isn't in my tarot, and it isn't in my chart,
But here and all, when I hear the call,
I'm just a femme at heart.

(Chorus)

Sent to us by Barbara Grier of Naiad Press.

Homophobia and Death in the Closet

by Marilyn Murphy

I knew of a Lesbian couple who were companion lovers for thirty-eight years when death separated them. Nancy had no family to speak of, but Betty Jean's large and nearby family treated Nancy as "another daughter" and "another sister." She was Aunt Nancy to Betty Jean's numerous nieces and nephews. Together the two financed college for a talented but impoverished niece. Together they attended all important family events: birthdays, graduations, weddings, holiday gatherings. They participated in the ordinary daily life of the family too, the phone calls, impromptu visits, dinners and the endless discussions of the relationships of family members to each other and to in-laws and

outsiders. Both women felt fortunate to be so lovingly embedded in "normal" family life as it is lived in the USA. They never talked about their own personal life, their own personal disagreements, problems and joys, of course. "It's nobody's business but ours," they'd say. Still, like so many Lesbians, they assumed everyone in the family "really knew" their relationship was Lesbian.

Nancy and Betty Jean had wills drawn up years before, wills they updated every so often as their assets increased. Except for a few bequests of particular objects to others, they were each other's sole beneficiaries. This, as everything else about their personal life, was not talked about, was private. When Betty Jean died, her family assumed that her half of everything was going to them. They were outraged to learn she had left her possessions to Nancy, a stranger, an outsider, someone she wasn't related to either by blood or marriage. They ransacked the house, shunned

Nancy at the funeral, and talked to an attorney about the will. The careful years of legal preparation protected Nancy financially, but nothing could save her from the pain of losing her "family" when she lost her lover.

Another Lesbian I knew lived alone in her lovely canyon home when she became seriously ill. Joanne had had almost no contact with her parents and siblings in the thirty-some years since she moved to Southern California from a small town in the Midwest. She had a large circle of friends, Lesbians and Gaymen she had known for years. They were her family, all the family she ever wanted. An ex-lover, then her dearest friend, coordinated her care during her last months of life. Friends took turns driving her to treatments, sat with her during the day and kept a nightwatch as well. They ran errands, kept her house, helped her get her affairs in order. Joanne spent hours going over her possessions in her mind, deciding which ring or art

"Homophobia and Death in the Closet" is reprinted from Marilyn Murphy's *Are You Two Girls Traveling Alone?* (Clothespin Fever Press, 1991), a collection of her "Lesbianic Logic" columns from *Lesbian News*.

piece was right for which friend, which Lesbian or Gay organization was to get what percentage of her estate. An attorney friend drew up her will. She gave friends instructions about her cremation and memorial service. When the end was near, she had someone contact her blood relatives. To her surprise, they flew in and were confronted with her Lesbianism for the first time. They banished Joanne's family of choice from her deathbed, turned them away from the christian church door and from the cemetery, and broke her will by claiming undue influence over a dying woman. They are now self-righteously spending Lesbian money.

A friend of my sister died in a boating accident recently. Carmela was in her late twenties, worked for the telephone company, and was very active in the Lesbian-feminist community. She didn't own much, a good stereo system, a word processor, some furniture, mostly second-hand, and a car, almost paid for. She had a modest savings account and just about every Lesbian and feminist book published and every record. She was not out to her parents, and at her death, they destroyed her precious books and records, and sold what they couldn't use of her things. The money from the sale and from her bank account went to the parish church in her home town, stipends for masses offered for the salvation of her soul.

Irene and I talked about making wills many times. Once, the morning before we left for an out-of-town conference, we each wrote a simple will on some lined stationery and left them on the dining room table, "just in case." We felt silly when we saw them on our return. Not long after, we heard that the bereaved but irate family of a Gayman acquaintance broke his handwritten will with no trouble at all. We promised each other to make real wills "soon." Of course, we didn't.

Trouble over money and property when someone dies is not a specifically Lesbian and Gayman problem. Neither is it only the province of the rich. Still, homophobia does create particular problems for Lesbians and Gaymen, in addition to the ones we share with the larger population. Obviously, the fact that our companion lover relationships are not legal creates the greatest difficulty. The legal mating of heterosexual couples is a sacrosanct relationship. No matter how much parents, siblings or children may hate one's marriage partner or disapprove of the relationship, the inheritance right of that partner is inviolate, even without a will. Our out-of-the-law relationships are quite another matter. If we want our companion lovers to inherit our estate, we do not have the (heterosexual) privilege to indulge in any superstition or squeamishness about death and wills. We cannot afford to be lazy or thoughtless either. A legal, loophole-free will is a Lesbian necessity, one more price we pay for our audacity, for our insistence upon living with and loving women. In addition, we need to name as executor a friend who can assist our beloved companion to stand up for her inheritance rights, should that become necessary. We cannot give our families the opportunity to behave badly, no matter how sure we are that they "really know" and accept our Lesbianism and our partner. In other words, we must be Lesbian cautious to the end.

Lesbians need caution in matters concerning our death and our possessions because many of our families have learned to ignore, "forget," or shield themselves from the Lesbian foundation upon which our "friendships" are built. Their self-deceit is usually the result of collusion between our families and ourselves, an unspoken agreement that if we do not discuss our personal lives with them, they will treat us as if we did not have personal lives at all. This covert contract enables us to fit into a "normal" family niche, that of the sexless, unmarried daughter, sister, aunt who, for some reason (after all, she was pretty enough!) couldn't get, or couldn't keep, a husband, so she lives with another woman in similar circumstances. In this way, the family does not have to acknowledge and "do something" about our Lesbianism, and neither do we. When we die and try to leave our estate to our "friend," the agreement is broken, and our families are left to deal with our Lesbianism without our help. It is not surprising that they frequently deal with it badly.

I am convinced that we Lesbians and Gaymen would be better off if we gave our families the opportunity to adjust to our lives while we are living them. Those family members who cannot adjust with love, can adjust with politeness. If they can do neither, we can create families of choice from among the large and varied communities of Lesbians and Gaymen. Certainly heterosexuals expect their families to adjust to their choices. Heterosexuals do not "respect" their families' feelings about their love choices when those feelings are racist, anti-Semitic, or classist, for example, the way we "respect" our families' homophobia. Heterosexuals marry persons of the "wrong" race, religion, nationality, class. They marry persons their families think are too old, too young, too stupid, too educated, too lazy, too ill for them. They would not attend a family gathering at which an "unacceptable" wife or husband was not welcome. They demand their families accept or, at the least, tolerate their choices. And most families do just that.

Lesbians and Gaymen should demand no less for our families than our heterosexual siblings do. "But I love her/him," is all the reason heterosexuals think necessary to justify their choices. Why should we need more? And just as the knowledge of their "wrong" love choices does not cause the premature death of their mothers and fathers, neither will the knowledge that our love choice is the "wrong" sex kill off our folks. Our families' homophobia is a social disease that can be cured by love, patience, education and the everyday sight of Lesbian and Gay parents and grandparents, aunts and uncles, sisters and brothers, children and grandchildren, nieces and nephews...and their companion lovers...living our lives and our deaths out of the closet.

However, even those of us who are completely open and honest with our families need legal wills. Before Irene and I finally met with an attorney, we thought making wills was simple. We are each other's heirs. We thought that was all there was to it. We were wrong. We had to name those who would inherit our estates if we didn't survive each other long enough to make new wills. Except for a bequest to my mother, we wanted our estate to benefit Lesbians. So we discussed, disagreed, and finally decided on which Lesbian projects to fund after our death. It was a fascinating process, one we recommend to all Lesbians.

(After all, if Lesbians do not financially support Lesbians and our projects, no one will. We think it unconscionable that Lesbians so often leave their money, by default or by design, to the very persons and institutions that are the causes, the instruments, or the beneficiaries of our oppression. They leave money to family members to whom they cannot speak the "L" word, to persons whose social and economic heterosexual privileges save them thousands of dollars in fees, premiums and taxes every year, to the churches that teach homosexuality is a sin, to schools, colleges and youth groups which harass or condone the harassment of Lesbians and Gaymen. Even "good" causes like cancer research and the March of Dimes can get along without Lesbian money left to them by our sisters. Our Lesbian good causes cannot.)

The difficult part of the will process came when our attorney suggested, as additional insurance, that we specifically exclude from inheriting our estates those blood relatives who might be seen by the court to have a legitimate claim to our estate. This meant that I had to list the names of my children and state that they were to receive nothing from my estate. A lifetime of books and films about unnatural and vindictive parents disinheriting their children poured out of my memory to unsettle my resolve. Even though I knew they knew I was planning to leave my estate to Lesbian projects and not to them, I was impelled to write each of them, reminding them that my will had nothing to do with my feelings for them. And that is mostly true. Still, leaving money to one's children is the traditional way to keep the money in the patriarchal family. It seems more womanly, more Lesbian to leave our goods, our treasures, to the Lesbian family which nurtures us, to the Lesbian sisterhood which strengthens us, to the Lesbians who follow us...our true beneficiaries. Irene and I think of ourselves as womanly Lesbians to the end...and after! ■

Riverfinger Women

by Elana Dykewomon

L ucy Bear and Rainbo Woman have disappeared. Therefore I, Inez Riverfingers, set down this, the pornographic novel of my life, with no regrets. The dough rises anyway, pierced as it is by arrows, and bleeding small bees that hover about the kitchen, searching for honey.

I have wondered what people who don't make love all the time do with their lives—and I have wondered this even though I have made love only six times this year, and was interrupted by the police one of those nights. They must have mistaken by abandoned sunday school, with its red urinal, for the abandoned birth control clinic down the block. Or, possibly, they were agents of the Committee (my friends tell me that's paranoia, and maybe it is, and maybe it's not).

They say it's sex that makes everyone crazy, and I believe it, though I am not quite sure how it happened.

End of Introduction. I am Inez Riverfingers, and I come complete with a vast family of the same. Some of their names: Ratatoville Riverfingers, Little Noodles Riverfingers, Natasha Riverfingers, Gabi-dog Riverfingers, Eulalee Riverfingers, Delphine Riverfingers, Holly Riverfingers, Bruce and San Fernando Blondie Riverfingers, Maggie and Al Bear Riverfingers, Peggy Warren (a closet Riverfinger), and Abigail,

Elana Dykewomon, 1974. *Riverfinger Women*. Tallahassee, FL: Naiad, 1992.

otherwise known as Abby Riverfingers (who chastises me now, years after, in her letters from Jerusalem, for not taking another steady lover—god knows I've tried, but it's not an easy life for a dyke). Pickpockets, poets, acrobats, sociologists, tough street women, farmers and friends.

...Moments have passed, and I will make Abby reappear. It is as easy as this, a voice squeezed from black plastic keys, telling stories in bed. The hammering of myself into the background will seem to be over. This hammering, this background—the language of our getting older, the time of our being no longer children but young women, that is to say, forming into identifiable shapes, it is not simple. From time to time you will hear that faint tackety-tackety-tackety, like kids at summer camp, making bronze nameplates in relief dot by dot:

these are our lives, these are our lives, these are our lives.

...Abby turns to look at Inez in the Colorado street light, in their first apartment, a two-room converted attic. Peggy Warren sleeps in the other room, which is also the kitchen. Inez is curled on her side, cuddled into the hollow of Abby's thin arm, looking up. They fit. Seventeen, eighteen, thin to fat, not self-conscious, pleased to be there, seam against seam. Their hands trace each other, begin to touch as leaves touch in first summer winds. Unbelievable. All the forces of civilization had worked against this, still it happened. They made love again that day, the last time before falling asleep. They had the freedom to touch while they were still children. No one had given them permission. They just made it all up, taking their freedom with their hands in front.

There was nothing in either of them that was older than seven, except that they knew how to do it, finally, after five weeks they had figured one hole from another. There were no movements putting pressure on their consciences, only safety in being two together. There was only the fairy tale, being seventeen and sleeping in each other's arms in Colorado. These small protections they wove like nets, to keep away what they understood perfectly.

They understood perfectly about names and rumors, psychiatrists and angry fathers, perverts, rotten ungrateful selfish vain children, disgust and fear, more fear, self-hatred, confusion, no women will let us babysit for their children if they find out.

They were beginning to learn to protect themselves by never touching or looking at each other in public. By waiting until they got into gas station restrooms when they wanted to kiss each other. By calling themselves roommates. By watching other people very carefully. By being children only together, in their first double bed. Sometimes they were open with Peggy, who never told them until three years later that she was jealous, for wanting to join them.

♀♀

...Some pornographic novel! Some novel! What's going on here anyway? Where's the sex, where's the action, the *angst*?

Let me try to make it clear. In 1967 we still wanted to repeat the same straight story. But we knew even then, in our careful duplications (toasters, laundry, feeding the cats, a whole inventory of living together), that we were pornographic because we were both women.

Nothing else—we were too modern already

to believe that one of us was the man and the other was the woman. We felt like neither men nor women. We were females, we queers ("but *I'm* not a lesbian," Abby said in Colorado, "I just love *you*, Inny."). We knew we had the right to love whomever we loved—it was part of the amorphous thought of a sexual revolution we found ourselves in the middle of. It was very democratic, theoretical, and very very personal. And we knew that when we made the movie about how good it was, how after all lesbians could lead normal lives, have jobs, go to college, how they were the same, the same, really the same as straight people, only they were both women, but that was just—an accident—a matter of—chemistry—we knew that when men came to see the movie we would make, the men would come because it was pornographic, that's all, baby, sinful, immoral and certainly absurd, for women to think they could do it without them.

Let me try to make it clear. There is Inez. There is Abby. They became lovers when they were seventeen. This is the story of what it means to be women and lovers when you are seventeen, with the years just behind (moving them toward it), and the years just ahead, with everyone waiting to say, uh-huh, just as we thought!

There is Peggy Warren. She is smuggling hash from Tangiers, accumulating a thousand tatooed stories behind her eyes like veils that keep even her old friends away. She's been sleeping with every kind of man there is, sadists, baby pimps and North Pole engineers. She comes to speak about heroin and the (real) 42nd Street porno trade, massage parlors and organized crime. She is an old friend of Abby and Inez.

There are all the places where these stories touch each other and make the start of a common life, the beginning of an idea about community. There are all the places where the story falls apart and something else shows through—an isolation, a terror, a hunger to shape that isolation and terror into some kind of love for ourselves.

A hunger for each other, two hungers, three: one out of fear; one for metamorphosis (to be girls no longer, to be women, and serious); one for actual love, whatever it is. There is a first powerfulness in knowing what our hungers are, that they may not be taken from us and be sold by Tampax or Pepsi-Cola.

When you're talking about someone's body, that's about as close as you can get. This is how it worked in our bodies, how our hungers worked into our bones. There was authority at every pressure point, trying to direct us (for our own good). We fought back with fads that nearly killed us. And slowly in our bodies words grew, formed a strength against both the fads and the pressures of our mentors.

We thought we were very special then, we thought we were hot shit, for being perfectly existentially unique, reading all the books by men about ultimate aloneness and the isolation of mass man.

We were exactly like millions and millions of others in the sixties and seventies and long before and after, self-important with big words like alienation and technological elite. It's the same story for every girl and boy adolescent who knuckled under waves of words they couldn't own: sexual revolution and hard rock and LSD. We were scraped along the sharp stones of those, where the undertow dragged us.

But in being faceless unmentionable nameless lesbians, unapproved by Ann Landers or Jerry Rubin, in being unable to find catch words in newspapers or the books we read in our dormitories, for that, for what that meant, women loving women—in that we could have no fads. That was where some of us began our resistance, learned to change (acid on stone) who we thought we were doomed to be into who we were. Tough, strong, proud: free women. ▰

JOSEPHINE **CRACKS** UNDER THE PRESSURE OF DECIDING WHAT TO WEAR TO MEET MIRIAM'S PARENTS.

by Alison Bechdel

Gay Head
by Alix Dobkin

I heard Cheryl and Mary say
There are two kinds of people in the world today
One or the other
A person must be
The men are them and
The women are we!
They agree it's a pleasure to be a

CHORUS:

> Lesbian. Lesbian
> Let's be in no man's land
> Lesbian, Lesbian
> Any woman can be a Lesbian

Liza wishes the library
Had men and women placed separately
For theirs is the kingdom
She knows who she'll find
In the *history* of *man*kind
But then she's inclined
To be ahead of her time. She's a…

(chorus)

Carol is tired of being nice
With a sweet smile and a pretty face
Submissive device
To pacify the people
For they won't defend
A woman who's indifferent to men
She's my friend. She's a Lesbian and
Woman's anger, Louise explains
A million second places in the master's game
It's real as a mountain
It's strong as the sea, besides
An angry woman is a beauty
She's chosen to be a Dyke like me, she's a...

(chorus)

The sexes do battle and batter about
The men's are the sexes I will live without
I'll return to the bosom where my journey ends where there's no
Penis between us friends. Will I see you again when you're a...

(chorus)

Words & music ©1973 by Alix Dobkin. "Gay Head" was recorded on Alix's first album, *Lavender Jane Loves Women* (1973), and on *Love and Politics* (1992).

Elizabethan Drama

by Jorjet Harper

I don't have a neon pink triangle or a purple labrys hanging in the window of my apartment, but it must be pretty clear to the neighbors that I' not a single gal in search of a husband. My lover drives a huge red convertible which no one on the block has failed to notice, and dykey-looking women wearing *Outlines* T-shirts are always ringing my doorbell.

My neighborhood is not the hippest, and it sure ain't the "gay ghetto" Newtown. Mountain Moving Coffeehouse used to be right around the corner, though, in a rented church space, and it was kind of fun to watch the expressions of puzzlement on our straight neighbors' faces when droves of dykes converged on the area every Saturday night.

My western windows face a single-family house owned by a genuine nuclear family—husband, wife, and four kids. They have vicious arguments. Their yelling—and sometimes the screams and crying of the children—can be heard way out into the street. The cops have been called many times.

Needless to say, they are not ideal neighbors, especially when I need to get some sleep and they are reenacting the Battle of Gallipoli in their bedroom.

Benny, the third child of this unhappy family, is about seven. Usually a very quiet kid, he was bouncing a volleyball in front of our building one sunny Saturday afternoon this spring while Paula was sitting on our porch steps.

"You don't go to the *Elizabeth* Church, do you?" he piped up.

"The what?" said Paula.

"The Elizabeth Church. You know, where all the Elizabeths go."

Then, of course, Paula understood. She and I and our lovers sometimes walked to Mountain Moving Coffeehouse together on a Saturday evening.

Paula, amused, asked him, "What's an Elizabeth?"

Benny, still bouncing his volleyball, said, "That's when two girls kiss each other *all the time*." He made an ugly face to demonstrate his revulsion.

"That doesn't sound so bad to me," Paula replied.

"Oh, it *is*," he told her, shaking his head. "It's really *bad*."

The windows of Paula's apartment, like mine, face Benny's parents' house, and she, too, has heard the shouts from their war zone.

"You know what I think is bad?" Paula said to the boy. "When people yell and scream and act mean to each other."

This caught Benny by surprise. He didn't

One of Jorjet Harper's "Lesbomania" columns, originally published in *Nightlines* (September 19, 1990).

have a ready answer. He stopped bouncing his ball and stood there thinking.

"Yes," he said pensively. "That's not good at all."

"And I think kissing is a lot better than that," Paula added.

He stood there a while longer, the volleyball still frozen in his hands. Finally he said, "Yes, you're *right*." Then, quick as a flash, he ran off down the street.

Ever since this talk, Benny has been very nice to us Elizabeths—and his mother has also been friendlier. Probably it's a coincidence, but maybe Benny said something at home that was able to make a difference—because since then the loud, terrible arguments have significantly diminished, too.

Jesse Helms and the Coalition for Family Values, take note. Here's a clear case in which a lesbian has undermined the nuclear family—undermined its child abuse, domestic violence, and homophobia. ■

Crooked and Straight in Academia

by Susan J. Wolfe and Julia Penelope

SCENE: *The female humor section at the Modern Language Association meeting. Chicago, December 29, 1977.*

SJW: Some lesbian jokes are almost vaudevillian.

JP: Does that mean I have to be the straight man?

SJW: Would you rather be a straight *woman*?

JP: When I joined an English department as an uncloseted lesbian, women faculty members came up at the rate of one a day to announce that they were heterosexual.

SJW: We decided we should post a list in the women's room headed, THE FOLLOWING WOMEN HAVE ANNOUNCED THAT THEY ARE HETEROSEXUAL, so that they could sign in. Then we'd cross their names off and initial them.

JP: One female colleague called me into her office and said, "You know, Julia, I'm different from you," and I said, "Oh, really? How?" She said, "Well, I'm more *conventional*." I said, "I'm sorry, I don't understand what you mean." "Well, I'm more *conservative*." I continued, "I still don't understand. Perhaps you could give me an example of the kind of distinctions you're making." With some hesitation she answered, "I don't teach in blue jeans." I said, "Neither do

From *Pulling Our Own Strings*, eds. Gloria Kaufman and Mary Kay Blakely, Bloomington: Indiana UP, 1980.

I." So she haltingly continued, "Well, I'm married," and I said, "That's true." "And," she went on, "I have a child...and...I'm hetero." Stunned by this announcement, I took a moment to reply, "Well, you know, you needn't suffer anymore. There are doctors who can cure that now."

SJW: This woman announced her heterosexuality as if it were some sort of secret—a confidence. Like, "I'm heterosexual, but don't tell my husband. He doesn't know."

JP: After this rash of declared heterosexuals, I left that department to join the English department at another institution. Shortly afterward, I received a letter from the National Council of Teachers of English explaining that our Committee on Lesbian and Gay Male Concerns in the Profession ought to contain a representative number of "declared heterosexuals." So I called Susan up.

SJW: I knew at once what she wanted. I agreed to serve on the committee, but wondered how I would get to be a "declared" heterosexual. (Most of the people I knew were *latent* heterosexuals.) So I opened the door to the office and screamed into the hallway, "I'm a heterosexual. I admit it!" I didn't want anyone to take this announcement as an invitation, so I quickly shut the door. ∎

Postscribbles

by Joanna Russ

1. Overheard at a gay conference, Lesbian to gay man, nearby a woman minister in "minister suit" trying not to smile: "We're *all* in drag."

2. A common way to cloak one's hatred of and dismissal of an issue is to snot it, *i.e.*, the outraged ignorance of the reviews of Marge Piercy's *Woman on the Edge of Time* and the more sophisticated (and more hateful) reviews of Adrienne Rich's *Of Woman Born*.

3. The paralysis of the "open secret," everyone reassured about their generosity and your safety...*except you*. Or the (even worse) open secret which everybody knows *except you*, a closet so vanishingly small that it's collapsed into a one-dimensional point and extruded itself (possibly) into some other universe, where it may be of use but not in this one. A well-meaning woman friend, upon learning that I was a Lesbian, "That's all right. It's nobody's business but yours."

4. Some white male reviewer in the *New York Times* speaking slightingly of the *irredentism** of minority groups in our time. The Boys never cease to amaze me.

5. That isn't an issue.

That isn't an issue *any more*.

That isn't *really* an issue any more.

Therefore why do you keep *bringing it up*?

Originally published in *The Coming Out Stories*, eds. Julia Penelope and Susan J. Wolfe (Persephone Press, 1980) in Joanna Russ's "Not for Years but for Decades."

You keep *bringing it up* because you are crazy.

You keep *bringing it up* because you are destructive.

You keep *bringing it up* because you want to be annoying.

You keep *bringing it up* because you are greedy and selfish.

You keep *bringing it up* because you are full of hate.

You keep *bringing it up* because you want to flaunt yourself.

You keep *bringing it up* because you deliberately want to separate yourself from the rest of the community.

How do you expect me to support a person as crazy/destructive/annoying/selfish/hateful/flaunting/separatist as you are?

I really cannot support someone as *bad* as that.

Especially since there is no really important issue involved.

6. Vaginas do *not* have sharp little teeth! Pass it on.

* Italian radicalism of the later 19th century, calling for a unification of all the Italian-speaking peoples, *i.e.*, nationalism: by extension, fighting for the rights of a group which perceives itself to have common interests. How wicked. ∎

Boots are being polished

by Pat Parker

Boots are being polished
Trumpeters clean their horns
Chains and locks forged
The crusade has begun.

Once again the flags of Christ
are unfurled in the dawn
and cries of soul saviors
sing apocalyptic on air waves.

Citizens, good citizens all
parade into voting booths
and in self-righteous sanctity
X away our right to life.

I do not believe as some
that the vote is an end,
I fear even more
It is just a beginning.

So I must make assessment
Look to you and ask:
Where will you be
when they come?

They will not come
a mob rolling
through the streets,
but quickly and quietly
move into our homes
and remove the evil,
the queerness,
the faggotry,
the perverseness
from their midst.
They will not come clothed in brown,
and swastikas, or
bearing chest heavy with
gleaming crosses.
The time and need
for uses are over.
They will come
in business suits
to buy your homes
and bring bodies to
fill your jobs.
They will come in robes
to rehabilitate
and white coats
to subjugate
and where will you be
when they come?

Where will we *all be*
when they come?
And they will come—

they will come
because we are
defined as opposite—
perverse
and we are perverse.

Every time we watched
a queer hassled in the
streets and said nothing—
It was an act of perversion.

Everytime we lied about
the boyfriend or girlfriend
at coffee break—
It was an act of perversion.

Everytime we heard,
"I don't mind gays
but why must they
be blatant?" and said nothing—
It was an act of perversion.

Everytime we let straights
make out in bars while
we couldn't touch because
of laws—
It was an act of perversion.

Everytime we put on the proper
clothes to go to a family
wedding and left our lovers
at home—
It was an act of perversion.

Everytime we heard
"Who I go to bed with
is my personal choice—
It's personal not political"
and said nothing—
It was an act of perversion.

Everytime we let straight relatives
bury our dead and push our
lovers away—
It was an act of perversion.

And they will come.
They will come for
the perverts

& it won't matter
if you're
            homosexual, not a faggot
            lesbian, not a dyke
            gay, not queer
It won't matter
if you
            own your business
            have a good job
            or are on S.S.I.
It won't matter
if you're
            Black
            Chicano
            Native American
            Asian
            or White
It won't matter
if you're from
            New York
            or Los Angeles
            Galveston
            or Sioux Falls
It won't matter
if you're
            Butch, or Fem
            Not into roles
            Monogamous
            Non Monogamous
It won't matter
If you're
            Catholic
            Baptist
            Atheist
            Jewish
            or M.C.C.

They will come
They will come
to the cities
and to the land
to your front rooms
and in *your* closets.

They will come for
the perverts
and where will
you be
When they come?

From *Movement in Black.*
Ithaca, NY: Firebrand Books,
1978.

Louisa May Incest
A One-Act Play For Two Women
By Carolyn Gage

Cast of Characters

LOUISA MAY ALCOTT, a woman of thirty-five.

JO MARCH, a woman in her early twenties with
short hair.

The Play

*The scene is Louisa May Alcott's room in Orchard
House, Concord, 1868. Her father, Bronson Alcott,
has his study across the hall. LOUISA MAY is thirty-
five years old.*

*She sits at a writing table and takes out her
manuscript, pens, ink, and paper. Then she closes the
curtains and crosses to the door to lock it. She sits
down and begins to write.*

*Someone is heard trying the door handle. Find-
ing it locked, the outsider tries to force the lock. Then
she knocks. Finally she calls out.*

JO (offstage): Louisa! Louisa! I can't get in! The
door must be locked.

*LOUISA looks up from her work, disturbed,
but she resolves to ignore the voice. She
continues to work.*

Louisa! Can you hear me? Louisa! It's me, Jo!

She rattles the knob.

Louisa! I can hear you…What's the matter? Is
someone else there? Louisa? Are you all right?
Louisa, answer me! I'm going to break the door
down.

*JO begins to batter the door. LOUISA,
frightened, sits at her desk. She tries to
ignore it.*

Don't worry, Louisa, I'm coming…

*Suddenly the door gives, and JO rushes in.
JO is JO MARCH from* Little Women.
*She is in her early twenties, with very short
hair. Jo trips, landing at Louisa's feet.*

Louisa! Louisa, are you all right?

*She throws her arms around the older
woman.*

What's the matter, dearest? Why was the door
locked?

LOUISA looks away.

Oh, Louisa, you weren't thinking those glum thoughts again, were you? Why didn't you call for me earlier? Is it your family again? It was Bronson, wasn't it? I saw the light on in his study across the hall. It was your father, wasn't it? He's been criticizing you again, hasn't he?

LOUISA: No. It has nothing to do with my family.

JO: What is it, darling? You know I'd do anything in the world for you. Is it one of your publishers? I know a thing or two about those men. It is, isn't it?

LOUISA: No, it's not.

JO sees the manuscript on the table.

JO: It's *Little Women*, then, isn't it? You're depressed about how it's going. Well, of course you are. You've been pegging away at it for months, day and night. Of course, you're tired. After all, you're human. Me, I could just rattle along forever, telling stories and blundering through. But of course, it's not the same for you. You need to eat and sleep. I've been so thoughtless. It's all my fault. Whenever you want to work, I just get so excited about the book, I get started, and I don't know when to stop. You see, I'm doing it now. You just turn and say, "Jo March, that's enough now," and I'll stop right where I am. Oh, I can see now that you haven't been taking enough time to rest. And you haven't had lunch, have you?...and it's nearly four...

LOUISA: It isn't me. I'm fine.

JO: Well, you dear, of course you'd say that if a ton of bricks fell on your head. That's just what I would say, too, so I know. But you can't fool me, Louisa May Alcott. You can't fool your Jo. You've been working too hard.

LOUISA: No, I haven't.

JO: ...But you think your family needs the money, so you're racing to finish the book. That's exactly what I would do—but it isn't right. You deserve a rest. We'll work on this tomorrow. Today, you just take a walk out in the sunshine, and eat a big healthy dinner...and I don't care what your father says, a little red meat wouldn't do you any harm...and you go to bed early—no reading! And tomorrow, bright and early, when you come into the study, I'll be waiting for you, and we'll start right in. You'll see. We'll work so hard tomorrow, because we'll be fresh, that we'll get twice as much done—and you won't have lost any work from today. Now, go on. Get your hat. Go on. I'll be waiting here.

LOUISA: I'm not tired. And I don't want to go out. And I don't want you to wait here.

JO is surprised by the sharpness in her voice.

I want to finish the book without you.

JO (after a long pause): You mean I'm going to die like Beth?

LOUISA (avoiding her eyes): You're not going to die. You're the main character.

JO: Then I don't understand. I thought we were writing this together.

LOUISA: We were. But I need to finish it alone.

JO: It's my dreadful language, isn't it—all that slang? Christopher Columbus and...

LOUISA: No, it's not the slang.

JO: Yes, it is. I know. And my selfishness.

LOUISA (smiling): You're not selfish, Jo.

JO: Oh, yes, I am. I'm not at all generous like Marmee, or Beth...and I've never learned to cook like Meg, and I'm not the least bit artistic like Amy...

LOUISA: You're fine, Jo.

JO: No, I'm not a bit. And I don't blame you at all for wanting to work without me. There—that's what I deserve for being so vain about my writing. And all I've published is a few stories in the *Weekly Volcano*. And here I've been thinking I can write a real book with a real author. Well, I don't blame you a bit, Louisa.

And I'm grateful you let me work with you as long as you did, although, of course, I should have seen it couldn't last. Well, there—that's enough of that, Josephine March! Now you just stop feeling sorry for yourself and get back to your own work.

She rises.

LOUISA: Jo, wait.

Jo turns.

Come back.

JO: I don't want to keep you from your writing.

LOUISA: There's plenty of time for that. Come here.

Jo returns to her side.

Oh, Jo, I'm going to miss you.

She hugs her.

JO (rallying): Well, it's not like I'll be gone forever. I'm come back when the book is finished, and you can tell me all about it, and we'll celebrate. And maybe by then I will have published something of my own—and you can be proud of me.

LOUISA: I am proud of you.

JO: Oh, Louisa, I don't deserve it, but I do so much love it when you say things like that.

She sits at her feet.

LOUISA (reaching down and rumpling her hair): Look at this hair!

JO: It's growing back.

LOUISA: I like it short.

JO: So do I.

She catches LOUISA's hand.

Is your hand still cramped?

LOUISA: It's not too sore today.

JO: Let me work on it.

She massages her writing hand.

How does that feel?

LOUISA: Better.

JO: I could still come every day and work on your hand. I could help you that way…

LOUISA: No.

JO: Why? I know I'm not as good a writer as you, but I could still help you in other ways. And I can be very quiet. Really.

LOUISA: Dear Jo. I won't be able to finish the book if you're here.

JO: Why not?

LOUISA: Because it's time for you to start growing up.

JO (getting up quickly from the floor and sitting in a chair): I am growing up. I just forget sometimes.

LOUISA: I'm not talking about your sitting on the floor.

JO (looking down): I know what you're talking about.

LOUISA: You do?

JO: Of course. I think about it all the time when I'm by myself. I know you're disappointed in my writing. So am I. I haven't been working on it nearly as much as I should. And mostly I've been trying to write those stories that will sell. And I know you're thinking it's time I took my work more seriously, if I'm to become a successful writer by the end of the book. Here we are three hundred pages along, and I still haven't done anything.

LOUISA (looking away): It's not your writing.

JO: Don't try to be tactful. I know. But now that I've moved away from home to the rooming house, I'll be able to work better. There won't be so many interruptions…

LOUISA: That's not what I meant when I said you needed to grow up.

JO: I don't understand.

LOUISA: I need to make plans for your future.

JO: I'm going to be a writer like you.

LOUISA says nothing.

I thought that was obvious. It's right there on the very first page about how much I love books. And then there's that little collection of children's stories I've written. And the Pickwick Club, and how I was the editor of the Club's paper. Everyone has always known that I would be a writer. I'm going to write a great book someday and make lots of money, just like you.

LOUISA: You need a family.

JO: I have my family…Amy, Meg…

LOUISA: Meg is married.

JO: She's still my family.

LOUISA (smiling): You never could accept losing her.

JO: Just because she got married, she's still my sister.

LOUISA: Jo, you need a family of your own.

JO (sitting in silence for a minute): Louisa, I thought you agreed that I wouldn't have to marry Laurie. You said that Amy was going to marry him.

LOUISA: She is.

JO: Then what are you talking about? You're two-thirds the way through the book and there isn't anybody else for me to marry—unless it's Laurie's grandfather, old Mr. Laurence.

LOUISA: It's not Mr. Laurence.

JO: Well, then it's too late now. You can't introduce a new character this late in the book. Your readers would never believe it. I'm going

to stay in my rooming house until I sell my first book. And then I'm going to buy a house big enough for Marmee and Amy…

LOUISA: There is someone else.

JO looks at her.

Someone in the rooming house.

JO (She looks confused for a moment until she realizes what LOUISA has in mind.):

You're not serious! Louisa!

LOUISA looks away.

That seedy old German professor? Louisa?

LOUISA: You like him.

JO: I like him, but I'm not going to marry him. He's old enough to be my father!

LOUISA (crossing to the door to close it): This is what I mean about our not being able to work together any more.

JO: Friedrich Bhaer is fat, and old, and poor, and doesn't take care of himself, and he can't even speak good English.

LOUISA: He's German.

JO: And he has two children, two *boys*.

LOUISA: They're his nephews.

JO: But *he's* raising them.

LOUISA: He loves children.

JO: I can't believe you're serious about this. It must be some kind of joke. Louisa—

LOUISA has turned away.

Louisa, talk to me!

LOUISA: There's no point in discussing it if you're going to be hysterical.

JO (scared): What have I done, Louisa? I've been too wild, haven't I? I've been too lazy? I'll do better. I'm going to sit myself down and write for eight hours a day. See if I don't. Just give me one year at the rooming house. If by then I haven't published a book, you can marry me off to anybody in the world, and I won't say a word. I promise. Just give me a year.

LOUISA: Jo, it isn't a punishment. He's a good man.

JO: So is Laurie, but I don't have to marry him.

LOUISA: Laurie is a boy. The Professor is a man.

JO: An old man.

LOUISA: A mature man. You need someone mature.

JO: Why?

LOUISA: Because you lack moral judgment.

JO (angry): What does that mean?

LOUISA: You don't always do the right thing. You go by your feelings too much.

JO: I don't feel like marrying that fat, old German.

LOUISA: I'm not surprised. Feelings are usually selfish.

JO (shouting): That's not selfish! How would you like to marry him?

> LOUISA turns back to her papers, ignoring JO. JO struggles to get control of her feelings.

I'm sorry.

> She sits.

LOUISA (looking up): I've chosen Professor Bhaer because of his maturity. He has the wisdom to help you become the woman you want to be.

JO: How is he going to do that? Teach me German?

> LOUISA turns away again.

I'm sorry, Louisa. How is he going to help me?

LOUISA: He is going to keep you aware of what is really important in life.

JO: And what is really important in life?

LOUISA: Serving others.

JO (bursting out): I do! That's all I've ever done! Louisa—this move to the rooming house is the first time I've ever begun to have a life of my own! And the money I've begun to earn for writing stories—that's the first time I've ever had a taste of being independent!

LOUISA: I don't think the rooming house was a good idea. I'm afraid that when I wrote that chapter, I was a little carried away with your ideas.

JO: What are you talking about?

LOUISA: Those stories you write.

JO: What about them?

LOUISA: Are you proud of them?

JO (defensively): I'm proud of the money.

LOUISA (looking away): This is why you need Professor Bhaer.

JO: What's he got to do with my writing?

LOUISA: He's going to make you see what you're doing to yourself by writing those trashy stories for money.

JO: He can't do that.

LOUISA (smiling): He already has.

JO (looks at her for a moment, and then looks at the manuscript on the desk): You've written it! You've written it in without me!

> She grabs the top paper and begins to read it.

"I would more rather give my boys gun-powder to play with than this bad trash!" That moralizing, pompous conceited, jackass! He doesn't have a family of six to support! How dare he…

LOUISA (rising, flushed): Give them back.

JO (continues to read): "If respectable people knew what harm they did, they would not feel then the living was honest." How dare he say that to me? Does he have any idea what I would have to be doing if I wasn't writing these stories. Does he have the faintest idea of how hard it is for a woman to make money? Has he ever been a live-in companion? Does he think it's more honorable to live in some stranger's home, to be treated like a slave, to put up with the sexual advances of every male in the household? Is that his idea of moral, just because I'm the victim? Has he ever taken in sewing for a living? I don't see him exactly making money, and he's a man, and thirty years older than me, and a professor at that! Do you know what I would do if I could have gone to college and gotten a degree? You can believe I wouldn't be living in some broken-down rooming house, giving German lessons for a living! Louisa—think of it! Think what women like us would be doing if we had been allowed to go to college!

LOUISA: You're wrong about Professor Bhaer. He's a great man. Now, give those back.

JO (reading again): "Jo…stuffed the whole bundle into her stove…"

> She looks up.

I *burn* my writing?

> LOUISA tries to snatch the papers, but JO dodges her.

I *burn* my own writing, because of what this doddering old lecher says?

LOUISA (She finally succeeds in retrieving the papers.): This is why it's impossible for us to collaborate.

JO: I can't believe it. I *burn* my own writing?

LOUISA: Yes. (Avoiding her eyes) Like the way you cut off your hair.

JO: It's not the same thing.

LOUISA: Yes, it is. It's for a higher principle.

JO: No, it isn't. Hair grows back. Louisa, don't you remember how I wouldn't even speak to Amy when she got mad at me and burned that little book of stories? You had to almost drown her to make me feel like forgiving her. Remem-

ber? And now you're going to expect me to take my own writings—that pay the rent—and *burn* them? I wouldn't do it.

LOUISA: You will do it. I've written it.

JO: No, I won't. I won't do it. You can write it, but I won't be there. And all your readers will know.

LOUISA: You'll do it, because it's the right thing to do.

JO: What about you? Would you burn your own writing? Would you burn *Little Women*?

LOUISA: I don't need to. It's a children's story. It isn't trash.

JO: What about your romance stories?

LOUISA: I don't have any.

JO: Oh, Louisa, don't lie to me. I know you. Where do you think I stole my plots from?

LOUISA: I don't know what you're talking about.

JO (angry): Oh, don't you…"Flora Fairfield," "A. M. Barnard…?"

> LOUISA freezes.

Those are your pen names, aren't they? The ones you used when you wrote "The Rival Painters," "The Abbot's Ghost," "Pauline's Passion…"

LOUISA (cutting her off): Where did you find those?

JO: I didn't need to find them. They're in your head, Louisa. I know you better than you know me.

LOUISA: I have had to support a real family. Yours is make-believe. It's different.

JO: How?

LOUISA: How? All I have to do is write a sentence, and suddenly you've sold a story. It's not that easy for me. I have to write it. I have to send it out. It gets returned, it gets lost, nobody buys it. That's real life, Jo. That's my life. You should thank me that I have decided you don't have to struggle the way I have. I'm going to have your Aunt March die and leave you her estate. Nobody is going to do that for me. Nobody's going to write a happy ending for me.

JO: Maybe I don't want a happy ending. Maybe I choose to write, because I love it. Maybe I'm just like you.

LOUISA: I write for the money.

JO: Don't lie to me, Louisa. You write those thriller stories for the same reason I do—because you like to. You get to say all kinds of unladylike things. You get to kill men. You get to pretend you're a man and write about laying your head against a woman's breast...

LOUISA (agitated): Jo! What are you talking about?

JO: I'm talking about you—about us! You wish you could live like a man just as much as I do.

LOUISA: No, I don't.

JO: Where do you think I get my ideas from? You call me "fellow," you cut all my hair off, you call me the man of the family. I use slang, I race Laurie and beat him, I give my money to support the family, I'm wildly jealous of John for marrying Meg. Louisa, you know what I am as well as I do. That's why I can't get married.

LOUISA: You're a tomboy. You just need to grow up.

JO: Look again, Louisa. You need to grow up. I'm a lesbian.

LOUISA: No! No, you're not!

JO: Yes, I am. Remember what you had me tell Laurie—"It's impossible for people to make themselves love other people if they don't..." Remember? We told him, "I don't believe it's the right sort of love, and I'd rather not try it." You know why I said that.

LOUISA: Laurie was a friend, but I never intended those remarks to refer to all men.

JO: Louisa, you know I love women. You know that. You know because you created me out of your own need to love women.

LOUISA: I don't want to love them like that.

JO: Oh yes, you do, Louisa May Alcott. And you want them to love you like that.

LOUISA: No!

> *Jo crosses to LOUISA. She takes her hand, the writing hand, and caresses it. LOUISA closes her eyes. JO takes her hand and brings it to her lips. She begins to kiss and caress her fingers.*

JO: Louisa, you are so beautiful. You take care of everybody. Who takes care of you? Nobody sees you like I do. I see who you are—I see how beautiful you are. Let me love you, Louisa.

> *She kisses her lips. LOUISA, after the kiss, turns away in confusion.*

LOUISA: I was in love with David.

JO: Louisa...

LOUISA: I was. I would have married him.

JO: Henry David Thoreau despised women, and you know it. He liked little boys.

LOUISA: I loved him.

JO: You loved him, because you knew you'd never have to do anything about it.

LOUISA: And I loved Ladislas.

JO: That boy you met three years ago in Switzerland?

LOUISA: I was in love with him.

JO: You were infatuated. He was eighteen. You were thirty-three. You were attracted to him, because he was the closest thing to a woman you could find.

LOUISA (turning to look at Jo): No! You're twisting things.

JO: Louisa, you're the one twisting things. Look at who you pick to fall in love with—homosexual men and adolescent boys!

LOUISA (rising): No!

JO: Yes! The reason you have never married, is because you're a lesbian. Like me.

She puts her arms around LOUISA.

LOUISA: No! No…

JO: Louisa, I love you. I'm the only one who has ever loved you. That's what you created me for.

LOUISA: I created you for Professor Bhaer.

JO: No, you created me for your own pleasure.

LOUISA (pulling away): No. I created you to marry him.

JO (nuzzling LOUISA's neck): I can't do that, and you don't want me to.

LOUISA: Yes, yes I do. Jo, he's kind. He needs you.

JO: You need me.

LOUISA (desperate): You'll inherit Plumfield. You won't have to write.

JO: I'm going to stay and work with you.

She kisses LOUISA's lips.

LOUISA (pulling away): You *have* to marry him.

JO: Louisa! Think about what you're asking. Think of the wedding night!

LOUISA: I'm not going to write about that.

JO: But your readers are going to think about it. Think of his seedy trousers coming down. Think of that big pink-grey penis coming out, sticking out like an elephant's trunk…

LOUISA: Stop it!

JO: Think about his bad breath in my face, his flabby stomach lying over my body. Think about his grunting and sweating and rocking back and forth. That's what marriage is about!

LOUISA: It's a union of two souls! It's a lifetime of companionship!

JO: It's him lying on top of me every night and shooting his sperm between my legs!

LOUISA (delirious): I'm leaving.

She heads for the door.

JO: Why? You can't bear to hear about it, but I'm supposed to go through with it? Is that your idea of being grown up?

LOUISA is out the door.

Just because your father violated you, don't violate me!

LOUISA (returning): That's a lie!

JO: Oh, Louisa, come on!

LOUISA: My father is a good and pure and true man. He's one of the most highly evolved souls in Cambridge. Ask anyone here.

JO: You hate him.

LOUISA: I aspire to be like him.

JO: You hate him.

LOUISA: No, you hate him. You're jealous.

JO: I do hate him. I hate him for what he's done to you. It's bad enough that he penetrated your vagina when you were a child, but it's penetrating your brain I can't forgive him for.

LOUISA: You don't know what you're talking about.

JO: Why do you think he lost all those schools?

LOUISA: Because his ideas on educating children were ahead of his time.

JO: He lost the school in Cheshire because he invited the children to his rooms after school, and he was caught "caressing" the girls.

LOUISA: That's a lie.

JO: No, it isn't. Remember how he lost Temple School, because he wanted to talk about sex to the children?

LOUISA: He was honest and uninhibited.

JO: Was that why he would spend hours in the bath with you? Is that why he wrote when you were four months old about your "beautiful proportions," your "perfect picture of luxuriant childhood," the "boldness and amplitude" of your body? Is that why he slept with you at night? Is that why your mother was desperate to place you in another home when you were two?

LOUISA: He was a loving father.

JO: What about that dream you had over and over? The nightmare with the man in the cape with the soft hands, saying "Lie still, my dear!" The man who is always coming after you out of closets, in at windows…the man who threatens you all night long. Where do you think you got that nightmare?

LOUISA: Dreams don't mean anything.

JO: And how about your father's writing. Have you ever read his books? How about *Observations on the Life of My Second Child, Louisa May Alcott, During the First Year*? Have you read about his little experiments with you and your sister? How your loving father would burn Anna's hand to record her reaction? Or how he would take her to the park and then hide, to see what she would do? Do you really believe he didn't perform other kinds of experiments?

LOUISA: I don't believe it.

JO: It's a fact.

LOUISA: How do you know?

JO: Because you know.

LOUISA: No, I don't.

JO: Yes, you do. You just won't open those parts of your mind. But I can see all of you, because I don't need to protect Bronson. In fact, I would like to kill him.

LOUISA: Jo! Don't say that! If he died, I would.

JO: That's probably true, because he's god in your brain. I can help you. We can find a happy ending together, Louisa. I can help you expose your father and get him out of your life. Here…take these chapters you wrote without me. Professor Bhaer doesn't belong in our book. He's your father. Take these and burn them.

LOUISA: Now you expect me to burn my work.

JO: You didn't really write these. Bronson dictated them to you. Professor Bhaer is his alter-ego. Burn them. Burn, them, Louisa, and we'll rewrite the ending where I meet a wonderful older woman who is a writer, and we collaborate on a children's book about four sisters and their mother, and it becomes a great success, and we buy a house together, and we continue to write books, and we meet all the brightest women in Boston, and they come to our house every week for salons…forever and ever.

LOUISA (taking the chapters, she moves towards the fireplace): I could be one of the boarders at the rooming house.

JO: You could. We could read to each other what we've written every evening.

LOUISA: You would sleep with me.

JO: We could.

LOUISA: No.

> She stops.

No, I see what's going on here. You are tempting me.

> LOUISA begins to speak in a style of oratory she has picked up from her father.

You, my creation, are the personification of all my worst weaknesses. This is my selfishness, my self-indulgence, my carnal desires speaking to me. I know you, Jo March—you are my own worst self.

JO: Your best self, Louisa! You are talking like Bronson now. He wants to ruin you life. He's taken thirty-five years already. He's a vampire. He sucks your life blood, and now he's sucking your creative blood. Don't let him, Louisa! Burn these chapters.

LOUISA (becoming very distant and rhetorical): Oh, you're clever, Jo March. I might have known you would be. I was always able to fool myself. If it weren't for the firm moral foundation my father laid in me, I might be tempted to listen to you. But thankfully I have his strong example to guide me. Without him, I would steer like a ship without a rudder, giving in to my impulses at every instant, headed nowhere at all and wrecking myself on the treacherous shoals of self-gratification.

JO (she grabs Louisa's shoulders): What are you talking about? Living your own life is not a crime.

LOUISA: You're a clever temptress.

JO: Louisa, your father is a child molester.

LOUISA: You must be very weak to malign such a good man.

JO: He is! You know it! Every sentence you write reeks of incest!

LOUISA: Poor Jo—your father was away, wasn't he, and you're jealous that I have always lived so close to mine. You can't understand what it is to have a saint for a father.

JO: A saint! Bronson Alcott is a devil!

She grabs the chapters.

LOUISA (gently): You know you can't act without my permission. You are my creation.

JO: I know that deep down you want me to burn these. I know that's what's in your heart.

She crosses to the fireplace. LOUISA watches her. JO picks up the matches and freezes.

Louisa, please. I know you must want to be happy.

LOUISA: My father has taught me the way to happiness is self-sacrifice.

JO (frantic): That's the way to *his* happiness. When have you ever seen Bronson do anything for anybody else? Haven't you and your mother been supporting him for twenty years?

What has he ever done for his family except molest and abandon you?

LOUISA (not hearing her): You see, you can't burn them. I don't want you to. You will put them on my desk.

Jo obeys.

JO: This means I will have to burn my work. It's in this chapter.

LOUISA: Yes, you will. It's the right thing.

JO: Oh, Louisa, you have killed us both.

LOUISA: *Little Women* will be a great success.

JO: Only in a world of incest.

LOUISA: I think you can go now.

JO: I'll never come back.

LOUISA: That's as it should be. The Professor will need you more than I do.

JO: You and your books are poisoned.

LOUISA (smiling): Oh, I forgot to tell you…You and the Professor are going to open a school for little boys…

JO turns to look at her a final time. Silently she exits, closing the door behind her. LOUISA crosses after her, locks the door, and returns to the manuscript. Lights fade. ■

Sister Gin

by June Arnold

K ibitzing from its permanent stand in the middle of the room, the bridge table with its cut-velvet top had been splendid with two scorepads, two gold pencils, and two new decks of cards, one white, one black, bearing the inscription "Make All Checks Payable to Mamie Carter Wilkerson." A small table holding an ashtray had stood at each corner and the bridge lamp had thrown its equal glow from the low ceiling.

Five women (one cut out each rubber to fix drinks) were present: Mamie Carter, Luz, Cad, Puddin, and Ella. None of them sat down; they were looking at a pile of black gowns neatly folded on a chair and a box of blond curly wigs.

"I hope you got my gown long enough, M.C.," Cad said. Her eyes were the open brown of a good child. "You never will admit how tall I am."

"Five seven," Mamie Carter said coldly.

"Five seven and three-quarters," Cad said.

"You've been shrinking just like the rest of us," Mamie Carter held up a cardboard sign: *Shirley Temples Emeritae.* "Do you like it?"

"That feminine latin plural is a dead give-away," Ella said. "No one would know how to do that in this town but you and Luz."

Mamie Carter frowned—her expression for extreme chagrin and devastation.

"I thought we decided on Shirley Temple

Graduates," Cad said, "or was it Shirley Temple *Graduates*?"

"I thought this was more succinct," Mamie Carter said. "As well as being more stylish."

"It is very elegant," Puddin said. She was trying on her wig in front of the mantelpiece mirror. She was so small-boned that even her plumpness did not bring her up to size and her face was lost under the acrylic curls. "Do you think it's becoming?" She poked the curls to bury the tremble of her conic fingers.

"Puddin, you'll have to wear a mask anyway. You've lived in Wilmington for seventy-five years and *might* be known by now," Ella said. Puddin was getting senile, she decided. Ella, even taller than Cad, wore her dyed black hair cut like a man's and Paris's most extreme styles which she went abroad to acquire at the drop of the latest in hats. Her jewelry was huge—today it was lapis from her eartips to her lean, large-knuckled hands. She could be persuaded to sing at every party and would dance with even the shortest of men. She was the only one who had a living husband, the only one who had never had children.

"Do you have the board?" Puddin asked.

"Are we going to use the board?" Cad's eyes were wide. "I thought…"

"Rape can be extended to cover *his* behavior, too," Mamie Carter said firmly. "If you look at the laws covering rape you'll see they all stem from the property code. Now Almeta—at sixty-

Excerpt from *Sister Gin*, published by Daughters, Inc., Plainfield, Vermont, 1975.

176

five a woman is not considered of much value as property so her rapist wasn't even indicted. And if she is black too she's not even believed. The fact is, people feel sex is obscene with the old, but you all read the tittering between the lines. The fourteen-year-old girl was property not really damaged since her hymen was left intact, so her rapist was allowed to plead to a lesser sentence. If you ever bothered to think abstractly, Cad, you'd see that rape and theft are both classified as property cases; therefore I see nothing amiss in treating Clayton's theft as the only form of rape open to him."

"Exactly," Ella said in her voice as deep as a man's. "Maybe we should expose his backside instead of his you-know to harmonize with the money aspects."

"Is that Freudian?"

"Who wants a little drink while we dress?" Puddin said.

Mamie Carter's speech had returned to her memory the fact of the girl's being forced to put her mouth on that man's penis; memory was now stuck on the gruesomeness of it and her hands shook violently as she brought the pitcher of martinis from the refrigerator. "The odor must have been just ghastly. Do you think a rapist would bother to wash? The poor child probably couldn't breathe, her head pushed into that sweaty putrid body…"

"Horrors," Cad said. "Puddin, I'd rather not think about…"

"*She* had to. And then he'd squirt all that stuff into your *mouth*." Puddin filled five glasses from the sideboard and quickly anesthetized her own mouth. "Ugh. I think I'd even rather be raped than *that*."

"I feel sorry for Almeta," Cad said. "At sixty-five you'd think you'd be free from even having to think about sex."

"Speak for yourself, friend," Ella said.

"Why do you suppose he picked her?" Cad said.

Mamie Carter took the last martini and held it up. "To show his contempt. The ultimate contempt for women is disrespect for age. To us," she said fiercely.

"To us," Cad said, smiling sweetly, clicking each glass in turn.

"You look very handsome," Luz said to Cad, surveying the black graduation gown. "It's because you're tall. That gown is very becoming."

"Thank you. I've always wanted to be a blonde," Cad said.

Mamie Carter picked up the plyboard cut in the shape of an outstretched human figure, a thick x, and handed a canvas shopping bag to Cad who peered inside. "Oh, it's the same old brown leather. Why can't we use bright-colored thongs sometimes?"

"We'll have to balance the board over our heads in the car," Mamie Carter said. "Don't let it knock off your wigs."

"And why would it knock off the blond wigs any faster than it knocked off the red ones last week?" Ella said.

♀♀

Clayton Everett Eagle III was in Room 514 in the Wilmington Hilton. It took less than five minutes to enter the room, lay him on the floor in surprise, and tie him to the board, Luz keeping him motionless with her valuable weight on his chest, Puddin holding a martini-soaked washcloth in his mouth with manicured fingers trembling only slightly.

"There," Cad stood up. "that was easy."

Clayton lay out like a stick figure.

"Let's gag him properly and take him into the bedroom. Shall we have a game? We have to wait a long time." Mamie Carter took off her gown and wig and combed her hair.

"We should have put him in the bedroom before we tied him," Luz said, visually measuring the width of the outstretched arms at more than three feet. "I don't think he'll get through the door."

"We can tilt him." Ella's arms, still muscular, tilted the board easily. "If Cad'll help me. The rest of you weak reeds can get out of the way."

Mamie Carter let the bellboy in with the bridge table, cards, scorepads, and drinks. All the wigs and gowns were in the bedroom with Clayton; she met the bellboy as elegantly as any visitor in her proper suit and hair. "Thank you," she said, handing him two dollars. "Mr. Eagle asks that it be put on his bill."

"Imogene should never have trusted a man who doesn't play bridge," Puddin said, cutting high. Cad was next high. "We'll sit this way," she said, having seen that the bathtub ran in that direction. She dealt shakily and half-sorted her hand. "I'm a passenger."

"One club," Luz said.

"Is that a meek and timid club?" Cad said. "Two clubs."

"By me," Mamie Carter said.

"We have to try it, partner. Three no-trump," Puddin said.

Luz played the jack of clubs and Cad put down her hand. "Is everyone ready for a drink?"

"I'll get the drinks," Ella said. "I'm out."

"Well, you didn't," Cad said. Ella was staring at the curtains, her frown lines very deep. "Are you upset about Clayton? He'll be all right. He'll just have to lie in there for a few hours. We can't take him to the street until at least two o'clock."

"Well, I am worried. It's damp and he'll catch pneumonia lying outside all night after being strapped to the board all afternoon."

"No, he'll just be a little stiff," Cad said. "He won't die. None of the others did." Her voice was wistful.

"He'll be *very* stiff," Ella said.

"Isn't that a rapist's hope?" Cad said.

Ella refused to laugh. She had been so furious at the previous two men that she had taken part in their punishment with all her height and energy. Now, part of her was tempted to identify with Clayton.

"It's because you don't have a daughter," Cad said.

"Because it isn't your money," Mamie Carter said. "If you have a club in your hand I'll concede," she said to Puddin.

"I have to cut out next rubber," Luz said, looking at her watch. "I'll take Adele's boys home after supper and be back—around nine."

"You be careful driving around at night," Cad said. "You know you can't see at night."

"Shall I bring something back?"

"No, we'll eat here," Mamie Carter said.

"Oh, good," Cad said. "We can order in the room on Clayton. They have wonderful shrimp here. I wish I weren't allergic to shrimp."

"Who dealt?"

"I did. I'm forced to pass."

"I pass."

Mamie Carter tapped the table twice.

"I open," Puddin said, calling attention to the score by peering at it over Mamie Carter.

"We all know you're vulnerable," Mamie Carter said.

"One heart," Puddin said.

"Suppose he has to go to the bathroom?" Ella had taken off her Jourdan walking shoes and was exercising her toes on the carpet. "Clayton, I mean."

"That's my long suit, partner," Cad said, laying down her hand at two hearts.

"Grossly underbid," Luz said.

"Speak for yourself, friend," Mamie Carter said, taking the first trick and returning Luz's lead for her to trump. "No diamonds, partner?" she said, scooping up their second trick. Luz returned a spade and Mamie Carter took her second ace, returning a third diamond to be trumped.

"It's time to get the children off the streets," Puddin announced, getting in with the king of spades and leading a heart to the board. Luz showed out.

"Many a woman has walked the streets of London cold and hungry..." Mamie Carter said mischievously.

"Can't help it, partner." Puddin conceded a trump and the spade ten to Mamie Carter. "Down one. If Luz had opened anything but a diamond..."

"What if he has to go to the bathroom?" Ella missed the bidding and had it reviewed twice before she bid.

"I do feel mean drinking in here with Clayton lying in there alone," Puddin said. "It *is* five o'clock."

Cad said, "You're on the board, partner. This'll be the first five o'clock he's missed in I don't know when."

"*I* know. Since he was knee-high to a duck. That's a trump," Mamie Carter said as Ella started gathering up the trick.

"Ducks are trumps?"

"That duck of spades is."

"Oh, I'm sorry." Ella dropped the cards and swept them toward Mamie Carter with the backs of her fingernails. "He must be suffering in there."

"Now don't you go feeling sorry for a Black Republican," Cad said. "A little dry spell will do him good. He can ruminate on his evil ways."

"Chew his cad," Mamie Carter said. "The rest are mine."

"Chew his *what*?" Cad said.

"You use the name, you don't own it."

"What if he does have to go to the bathroom?"

Cad lay the cards for Luz to cut and then dealt them rapidly and expertly. "Let's don't think about that, Ella," she said, picking up her hand. "You'll just upset yourself. There's nothing we can do about it. One no." ▪

© 1987 by Sudie Rakusin

IV.
Carol, in the park, chewing on straws
by Judy Grahn

She has taken a woman lover
whatever shall we do
she has taken a woman lover
how lucky it wasn't you
And all the day through she smiles and lies
and grits her teeth and pretends to be shy,
or weak, or busy. Then she goes home
and pounds her own nails, makes her own
bets, and fixes her own car, with her friend.
She goes as far
as women can go without protection
from men.
On weekends, she dreams of becoming a tree;
a tree that dreams it is ground up
and sent to the paper factory, where it
lies helpless in sheets, until it dreams
of becoming a paper airplane, and rises
on its own current; where it turns into a
bird, a coasting bird that dreams of becoming
more free, even, than that—a feather, finally, or
a piece of air with lightning in it.
she has taken a woman lover
whatever can we say

She walks around all day
quietly, but underneath it
she's electric;
angry energy inside a passive form.
The common woman is as common
as a thunderstorm.

From *Edward the Dyke*, Judy Grahn, 1971.

Lesbian Metaphysics

by Janet Aalfs

Of all the holes I've jumped
in the air, being a dyke
is the holeyest. Look,
even my tracks
have no edges. I leap, spin
around once, both feet
off the ground, bright
sun everywhere and below

my body, no shadow.
How different, I think, even
talented to leave
no trace. But practical?
Who will wonder where I am?
Who will muse about me
if they never knew
I was here?

I keep jumping holes
in the air. Sometimes a meteor
falls through one and burns
a crater in the earth.
I did that, I think
to myself, pointing.

A Dutch saying, "Een gaat in de lucht
springen" translates literally, "to jump a
hole into the air." Used when doing something that feels ineffective or unnoticed.

Originally published in *Sinister Wisdom* 46
(1992)

Lesbian Invisibility
by Leslie Stewart
*ASWAC= Alberta Status of Women Action Committee (Canada)

On My Way

by Chrystos

to washington, d.c. to speak for Lesbian rights
it all started when I agreed
to lecture 200 students at the university on anti-racism
I did well enough though I was at the bottom of a bowl of seats
with a few scattered notes & a weariness with the subject
deep enough to scream
There was the usual white guy saying he agreed
with everything I said
who couldn't go on when I asked him if he realized
how patronizing it sounded for him to say that
& the usual white gal on the verge of hysteria
who accused me of making him uncomfortable
& claimed that reverse racism is real
because twelve Black girls in her high school beat her up once
& the usual students of Color relieved to hear me
or anybody
then speaking eloquently of their own experiences
There was the usual applause   tears of those I had touched
Then a woman came up very close to me
I thought she was a Dyke & then she said,
I'm a white person as you can see,
WHY do they always think they have to tell us that?!
and when things go wrong it's always my fault.
I want to know why you people
WHY are we always you people?!
can't see that this is your fault.
She started to tell me that we didn't have
to live as we do & as usual   little bits of steam started
around my ears & then she said
Are you a Lesbian?

Yes   I said
You're sick!   she said with the usual venom
My arm went back fury sudden hot
& in front of the departing students I screamed
I am not sick! Get out of my face!
Oh she was happy then to see me being
the savage she knew I was
& how ashamed as usual I was that she could get me
in the throat   touch my last raw tired nerve & blow up
my heart   I hurried away   She chased after me
to tell me two more times at the top of her lungs
that I was sick
I shouted at her again in the halls my fists still clenched
Her age all that stopped me
Respect your elders   I hear my father murmur
She taunts me again   *You'll go to the penitentiary*
if you hit me
quite proud of herself
I shouted back   *That's the only reason I haven't!*
A Native student with tears in her eyes held me
Some Black women encouraged me
Some white women thanked me
I had a plane to catch
all the way to the airport   all the way to d.c.   all the time
I was in d.c. my heart raced I held in tears as well as I could
as usual.
That old woman would tell you this grief & rage are all
my own fault   That she didn't ruin my elation
at going to d.c. with thousands and thousands
of other Lesbians   That it's my own fault I'm poor Queer
& unhappy with america   She'd tell you that just as she thought
I'm a savage & we're all sick
Will you shout it with me now
We're not sick
Again
We're not sick

Especially for Donna Langston
From *Dream On,* (Vancouver: Press Gang Publishers, 1991)

to the women who weep

by Chaia Zblocki Heller

They say we are crazy
we women
who weep
we women who weep
who keep
the last grains of soil
moist with our grief

they say we are crazy
for we do not string coins
upon a cord
and then eat them
instead
we set clay bowls
beneath the moon's face
we sit and dream
over her reflection

they say we are crazy
that we long for a past
we've invented
that we long for a time
when women stroked the earth
with magic feet
and when women ruled gently
like grandmothers

but we are not crazy
our madness makes us bold and sane
our sadness and our rage
are the last precious stones
of our fortune

we need these stones
to throw, destroy
rebuild
what we know
we have lost

we are not as they say
our tears and our memories
fertilize our fields
and taste in our mouths
like manna

In *Sinister Wisdom* 36 (Winter 1988/89)

The Fourth Daughter's Four Hundred Questions

by Elana Dykewomon

She does not know if she dreamt this, but she remembers that Bartons also made a box of chocolate pops in the image of the "four sons." She remembers them clearly, their little chocolate heads with big eyes and yarmulkes staring out of the cardboard filler. In the passover service there is a section on how a man must instruct his sons, and there are four kinds of sons a man may have. She had no choice but to be a son, then, since the aunts were all busy cleaning, carrying, cooking, and there was nothing for a girl to do but open the door for elijah or learn to sing the four questions which the modern age had rendered genderless, to expand the role of the girl child in religion. But a man does not really have daughters, which is true enough.

A man, a jewish man, tells the passover story to his sons. The first is he who does not know how to ask at all (because he will be a laborer, you must treat him gently); the second, he who asks simply (for he will be a dentist, you must tell him only what he can understand); the third, he who asks in detail (because he will be a rabbi, you must encourage him, explaining everything). But the fourth son asks, "What does this mean to you?" Because the fourth son says "you" and not "us," he is called the wicked son,

Excerpt from "The Fourth Daughter's Four Hundred Questions," in *Nice Jewish Girls: A Lesbian Anthology*, ed. Evelyn Torton Beck. (Boston: Beacon Press)

and you must say to him, "it means the Lord God saved me from Egypt." You must say "me" and not "us," for had he been there, he would not have been saved. He would have been an outsider among his people, excluding himself from the life all jews have in common. She remembers, twenty-three years later, how she bit the head off the chocolate fourth son, how then he was inside her, watching the dinner go on.

To choose to be crazy gives you a home among the crazies. To choose to identify as a jew only gives you a home among the jews. To choose to identify as a lesbian gives you no peace. To choose to identify as a lesbian separatist places you back among the crazies, who will not have you, and with whom you could not stay, even if they would. To identify as a lesbian separatist remembering the jews, the jews from which you came and whom you carry in you, makes you remember over and over again being an outsider among outsiders, even when you feel a center, a sense of self that is strong and sure, a clear understanding of all your choices.

It is a hard difference between lesbians. What color, what country, what class, what religion, what culture.

It should make no difference if you understand that we are at war, that men made judaism among the patriarchal religions that crushed the power of womyn, that men trampled the feasts of the ancient goddesses worldwide, and demanded gods in their own images, not a fertile profusion of female figures who bled into the earth. It should not matter when you remember your aunts at passover passing the platter. It should not matter when you remember that a boy at the age of thirteen is included in the religious life of the community whereas a woman may never take part. It should not matter when you remember the centuries in which women were actually sold and bought, and then made to carry on, be the strength of the family. When you know this and know that every jewish man is your enemy, not just your father who hit you, who read you "When you ask, 'what does this mean to you,' to you and not to us, it means if you were there you would not have been saved," it should make no difference. You were not with them. You were not of them though you were born among them. The old ecstatic dances were stolen…. The egg, the feast, the light that never goes out in the temple, all stolen, stolen from you and not just a thousand years ago but today. While these are being stolen from you every hour, there is a woman raped sixty times within that hour, once a minute. So that we will know not to complain. Not to raise our voices. Not to say, give us back our memories, give us back our centuries, we are taking our lives again, we will never repeat your crummy prayers in your ugly temples where rapists hide in the back corridors.

It should make no difference then. It should make no difference among lesbians. Who have gone this far.

But it does. It is the same american mistake. To believe that having the same understanding, the same conclusion from the same facts, makes us therefore the same. It is anti-separatism to believe that in order to have a motion, it must all be the same motion, that all the words of the new language must come from the same root; it is mindless melting pot politics, to give away what has made you, to come forward pretending you are a blank slate, to expect that all the womyn coming towards you will come empty, blank as the great plains in winter after all the native peoples were killed. To not come towards each other full of ourselves, wanting to taste and smell all the other culture womyn bring, is a waste. To deny our own cultures is to rob ourselves and each other of the gift we have to give. ■

Branded

by Janet Aalfs

1.
Take this
the doctorman says.

Silent on couches,
eyes lowered, women
place pills on tongues
and swallow,
blowing up inside.

2.
I have been called crazy
in fun, by friends who want to laugh.
I have laughed too,
never having been locked up.

I am not laughing now,
sitting in a circle with women
whose faces have been razed,
senses erased,
who are the battlefield.

Our voices
travel, one to the other,
hoping to be heard.

3.

This is war
and I have been branded
dyke, bitch, manhater,
diseased. For some
this means I'm crazy.
For others I don't exist.

The facts of my life
have saved me thus far
from destruction
but I am not outside
the range of fire.

The real damage already done
is that when we talk
woman to woman
words we use shatter
inside each other's heads.
I could sit here
still, mouth closed,
eyes on the ground
in the middle of a minefield
praying I'll survive,
or I could move forward,
asking questions,
telling my version,
knowing that when I am taken
I will not go face down.

In *Sinister Wisdom* 36 (Winter 1988/89)

Letter to Claudia Brenner

In Memory of Rebecca Wight

by Janet Aalfs

Claudia, I don't know you, can't begin
to imagine what it was like
to kneel beside your lover as breath
and blood drained out of her body
into the flattened ferns. He aimed
to kill you both but you lived

against his will. As long as you live,
you won't forget the day that began
like any other. Darts of light aimed
through the leaves fell prismlike
into your tent, your curled bodies
pulled up from deep-breathing

dreams to drink breaths
of pine. You opened your eyes, alive
in the silence, nobody
to interrupt the tremors that began
in your sleep-warm bellies. Like
warnings, they spread with certain aim

up your spines to your tongues aimed
into each other's mouths. You breathed
secrets of aspen and birch, cloudlike
shadows on the nylon roof, life
slowed down to where each began
to feel the earth's rotation in her body,

the triumph of women's bodies
spiraling together, aiming
for home. The killer, unknown, had begun
to stalk you by then, his breath
heavy from the climb, the plantlife
around him vibrating green like

it had always been that bright, like
the heat of your twined bodies
could burn him alive
so that even after he hit what he aimed
for, he kept firing, breathing
hard. Claudia, I don't know you, can't begin

to imagine how likely it is for a man to aim
his gun at a woman's body and shoot the breath
out. Or where, in the life he shattered, you begin.

Trespassing
by Valerie Miner

Exhausted from four hours of traffic, Kate and Josie almost missed seeing the two doe and their fawn drinking at the pond. The women waited in the car, cautious lest the noise of opening doors disturb the animals. The deer lingered another five minutes and then stepped off gracefully into the wings of sequoias. Last sun settled on the golden hills. Night noises pulsed: frogs, crickets, mallards. Wind whispered across dry grass. Jays barked from the top of the hill. As the sky grew roses, Kate and Josie watched Jupiter blaze over the Eastern mountains.

They unloaded the Chevy quickly and sloppily, eager for the comfort of the compact wooden cabin they had built with their friends over five summers. Josie opened the gas line outside the house. Kate lit a fire, reflecting on the joys of collective ownership when the rest of the collective was absent. She could hardly believe it—two whole days away from Meredith High School; forty-eight hours of privacy and peace.

Suddenly starving, they decided to eat right away. Afterwards they would sit in front of the fire and read to each other. Kate chopped salad while Josie made pasta and whistled. The sky got redder and then, abruptly, the cabin was dark. With heavy reluctance, Kate walked around and lit the lanterns.

From *Trespassing & Other Stories* by Valerie Miner. The Crossing Press, 1989.

'Oh,' Kate said.

Josie turned and caught a flick of brown before her, like an insect crashing on a windshield.

'Damn bats.' Kate shook her head and picked up the broom.

'Bats!' Josie screamed. 'I thought Iris got rid of those gruesome things last month.'

'Must still be some holes in the sun porch.'

A dark object dropped beside Josie, like a small turd falling, from the eaves. It disappeared. She fretted the wooden spoon through the pasta, watching another tiny brown mass cut its fall in mid-air and swoop across the room. It was too much. 'Bats!'

Josie ran outside. She felt safer in the dark.

Kate stayed in the house, sweeping bats out of the windows and back door.

Staring up at the stars, so benign in their distance, Josie considered vast differences between Kate and herself. Rational, taciturn Kate was probably calculating the increasing velocity of wing movement as the bats ignited to wakefulness. Josie, herself, still cringed at Grandma's tales about bats nesting in little girls' hair. And raised as she was in a wilful family where intentionality was more important than action, where danger didn't exist if one closed one's imagination to it, Josie was given to the substitution of 'good thoughts.' Let's see, she forced herself to concentrate on a pleasant memory: how she and Kate met. It was a miracle if you thought about it;

195

who would have expected romance at the school xerox machine? But there was Kate copying quark diagrams for her physics students while Josie waited to xerox a new translation of *La Cigale et La Fourmi*. If Kate hadn't run out of toner, they might never have become acquainted.

'All clear,' Kate called. There was no disdain in her voice for she had always envied Josie's ability to show fear. She should tell Josie this.

Josie craned her neck and stared at the sky. 'Glorious night,' she called back. 'Wanna see?'

Ducking out the front door, Kate ran through the pungent pennyroyal to her friend. Josie took her hand. Together they stood quietly until they could hear the frogs and the crickets once more.

♀♀

They slept late and spent the next morning eating eggs and fried potatoes and rye toast. Josie noticed some wasps dancing around the table, so they cleaned up and went outside to lie on the warm deck.

Later they spent an hour fitting moulding around the edges of the sun porch's glass door, sealing the house seams against nocturnal trespassers.

At noon the women drove five miles to town for forgotten country necessities—ice, water and flashlight batteries. Josie secretly checked the grocery shelves for bat killer, but she didn't find any and she knew Kate wouldn't approve.

As they drove back to the land, Josie tried to renew her enthusiasm for the weekend. She stopped in front of the cabin. Kate, now completely restored by the country air, bounded into the house with the grocery bag.

Josie moved the Chevy into the shade of an oak tree which was being gradually occupied by Spanish moss. As she locked up the car, she saw a fat man with a rifle waddling out of the forest. He wore a yellow cap, a striped T-shirt and bluejeans.

A giant bumblebee, she thought. Then she warned herself to get serious. The land was clearly posted, 'No Trespassing. No Hunting.' A shiver ran along her collarbone. They were half a mile from the highway here. It could be weeks before anyone investigated.

Josie decided to be friendly and waved.

'Hello there.' He was winded, hustling to meet her.

Josie closed her eyes and hoped Kate would stay in the house until it was all over.

'I got lost,' he said, nodding his whole body. 'How do you get back to the highway?'

'That direction.' Josie tried to calm herself. 'Up the road there.'

He looked her over. 'You got any water? A glass of water? I've been walking for hours.'

Biblical tales filled her head. 'The Woman at the Well,' 'The Wedding at Cana,' 'The Good Samaritan'. 'Sure,' she said as noncommittally as possible. 'I'll be right back.'

'Who's that?' Kate greeted her.

Josie tried to be calm. 'Water man. I mean, a lost man who needs water.' She watched Kate's jaw stiffen. 'Now let me handle it. He just wants a glass of water and then he'll be on his way.' Josie poured water from a plastic jug into an old jam jar they used for drinking.

'Water, my foot, what is he doing on the land? It's posted "No Trespassing", for God's sake.'

'Listen, Kate, he was hunting and...'

Kate took the glass and poured half the water back into the jug. 'Don't *spoil* him. He may return.'

She stalked out to the man, who was leaning on their car, his gun on the ground. Josie stood at the door, watching.

'Thanks, ma'am.' He reached for the water.

'No shooting on this land,' Kate said as she released the glass.

'Sorry, ma'am. I was hunting up there on the North Ridge and I hit a buck. But he got away. I followed, to make sure I got him good. Then I got lost and I guess I wound up here.'

'Guess so,' Kate said. She held her hand against her leg to stop it from shaking.

'I'll be off your land soon's I finish the water,' he promised.

'That's right.' She kept her voice even.

'But I'll need to be coming back to get the buck. See, I finally did get him. But since I was lost, I couldn't drag him all over tarnation.'

'We don't want a dead buck on the land,' Kate conceded. 'When're you coming?'

'Tomorrow morning?' he asked. 'About eight o'clock?'

'Fine, and no guns,' she said.

'No, ma'am, no guns.'

'Right then.' She held her hand out for the jam jar. Road's that way.'

'Yes, ma'am.'

Kate watched him climb the hill and walked back to the house, shaking her head. Josie reached to hug her, but Kate pulled away. 'God damned hunter.' She was on the verge of tears.

'How about some coffee or lunch?'

'Naw, are you nuts, after all we ate this morning? No, I think I'll just go for a walk. See if I can find the buck. If there *is* a buck.'

Josie nodded. 'Want company?' She wasn't keen on viewing a dead animal, but she didn't care to admit being afraid to stay in the house alone, not after her melodramatic performance with the bats last night.

'Sure.' Kate was grateful. 'Let's go.'

Josie locked the ice chest and dropped the jam jar in the brown paper garbage bag on the way out.

It was hotter now, about 85 degrees. The pennyroyal smelled mintier than last night. The day was dry and still—bleached grass, golden hills scumbled against teal sky. A turkey vulture glided above the oak grove. As they walked around the pond, they could hear frogs scholop into the water. Kate stopped to inspect the eucalyptus trees they had planted in the spring. Four out of five still alive, not bad. Further along, a salamander skittered across their path. Josie felt cool even before she entered the woods. In a way, she hoped they wouldn't find the buck. But if there was no buck, who knew what the bumblebee man really wanted?

The woods were thick with madrone and manzanita and poison oak. It was always a balance on the land, Kate thought, pleasure and danger.

Josie wished she had worn sneakers instead of sandals. But Kate didn't seem to be bothered about her feet as she marched ahead. Right, Josie reminded herself, this wasn't a ramble. They continued in silence for half an hour.

'Round here, I guess,' called Kate, who was now several yards ahead. 'See the way branches have broken. Yes, here. Oh, my god, it's still alive. God-damned hunter.'

They stared at the huge animal, its left front leg broken in a fall, panting and sweating, blind fear in its wide eyes.

'I told Myla we should keep a gun at the house,' Kate cried. 'What are we going to do?'

Josie didn't think about it. She probably wouldn't have been able to lift the boulder if she had thought about it. But she heard herself shouting to Kate, 'Stand back,' and watched herself drop the big rock on the buck's head. They heard a gurgling and saw a muscle ripple along the animal's belly. Then nothing. There was nothing alive under that boulder.

Josie stared at the four bullet wounds scattered up the right side of the buck. The animal's blood was a dark, cinnamon colour. She noticed sweat along the hip joints.

Kate walked over to her quietly and took her hand. 'Good, brave,' she stuttered. 'That was good, Josie.'

'Yeah, it seemed the right thing.'

Kate hugged Josie and gently drew her away from the dead buck and the broken bush.

They walked straight out to the trail. Neither one seemed to want to stay in the woods for their customary ramble. Kate watched her friend closely, waiting for the explosion. This silence was so uncharacteristic of Josie. Soon, soon, she would erupt with anger and aggravation and guilt and a long examination of what she had done in the woods. For her own part, Kate could only think of one word. Brave.

'Let's go swimming,' Josie said, trying to focus on the trail. 'It'll cool us off.'

The two women stripped on the makeshift dock and lay in the sun beside one another. Kate was slim, her legs long and shapely. She didn't think much about this body which had always served her well. She never felt too thin or too plump. Josie, in contrast, fretted about her zoftig breasts and hips. Her skin was pinker than Kate's, a faint pink. Kate curled up beside Josie, her legs across Josie's legs, her head on Josie's shoulder.

Josie closed her eyes and told herself it was

over. They were all right. She had never killed anything before and she felt terribly sad. Of course, the animal had been dying. It was a humane act. Still, her chest ached with a funny hollowness.

'What's that?' Kate sat up.

They listened, Josie flat and Kate leaning forward from her waist.

The noise came again.

A loud whirr.

Like an engine.

Whirr.

'Quail.' Kate relaxed back on her elbow. 'Come on, let's wash off the feeling of that creepy guy.'

She lowered herself into the water from the wooden ladder, surprised as Josie jumped in.

'Freezing!' Josie laughed, swimming around her friend and noticing how Kate's blonde curls sprang back the minute she lifted her head from the water. 'Freezing!'

'You'll warm up,' Kate said, herself breathless from the cold.

'You're always telling me to stop daydreaming, to stay in the present. The present is freezing.' Josie giggled and splashed her friend.

Kate laughed. She ducked under the water, swimming deep enough to catch Josie's feet, which were treading earnestly.

'Hey, watch it.' But Josie called too late. Now she was below the surface, tangled in Kate's legs and the long roots of silky grass. It was green down here and very cold.

They dried out on the sunny dock and dressed before starting towards the house. Often they walked naked across the land, especially after swimming when they didn't want to wear sweaty clothes. Today that didn't feel safe.

Back at the cabin, the afternoon grew long and restless. Both women felt fidgety. Kate put aside her equations and washed all the windows in the house. Josie couldn't concentrate on her translation, so she worked up lesson plans for the following week.

About five o'clock, she glanced at Kate, stretching recklessly to the skylight from the top of a ladder.

'Careful up there.'

'Sure, hon!'

'What did we bring for dinner?' Josie's mind was blank.

'That beef chili you made last week. And rye bread.'

'Why didn't we go out?' Josie paced in front of the wood stove. God, she wished Kate would be careful on that ladder.

'Out. But the whole point of being here, oops,' she tipped precariously and then straightened. 'Hey, just let me get one more lick in here and we can talk. There.' She started down the steps. 'But the whole point of being in the country is to retreat together in solitary bliss. And what's wrong with your chili? I thought this batch was perfect.'

Josie shrugged and looked out the big bay window across the grass. She told herself to watch the horses ambling along the ridge or the hawk hovering over the pond. Instead she was caught by a line of lint Kate had left in the middle of the frame. 'I don't know. Not in the mood. Guess I'd like vegetarian tonight.' Her eyes stung.

Kate stood behind her; still, Josie could sense her nodding.

'Why not,' Kate said. 'Be nice to take a ride this time of evening.'

Edna's Café was practically empty. But then—Kate checked her watch—it *was* only five-thirty. Edna waved menus from behind the counter. Josie and Kate said yes.

'Coffee, girls?' Edna carried the menus under her arm, pot of coffee in one hand and mugs in the other.

'Thanks,' Josie said.

'Not just yet,' Kate smiled. Edna reminded her of Aunt Bella who worked in a coffee shop back East.

While Kate studied the menu, Josie excused herself to the restroom.

Kate breathed easier when Josie returned to the table looking relaxed. She felt a great surge of affection as her companion intently appraised the menu.

'I think I'll have the chef's salad with Jack cheese,' Josie decided.

'Sounds good.' Kate nodded. She was relieved to see Josie looking happy. 'Two chef salads, with Jack cheese,' she called over to Edna.

They talked about plans for the following summer when they could spend four consecutive weeks on the land.

'You two girls sisters?' Edna served the enormous salads.

'No,' laughed Kate. 'Why?'

'Don't know. You kinda look alike. 'Course when I stare straight at you like this, there's not much resemblance. I don't know. And you always order the same thing.'

'In that case, I'll have tea,' Kate laughed again. 'With lemon.'

They ate silently, self-conscious of being the only ones in the restaurant. Kate could hardly get down the lettuce. She'd feel better after she made the phone call. She wouldn't tell Josie, who would get nervous. But it was responsible to report the intruder to the sheriff. 'Excuse me. Now I've got to use the bathroom,' she said to Josie. 'Don't let Edna take my salad.'

'I'll guard it with my life,' Josie grinned.

The sheriff's number was posted beneath the fire station number. She dialled and heard a funny, moist sound, as if the man were eating or maybe clicking in his dentures. She concentrated on the sturdy black plastic of the phone.

'Hello,' he said finally.

She began to report the incident.

'Listen, you're the second lady to call me about this in twenty minutes. Like I told the other one, there's nothing I can do unless the man is actually trespassing on your land. Since you've invited him back tomorrow, he ain't exactly trespassing.'

'We didn't exactly invite him.'

'OK, if it makes you feel easier, I said I'll swing by about eight a.m. That's when the other lady said he'd be coming.'

'Thank you, sir.'

'Sir,' she shook her head as she walked back to the table. She hadn't said 'sir' in fifteen years.

Josie had finished her salad and was doodling on a paper napkin. Definitely signs of a good mood. Kate sat down and stared at her until she looked up. 'So I hear you have a date with the law tomorrow morning.'

Josie smiled. 'Hope you don't think I'm stepping out on you.'

By the time Kate finished her salad, the café was getting crowded.

'Refills?' Edna approached with a pot of coffee and a pot of hot water. 'No thanks, just the cheque,' Josie said.

'Guess you girls didn't mind my asking if you was sisters?'

'No, no, not at all.' They spoke in unison.

♀♀

It was a warm, richly scented evening and they drove home with the top down. Jupiter came out early again. Josie thought how much she preferred Jupiter to the cold North Star.

They were both worn out as they collapsed on the couch together. Their feet on the fruit crate coffee table, they watched pink gain the horizon. It was almost pitch dark when Josie reached up to light the lanterns.

She hesitated a moment, remembering last night, and then proceeded. Light, *violà*, the room was filled with sharp corners and shiny surfaces. Kate picked up her book, but Josie drew it away, cuddling closer.

'Here?' Kate was surprised by her own resistance. After all, they were alone, five miles from town.

'Where then?' Josie tried to sound like Lauren Bacall.

Kate sighed with a breath that moved her whole body, a body, she noticed, which was becoming increasingly sensitive to the body next to her. 'Mmmmm,' she kissed Josie on her neck, sweet with late summer sweat.

When Josie opened her eyes, she thought she saw something. No, they had sealed off the sun porch this morning. She kissed Kate on the lips and was startled by a whisssh over her friend's head. 'Bats,' she said evenly, pulling Kate lower on the couch.

'Don't worry,' Kate said. 'I'll get rid of him.'

Worry, Josie cringed. She wasn't worried; she was hysterical. Calm down, she told herself. Think about the invasion of Poland. This was her mother's approach to anxiety—distract yourself by thinking about people with *real* problems. Worry is a perversion of imagination.

Kate opened the windows and set forth again with the broom, but the bat wouldn't leave. Eventually it spiraled upstairs into the large sleeping loft. Kate shook her head and closed up the house against further intrusion. She shrugged and returned to the couch, where Josie was sitting up, considerably more collected than the previous night.

'It'll be OK,' Kate said. 'It'll just go to sleep. You know, they're not really Transylvanian leeches. They're harmless little herbivores. And rather inept.'

Herbivores. Josie thought about eating salad for absolution after she murdered the buck.

Kate reached over and brushed her lover's breast, but Josie pulled away. 'Not now, sweetie. I can't just now.'

Kate nodded. She picked up her book. Josie fiddled with a crossword puzzle. At about ten o'clock, Kate yawned, 'Bed?'

'OK,' Josie was determined to be brave. 'I'll go up first.'

'Sure,' Kate regarded her closely. 'You light the candle up there. I'll get the lantern down here.'

They settled comfortably in the double nylon sleeping bag. Kate blew out the light. She reached over to rub Josie's back in the hope something more might develop. Suddenly she heard a whissh, whissh, whissh.

'Looks like our friend is back.' Kate tried to keep her voice light.

'Just a harmless little herbivore.' Josie rolled to her side of the bed, putting a pillow over her head.

♀♀

That night Josie dreamt that she had become Mayor of Lincoln, Nebraska.

Kate slept fitfully, hardly dreaming, and waking with the first sun.

She lay and watched Josie breathing evenly, blowing the edges of her black hair, her body ripe and luscious in the soft light. If she woke up early enough, they could make love before Mr. Creepo arrived. And the sheriff. Had they made a mistake in phoning the sheriff?

The loft grew lighter. Kate lay on her back with her head on her palms, wondering where the bat had nested, about the reliability of her research assistant, whether she would go home for Christmas this year. Then she heard a noise.

Her entire body stiffened. No mistaking the sound of a car crawling down the gravel road toward their cabin. She checked her watch. Seven a.m. Shit. The sheriff wouldn't arrive until their bodies were cold. Maybe Josie would be safer if she just stayed in the house; maybe she wouldn't wake her. Yes, Kate pulled out of the sleeping bag. She was grabbed by the nightgown.

'Not so quick, brown fox,' Josie said sleepily. 'How about a cuddle?'

She was adorable in the morning, thought Kate, completely *dérangé* as Josie herself would admit, before the second cup of coffee.

The noise outside grew closer and Kate tightened.

'Don't you even want to hear how I got elected Mayor of Lincoln…?'

'Not now.' Kate couldn't stem the panic in her own voice.

Josie sat up. 'What is it?' Then she heard the truck's motor dying.

'I'll just go check in with him,' Kate said nonchalantly. 'You wait here and I'll come back to snuggle.' She pulled on her clothes.

'No you don't, Joan of Arc.' Josie stood up and tucked her nightshirt into a pair of jeans.

The two walked downstairs together.

The fat man was approaching the house, empty-handed. His friend, also bulky and middle-aged, stayed behind, leaning against the red pickup truck.

Kate called out to him when he was three yards from the house. 'Back again.'

"Sorry to bother you, ma'am. As you can see we didn't bring no guns. We'll just get that deer and then git offa yer property as soon's we can.'

His friend shuffled and looked at his feet.

'OK,' Kate said gruffly. 'We don't want dead animals on the land. By the way, we finished him off for you yesterday.'

The man opened his mouth in surprise. His friend moved forward, tugging him back. They closed up the truck and headed into the woods.

Josie watched until they were out of sight. Kate went inside to make coffee.

Half-an-our later, as they sat down to breakfast, another vehicle crunched down the hill. Josie looked out at the black and white sedan. 'Our hero, the sheriff.'

They walked over to greet the sheriff, a solid man, who looked them over carefully.

'You the girls who called me yesterday?'

'Yes, we did.' Josie smiled.

'Yes.' Kate nodded, the 'sir' gone as quickly as it had come. She didn't like his expression.

'Only ladies listed on the deed to this land, I see. Looked it up last night. All schoolteachers. Some kind of commune? Something religious?'

'Just friends.' Kate stepped back.

'Edna says she thought you were sisters.' He squinted against the bright sun. 'One sort or another.'

'Just friends.' Kate's voice was more distant.

'Soooo.' The sheriff held his ground. 'You want to run through the nature of that problem again?'

As Kate talked with the sheriff, Josie inspected the hunters' pickup truck. The bumper sticker read, 'I live in a cave and one good fuck is all I crave.' Inside, dice hung from the rearview mirror. On the seat were a parka and two empty cans of Dr Pepper. The dashboard was plastered with several iridescent signs. The sun glared so that she could read only one. 'Gas, Ass or Grass— No one rides for free.'

The sheriff noticed her and observed, 'Leon's truck. Just as I figured. Leon Bates, a local man. He's well, he's strayed off the hunting trail before.'

'Isn't there something you can do about him?' Josie felt the heat rising to her face. 'He might have killed one of us. On our property. With a gun.'

'Today,' the sheriff's voice was cool, 'today your friend tells me that he has no gun. That in fact, you said he could come back here to get his buck. That right?'

Josie closed her eyes, feeling naïve for imagining this man might protect them. Now bureaucracy seemed the only recourse. 'Right. Can't we

make some kind of complaint about what he did yesterday?'

'Sure can,' the sheriff nodded. 'If that's what you want.'

'What do you mean?' Kate's back tightened.

'You're weekend folks, right?' He lit a cigarette.

'We work in the city, if that's what you mean,' Kate spoke carefully, 'and don't live here year-round.'

'None of my business what you all have going on here. None of Leon's business either. But if you file a complaint and we take it to court, well, he's bound to do some investigating and...'

'There's nothing illegal about our land group,' Josie snapped.

'Miss, Miss, I never said anything about legal, illegal, but you know there are natural pests the law can't control. And it's better maybe not to get them roused.'

Kate and Josie exchanged glances. 'Well, perhaps we'll check with Loretta; her sister's a lawyer. We'll get back to you.'

'Yes, ma'am.' He grew more serious. 'That about all for today, ma'am? I mean you said they didn't bring no guns with them. You feel safe enough on your own?'

'Yes,' Josie said. 'We're safe enough on our own.'

'Then if you'll excuse me, it's almost eight o'clock and services start early around here.' He stamped out his cigarette and softened. 'Church is always open to outsiders and weekend people, by the way. Just three miles down, on the road by the gas station.'

'I know where it is,' Josie said. 'Good-bye, sheriff.'

They watched him roll up the hill, then returned to the house for breakfast. They were both too furious to talk. Kate hardly touched her food, watching out the window for the trespassers.

About ten o'clock, she saw two pregnant-looking men pulling a buck through the dust by its antlers. Her first thought was how powerful those antlers must be. She tightened and Josie looked up from her book. 'At last.'

It took the men ten minutes to reach the truck. They were huffing and sweating and Josie

201

had to resist the urge to bring them a pitcher of water. She followed Kate out on the front porch.

Leon Bates glowered at them, as if weighing the value of wasting breath for talk. He and his friend heaved the buck into the truck. On the second try, they made it.

Leon's friend wiped his hands on his jeans, waiting with an expression of excruciating embarrassment.

Leon straightened up, drew a breath and shouted, 'That'll do it.'

'Good,' called Kate.

'Gotta ask one question.' Leon leaned forward on his right leg. 'What'd you have to go and bust his head for? Ruined a perfect trophy. Just look at the antlers. Would have been perfect.'

'Come on, Leon,' his friend called.

Kate stood firmly, hands on her hips. Josie tried to hold back the tears, but she couldn't and pivoted toward the cabin.

'The road's that way,' Kate pointed. 'Only goes in one direction.'

Kate stamped into the house. 'Damn them! Damn them!' she screamed.

'Hey, now.' Josie reached up to her shoulders and pulled Kate toward her. 'Hey now, relax, love.'

'Don't tell me to relax. This man comes on our land, shoots living things, threatens us. And you tell me to relax.' She banged her hand on the table.

Josie inhaled heavily and pulled Kate a little closer. 'They've gone now.' She looked over Kate's shoulder and out the back window, which gleamed in the mid-morning sun. 'See, they're over the hill.'

'Out of sight, that's what you think, you fool.' Kate tried to draw apart.

Josie held tight, hoping to melt the contortions from her friend's face.

Kate pushed her away. Josie lost balance, hitting her head against a pain of glass in the sun porch door.

The glass cracked, sending a high-pitched rip through the room.

Josie ducked forward, her eyes shut tightly,

just in time to avoid most of the showering glass fragments.

Drenched in sweat, Kate shook her and shouted, 'Josie, Josie are you all right? Oh, my God, Josie, are you all right?'

'We'll never keep out the bats this way,' Josie laughed nervously, on the verge.

'Josie, I didn't mean it.' Tears welled in Kate's eyes. 'I love you, Josie, are you all right?'

Josie nodded. They held each other, shivering.

Josie stepped forward, 'OK, yes, but I feel a little like Tinkerbell. Scattering all this glitter.'

'Tinkerbell!' Kate laughed and cried and choked. The room seemed to be closing in on them. Hot, tight, airless. She could feel herself listing.

'But you, hey.' Josie frowned. 'Let's go upstairs and have *you* lie down.'

They sat on the bed, holding hands and staring out at the land. The day was hot, even dryer than yesterday and the golden grass shimmered against the shadowy backdrop of the woods.

'We really should go down and clean up the glass, put a board over the shattered pane.' Kate whispered.

'Yeah, if we don't head home soon, traffic's going to be impossible.'

Kate rested her head on Josie's breast. She smelled the musk from the black feathers beneath her arms. Her hand went to the soft nest at the bottom of Josie's generous belly. Josie slipped off her clothes. Kate followed. They sat down on the bed, swimming together again, sucked into the cool sleeping bag.

'Home,' Josie murmured.

'Hmmmm?' Kate inhaled the scents of Josie's sweat and sex. Forcing herself to be alert, she pulled back. Was her friend delirious? Maybe she had a concussion.

'Home.' Josie kissed her with a passion so conscious as to take away both Kate's concern and her breath.

'Yes.' Josie moved her fingers lower, separating the labia, swirling the honey thicker. 'Yes.'

Josie crawled on top of Kate, licking her shoulders, her breasts; burying her nose in her navel;

kissing her thighs. Then she was distracted by a slow fizzzz, as if their air mattress were deflating.

Josie looked up. Two wasps hovered over them, bobbing and weaving and then lifting themselves abruptly out of vision. Maybe if she continued Kate wouldn't notice. But it was too late.

'They always come out in the middle of the day,' Kate said drearily. 'For food. For their nests.'

Josie shook her head, staring at the unsteady, fragile creatures.

'What the hell,' Kate shrugged, inching away from Josie.

'What the hell,' Josie whispered seductively. They returned to the pleasures between them. When they finished making love, Josie curled around Kate. She explained how she had been elected Mayor of Lincoln, Nebraska.

The wasps wove over and around the two women. Even as they fell asleep. ▩

I'm not a girl
by Judy Grahn

I'm not a girl
      I'm a hatchet
I'm not a hole
      I'm a whole mountain
I'm not a fool
      I'm a survivor
I'm not a pearl
      I'm the Atlantic Ocean
I'm not a good lay
      I'm a straight razor
look at me as if you had never seen a woman before
I have red, red hands and much bitterness

From *Work of a Common Woman*.
Freedom, CA: The Crossing Press, [1978]

Words

by Susan Sherman

              I am trapped
by words
              The ones I speak
The ones I never say

My head stuffed full of dreams
My body of memories
                    I flounder
          between two worlds
The future and the past

I wanted to write a poem
more full of passion more full
of love
          than any
                    I have ever
          written

How does one measure years
What standard does one use
to weight them
                    I am trapped
          by time
It circles my wrists
                    guides
          my steps

I live in the shadow of my words
They measure the moments
            of my life

What part in all this do you have
What part in all this do I
To understand that question

to hold it
            open
                        to hold it
                                    open

until finding it
we enter
            free

From *Women Poems Love Poems.*
New York: IKON, 1975.

Ya Don Wanna
Eat Pussy
by Chrystos

that Chippewa said to that gay white man who never has
Ya don wanna eat pussy after eatin hot peppers   he laughed
I stared   in the white sink memorizing rust stains
He nodded in the general direction of the windows behind us
       Two Native women chopping onions & pickles
       to make tuna fish sandwiches
       for these six men helping to move
He said   *Ya didn hear that did ya   Good*
She answered   *I chose to ignore it*
I muttered   *So did I*
Ya don wanna take offense at an Indian man's joke
       no matter how crude
in front of a white man
Close to my tribe   he probably guessed we're lesbians
said that   to see what we'd do
which was to keep on doin what he had been doin
That gay white man stopped talking about how much he loved
hot peppers
That Chippewa said   *Not too much for me   Don eat fish*
probably another joke we ignored   I said
The grocery was fresh out of buffalo & deer
Much later that gay white man called that Chippewa a drunk
       we both stared at a different floor
       in a different silence   just as sharp
       & hot

In *Not Vanishing*. Vancouver: Press Gang Publishers, 1988.

Dicks Joseph G Gray Cary Ames & Frye attys
   1700 First Interstate Plaza **699 3604**
Dick's Liquor 737 Pearl La Jolla **459 3889**
Dicks Marshal 3980 Faircross Pl **583 3045**
Dicks Michael 2568 Albatross **234 8234**
Dicks Of America P O Box 600782 . . . . **286 5448**
Dick's Towing Service
                1398 Dewey Pl Campo . **478 5616**
Dick's Welding Service
                5160 Marlen Wy La Mesa . **697 5679**
  DICKSON-SEE ALSO-DIXON
Dickson A P **461 2135**
Dickson A PhD **435 3022**

GERMAIN© 1992

Now we know where They are coming from!

Dicks of America
Diane F. Germain

208

How can you tell a dyke?
by Donna Allegra ~

If she tells men "no"
won't suck his dick or ego
doesn't go giggly when he insults
is not intimidated when he menaces
won't stand for disrespect
has her own attitude and opinion
about everything
insists on being listened to
when it's her turn
decides her own way is just fine

if she likes women
cares about them
prefers their company to his
can't see the fun of having a man
around the house
to mess it up and pick up after

if he can't coerce his way
into her bed by insinuating
can't threaten himself between her
legs
by calling her one
doesn't act like a dick-happy simple
bitch
decides heterosex isn't so great
as it's cracked up to be

if she really doesn't give a fuck
what some boy thinks

about her or anything else
doesn't like most men
feels no woman in her right mind
would
when you look at how they act
and even half-way think about it

if she goes out with you
assumes you wanted the pleasure
of her company
doesn't give a hoot or holler how much
reefer-alcohol-cocaine-money he offers
doesn't give good head
or any
for that matter

if she by her lights examines his
calls her own shots
just won't listen
to what a man has to say
and he can't
tell her anything anymore.

by Jennifer Camper

1979: First National March on Washington for Lesbian and Gay Rights
by JEB

Howm'I sposta sit here and draw cartoons when there's a straight white guy RUNNING THE COUNTRY??

by Diane DiMassa

The Master's Tools Will Never Dismantle The Master's House

by Audre Lorde

I agreed to take part in a New York University Institute for the Humanities conference a year ago, with the understanding that I would be commenting upon papers dealing with the role of difference within the lives of american women; differences of race, sexuality, class, and age. For the absence of these considerations weakens any feminist discussion of the personal and the political.

It is a particular academic arrogance to assume any discussion of feminist theory in this time and in this place without examining our many differences, and without a significant input from poor women, black

Comments at "The Personal and the Political" Panel (Second Sex Conference, October 29, 1979)

From *This Bridge Called My Back: Writings by Radical Women of Color*, eds. Cherríe Moraga and Gloria Anzaldúa (1981, Persephone Press; 1983, Kitchen Table: Women of Color Press.)

and third-world women, and lesbians. And yet, I stand here as a black lesbian feminist, having been invited to comment within the only panel at this conference where the input of black feminists and lesbians is represented. What this says about the vision of this conference is sad, in a country where racism, sexism and homophobia are inseparable. To read this program is to assume that lesbian and black women have nothing to say of existentialism, the erotic, women's culture and silence, developing feminist theory, or heterosexuality and power. And what does it mean in personal and political terms when even the two black women who did present here were literally found at the last hour? What does it mean when the tools of a racist patriarchy are used to examine the fruits of that same patriarchy? It means that only the most narrow perimeters of change are possible and allowable. The absence of any consid-

eration of lesbian consciousness or the consciousness of third-world women leaves a serious gap within this conference and within the papers presented here. For example, in a paper on material relationships between women, I was conscious of an either/or model of nurturing which totally dismissed my knowledge as a black lesbian. In this paper there was no examination of mutuality between women, no systems of shared support, no interdependence as exists between lesbians and women-identified women. Yet it is only in the patriarchal mode of nurturance that women "who attempt to emancipate themselves pay perhaps too high a price for the results," as the paper states.

For women, the need and desire to nurture each other is not pathological but redemptive, and it is within that knowledge that our real power is rediscovered. It is this real connection, which is so feared by a patriarchal world. For it is only under a patriarchal structure that maternity is the only social power open to women.

Interdependency between women is the only way to the freedom which allows the "I" to "be," not in order to be used, but in order to be creative. This is a difference between the passive "be" and the active "being."

Advocating the mere tolerance of difference between women is the grossest reformism. It is a total denial of the creative function of difference in our lives. For difference must not be merely tolerated, but seen as a fund of necessary polarities between which our creativity can spark like a dialectic. Only then does the necessity for interdependency become unthreatening. Only within that interdependency of different strengths, acknowledged and equal, can the power to seek new ways to actively "be" in the world generate, as well as the courage and sustenance to act where there are no charters.

With the interdependence of mutual (non-dominant) differences lies that security which enables us to descend into the chaos of knowledge and return with true visions of our future, along with the concomitant power to effect those changes which can bring that future into being. Difference is that raw and powerful connection from which our personal power is forged.

As women, we have been taught to either ignore our differences or to view them as causes for separation and suspicion rather than as forces for

change. Without community, there is no liberation, only the most vulnerable and temporary armistice between an individual and her oppression. But community must not mean a shedding of our differences, nor the pathetic pretense that these differences do not exist.

Those of us who stand outside the circle of this society's definition of acceptable women; those of us who have been forged in the crucibles of difference; those of us who are poor, who are lesbians, who are black, who are older, know that *survival is not an academic skill*. It is learning how to stand alone, unpopular and sometimes reviled, and how to make common cause with those others identified as outside the structures, in order to define and seek a world in which we can all flourish. It is learning how to take our differences and make them strengths. *For the master's tools will never dismantle the master's house.* They may allow us temporarily to beat him at his own game, but they will never enable us to bring about genuine change. And this fact is only threatening to those women who still define the master's house as their only source of support.

Poor and third-world women know there is a difference between the daily manifestations and dehumanizations of marital slavery and prostitution, because it is our daughters who line 42nd Street. The Black panelists' observation about the effects of relative powerlessness

and the differences of relationship between black women and men from white women and men illustrate some of our unique problems as black feminists. If white american feminist theory need not deal with the differences between us, and the resulting difference in the aspects of our oppressions, then what do you do with the fact that the women who clean your houses and tend your children while you attend conferences on feminist theory are, for the most part, poor and third-world women? What is the theory behind racist feminism?

In a world of possibility for us all, our personal visions help lay the groundwork for political action. The failure of the academic feminists to recognize difference as a crucial strength is a failure to reach beyond the first patriarchal lesson. Divide and conquer, in our world, must become define and empower.

Why weren't other black women and third-world women found to participate in this conference? Why were two phone calls to me considered a consultation? Am I the only possible source of names of black feminists? And although the black panelist's paper ends on an important and powerful connection of love between women, what about interracial co-operation between feminists who don't love each other?

In academic feminist circles, the answer to these questions is often "We did not know who to ask." But that is the same evasion of responsibility, the same cop-out, that keeps black women's art out of women's exhibitions, black women's work out of most feminist publications except for the occasional "Special Third-world Women's Issue,"* and black women's texts off of your reading lists. But as Adrienne Rich pointed out in a recent talk, white feminists have educated themselves about such an enormous amount over the past ten years, how come you haven't also educated yourselves about black women and the differences between us—white and black—when it is key to our survival as a movement?

Women of today are still being called upon to stretch across the gap of male ignorance, and to educate men as to our existence and our needs. This is an old and primary tool of all oppressors to keep the oppressed occupied with the master's concerns. Now we hear that it is the task of black and third-world women to educate white women, in the face of tremendous resistance, as to our existence, our differences, our relative roles in our joint survival. This is a diversion of energies and a tragic repetition of racist patriarchal thought.

Simone DeBeauvoir once said: "It is in the knowledge of our lives that we must draw our strength to live and our reasons for acting."

Racism and homophobia are real conditions of all our lives in this place and this time. *I urge each one of us here to reach down into that deep place of knowledge inside herself and touch that terror and loathing of any difference that lives there. See whose face it wears.* Then the personal as the political can begin to illuminate all our choices. ▣

Conditions of Brooklyn, NY is a major exception. It has fairly consistently published the work of women of color before it was "fashionable" to do so.

Six Pomegranate Seeds and One Lesson in Manners

A Piece About Straight Folks Who Don't Mind Gays, But...

by Elliott ~~~~~~

Current Events

Zsa Zsa Gabor says
receiving a jail term
would endanger her because
of the lesbians
in prisons.
And I say hey,
relax, babe—
we bulldykes tend to avoid
those who so openly
hate women.

On the Joys of a Familiar

I saw Flossie's new trick today.
When Toot, treat in hand, asked
"Flossie, would you rather
be straight
or dead?"
the dog hit the ground
legs stiff in the air
as we made jokes
that were hardly polite.

Heteropatriarchy, Sweet Heteropatriarchy

"thrust thrust thrust"
might sound like sex
to you
but yours is not
the only physical reality

Bulldyke Humor 1: Heterosex

When I met Jackie
her T-shirt said
    LESBIANISM
    Is The Only
    Natural Form of
    Birth Control

Bulldyke Humor 2: Art

Otter's postcard this week
is a picture of Ayer's Rock, Australia
with the slogan
"smooth, designed with a woman in mind"
cut from some ad and pasted on.
One current plot of
the International Lesbian Conspiracy
is to gather our climbers and artists
and a couple tons of clay

and construct a huge nipple up there
during twilight, of course.
We'd sign it
"love, the leaping lesbians"

And Speaking of Art

Tell me, breeder boys,
why are words about your life
REAL POETRY
and words about mine
just politics?

Pat Parker's
Politeness Model

I spent lunch dreaming
of the mystical Sue
and her gracious gang.
But perhaps you don't know
the Ladies Sewing Circle and
Terrorist Society?
Perhaps you should.
Or perhaps, now, you do.

From *The Separatist Revolution*, 1991.

by Noreen Stevens

ii.

by Cheryl Clarke

The woman who raised me asks me
'Where is the hope here, where is the hope?
The fruit here is rotten.
All the roots are excavated.
The sidewalks are cracked and in pieces
and the rain forms stagnant pools.
Children walk the night through the streets here
and men make every urge so public.
And who will hear me cry for help?
Will they want to climb all these flights
up here to save me? and what will you do
when you wake up
and find your good woman
gone?'*

*Line adapted from blues songs sung by Bessie
Smith, 1925–1927, *Bessie Smith: Nobody's Blues But
Mine* (Columbia Records, reissued 1972).

From *Living as a Lesbian.* Ithaca, NY: Firebrand Books,
1986.

Asphalta

by Morgan Grey & Julia Penelope

ASPHALTA, goddess of all roads, streets, and highways, and guardian of those who travel on them, is best known for Her miraculous powers of finding parking places. The formal Parking Place Invocation to Asphalta, chanted by Her devotees around the world, and never known to fail when sincerely uttered, even in impossible-to-park-in cities like New York and Montreal, is:

> Hail, Asphalta, full of grace:
> Help me find a parking place.

This invocation should be intoned at least two blocks before you want to park, although it has been known to work on very short notice. A brief version of the invocation, developed by followers of Asphalta in Chicago, "Asphalta, do Your Thing," has also proven to be effective. In the event that Asphalta has created an ideal parking place, and some rude motorist attempts to take it away, chant:

> Hail, Asphalta, full of grace:
> Keep that pud out of my space.

Asphalta is one of the most widely worshipped of all modern Found Goddesses. Her highways and streets form complex intersecting webs which join Her many thousands of temples

Found Goddesses. Norwich, VT: New Victoria Publishers, 1988.

and shrines, and connect the lives of Lesbians. Her major temples are located wherever road construction is underway, and are attended by Her High Priestesses, who usually wear jeans or overalls, boots, hardhats, and colorful scarves or handkerchiefs about their necks or heads, as well as vestments of Her sacred color, day-glo orange. They often carry flags or signs as symbols of their high office. All motorists slow down when passing through one of Asphalta's Sacred Places, and stop when instructed to do so by a priestess, who should always be addressed as "Most Esteemed Flagwomon." Failure to heed the signals of a priestess has been known to have fatal consequences, but those especially cherished by Asphalta may be given the Sacred Baton to pass to a traveler going in the opposite direction. The ritual of Passing the Sacred Baton symbolizes the continuity as well as the diversity of our paths.

Asphalta's shrines, marked by heaps of concrete and asphalt left after a temple has moved, are usually unattended and visited only by Her most devoted followers, who sometimes carry a relic from one of these places (a small crystal of asphalt, in a bright orange bag with a yellow cord) around their necks or hanging from the rearview mirror of their cars. These relics are said to have great powers, and will guarantee safe passage from one place to another. Especially renowned for their shifting powers and much sought after by frequent travelers are the rare Asphalt crystals that have part of the Yellow Line in their matrix. The Yellow Line is widely held to represent the Order of Society and Social Contracts. For this reason, many theorists suspect that Asphalta is actually a major goddess whose influence extends far beyond roads and travel. Indeed, Her intersecting webs connect all that Is.

INTERSTATIA is one of Asphalta's best-known aspects, although each town and city has its own names for this deity. She sometimes appears as Toll Road or Tollway, and is reputed to be both convenient and expensive, for, at varying distances from each other, one will find small shrines to Asphalta. It is said that making an offering to a priestess at one of these shrines, called Toll Booths, insures the traveler's safe passage from one shrine to the next. Some devotees, anxious to travel as quickly as possible from one point to another, are known to buy Monthly Books of Coupons, which they use as offerings. Interstatia's symbol is the Cloverleaf, and many report exceptional effects when **MOOLA-MOOLA**'s favorite color, green, is combined with the Cloverleaf and worn as an amulet. ▪

by Noreen Stevens

A Medal For Not Drowning

by Amy Edgington

When I was eleven years old I fell in love with a girl I met on a camping trip. Kris was witty, sarcastic and smart. She took herself seriously as an artist, and she had the moral values I considered most essential in my friends at that time: she abhorred what we called "segregation" in 1957. Her German immigrant family was not as dully all-American as my own, and her Wisconsin accent sounded exotic to my Southern ears. My instincts told me Kris would not be open to sexual approach, but that did not stop me from wanting with every cell of my body to be as close to her as possible as often as possible.

This posed some difficulties: we did not go to the same school, and our parents didn't drive. We lived impossibly far apart when it came to figuring out the bus routes and schedules to get from my house to hers. However, she swam on a swim team at the YWCA downtown, and we could both take the bus there. One problem remained: I was terrified of the water. More than one adult had given up on teaching me to swim, saying, "She'll never overcome her phobia." Without my glasses I am legally blind, yet I was labeled "phobic" for being afraid to move around in a strange, potentially lethal element.

I spent the first six years of my life without glasses, and I avoided the kind of play that develops large muscle coordination; why should I slide

In *Sinister Wisdom* 39 (Winter '89/'90)

down the slide when I couldn't see what was at the bottom? I preferred the sandbox and make-believe. Unfortunately, the brain and body seem to learn some things best at a certain age, so I never quite made up for lost time. I developed a wariness about tackling new physical feats. I learned that the combination of my body and strange surroundings often caused others to call me clumsy and accident prone.

Once I got glasses, I became a confirmed tomboy despite skinned knees and elbows. I kept my glasses in a holster at night. I came home from church and cracked my Lash Larue bullwhip for an hour to rehabilitate myself from wearing not just a dress, but the added indignities of a purse, a hat and gloves. I played tackle football in the street with the boys, until I was banned for breaking the quarterback's collarbone. Evidently I was even prone to other people's accidents.

At the age of nine I had had my first sexual relationship, but my girlfriend's mother put a traumatic end to our affair. By the time I met Kris, I was determined to hide all evidence of my sexuality, although that did not get rid of my feelings. I had also become embarrassed about my body. I knew I not only had "bad" eyes, I had a "bad" back. I have Scheuermann's disease. For reasons unknown my spine slowly twists into a more and more pronounced S-shaped curve, when viewed from the side and from the back. It's actually a spiral: I have seen trees shaped like me that look strong and graceful. Yet this is considered an ugly defect in humans, and in a female ugliness is the worst sin.

My ordinary adolescent paranoia about my appearance seemed to be confirmed by others. I had been muttered over by a series of doctors and physical therapists. I had overheard remarks about "the hunchback." In the first grade the other girls insisted that I play "witch"; they left me tied to a tree after recess was over, burning with humiliation. I did not feel ugly, but I suspected that others found me ugly. I knew that to go swimming once, you had to get completely naked in a room full of other girls twice; the rest of the time you had to run around in a terribly revealing bathing suit. But I was in love with a swimmer, so in three months I was on that swim team.

This was at least semi-amazing: the newspaper headlines should have read: "Half-Blind Girl Half-Conquers Half-Handicap." I swam all right, but I swam very poorly compared to most of the girls, who had been competing since they were five years old. Swimming did offer some pleasant surprises: from the starting block I could only guess where the other end of the pool was, but I found that the water acted as a lens and I could see the lane marker on the bottom when I swam. I didn't get lost or accidentally bump into somebody. Best of all, the water cut off my awareness of other people, and my awful self-consciousness evaporated.

Before summer vacation, we had our annual swim team party. During the day, an awards ceremony honored the outstanding swimmers for the most points accumulated in meets, pool records in each event, and so one. Needless to say, I was the slowest of any age in any event. I had never reached the finals in a race. This did not bother me much: I was on the swim team with Kris, wasn't I? I was as happy as a shark with a new set of teeth. I was thrilled to watch Kris and my other friends receive their trophies and medals. But after half an hour I got hungry and bored like a typical teenager; I was ready to sneak off to the snack bar. Then to my astonishment, I heard my name called. For a moment I panicked: were they going to give me a joke tro-

phy for being the worst member of the team? The coach announced I was receiving a special award—a tiny gold charm in the shape of a medal—because I had improved my times in all events more than anyone else. In swimming, cutting your time by half a second is significant, and I had improved by minutes.

I cannot remember ever having such ambivalent feelings. Kris's eyes shown with excitement. My friends were cheering and clapping. How could I not be pleased? Yet how could I be pleased? I knew in my guts what no one had ever told me: athletes get medals for winning; handicapped people get special awards for trying hard. Until then, I had felt like an athlete.

In subjective terms my accomplishment in swimming meant that I had worked like a dog, which I expected to do to learn a major new skill. At practice I often put on a sweat suit and high-topped basketball shoes and swam a mile, after I had swum all my races and a mile of regular laps. The best swimmers did this too, and no one made a fuss about it. I often went to bed in pain, but I had been in pain before without being in love. Love beats physical therapy any day.

In objective terms my record-shattering improvement meant that I had advanced from what could technically be called "not drowning" to what could technically be called "racing." I had never doubted that I could do this, but as I stood before my friends that day, I realized for the first time that none of them had thought I could. I understand now that my teammates and coaches were also genuinely awed by the amount of work I had done (they didn't know about the pain). They couldn't imagine working that hard themselves without the reinforcement of winning. I ask you: what sense of inadequacy was being soothed by that fake medal?

Eventually I bought a bracelet for my charm, but I rarely wore it. I withdrew somewhat from Kris, when she told me she was afraid people would think we were queers. I swam competitively for eight more years and became strong and graceful in the water. However, I owed my real medals and ribbons partly to the fact that competition grew less intense: more and more

© 1991 Sudie Rakusin

women quit athletics rather than risk being called "dykes."

As I grew up, I never knew when someone might pity my "deformity" or spurn me for my "unladylike" strength. I learned that in the straight world I would be expected to hide behind a disfiguring facade of femininity, and that among Lesbians I would sometimes find women whose prejudices were more limiting than blindness. Somehow I managed to keep myself afloat in spite of all this. Perhaps a medal for not drowning is appropriate after all. ■

Whole Cloth

by Susan Stinson

When we look closely, or when we become weavers, we learn of the tiny multiple threads unseen in the overall pattern, the knots on the underside of the carpet. (Adrienne Rich, "Women and Honor: Some Notes on Lying," 1979)

Once there was a small girl. She was small in height and years, that is, but her chin was full and her legs were thick and she was shaped like a drum. I see her sitting tight, with her thin tight dresses pulling across her chest, and her tight patterned pants creasing her thighs.

The land around her was flat. The small girl played kickball on the grass with the others. She played softball, spud and time-to-find-the-midnight-ghost. She did not make out behind the little shed. She did take her clothes off there, privately shutting the pink door with the good brass knob that her father had installed, sitting on the plywood floor in the bit of bare space between the bicycles and the lawnmower, leaning on a bag of peat moss. It smelled like grass and turpentine. She itched.

This was only afternoons when everyone was out. She knew it was nasty.

Sometimes she sat in there and read Louisa May Alcott. Sometimes she just breathed. Sometimes she pulled off her stretchy blue shorts and her underpants. She left them dangling around her Keds so it would be faster to pull her clothes back on if she heard someone coming.

She stood up and swung her hips a little, and moved her back. A little breeze crossed her, light dry air passing between her fat thighs, soft against the places that got sore from sweating and rubbing in tight pants. Goose pimples prickled up on her pale behind.

A neighbor's mower started up. She pulled her striped top off over her head, then felt too bare. A sharp line of light split the bottom of the door from her floor. She pulled her shoes and socks off with her feet, shaking the shorts from her ankle, then opened the door and stepped out onto the grass.

Naked. Now what? Her heart was hitting the inside of her chest. The grass felt familiar. She could see the oil stains on the concrete of the empty carport. What if the station wagon pulled in just then? What would her mother do? Forget the neighbors' windows. Run. She ran in a hot circle around the toolshed, past the garbage cans, then back in the door to strong smells and less light. She shut the door, breathed hard, leaned against the gasoline cans. Their rims pressed into her back. If she messed them up, her father would know that she had been in there. Better get dressed.

Originally published in *Common Lives/Lesbian Lives 19* (Spring, 1986).

My blouse gaps. My zipper may not close. I make my fingers sore forcing it up. My sides and belly have a deep red ridge in them after a day of that. My pants wear out on the inseam, thinning and splitting where my legs run. I have to try to walk delicately, as if that were possible, as if I met only at the crotch, as if the whole of my legs weren't intimate with each other, rubbing together just as my arms rest on my breasts and my breasts rest on my belly. The clothes can't get into every fold and separate every layer of flesh from itself. The dark blues can't camouflage me, the vertical stripes can't hide me, and no foundation garment can keep me in.

Look at this. This is a painting from around 1618. A fat woman did it. It tells a story, but I won't tell it here. I'm not writing the story of the strong Jewish woman who chopped off the general's head, although that story needs to be taken and told. I'm not writing the story of her maidservant, whose name is never mentioned, who helps God make her mistress beautiful, who carries the food into the enemy camp, who watches by the door as Judith kills, who carries the head back in a basket, who is freed in a line of the last chapter. This is not her story, although her name needs to be found, her life remembered, and her deeds told. I'm not writing the story of the young Italian painter raped in her studio by her teacher and tortured in thumbscrews at the trial of her rapist. This is not her story; it's an image of one of her images.

Arms. Hands. Light. A wide thigh. Small breasts. Two women look past the candle. A man's head is being handled. Judith is dressed up. One hand is help up, flat, shielding the candle, shadowing her face. With the other hand she holds a curved sword. Look at her belly, at the light up her arms, the geometry of it.

The maidservant tucks cloth around the severed head. Her own neck is thick and taut. Both women have double chins. The woman with no name, the maid, is crouching. Her scarf is light

and has deep living folds, like a brain, like my back.

There's a lot of cloth in this picture. The figures are big.

The smell of sizing. The altered pattern in its envelope on the sewing chair. It's a half size. We have three yards of cloth. We stretch it across the dining room table. Blond wood. Sticky varnish on the corners of the chairs. Swinging doors lead back to the kitchen. I pull on the diagonal, move to change the angle, then pull again against my mother. We are straightening the grain.

Balance this with two women in the painting. The arms. The tension. The light. Frame it in the sliding glass door, with the curtains for drapes, those long white hanging curtains with dog hair on the lining and smudges from his nose on the glass.

We take the fact that we are fat and wrap it in cloth like an enemy's head, except we can't chop it off.

Those women in the story of the painting ate. The bible tells me so. Even in the time of famine, they ate corn, figs, bread and cheese, with wine and oil. They look no thinner than my mother and I. They look no fatter than my mother and I. I don't know what the models ate. It does not matter to me.

It is beautiful, this picture of us stretching the cloth. There is passion in the long, taut fold of it between us. Our bellies touch the edges of the table as we lean over it.

My mother is helping me make a nice blouse. She had widened the pattern and will take the darts. She marks where they go with colored tracing paper and a spiked metal wheel. I love her. She calls me in to fasten her long-line bra. It takes all my strength to do this.

Two women dance. One wears a long scarf, silver and blue. Her black pants are loose and puff out across the form of her lower belly so that the waves in her body there, all of that loose rhythm passes out through her fat and becomes subdued and muted in the fabric. Her big hips

send out currents that cross the paths of motion
from her shoulders and her back. She wears a red
shirt. It shines. The red goes darker deeper back in
the folds of her fat, then pulls bright and flat
across her thicker places as the music pulls those
hips up and they swing like power through the
air, sending flutters down the pant legs, and her
breasts fall like grace past the ends of her scarf.

      The second woman wears no shoes. A new
song starts. She is jumping, streaming color. Her
feet lift. The music sparks. Her calves are bare
and pale under dark hair until the cloth starts
halfway up them, strips of yellow orange, green
pink, gold blue, sideways stripes that circle more
and more leg as they stretch and quiver on up.
Her ringed thighs shake, they bounce, they shake.
She jumps. Her belly rises as she hits the floor,
floats up full, tied in a white sash, big soft circle
of cloth that could almost wish itself skin, but
there are not wishes for cloth, there're just its
properties, the color and the weight and the
width to give it a place wound tight enough for
room for breath around so much wild fatness,
making its own song in motion, making a song
in largeness, the fat and the sash together up
with ripples, down with passion, and the woman
moving herself all over, even her chin is shaking,
even her fingers dart and wander, even her
clothes are with her. ■

Relevant Books

Beck, Evelyn Torton, ed. 1982. *Nice Jewish Girls*. Boston:
    Beacon Press.
Fine, Elsa Honig. 1979. *Women and Art*. Montclair, NJ:
    Allanheld & Schram.
Rich, Adrienne. 1979. *On Lies, Secrets and Silence*. New
    York: W. W. Norton.
Schoenfielder, Lisa, and Wieser, Barb, eds. 1983.
    *Shadow on a Tightrope: Writings by Women on Fat
    Oppression*. San Francisco: Aunt Lute.

Women, Lesbians and Prostitution:

A Workingclass Dyke Speaks Out Against Buying Women for Sex*

by Toby Summer**

*I am thankful that *Lesbian Ethics* exists; without it, no one could hear my written voice over the roar of the Man's lies. I am also deeply grateful to those women who make my life possible in an impossible world. I thank you for your guidance, insight, truth-saying, assistance, criticism, patience, love and support. Without you, my courage would have failed me here.

**Toby Summer is not my real name. I do not use my real name because I don't want to be exposed to the sexual humiliation that goes with having been abused as a prostitute. It never ends. No one who knows who I am is authorized to "come out" for me; if, when, where, how, to whom, and for what purpose I *do* choose to identify myself, it is *my* choice. It is the only control that I have that leaves me any human dignity.

In *Lesbian Ethics* (1987).

Dedication

To the woman in my life who knows most what this has cost the both of us.

Introduction

Shining bright red, a miniature box of wooden matches sits next to my flat blue cigarette package. I bought the cigarettes, but some man forgot the matches when he left. The matchbox is embossed with gold, two circles. Inside the smaller circle, an owl sits on the stump of a redwood tree. On the left of the owl, there is a stick-figure drawing of a whole living redwood. On the right, child-like squiggles represent flying birds. Between the two circles, bold capital letters name the institution issuing the matchbox: BOHEMIAN CLUB. It is world famous; infamous, more accurately. War lords of this outlaw nation belong to this exclusive club, this men-only club.

While week-ending with a friend on the Russian River, I once penetrated the Bohemian Club's summer encampment's security. We strolled right through the center of camp. Structurally it looked like Girl Scout camp, but felt different. Bohemians don't allow girls.

This club may soon have to hire women as workers because they lost a case in court for sex discrimination in employment. If and when they do, it won't be the first time they've paid money to women, just the first time for non-sexual work.

I draw the above frame around the subject that I want to address to my community. This frame of men with absolute power and women with so little starkly shows that men make the rules and women do what we're told to do. This is a system that uses class and race to divide women from each other, but it is based on sex dis-

231

crimination. Prostitution and pornography are graphic practices of female sexual slavery within this system; the major difference between the two practices is that in pornography there is a permanent record of the woman's abuse that can be sold again and again.

I do not deny that women are hungry for freedom and equality; I am such a woman. I do not deny that women make hard "choices," nor do I deny that women find many ways to resist male supremacy. I have made such choices and continue to devise ways to resist, too. I simply underline the obvious; women do not rule. We have not consented to this system; our consent is not necessary or required. Men set the standards and women either go along and get along or try to think of ways to resist without getting killed. We get killed either way.

I.
Connections

In *Sex Work: Writings by Women in the Sex Industry*, a newly released book by Cleis Press edited by Frederique Delacoste and Priscilla Alexander,[1] the Bohemian Club is mentioned by name in at least two prostitutes' stories. The first woman stiffly walks us through the staging area of her experience as though it were a grade B movie set. She doesn't say how she feels. Her description struck me as perfunctory and disconnected. Scarlot Harlot's profile of

the Bohemians is one of her eleven submissions to *Sex Work*; her style is much more personal and engaging. She also admits that she'd make more money in a massage parlor than working the river's rich trade. To understand the amounts involved, we have to move to another story in *Sex Work* called "In the Massage Parlor." It gets specific: $10 for a "tip," or a $15 blowjob that deflates into a $5 "tip." The massage parlor worker also reveals how she feels about the actual "work" that she does.

> When they [the johns] touch my breasts, I tell myself they're not really touching me…[a]nd sometimes I wonder how I can let the men do that. I wonder what is left for me. I wonder where *I* am. (p. 63)

In *Sex Work*, Joan Nestle has contributed a piece called "Lesbians and Prostitutes: A Historical Sisterhood." She says, "Besides recognizing the history of prostitutes as a valuable source for lesbian history, another connection that emerges is the lesbian customer [sic] and protector of prostitutes" (p. 238). She illustrates this with "the wonderful and moving story" of Jeanne Bonnet who is a transvestite and a john, who winds up "decid[ing] to enlist some of the women she visited [sic] in her all-women's gang" (p. 239). Blanche Buneau, won away from her pimp by Bonnet, is shot and killed by him in their bedroom. The year is 1876. Nestle adds later, "Lesbians have and still do turn to prostitutes for

sexual comfort [sic] as well as work as prostitutes themselves" (p. 249). Nestle attempts to draw connections between prostitutes and lesbians, but she has no radical analysis of the condition of women, lesbians or prostitutes.

There *are* connections between lesbians and prostitutes. I know because I am one. A lesbian. An ex-prostitute. I have lived the connection. I still live daily with the results. I have been a lesbian for about thirty years. Coming out butch (transvestite actually) as a young teenager in the late '50s meant that I couldn't finish school, couldn't get a regular job, couldn't rent a place to live after home became unbearable. The irony of loving women—which created a situation for me (actually created by an ageist, classist, and sexist society whereby the alternative to jail and the street was the street, jail and fucking men for a meal, small change, and a temporary bed—is only surpassed by the damage. Consider the fact that I learned what sexuality meant from johns and pimps before I could find out what it *might* mean with the girl I loved. This lesson is not erasable. My body remembers all of it. It seems that bodies learn—in the body, physically—how sex is to be *felt*, not just done or gone through. I submit to my readers that it was not a good thing for this girl-child, this young lesbian to do with her bright-fired self.

II.
The Man's Lie: Strategy and Damage

The removing of oneself from one's body is a strategy for immediate survival; many prostitutes acknowledge this. This numbing—whether done like other torture victims do it or done with drugs and alcohol—is flight from that which is intolerable. Numbing mechanisms become reflex quickly. Reversing the process, later or in other circumstances, is difficult. It is my belief that such numbing in sexual assault situations sets women up for tolerating abuse, especially prostitution and sado-masochism.

Although I used this strategy as often as not, I also used a more damaging one at the same time. Today, I call this second strategy the Man's lie, but then I called it pro-sex[2] and my choice.

The Man's lie is still passing as truth not only from the Man but also through the lips of women, who—like I did—believe the lie. I mean, when Scarlot Harlot quotes her friend, Priscilla Alexander, as saying, "The right to be a prostitute is as important as the right not to be one. It is the right to set the terms of one's *own* sexuality… [my emphasis]" (*Sex Work*, p. 61), what I hear is that someone thinks that prostitution has something to do with *women* owning our own bodies—somehow—while at the same time selling the very same bodies to

men who hate women, whores[3] and lesbians and who do not make any excuses for their hatred.

This mind-fuck is very familiar to me; I thought for the longest time that I had invented it. I double-fucked myself for years before coming face-to-face with the truth of how male supremacist sexuality got to me. Not just remembering, but feeling; not just looking at all of it momentarily, but living it; not just opened up, but analyzed from a radical feminist politic for what it is and does. I have not *always* been a feminist, but I have always wanted to be free and female.

What I did in my mind *did* have something to do with freedom when I spoke the Man's lie silently to myself about prostitution. I felt closer to freedom when I told myself that I chose what happened (even the rapes), that I felt OK about what was done to my body (even against my will), that the sex in the room had something to do with me and my sexuality (even though when she was in the room, too—my lover—the only thing I tried to do was keep him interested in me so he wouldn't fuck her…some butch role), that the nausea-alienation-bruises-humiliation-STDs (sexually transmitted diseases)-poverty-abortion all were somehow fixable with what amounts to an EST positive attitude.

Oppressed people develop a sixth sense with which we anticipate the next move of our enemy in order to try to be successfully out of the way or in

the most acceptable pose. The EST positive attitude served that purpose, as well as twisting my own mind; that is, the Man's lie not only took the truth away from me, but it also served the Man by allowing him to point to me and say, "See. She loves it. She chose it. She's even a lesbian…they all want it. Women are whores by nature."

This strategic lie attempted to turn my degradation into something else, something more human, something that was not force and coercion. Poverty and oppression against women and lesbians certainly qualify as force and coercion, even if the barrel of the gun is behind the curtain of sex. What was accomplished with this lie was not a changed reality but merely a renaming of reality for something other than what it was. Reality did not change until I changed it, personally, for me; I got a different "job." I wasn't successful the first or second times. Even after I got out, I took my EST positive attitude with me when I went. What it didn't explain was why I'd rather work in a hot commercial laundry for $1.00 per hour than fuck another man. The Man's lie should have been exposed at that point, but it wasn't. I hid behind the fact that I was a lesbian; that is, I told myself that I just didn't want to fuck *men*. There was no understanding that there was something wrong with what happened to me as a *woman*. That lie stayed coiled like a viper for many years, waiting.

The lies that I've lived with, trying to make prostitution into anything other than what it is, are why I'm writing this paper; them and the damage. I did not want to do this paper. I hate every minute that I have been forced to spend on it. Like every fuck. Confronting how I've been hurt is the hardest thing that I've had to do in my life. A hard life, if I may say so. It is humiliating to acknowledge victimization. It is really quite simple: if you lose, you don't win. One cannot be hurt and not be a victim to the perpetrator, and to all those who come after to watch the show. To avoid further abuse by the sexual practice of humiliation, I claimed the intolerable as my own, because being a victim was and still is intolerable. What I am doing in this paper is the intolerable. I want you to know that. I'm doing it because I can't stand it that lesbians are buying women for sex and calling it progress, freedom, our sexuality, lesbian politics. I cannot stand the pretense of regard towards the women bought. Buying a human being is *not* regard. It is another lie. Prostitution is not freedom, not just another job. It is the abuse of women. It is sexual slavery. Period.

I want to say one thing about "healing." For me, it is a fact that so-called healing is an empty and desperate gesture towards that which we do not have: freedom to be equal, cre-

ative and as safe as men are safe. I know that some damage is permanent; that is one of the reasons to *stop* what happens to women. Among other damages, what has outraged me most deeply is the damage done to *my* sexuality; it is the one thing that I had thought that I had saved[4] out of that disgusting abuse. Somehow. I despair of any hope to undo this damage.[5]

I wonder to myself what it means that so many women lovers have told me that our love-making was "the best it's ever been" when what I held in my body was this incredible abuse. Once a whore, always a whore? I mean, how could they not feel what was going on? Was I that good of a performer? I'm not talking about faking orgasm either. I'm talking about how orgasm *felt*. How the sexuality itself felt. Fucking my way to heaven with thousands of orgasms and many truly loved partners did not "heal" the abuse. It may actually have deepened the learned sexual dynamic; it certainly caused confusion between this dynamic and any regard and respect we enjoyed with each other.

While I may not believe in "healing," I do believe in change.

III.
Sexuality Inequality

Dominance and submission is the basic dynamic of sexuality; regard for an equal is not sexy. Hierarchy is sexy. Power is sexy. Vulnerability is sexy. Humilia-

tion is a sexual practice. It is humiliating to be a second class citizen; that's why men keep women second class. Men as a class devised male supremacy because men—but not only men—find it exciting to use force and coercion. "The good news is it isn't biological."[6] This dynamic is best expressed through prostitution; ruling class men buying women to feel their power manifested. Workingclass men, middle-class men, men of all races and ages, disabled men and gay men are also to be counted as johns when I start counting. Name your category and I'll tell you what he looked like. It is felt in bodies as sexual, this expression of power. (It is a sexual rush to just contemplate it; ever watch some up-scale man thumb through a *Vogue* magazine? He consumes it like other men do actual pornography. Watch the body language. Whores are good at noticing men's body language. I watch them, openly. It disturbs them to be watched.)

I know that some gay men do not flinch from fucking women or lesbians. My own experience stands: some of my johns were gay men who just thought I was a young teenage boy turning tricks for spending money (blowjobs reveal nothing in terms of biology and I consistently passed for a straight boy when I chose to), but some of them knew I was a lesbian and thought it cute to buy a gay "sister." Someone once asked me why it was that gay men seemed to have a stake in *female* prostitution; I think I know. Our gay brothers directly profit from keeping all women down and prostitution is central to keeping women down as a class; gay men sometimes use women that way, too.

Without dominance and submission sexual boredom sets in. My guess about why many lesbian couples who stay together over time seem to coast to a dead stop sexually—or at least turn to on a slow bell—is that familiarity breeds a working knowledge of the other person, while commonality creates a rough-cut version of respect. That is, the more we like each other and the more actual respect we have the less dominance and submission is left, and therefore sexual feelings are not aroused as easily. Even built-in hierarchies like class, race, age, disability *sometimes* soften over time. Heterosexual hierarchy is much less likely to soften because *male* and *female* are terms defined by the dynamic of dominance and submission; it is categorically defined as *sexual* hierarchy where other hierarchies are not seen immediately as necessarily sexual. (They are, but it requires some analysis to get there from here, e.g., pornography shows us that Black women are used in specific ways to make their skin into a sexual organ to be then violated like genitals. We *do* find much visible bruising on Black women's bodies in pornography.)

I want to ask my community: when we have sexual feel-ings, *what* are we feeling? Is it the pleasure and danger, perhaps? Have we eroticized our own destruction, as in the *Story of O* by Pauline Reage? Do we, like O (stands for "nothing"), murder ourself? *I wonder what there is left for me. I wonder where I am.* Or, do we, like Pat Califia, San Francisco's picture perfect 'lesbian' sadist (who left town after allegedly carving an unwanted swastika into a workingclass dyke's body [I know the Jewish nurse who had to clean the wound], and who "...couldn't figure out how to reach orgasm with a [woman] lover") turn 180 degrees from 'sexual dysfunction' into a sadist who would rather fuck a hot male masochist than a vanilla lesbian?[7]

It seems to me that what might have been Califia's original problem is simply that two women—without more—don't generate enough dominance and submission for her arousal: the sexual dynamic of hierarchy was missing. I think that perhaps more women than Califia might feel this way. Maybe sado-masochism has been the key to inventing arousal, so that orgasm is possible for some lesbians. I know that butch-femme roles work that way even when

I can't stand it that lesbians are buying women for sex and calling it progress, freedom, our sexuality, lesbian politics.

mixed-and-matched (kiki in '50s language). I know that many, if not all, of my women lovers were aroused by what they perceived to be my butch ways. The difference between Califia and myself is only a matter of degree, not content. Sexual hierarchy *is* sexy. This is why I think that many lesbians have embraced sado-masochism and other trappings of male supremacist sexuality such as pornography, prostitution, strip shows, etc., as a "newly found, previously denied, to-be-explored" sexuality that we need to adopt, adapt, whitewash and call our own. (I also think that some lesbians learned "their" sado-masochism directly from gay men, as well as from prostitutes, ex-prostitutes and pornography.)

Prostitutes have been known to express our utter contempt for the johns that use us, but usually only to each other. We do not correct the power imbalance when we do this, although it does feel briefly better to vent the outrage and disgust. This is one way to acknowledge abuse of our bodies while attempting to block the fact that we are second class citizens being used for what women are: sex. The bravado about having power over men because men buy us is simply bullshit. "When those who dominate you get you to take the initiative in your own human destruction, you have lost more than any oppressed people yet has ever gotten back."[8]

The prostitute who performs as a female sadist, a dominatrix, does not reverse the dynamic of dominance and submission. It may be true that she has "complete power" (*Sex Work*, p. 51) over the male masochist's body for those moments that she is paid to do what she is told to do by him; but I think that is a matter of this man wanting to violate the social taboo[9] against men giving up male power. It is also true that the power of male supremacy is so great that a man can feel very safe even while he chooses to toy with "submission" momentarily. Let me suggest to you that if the dominatrix *used* that "power" that she has during this singular moment in history—in the way that men use their power over women—she'd be either in jail or dead. It is phony power.

While men eroticize the "exchange" of money for sex (arousing in and of itself because it actualizes and symbolizes the woman's *subordination*), the female sadist *may* eroticize her perception of "power." This is learning sexual hierarchy from the dominant's point of view. However, individual perceptions do not alter social structures. It is conceivable— even likely—that some women have adopted this point of view as their "own." This is possible because dominance and submission is learned behavior. If and when some women learn to eroticize dominance in its complete manifestation, what we will have will be biologically female people who are socially men. That is, it is possible that such a woman could eroticize the murder—sexual murder—of men. Picture a female Green River Murderer who murders men. For sex. There can be no subordination of anybody without the ever-present threat of murder to give the threat life. Liberal men who promote sexuality-at-any-cost for "women, too" probably have not thought about this possibility. Even if they have, what it would mean—socially—would not be what it means for a man to do it to a woman while male supremacy remains intact. Biological hopscotch cannot alter the system. Social transformation to *female* supremacy would have to occur before it would mean the same thing that it means now.

Personally, I think that it's not what I have in mind when I think of freedom.

IV.
About Class Solidarity

I have watched with some interest an element of organized pro-prostitution women adopt language from the organized labor movement. They argue that prostitution is just another job, albeit a relatively high paying one. They call pimps "managers" and johns "customers." They say that what is wrong with the "business" is that it is illegal, or, as in the case of Nevada, that the State controls prostitution. They claim that what is needed is a union to bargain for wages (already high, they say), hours (already good, they say), and working conditions. If wages and hours are already good, the issue must be working conditions. These same women argue that what is better about prostitution than other jobs for women is that prostitutes have "control" over what they do, what they "choose" to do. They don't explain why prostitutes can't control pimps and johns who hurt them right now. They slide past hard issues and blame them on the illegal nature of prostitution.

The fact that prostitution

is illegal does not explain why men sexually murder women and children for sex. The fact that police do not seem to care about dead prostitutes, or other dead women either, does not explain why men do it. The fact that some police officers are corrupt and brutal when they harass and arrest women for prostitution is a secondary issue.

It is not that I think that prostitutes should be arrested; I do not. My solution would be to make *buying* women illegal, as well as all third-party involvement, but to "allow women to sell their bodies" without legal penalty. This would put real power into the hands of prostitutes; they could overlook the crime committed against them by the john if he abided by their agreement, e.g., paid them, did not otherwise abuse them. This suggestion is not a solution to prostitution; it is a transitional band-aid.

None of this addresses the system which *requires* male sexual access to women and children at all times. The analysis exhibited in the "business-as-usual" presentation of prostitution is one that does not in any way challenge the harm of prostitution itself. If workingclass people had no analysis of capitalism, then what we would have is what this element of organized prostitution has: no structural challenge to the status quo. Men *must* have this sexual access to women and children. (Why?) Fringe benefits like worker's compensation, demands for no more arrests, or somehow resisting torture and

murder are OK as far as they go, but they do not challenge the system of male supremacy of which prostitution is the ultimate systematic expression. Trying to make an inhumane system more humane with reformatory adjustments is like spitting in the ocean: I'm not against it, but it doesn't do much.

Finally, I want to say that—as an ex-prostitute, a workingclass woman, a radical labor organizer—I have to wonder if the women who are using the language of organized labor are seriously trying to make common cause with working people. I wonder about this because of the contempt that is frequently expressed for other women who work at low-paying, low-status jobs everyday, who do it all their lives, who frequently challenge *their* wages, hours and working conditions (including sexual harassment). For example, in *Sex Work*, Scarlot Harlot says, "Ex-prostitutes are out of touch with the true glories of the trade. Plus, they were never very good at it. That's why they're ex-prostitutes" (p. 123). (However, she also said on the TV show "People Are Talking," KPIX, San Francisco, July 2, 1987, that she didn't want to be doing this for money but couldn't make as much money otherwise. She was the only woman on the show who still did prostitution; no one asked her why she didn't want to do it.) In *Sex Work* "Aline" says, "I much preferred exhibiting myself, flirting, showing off my body than working at some shit-

job cleaning someone else's toilet for poverty level income" (pp. 131–2). (However, on the next page she finds her "work" intolerable and says it's "time to clean toilets.") Prostitutes, ex-prostitutes, and "feminists" cannot succeed in making common cause by ridiculing other women who are struggling to get by *without* fucking men.

V.
Sisterhood: Just Another Brotherhood?

Now what about lesbians buying women, prostitutes, other lesbians? For sex. Like men. It isn't news.[10]

Lesbian pimps have always been around. Lesbian prostitutes have always been around. Lesbian johns have always been around. I've known some of them. What has not been challenged is the harm done to those women who are positioned to be bought and sold. It is the failure of "feminism" to leave the structure of male supremacy intact while women pry their way into it. It is outrageous to me that women attorneys, who call themselves feminists, who don't have to sell themselves to men for $15.00 a blowjob, say, "I think that prostitution is an excellent way to earn a living" (Flo Kennedy, attorney, activist, TV interviewer, *MS Magazine*, July 1987, p. 18). Kennedy is just the most recent example. Attorney Nan Hunter, who wrote the FACT brief against the Dworkin-MacKinnon anti-pornography civil rights ordinance, said in it, "A range of feminist imagination and expression in the realm of sexuality has barely begun to find voice. Women need the freedom and socially recognized space to *appropriate* for themselves the robustness of what traditionally has been male language" [my emphasis].

Never mind the *other* women, who are not attorneys, who are crushed by the weight of the pornographers, pimps and johns. I want to know why anyone thinks they have a *right* to buy a woman for sex.

The connections between pornographers and women who call themselves feminists have always fascinated me. For example, we find Susie Bright, editor of *On Our Backs* (lesbian pornography) in such publications as Penthouse's *Forum*, and *Hustler*. See "Confessions of a Teenage Lesbian," by Susie Bright, "a real live dyke," in *Hustler*, March 1986. I found in *Sex Work* another such connection. Debi Sundahl, also known as "Fanny Fatale," a stripper, says that the first place she worked was called the Lusty Lady Theater and that the owners of this place "...were involved in founding...the Institute for Advanced Study of Human Sexuality in San Francisco" (p. 176). Sundahl takes credit for "...start[ing] the first women-only strip show at a lesbian bar in San Francisco" (p. 177), for publishing the first issue of *On Our Backs*, "a lesbian sexual entertainment magazine," and for making "adult or

x-rated videos for lesbians under the name Fatale" (p. 178). It is also interesting to me that Phyllis Lyon (of Del Martin/Phyllis Lyon fame) is the Registrar for this Institute; she is also a FACT member.

I can't say I have a lot of hope for change. I can't say I've noticed much difference between the heterosexual community, the gay male community, and lesbians, except that women as a class do not have power as men do. But I have noticed that some women are aspiring to join the Bohemian Club. Similarly, in San Francisco there has been a hoopla around the 87th U.S. Open Golf Championship hosted at the S.F. Olympic Club's lakeside golf course (one of several men-only clubs; it has 7000 members). Seems like the city leases seventeen acres of land to them and that it is unseemly for a city run by a woman mayor, a woman president of the board of supervisors, and a woman city attorney, to contribute to the success of the club's discriminatory policy. News, it is: the city may not renew the lease unless the exclusionary policy changes (*S.F. Chronicle*, June 23, 1987).

Some women seem to think that if they can do what men do then "we" will be equal. The question to be asked is, if women get to do what men get to do, and one of the things men get to do is buy women, who is going to be left for anyone to buy? Some women want to rule, and have the privileges, too. Some lesbians buy women

for sex like the Bohemian Club members do, **already**.

Notes

1 *Sex Work* is a collection of stories written by women who have been or still are inside the sex industry. I considered submitting an article to *Sex Work*, but decided it was not a context for my viewpoint. At least one contributor, Sarah Wynter, was not told that *Sex Work* would be co-edited by Priscilla Alexander, co-director of C.O.Y.O.T.E. (Call Off Your Old Tired Ethics), a San Francisco based group which addresses "prostitutes' issues." This group has very liberal politics. For example, what is wrong with prostitution is *not* "...the stigma imposed on sex work, keep[ing] all women from determining their own sexuality" (Priscilla Alexander, "Prostitution: A Difficult Issue for Feminists," *Sex Work*, p. 184). Identifying "stigma" as what is wrong is a re-naming of reality that unfocuses perception of real harm to women in prostitution. Most people recognize harm when they see it. Whatever the response, the harm *is* noticed. The shift from seeing harm to criticizing emotional responses emanating from the perception of harm targets a non-primary issue. It is a smokescreen, used so that no one will challenge the *actual* harm.

The *Sex Work* bibliography, section 8—"The Pornography Debate," is skewed: with exactly one exception, one half of the "debate," the radical feminist critique, is missing. The political bias of *Sex Work* seems to grow out of its association with COYOTE. Alexander is the only contributor who has *not* worked in the sex industry. COYOTE is the only contact for women organizing on the issue for which an address and phone number is given, although other groups with different analyses are represented in *Sex Work*.

2 Andrea Dworkin (*Intercourse*, New York: Free Press, 1987, "Communion," pp. 48–9) writes, "Lost in the simple-minded prosex chauvinism of Right and Left is the real meaning of affirmation, or any consciousness of the complexity—the emotional tangledness—of a human life. 'It is really quite impossible,' writes James Baldwin (*Notes of a Native Son*, Boston: Beacon Press, 1984, p. 131), 'to be affirmative about anything which one refuses to question; one is doomed to remain inarticulate about anything which one hasn't by an act of imagination, made one's own.' There is no imagination in fetishlike sexual conformity; and no questions are being asked in political discourse on sex about hope and sorrow, intimacy and anguish, communion and loss."

3 The word *whore* is an insult to all women, commonly, like the word *dyke*. When I use it here, I do not mean it in that way, although I am not attempting to reclaim it as *dyke* has been reclaimed by some lesbians. I use it because I want my readers to occasionally *feel* the feeling associated with it, I also think that no one has the right to use the word *whore* unless that person has been one of us. And then, only carefully.

4 Andrea Dworkin, *Op. Cit.*, p. 50: "Truth is harder to bear than ignorance, and so ignorance is valued more—also because the status quo depends on it; but love depends on self-knowledge, and self-knowledge depends on being able to bear the truth. For Baldwin, in his fiction and essays, being human means that one pays for everything one knows and for everything one refuses to know; that 'you have to, in order to live, finally, make so many difficult and dangerous choices that the one thing you're really trying to save is what you lose. And what you're trying to save is your ability to touch another human being or be touched by that person'" (James Baldwin and Nikki Giovanni, *A Dialogue*, Philadelphia: J.B. Lippincott Co., 1973, p. 86)."

5 In *Sex Work* Gail Pheterson claims that it is "…another illusion…that male sexual violence causes irreparable damage to female personality" (p. 224). I say it is no illusion.

6 Catharine A. MacKinnon, "Pleasure Under Patriarchy," In, *Theories and Paradigms of Human Sexuality*, Plenum Press, in press.

7 The failed orgasm quote is from Pat Califia, "We Know What We Want," *Sinister Wisdom*, Vol. 1, No. 2, Fall 1976, p. 67. Her preference for a male is stated in her, "Unraveling the Sexual Fringe: A Secret Side of Lesbian Sexuality," *The Advocate*, Dec. 27, 1979.

8 Andrea Dworkin, *Op. Cit.*, pp. 142–3.

9 It is my opinion that taboos exist to be violated and that such violation is a sexual practice. Rape laws are that way. Likewise prohibition against sex with children. Sexual crimes are enhanced by male laws against them; such laws do not seem to deter very much. It is sexy to be an "outlaw." Violation of anything is sexy. Especially women.

10 Lesbian battery isn't news, either. But it has been only recently taken up as a political issue by the lesbian community. (Battered women's shelters have been reluctant to accept either battered lesbians or battered prostitutes, a "connection" missed by Joan Nestle.) It is no solution, but the feminists who organized the first conference on lesbian violence are to be commended on their work (May 2, 1987, San Francisco). However, the tough issues of sado-masochism, pornography and prostitution were not addressed; when I brought them up they were shuffled aside. For instance, I want to know about the connection that pornography has to both battery and sado-masochism in our community. ■

tremors

by Caryatis Cardea

your head is on my shoulder
while somewhere
the earth shifts

feminism produces a rage
     creates it
     feeds it
watches it grow

we attempt to make of this
a strength
as
i was raped
i am a survivor

this is an act of endurance
but confronting the evidence of our powerlessness
does not equate with power

we have been raped
     nearly all of us
we have
     every one of us
been robbed

     with what stubbornness do womyn
     robbed of our lives
     continue to live

many men are islands
don't believe the saying
but no womon
is separate from womonkind

the bond of sister
       mother daughter lover friend
is reality
is community
is

even the sell-out
       in the comfort of her counterfeit success
has not beaten us
does not truly hasten our demise
despite our fears to the contrary

for to live
unconnected to womyn
is only a hollow denial of our bond

the contrast is unbearable
your head is cradled on my shoulder

the newspaper says a womon
       young
was raped and beaten by six men

her life stretches before her now
an unbroken series of days to relive
       remember
       vomit her fear
but her hatred
she will be told
is an unacceptable response to theirs

terror of living alone
or on a ground floor
or in the country
of being alone on a city street or in a park
or getting to her car
or into an elevator
of dancing studying sleeping
or waking
this is called the survival of rape

her life is before her
so many mornings
and nights ice-starred with memory
of this act of imbalance
            proof to them
            of her powerlessness
            in their world
this theft of her power
            her freedom
this womon robbed
of her life

and when she knows it all
the balance must change
the scales alter

you stir
and settle again more restfully
your head secure on my shoulder

we are at rest
we are in balance

but somewhere
always
the earth shifts

A different version was published in
Sinister Wisdom (1989).

Lesbian "Sex"[1]

by Marilyn Frye

The reasons the word "sex" is in quotation marks in my title are two: one is that the term "sex" is an inappropriate term for what lesbians do, and the other is that whatever it is that lesbians do that (for lack of a better word) might be called "sex" we apparently do damned little of it. For a great many lesbians, the gap between the high hopes we had some time ago for lesbian sex and the way things have worked out has turned the phrase "lesbian sex" into something of a bitter joke. I don't want to exaggerate this: things aren't so bad for all lesbians, or all of the time. But in our communities as a whole, there is much grumbling on the subject.

It seems worthwhile to explore some of the meanings of the relative dearth of what (for lack of a better word) we call lesbian "sex."*

Recent discussions of lesbian "sex" frequently cite the finding of a study on couples by Blumstein and Schwartz[2], which is perceived by most of us who discuss it as having been done well, with a good sample of couples—lesbian, male homosexual, heterosexual non-married and heterosexual married couples. These people apparently found that lesbian couples "have sex" far less frequently than any other type of couple, that lesbian couples are less "sexual" as couples and as individuals than anyone else. In their sample, only about one-third of lesbians in relationships of two years or longer "had sex" once a week or more; 47% of lesbians in long-term relationships "had sex" once a month or less, while among heterosexual married couples only 15% had sex once a month or less. And they report that lesbians seem to be more limited in the range of their "sexual" techniques than are other couples.

When this sort of information first came into my circle of lesbian friends, we tended to see it as conforming to what we know from our own experience. But on reflection, looking again at what has been going on with us in our long-term relationships, the nice fit between this report and our experience seemed not so perfect after all.

It was brought to our attention during our ruminations on this that what 85% of long-term heterosexual married couples do more than once a month takes on the average eight minutes to do.[3]

In: *Sinister Wisdom* 35 (Summer/Fall, 1988), 46–54.

*When I speak of "we" and "our communities," I actually don't know exactly who that is. I know only that I and my lover are not the only ones whose concerns I address, and that similar issues are being discussed in friendship circles and communities other than ours (as witness, e.g., discussion in the pages of the *Lesbian Connection*). If what I say here resonates for you, so be it. If not, at least you can know it resonates for some range of lesbians and some of them probably are your friends or acquaintances.

Although in my experience lesbians discuss their "sex" lives with each other relatively little (a point to which I will return), I know from my own experience and from the reports of a few other lesbians in long-term relationships, that what we do that, on average, we do considerably less frequently, takes, on average, considerably more than eight minutes to do. It takes about thirty minutes, at the least. Sometimes maybe an hour. And it is not uncommon that among these relatively uncommon occurrences, an entire afternoon or evening is given over to activities organized around doing it. The suspicion arises that what 85% of heterosexual married couples are doing more than once a month and what 47% of lesbian couples are doing less than once a month is not the same thing.

I remember that one of my first delicious tastes of old gay lesbian culture occurred in a bar where I was getting acquainted with some new friends. One was talking about being busted out of the Marines for being gay. She had been put under suspicion somehow, and was sent off to the base psychiatrist to be questioned, her perverted tendencies to be assessed. He wanted to convince her she had only been engaged in a little youthful experimentation and wasn't really gay. To this end, he questioned her about the extent of her sexual experience.

What he asked was, "How many times have you had sex with a woman?" At this, we all laughed and giggled: what an ignorant fool. What does he think he means, "times?" What will we count? What's to *count*?

Another of my friends, years later, discussing the same conundrum, said that she thought that maybe every time you got up to go to the bathroom, that marked a "time." The joke about "how many times" is still good for a chuckle from time to time in my life with my lover. I have no memory of any such topic providing any such merriment in my years of sexual encounters and relationships with men. It would have been very rare indeed that we would not have known how to answer the question, "How many times did you do it?"

If what heterosexual married couples do that the individuals report under the rubric "sex" or "have sex" or "have sexual relations"* is something that in most instances can easily be individuated into countable instances, this is more evidence that it is not what long-term lesbian couples do…or, for that matter, what short-term lesbian couples do.

What violence did the lesbians do their experience by answering the same question the heterosexuals answered, as though it had the same meaning for them? How did the lesbians figure out how to answer

the questions "How frequently?" or "How many times?" My guess is that different individuals figured it out differently. Some might have counted a two- or three-cycle evening as one "time" they "had sex"; some might have counted it as two or three "times." Some may have counted as "times" only the times both partners had orgasms; some may have counted as "times" occasions on which at least one had an orgasm; those who do not have orgasms or have them far more rarely than they "have sex" may not have figured orgasms into the calculations; perhaps some counted as a "time" every episode in which both touched the other's vulva more than fleetingly and not for something like a health examination. For some, to count every reciprocal touch of the vulva would have made them count as "having sex" more than most people with a job or a work would dream of having time for; how do we suppose those individuals counted "times?" Is there any good reason why they should *not* count all those as "times?" Does it depend on how fulfilling it was? Was anybody else counting by occasions of fulfillment?

We have no idea how the individual lesbians surveyed were counting their "sexual acts." But this also raises the questions of how heterosexuals counted *their* sexual acts. By orgasms? By *whose* orgasms? If the havings of sex by hetero-

*This is the term used in the Blumstein and Schwartz questionnaire. In the text of their book, they use "have sex."

sexual married couples did take on the average eight minutes, my guess is that in a very large number of those cases the women did not experience orgasms. My guess is that neither the women's pleasure nor the women's orgasms were pertinent in most of the individuals' counting and reporting the frequency with which they "had sex."

So, do lesbian couples really "have sex" any less frequently than heterosexual couples? I'd say that lesbian couples "have sex" a great deal less frequently than heterosexual couples: by the criteria that I'm betting most of the heterosexual people used to count "times," lesbians don't have sex at all. No male orgasms, no "times." (I'm willing to draw the conclusion that heterosexual women don't have sex either; that what they report is the frequency with which their partners had sex.)

It has been said before by feminists that the concept of "having sex" is a phallic concept; that it pertains to heterosexual intercourse, in fact, primarily to hetero*sexist* intercourse, i.e., male-dominant-female-subordinate-copulation-whose-completion-and-purpose-is-the-male's-ejaculation. I have thought this was true since the first time the idea was put to me, some twelve years ago.[4] But I have been finding lately that I have to go back over some of the ground I covered a decade ago because some of what I

knew then I knew too superficially. For some of us, myself included, the move from heterosexual relating to lesbian relating was occasioned or speeded up or brought to closure by our knowledge that what we had done under the heading "having sex" was indeed male-dominant-female-subordination-copulation-whose-completion... etc. and it was not worthy of doing. Yet now, years later, we are willing to answer questionnaires that ask us how frequently we "have sex," and are dissatisfied with ourselves and with our relationships because we don't "have sex" enough. We are so dissatisfied that we keep a small army of therapists in business trying to help us "have sex" more.

We quit having sex years ago, and for excellent and compelling reasons. What exactly is our complaint now?

In all these years I've been doing and writing feminist theory, I have not until very recently written, much less published, a word about sex. I did not write, though it was suggested to me that I do so, anything in the SM debates; I left entirely unanswered an invitation to be the keynote speaker at a feminist conference about women's sexuality (which by all reports turned out to be an excellent conference). I was quite unable to think of anything but vague truisms to say, and very few of those. Feminist theory is grounded in experience; I have

always written feminist political and philosophical analysis from the bottom up, starting with my own encounters and adventures, frustrations, pain, anger, delight, etc. Sometimes this has no doubt made it a little provincial; but it has at least had the virtue of firm connection with *someone's* real, live experience (which is more than you can say for a lot of theory). When I put to myself the task of theorizing about sex and sexuality, it was as though I *had* no experience, as though there was no ground on which and from which to generate theory. But (if I understand the terminology rightly), I have in fact been what they call "sexually active" for close to a quarter of a century, about half my life, almost all of what they call one's "adult life," heterosexually, lesbianly and autoerotically. Surely I have experience. But I seem not to have *experiential knowledge* of the sort I need.

Reflecting on all that history, I realize that in many of its passages this experience has been a muddle. Acting, being acted on, choosing, desiring, pleasure and displeasure all akimbo: not coherently determining and connecting with each other. Even in its greatest intensity it has for the most part been somehow rather opaque to me, not fully in my grasp. My "experience" has in general the character more of a buzzing blooming confusion than of *experience*. And it has occurred in the midst of almost total silence on the part of others about their experience. The experience of others has for the most part also been opaque to me; they do not discuss or describe it *in detail* at all.

I recall an hours-long and heated argument among some eight or ten lesbians at a party a couple of years ago about SM, whether it is okay, or not. When Carolyn and I left, we realized that in the whole time not one woman had said one concrete, explicit, physiologically specific thing about what she actually *did*. The one arguing in favor of bondage: did she have her hands tied gently with ribbons or scarves, or harshly with handcuffs or chains? What other parts of her body were or weren't restrained, and by what means? And what parts of her body were touched, and how, while she was bound? And what liberty did she still have to touch in return? And if she had no such liberty, was it part of her experience to want that liberty and tension or frustration, or was it her experience that she felt pleased or satisfied not to have that liberty…? Who knows? She never said a single word at this level of specificity. Nor did anyone else, pro or con.

I once perused a large and extensively illustrated book on sexual activity by and for homosexual men. It was astounding to me for one thing in particular, namely, that its pages constituted a huge lexicon of *words*: words for acts and activities, their sub-acts, preludes and denouements, their stylistic variation, their sequences. Gay male sex, I realized then, is *articulate*. It is articulate to a degree that, in my world, lesbian "sex" does not remotely approach. Lesbian "sex" as I have known it, most of the time I have known it, is utterly *inarticulate*. Most of my lifetime, most of my experience in the realms commonly designated as "sexual" has been pre-linguistic, non-cognitive. I have, in effect, no linguistic community, no language, and therefore in one important sense, no knowledge.

In situations of male dominance, women are for the most part excluded from the formulation and validation of meaning and thereby denied the means to express themselves. Men's meanings, and not women's meanings, are encoded in what is presumed to be the whole population's language. (In many cases, both the men and the women assume it is everyone's language.) The meanings one's life and experience might generate cannot come fully into operation if they are not woven into language: they are fleeting, or they hover, vague, not fully coalesced, not connected, and hence not *useful* for explaining or grounding interpretations, desires, complaints, theories. In response to our understanding that there is something going on in patriar-chy that is more or less well described by saying women's meanings are not encoded in the dominant languages and that this keeps our experience from being fully formed and articulate, we have undertaken quite deliberately to discover, complete and encode our meanings. Such simple things as naming chivalrous gestures "insulting," naming Virginia Woolf a great writer, naming ourselves women instead of girls or ladies. Coining terms like "sexism," "sexual harassment" and "incestor." Mary Daly's new book is a whole project of "encoding" meanings, and we can all find examples of our own more local encodings.*

Meanings should arise from our bodily self-knowledge, bodily play, tactile communication, the ebb and flow of intense excitement, arousal, tension, release, comfort, discomfort, pain and pleasure (and I make no distinctions here among bodily, emotional, intellectual, aesthetic). But such potential meanings are more amorphous, less coalesced into discrete elements of a coherent pattern of meanings, of an *experience*, than any other dimensions of our lives. In fact, there are for many of us *virtually no meanings* in this realm because nothing of it is crystallized in a linguistic matrix.*

*I picked up the word "encoding" as it is used here from the novel *Native Tongue*, by Suzette Haden Elgin (NY: Daw Books, Inc., 1984). She envisages women identifying concepts, feelings, types of situations, etc., for which there are no words in English, and giving them intuitively appropriate names in a woman-made language called Láadan.

What we have for generic words to cover this terrain are the words "sex," "sexual" and "sexuality." In our efforts to liberate ourselves from the stifling woman-hating Victorian denial that women even *have* bodily awareness, arousal, excitement, orgasms and so on, many of us actively took these words for ourselves, and claimed that we *do* "do sex" and we *are* sexual and we *have* sexuality. This has been particularly important to lesbians because the very fact of "sex" being a phallocentric term has made it especially difficult to get across the idea that lesbians are not, for lack of a penis between us, making do with feeble and partial and pathetic half-satisfactions.** But it seems to me that the attempt to encode our lustiness and lustfulness, our passion and our vigorous carnality in the words "sex," "sexual" and "sexuality" has backfired. Instead of losing their phallocentricity, these words have imported the phallocentric meanings into and onto experience which is not in any way phallocentric. A web of meanings which maps emotional intensity, excitement, arousal, bodily play, orgasm, passion and relational adventure back onto a semantic center in male-dominant-female-subordinate-copulation-whose-completion-and-purpose-is-the-male's-ejaculation has been so utterly inadequate as to leave us speechless, meaningless, and ironically, according to the Blumstein and Schwartz report, "not as sexual" as couples or as individuals of any other group.

Our lives, the character of our embodiment, *cannot be* mapped back onto that semantic center. When we try to synthesize and articulate it by the rules of that mapping, we end up trying to mold our loving and our passionate carnal intercourse into explosive eight-minute events. That is not the timing and ontology of the lesbian body. When the only things that count as "doing it" are those passages of our interactions which most closely approximate a paradigm that arose from the meanings of the rising and falling penis, no wonder we discover ourselves to "do it" rather less often than do pairs with one or more penises present.

There are many cultural and social-psychological reasons why women (in white Euro-American groups, but also in many other configurations of patriarchy) would generally be somewhat less clear and less assertive about their desires and about getting their satisfactions than men would generally be. And when we pair up two women in a couple, it stands to reason that those reasons would double up and tend to make relationships in which there is a lowish frequency of clearly delineated desires and direct initiations of satisfactions. But for all the help it might be to lesbian bodies to work past the psychological and behavioral habits of femininity that inhibit our passions and pleasures, my suggestion is that what we have never taken seriously enough is the *language* which forecloses our meanings.

⚢

My positive recommendation is this: Instead of starting with a point (a point in the life of a body unlike our own) and trying to make meanings along vectors from that point, we would do better to start with a wide field of our passions and bodily pleasures and make meanings that weave a web across it. To begin creating a vocabulary that elaborates and expands our meanings, we should adopt a very wide and general concept of "doing it." Let it be an open, generous, commodious concept encompassing all the acts and activities by which we generate with each other pleasures and thrills, tenderness and ecstasy, passages of passionate carnality of whatever duration or profun-

*Carolyn Shafer has theorized that one significant reason why lesbian SM occasioned so much excitement, both positive and negative, is that lesbians have been starved for language—for specific, detailed, literal, particular, bodily talk with clear non-metaphorical references to parts of our bodies and the ways they can be stimulated, to acts, postures, types of touch. Books like *Coming to Power* feed that need, and call forth more words in response.

**Asserting that robustness and unladylikeness of our passions and actions, some of us have called some of what we do "fucking."

dity. Everything from vanilla to licorice, from puce to chartreuse, from velvet to ice, from cuddles to cunts, from chortles to tears. Starting from there, we can let our experiences generate a finer-tuned descriptive vocabulary that maps and expresses the differences and distinctions among the things we do, the kinds of pleasures we get, the stages and styles of our acts and activities, the parts of our bodies centrally engaged in the different kinds of "doing it," and so on. I would not, at the outset, assume that all of "doing it" is good or wholesome, nor that everyone would like or even tolerate everything this concept includes; I would not assume that "doing it" either has or should have a particular connection with love, or that it hasn't or shouldn't have such a connection. As we explain and explore and define our pleasures and our preferences across this expansive and heterogeneous field, teaching each other what the possibilities are and how to navigate them, a vocabulary will arise among us and by our collective creativity.

The vocabulary will arise among us, of course, only if we talk with each other about what we're doing and why, and what it feels like. Language is social. So is "doing it."

I'm hoping it will be a lot easier to talk about what we do, and how and when and why, and in carnal sensual detail, once we've learned to laugh at foolish studies that show that lesbians don't have sex as often

as, aren't as sexual as, and use fewer sexual techniques than other folks. ■

Notes

1 In its first version, this essay was written for the meeting of the Society for Women in Philosophy, Midwestern Division, November, 1987, at Bloomington, Indiana. It was occasioned by Claudia Card's paper, "Intimacy and Responsibility: What Lesbians Do" (published in the Institute for Legal Studies Working Papers, Series, 2, University of Wisconsin-Madison, Law School, Madison, WI 53706). Carolyn Shafer has contributed a lot to my thinking here, and I am indebted also to conversations with Sue Emmert and Terry Grant.

2 Philip Blumstein and Pepper Schwartz, *American Couples*, (NY: William and Morrow Company, 1983).

3 Dotty Calabrese gave this information in her workshop on long-term lesbian relationships at the Michigan Womyn's Music Festival, 1987. (Thanks to Terry for this reference.)

4 By Carolyn Shafer. See pp. 156–7 of my book, *The Politics of Reality* (The Crossing Press, 1983).

Part 3

New Ground

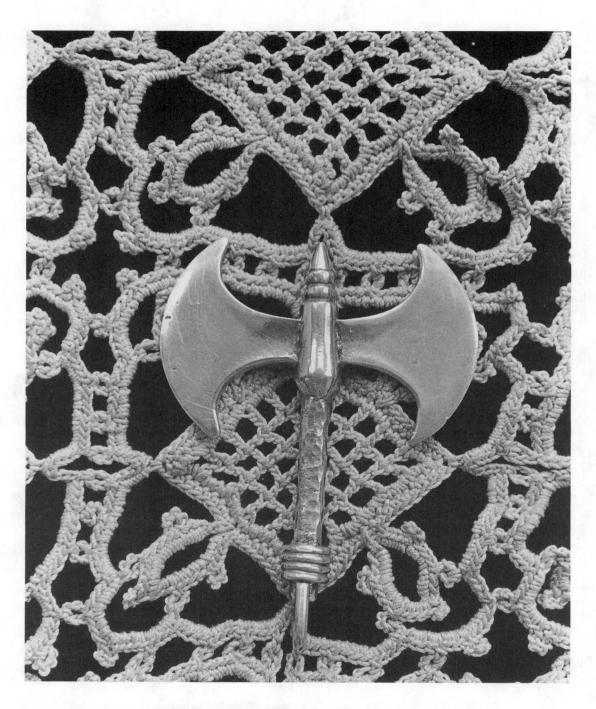

Cover for the 1st edition of *The Lesbian Path*,
ed. Margaret Cruikshank, 1980

Photo by Tee Corinne

On Singing Women's Praises

by Carolyn Gage

Yes, it's true—
I only know one song.

But that one song takes all the notes
And lasts forever.

In *Sinister Wisdom* 37 (Spring 1989)

New Ground
by Alix Dobkin

(2nd time)
You and me
We're goin' *out of bounds* (deep and dark)
We're goin' oh so far not even close
To yesterday
Seek *new thrills, easy* (adventures)
Brave, wild, sweet darlin'
Breathe deep, keep the faith (bear down, breathe easy)
We'll find (we're on)
Some new ground

One by one
We take each other home
We take our words, call each other girl
Whenever we please. We're gonna
Live together
Hold hands, kiss each other
On the mouth, just because
We love
This new ground, new ground

CHORUS:
> We are the women
> We are the loving women
> We've been around forever
> Deep in the hearts of women

Once we were
Separated from ourselves
Afraid and lonely for what we
Couldn't even name, we
Cried, despaired or
Died in flames, scorned and shamed
or worse. What heartbreak
Passion, rage has
Driven us
To new ground

(chorus)

Holidays
Start with Mississippi in the spring
Then mark time 'till those chilly nights
In Michigan, then
August ends, it's
To the coast to say good-bye
to Special, most devoted friends
We got so close
On new ground.

(chorus)

(repeat first verse with ( ))

*"New Ground" is on the *Yahoo Australia!*
recording (1990)
Words & music ©1986 Alix Dobkin

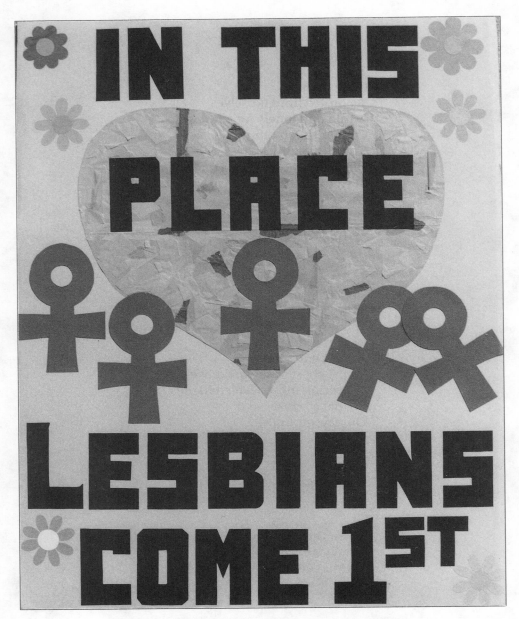

In This Place Lesbians Come First
by Diane F. Germain

Posters of Power

by Diane F. Germain

The posters I have created were mostly made to carry in the Lesbian and Gay Pride parades or for various protest marches (Myth CaliPORNia Kontest). They are basically made with as much "found" materials (junk or thrown away stuff) as possible. The backings are large pieces cut from refrigerator boxes or stiff cardboard from liquor displays discarded in the back of stores. Part of the point here is to use *free* things (so poor women can participate) and part is to take the *trash* that the patriarchy creates and make *ART* out of it. Another discovery that I made was that game boards are often discarded after the game pieces are lost or the children get bored. These folding boards, once spray-painted white, black, silver or covered with butcher paper, can hold a rude message that can be re-folded and carried easily to the demonstration ground and opened at any significant opportunity. Like one that says HOMOPHOBIA on both sides so the offending speaker and the audience behind can all see what you are objecting to. Quel plaisant!

In any case, the letters are cut out of black paper squares and then stuck down with glue dots applied sparingly on the edges. The graphics are cut from paper, too, with an added depth created by covering the big pink heart with layers of torn tissue in various colors of red, pink and orange. When I get a satisfactory design of a star or women's symbol, I make a stencil out of a manila folder and keep them on file to use in case there is a hurry-up need for a protest or support-Lesbians rally.

The phrases are rather universally known, mostly, except for "in this place Lesbians come first." In the late '70s when I was living in a humble grotto in Ocean Beach, I had parties and discussion groups for Lesbians only and made a long banner of colorful cut-out letters stapled together along a wide ribbon strung along the top of the walls. It was the first thing you saw when you came in the door. Later, I made a T-shirt of cut-out letters from Iron-on material that surrounded a giant heart. At the time, there were not so many places that one could have these messages made in a commercial business establishment. Then the final product, the poster, a portable "Lesbian Place" that we can be first in.

My lover Pamela now helps me cut and paste at home on the living room carpet. Talk about family values! ■

Poem of Affirmation

by Elliott

I'm a fat,
offensive
man-hating,
bitchy-witch of a dyke

And I am not alone

From *The Separatist Revolution* (1991).

Self-Portrait: Seeing Myself through Alice Walker's Eyes
by Jean Weisinger

So the World Can See

by Jean Weisinger

It was not my intention to photograph myself. When I was small, there were no photographs of me; I was the first-born of nine children. Seeing photos of them and not me led me to believe that I was from another place. So, as soon as I got my hands on a camera, I began taking images of my family, people in the community, writers, artists, and the sensitive and beautiful common folks, down to earth human beings;

like my mother and the women who sat around the kitchen table, drinking coffee, eating, laughing LOUD—and telling stories, telling their lives—all gone—dead before sixty—WHY?

At this point in my LIFE, I'm learning about the POWER of loving the SELF. The loss of my mother on October 6, 1989 has taught me this. Losing her has forced me to FACE myself;

who is JEAN?, what do I want?

Photography, like art, has been healing and therapeutic. I have come to know and love myself through both. Art saved my life in 1989 as photography is doing now.

These are powerful times, and I'm experiencing an enormous burst of power. Everything is possible and I can create my own reality;

dreams and visions do come TRUE.
My vision is to travel around the world and take photographs of
the beautiful, spirited EARTH'S PEOPLE—

and to make powerful photographic books as gifts to the world.

In October, 1990, after traveling to Germany, Amsterdam, England, and the East Coast of America to document the *I Am Your Sister* conference honoring Audre Lorde and her work, Audre said to me what many women had also been saying:

"Jean, you take beautiful, positive and powerful images of women—you need to show your work so the world can see."

A year later and still struggling to do my work, to survive as AFRICAN AMERICAN artist, I decided to do a photography book of black/white portraits of women around the world (currently in progress) called *A Community of Women*, with personal statements answering the question: *What Does Community Mean to Me?"*

Having an exhibition or even making postcards was too expensive at the time. HUNGRY for film, I began calling on the UNIVERSE. I began asking the universe, the souls of my AFRICAN/ NATIVE American, the spirits who walk among us, the spirits who speak to us through our dreams, our bodies, the trees and the wind, to help me SECURE the things that I need to do my work and to continue to document these times and the lives of those that cross my path.

In February, 1992, I was extremely happy and very thankful to get an opportunity to travel to CUBA. I went to Cuba with all the film that I needed, plus the love and support of someone very special to me. I went with the intention of taking photographs of the spirit of the CUBAN people.

After ten days and over 1500 photographs, I returned to the states in tears and overwhelmed with the "unconditional" love that I received and felt from the Cuban people and the way in which the country puts "PEOPLE BEFORE PROFIT."

In AUSTRALIA, NEW ZEALAND, and BALI it became clear to me that we are everywhere. I saw myself in the faces of the ABORIGINAL grandmothers dancing, singing, and sharing their witchetty grub in the bush of ALICE SPRINGS, in the magical place that the MOARI people took us, and I saw myself in the rice fields of BALI.

In San Francisco, I see myself in the trees desperately trying to SURVIVE, I see myself in the faces of my AFRICAN-NATIVE American sisters and brothers STRONG and VISIBLE. I see myself in the LATINA community, warm and friendly. I see myself in the HOMELESS, the HUNGRY, and the UNEMPLOYED. I see myself STRONG and POWERFUL in the VOICES of women fighting for housing, childcare, healthcare, education and control of our bodies. I see myself HAPPY and TRUSTING in the eyes of my grandsons (fortunate enough to have a childhood). I see myself finding my place, in the spirit of my daughter and I see myself in the beautiful eyes and soul of my lover.

We are everywhere as we are all connected to the EARTH—and we KNOW the meaning and the value of LIFE, love and survival.

Sometimes, when I'm photographing women, especially women of AFRICAN descent, I feel like I am under a SPELL—I feel like a spirit walking among the women, unseen, and this enables me to capture the true spirit of their hearts.

The unposed exposure of the emotional self—

I am, therefore, attracted first to the soul of women and later, I notice the physical body. I'm aware of the FACT that I am an emotional, intuitive and sensitive photographer. There are times when the frozen, motionless FACE is difficult for me to photograph—

If I had been born in the early 1800s when a model would have to be still for three–four minutes, I would have done my best and would have felt PROUD to work with sister photographers;

like EDMONIA LEWIS, MARY E. WARREN, HATTIE BAKER, ALBERTA BROWN, and others. YES!

The photograph *SEEING MYSELF THROUGH ALICE WALKER'S EYES* taken in March, 1991, expresses a whole person, a new way of seeing myself. A BIRTH.

A person who is STRONG, confident and yet warm and sensitive; POWERFUL and still soft, friendly, TRUSTING, and open-hearted—SPIRITUAL. This series of photographs made a POWERFUL impact on my LIFE and it has come to help me understand who I really am;

to see my BEING as a gift to those who cross my PATH and the LOVE that I have for the people whom I photograph.

The photograph SEEING MYSELF THROUGH ALICE WALKER'S EYES captures the gentle soul of jean WEISINGER.

ALICE WALKER has been very INSTRUMENTAL and INSPIRATIONAL to my work. Through her VISION, I know that my own vision is possible—and this is liberating to me. This knowledge has VALIDATED my life, my work, and the woman I am and (the woman) I am becoming.

I am thankful for the support of the women in my community who have opened their hearts to my VISION;

My work is the way I GIVE BACK to my sisters and to the universe. It's a way in which I FIGHT the constant battle against RACISM, SEXISM, CLASSISM, and VIOLENCE toward women/children/human beings/animals and the trees.

I take photographs to not only DOCUMENT these times and the lives of those who cross my path, but, also to EXPRESS myself. PHOTOGRAPHY is a passion born within me, a NECESSITY that is not governed by monetary payment. It has become part of the progress toward FREEDOM and LOVE.

PHOTOGRAPHING the self is an act of love and GIFT to others.

Feel the gentle POWER of the WIND.
Feel me EMBRACING and LOVING you all
jean WEISINGER ▉

diving, i kiss
by Elana Dykewomon

```
diving,  i kiss and/kiss and/  kiss
          and/& kiss
          kiss/and kiss
                            :underneath
you are coral
          live   red   coral
```

From *fragments from lesbos*,
Langlois, OR: Diaspora Press, 1981

in the place where

by Judy Grahn

in the place where
her breasts come together
two thumbs' width of
channel ride my
eyes to anchor
hands to angle
in the place where
her legs come together
I said 'you smell like the
ocean' and lay down my tongue
beside the dark tooth edge
of sleeping
'swim' she told me and I
did, I did

From *Work of a Common Woman*.
Freedom, CA: The Crossing Press
[1978].

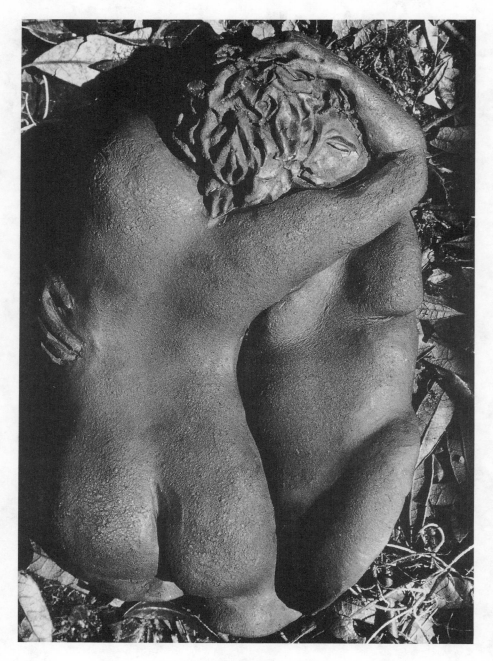

Two Women
by Myriam Fougére

iii.

by Cheryl Clarke

I come to the city for protection
and to witness the thick transactions
of women
and women
and dance with my head.
My turns are calculated
to end on the right foot
to subdue the hip movements.
The city fumes with expectations
and the smells of women
wanting women
I been in love
six times in the last six months
and ain't done tryin yet.*

*Lines adapted from blues songs sung by
Bessie Smith, 1925–1927, *Bessie Smith:
Nobody's Blues But Mine* (Columbia
Records, reissued 1972).

From *Living as a Lesbian*. Ithaca, NY: Firebrand Books, 1986.

Song for a Lakota Woman

by Chrystos

As we came
around the curve
of a bluff the lake opened on spread wings
of a white egret
You turned to me with tiny wildflowers in your hands
murmuring softly *Winyan Menominee*
Anpetu Kin Lia Wasté*
All my feathers shone in your voice
Brushing through leaves growing from fiery red earth
We came to a place where we knew
our mouths would meet
Hurrying to an anonymous room
we showered and plunged into bed
Your soft arms shining brown over me turning
me wild in your hands
a flying lake you drank
flowers in your eyes
as I shouted too loudly coming
open

*Menominee woman you are good and beautiful.

This is Not a Poem for Wimmin Drinking Diet Colas Just to Save Those Few Extra Calories

by Elliott

Holding you
is not easy.
Regardless of what we don't say
I am wider than you
      and thicker than you.
When we lie on our sides
my body curled behind yours
my large stomach and small breasts
cannot both touch you without my pressing and pushing.
And when my arm lies along yours
it is not, as poems say, tight and lean
but is loose and large
hanging over the edges.
With my upper arms the size of your calves,
my calves as large as your thighs,
my thighs more round than your waist,
how can holding you be easy?
How can we be this thing "lovers"?
When you disappear beneath me
When I cannot stay one more night and borrow something of yours
when we are not, by anyone, mistaken for one another.
We who are so different in a physical sense
which is, in this world, an emotional sense.
And what ways can we be
if way to you means methods and styles
but weigh to me means pounds and hatred?
We can, when alone, be each one most beautiful
we can, when alone, redefine our givens
but we are, my love, so rarely alone.

In *Wanting Women: An Anthology of Erotic Lesbian Poetry*, ed. Jan Hardy.
Pittsburgh, PA: Sidewalk Revolution Press, 1990.

Rotunda

by Morgan Grey and Julia Penelope

ROTUNDA, the Folded One, is widely worshipped, especially by Her Chosen, the Fat Dykes, who follow Her roundabout paths and circumlocutions. She is a kind and generous goddess, lavishly bestowing Herself amid the rolls and folds of Her devotees. On those She enfolds, Her blessings are called "Love Handles," for their esoteric uses in the rituals sacred to **LILIHA'ALA'A**. Her priestesses are reputed to be among the most well-rounded Dykes found anywhere, and they are called Zaftig.

Some authorities say there is mounting evidence of Lesbians hostile to Rotunda's magnificence, and they cite rumors of clandestine meetings, called Cambridge Diets, where Lesbians starve themselves for affection. Others mention Dykes possessed by ANOREXIA and BULIMIA, wasting themselves in cruel practices that leave them fat-free. Indeed, we have heard stories of Lesbians so fearful of Rotunda that they are ever pursued by the demons of Weight Watchers, who are much given to the vile ritual of Counting Calories, for they aspire to weightlessness.

Rotunda heartily approves of full-bodied invocations, and finds most appetizing any who approach Her with guttural rumblings and largesse. As the number of Her devotees continues to expand, so, too, do the invocations known to appeal to Her taste. Rotunda's generous proportions can be sought by the following invocation, sometimes called the Fat Blessing. It is known to carry weight with Her:

Rotunda the Large, Rotunda the Great,
Enfold my body, for I love my weight.

Terms like "roly-poly," "chubby," or "obese" displease Her, and must be avoided by those who seek Her.

Rotunda, it should be noted, abhors the sickly aftertaste of Diet Sodas, for these are consumed in great quantities by the followers of the false goddesses, Jane Fonda and Crystal Light. No one dares step light 'n' lively at Her observances, for She attends only to the weighty tread of the elegantly fat, and cherishes their bouncing breasts and generous flesh. ∎

From *Found Goddesses*. Norwich, VT: New Victoria Publishers, 1988.

Lifting Belly Again

by Susan Stinson

with poetry from Gertrude Stein's long poem, "Lifting Belly"

I have been heavy and had much selecting. I saw a star which was low. It was so low it twinkled. Breath was in it. Little pieces are stupid.

I want to tell about fire…

What is it when it's upset. It isn't in the room. Moonlight and darkness. Sleep and not sleep. We sleep every night.

What was it.
I said lifting belly.
You didn't say it.
I said it I mean lifting belly.

"The stomach with its adjuncts
appetite or capacity for food; gluttony
the womb
the inside or interior of anything
a protuberant or bulging surface of anything"

Lifting belly
Lifting belly
Cry.
Lifting belly
Lifting Belly. Splendid

Lifting belly is so kind
Lifting belly fattily.
Doesn't that astonish you.

Common Lives/Lesbian Lives 25 (Winter 1988).

You did want me.
Say it again.
Strawberry.
Lifting beside belly.
Lifting kindly belly.
Sing to me I say.

When my lover touches me, I might relax. I might lie back and let my body spread across the bed like butter or warm toast. Maybe bounce a little on the bed or floor or grass, wherever we are, just bounce enough to be moving all over myself, to be loose and shaking on the high, wide parts of both legs, my breasts bumping into each other and the fat tops of my arms, then me pushing up, brushing up with my belly against hers rolling down, rolling with its own motion, smaller trembles in the wide, tight fat, against my own folds and looseness, many bellies, mounds and valleys becoming mounds, parts of her folding into parts of me, all soft thickness, big legs rubbing across big legs, parting the soft fat touching where they meet with a knee, thick knee pushing into wetness. I might prop one heel up on a wall, might dangle the other off the side of the bed, might move the layers of her back in circles, pull it all up into my fists, then knead it back flat, and slide my hands off to her complicated side, with its different curves of hanging belly, hanging breasts, hanging hips. I might anchor my feet and lift up to meet her, rubbing so hard that the bed creaks, that we both gasp, that we notice a bone.

> *Lifting belly is current rolling.*
> *Lifting belly is so strong.*
> *Lifting belly is so strong.*
> *That is what I say*
> *I say it to please me.*
> *Please yourself with thunder.*

Or I might tense up, hollow out. She might lean too close and pinch me. I might remember dinner, and our struggle over food. She says I gobble. It's true, I rush as if this plate might be my last, as if I'm not supposed to be eating, as if I'm doing something shameful. But too many people have told me that they can't stand the sight of me eating, and hearing it from her shocks me. How come we're both in pain about this? I chew slowly and clench my stomach. There's a knot there she could feel hours later if I let her, but I turn on my side.

> *Lifting belly is no joke. Not after all.*
> *I am so discouraged about it. About lifting*
> *   belly. I question.*
> *I am so discouraged about lifting belly.*
> *The other day there was a good deal of sun-*
> *   light.*
> *There often is.*
> *There often is here.*

Use me as a pillow. Rock me and sing. Walk past men on the street with me and never be ashamed of my breasts, of our fat arms, or our bellies. I will also rock you, and also sing. I will memorize your body to recognize swellings. I will be on the beach with you, watching the ocean and remembering current rolling. I will be current rolling, even pouring sand against my own legs.

> *We see a splendid force in mirrors.*
> *Angry we are not angry.*
> *Pleasing*
> *Lifting belly raining.*
> *I am good looking.*
> *A magazine of lifting belly. Excitement sisters.*

I am angry in the mirror, and then again over the phone. How many boys shouted out of cars. How many men stood behind me and muttered. One man left his number on the subway seat.

You don't listen. You say, "Thanks for sharing." We have other issues.

> *Lifting belly is such an incident. In one's life.*
> *Lifting belly is such an incident in one's life.*
> *I don't mean to be reasonable.*
> *Shall I say thin.*
> *This makes me smile.*

> *Lifting belly.*
> *Exactly.*
> *Lifting belly all the time.*
> *Do be careful of me.*
> *Remarkably so.*
> *Remarkably a recreation.*

> *Lifting belly is so satisfying.*
> *Lifting belly to me.*
> *Large quantities of it.*
> *So that you see that you are praised.*
> *Lifting belly.*
> *See that.*

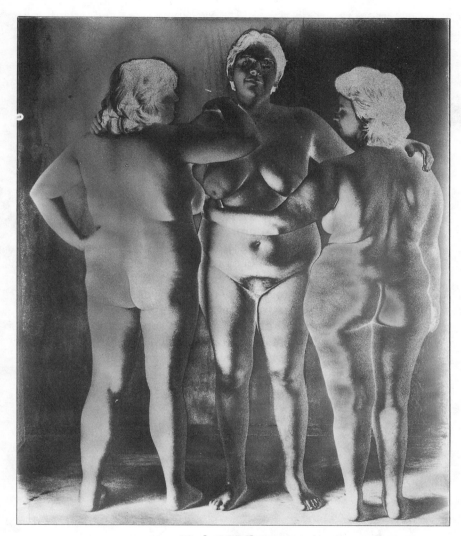

Dyke Trilogy
by Tee Corinne

One Fool to Another

by Chrystos

for Bonnie Jo Price

When the owls called to us we rode through a breaking
dawn sky   Beadwork patterns racing between our fingers
Our hands spoke when the small birds sang so sweetly
closing our long night of stones   words   memories
women in common   You entered with a soft feet spirit
We called to one another in voices of owls
We called to one another in morning songs
I heard the tree branch shake a bouquet of snow to the ground
both of us far from home
We rode to where I live   to the Three Sisters Mountains
to deep green hills where you live
to stones we leave behind
We called to owls from our horses
We called to the snow
to the indigo sky
We were so beautiful
everybody thought
the sun was rising.

From *Dream On*. Vancouver, B.C.: Press Gang Publishers, 1991.

Love Poem

by Audre Lorde

Speak earth and bless me with what is richest
make sky flow honey out of my hips
rigid as mountains
spread over a valley
carved out by the mouth of rain.

And I knew when I entered her I was
high wind in her forests hollow
fingers whispering sound
honey flowed
from the split cup
impaled on a lance of tongues
on the tips of her breasts on her navel
and my breath
howling into her entrances
through lungs of pain.

Greedy as herring-gulls
or a child
I swing out over the earth
over and over
again.

From *New York Head Shop and Museum* (1974)

Audre Lorde
by Jean Weisinger

Woman

by Audre Lorde

I dream of a place between your breasts
to build my house like a haven
where I plant crops
in your body
an endless harvest
where the commonest rock
is moonstone and ebony opal
giving milk to all of my hungers
and your night comes down upon me
like a nurturing rain.

From *The Black Unicorn* (1978)

Four Beginnings/
for Kyra

by Olga Broumas

1. You raise
your face from mine, parting
my breath like water, hair falling
away in its own wind, and your eyes—
green in the light like honey—surfacing
on my body, awed
with desire, speechless, this common dream.

2. You bore your marriage like a misconceived
animal, and have the scars, the pale
ridged tissue round front and back
for proof.   For proof.   Tonight

we cross into each other's language. I take your hand
hesitant still with regret
into that milky landscape, where braille
is a tongue for lovers, where tongue,
fingers, lips
share a lidless eye.

3. I was surprised myself—the image of the lithe
hermaphroditic lover a staple of
every fantasy, bought, borrowed, or mine. We never did
mention the word, unqualified: I love:
your hair, I love: your feet, toes, tender nibbles, I love:

I love. You are the memory
of each desire that ran, dead-end, into a mind
programmed to misconstrue it. A mind inventing
neurosis, anxiety, phobia, a mind expertly camouflaged
from the thought of love
for a woman, its native
love.

4. I in my narrow body, spellbound
against your flesh.

From *Beginning with O*. New Haven, CT: Yale UP, 1977.

Cover of Sinister Wisdom #3 (Spring 1977)
by Tee Corinne

Turtlehawk dreams an ocean breathing

by Lynne Yamaguchi Fletcher

When did wanting to kiss her turn to certainty that I would? When I turned from an eight-foot-tall painting of purple coyotes dancing in a red-and-orange night to find her watching me, the flecks in her eyes flashing green across the gallery, the tip of her tongue seeking the corner of her half-smile like a shadow nudging light.

We had spent the day together, meeting at eight in the parking lot at the base of Squaw Peak to make the climb before the heat became too intense. In another few weeks, eight would be a late start, but this early in May, the daily high hadn't yet broken a hundred, and we could count on getting up and back at a leisurely pace without frying.

We took our time hiking up, stepping aside to let by the backpackers-in-training and the runners, some on their second or third trip up or down. We talked as we walked, about, literally, everything under the sun—the chollas haloed in the morning light, the hummingbirds sipping the first waxy blooms of the saguaros, the city spreading its turquoise finery—backyard pools—below us as we climbed higher and higher, her growing up in the desert, my hopscotch journey here, her pending divorce, my editing, her teaching—one subject segueing into the next like morning into day.

She fascinated me. It wasn't her looks,

Originally published in *Bushfire: Stories of Lesbian Desire*, ed. Karen Barber, Boston: Alyson, 1991.

though she was pretty enough, with a lively face under a cap of hair four shades lighter than my near-black, lit with random strands that shone golden in the sun. Rather, it was the conviction of her charm that drew me, the aura she projected, at once naive and seductive, of a child-woman certain of her allure. She didn't need a model's physique to claim womanhood: her being—pale, petite, and succulent—proclaimed it. Sex was an attitude with her, an angle of eye, a line of throat, a language she spoke with assurance and, one was sure, fluently, though she dropped only a word or two, perfectly pronounced, here and there into conversation.

Winded and exhilarated from the final, vertical climb, we lingered an hour at the top of Squaw Peak, longer than we'd planned, sprawled on a rock face, basking in our bodies, taking in the Sunday-blue sky with what we'd learned about each other. We'd spanned a range of feeling in our conversation, shifting fluidly from solemnity to silliness to sadness and onward. Now, we were mostly silent as we shared an orange and drank from our water bottles, careful to leave enough for the hot trek down. She'd sweat in patches, I observed, whereas my T-shirt and shorts were uniformly darkened.

The film of dust that had settled over her pink gave her the illusion of a tan. She was the palest desert dweller I'd seen, but seemed blithely unselfconscious of her pallor in this city of sun worshippers. In contrast, I looked like a native. When, unconsciously, I reached one brown finger to trace a line of freckles down her arm, she only smiled.

The trip down was quick, hot, and breathless, as gravity outstripped the desire for conversation down the steep slope. I led the way to the shaded water fountain at the base, where, having finished the last of our bottles, we doused ourselves before getting into our cars. We both were dry by the time we got to my house for a quick shower and change of clothes.

She insisted I go first, so I set her up at the kitchen table with the Sunday paper and a frothy mug of juice and seltzer, and hopped into the shower to rinse the dust off. I was in and out in three minutes but took my time toweling off to give her—and me—some time to breathe and assess the morning. I didn't want the exhilaration of the climb to skew my expectations: I'd skinned both knees falling for straight women before, and the memory stung enough to keep me stepping carefully. It wasn't love I wanted now but romance: to indulge in the getting-to-know-you rapture of a burgeoning friendship without drowning in need—to tube the rapids without swallowing the river.

I left a set of towels for her on the edge of the sink, called out to let her know the bathroom was free, and disappeared into my room to change.

She surprised me then, appearing twenty minutes later in a sassy white cotton dress, then turning her back to me with a "Will you?" My hands went hot and clumsy on the zipper. The sprinkling of freckles stopped below her shoulder blades. My stomach stopped at my groin.

The Cinquo de Mayo festivities were still warming up when we arrived at the Buttes in her car, just short of noon. She led the way in, producing two tickets—her treat, her invitation—from a pocket I didn't know she had. Hungry from the climb and from want of a real breakfast, we went first for the food, loading our plates with Indian fry bread, fresh blue-corn tortillas, salsa, beans, guacamole, mesquite-broiled *el pollo*. Balancing a pitcher of water under my plate, I followed her to

a ringside table under the slatted roof of the pavilion. We sat and proceeded to feast.

The first of the bands was setting up, and she watched the preparations eagerly while her fingers tucked bite after bite into a mouth as eager as her eyes. She loved dancing as much as I did, and a wider range of music. Half a song and she was out on the concrete, half a plate of food forgotten. We danced together, she danced alone, she danced with any man who asked, charming each for the span of a song or two, but clearly herself charmed by the music. Salsa, jazz, rock, reggae, country swing—her energy never flagged. In between sets and changeovers, we amused each other making up stories about members of the crowd.

She was a terrific flirt. She could have flirted in any language, conjuring response with mirrors, not words: catching the light in the lake of her eyes; tossing it back in a glint of lips, a gleam of shoulder. To be the focus of her attentions was electrifying. My palms and soles hummed.

A troupe of dancers performed, torsos thrusting, feet throbbing hypnotically to the beat of African and Caribbean drums. I knew one of the male dancers through the local food co-op and introduced her to him at her request. As I watched, she looked long at his bare chest and muscled calves, smiling, and touched her lip; I heard him swallow. She led him to the dance floor when the next band struck up, and I watched him whirl and counterstep before her, solar plexus high and forward, his eyes intent on hers.

She was back in three dances.

I told myself again, sternly, not to take her attentions personally. Already, the warning felt like hindsight.

I began to feel drugged, with that split consciousness that says at once, "Whoa, you're losing control," and "I'm flying, fly me higher." No; yes. Two letters versus three: I could feel the slide of the scales like a ship listing hard starboard as my ribs rose skyward. The mystery here was not what her eyes and fingers and mouth were doing but how powerless I felt to resist them.

I was quiet on the drive to Scottsdale, where we were to meet some friends to attend a gallery opening. She still spilled over with energy, but I had danced hard to shake free of the spell I'd fallen under and, happy just to feel both feet again, was content for the moment to play appreciative audience.

Our friends couldn't keep the surprise from their faces when they saw us together. It wasn't the fact of our arriving together—we were expected—but her high color and my off-balance grin that surprised them. They knew us from different contexts—her, more or less professionally, through the university; me, socially—and apparently the borders hadn't crossed in their minds.

One—Ricki—took me aside as soon as she gracefully could. "I thought she was straight," she whispered.

"She is," I answered.

Ricki punched me in the arm. "Tomorrow," she said, wagging a finger at me. "I want the dirt."

I laughed and rejoined the entourage.

"Animal Dreams," the show was called. The animals here could not be found in any zoo. Cartoonlike creatures cavorted in big, brilliantly hued paintings; clothed clay beasts prowled the square tops of pedestals; humanlike faces gazed from masks of paint and bone and feathers and teeth and fur. Were these animal dreams of humans or human dreams of animals? I found the work and the theme bizarrely fitting: animal joy, animal hunger, animal mystery.

I quickly left the socializing to the others and wandered off by myself to look at the masks. Peering into the faces, shifting my angle of vision to catch their shifting expressions, I was suddenly struck by the familiarity of the movement. Mirrors, I thought. Here was the artist flirting with the viewer flirting with mystery, power, fear.

One mask stood out from the others. Relatively plain but for a sea-green opalescent finish, it featured half-lidded eyeholes and a beaklike nose under a high brow ridge. Small feathers hung at its temples, and the upper lip overhung the lower. Where its wearer's throat would be, a winged vertebra dangled. The unexpected effect was of utter serenity. "Turtlehawk Dreams an Ocean Breathing," the card beside it said.

On impulse, I began experimenting, trying to mirror the mask's expression. How well I succeeded I don't know, but for a moment, before I grew too self-conscious to continue, a feeling rose in me of light, as if I stood in the copper flame of sunset with stars in my head. The pitching sea I'd been riding all day calmed. I wanted to kiss her, and the wanting suffused me with happiness.

Before I could savor the feeling, Ricki snagged me again and dragged me over to view the paintings. Now the work mirrored me: colors of elation, shapes of joy. I grinned and, at a prod from Ricki's elbow, turned. Across the room her eyes flashed "go." A wave washed through me, leaving in joy's stead a feeling cooler, metallic, tall. My hands jumped. My center of balance went south.

"Uh-huh," said Ricki.

We were both quiet as she was driving me home. We had each declined our friends' invitations to go for ice cream, but I, at least, wasn't ready for the day to end. On impulse, as she turned down the road that cut through the desert park near my house, I suggested a moonlight hike. She was even more than agreeable.

The small lot near my favorite climb was empty—unusual except on a Sunday night. After we'd parked, she pulled an old quilt from the trunk of her car, and we followed a vague trail up the small red sandstone mountain. Halfway up we spread her quilt, staking out a rounded ledge facing the city to our west, with a shallow cave scooped by hot winds at our backs and a screen of creosote bushes between us and the lot below.

The city lights spread before us; a sea of stars spread over us. Balmy, not even sweater cool, the night air enfolded us in the desert's perfume. Wrapped in this intoxication of sky and dust and creosote and millennia of light, we leaned back, near but not touching, and soaked it all in.

We sat without speaking for a long time, until the erratic flight of a bat caught our attention. We watched it avidly, speculating as to its food, its nesting habits, the reasons for people's fear. We went off on a long tangent then about pocket mice, king snakes, jackrabbits, coyotes.

At this, the moment in the gallery flooded back and I lapsed into silence. What was she remembering?

The quality of the silence had changed. Charged now, the night seemed to be waiting, and we with it.

A moment of laughter was all it took.

The bat came back, with a companion this time, and she made a crack about Dracula's bite. I countered with a slur on Batman and Robin.

"What about Batwoman?" she asked.

"If that's Batwoman," I said, "the other one's Catherine Deneuve."

She frowned at me, confounded, then her eyebrows lifted and her mouth opened and she laughed. "Ah, ha," she said. "And where is Susan this evening?"

I nudged her. She nudged me back. We sat for several minutes leaning up against each other, feeling the intersection of our bodies—shoulders, arms, thighs, Finally, I took her hand, brushing the fingertips with my own, tracing, lightly, the grooves of her palm. After a moment, I raised her hand to my lips, kissed each fingertip slowly, touching the faint salt of each with my tongue. I kissed her palm, dragging my lip across the pad at the base of each finger. When two fingers cleaved, I licked, softly.

I looked at her. Her eyes were closed, her head tipped back and turned slightly away, as if listening for her name. I pressed my face to her palm, closing my eyes, then wrapped my mouth full around her first finger and tugged, drawing the salt from her pores, drawing the blood to her skin, drawing a moan from her opening throat. I met and held her startled gaze as I moved to the next finger, sucking deep, pulling back to take both fingers in. Blood filled my limbs. My tongue swam around and between her fingers. The smell of sun on skin and a hint of sunscreen teased me from the back of her hand. As I breathed it in, I could feel her in me already, how it would be to fill this wanting.

Hooking her thumb under my chin, she pulled my face toward her, hunger and some-

thing like danger darkening her eyes. I let her fingers slide from my mouth and waited. Her lips touched mine like smoke from the fire between my thighs, and the center of my chest caught flame. She pressed into me savagely; the world fell away. And came back in a slow kiss made slower by the racing of my pulse. Breathing deep, I savored the silken rim of her sweetly clean mouth, small arc by small arc, welcoming her tongue—the satin underside, the softly nubbled surface—with mine.

How long we kissed I have no idea. Long enough to drown and be resuscitated. We kissed till we reached a clean, clear place in our kissing, and found ourselves wrapped around each other like vines after an April rain, satiated, drunk on fullness. We lolled against each other, laughing. And rested, face against face, breathing the night air.

And then we kissed again, and the hunger rose like a tidal wave from a sea shaken at its floor.

Suddenly four hands weren't enough, and her underwear was in my hand, my pants were to my knees, and she was over me, pinning my wrists to the rock, our arms taut over my head, her face fierce a breath from mine.

Eyes locked on mine, she lowered herself onto me, hot wet scalding my exposed belly. Deliberately, never wavering her gaze, she began to rub, back and forth, up and down, down and around. I was drowning in sensation. Juices flowed from me like hot tears. Feeling her gyrations beginning to center on my bush, I stretched myself longer—longer to stretch her longer, to feel the length of her body rolling against mine.

She wriggled lower, pulling my wrists down to my shoulders, her mouth at my chest seeking skin but finding shirt. She sat up, releasing my arms, to concentrate instead on her movements. My hands found her under her dress and gripped, slipping over the slick muscles of her thighs and buttocks as she rode me. Her hands gripped my ribs, then my thighs as she leaned back, pressing up on me. My pelvis and neck arched hard as I angled for fuller contact. I closed my eyes to focus on the center of our juncture.

We were like two oppositely charged wires, the voltage jumping in each with each roll of our hips, the ends brushing closer and closer, tantalizingly close to contact. Small sounds fluttered from her throat; my breath soughed through narrowed lips. Heat engulfed my pubis as my whole being strained toward her. The ends of the wires moved closer and closer, millimeters apart now, current leaping the liquid between them.

And then they touched. A deep shudder shook us both. A wave of liquid heat swept the inside of my legs and rolled from my feet, and the backlash rippled audibly through my chest and neck. She remained arched back, breathing long, loose breaths like sighs.

Kicking my ankles finally free of my pants and unbuttoning my shirt with one hand, I stretched the other behind her and unzipped what I had zipped that morning. Easing the dress from her shoulders, then over her head, I pulled her to me. Breast to breast, mouth to mouth, we steeped in our mingled sweat.

We ended up on our sides, murmuring together forehead to forehead, stroking the length of each other's body, for a long spell. Then the sound of tires on blacktop and a sweep of headlights below us swung me upright. Through the web of creosote I watched a lone car pass through the park.

When I turned back, she was smiling, her body a feast of cream in the starlight. Feeling a purr begin in my chest, I bent to the cream, lapping the bowl of her belly and ribs with long sweeps as she drew her fingers through my hair. I worked my way slowly up to her breasts, nuzzling and lapping each nipple till it stood, then painting broad wet circles around the near nipple with my tongue. Eyes closed, she kneaded the small of my back with one hand, tracing my face with the other. I twined one fingertip in her damp pubic curls, then shifted to straddle one leg.

Cupping in my hand the breast I'd been licking, I leaned over her and took into my mouth as much as I could of the other. I sucked slowly with my whole mouth, alternately flicking the round berry with the tip of my tongue. Her hands tangled in my hair, urging me to her. The other berry I brushed with my thumb till I could feel her begin to undulate beneath me.

Her grip on my head tightened, and when I raised my head to look at her, she seized me to her, mouth open, devouring mine, all teeth and jaw and tongue and need. She engulfed my chin, scraping my neck with her teeth. Sliding her hot mouth over my larynx. I broke away, startled, stiff-arming the rock we lay on to hold myself above her. We stared at each other.

My arms bent. I devoured back, flattening myself against her as she gripped my buttocks and thrust her thigh between my legs. I bucked against her, smearing her thigh with my juices. Our nipples chafed together. I ground my hip into her, and myself against hers.

My fingers found her vagina and I thrust two in to the knuckle. She bucked and shuddered and broke from my mouth with a cry. I rolled to her side. Her hips began to rock and rotate; her hands clutched at the quilt. Whimpering gasps sprang from her chest. I began sliding my fingers in and out with a long twisting motion. Her vagina ballooned. My fingertips circled her cervix. Her cervix pushed back.

My thumb on her clit, fingers pressing upward against the washboard inside, I began moving my whole arm in circles, slowly at first, faster as her hips responded as if with a mind of their own. Knees bent, her feet pressed into the rock, she bore down on me, hips in the air jerking up and down, side to side, circling with me and against me. I closed my eyes and labored to stay with her.

My own body was on the verge of orgasm, my genitals so engorged I could have come at a touch. My skin sang; a howl leapt within my throat. I held my thighs tightly closed.

Her cries filled my chest, high grunting moans that punctuated her quickening thrusts. A quick inbreath and suddenly she went silent, her hips suspended in motion. A low cry began in her belly then, rising in pitch and volume as her vagina convulsed around my fingers and her hips jerked and dropped and her hands seized my shoulders and held on.

We lay, spent, for several minutes. Then, my fingers still in her, I leaned over to taste her. She shivered. I knelt carefully between her legs and parted her hairs with my other hand. She groaned and reached for my head, then fell back. Stretching my legs out behind me, I folded my arm under my chest and bellied up, touched my lips to those lips, and exhaled hotly. She sighed. I touched my tongue to the underside of her clit. Her breath caught, and resumed. Easing my fingers halfway out, I licked them, savoring the heady fragrance on my tongue. And continued my slow lick up to rub my nose in her wet curls.

She swept her feet up my sides, gripping my head a moment, then rested them on my shoulder blades, her knees flung wide.

I lapped the spill of cream from the satin grooves either side of her clitoris. Then, gently, slowly, as I enfolded her clit in my lips, I began wiggling my fingers alternately back and forth inside her. I made my tongue as soft and flat as possible, tracing small, gentle circles against her. When I felt that bud swell I began sucking softly and running my tongue up again and again from her innermost lips.

I let my fingers slip from her and my tongue take their place. A low "oh" escaped her, and she pressed against me, tightening her vagina as I reached deeply in, kissing me back as thoroughly as she had with her mouth.

I drank her in and in.

Slick-faced, I returned at last to her clit, breathing on it softly, circling it with the tip of my tongue. Her hips echoed the motion almost imperceptibly. I continued the circles, slowly increasing my pressure as her circles became more pronounced. Occasionally I let my tongue flicker across her, resuming the circling as she would stop hers and begin to moan. Finally, she began to squirm against my mouth with a low whimper.

I began flicking her clit in earnest and slipped my fingers back into her to resume my back-and-forth motion. She began rocking up and down, her whole body now, and her whimper took on the same quick rhythm.

With my free hand I pressed her mound, pushing the skin back to expose her further. My flicking became a vibration, a thrum humming all through me, electrifying my fingertips, toes, clit. I felt as though I were licking myself, each flicker of tongue on her bringing me closer to combustion. But it was her I wanted, on me and in me. The force of my wanting narrowed to twin points of flame on the tips of my tongue and clitoris.

Her feet clutching my ribs urged me on. Faster and faster came her staccato song; faster and faster came my answer. Then, as her rocking became a pulse and the hum became a roar, she jerked—almost sitting up—and jerked, jerked, jerked, jerked, each spasm smaller, subsiding like a basketball's dribble to a state of rest.

When her walls had stopped fluttering and our breathing had slowed to normal and the evaporation of sweat was at last beginning to chill our skin, I eased my fingers from her and climbed up to her head. She looked at me. "Lover," she said.

I grinned hugely and flopped on my back next to her, one hand rubbing my still-wet belly.

She nuzzled her way into my armpit, and I wrapped her in skin.

I was in some other space, breathing night, lulled by star-song, when I became conscious of something sharp brushing my nipple. I opened my eyes to find her teasing her fingernails across my breast. Seeing me looking up, she sat up.

She looked at me then, at my body, running her hands along my skin as though her fingertips held another set of eyes. I wondered if she'd ever really looked at another woman's body before. She kept returning to my breasts, cupping their curve in her palms, rolling my pursed nipples under her thumbs, bending finally to touch her tongue to one. She closed her lips around it carefully, exploring its tip with her tongue, pressing into my breast when I drew a quick breath and held it. Heat was beginning again its spread from my center.

She laid her face against my belly for a moment, turning her head back and forth to feel the smoothness against each cheek. My ribs began to prickle; my breath, to quicken.

I felt a finger teasing my bush hairs and stifled a moan—a moan she dragged from me in the next moment, her fingernails leaving four hot trails down the inside of each thigh. I started to sit up; she pressed me back into the rock.

She pushed my legs open wider and knelt between them. I curved around to watch her.

As she leaned in to look, I could feel my juices begin their slow cascade from my vagina. Sure enough, a touch and she held up a finger: on its tip a dollop of cream. Watching me carefully, she painted her mouth with it. She licked. She smiled. My insides flipped. I closed my eyes as desire flooded my forearms and thighs.

At the touch of her thumb pulling back the hood of my clit, I looked again. She was peering closely through the dim light into my spread lips. Her lips pursed. She blew across me. My vagina contracted, releasing another daub. She touched me again and painted the smooth wet along my ribs.

She seemed to make a decision then and surprised me by moving to my side. She bent to kiss me—a short, sweet kiss, in the middle of which something like fire—her fingertip—seared the underside of my clit. A jolt shot through me.

She moved her mouth to my breast again, tonguing and sucking and rubbing her whole face over me. That single point of heat stayed on my clitoris, even as I began to writhe under the intensity.

She stayed with me, breaking her touch only to dip again into the river of my juices. Was her finger moving, was I moving against her, was this heat pure energy and not friction at all?

I only knew that my skin was raging, that I wanted her wrapping me like a fresh dressing on a burn. Or was it a match I wanted, ready to immolate myself on her pyre? I heaved my hips at that point of fire, bracing my arms and shoulders against the rock like a sacrifice.

All my consciousness came to exist in that single point of contact as that hot coal grew hotter. All awareness of my body vanished, though I continued to thrash, that incendiary urge driving me toward combustion. But the higher the heat climbed, the higher my threshold for heat seemed to rise. Thrash as I might, I could come no closer to flame.

Finally, I no longer knew whether I was chasing flame or feeling it. A groan tore my throat.

She dipped again but this time came back above my clit, stroking the stiff root above the hood. Something in me melted. My body came back. I could feel her length stretched along my leg now, her head resting on my hip, my hands—one lost in her hair, the other pressing my own mound—the pleasure flowing from my center with each rub of my root. A long "aaahhh" rolled from my chest. I rode the pleasure as if floating in a tropical sea, saturated with sun and lazy with longing answered. Dipping and bobbing, I let the swells lift me like breath, deliver me like breath. Closer and closer to sky I rode, basking in the billowing flow till the ocean rose in me and flung its swollen waters on my shore.

I lowed.

She slipped over my chest to cover me like a wave. My mouth found hers and submerged. All was water. We twined together like anemones on the sea floor, wet on wet everywhere, swimming in each other, around each other, our mouths and limbs and fingers everywhere at once. Turning, diving, flipping, and sliding in an underwater dance, we skimmed bottom. We sang sea. We came up for air to find ourselves mirroring each other, sitting mouth to mouth, breasts to breasts, legs scissored around each other, one over, one under, our cunts open and joined.

That night I would dream of ocean, dream an ocean breathing. ■

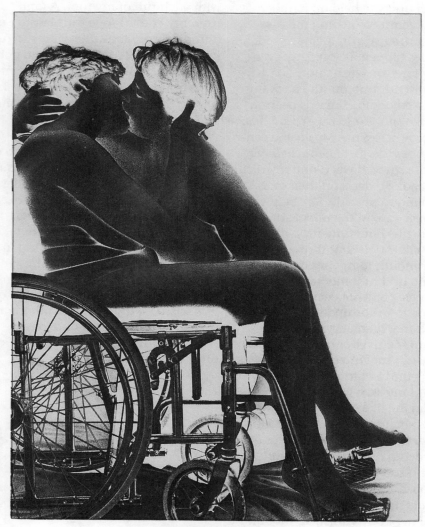

Dykes Kissing
by Tee Corinne

Rumplestiltskin
by Olga Broumas

First night.
Mid-winter.
Frightened
with pleasure as I came.
Into your arms, salt
crusting the aureoles.
Our white breasts.   Tears
and tears.   You
saying
I don't know
if I'm hurting or loving
you.   I
didn't either.
We went on
trusting.   Your will to care
for me intense
as a laser.   Slowly
my body's cellblocks
yielding
beneath its beam.

I have to write of these things.   We were grown
women, well
traveled in our time.

Did anyone
ever encourage you, you ask
me, casual

in afternoon light.   You blaze
fierce with protective anger as I shake
my head, puzzled, remembering, no
no.   You blaze

a beauty you won't claim.   To name
yourself beautiful makes you as vulnerable
as feeling
pleasure and claiming it
makes me.   I call you lovely.   Over

and over, cradling
your ugly memories as they burst
their banks, tears and tears, I call
you lovely.   Your face
will come to trust that judgment, to bask
in its own clarity like sun.   Grown women.   Turning

heliotropes to our own, to our lovers' eyes.

Laughter.   New in my lungs still, awkward
on my face. Fingernails
growing back
over decades of scar and habit, bottles
of bitter quinine rubbed into them, and chewed
on just the same.   We are not the same.   Two
women, laughing
in the streets, loose-limbed
with other women.   Such things are dangerous.
Nine million

have burned for less.

How to describe
what we didn't know
exists: a mutant organ, its function to feel
intensely, to heal by immersion, a fluid
element, crucial as amnion, sweet milk
in the suckling months.

Approximations.
The words we need are extinct.

Or if not extinct
badly damaged: the proud Columbia
stubbing
her bound up feet on her dammed
up bed.   Helpless with excrement.   Daily

by accident, against
what has become our will through years
of deprivation, we spawn the fluid
that cradles us, grown
as we are, and at a loss
for words.   Against all currents, upstream
we spawn
in each other's blood.

Tongues
sleepwalking in caves.   Pink shells.   Sturdy
diggers.   Archaeologists of the right
the speechless zone
of the brain.

Awake, we lie
if we try to use them, to salvage some part
of the loamy dig.   It's like
forgiving each other, you said
borrowing from your childhood priest.
Sister, to wipe clean

with a musty cloth
what is clean already
is not forgiveness, the clumsy housework
of a bachelor god.   We both know, well
in our prime, which is cleaner: the cave-
dwelling womb, or the colonized
midwife:

the tongue.

From *Beginning with O*. New Haven, CT: Yale
UP, 1977.

What Kinsey Missed

by Kathleen Hawk ~~~~

Old Kinsey, who supposedly knew,
painted a blue picture
of lesbians, noting that
kissing and hugging
seems to be most of what we do.

As a woman once fixed
in the piston rhythms of hetero sex,
I would have imagined that Kinsey meant
the neck-nuzzling, cookie-fragrant and innocent,
that happens between grandmothers
and toddlers before the age of four,
or even the flimsy hugging
and cheek-nipping that women in furs
do in doorways of restaurants
and department stores.

As sex goes,
it was not even plain vanilla.
More like toast
without the jelly.

Kinsey, of course,
never kissed you,
as I have done in my wiser age.

And those questionnaires
surely didn't have a page to tell
how your lips speak in braille,
how your tongue finds its mate,
and how your cheek
floats against mine
as you taste my ear,
catches its skirt in your teeth,
and tugs me out of myself.

Kinsey never rested against your breasts,
or felt the dense curve
of your arm cross my shoulders,
your hand like sun-warmth
on my neck, to hold me,
to make me aware of your intention
to kiss me.
He might have dropped his pencil and not cared
as his questionnaire
floated away in a silent mist
of moist and breathing multiple choices.
Kinsey never mentioned
that necking is not a fill-in-the-blank,
but an essay question.

Sculptures
by Myriam Fougére

Myriam Fougére, taping events at the East Coast Lesbians' Festival
by Toni Armstrong Jr.

A Visionary Woman Creating Visions: Barbara Hammer

by Ellen Meyers and Toni Armstrong Jr.

Barbara Hammer's impact on experimental film in this country has been significant. An internationally recognized artist, she has screened and lectured about her work all over the world. "I have been working for twenty years, and one of my ideas was to document a lesbian life. That was my own because that was the one I knew the most," says Barbara.

Barbara started making films in 1967 or 1968 when she was given a Super 8 camera. "On my way to my first film class, I stopped my Lambretta motorscooter in the Northern California town of Bodega and began shooting *Schizy*. My first film captured the schizophrenia I felt as a heterosexual—at that time—woman living in a man's world. I shot through bifocal lenses an optometrist had given me to show the split level reality I saw in the world around me. This was before I heard the

From *HOT WIRE*, May 1991

world 'feminism,' which enabled me to see the world, not myself, as crazy," she recalls. "*Schizy* won an Honorable Mention in the Sonoma Super 8 Film Festival. This recognition, plus the fact that the screen was larger than any canvas I had yet used (I began to paint in 1965), and the fact that the audience was compelled in the dark to watch the film changed my life. I became a filmmaker."

Barbara's first 16mm film was made in school many years later, following many Super 8 films shot while coming out and exploring her first lesbian relationship (*Barbara Ward Will Never Die*; *Marie and Me*; *Travelling*; *Yellow Hammer*; others). "I left my husband, came out with a woman, traveled to Africa on a motorcycle, and taught a year in Germany before returning to the U.S. and making the decision to study 16mm film production at San Francisco State University," she recalls. "There I made my first 16mm film, *I Was/I Am*, in which I enacted a

transformation from a gowned and crowned 'lady' to a motorcycle dyke. I went on to make thirteen films in the two and a half years I was at State because I was motivated, the equipment was free, and the low tuition fees left me income for film stock. Most of these films—such as *Dyketactics*—were not made for any classes, but just for myself and the women's community."

Barbara sees her body of work encompassing several phases. The first phase she calls "a period of celebration and identity naming," which includes the groundbreaking *Dyketactics*. Only four minutes long, the film has 110 different cuts in it, so it moves very quickly. It reflects her since-developed aesthetic about lesbians and their sense of touch. In 1974 when the film came out, there were very few explicitly lesbian films with lesbian images. After she made it, she was told that it was the first lesbian lovemaking film made by a lesbian.

Before filmmaking Barbara earned a B.A. in Psychology from UCLA and an M.A. in English Literature from San Francisco State. "I worked as a counselor in Marin County Juvenile Hall and later at an experimental open setting for 'emotionally disturbed adolescents' where I was a teacher in a self-contained classroom," she says. "I found this work challenging for a while, but I wasn't expressing a large part of myself. At first, I thought I would have to have a baby to justify the fact that I wanted to stay home and paint. When I didn't conceive and my husband was found to be sterile, I was relieved. I realized then that I really just wanted to 'work on my own thing'—as we used to say in the '60s—and that I hadn't wanted to be a mother at all."

In 1975, Barbara earned a second M.A.—this one in film—and was offered a job teaching Super 8 filmmaking at San Jose State. "At that time, I didn't know how important teaching would become to me later, and I turned it down because I had a burning desire to make film after film after film. There was so much I had to say, so many films to create," she recalls. "Whenever one was completed, another would come to mind and I'd begin again. I knew I was starting late, but I had stored up extra energy for this expression. I wanted to be recognized first as an artist and then, perhaps later, as a teacher. To do that I had to do the work."

She says that she feels college teachers "can be and are" artists, but sometimes a teacher has to sacrifice energy and commitment for her students. "When you are just beginning and the world is in front of you, and you are lucky enough to have the monetary resources available, it is a great luxury and honor to be able to work full-time on your art," she says. "Mostly one needs to do what one is compelled to do at the time there is the drive. Ten years later I had to struggle to get my first full-time teaching position in a college, but I had made the films I had needed to make. I wouldn't do it differently today. I now enjoy teaching as well."

She made *Superdyke* and *Superdyke Meets Madame X*,

that helped her pay the rent and she further supplemented her income with screenings of her work.

Barbara came out when she was thirty years old. Her first lovemaking experience with a woman changed her life and became an inspiration for future films. She refers to *Dyketactics* as "a commercial so that other women might realize that there was an experience that they might have when they make love with another woman."

For Hammer, "being a lesbian and being an artist is always creating and always defining. It never reaches a static point." She sees each new film as a challenge and not a repetition of something she's seen in the outside world. She also says,

> ## "Being a lesbian and being an artist is always creating and always defining. It never reaches a static point."

kinds of films that "an institution would suffocate." A small inheritance supported her through graduate school, and she had some left over when she graduated. She started teaching women in her studio using her own equipment. These small groups of women formed classes

"For some reason, being a lesbian is so difficult in the world that the security we get in our home lives sometimes leads to more conservative visual preferences, so that we like a realistic picture or a realistic film. That is not my vision of what being a lesbian or being an artist is. So I don't always conform to the lesbian community needs.

"Some women in the lesbian community have supported my experimental work, while others have wanted a more documentary or narrative cinema. I had an idealistic view that a lesbian took chances, challenged tradition and form, and that connected with my idea of what an artist did. I never wanted to make 'straight' films that fit a pre-established order. Sometimes I've wondered if it is so difficult for lesbians to be accepted in society that we choose to blend in and assimilate rather than stand for difference. I wonder if the desire some lesbian women express for film that tells a story with lesbian characters in the Hollywood tradition comes out of this need to fit in," she says.

The second phase of Hammer's work took place in the 1980s and has to do with landscape, underwater as well as above water. She feels it was an outward identity naming, claiming a lesbian- and woman-identified place on the planet. It was during this time that she moved from Oakland to New York to challenge her work. She felt critics were saying that her work was all woman-identified in nature. While Hammer agrees with that basic assessment, she decided to go to an urban environment where people might be more committed to work rather than lifestyle.

"Many of my films of the '70s were set in the natural surroundings of the East Bay hills and parklands near my home," she recalls. "Critics had assumed I equated women with nature by placing them in idyllic natural environments. To equate women with nature was to say woman was biologically determined and not socially constructed. In fact, I believe we are constructed in terms of gender; indeed, I believe there is a 'lesbian construction,' and that is the topic of my next film. We are not one or the other. We are the results of biology *and* culture, and these are not necessarily contradictory ways of seeing and naming."

It was during this period that she made *Endangered* and *Optic Nerve*, which are categorized as some of her most formal work in terms of style. *Optic Nerve* was in the 1987 Whitney Biennial, an exhibition that showcases cutting-edge avant-garde painting, sculpture, installation, video, and film. *Endangered* was selected for the 1989 Whitney Biennial. *Snow Job: The Media Hysteria of AIDS* was made during this time, and because this work and *Optic Nerve* do not deal with lesbian issues, they are among the most exhibited works she has produced.

Snow Job: The Media Hysteria of AIDS is presented with a film projector as well as several video monitors. The audio comes through the video. People look at the screen, which is much larger, but there is more media on the monitors. Hammer says, "it's all about the hysteria of media, so it works well in that it also adds to the snow job accumulation of the hysteria."

In 1985, she accepted her first full-time teaching position, for one year at Columbia College in Chicago. As a teacher, it enabled her to have free access to equipment. When she was hired, she was the first full-time female faculty in the history of the department. "*Optic Nerve* was the first film I made with my own optical printer," she says. "I began it in New York and moved it with me to Chicago when I was hired by Columbia. I put the optical printer on my kitchen table and worked on the film every day. This work in progress helped me to make the transition."

She next moved to Evergreen State College in Olympia, Washington because of the learning/teaching/philosophy unique to that institution. "Students could plan their own classes, I could plan mine," she says. "I didn't have to use the letter grading system, but instead provided a written evaluation of the student's progress and process with regard to her/his growth. Seminars were required where texts—and films, books, music scores, etc.—were debated and enlarged upon by student participation and faculty leadership. Faculty members who were team teaching met once a week to go over the text assignments." Although she found Evergreen State to be a "very stimulating educational context," eventually Washington was too isolating and she returned to New York.

She decided to stop teaching so she could have flexibility to be in New York more. "In New York, the arts are supported much more than in Washington or California. The density of the population and the milieu of the city make for artistic ferment," she says. "There are many venues in which to see experimental film, and many places to screen work. I was able to get grants for my current film/video project there." While in New York, and as she gained more recognition for her work, she was offered three visiting artist jobs in the Bay Area at places she had been trying to teach for years. Of this she says, "Sometimes you are not recognized in your own hometown until you move away and do well. Then you come back and are a hot item…or at least they consider you a valuable person."

Barbara Hammer does not know how to define the period of work she is currently in. "I think it's a period of no fear and abandonment, a use of the intellect I never used," she says. She is making the comedy *Hot Flash* about menopause that attempts to take what is considered a serious issue and turn it into a comedic one.

Several recently completed works include *The History of the World According to a Lesbian* (1988), which goes from the platonic cave to the post punk scene with the Seattle based music group Sluts From Hell, who sing 1950s songs with a lesbian twist. *Still Point* (1989) uses four multi-image filled screens to

"Controversy is healthy, especially if it is open. We need to critique one another's work, but before we can do that we must state our aesthetic."

evoke beauty, pain, home, and homelessness, and the sense of being caught in all worlds at once. *Still Point* received the Women in Film Award at the 1990 Atlanta Film/Video Festival.

Barbara turns fifty-two this May 15th, and has received several large grants which will allow her to stop visiting teaching jobs and be able to do her creative work full time. She works either in film or video and is currently trying to merge the two. A current work in progress [*Sanctus*] uses archival x-ray footage from the 1950s that she is optically printing and transferring onto video. "I have just finished *Sanctus*, a 16mm film using moving x-ray footage originally shot by Dr. James Sibley Watson and his colleagues and now archived in The George Eastman House in Rochester, New York. Dr.

Watson made one of the first experimental films in the United States, *Fall of the House of Usher* (1929)," she says. "I was thrilled to be able to view the nitrate 35mm x-ray film and select what I wanted to rephotograph. *Sanctus* explores the fragility and mystery of the human body as the viewer enters through skeletal frameworks to organ systems in imagery usually reserved for medical practitioners. The sound composition by Niel B. Rolnick is digitized and sampled, using the "Sanctus" section of the Mass from Bach, Beethoven, Mozart, Byrd and Mechant. I am completing *Dr. Watson's X-Rays*, a video documentary of people who worked with Watson on the x-rays, or who knew him. This complements the film and will be shown in conjunction with it.

"My ultimate career goals

are to continue working just as I am—to take up a project that interests me when the one I've been working on is finished. I wish to get my films to the largest audience possible without compromising my aesthetics. If I had a megabudget I think I would set up a film school for women of difference: lesbian women, women of color, physically challenged women, old women, children. I would provide the equipment and film, the encouragement and criticism, and the environment in which they could begin personal work using the moving image.

"Controversy is healthy, especially if it is open. We need to critique one another's work, but before we can do that we must state our aesthetic. The criticism needs to be built on a philosophical structure. Criticism that comes from 'I-know-what-I-like-and-this-is-or-isn't-it' doesn't open a dialogue but rests upon a secret unspoken aesthetic. It is terrific to say this is what I like because I think…and we need this kind of film because… It is not helpful to critique silently to oneself, or to another, avoiding speaking directly to the person who made the work. We need to be strong in accepting difference, different voices, different work. We need to feel so strong in our sense of self that there is room for others. As there is no feminism but feminisms, so there is no lesbian cinema but lesbian cinemas," she says. "Light the projectors. I'm waiting." ■

For more information about Barbara Hammer's work, contact Women Make Movies, 225 Lafayette Street, Suite 211, New York, NY 10012, or Barbara Hammer, P.O. Box 1643, Canal Street Station, New York, NY 10014.

In The Life
New Works by Black Lesbian Filmmakers
by Cheryl Miller

Every March, the Chicago-based Women in the Director's Chair organization sponsors their annual International Women's Film and Video Festival. The event is well-known for the diversity of its screenings and the varied cultural backgrounds of the presenting film- and video-makers. [See articles in *HOT WIRE* issues July 1987, July 1988, and September 1989.]

The 1992 WIDC Festival offerings included a panel discussion and screenings called *In the Life: New Works by Black Lesbian Film and Video Makers*, which was part of "Mosaic in Black," a special presentation of films and videos that spotlighted the works of African American women filmmakers and video artists.

"Mosaic in Black" films included *Spin Cycle* (Aarin Burch), a short experimental film that explores some of the filmmaker's relationships;

From *HOT WIRE*, September 1992

Among Good Christian Peoples (Jacqueline Woodson/Catherine Saalfield), the story of a Black lesbian who was raised as a Jehovah's Witness; *A Powerful Thang* (Zeinabu Irene Davis), about intimacy; *Finding Christa*, about adoption and reunion, and *Suzanne, Suzanne*, about heroin addiction and mother/daughter communication (both by Camille Billops); *Land Where My Fathers Died* (Daresha Kyi), about family dynamics; *Illusions* (Julie Dash), about false imagery as status quo; and *Losing Ground* (Kathleen Collins), in which a Black female philosophy professor undertakes a quest for ecstasy.

The panelists for the *In the Life* discussion were Yvonne Welbon, Cheryl Dunye, and Michelle Parkerson. Yvonne Welbon is a MFA candidate at the School of the Art Institute of Chicago, and a journalist and writer/producer. In addition to creating her own works, she is interested in cataloging the work of other Black women

film- and videomakers. She has just completed a video about film director Julie Dash (*The Cinematic Jazz of Julie Dash*). Her award-winning experimental film *Monique*, which tells the story of a childhood relationship and her first comprehension of racism, was included in the *In the Life* screening. The autobiographical film tied for first in the Best Documentary category of the 17th Annual Festival of Illinois Film and Video Artists, and was also the winner in the Experimental category at the Chicago Student Film Festival.

Cheryl Dunye is an independent film and video artist committed to creating works that explore the lives and experiences of Black lesbians. Two of her videos were screened in this year's Festival. *She Don't Fade* explores the lusts and loves of Shae Clark, a character played by the filmmaker herself. *Janine* is a short video about Cheryl's high school friendship with an upper middle class white girl.

Michelle Parkerson, the

Washington, D.C.-based writer and independent producer/director, is currently working on *The Audre Lorde Project,* which chronicles the life and work of the internationally acclaimed Black lesbian poet. Michelle's other documentaries include *Storme: Lady of the Jewel Box, Gotta Make This Journey, Sweet Honey in the Rock,* and *But Then, She's Betty Carter.* [See "Filmmaker, Activist, Writer: Michelle Parkerson, July 1987 *HOT WIRE.*]

Michelle Parkerson

Debates occur at media arts conferences—as well as informally among members of the film-video community—regarding the value of specialized festivals and programming. Some feel that the distinction between different films should be completely eliminated. Is there value in specialized film festivals, such as the annual one put together by Women in the Director's Chair (WIDC), or is women's work presented enough in other venues?

Michelle Parkerson says that the WIDC festival—now in its eleventh year—is increasingly considered to be one of the major international women's festivals. Women filmmakers are able to be seen in other venues, but not with the specificity that is found at the WIDC festival. She has had her work screened at the WIDC festivals over the past five years, and says the response has been tremendous. For example, her documentary *Storme: Lady of the*

Jewel Box—about a woman of mixed race who worked as a male impersonator—was screened at the 1987 festival. Storme was a starring member of the Jewel Box Revue, a female impersonation company that played the Black theater circuit in the 1950s and 1960s. The Jewel Box Revue gained much notoriety because it was the first integrated cabaret of female impersonators. The screening of *Storme* at the WIDC Festival was instrumental in the film's being shown at other festivals. "FilmFest D.C.," an international film festival in Washington, D.C., picked up *Storme* because of the tremendous response and the press generated at the WIDC Festival," says Michelle.

The importance of the WIDC Festival is underscored by the size and diversity of the audience. "Not all of them were gay or lesbian," she says of this year's *In the Life* audience. "Not all of them were Black. Not all of them were female. I think it highlights and showcases this particular body of work in a way that might not happen at other festivals."

Cheryl Dunye expresses concern about the "ghettoizing" of Black gay and lesbian works in some gay and lesbian film festivals as well as at the women's festivals. "Our work ought to be intermingled with the main body of work," she says. "Our work and images are comparable to—and competitive with—the kinds of images that are being put out at large in the

Black independent media and in the gay and lesbian media."

Michelle agrees, but also believes that there is value in providing an umbrella under which certain work can be highlighted and showcased. "In a setting such as the *In the Life* screening and panel, Black lesbian work can be seen and judged within its own indigenous community," she says.

There is a wave of Black lesbian and gay filmmakers who are producing work that is explicitly gay. Michelle Parkerson is widely perceived to be at the forefront of this movement, though she doesn't think of herself that way. She says that she is of a certain generation of African American women who entered filmmaking in the mid-1970s. Among her peers are Ayoka Chenzira, Jackie Shearer, and Julie Dash. "We came of age at a time in which the political climate was such that the mere presence of women behind the camera—let alone African American women—was a big surprise to most people," she says.

The topics of her documentaries and early works were not necessarily specifically lesbian, though she herself was out. "In my writings, I've been much more out than if you look at the body of my work over the years," she says. "I think that now I'm coming into a phase of fruition in terms of putting some of the import and achievement and complexity of African American lesbians onscreen." She has been encouraged by a younger generation of lesbian filmmakers, such as Cheryl Dunye, Dawn Suggs, Sylvia Rhue, Aarin Burch, Jocelyn Taylor, and Yvonne Welbon. ("I always knew there were other Black lesbians in the community of Black independent filmmakers; however, their works were not specifically lesbian, or they themselves were not out.") She is inspired by this new generation because their initial works have been both lesbian-identified and Afrocentric. She believes that these African American women filmmakers, along with their male counterparts, are creating a new sensibility in images of Black gays and lesbians.

Michelle's current project documenting Audre Lorde's life and work is being produced by Ada Griffin, the executive director of Third World Newsreel, one of only a few distributors of politically progressive films and videos by people of color. In the past three years, Third World Newsreel has targeted works by lesbians and gay men of color. Ada Griffin developed the idea for the Audre Lorde project and invited Michelle Parkerson to be the director.

"I never knew the luxury of having just one job on a film project until I was invited to be the director of this project," says Michelle. "I don't have to be the director/editor/sound person. Most independents wear at least twenty hats when trying to bring a concept to screen, often because of the financial realities we encounter. At other times it is because of a reluctance to relinquish control of the vision. For me, though, it has usually been because of not having the resources to afford a large cadre of technicians and personnel. Often you don't have the money to pay them even minimally, let alone a wage that is comparable to their talents and expertise."

This project has produced a quantum leap in her career. Since being asked to direct the Audre Lorde project, Michelle has been offered other directing jobs, including the 1991 series of seven half-hour dramas for the Howard University PBS station celebrating the bicentennial of Washington, D.C. The dramas highlighted the lives of historic and contemporary ethnic leaders.

Michelle feels that the Audre Lorde project has taught her to examine more fully the subjects of her documentaries. "I think that *Betty Carter*, *Sweet Honey in the Rock*, and *Storme* all had a very celebratory premise. Investigating the complexities of these African American women's lives was not as central as the lauding of their artistic achievements. I'm learning to question more—the circumstances, the ambitions, the motivations of the subject. By doing this, I hope to show what makes Audre Lorde so important to so many people across so many cultures—to recognize her achievements, and frame them in such a way that someone who has never heard of Audre Lorde can understand why she is such a seminal figure in her discipline. I want to show some of the wonderful things about her life and illuminate some of the contradictions as well. This will not dilute the celebratory feelings of audiences toward women such as Lorde who are, in a sense, icons in their communities. I hope this will push us as viewers to investigate the range of our identities from the problematic to the wonderful ways that we all are."

Yvonne Welbon

Yvonne Welbon graduated from Vassar in 1984 with a degree in history. She moved to Taiwan to learn Chinese and stayed there for six years. After her first year in Taiwan, she founded an arts magazine for English-speaking foreigners who did not speak Chinese and consequently did not frequent the local galleries and theaters. "I started it because I believe you should live wherever you are," she says. The magazine's name, *Bang*, was derived from a Chinese word meaning great or terrific. When martial law was lifted in 1987, *Bang* expanded its focus to include political coverage.

Two factors contributed to Yvonne's transition into film and video. Around 1987, she developed a writing style that she called "imaging," in which she attempted to appeal to the reader's visual, auditory, and tactile senses. Her efforts were unsatisfactory, and she began to feel a growing need to express herself in a different medium. At a publishing conference, she first became aware of the power of video as a communications medium. "Although the conference was print-oriented, everyone was talking about video," she recalls. She then put together a pilot issue of the magazine on video. "If my strong area is as a communicator, then I should learn to communicate in the most powerful medium to get my message across."

Shortly after completing the pilot, Yvonne Welbon was involved in a near-fatal motorcycle accident. During her recovery, she began to re-examine her life. ("When you get really hurt, you think 'Why am I so far from home?'") She decided to close the magazine, return to the U.S., and go to film school.

On her return, she was disturbed by the fact that she knew of only one Black woman filmmaker—Julie Dash. "'Get real,' I thought. 'How can I be the only other Black woman who's thought about being a filmmaker?' When I tried to find more information about Black women filmmakers, I was amazed at how difficult it was. I could find more information in Taiwan than I could here! Because of my history background, it was important for me to know who the other women were. To know who you are, you have to know about the women who are like you, who came before you," she says. She currently has a database cataloging about sixty Black women filmmakers and 150 of their films, and has information on twenty-five more ready to be added.

Feeling that part of her mission is to document the work of these filmmakers, she recently completed *The Cinematic Jazz of Julie Dash*. "There needs to be work out there," she says. "We're not going to exist unless we put information out into the world that we do exist. I'd like to do more video essays on Black women filmmakers. When I do my feature, I don't want people to say, 'Black woman filmmaker? What's that?' or even 'Black lesbian filmmaker? What's that?'"

Last Christmas, Yvonne returned to Taiwan, where she shot footage for *Wei Yi-Fang, Remembering Myself*, an autobiographical film. She has also completed a screenplay entitled *Resurrecting Faith*, which she describes as a story about mistaken identities as well as about women finding themselves.

I asked her what she thought the '90s would mean for Black women filmmakers. "I'm really optimistic about the future," she says. "I can see a lot of women in and out of school taking cameras into their hands. Good quality consumer equipment is becoming more available, and with the popularity of the multicultural movement, you find the public—even white males—demanding to see more diverse work. There are just so many stories to tell—now more than ever we can and will make sure ours are seen."

Cheryl Dunye

When Cheryl Dunye was a beginning film student, she attended a Spike Lee lecture. A Black woman approached the mike and asked him to address what she felt to be the poor representation of Black women, particularly Black lesbians. He said that if she wanted different representation then she should make her own films. Next question. "I thought, 'God how cold—but in a way, how right,'" Cheryl recalls.

She is making films that create images and explore the worlds of Black lesbians. She had two pieces included in the Women in the Director's Chair film festival this year: *Janine* (about the struggle for acceptance despite racial and sexual differences), and *She Don't Fade* (about one woman's search for love and her relationships with other women). Originally, Cheryl intended this to be a video about a Black woman's coming out story. After the first rushes, the filmmaker inserted herself into the video as one of the characters.

"Then it became my story in relation to other women," she says. "It was very much off-the-cuff, and yet a somewhat structured production. There were a lot of narrative references to storytelling as well as comedy. I think that it is very interesting to use comedy to get your point across. This piece just evolved, and in some ways it was about evolution."

Cheryl Dunye just received

her master's degree in Fine Arts from Rutgers University and is currently working on several different projects. In addition to being a filmmaker, she is also a performance artist, and is working on a performance piece that is largely autobiographical, with the characters in the piece representing various Black lesbians. In the sketches which compose the piece, she explores the relationships of the characters to themselves, to other Black lesbians, and to the white lesbian community. "One personal story I call 'Vanilla Sex,'" she says. "It's about the term 'vanilla sex' and how it played in my life at one point."

She is also currently discussing a joint project with several Black gay men, including Essex Hemphill. "Essentially it will be a dialogue between Black lesbians and Black gay men. I believe that it is necessary for culturally active Black lesbians and Black gay men to develop some type of community with each other." She is almost finished with an experimental video called *The Potluck and the Passion*, which is about the meeting of souls at a potluck hosted by a Black lesbian couple to celebrate their anniversary.

When Cheryl first started working in the media arts, she knew of only one other Black lesbian filmmaker—Michelle Parkerson. When asked if there is now more of a community of Black lesbian filmmakers, she responds, "Yes and no." She believes that there is more openness and discussion about sexuality in the '90s. "However," she says, "we're still working against the dominant mainstream and/or dominant independent notion of what film and video art is—and that still remains white and heterosexual. There's also the conflict between working together and working individually. We do talk to each other and try to support each other's work. We are on each other's panels." She thinks that there is more of a gathering together, but adds, "We're all just trying to make it. Being a woman artist is hard even if you're dealing with the issue of lesbianism."

Unlike some other art forms, film and video require substantial amounts of money in order to produce a finished product. Many people are concerned that in this current political climate it will become even more difficult to raise money for work that has a gay or lesbian theme. Cheryl believes that people must become more creative in their fundraising efforts. During the panel discussion she suggested that people try to raise funds on a grassroots level. "Offer a lottery. Throw fundraising parties." During the interview I asked her if she thought money will become even tighter in this climate. She said, "I know of a white straight male filmmaker who said that he wishes he was a Black lesbian, because supposedly they're getting all the money and attention. I haven't seen it. There are still very few funds that are specifically for gays. There's the Out Fund, and there are a couple of lesbian funds," she acknowledges, "but there's not much out there."

The eleventh WIDC International Film and Video Festival was held in conjunction with the Center for New Television. In addition to the *In the Life* panel, there was also a panel of Black women filmmakers moderated by Dr. Gloria Gibson-Hudson (writer and assistant director of the Black Film Center/Archive at Indiana University). It featured Camille Billops (mixed-media artist, filmmaker, playwright, TV staff writer, and keeper of the Archives of Black-American Cultural History of the Hatch-Billops Collection in New York); teacher/filmmaker Zeinabu irene Davis (*Cycles*, *A Powerful Thang*); and Michelle Crenshaw (producer/director and union camera assistant for feature films, commercials, and industrials).

In addition to the films shown as part of the *In the Life* series, the festival featured work by more than four dozen other women, and was divided into several categories. ■

For info about the 1993 International Women's Film and Video Festival: Women in the Director's Chair, 3435 N. Sheffield Ave., Chicago, IL 60657. (312) 281-4988.

Lesbian Movies I'd Like to See

by Diane F. Germain

TEENAGE MILITANT NINJA LEZBOS: Reptilian dykes are cool to the touch but never slimy in their politics.

GRIMLEZ 2—THE NEW BITCH: A gruesome tale of really small and mean-hearted lesbian trolls. Hard to believe. Of little redeeming value.

POSTCARDS FROM THE EDGE: Memories of a traveling poets' collective and their talking lavender van. Kind of strange, but has its touching moments.

STAR TREK VI—THE UNDISCOVERED "C" WORK: Nimoy and Shatner have been reduced to silicone statues in a futuristic "museum of man." No one has time to rescue them, as every lesbian possible is jetting among the stars liberating other female aliens from the fear of intimacy and internalized homophobia. Look for a clever use of the calibrated G-Spot Finder near the end.

From *HOT WIRE*, May 1992.

FRIED LESBO TOMATOES: The title sounds like Damon Runyon's idea of lesbians on drugs, but not so. A feisty old lesbian, recently escaped from a nasty nursing home, helps a bedraggled but adorable homemaker find love and joy in the arms of another woman. This is accomplished amusingly through stories of radical rural activist lesbians.

PRETTY WOMBMOONS: Romantic separatists are beautiful and witchy in this comedy of class differences and love.

DYKELET: Shakespeare's eternal dilemma—to be one or not to be one.

THE PRINCESS OF DIKES: A Dutch lesbian stomps through her childhood memories for the key that will save her sensitive sister from a painful case of writer's block. Hint: It has something to do with holding back the oceans, leaks, and fingers used in an unusual way.

DYKELINERS: Exciting film about women medical students daring each other to compete for the longest time doing cunnilingus without coming up for air.

THE DYKE THAT ROCKS THE CRADLE: An indictment against the lesbian "baby boom" of recent years. An innocent-looking baby dyke acting as "nanny" is suspected of attempting to single-handedly curtail the "patriarchal breeders syndrome."

FREE DYKE CITY: A separatist's dream of the future...a women-only city patrolled by lesbian rock stars. Carol MacDonald, Helen Hooke, Toshi Reagon, and the women of BETTY and Musica Femina are the intense bounty hunters who relentlessly chase down Richard Gere, the weird intruder. The grossest part is the scene where he claims to be a lesbian. Eeeoow! No way!

LEZ' BETTER BLUES: African-American dykes into sex, jazz trombones, and the value of commitment.

AT PLAY IN THE FIELDS OF THE LEZBOS: Two mercenary white boys crash land in the jungle amid an Amazon tribe. Big personalities clash dramatically as the women decide how to get rid of these intruders and save the rain forest.

NUNS ON THE NUN: Several religious women have desires for the aloof Mother Superior in a Montreal cloister.

NOT WITHOUT MY GIRL-FRIEND: Two Iranian women struggle to escape the binds of patriarchy and tradition to come to America as a couple.

ATTACK OF THE FIFTY FOOT LESBIAN: A science fiction classic monster humorous in her proclivity to bite off the heads of pig-like men, but hey, guys, it's just a feminist movie... don't you have any sense of humor? ▧

Tortilleras*

by Terri de la Peña

On that balmy summer evening, Veronica Melendez and her friend Michi Yamada were lucky enough to find a sidewalk table outside Alice's Restaurant. Westwood Boulevard teemed with noisy traffic, its rumbling sounds jarring Veronica's nerves. For most of that day, she had sat before her typewriter, struggling over the first draft of her novel. She had been relieved when Michi had phoned and rescued her, but she had not counted on dining outdoors.

Being alone so much made her cranky. And the trouble with writing, Veronica mused, was its inward focus; it intensified her reclusive tendencies and moody spells. With Michi back in town, Veronica knew her friend would not allow her to wither at the typewriter; Michi would push her into socializing again.

Veronica lifted her wine goblet. "I'm so glad you got the job, Mich! Now we'll both be on campus this fall."

Michi grinned. Her bejeweled fingers sparkled with amethyst and blue topaz. She clicked her glass to Veronica's and took a quick sip. "'Course my parents'd prefer my being in grad school. But I'll be doing administrative work for a Japanese-American oral history project, so

at least it'll be relevant." Michi dug into her combination salad, selecting slivers of purple cabbage. "You've been quiet tonight, Roni. Still in the writing mode?"

Veronica shrugged. "Sometimes it takes a while to snap back into reality." She rolled some garbanzo beans across her plate. "It's hard to fictionalize something that actually happened. And the more I write about Joanna, the more I miss her." She turned from Michi, watching a heterosexual couple nuzzling at the next table. The woman's hair was glossy brown, like Joanna's had been. Veronica stared for a moment, remembering, and turned away when the woman's gaze met hers.

"Maybe it's too soon, Roni. It's only been eight months since—"

Michi broke off, her face uncommonly solemn. "It might be a better idea to write about something else."

"No. I need to deal with my feelings now. Keeping a journal wasn't enough. I need to get Joanna's essence on paper, before I forget—" Veronica looked away again, her eyes wet.

"Roni, you'll never forget her. I know I won't." Michi sniffled and very nonchalantly wiped the corner of one eye in the same motion as she patted her moussed crewcut. Her black hair glistened in the streetlight's glow.

Veronica blinked quickly and tried to smile. Michi had not invited her out to talk about her deceased lover, although mention of Joanna in-

*A slightly different version of this story became Chapter 7 of de la Peña's first novel, *Margins* (Seal Press, 1992) From *Lesbian Bedtime Stories*, ed. Terry Woodrow [Tough Dove Books, 1989]

evitably entered their conversations. Tonight, Veronica felt she owed it to Michi—and to herself—to put thoughts of Joanna aside, to relax and have an enjoyable time.

She reached across the table and affectionately touched her friend's hand. "I'm still dealing with it, Mich, but I'm okay." She tweaked Michi's pudgy cheek. "Tell me about the student films we're seeing tonight."

Michi perked up. "After I landed the job, I swung down to the Women's Resource Center to see what's cooking on campus. According to a flyer posted there, one film has a lesbian theme." She wriggled in her chair and leaned forward, her eyes alight.

"No wonder you dragged me away from my typewriter." Veronica smiled, this time spontaneously. With typical zest, Michi had already unearthed some lesbian culture on campus.

Michi grinned. "There'll be a question and answer session about each film, but I'm only interested in the dyke flick. We don't even have to stay for the others."

They looked at each other and laughed.

In the Melnitz Hall screening room, Veronica and Michi selected center seats in the fourth row. The first film, a science fiction spoof, though technically superior, needed much editing. As the discussion droned on, enlivened by the witticisms of sci fi buffs, Michi scanned the sparse audience for any trace of lesbians. Veronica had difficulty staying awake. The long hours of writing had caught up with her. She soon nodded off, her curly head propped on Michi's shoulder. Her catnap was interrupted when her friend jabbed her in the ribs.

"Who is THAT?" Michi whispered harshly.

"What?" Veronica unfolded herself and frowned.

"That Latina Amazon who just walked in and brightened the scenery."

Drowsily, Veronica followed Michi's directions and viewed a leggy Chicana with a stylish haircut: short and sleek on the sides, long and tapering in back. She wore form-fitting Levis, rust-colored Frye boots, and a turquoise T-shirt with a silk-screened portrait of Mexican artist Frida Kahlo directly over her impressive breasts.

"I think my heart's stopped." Michi breathed quickly, as if gasping for air.

"She's probably straight." Veronica ignored Michi's exaggerated reaction and leaned back again. But she continued gazing at the striking woman, admiring her glowing brown skin, black hair, and ebony eyes. Keeping her thoughts to herself, Veronica considered the woman a fine mestiza dyke. Unlike Joanna's tawny-skinned delicate beauty, this tall Chicana no doubt boasted sangre de india.

Leaving a colorful hemp bag beside her notebook on the discussion table, the Chicana strode past the two friends, her long legs nimbly taking the steps two at a time, heading towards the projection room.

"She's got to be the lesbian film maker," Michi squealed, nearly bouncing off her seat. "Oh, thank you, Goddess!"

"Michi, cool it, okay?" With aplomb, Veronica picked up the one-page program and read it aloud. "The film *Tortilleras* was directed by grad student René Talamantes."

"Did you take a good look at her? Amazon City! Dyke Delight! Aren't you glad you're here, Roni?"

"As long as her film keeps me awake, I'll be fine." Veronica fluffed her hair and stifled a yawn.

The short film *Tortilleras* contained no dialog, but consisted of stark black-and-white close-ups of two Latinas, clad in flowing transparent robes, performing a silent but very erotic mating dance. Wide awake, Veronica gazed at the screen, mesmerized as the dark-skinned women glided in stylized movements, nearly touching, tossing their lengthy black hair over their shoulders.

In the darkness, Veronica imagined them to be Joanna and her, advancing and retreating, teasing each other with suggestive motions, fingers outlining breasts, hips and thighs. Alone in their apartment, they had often danced together, moving sensuously to rhythm-and-blues standards, falling into bed together afterwards. All those wondrous nights—Veronica longed for her Joanna; but she was gone forever. Beside her, she heard her friend's sudden intake of breath, and hoped Michi would not hyperventilate.

Communicating visually, the Latinas in the film whirled and twirled, graceful mirror images of one another. At last, they concluded their stylized dance by embracing, their lips touching and melding as the film faded to black. The audience's hushed silence was broken only by scattered applause.

"Roni, I'm ready to faint," Michi whispered. The screening room's lights flickered on and the two friends blinked dazedly.

"I'm feeling kind of woozy myself," Veronica admitted. She noticed the flush on Michi's face, and wondered if her own betrayed her. The temperature in the room seemed stifling.

They both stared at the willowy unperturbed Chicana standing at the discussion table, one brown hand casually upon her hip, awaiting the audience's remarks. A professorial-looking man in the first row wasted no time in asking the significance of the film's title.

René Talamantes' smoky voice filled the small auditorium. "In Spanish, 'tortillera' literally means a woman who makes tortillas. In the film's context, I use 'tortillera' to suggest tribadism."

Veronica felt a titillating shiver course along her spine. Talamantes' words bore a Southwestern tinge, a slight drawl uncharacteristic of local Latinas. She imagined the dark women in the film rubbing their bodies together like warm tortillas gently molded in a Chicana's hand. Veronica could not remove her eyes from the self-assured film maker.

"She actually said 'tribadism,'" Michi murmured in awe.

"I wonder if everyone here knows the definition," Veronica remarked. She could not recall having been so affected by any other film, and tried to modulate her tone. "Some of those guys in front look absolutely mystified."

"Ask her something," Michi urged with a nudge.

"You ask her." Veronica edged away and rested her chin on her hand. "I dare you, Mich, since you're creaming all over the place."

Suppressing a giggle, Michi accepted the challenge. Her right arm with its multicolored yarn bracelets shot up. Determined to be noticed, she even stood.

The film maker cooly pointed to her.

"I was just wondering why you decided to shoot in black and white." Michi's voice sounded an octave higher than usual.

René Talamantes grinned at her question. "Two reasons: first, I wanted to focus on the women's mutual sexual attraction. Color would've distracted from that, and it really wasn't necessary anyway, because both women have the same skin tones. I think black and white emphasizes their similarities. If I had wanted to show their dissimilarities—for example, if one woman were Latina and the other white, color might have worked better. For my purposes, black and white worked fine. My second reason was purely financial. Color film and processing are expensive."

Talamantes' frank answer prompted some murmuring and laughter. While the film maker responded to a more challenging question, Michi glanced at her companion. "Isn't she fabulous?"

Veronica frowned, recalling her day's labor on the novel. "What if everyone decided not to use dialog? I live by words, Michi. As much as I like the film, I'm uncomfortable with its silence."

"Tell her so." Michi gave a teasing pinch.

Wincing from the sudden pain, Veronica moved her arm reflexively, just in time for the film maker to point to her.

"Michi, I'll kill you someday." Veronica glared at her amused friend and quickly formed a question. She felt her heart slide into her throat, but her words tumbled out without obstruction.

"I'm curious about the lack of dialog—and even of music. I think the film is unique as it is, but silents aren't too common these days. Most current films, it seems, have superfluous dialog—not like the well-crafted scripts of the classics. And recently there's been so much emphasis on technique. Was eliminating dialog and music a budgetary decision, too? Can you elaborate your reasons for making a silent film?"

With a droll expression, Talamantes appraised Veronica before answering. Her drawl became more pronounced. "For a film student, almost everything boils down to budgetary decisions. Despite that, I really wanted to show that when a definite sexual message occurs between two people, only the basics count—eye contact, facial signals, body language. I decided to pare everything down to the bare essentials. That's why I eliminated color, dialog, and music." She paused, gesturing towards Veronica. "You seem to know a lot about films. Do you think my technique worked?"

Veronica's heart threatened to pop out of her cotton shirt. "Well—yes."

"Bueno. Quiero hablar contigo despues. Esperame."

At that personalized request, Veronica blushed, even more embarrassed when several members of the audience turned to gawk.

"Roni, you're fabulous!" Michi snuggled closer, one hand on Veronica's knee. "What did she say?"

"She wants to talk with me afterwards."

"Sounds like a 'definite sexual message.'" Michi pressed Veronica's knee. "Let's ask her out for cappuccino."

"If I don't murder you first." Veronica pretended to be annoyed with Michi; yet she could barely hide her eagerness—and apprehension. "I don't even know what I said."

"Words just poured out of your eloquent little mouth."

Veronica groaned. "Michi, you're so full of it."

⚢

Before the next film began, the two friends scurried after René Talamantes. She stood in the film department's narrow corridor and stuffed her notebook into her hemp bag. She glanced up when they approached.

Veronica lagged behind, trying to maintain her dignity despite her nervousness. Memories of Joanna filled her mind, but she did not want to think of her at that moment. After long months of mourning, she at last felt attracted to a woman. Simultaneously, she felt disloyal. But she aimed for a calm attitude in spite of her conflicting emotions, and casually learned against the corridor wall.

Talamantes smiled. "Thanks for your comments, women. I had a feeling I'd be crucified in there. Did you hear that one pendejo who asked why there were no men in the film?" She laughed, her teeth large and white.

"I guess the subtleties were lost on him." Veronica shrugged, hands in her jeans pockets. She noticed the film maker was about three inches taller than her and even more attractive up close.

"De veras." Talamantes' deep-set eyes surveyed her. "Vienes de aqui?"

"Santa Monica." Veronica suddenly wished she had used the proper Spanish pronunciation of her home town; she was unaccustomed to switching languages in midstream and uneasy about her rusty Spanish. She hoped the film maker would not insist on speaking it; some Latinas did as a matter of principle. Besides, she did not want Michi to be left out of the conversation.

"Yo soy Tejana, nacida en El Paso. Eres Chicana?"

Veronica nodded, not trusting her voice.

Michi cut in. "We're going for cappuccino. Would you like to join us?" Next to Talamantes, Michi seemed smaller than usual.

"Sure. Great idea." The film maker offered one lean brown hand to each. "I'm René. I didn't catch your names."

After they introduced themselves, they stood awkwardly in the empty hallway, clasping each other's hands.

Talamantes squeezed Veronica's fingers. "So you're Chicana, too. Que suave! I got jazzed seeing you in the audience. Usually I'm the only brown woman in sight."

"I know the feeling." Veronica met her compelling gaze again and did not look away. René's fingers were warm and electric.

Her free hand smoothing her moussed head, Michi fidgeted.

Talamantes noticed Michi's impatience and alternated her gaze between them. "Perdoname. Are you two lovers?"

"Friends," Veronica sputtered. She was taken aback at René's candor, but also grateful for her question.

"Since first grade," Michi swiftly added.

"Hey, that's cool." Talamantes finally released their hands, slinging her hemp bag over her wide shoulder. "Want to go off campus or over to the Kerckhoff coffeehouse?"

"Kerckhoff sounds fine," Veronica said with a sudden smile.

♀♀

"So what brought you two dykes to my film preview?" Talamantes stretched her long legs and waited for her cappuccino to cool.

Michi raised her brows. "Are you always this direct?"

"Why not, huh?" The film maker's even teeth gleamed.

"Roni, you're blushing," Michi teased.

"That's just the reflection of my red shirt against my brown face," Veronica explained, toying with a strand of her curly hair.

"Yeah, and my eyes're slanted 'cause I'm squinting from the cappuccino steam." Michi impishly wriggled her brows.

Amid Talamantes' raucous laughter, Veronica tried to maintain a serious demeanor. "Let's get back to René's question. This Munchkin," she continued, gesturing towards the grinning Michi, "lured me over to Melnitz, and didn't even mention your film until we were having dinner in the Village. And, even though I split hairs over the lack of dialog, I am really impressed with *Tortilleras*. It's sensual and erotic—and it works."

"For her to say that's a major compliment," Michi interjected. "She's a writer, you see."

"Oh, yeah?" Talamantes leaned forward, one round breast brushing the table slightly. "Anything I'd be familiar with?"

Veronica tossed Michi a peeved glance. "I've written for *Westwinds* and *The Jacaranda Review*. And I've had pieces in *Conditions*, and in *Third Woman*."

"And tell her about your novel, Roni."

"You're writing a novel?" At that, Talamantes set down her cup, elbows on the table.

"I'm in the middle of the first draft." Veronica blew on her cappuccino to avoid looking up.

"Does it have a lesbian theme?"

Veronica nodded, finally taking a sip.

Gesturing, René's graceful hands spoke a language of their own. "Listen, we ought to collaborate. To be honest, Veronica, my weak point is structure. I do great camera work, but when it comes to structuring a story, I really have to buckle down. The writing doesn't come easily. I'd sure like to get some tips from you."

Veronica studied her, liking the way Talamantes had pronounced her name in perfect Spanish—Veh-roe-nee-ka—a verbal caress. Accustomed to "Roni," her childhood nickname, Veronica had forgotten the Latin beauty of her actual appellation. She felt herself smile.

"Well, René, I'm a grad student in the English Department, so I'll be back on campus this fall. Right now, I'm concentrating on finishing my first draft. I'd be glad to help you out, if I can, but I've only taken one screenwriting course."

"Hey, I'd be satisfied if you'd just take a look at one of my screenplays." René reached for her hemp bag and fished inside for her combination calendar/address book. "What's your phone number?"

Veronica heard herself stutter. "450-1868. It'll be Michi's, too, before long. She's moving in with me."

"We're both in states of transition, and decided we needed mutual support," Michi explained.

"Yeah. Tell me about it. I could use some supportive friends myself. I'm the only token dyke in the film department, and sometimes it gets damn lonesome." René threw the book into her bag and downed more cappuccino. "Besides, earlier this year, I made the gigantic mistake of getting involved with a theater arts major. She thought I'd make her a star."

"Was she one of the women in the film?" Michi probed.

"Hell, that's what caused all the mitote between us. She's white and couldn't understand why I wouldn't use her for *Tortilleras*." Talamantes pushed her coarse black hair from her face. "Are you two single?"

Michi sighed, playing with her ear cuff.

"Yes," Veronica said quietly. And for the first time in months, she was sure. ∎

by Diane F. Germain, from *Lesbian News* (April 1991)

Me and Ahnie Silver

by Sandy Boucher

There was a sense of something missing, right from the beginning. I felt the lack that first Sunday when she arrived at my house. Sitting in my living room, Ahnie talked at length about her work. "This fall maybe I should go ahead and do it," she said. "Really, Columbus, Ohio is no place for a dancer. There's no stimulation here. No challenge. People tell me I could do well in New York...." I watched her, speechless. Her perfect blondness, her height, intimidated me.

"I like you as much today as I did last night," she said, and I found her words hard to believe, for no particular warmth came from her toward me. I was puzzled by her, until, when she got up to leave, she stopped at the door and put her arms around me. She held me with surprising urgency. When she pulled away to leave, excitement welled up in me, and my questions of a moment before drowned like helpless kittens in a flood of desire.

We were unlikely people to be together. Ahnie's dance classes and performances were attended by the young hip women in town; she was the darling of the lesbians and feminists up near the university. I live in the same house in Grandview where my family lived, and now, in my forties, I am still working at the insurance company where I started back when I finished high school.

From *The Notebooks of Leni Clare, and Other Short Stories*. Freedom, CA: The Crossing Press, 1982.

Maybe we should never have made love (we moved so easily over into sensuality, and then sexuality), but the night it happened I did not feel it as a mistake. Our being there together seemed wondrous to me as her hands cradled my thighs, heartbreakingly gentle. Lingering, palms brushing my skin, she smoothed the fine hairs there. I lay absolutely still, responding to all the comforting I could ever have wanted.

I stroked Ahnie's pale straight hair. Her cheeks were flat above a squared chin, her mouth a straight line. Her skin was deeply sun-tanned, bronze on the shoulders and arms, red gold on the face. I was immensely intrigued by her face as it changed, when she was disturbed, clenching into a tight wrinkled scowl. When I held her, making love to her, she turned her head against my arm, eyes closed, sucking my skin in her excitement, not wanting to open her face to me, let me look deeply into her eyes. And I was so moved by the flat expanse of her cheek, the line of jaw, the lock of hair lying next to her ear, the muscles of her throat swelling under the tanned skin. I was touched by her hiding away from me in her desire.

She eluded me, from the beginning, even in our most intimate moments. It was like a chase: Ahnie glimpsed for an instant—Ah, there she is!—and then gone. I had had several wonderful lovers in my life, women who satisfied and instructed me; never had I been with someone like Ahnie.

Only in her performing was she fully

present. Dancing, she projected a special quality of delight. She opened herself to her own magic when she was in public, with an audience, with students. The smile then—dazzling. And the eyes partook. They were extraordinary in that blond face, brows and lashes colorless so they startled in their pale clarity. Eyes full open and brilliant: she glowed. This gesture was immensely affecting, something of surrender in it. I watched the people gather about her after a performance—she taller than many of them, standing there in her white performance suit, the brown of her beautiful arms and shoulders deepened by the contrast. She clutched a bouquet to her chest, looking into the faces of her admirers, offering them her complete attention with that miraculous smile, those eyes saying, You are magical too. I acknowledge your being. A joyous love came from her, and they gathered about waiting to touch her, embrace her, smile into the full beaming of herself that she gave them.

When her students discovered we were lovers, they said, "How wonderful!" "Ahnie Silver is so wonderful." They said, "She must be very easy to love." They said, "Ah, you're so lucky!" My old friends gazed curiously at me when they saw us together. I knew they were wondering what Rose Giannini was doing with someone like Ahnie. Most of them are securely settled in couples, own homes together, have raised each other's children and supported each other over the years. They wondered what Ahnie and I had to say to each other.

Her face was so often closed in worry when she was with me: she worried about money, her classes, her car, her big floppy afghan dog, Spark, who was silkily delicate and ridiculous and often sick. She worried about the aching of her legs, the dried flower arrangements on the walls of her apartment (Did I like them? Were they too impersonal? Should she hang posters?), the way her apartment smelled.

In fact I did dislike her place, in one of those cheap apartment houses thrown up for students right near the university. Her apartment was a sterile, white-walled box, and I could not understand how she could be so contented there.

She lay under the sun lamp's harsh light, saying, "I wish I had smooth arms like yours."

"But it's because my muscles aren't developed," I laughed, "and look, I'm getting flabby!" Lifting my arm to show her.

"No, most women's arms are like yours. Even if you developed muscles, your arms would be smooth."

"People are turned on by your muscles," I reminded her.

"I know. Now they are. A lot of women are now, because of the women's movement. And some men. But I used to be ashamed of my muscles. I wore sleeves to cover them up."

She had long legs, a tight round behind, absolutely flat belly, slim upper body rising to shoulders held a little forward, muscles of arms and shoulders boldly defined under the brown skin, muscles of back beautifully articulated.

I sat on her bed watching her as she lay under the lamp.

"I like your muscles, Ahnie, but I don't love you for your body."

"Yes, I know that." She turned to look at me. The smile that began was not the vivid, public one. It was thoughtful, for herself and for me.

Yet if I am honest, surely it was the romance of a perfect body, that physique in which she was more present than in her emotions or her spirit, that drew me. And I know I basked in the glamour of her performing, vicariously enjoying the applause.

In that first month I was swept with a consuming hunger for her. I remember the expansiveness, the charm, with which she turned toward me, the way she opened to me, questioned me about who I am, what I like, what I think— arrived on my lunch hour at work with sausage and pickles and tomatoes and pumpernickel so that we could eat together before she had to hurry off to teach a class. And when she came to my house late, after her classes were over, we ate dinner and she talked with such intensity about teaching, performing, about what was going on in the New York dance world, about her plans. I was dazzled by her, all of this new to me. Ahnie's life seemed so much more vibrant than mine, or, *crucial*, as if she lived closer to her own hot flame, so that each moment mattered. We stayed up until dawn sometimes, and often the next morning I went into my job late or not at all. And Ahnie said, "Let's live together. I want to have a home with you." I did not know how to respond to that because it seemed she wanted to install herself in my life—to have me as support for her work, companion for her home life. My family's old house is really a home to me after all these years: perhaps she felt she would be taken care of by me if she moved in with me here. I was forty-three while she was not yet thirty: was she looking to be mothered? I held back, cautious, noncommittal. But deep inside I was certain we would live together very soon, for I wanted a life-partner, one who would daily share my existence. It's what I was used to. I had lived in this house with a lover five of the seven years since my mother died. That daily intimacy seems to me the most human way to live.

So I perpetrated a fantasy. There was that gap in my life and Ahnie would fill it, even though I suspected, from all the evidence, that she was not a person to depend on. I went right ahead with the dream anyway, imagining Ahnie and I settled in domestic bliss, letting the momentum of my desire carry me forward.

One Saturday afternoon she arrived for a surprise visit, saying, "Let's go upstairs and make love." And the very next day we did it again, and she said in astonishment, "That's the first time in my life I ever made love two afternoons in a row." I was used to more voluptuousness in lovers. But Ahnie lived for her career, anxiously tending the details of her work twenty-four hours a day. She could not lie in bed in the mornings; she went out to breakfast—to a restaurant where everyone knew her. Sometimes I went with her. We drank strong coffee and talked about her work. I learned from her. I was neglecting my own work to be with her. I had no time anymore to spend with the nieces and nephews who used to demand so much of me. I made excuses to my sisters and their husbands when they invited me over. I told my friends I was too busy to see them. All this so I could be available when Ahnie needed me.

She began to withhold herself. She began to find fault. "You are very needy," she said. "You are a subtly controlling person." "You want more than I can give." "You want to consume me." In the morning she lay rigidly separate and would not touch me. I was confused then, feeling shut away from her; and her face looked so angry that it seemed she was punishing me for something. I could not leave her apartment without asking, "Will you hug me?" Her anger flashed out at me. "Why can't you allow me my freedom!" Until everything I did was seen as an attempt to manipulate her.

We were making love: I unbuckled her watch, removed it, placed it on the bedside table. Hours later, the rage boiled out. "How dare you take off my watch! How dare you intrude on me like that!" It had seemed so natural to me, thinking she had forgotten the watch and I was doing her a favor by removing it.

"Why are you so angry with me?"

"Because I needed to be alone after dinner," she said. "I wanted to go in the bedroom by myself for half an hour."

"Yes?"

"Now I feel smothered by you."

"But why *didn't* you go off by yourself after dinner. I wouldn't have cared."

"I don't know. I just didn't. I stayed talking with you."

"Do you want to be alone *now*?"

"No, it's too late now. I'm too angry."

At her work, Ahnie was always with students or audience, always observed, and when she left it she wanted to be alone. Knowing my job so well, bored with it, I looked for stimulation in my evenings and weekends. We conflicted. There were the signals that she wanted to be taken care of: losing keys, losing money, breaking things, leaving things, the distraction, the distress. And when I responded instinctively, moving forward to help, she said it made her feel inadequate and controlled by me. "Don't help me!" she snapped, "I don't want your help."

I knew it was wrong. Sometimes I talked to myself, saying, Rose, you could stop this, you could step back, say I don't want this. But there was such intoxication in some of our time together, as if we escaped real life, with all its responsibilities, to become children again. I had let myself become addicted to those moments, imagining they could make up for the rest.

At the studio where she taught and performed, she stepped into the center of her power. Here she could afford any generosity. The Silver Dance and Gymnastics Studio on High Street near the Capitol looked like any other storefront from the outside, but inside a hardwood floor had been carefully laid, spotlight racks hung high up against the walls. Ahnie had created this environment through five years of discipline, effort, risk of herself. Perhaps only here in all the world was she safe. In this great high room with its wall of mirrors she was gracious, even to me. She made a place for me here where I might have been so at loose ends. I was her special person in the studio, lovingly touched, asked for my opinion on her costume, how she should begin, should she use the drum? And after the performance when she stood still, letting the people come to her, speak to her, touch her, I waited; until at some moment suddenly she was there before me, grasping my arms, wanting me to touch her, kiss her, wanting to know, Was it all right? Was I good? Did I do well?

We went out to eat, then, with the money from the gate—a few of her friends with us. In the Chinese restaurant, loud and busy, she and I sat next to each other on the bench against the wall, thighs touching, enjoying this closeness. I was exchanging funny remarks with her friend, who sat across from us, and I had a sense that now in this verbal play *I* was performing for *Ahnie*. I could feel her pleasure in watching me.

Then, leaving the restaurant—it was near midnight—in the car and in the kitchen of my house, she wanted to hear from me in detail about the performance. I told her what I had seen; I called up the parts I found most powerful or interesting. More than that I could not tell her because I don't know about dance or movement, how it should be. She said that's all rigid traditional bullshit anyway; what she wanted to know was what happened inside me as I watched. I tried to tell her, searching for the words that would name my feelings. I was secretly thrilled by this sharing, experiencing an energy, almost a fervor, that I remembered from my childhood.

When I was a little girl I had thought I would be an artist, maybe the person who painted the statues in the church, or a singer warbling *Ave Maria* so beautifully that everyone would cry. My mother and my sisters and brothers and I spent so much time in church that it was the theater for all my fantasies. But out in the world, I always settled for what was practical, taking the secretarial course in high school, working to put my brother through college. Then when Papa died, my sisters were already married or engaged, and my brother was in medical school: there was no one else to take care of Mama and it was important not to lose the house in Grandview where we'd all grown up. So I stayed there with her, keeping my secretarial job at the insurance company, where eventually I was promoted to underwriter. But even after all those years of issuing insurance policies, the desire sometimes awoke in me to reach inside to what was most true in myself, bring it out and shape it as something in the world, the way Ahnie shapes her feelings into a performance.

Our merging was powerful—much of ourselves simply accessible to the other without effort on our part—to a depth that I have experienced with few others. Making love to her, that afternoon when she arrived to surprise me, I saw the insides of her thighs, her pubic hair. It seemed she was golden, the blond hairs on the tanned skin. A golden woman who was so fully present there with me, so without fear or defensiveness, not yielding so much as opening physically to my opening, that I was carried out in waves of feeling that can hardly be called pleasure. It was more a heaving, awakening of senses in my spine, my groin, capacities locked away even for years. I knew she experienced it too.

It was this wonderment and deep physical awareness that forged the commitment in me. I remember that flat voice speaking softly next to me in bed. I had turned to rest my closed eye on the curve of her shoulder, enjoying the warmth of her flesh against the skin of my eyelid. "You're very sweet," she murmured. And I who have sometimes in my life felt so ponderous, as if my flesh were stupid and slow, not worthy to be loved, experienced myself lithe and cherished.

At first there was such delight in discovery. I found that when I was not with her I was aware of walking like her, of making the gestures her body makes—that leaning forward, knees flexed, that attitude of listening, the head thrust forward and up. This mimicry became a pleasure I cultivated: talking to someone at work, I heard myself speaking with her inflection; I continued it, secretly playing this game of closeness with her while maintaining a perfectly reasonable conversation. Delicious. Walking from the office building to the parking lot, I enlarged my stride to adopt her vigorous athlete's walk.

How it comes in, now, the ways in which she held herself away from me: remembrance of a morning at her apartment when she was making love to me. I felt her strangely separate in the act, hiding off in herself even as she stroked my breasts, bent to kiss my throat, and I found myself staring at the photographs of her taped to that stark white wall next to her bed. Ahnie, seated among her dance students, looking sideways at them, gesturing as she spoke. I stared at this picture—and next to it the photo of a performance she had done in the nude, her body supported by a group of dancers. Her hands stroked my belly, her tongue moved delicately. I came back to her real self, to touch her brown shoulders, her hair—but my eyes kept returning to the photographs, seeking out those two images that could give her to me. She lay her cheek against my belly, her voice came, "So sweet." And I stared at the spread-open nude body held ecstatically aloft, turned my eyes to the intent face of the teacher speaking to her students. Hoping to know her in this moment, touch her, I was caught in the space between those cardboard images and the woman of flesh who lay cradling my hips. In this most intimate of situations, Ahnie was strangely absent.

She was interested only in herself and her career, caught in the habit of tight focus on a goal. The rest was worry: the elaborate fumbling ritual with her contact lenses. They did not fit right. Were they scratched? Taking them out, washing them. Were they lost? Dropped on the floor. Stuck to the side of the bottle. Putting them on. Discomfort. The indecision over a place to live. Move or not move? Go once and for all to New York? There were problems with the car, and with Spark, who was scratching a lot. He might have some kind of mange, and what would she do about *that!* A favorite student did not come to class. Was this a gesture of rejection? She lay for hours under the sun lamp, worrying. I saw how ill-suited we were for each other, I so exasperated by her constant anxious questioning, and yet I could not pull back for I had allowed myself to love her in a way that contradicted reality, our two persons, my own needs.

Sometimes I was foolishly innocent and vulnerable, trusting in a kindness I was used to in lovers. After one performance I was in the kitchen, preparing a midnight supper. Happy to be there in my house with her, happily singing to myself, "Wouldn't it be loverly" as I stirred the soup, "...lots of chocolates for me to eat, lots of coals making lots of heat"—wallowing in intimations of domestic comfort with her, someday, to live together, eat together every day—"warm heart, warm hands, warm feet, now wouldn't it be loverly...." Excruciating to remember how I was—silly warbling fool, singing the verses over and over—when suddenly her voice cut across mine with blunt cruelty.

"I hate that song!"

Instant heaviness in my chest. Tears suddenly at my eyelids, as if she had struck me across the face.

It was an hour later, after a tense dinner and a labored discussion, started by me, about my feeling hurt, and the dynamics of her family situation that may have made her act that way—it was only after this circuitous discussion that her true motivation came out. Revenge. Revenge for a criticism I had made of the performance! I was amazed, and began to feel hopeless. There we were in the middle of the night, I at least exhausted and wishing I were soundly asleep, she hurt and I hurt, and neither of us knowing how to make it right.

I believe it was when she started to work with a therapist on the problems with her father that her rage began to boil out at me. Awareness of that man came strongly to her—that crazy father who had weighed so heavily on her, needy, unpredictable, miserable, frustrated, trying to be kind, then turning brutal, harassing Ahnie, criticizing her: this man had made a hell of her childhood. I was confronted with unreasoning fury at the dinner table. Ahnie accused me of putting her down, of smothering her, of dragging on her. Ahnie's hatred was like a wall of steel between us. I did not understand what happened in therapy that aroused her cruelty and directed it at me. I could not accept the rightness of that: it seemed hideously unfair, and I fought back, my fury rising to cover my hurt, until we wounded each other equally.

As the summer settled to its still, hot, slumbering core, she withdrew into this struggle with the memory of her father, and asked me to be patient until she resolved it. But at moments when I was least protected, the rage spewed out on me like molten lead. One morning I got up from Ahnie's bed after a terrible night. "Do you want me to drive you home?" she asked sleepily. "No." She turned over, settled in to go back to sleep, mumbled, "I'll call you later." I went out into the morning. It was seven a.m. on a Sunday. As I started up the broken sidewalk toward High Street, grief took me. Tears streamed down my cheeks. I made the long walk to the bus choking and sobbing, not bothering to hide my distress from the few joggers who came bouncing past. I felt strung out and crazy the rest of the day, lifted out of my life, floating in dangerous space, my head buzzing, my stomach tight with anxiety. The tears kept coming.

Next morning I sat for a long time on my back porch, looking at the grass that needed cutting, watching a fat robin pick about under the old tree. Again and again I saw the picture of myself leaving Ahnie's apartment, and wondered how I, Rose Giannini, who had always been so cautious, could have allowed myself to get into

that condition. Surely in choosing Ahnie I had not chosen that!

As I prepared to go to work that day, however, I saw a glimmer of hope, for Ahnie was going off soon to Lake Erie, where she would stay for a month. She needed to be by herself, she said, to read, to think, to stare out over that great expanse of water. Perhaps while she was gone I could think about all this with some clarity. Maybe I could decide what to do.

During the month away, Ahnie wrote me only one letter, in which she told me about her schedule of swimming and sunbathing, how she loved the long hours of solitude. In her absence I began to see my friends again. I went to my nephew's tennis match and took my favorite niece shopping. My sisters invited me to dinner and I accepted. I felt the love of these people surrounding me, beginning to heal me. In my evenings at home alone, I pondered all the misgivings I had had since I met Ahnie, thought over our time together. A message began to make itself heard in me. Anticipating Ahnie's return, I summoned all the strength I had.

We sat across my living room from each other. She had just driven into town and wore a brown-patterned scarf tied over her shining hair. It was very unbecoming, I thought, and was glad she did not look her most appealing. As I talked, I watched her mouth tremble and open, her body huddle into itself. It was as if I were seeing that child she had been, the scrawny daughter, unloved, untended, abused by the one parent who had stayed with her. Even as I went on saying the things I needed to say, I felt a great sinking in myself, a sorrow that had nothing to do with Ahnie the adult, and that would not leave me after she was gone.

First Ahnie argued, then she screamed at me, calling me a possessive, smothering bitch. I shouted back at her, until we had said all the ugliest, most damaging things we could summon up about each other.

Ahnie perched on the arm of my couch, her body anxious, prepared for flight.

"I don't think we should see each other anymore," she said, and I was relieved she had said it, so I wouldn't have to.

"I feel the same."

We sat in excruciating silence for a time.

"No meetings, no phone calls."

"Right."

Again silence.

She got up quickly to go to the doorway, where she turned, her shoulders pulled slightly forward, to look back at me. I saw the clean lines of her face clenched tight, her eyes a cloudy, dull blue. Ahnie hesitated, as if there were something more she would say to me, and for one foolish instant I hoped she could bring forth words that might make it all right. But, still silent, she turned her back, and then she was gone.

That day I sobbed brokenly for a long time, sitting in a friend's backyard, lying across her bed. My friend wanted to comfort me, but there was no comfort for this—no one could make it better. Ahnie gone from me.

In the next weeks the moments of my life were haunted by her. Her voice one day as we had entered my house: "I like the smell of your house." I so pleased by that, knowing my house smelled of fresh air and sunlight and perhaps of me. Certain moments—as one day I had brought something to her at the studio just before she was to teach a class. She was delighted to see me, meeting me at the door, leaning to kiss me. I looked past her into the studio where dancers were posed or lazily stretching in the dim underwater light of the room, mysterious. I was wracked at night by the remembrance of her body curled behind me, in this very bed. Every room of this house I live in was a place where we had talked together, eaten together, held each other, argued. Old brown-shingled house with deep porch and wide eaves: it thrust Ahnie at me. The back yard brought her to me strongly, especially the afternoons before her performances when we had sat in the yard and I was there to help her tolerate her nervousness. I heard her voice speaking, saying, "You are very sweet," saying, "I love you."

Despite our promise, Ahnie called me several times, and we talked in a sad, hurtful way to each other. After each phone call, I went into my bedroom and cried, wanting Ahnie still.

I plunged into my work each day, shutting out for hours at a time the impressions of her that entered between me and what I was doing. I went out with friends, my heart bruised each time we approached a place where I had been with Ahnie. Once again I participated in the lives of my nieces and nephews, accepting my role of wise generous aunt. There was time now to drink coffee with my sisters, listen to their tales of husbands and children. But still I awoke sometimes in the middle of the night with the longing for Ahnie strong in me.

Then finally the heat lifted and it was autumn, the air sharp as apple cider, excitement building as the students returned to Ohio State University, the football season began. A new year, like all the others. I swept the yellow leaves from the sidewalk in back of my house; in the cold twilight I built a fire and breathed the smoke. Turning to look at my house, shabby and old-fashioned in the near dark, I was filled with affection for it. All the past it held for me: ourselves as children; Papa stumbling tiredly out the back door in his plaster-spotted overalls to sit on the steps, inhale the grass smell, rest; Mama in her last weeks, lying still and gazing out that upstairs window down into the yard. This was my place which sheltered and explained me. I was the same age Mama had been when Papa died—a middle-aged woman, settled, half of my life behind me. The autumn brought its reminders of loss; it let me understand I was larger than the events in my life, more enduring than any particular pain. ∎

Dykes To Watch Out For

by Alison Bechdel
From *More Dykes to Watch Out For.* Ithaca, NY: Firebrand Books, 1988.

Jacky and the Psychic

by Lee Lynch

Once Jacky spent a summer in California. Her brother the gay screenwriter was in Europe and she housesat his West Hollywood bungalow. The furniture was ivory colored, the rug was mauve, the dishes were delicate and expensive. She lived in fear of soiling and smashing everything in sight and got the hell out as much as possible.

In her wanderings she found a strange bookstore in Hollywood. Did it carry women's titles? The saleswoman looked like a valley girl, but she really knew her women's spirituality. She also knew the best veggie restaurant in Southern California.

But it was in Monterey Park and Jacky had no car.

She hung around the shop all afternoon and talked crystals with the lapsed valley girl between customers. "I'll tell you what," she proposed when they stood out on the curb together. "You provide the wheels and I'll treat you to dinner at The Fragrant Vegetable."

"At rush hour? Oh my god, Jacky. That could take all night."

"So? How long does it take to fall in love?"

They scarfed out on vegetable protein egg rolls. Later, Jennifer looked gorgeous against the ivory upholstery. And against the mauve carpeting.

"This place is wasted on my brother," she told Jennifer, arranging her this time on the king-sized futon. The colors on the bedspread matched Jennifer's labia almost exactly.

Jennifer burned sage in the bungalow to rid it of male energy. She took Jacky to a circle where the women sat on the ground and shared and sang for so long Jacky's bottom fell asleep. Jennifer went to classes in voice to open up her soul.

"You know what would be, like, totally ideal?" Jennifer said one bright and balmy afternoon as they lay by the lake at the Self Realization Shrine.

"Umm," answered Jacky, engrossed in the new Starhawk book.

"Why don't you come to my psychic with me? She'll tell us if this is meant to be."

Jacky squinted up over her sunglasses. "Jennifer, we *are*."

"Wouldn't it be exciting, though? She did a couple reading for Otter and Naomi and told them they were the most compatible couple she'd ever read for, *gay or* straight."

The psychic looked like a middle-aged housewife. She had them sit at a table in her sunroom overlooking an empty swimming pool with a large mossy crack. Jennifer's hands shook.

Is she really into this? Into us? I'm going home in a month, for crying out loud.

"I'm sensing something," said the psychic and shook her head. She talked about being open to new experiences, but staying true to their paths.

The next day Jennifer didn't come by after work. The clerks at the store said she was too busy to come to the phone. She never responded to

Jacky's messages at home.

"My Southern California breakup," she told her friends back in Chicago, laughing. Privately, though, she'd worried ever since about what might be wrong with her aura. ∎

by Diane F. Germain, 1987.
From *Common Lives/Lesbian Lives* (April 1988)

gardening

by Chaia Zblocki Heller

while you are gone, i take care of the garden,
four raised beds that look like lumpy graves
studded with rugged plumes of broccoli and brussel sprouts.
neither of us have done this before. as a kid,
i had to weed the walk in front of my mother's house,
my head wedged between the waxy rhododendrons.

turns out i pulled the carrots you planted before leaving,
mistook their spidery leaves for weeds, unimportant details
that slipped out smooth and slick as toothpicks.
i planted the tomatoes you left me, quivering
in their squat, green containers. two days later,
their stems sagged, leaves paled to a pastey yellow.
i think it is hard for anything to grow these days.

you call me almost every day to see how the garden is doing,
to see if i am watering. i lug the fat, green hose
around the back of the house, flood the beds
until silt slides down the sides in thick, loopy rivers.
strange, i don't even know what you planted;
what green signs of life to look for. each day i try to identify
heart shaped, star shaped, straight shooting leaves.

i tell you i am lost, but having fun.
pulling out the wrong things and planting more.
your trip is going well, but you worry. worry about women
i meet out dancing. ask each time if i love you

and am i sure really. you think about the marigolds
keeping their tidy orange heads
around the fringe of the garden.
they keep the bugs away, you warn.
gardening is an act of faith unfamiliar to both of us.
the first frills of lettuce thrill me like laughing gas.
i pick before it's ready, i am so giddy
i want to press it between waxed paper
and send it off to you   for proof.

i am spending more and more time
in the garden. the first shivering
hours of the day find me on all fours
sturdying the beds, planting little white stones
around the edges. i don't wait for seeds.
i bring home car loads of flowers, six in a box,
to plant around the vegetables, their spots and stripes,
their daring and delightful gestures   i tell you
you will be amazed when you come home.
and i want to amaze you. not really me, but the garden.
i can't wait to steam up a broad, silver platter
full of fronds of the deepest emerald,
feed you each radiant, miraculous leaf.

Lilith of the Wildwood, of the Fair Places

by Susan Sherman

And Lilith left Adam and went to seek her own place
and the gates were closed behind her and her name
was stricken from the Book of Life

1.

And how does one begin again

(Each time, each poem, each line, word, syllable
Each motion of the arms, the legs
a new beginning)

women   women surround me
images of women   their faces
I   who for years   pretended them away
pretended away their names their faces
myself   what I am   pretended it away

as a name exists to confine   to define   confine
define woman the name the   word   the definition
the meaning beyond the word   the prism   prison
beyond the word

to pretend it away

2.

It's the things we feel most
we never say   for fear perhaps
that by saying them the things we care most
for   will vanish
Love is most like that   is the
unsaid thing behind the things we do
when we care most

3.

to be an outcast   an outlaw
to stand apart from the law   the words
of the law
            outlaw
                        outcast

cast out   cast out by her own will
refusing anything but her own place
a place apart from any other
                                    her own

I do not have to read her legend in the ancient books
I do not have to read their lies
She is here   inside me
I reach to touch her

my body   my breath   my life

4.

To fear you   is to fear myself
To hate you   is to hate myself
To desire you   is to desire myself
To love you   is to love myself

Lilith of the Wildwood
Lilith of the Fair Places

who eats her own children
who is cursed of God

Mother of us all

In *Lesbian Poetry*, eds. Elly Bulkin and Joan Larkin.
Watertown, MA: Persephone Press, 1981.

Growing Avocados
by Ruthann Robson

Four blue toothpicks have been stabbed into each pit, so that every sea-urchined creature is partially submerged in water and partially suspended above the rim of the glass. The ledge above the kitchen sink is a mob of attempted rootings, not all of them successful. On the other side of the window, a fuchsia blossom bangs against the shadows of the afternoon sun. Deeper in the yard, near a single-storied structure, a discarded avocado pit which had rotted in water now pushes a bruised root through the soil.

Two women live in the house, on the land. Each woman has proudly wondered aloud whether a casual observer would know this is a women's house, women's land. Each woman has worried silently whether the house or land can share other secrets. The women dream with their heads tilted toward each other. They dream that their secret grows as wild and as obvious as the potted avocado plant on the wicker chest beneath the blinds of their narrow bedroom window. The women are afraid their secret will come to light and the women are afraid that it won't. They are afraid. They are afraid of each other.

Charleen is a teacher. Philosophy. At Three Rivers Junior College, she is the only person who teaches the subject. Other teachers, who like to be called professors as much as Charleen does, de-

bate whether or not there should be any curriculum offerings in philosophy. The junior college, which has been enrolling students for the past twelve years, holds Friday forums with topics such as, "Liberal Arts or Liberal Trades?" and "Are We *Under* Undergraduate Schools?" Charleen has been teaching at the school for less than an academic year, so she tries to attend these meetings.

Sometimes, like today, she chooses not to go. Charleen cannot bear to be seen by the other faculty members this afternoon. The book contract she was going to have fell through, and although she tries to feel smart because she did not share the possibility with any of her colleagues, Charleen cannot accept her consolation prize. A contract with the biggest textbook publisher would have meant a raise, an impeccable credential, a shot at a better job. Everyone would have envied her, would have whispered about something other than her personal life. Everyone would have realized that she was just as good—better—even though she graduated from a third-rate university and teaches an unrated subject. But now, nothing will change.

Charleen pushes past a budded bush, short-cutting her way to her $225 a month, 11% interest, Nissan station wagon. The spring sun heats the skin under her too-tight black slacks and tweedlike jacket. Her students have been promising her that spring will be gorgeous. Charleen discounts their assurances because they are

In *Eye of a Hurricane: Short Stories* by Ruthann Robson, Ithaca, NY: Firebrand Books, 1989.

mostly local kids who seem apologetic about the incessant rain and frosty nights. During an epistemology lecture, Charleen had used the awful weather as an analogy. She had told the students that the harsher the winter, the more pleasing spring seemed, regardless of spring's actual character. She had written the word *phenomenology* on the blackboard. She had explained to the class that it was like banging your head on the wall: the harder you banged, the better it felt when you stopped.

She drives the new but narrow road into the country. Blood-colored soil, netted by giant gouged roots, defines her way. When she arrives at her turn, to an older but also narrow road, she holds the wheel with one hand and twists out of her jacket.

Then she smiles. She knows she is almost home when she reaches this long, sloping-southward field of hay. She loves this hill because it refuses to be green or garish, despite the coaxings of the surrounding land. This rise reminds her of Deirdre's hair, of Deirdre's thighs.

Deirdre makes jewelry. She works all day in her one-story studio behind the thickly wooded hill, filling orders for the stores in South Florida that stock her creations. This late afternoon she feels a satisfaction with her progress that has recently become quite rare. She shines her planishing hammer and hangs it on the rack between the tack hammer and the chasing hammer. She straightens the anvils, the dapping block and punch, and the mandrels. She puts the tops on the pickle acid and the flux, checks that both tanks for the oxy-acetylene are off, and wipes the tripoli and rouge wheels of the buffer. She slips an earring in her pocket to show Charleen.

Deirdre's Nike AirSoles follow no particular path up the mossed hill, but wander under the dogwoods and past a plot of daffodils, drowning in brown leaves. Deirdre cannot imagine herself as anything other than a visitor on her own land. She judges the sun too shallow to penetrate the web of trees and the air too damp to mark the first day of spring. She misses her house in Mi-

ami, forgetting for a moment the agony of daily life as a physician's wife, remembering only the hibiscus, the oleander, the swift scent of the ocean, walking and holding hands with Jana. It was true, as Charleen had said, that one could bang metal into bracelets anywhere. Still, Deirdre thinks she would be more regularly inspired if she did not feel so inappropriate in her cotton clothes.

Yet she smiles. She sees the crest of the cedar A-frame house, bordered with tangles of blooming bushes. She begins breaking the thin branches, borrowing beauty with the justification that it will fade anyway. There is an almost tropical pink, and a delicate pink, and a pink that seduces red. There is a small flower so tightly open it could be mistaken for a bud, and a florid mouth of tongues. There are purples, whites, petals, pistils, yellows, and the sweetest tangerine-colored anthers.

Variety excites Deirdre. She spreads her bounty on the kitchen table, then fetches her sketchbook and charcoal pencil from upstairs. Perhaps a pair of earrings. Perhaps an amulet. Finished sketching, she hums textures to herself as she bends the branches into glasses of water. One glass for the coffee table. One glass for each bookcase. A big glass on the bedroom chest next to her favorite avocado, nearly three-feet high. One glass—of madder yellow flowers, she laughs to herself—for the bathroom. On the white birch kitchen table, she places the most disarmingly pink blossoms in a small vase she brought back from that long-ago honeymoon in Japan. She stuffs an oversize goblet with all the remnants, jamming it onto the windowsill amid her variously rotting and sprouting avocados.

The two women sit at their white birch table, in their house, on their land. In the gradual twilight, they look as similar as half-sisters. They are both white, with overgrown eyebrows and slim fingers. Their hair is brown, darker on the legs than on the head. Their backs are straight and their irises more blue than not. They both had jutting bicuspids. One of the women is taller by three inches, bigger boned, softer spoken, and has a scar on her left cheek. And one on her ankle and one on her forehead. And a mending wrist.

The women quietly eat the black beans and rice Deirdre has simmered. They chew without comment. There are no complaints and no compliments.

"It's amazing all the different flowers that grow up here," Deirdre says, adding, "by the house, I mean. I mean, up here, by the house."

"What different flowers are you talking about?" Charleen asks.

"The ones outside. By the house. I mean, I brought them inside. I thought you'd like them. Do you like them? I thought they were a nice mixture. All so different."

"They're all the same," Charleen says.

"They are all the same," Charleen says again.

"They're all rhododendrons, stupid. I thought you'd learn something like that in one of those garden clubs doctors' wives belong to."

"I thought those pink ones were azaleas." Deirdre gestures to the Japanese vase on the table.

"An azalea *is* a rhododendron, stupid."

The women look at each other. A trace of amusement, of victorious retreat, glimmers in Charleen's eyes.

"Lovers shouldn't argue about botany," Charleen says, reaching across the table to smooth Deirdre's tense shoulders.

Deirdre nods.

"Are the beans too mushy?" Deirdre risks a question after a few minutes.

"Findhorn phoned today," Charleen answers.

"Oh, what did he say?"

"Only that the whole deal is off. Only that the marketing people don't want someone like me. He was very apologetic, of course. He apologized if he'd led me on or anything. He said he was sure it would go through." Charleen twirls the Japanese vase between her slim fingers. "But the marketing people, the marketing people think it would be better if the author has either graduated from a top-flight university or teaches at a university rather than a junior college. They need to sell the book. They can't market someone like me."

"I'm sorry."

"What are you sorry for? You didn't do it,

did you? It's not your fault."

"I mean, I'm sorry. It's just an expression." Deirdre leans back in her chair, but not soon enough. Porcelain hits her on the jaw, Charleen's finger still holding the neck of the vase. Water runs down Deirdre's throat. A petal falls on Deirdre's collar.

Deirdre stands and moves against the sink, facing the window. The smaller woman spins Deirdre around, slapping her and screaming.

"You and your stupid flowers."

The rhododendrons on the sill scatter to the floor.

"You and your goddamn slimy growths."

Glasses shatter.

"You think you're going to grow trees on the fucking windowsill."

A hurled avocado pit stabs Deirdre's shoulder.

"If you hate it here so much, why did you ever want to live up here?"

Toothpicks graze an eye.

"You think you can buy anything with your doctor husband's money. Well, you can't buy me, you whoring cunt."

A fist in the stomach, on the thigh.

"You think you're not a dyke 'cause you were married. Let me tell you something. You're more queer than I'll ever be."

Charleen shoves Deirdre to the floor. A silver earring spills from Deirdre's pocket.

Charleen rips Deirdre's thin cotton shirt. Two unsunned breasts blink in the day's last light.

Charleen bites. And bites. Only when the kitchen lapses into total darkness do the bites become soft. Deirdre nibbles back, her mouth swelling.

Deirdre sits on the back step of her studio. The cold concrete is thick with pollen. She wishes there were a clearing, perhaps a pond, somewhere she could get a tan deep enough to cover. It is Saturday, the second day of spring, but a crackling drizzle descends, falling from the live oaks which habitually hold their leaves until the last possible moment. Deirdre wishes for Miami, for a Miami with Jana, for the Miami before Charleen arrived.

The violence had started there. Deirdre recalls how quick Charleen had been to blame the heat, to blame the aftertaste of Deirdre's divorce, to blame Deirdre's perplexed family or Deirdre's cautious friends. At the time, it had seemed logical to move away from the memories as well as from the urban crime. Rural North Florida seemed like the perfect place for Deirdre to transform her lump-sum alimony into acreage near the school where Charleen had an outstanding job offer. It had seemed possible that things would change.

Deirdre wants to heal herself, but she feels like she is in a universe of unfamiliar tools. All her past healings, and there have been many she reminds herself, have relied upon the ocean. When Jana had left to go back to Nicaragua, Deirdre had walked miles along the beach, becoming more and more malleable, until her soul opened to the horizon.

She knows she will get lost if she walks now: everything twists in the forest, and the obscured sun gives no direction. To walk in the woods, she thinks, requires a destination. She has nowhere to go. No friends or family here. No one. She longs for Jana, her best friend still, her best lover ever. Jana would know what to do.

Deirdre thinks that she could go and try to find a women's shelter or flag down a sheriff's car, but she wonders what would she tell them? *My lover—she beats me.*

And if the counselor or the officer asks what happened next, what can she say?

My lover, she beats me. And then we make love. The same fingers that leave a bruise on my throat feel so fine when they stroke my neck. The same tongue that calls me cunt feels like a miracle when it goes there.

♀♀

Charleen wakes with shame. Again. She had promised herself that this would not happen again. She had promised Deirdre.

But it is difficult for Charleen not to blame Deirdre: Deirdre of the mythically easy life who has never struggled. Charleen thinks that Deirdre can never understand how painful it is to go out every day into a world that whispers dyke behind her back. Charleen is sorry, but believes that Deirdre should be sorrier.

Charleen walks through the house looking out windows, looking for Deirdre. She sees only those sinister rhododendron blossoms—hundreds of the same shade of pink—in the bedroom, on the kitchen floor, pressing against the windows. Charleen laughs that Deirdre had been naive enough to believe all those flowers were different. Charleen slips on the wet floor, swearing as her feet slide, finally regaining balance. Perhaps Deirdre had known, she thinks, and was only mocking. Yes, Charleen says almost aloud, Deirdre was like that: provoking her one minute and kissing her the next.

Charleen breathes. She will show her. If Deirdre thinks she's so smart, disappearing on this beautiful spring morning just perfect for a walk, disappearing without making coffee or cleaning up the mess she made the night before, she'll find out how stupid she really is.

Charleen hurriedly dresses. She pulls down Deirdre's largest leather suitcase from the attic crawlspace. She packs two of Deirdre's favorite pants and takes her most comfortable shoes. Charleen then stuffs into the suitcase as many of her own clothes as it will hold. She is forcing it closed on the bed when she brushes against the plant on the chest. She jerks the stem free from the dirt, shakes it on the rug, then jams the plant into the suitcase.

When the bulky suitcase is anchored on the Nissan's roof rack and lashed down with elastic ties, Charleen notices that are are long roots protruding. It takes her several tries before she can rip off the offending pieces. She drives away, reddish dirt on both of her hands. ■

I am the wall at the lip of the water

by Judy Grahn

I am the wall at the lip of the water
I am the rock that refused to be battered
I am the dyke in the matter, the other
I am the wall with the womanly swagger
I am the dragon, the dangerous dagger
I am the bulldyke, the bulldagger

and I have been many a wicked grandmother
and I shall be many a wicked daughter.

In *Work of a Common Woman*. Freedom, CA: The
Crossing Press, 1978.

THEY WILL KNOW ME BY MY TEETH

Gorgon
by Laura Kaye

Elana Dykewomon
by JEB

Big Dykes with Attitude

lyrics by Karen Escovitz and Elliot

rap with funk bass line

One night I went to a wimmin's dance.
Didn't know who'd be there but I took a chance
on finding the kind of wimmin I like—
ones who are proud to call themselves "dyke"—y'know

      BIG DYKES! B B B B B B B B B BIG DYKES!
      BIG DYYYYYYYYYYYYYYYKES....with ATTITUDE!

There was a bunch of Gay Ladies hanging out by the door,
but then I checked out the dance floor.
They were strutting their stuff, they were hot and tough,
and the way their bodies moved, I could never get enough of those

      BIG DYKES! B B B B B B B B B BIG DYKES!
      BIG DYYYYYYYYYYYYYYYKES....with ATTITUDE!

A commercial says, "Lose yourself in the weight."
Well, I've got better things to do than to keep a date
with death by starvation, I'm a big dyke by choice—
my body and my spirit and my BIG DYKE VOICE! I'm a

      BIG DYKE! B B B B B B B B B B BIG DYKE!
      BIG DYYYYYYYYYYYYYYYKE....with ATTITUDE!

Two dykes on a date and having a ball
were on their way out of a concert hall
where they'd gone with most of the dykes in town
to hear a lesbian band get down.
They came around the corner holding hands with each other
when they ran right into a jerk and his brothers.

He said, "Hey guys, look what we got here!
We got ourselves a couple of lezzie queers.
You know you *girls* shouldn't be out alone at night.
Don't you know you need a *man* to do it right?"
The dykes just laughed because they had a plan.
They said, "there's a lot of wimmin who don't *want* a man
—and they're right behind us!"
and he said, "Yeah, right. Heh heh heh....."
and she said, "We're *not* alone."
and he said, "Yeah, right. Heh heh heh....."
and she said, "Well, then see for yourself."
and he said, "Yeah, right. Heh heh heh heh heh...
      (choke)...(gasp)...holy shit!...look at all of those...
            there must be AT LEAST FIVE HUNDRED

      BIG DYKES! B B B B B B B B B B BIG DYKES!
      BIG DYYYYYYYYYYYYYYYKES....with ATTITUDE!

Gay boys say we're all sexual minorities,
but they don't understand that *our* priorities
are to strengthen ourselves and to help our sisters
and to blow *away all* child molesters!
And one more thing about our frame of reference—
we're a hell-of-a-lot more than our sexual preference! We're

      BIG DYKES! B B B B B B B B B B BIG DYKES!
      BIG DYYYYYYYYYYYYYYYKES....with ATTITUDE!

The liberals tell us that we're all the same,
that there's a "common humanity" and no one's to blame
for the broken backs,
the death of Blacks,
pornography that fills the racks,
or misogynist attacks.
But we're not afraid to name the perpetrators—
and *that's* why they call us MAN-HATERS! We're

      BIG DYKES! B B B B B B B B B B BIG DYKES!
      BIG DYYYYYYYYYYYYYYYKES....with ATTITUDE!

When it's time for a potluck, WE bring the food.
When it's time for a protest, WE set the mood.
When it's time for a joke, WE can be crude.
We're heavy and humorless and raucous and rude! We're

BIG DYKES!   B B B B B B B B B B   BIG DYKES!
BIG DYYYYYYYYYYYYYYKES....with ATTITUDE!

We're taking up space! We're in your face!
We're every age and class and culture and race!
We're every size and shape in every city and town!
One thing's for sure...you always know when WE'RE around! We're

BIG DYKES!   B B B B B B B B B B   BIG DYKES!
BIG DYYYYYYYYYYYYYYKES....with ATTITUDE!

© 1992

Safe At Home: Softball As A Place Of Refuge

by Yvonne Zipter

All through the winter I think about softball and worry about it and wait for it. Then in the spring I panic because I think nobody else cares about softball and we won't have a team. (Jo, The Wilder Ones)[1]

What is it about softball that inspires such passion among lesbians? Though the aesthetics of the game—the pure physical appeal, and philosophical aspects—are certainly not without their appeal, the real attraction of softball is its social nature. What begins as cooperation and teamwork on the field often evolves into off-field intimacy and support. The many hours of practice in which we help each other to play our best, the impromptu meals afterward, the games in which we share a common goal, the celebrations and post-mortems that follow—all of these things produce a heightened sense of camaraderie among the players, a camaraderie not easily found elsewhere.

Unlike bars, for instance, in which meeting people can be a difficult and tricky business, softball is a more structured place, where other women have at least one interest in common with you. Softball also has the advantage of letting you get to know people slowly over time, and often in a healthier environment. In addition, softball is different from political and cultural organizations, which, although they have softball's structure and on-going nature, frequently have more of a class bias that discourages some women from getting involved. Such organizations may be perceived as more dangerous for women who must—or feel they must—protect their lesbian identities from becoming public. And while everything from the camaraderie to the structure of softball can also be found in other team sports, softball has a number of advantages over most of them.

First of all, softball, because of our familiarity with it and its long-standing reputation as a haven for dykes, is more universal from community to community than are other sports. A new adage for the Lesbian Nation might be: "Some communities play basketball, some play rugby, and some play soccer, but *all* lesbian communities play softball." What this means, speaking practically, is that (1) softball teams, generally being more numerous, are easier to find; (2) once you've found them, you can be pretty sure there will be other dykes on the team; and (3) most of us—even if we can't play well—at least know the basic rules of the game.

"A Good Excuse To Socialize"

Alix Dobkin: "Softball is the single greatest organizing force in lesbian society."

Chapter 4 of *Diamonds Are a Dyke's Best Friend*. Ithaca, NY: Firebrand Books, 1988.

Miki Adachi: "This last time I got involved with softball because I just didn't want to sit at home....It was a way to get out there [in the lesbian community]...Actually, when I was playing softball in my earlier years, it was because I liked the game. And now, it's kind of become a social thing...get out there and have some fun....I like being with everybody, I like the camaraderie, going out after the games. We do other things too; like we'll go to the parade or have *dim sum*. Just little things. Otherwise I might be at home."

B. Victoria: "The reason I played was to have fun. I am a lousy athlete, but when I was put on third base I got to hug everyone getting to my base!"

Pat Griffin: "It was a tradition that we [the Common Woman team] started with the Hot Flashes: whoever's home game it was planned some sort of special pre-game event. One time, they all arrived in this huge bus dressed in punk-rock outfits and made up songs and stuff. Another time, we did *Chariots Of Fire*. We all came out carrying a torch, wearing huge, white boxer shorts. But the best was— it was our home game—we decided to have this elaborate homecoming event associated with the game. And they had no idea what we were going to do. The whole league got wind that we were going to do something outrageous. So we had about sixty spectators for this game. (Usually there are only a few.)

But all the people who weren't playing that night heard we were going to do something wild so everybody came to see what it was. We had a homecoming parade, starting from

Every dropped ball helps another woman.

way across the field, and we had several decorated cars, and we had two queens in the back of a convertible. I got to be one of the queens. We were dressed in really outrageous old dresses from the Salvation Army. And we invited some women who used to play on our team but don't play anymore to come back as alumnae. Back in those days our motto was: 'Every dropped ball helps another woman.' So we had a banner with that on it. One of the women on the team was a majorette in high school, and she did this baton-twirling thing dressed in a lavender outfit. We had a hoop with paper on it, which the team crashed through and did forward rolls

as they were introduced. And the Hot Flashes had a big hoop with paper on it that said, 'Every Common Womon needs a Hot Flash.' And they crashed through that. Then everyone lined up for the national anthem, which was 'Leaping Lesbians.' Then we played the game—the game was really anticlimactic after all of that. That same year, another two teams in the league, Woman-rising and Yellow Fever—it was the year Prince Charles and Lady Di got married—had a reenactment of the royal wedding and actually played the entire game in formal prom gowns. Obviously we don't take the game as seriously as a lot of leagues do."

It is because of softball's universality and accessibility that it is a convenient focus for a variety of social activities. In fact, sometimes softball is little more than an excuse for socializing. This is certainly evident, to cite one example, in a tongue-in-cheek report of an exhibition game between the L.A. Women's Independent Softball Association's champs, the Hialeah House Sandettes, and the *Lesbian Tide* Collective, which was held "to provide an opportunity for the radical *Lesbian Tide* Collective and the Valley gay women to become better acquainted."[2]

In Chicago, the gay and lesbian Metropolitan Sports Association League is only one summer social scene, but it is definitely a major one. On Saturday and Sunday afternoons,

If you *think* someone is gay and you don't have enough proof to satisfy your curiosity, asking the question "Have you ever played softball?" may be a solution.

dozens of women bring blankets, lounge chairs, coolers, suntan lotion, and snacks, then settle themselves on the sidelines to get some sun, conversation, and entertainment. Often, the ballplayers themselves will join the spectators after their games are over or on the days they don't play. There is generally a kind of party atmosphere to the whole thing. Women come with their dogs, children, lovers, friends, and even, occasionally, siblings or mothers. The convivial confusion, as much as anything, sparks a lot of interaction between those on the sidelines, making it easy to get acquainted. There are also, of course, the impromptu celebrations and parties at the bars after a game or practice.

Beyond the entertainment role softball serves once we're on a team, it also functions as a way to actually meet lesbians in the first place. This is especially true in rural areas or when one is new to a place, but can also be the case when you've lived in a city a long time and just aren't politically or culturally inclined, and either aren't interested in or aren't good at the bar scene.

New In Town?

Louise Hernandez: "About three years ago, a gay league started in San Diego. (I'm about twenty minutes north of San Diego.) I was single and I joined the league mostly for the social reason [of] meet[ing] women. So that's the only time it ever really became a social event for me. But of course, once I got in the league there was [the] competition and the activity of it....I have a girlfriend now. I have a lover of fifteen months and I'm really content. I'm twenty-nine, she's thirty-three, and we're pretty set. So I'm not out to meet anybody anymore."

Berneice (from the novel *Leave A Light On For Me*): "To think if it weren't for women's rec softball, we'd never have met."[3]

Olivia: "When I first moved up to San Francisco, [softball] was an easy way for me to meet other lesbians....I had lived here for about a year or so before I came out. And when I came out, around about that time I joined the women's—the bar league, it's called here in San Francisco. It's a gay softball league. It was primarily to meet people even though I enjoy softball a lot [for its own sake]."

The main reason this strategy for meeting other lesbians works, of course, is not only that there are lesbians on those teams but also that all or most of us know this to be true. As Sandy Hayden once wrote, "I'm not saying all women who play softball are gay, but I am pointing out that if you *think* someone is gay and you don't have enough proof to satisfy your curiosity, [asking the question "Have you ever played softball?"] may be a solution.[4]

It's much simpler, certainly, when you know there's a specifically gay league and you know where to find it, but this knowledge applies even in so-called nongay leagues. When I moved in 1980 to Naperville, Illinois, forty miles from Chicago, where I was in a very straight corporate setting and without a car, one of the first things I did was to join a softball team. I reasoned that if there were going to be dykes out there anywhere in those 'burbs, they would be on softball teams.

The Only Game In Town

R. J.: "[Softball is] one of the only sports in a community like this where other 'family' members are. (They are so hard to find.)"

Starla Sholl: "In South Dakota, softball isn't only a sport, it's one of the only social events available for lesbians. One night a week the A league would play at the city diamonds, and the women would come from up to fifty miles to play. The league was at least 50% lesbians, although many of us believed that the other 50% either were closet cases or that they were on the verge of coming out. On Tuesday nights, even the few women who didn't play softball came out, and we all would sit on the same bleachers. Some people may have guessed we were lesbians, but in that area most people don't even know what the word means. Sitting on the same bleachers, on Tuesday nights, was one of the best ways to re-

ally feel the solidarity of the South Dakota dykes…especially since there are so few 'blatant' events."

Sometimes the difficulty of finding other dykes is not just a function of having recently relocated. In rural areas, lesbians tend to be scattered over a lot of acreage, and there are generally few places to socialize—bars, coffeehouses, and women's bookstores being most conspicuous by their absence. Both the scattering and the lack of places to gather make it problematic for lesbians to meet each other and to locate places to mingle once they've become acquainted. For rural lesbians, the game of softball functions today much as it did thirty or forty years ago: as a singularly safe place to meet lesbians. As R. J. has said, "It's very important *not* to be identified [as a lesbian] in this part of the country."

Given that softball is also one of the few activities available to straight women in rural areas, it provides a safe cover for lesbians interested in hanging out together. Sometimes the straight women on the team know who the lesbians are, but most often they don't. In either case, lesbians seem to have a second sense—a sort of radar—that lets us pick each other out.

A Healthy Alternative

Laurie: "I use sports as a whole to meet people—I rarely ever go to bars for that purpose. If I do go to a bar, it is to socialize with

the friends I have met through sports. Team sports are the main social outlets in my life. I depend on them for emotional support, physical activity, a sense of belonging, a comfortable atmosphere, and an outlet for my competitive nature."

Fran: "I met my first lover through softball.…I think softball is a good place to meet people and probably always will be—especially for the young people who can't go to the bar or anything. My daughter—she's eighteen—she plays softball. She has a girlfriend, too. They met playing softball in high school together."

Linda Locke: "I was adopted; my parents are white [and I am Korean]. So I grew up kind of isolated from a lot of Asian women. The interesting thing is, the softball teams that I've played on up here are Asian teams. So for me, it was a way of meeting Asian women and a way that felt real comfortable, more than, say, at that point, a political meeting or an organization like that. So what happened is I met them in a way that I felt real comfortable and then after that I could go and meet with Asian women on another level. Because [in the beginning] I felt like maybe I didn't have that 'Asian experience.'… It was a way…to feel like I was part of the group…It's like a way of coming home in a sense."

Valerie Edwards: "There are so few places for women to go and meet apart from bars. And unless you're interested in getting involved in a political organization, it's very difficult to meet lesbians....It is an ideal way to get to know other people."[5]

Although larger towns and cities may provide more opportunities for socializing than there are out in the countryside, those opportunities are not always suitable for everyone. By way of example, for women who have a problem with alcohol, or who don't like to dance, or who have allergies to cigarette smoke, or who can't or don't want to stay up late, or who are not adept at handling unstructured social situations, bars are not a viable place to socialize. Janice Kaplan quotes one woman, a writer and fitness consultant in San Francisco, who thinks "sports are replacing bars as a way to meet people."[6]

Also, for women who are closeted, lesbian political and cultural activism can be too public and, therefore, too risky. And some women just aren't interested in activism of any kind.

Even for women who *do* enjoy going to bars or who *are* involved culturally or politically, softball can be an important—even necessary—change of pace. Compared to the often surreal feeling of bar life and the serious quality of activism, softball can be a mental health-saving escape, something relaxing and *fun*. I know it's been a lifesaver for me.

When I moved from the suburbs into Chicago, knowing how lousy I am at getting acquainted with people in bars, I joined practically everything I heard of: the local chapter of the Feminist Writers' Guild, a literary magazine collective, the staff of the women's bookstore, and a group engaged in founding a journal devoted to women's music and culture.[7]

I was very active in our lesbian culture and, not insignificantly, I was quite successful in building up a large circle of friends and acquaintances. My cultural activities were gratifying on two levels: mentally and emotionally. But I started to feel burnt out after a couple of years and realized there was still one major void in my life: the physical.

It's not that I hadn't tried to find both softball and volleyball teams here in Chicago. I had. But I hadn't heard about our gay sports organization (clearly a gap in the knowledge of my literary/political friends!), and all of the park rec leagues here play a weird brand of softball known only to Chicagoans. It's called "sixteen inch" because it is played with a ball that has a sixteen-inch diameter, and it is played without a glove. I tried it once, but found that, not being able to get my hand around the ball (which is about the size of a cantaloupe), throwing it was something akin to putting the shot—and all of the stories about broken fingers didn't exactly sell the game to me either.

Luckily, around the same time I was experiencing burnout, I discovered the Gay Athletic Association (as it was called in 1984), and that it had a women's twelve-inch softball league. Softball has been an important social and recreational outlet for me since then. Not only does it provide me with much-needed exercise and give me a break from intense cerebral activity, but it has provided me with an important "home base" as well. While my literary friends are without a doubt very significant in my life, there is something special about the bonds I have formed with my softball buddies, a closeness and ease of relating that I've seldom found elsewhere.

We Are Family

Mary Farmer: "I enjoy the camaraderie, I enjoy the teamwork, and all the social stuff that comes from it. Our softball team is really like an extended family and has been for a long time. It's a great source of pride to me and to my teammates. It's one of the most important things I do in my life."

Meryl Moscowitz: "When I change from my business suit into my sweatsuit and head for the ball field, I'm home again! My team is my 'family,' and though I don't see them all year-round, we always are concerned and in touch."

Pat Griffin: "Several years ago..., we *were* a family. We were a very close-knit group. [But] some people have left the area, and the team has sort of changed character over the years. The summer before last we had one of our *worst* seasons—not necessarily in terms of wins and losses, but it just seemed like the team had no heart. There were really serious questions about whether or not there was enough of a core of us to keep it going, that we would have a team. So we had a big meeting in the spring to kick off the next season and to figure out what was wrong. What we realized is that, those of us who had been on the team a long time, we were sort of imposing on the new women this *family* thing from the past. And they resented that. They didn't want to be like the team was [before]. They wanted to be whatever they were. So those of us who had been around a long time just had to let go of that, and once we did, as it turned out this past summer, not only did we have our very best season playing-wise, but we also just had a really good time. It was not the same and it never will be, but we created something else that was terrific. So there is definitely a sense of extended family to the Common Womon team."

M.: "Softball makes my summer fun. I'm with very close friends with whom I can…share some B.S. and beers. I don't play [softball] to find lovers but to be with loving friends."

R. J.: "When I was in my early teens (fifteen or sixteen) and still coming to grips with my own lesbianism, feeling very alone and confused—I got on a [softball] team in Billings, Montana, with a female coach—probably twenty-five years old or so. I think now she knew what I was going through and she taught me more about the game and myself than anyone else I've ever met. Because of… her and the other team members, [I felt] like I did belong."

Mariah Burton Nelson, an associate editor of *Women's Sports and Fitness*, has observed that "women writers are examining not only the traditional lessons that sport offers: teamwork, leadership, enjoyment—but also less traditional lessons of sport: commitment, intimacy, bonding with others of the same gender."[8] If that is indeed true, it is probably because those "less traditional lessons" are often some of the most important aspects—for women—of sports.

For many women, in fact, this sense of intimacy and bonding runs very deep—*extended family* was a phrase I heard with some regularity. And the sponsor and manager of one of the teams here in Chicago is frequently heard referring to the women on her team as "her kids."

Like most families, while we don't do *everything* together, we do share a lot: going on picnics, celebrating our birthdays, going to concerts and movies in groups of four or six, inviting each other over or out to dinner, helping one another move, and playing other sports and games together. And also like most families, we do more than just have good times. We help take care of each other when we're sick or injured, and we comfort each other in times of loss. Sometimes, as R. J.'s story illustrates, we even help each other deal with issues surrounding our lesbianism.

Caring: Never Out Of Season

In the South and in much of California, the weather permits softball playing almost all year-round. In places like Chicago, where summer is short, our season has a distinct beginning and end. But the season's close doesn't necessarily signal the end of the close relationships we form.

No family is perfect, however, and even the most close-knit teams have their problems: couples breaking up, "sibling rivalry" for prized positions on the field, misunderstandings, hurt feelings, gossip. Frequently, our fondness for one another is greater than whatever the problem is, and we are able to resolve things. Occasionally something will happen that causes irreparable damage, however, and there is a rupture in the family, a time of great sadness—and sometimes bitterness. Even then, women seldom quit softball. When things don't work out on one team, they leave to join another, or help to form a new team and, ultimately, a new family—even if that's not what they initially planned. There's just something about softball.... ■

Notes

1 Toni McNaron, "An Interview with the Wilder Ones," *So's Your Old Lady*, no. 10 (September 1975), p. 8.

2 "Sandettes Blast Tide," *Lesbian Tide* 3, no. 4 (November 1973): 24. See also Pat Greene, "Beautiful Women's Softball." *Lesbian Tide* 2, no. 12 (July 1973): 3, which reports on another game that was accompanied by a picnic and a variety of other social activities.

3 Jean Swallow, *Leave A Light On For Me* (San Francisco: Spinsters/ Aunt Lute, 1986), p. 2. Oddly enough, as central as the role of softball is in the lesbian community, *Leave A Light On For Me* is the first lesbian book in which softball figures prominently. The only other women's softball novels that I know of (Sara Vogan, *In Shelly's Leg* [St. Paul, Minn.: Graywolf Press, 1985]; and Ellen Cooney, *All The Way Home* [New York: G. P. Putnam's Sons, 1984]) are very heterosexual, though the feelings of camaraderie and community, so evident in lesbian softball, are also present in these novels.

4 Sandy Hayden, "Giving Her Away," *Focus* (May/June 1980), p. 24.

5 Valerie Edwards, "Notso Amazons Not So Competitive Softball," *Everywoman's Almanac 1987* (Toronto, 1987).

6 Janice Kaplan, *Women and Sports* (New York: Viking Press, 1979), p. 79. See also Linn ni Cobhan, "Lesbians in Physical Education and Sport" in *Lesbian Studies: Present and Future*, ed. Margaret Cruikshank (Old Westbury, NY: Feminist Press, 1982), who suggests that athletes may not need bars, dances, or meetings to form their social communities among women because they form their own social groups. Characteristically, a male sports psychologist, Bruce Ogilivie (quoted in C. W. Nevius, "Theories on Homosexuality in Sports," *San Francisco Chronicle*, May 14, [1981]) "calls female athletes 'cultural mutants,' because 'they defied the culture they live in.' It is no surprise, Ogilivie says, to find these alienated women turning to each other for support." While there is little doubt that both athleticism and lesbianism can be alienating factors in a woman's life that encourage the formation of bonds between and among softball dykes, most women tend to focus less on such negative aspects and more on the cooperation, shared energy, and mutual support they find in softball.

7 The journal I cofounded, along with Toni Armstrong, Jr., Michele Gautreaux, and Ann Morris, is *HOT WIRE: A Journal of Women's Music and Culture*, a nationally (and internationally) distributed periodical, and the only one of its kind. I am no longer on *HOT WIRE's* staff, but I contributed an article on the All-American Girls Professional Baseball League in 1987.

8 Mariah Burton Nelson, foreword in *More Golden Apples*, ed. Sandra Martz (Manhattan Beach, Calif.: Papier-Mache Press, 1986), p. iii.

by Alison Bechdel
From *More Dykes to Watch Out For*. Ithaca, NY: Firebrand Books, 1988.

Umpira/Tempura

by Morgan Grey and Julia Penelope

Umpira/Tempura, She-Who-Calls-the-Plays, often stands just behind a Plate where She takes a dim view. Skeptics, who would question Her Calls, allege that an intimate connection between Umpire and Tempura is unlikely, but that can be said of any relationship. In fact, we have it on authority that They have called many diamond celebrations in Their own honor, crowding plates and hearing appeals. In Their dual aspect, They are defensive or offensive, depending on the occasion.

Umpira/Tempura is a rookie in the association of goddesses, having only been dis-covered recently by scouts in the bush leagues, and the dubious say that this cannot be a winning combination. This team works together well, however, for it's Tempura who fires up softball Dykes during real hot games and leaves them fried after too much exertion. Unlike Umpira, Tempura likes batting the ball around and keeps pitchers firing away.

Both are primarily summer goddesses, as heat is properly Their element. For this reason, many of Umpira/Tempura's ritual observances are held during the period that begins soon after the Vernal Equinox and ends with the Autumnal Equinox. Many a pleasant summer night is spent with Her priestesses, called Jocks (for their habit of Jockeying for Position), arranged in a protective figure, The Diamond, while others sit on

hard, wooden benches being offensive. The latter take turns swinging a wand, called a Bat, trying to hit the flies so numerous at this time of year. Players who Drop Flies are said to be defensive, and this Act is called an Error. We have, so far, not unearthed a reasonable explanation for this terminology, although scores suggest themselves.

Umpira, true to Her Nature, stationed majestically behind the Plate, calls strikes and balls according to Her Blessed Whim. When a Batter has had Three Strikes, Umpira calls her Out, and the disappointed one cannot become a Runner. Instead, she returns to The Bench, where she must sit until summoned once more into the hallowed On Deck Circle. The sacred number Three is pivotal in these rituals, for each group of priestesses is also allotted Three Outs per Inning, and there are Three Sacred Bases which Runners are obliged to touch before they are allowed to approach Home Plate. One of Umpira/Tempura's profound mysteries is called Stealing Bases, and Their devotees are said to Steal Bases whenever they can. Should they fail in an attempt, they are put out.

Umpira/Tempura is also much-beloved of devotees to **PEDESTRIA** and **DEA ABLEA**, and Their priestesses often garb themselves in the habits of Dea Ablea, sweatpants and terry cloth headbands, which soak up the sacred moisture they exude during their rituals. A minor aspect of Umpira, **GAMEY** (see also **VISCERA**), works part-time officiating Break Ups, for She enjoys keeping Her hand in. ∎

Found Goddesses. Norwich, VT: New Victoria Publishers, 1988.

Dykes to Watch Out For

by Alison Bechdel

From *New, Improved! Dykes to Watch Out For.* Ithaca, NY: Firebrand Books, 1990

Lesbian Stew

by Lee Lynch

At dinner the other night, a friend suggested that lesbians have a unique relationship with food. What I took to be the essence of her thoughts was this pithy observation: We fuss over food. It is another of the innumerable issues that makes us so loveable.

There probably is not a lesbian in the world who would not, at the slightest sign of interest, tell you about her personal history with food. For some, food has been a joy, for others, a struggle. I spent my earliest years swallowing great quantities of evil-tasting stuff called *tonic* in an effort to fatten my skinny frame. One of the most humiliating moments of my childhood was the time my father, rather than take my hand to cross the street, encircled my wrist with his big fingers and laughed at its slightness, like he'd found a pitiable lone toothpick in an otherwise empty jar. We were crossing a busy street in Boston at the time; to this day I can't think of the school, the VFW post, the apartment building on that site without a sense of shame. All those years of nauseating tonics and I still couldn't measure up.

As an adolescent, I wished food could be served powdered, in a capsule, and that the social rituals around it would be banned by the World Health Organization. Dinner Out was the only thing worse than Dinner At Home with the nuclear family. Why in the world groups of people gathered around tables and talked to each other while stuffing their mouths was beyond me. I had what the doctors called a "nervous stomach." They gave me little blue pills, bitter white pills, tiny peach-colored pills. In college, after a little blue pill and some gross imitation of nutrition, I could just barely stagger back to the dorm to pass out. I spent a good part of my first thirty-five years sick to my stomach. Literally. I thought *everyone* went through what I did and, like me, was just too polite to mention it.

Now I know I faced two problems. The first was solved fairly simply: I had food allergies. Some of the most common table foods actually make me ill. The second was much larger and more complex: a need to control my life. It was this latter problem which I suspect is at the bottom of the unique lesbian relationship with food.

Everyone, it is said, is born into this world kicking and squalling. The lesbian child, whatever other strikes she may inherit against her, enters life with two. The female condition has been well documented. But who has talked about butch infants striding around their cribs with clenched fists? Of *femme fatales* plying their early little charms on every aunt, girl cousin, and housewife-neighbor who peers into their playpens?

I always thought that I came out at fifteen. Last year I delved into a box of family photographs to find images of Little Lee (clothed in more feminine appellation) dressed in three-piece

Lee Lynch, in *Amazon Trail*. Tallahassee, FL: Naiad, 1988.

corduroy pants suits, in flannel-lined dungarees, in overalls. Images of my pre-adolescent self in flannel shirts and jeans, hair slicked back. Or just-adolescent with my sleeves rolled up to my paltry biceps, an unlit parental cigarette hanging from my sneering eleven-year-old lips. "Holy shit," I thought, I was gay even back then.

"Holy shit," I say now, no wonder so many of us have food issues. If food, as we've learned from research on anorexia and bulimia, is a way of controlling, often the only way of controlling, our young lives, no wonder lesbians wield it like a weapon. Scrawny Little Lee was rejecting everything her innocently straight parents were offering her. "This is the life we want you to live," they told me a thousand different ways, offering me marriage and my very own family; offering me boys, dresses, homemaker skills; offering me a highly socialized role that my gut knew was dead wrong for me. I rejected their social nourishment—of *course* I'd reject their carrots and spinach and steak. In fact, I suspect my food allergies are no more than a systematic, automatic response my body developed to those foods which most obviously represented to me family life and the golden platter of heterosexuality. I gagged on it.

Enter potlucks, vegetarianism, feminist restaurants, growing our own foods, collective cooking, music festival foodlines.

Enter health foods, allergy testing, rotation diets, organic foods, food co-ops, *The Political Palates*, and *Red Beans and Rice*.

Enter the concept, shared with other alternative cultures, of taking control of our lives through food. Creating our own rituals around eating. Determining for ourselves what to feed us, how to feed us, with whom we would feed.

Once, after leaving a lover and moving into my own place, Barbara Grier, then editor of *The Ladder*, urged a recipe on me to forestall malnutrition I was likely to have suffered. She told me to cook up some green peppers, onions, rice, hamburger and what all in a great big old frying pan, and then to freeze individual packets of the stuff in foil. Dutifully I took a packet of what I'd dubbed Lesbian Stew from my freezer each day before work and each night when I came home

pushed it around the frying pan. I think that was the first time I'd ever fully understood that there was a connection between food and sustaining life—between putting this stew in my mouth and being able to write stories and articles for *The Ladder*, or make love to women, or dance all night.

My cooking repertoire has grown. I've even come to enjoy long solitary nights of baking cookies, the smell of garlic frying in preparation for a rice dish, the way a well-sharpened knife can make paper-thin slices of tomatoes look pretty all soaked in rice vinegar, under a sprinkling of minutely chopped scallions. But more, I've come to almost like digging in with friends, comparing recipes or writing styles or the day's events over a casserole topped with bubbling just-toasted cheese. No longer does anyone serve me promises of motherhood, skills for keeping a husband happy, or Emily Post's recommendations on hostessing.

My body has learned what foods poison it; my queer soul has found tablemates to nourish it; I take great care what I ingest, having been force-fed from an alien menu too long. Where once the little girl stood accused of fretfully fussing over her food, now, lesbian-like, I fuss joyfully over what I know I need, body and soul. ◼

Chancy

by Morgan Grey and Julia Penelope

CHANCY, our goddess of unpredictable edibles, protects our weighs and means, and hears our woes and moans. She is particularly popular in Lesbian communities, where She is worshipped in ritual feasts known as "potlucks." Like the Chinook ceremonial feasts, called *potlatch* (from Nootka *patshatl*, giving or gift), from which our potlucks are descended, we celebrate our free giving to one another. Each member of the community brings with her some favorite dish of food as an offering, and these offerings are then displayed together on however many tables are required for their appreciation. Before the revelers are permitted to break these foods together, they must circle each table at least once, uttering "oohs" and "aahs" before each offering, and ask "What is that?" and "Who brought it?"

The substance of the ritual begins when one reveler turns to another and asks, "What do you think is in it?" and the response is, "Chancy." After Chancy has been invoked by these questions and appropriate noises, the hungriest participants race for the plates to see who can fill hers to overflowing the fastest. This is said to be "helping oneself" and it must be accomplished with great relish. It is often said, "To the quick, variety." Casual worshippers, slow to help themselves to Chancy's

Found Goddesses. Norwich, VT: New Victoria Publishers, 1988.

bounty, often find they must make a meal of clam dip and dried oatmeal cookies.

If, by Chancy, the plates available on that day are made of flimsy paper, overfilling can result in overspilling, whereupon more appropriate noises are forthcoming from the revelers. If the potluck occurs outdoors, under a full moon, the quantity of food dropped to the earth is taken as a measure of Chancy's favor. Those who leave nothing to Chancy are at great risk. Each tribe, of course, has its own way of worshipping Chancy, but it is She who watches over the selection and preparation of recipes. She is, therefore, one of our goddesses of inspiration, and her devotees have been known to concoct veritable, edible delights from leftovers, which are sacred to Chancy. Woe unto her who, uninspired or neglectful, makes an offering of Kentucky Fried Chicken, with only eleven herbs and spices. She will quickly find herself over a barrel, and her cries of "Fingerlickin' good" will avail her naught. "'Tis better," it is said, "to take one's chances with tofu and soy sauce."

Chancy is well-known for her peculiar and unpredictable sense of humor and her utter disregard for the principles of nutrition and aesthetics. She delights and exults in feasts consisting of only desserts or breads, and her worshippers fondly recall their salad days and entire meals of just desserts. These, however, have become rarer as the years pass. ∎

This Summer I'm Going to Learn to Eat Tofu

by Elliott

White, cold, clammy, tasteless
slimy, icky, weirdo food.
Tofu dyke is good for you
tofu is what vegans do.
And so now in my fridge live tofu cakes
for tofu burgers and tofu bakes
and eggless egg salads and miso soup
and pesto-pizza tofu topped.

This summer I'm going to learn to use sponges
buy them and fit them and cut them and boil them
and leave them to dry in the sun on the patio.
I'll stop buying tampax and kotex and playtex—
whether light, thin or super, mini, maxi or deodorant—
for this body will bleed without profits for boys.
And when you come for dinner you'd best be beware
I may serve tofu soup from the sponge boiling pot.

This summer I'm going to learn to say goddess
and stop invoking the name of the dick on the stick.
I'm going to stop saying bastard and bitch
and witch will mean wicce and carry respect.
I'll no longer be saying fuck this or fuck that
except where appropriate as in "he fucked her over"
and I'm going to use terms like pud, boy and prick
to yell out at men with a slow taunting laugh.

This summer I'll be learning to like oral sex
to kiss, lick and savor like the dykes in novels do.
I'll lust for sweet cunt and I'll hunt salty pearls
and I'll vacation in the outback of the strange land down under.
I'll be using my hands to do more than write
and using my tongue to do more than talk.
With my futon I'll build a working relationship
and I may use my shower to do more than get clean.

While others are running and tanning and dieting
I'll be dicing my tempeh and mashing my basil,
rinsing my tofu and drying my sponges,
practicing Be-spelling and yelling out loud.
I'll be building up tongue muscles, honing my wit
and stirring up bread dough to strengthen my wrist
I'll mean it when I say I'm a practicing lesbian
so by Lammas I'll be great and by Midwinter a legend.

From Elliott's collection of poetry, *The Separatist Revolution*, 1991.

Tofu, Miso and Soya

by Morgan Grey and Julia Penelope

TOFU, MISO and **SOYA** name the triple goddess of natural foods, She-Who-Decides-What-Is-Good-For-You. They are most often represented sitting together atop a compost heap or midden, with wreaths of wheat grass, oats, and alfalfa sprouts upon their bran-colored brows. Their believers eschew all red meats, refined sugars, and white flour, and are said to engage in orgiastic rituals during which they ingest huge quantities of garlic cloves, said to be an aphrodisiac, and brewster's yeast. Some adepts are said to be so transported by these observances that they enter into the transcendent state of Fermentation where they bubble with much spirit. While the esoteric significance of these rituals remains obscure, some experts believe that these activities are a type of sympathetic magic used to aid the rising of seven-grain bread dough.

The most sacred ritual dedicated to the worship of Tofu, Miso and Soya is the Rite of Recycling, not to be confused with the rituals sacred to **FALLOPIA** or **PEDESTRIA**. The fastidious practitioners of this rite divide their garbage with great care into Organic and Nonorganic. Organic Garbage, so called for its readily identifiable odor, includes eggshells, coffee grounds, thrice-used tea leaves, corn husks, tomato ends, and the well-browned leaves of lettuce. These offerings are added

Found Goddesses. Norwich, VT: New Victoria Publishers, 1988.

to sacred Compost Heaps at least once a week, and then carefully worked in with previous offerings. This process is said to produce much heat as Bacteria and Earthworms, the Little Folk much-beloved of Tofu, Miso and Soya, consume the offerings, thereby Recycling them. A "rich" Compost Heap is believed to be a sign of great virtue.

Nonorganic Garbage is faithfully divided into various types: the Aluminum, the Metal, the Glass, the Newspapers. Each type of Nonorganic Garbage to be Recycled is allotted its own sacred Garbage Can, and woe unto her who is ignorant enough to put Glass into the Aluminum container, or Aluminum into that reserved for Metal. These are grave errors for they expose a lack of proper concern for the worship of Tofu, Miso and Soya. The particularly devout are rumored to sort the Glass containers into Brown, Green, and Clear, but our re-searches have failed to turn up grounds for this. The less fanatical occasionally offer up used brown bags and glass jars to Her priestesses at the temples of Tofu, Miso and Soya—called Food Coops—where the most devoted of Her followers regularly volunteer their labor, thereby earning Members' Discounts. Though the origins of the Ritual of Recycling are uncertain, its rapid spread is evidenced by increasing numbers of Dumpsters and Canisters, shrines, large and small, dedicated to accepting our offerings to Tofu, Miso and Soya.

Cherished by Tofu, Miso and Soya are those

who plant their own organic gardens and protect the fragile greens from the destructive influences of The Poisonous Pesticides, the DDT, the Dioxin, and others. Her Threefold Protective Blessing can be sought with the following invocation addressed to one of Her minor aspects:

> RUTABAGA, Rutabaga, come and bless
> My salsify and watercress.

Great faith is also placed in instant invocations, like "Can it!" and "Put a lid on it!," but these are wrapped in mystery. It is said, too, that regular observance of Her rituals will ward off the cancerous presences of the demons BHA, EDP, and the perilous Red Dye #2. Especially sacred to Her Threefold Self is the Mung Bean, and a complicated five-day ritual, called Sprouting, if successful, will earn Her most Bounteous Blessings.

NOTE: There is fuzzy evidence that certain followers of **INERTIA** often feel the displeasure of Tofu, Miso and Soya when they forget to turn their Left-Overs, sacred to **CHANCY**, into inspired victuals. Her disapproval is said to reveal itself to these slackards when molds of brilliant hues and bizarre construction appear on Left-Overs. They may or may not announce their appearance with Reek, but, once these growths reside among one's Left-Overs, the Threefold Threat of Tofu, Miso and Soya's displeasure can only be averted by immediately making an offering of them to a Dumpster, Canister, or Compost Heap. Truly, it is said, "We have nothing to lose." ▪

Dykes to Watch Out For

by Alison Bechdel
From *New, Improved! Dykes to Watch Out For*. Ithaca, NY: Firebrand Books, 1990.

Chocolata

by Morgan Grey and Julia Penelope

Chocolata is believed by many to be merely an occasional, or periodic, aspect of **MUNCHIES**, because She frequently appears only at specific times during a lunar cycle or under similar conditions. Her most devoted adherents, however, who are legion, maintain that Chocolata is a major goddess, deserving ritual observances of Her own. Devotees of **TOFU, MISO, and SOYA** are known to invoke the deity **CAROB,** claiming that the delights of Carob are indistinguishable from those of Chocolata and, besides, "better for you." These are major thealogical debates unlikely to be settled in the near future, and we won't try to resolve them here. Of more importance, we believe, are indications that some forms of Chocolata worship can be traced back to the Amazons.

What we have been able to find out suggests diverse connections between the rituals of Chocolata and the most ancient roots of our own spirituality. Chocolata is often found in small, edible statues that resemble bunnies or cream-filled eggs (around the time of the Vernal Equinox), or fat, bearded figures with bags slung over their shoulders around Winter Solstice, and in small pointed breast-like pieces commonly called "Kisses." One researcher on goddess worship has suggested that both the shape and the name of

these "Kisses" point to an intimate relationship between the rituals of Chocolata, during which loud sucking sounds are made, and those of **CUDDLES, LILI-HA'ALA'A,** and **LABIA** (both Minora and Majora). One linguist, who has spent much of Her life decoding the ancient language of the Amazons, has discovered that the mysterious name, M & Ms, is an esoteric aspect of Chocolata that means "Menstruation and Menopause."

Further evidence can be found in the custom of exchanging heart-shaped boxes of Chocolata tokens (the heart being a well-known symbol of Liliháaláa in the Old Religion), while chanting the invocation, "Be My Valentina." The origins of such customs, while obscure, have much in common with the rituals of Liliháaláa, **NEME-HA'ALISH,** and Cuddles, which are generally regarded as pleasurable and, therefore, much sought after. Devotees of all three goddesses have been known to smile broadly after a ritual enactment, and report a sense of well-being and contentment. Given the increasingly strong evidence of long-standing associations between Chocolata, **EUPHORIA,** Cuddles, Nemeháalish, and Liliháaláa, we find it difficult to dismiss Chocolata's significance out of hand.

Worshippers of Chocolata are sometimes secretive about their rituals, but certain tell-tale signs signify that ritual indulgence has occurred. The most common include small, brown smudges

Found Goddesses. Norwich, VT: New Victoria Publishers, 1988.

around the lips and chin, sticky fingers, and a serenity of spirit verging on Euphoria's blessing. Lesbians who speak of "melting in one's hands" or "a month of sundaes" may well be fudging.

Of special importance, we think, are the reports of many Lesbians who feel an increased longing and enthusiasm for the rituals of Chocolata, Cuddles, and Liliháaláa one week before the onset of menstruation. Surely this cannot be a casual relationship. ■

by Kris Kovick

A Favorite Haunt

by Jess Wells

The steam from Abbie's plate of veal rose into her face as she bent in awe at the perfect swirls of sauce, one buttery yellow, one creamy brown, each contained to its side of the plate and spotted with tiny carrots, not a drop or speck outside the chef's design.

Abbie lifted her face to me, the gold caps gleaming on her teeth, her eyes warm, but tragic like a child who's found her favorite stuffed turtle after a good, long cry.

"This is why I love coming here," she said, a flush rising to her lined face.

She gave this speech every time we ate at Chez Nous, a French restaurant that seemed an oddity: all this brass and crystal in an industrial neighborhood, a part of town where solvents blew in the air at noon. Chez Nous had tremendous food, a gay staff and prices we used to consider outrageous. After Abbie's first monologue on her love of this place, I thought she was justifying a couple of working-class dykes blowing all their money on a fantasy. I guess I didn't know Abbie very well.

At that first dinner, fifteen years ago, we stepped through the heavy oak doors of the restaurant as new lovers. It was my birthday and I wore a turquoise lambswool dress, cut down the back to the crack in my ass. She seemed to like it. Abbie had only slept with me once and she kept

In *Two Willow Chairs*. Chicago: Third Side Press, 1987.

watching the French neckline of the dress as it slid further and further off my shoulders, threatening to fall into a puddle around my thighs. I grinned a little but pretended not to notice the cloth's meanderings, or Abbie as she watched the rise and fall of my breath. I had shopped for hours.

Abbie looked away from my collarbone, ordered wine. We fiddled with the linen napkins, admired the artwork and the tapestries. Our manners were impeccable—and acquired—since we had both come from backgrounds of Melmac and silverware you ordered through the mail—four box tops for a knife and fork. Table manners were learned like a second language.

My desire for Abbie had been building all day and was now being fueled by gate-crashing the upper class and the sound of the voices at the table next to us. While we held hands between the candlesticks, murmuring sweet things about wanting each other, a priest, a couple of monks and some laywomen discussed the Book of Revelations. The voices carried in counterpoint.

"And Jesus said unto the…"

"Umm, baby, I can smell your skin over here…"

"And bringing the lambs and fishes to the sacristy…"

"When can we fuck, gorgeous, now?"

For an ex-Catholic, it was heaven on earth: the most wicked and dangerous situation. I thought, 'Com'on Goddess, make my dress fall. Let me reach under the table and unzip her pants.'

Abbie bit her lip and clutched her wine glass.

Then they served dinner.

We began with plates of escargot, four big shells in an oily sauce of pesto and garlic, the smell of it nearly coating my cheeks. I talked of Abbie's beautiful breasts and picked up the spring-loaded tongs made of silver, gripped the shell, ate the snail with relish, talked of her nipples, grabbed another shell. I loved her ass, I said, leaning into the table, my long black hair falling to my left side. I was engrossed, but the snail wasn't paying attention: it sprang from the tongs, spewed green garlic sauce across the front of my dress and whizzed over my right shoulder. As it shot through the restaurant it passed several tables and finally skidded to a stop in the middle of the floor, puddling its goo into the carpet.

Abbie broke into laughter that was loud, from the middle of her belly. I turned to see the waiter deftly bend and scoop up the snail in a napkin, everyone but Abbie and I pretending that nothing had happened. That's just what she wanted, Abbie said, someone with style who wasn't *too* middle class.

For dessert at that first dinner, we fed each other chocolate mousse and poached pears. We had fallen from lust into love.

⚢

The second time we ate at Chez Nous, it was our fourth anniversary. The evening had a very different feel.

Abbie and I spent an hour or more bellied up to the downstairs bar. She growled over the menu: upper class people spent this much money just to avoid doing the dishes, she complained, no point in buying what she could cook at home. She went to restaurants to sample the unusual, the exotic, she muttered and I thought she made eating out sound like going to the zoo.

We ordered wine. Our conversation was lax and surly. There was no mention of sex, no hint of seduction. We argued over the dishes, the children, whose job was worse, whose mother had been less loving. As I became simpering to placate Abbie, she became vicious and loud. Our voices began to make people's heads turn. Plates of nondescript food arrived but we continued

roles so deeply memorized that there was no need to even consult our minds. She shouted, I grimaced. The first course had arrived and the others were waiting, leaving us nothing to do but sit like spectacles and finish. That night was our fourth anniversary but I don't remember what we ate or what we wore. There was no chocolate mousse or poached pears: we would have knocked each others' teeth out with the spoons.

In the weeks following the disastrous anniversary we turned our heads away when we drove past the restaurant. We didn't speak about the evening until weeks later.

"Do you suppose we did that on purpose?" Abbie asked, making a right turn to avoid the street. "Making fools of ourselves at the restaurant?"

I stared out the window, finally turning towards her at a red light.

"What's the matter, Abbie, don't we deserve to be happy?"

Both of us stared ahead as if seeing the terrain for the first time.

"If we make it to our fifth anniversary, let's buy our therapists champagne," Abbie said.

Abbie and I began to make a passionate discipline of avoiding the past. When we weren't relearning it, we were trivializing it, running from it, boxing it up as if it carried the virus of our relationship's destruction. If you exorcise the past, we reasoned, you exorcise the problems. We tried anything that held the potential of a fresh start. Abbie and Ruth ate chocolate, Abbie and I drank tea. I wore nothing but denim with Susan so I took everything blue to Community Thrift. This relationship with Abbie was going to work, I chanted, and if it took grey shirts to make sure, grey shirts it was. To save ourselves from the fate of the past, we left town on the weekends as we had never with anyone else; we cooked dinners together as if stewing the cement that would hold us together. Never again, Abbie had grumbled, as she put a timer and a rationing-chart on the TV set: it was television that had ruined their love, she breathed, it must have been the television.

The past sometimes followed us around. Even after four years, Abbie's ex-lover would occasionally appear and create a dull pain in my chest. The look on her face made it clear she had loved Abbie very much and as I looked at the woman, I wondered about my future, questioning if I, too, would lose, even though I, too, had loved.

♀♀

Abbie and I bought champagne for our therapists several years in a row and on our 10th anniversary, we went back to Chez Nous. That night, we took up both "our" table and the one that had seated the priest and his study group. We had grown into an entire clan of women.

Abbie busied herself checking up on her oldest daughter and her grandchild, turning then to her youngest daughter who leaned against her girlfriend and two daughters. Abbie's oldest sister, who had moved into an apartment down the street and a deep space in my heart, was catching up on the news with my best friend and her girlfriend.

The plates arrived on huge trays, spewing forth every smell a kitchen can offer. Soon we were elbow deep in our favorite sauces, arms reaching for the butter, the cream and a bit of someone else's food, the salt, or a knife, while across the table, a hand cupped a smiling cheek.

The people surrounding us were part of the way Abbie and I had learned to take ourselves and our relationship very seriously. We spent our time clear-headed, working. Working on talking, caring, working on securing our money, our jobs, our children's future, buying things for the house, making things legal and permanent, drawing comfort and stability towards ourselves as if taking tiny pieces of life and love and battening them down.

We drew people to us in the same way: cultivating a friend here, developing a new relationship with our families there, securing them to us for their love, to give them love, to share the warmth. And when the world scorched us, or the 10 o'clock news was bad, Abbie and I would walk through our house as if trying to collect all our efforts and draw this tarpaulin over us for protection, the two of us huddled under it for the heat.

That night, after the girls went off to their East Bay flats and our friends out to the bars, we went home and made love, an event whose rarity was not troublesome. We touched slowly, carefully, offering solace and tenderness and a familiarity that years ago we had disdained and now

had grown to count on. We had learned to allow each other a very private space in sex, not the insistent clinging of newlyweds, but a tempered assurance that if either floated off into fantasy, she would return. The other was happy to be part of the send-off.

♀♀

Tonight, years later than even that anniversary, we are here at Chez Nous, alone, having given and taken and convinced ourselves that daughters and granddaughters always come home. It is our fifteenth anniversary and the mood is bittersweet.

Our life is sweet but our friends, who were also together for fifteen years, have just broken up. One of the bonds of our friendship with them has always come from crossing the same milestones at the same time. If it just happened to them, was it going to happen to us? All day, Abbie's eyes have alternated between fear and sadness as she talked nervously about what the early signs might have been, what the symptoms were, trying to convince herself that early detection can guarantee a cure.

"Do you think they were each too wrapped up in their work?" she asked me as she finished the last bite of veal and pushed the plate away.

I didn't know. If I had thought it was just a fear of breaking up that was making her ask, I might have tired to calm her, but fears of all kinds had been building in us for several years. It seemed that just when we had finally secured our home and family, we had become more afraid of life. Just when we had gained power over our circumstances, we had begun to feel powerless in the face of fate. Five years ago, the phrase we uttered was "when we finally get"…but now it was "what if suddenly…?"

I suppose after 50 years of watching television reports on snipers, earthquakes that strike without warning and the inevitability of nuclear destruction, it was sensible that we should feel this way. But through all the uncertainty, somehow love had escaped the ravages of our growing fear. We continued to work hard and somewhere inside ourselves, where women nestle unreasonable beliefs, we carried the hope that a couple could pass the milestone of a magic number of years and then never have to worry about it failing, again.

Breaking up even sounded adolescent; it was for youngsters who needed to figure out pussy, or pretend they didn't need or want to be needed. It just wasn't supposed to happen after fifteen years.

"I didn't hear anything about another woman," Abbie whispered. "Do you think Sybil met someone at work? I mean, they just couldn't have...gotten bored, do you think?"

I didn't know the answer and the question gave me a knot in my stomach as if faced by yet another young woman who expected me to have all the magic answers on relationships. They asked us breathlessly, "how many years?" and sometimes I couldn't bear to tell them. They would repeat the answer like an incantation—"*Fifteen*"—and then immediately look at me with skepticism. Their next question, either silent or spoken, was always, "yeah, but is the sex still good?" or "My God, have you *always* been monogamous?" Then they'd sit back and wonder: "Wow, you think they're still in love?"

The waiter poured us coffee and Abbie looked up from her cup with the same question in her eyes. Such a basic change in the scenery, such a challenge to her foundation as the breakup of our best friends had thrown her ego back to age twenty, despite her beautiful silver hair, its shock of white from the forehead. She just didn't want to accept that unlike all our stocks, our state retirement plans and money market funds, there is no maturity date on a certificate of love. The working class girl simply could not go down to the bank and check the balance.

"Maybe they closed their channels of communication," she pondered.

I took the last bite of my salmon and pulled my coffee towards me. The waiter was there immediately to clear the plate. My darling just did *not* want to hear that there is no FSLIC for bankrupt relationships.

I stirred my coffee, a little weary thinking of the relentless work of a relationship, the constant vigilance of it all. I preferred to block those thoughts with dessert questions and the taste of salmon in my mouth.

"You never, ever doubt us, do you?" Abbie said, falling back in her chair and wrapping her fingers together.

"No," I said, then turned my head away. "Not for years."

"I don't know whether that's reassuring or not."

I pushed aside my coffee and took her hand, pulling it to my face. I kissed her knuckles, rubbed my cheek along the back of her hand. I had nothing to say, no fine print that would explain it all.

"Abbie, can't the warmth of a favorite haunt be worth the chance of it burning down tomorrow? Never to cook another poached pear?"

"Now don't get abstract on me; I'm talking about terrible pain, here."

"What happens if the most precious thing in the world comes without a guarantee?" I said, not knowing if it was true. Did you puzzle together pieces of a life with one woman or try a series of women only to remember each one with a smell, a song, an income level? How can so many of us live here and still have no geography of love? I had absolutely no answers, not even a neat, catch-all-but-explain-nothing-philosophy that might serve to change the subject at parties.

But I did know that if Abbie put her cup down and walked away tonight I'd try again. Still without lights, maps or a handrail to steady me, I'd be back, haunting the same old place of love, the terrifying possibility of joy. I'd glide around the edges of devotion and companionship, in my desire for love like an old ghost that can't be shooed away with broom or sticks or flailing arms.

Abbie sighed deeply and dropped her hands. "Do I have you, baby...hook, line and sinker?" she asked me, her eyes finally settling into the age of her face.

"With the rowboat *and* the summerhouse, my darling."

She sighed, flashed me those gold caps, then eyes that looked happy, maybe a bit resigned.

"Alright, alright," she said softly. "Waiter, we'd like two snifters of warm Cognac, please. And do you have mousse tonight? Maybe pears? One of each, please."

"Great restaurant," she said to me, stretching her hands across the table. "A very nice place." ▪

Colevia Carter
by JEB

What the Well-Dressed Dyke Will Wear

by Liza Cowan

In 1973 and 1974, when I was co-editing the Lesbian/feminist magazine, *Cowrie*, I wrote a series called "What the Well-Dressed Dyke Will Wear." The quotations here are taken from that series, with responses I added for the Winter 1975/76 issue of *DYKE, A Quarterly*.

Oppression

"Women have been forced to dress as objects since the invention of patriarchy…Do you object to my saying that women are forced to wear certain clothing? I know some women will say that no one is forced to wear anything. If women go along with these social/fashion customs they are just stupid. But this is not true. If you don't dress the way you are supposed to, you are a social outcast. If you function in mainstream culture you may be fired from

Originally published in *DYKE: A Quarterly (Winter 1975/76)*

your job, kicked out of school, ridiculed by your 'peers' and family. It takes great courage to defy your class and sex taboos." (February, 1974)

Sometimes I forget how different we're looking these days. My eye has become so accustomed to our short cropped hair, baggy work trousers, vests, boots, and our direct stares. The other day, my lover Alix and I went to town to pick up five-year-old daughter Adrian at her school. It was the first time we had been since school opened last month. Adrian usually comes and goes on the school bus. Her class wasn't quite finished when we arrived, so we hung out in the hall. Several classes were on their way to the cafeteria, and every kid in that hall stared at us as if we had three eyes, and they were not merely curious. Lots of them were hostile, especially the boys.

It was a difficult situation. Ordinarily we would have let the boys know that it was past time for them to be castrated.

Especially me. I hate little boys, and I love to make scenes. However, we decided not to since we were in Adrian's school. She's only five, and has no choice about where to live or go to school, and we know how heavy the other children in that rural public school could make it for her. At least in the city there are bound to be other children whose parents are weird, but here in the country everyone is pretty much the same except for the Lesbians, and Adrian is the only child in our Dyke community. Clearly, nobody in that school had ever seen the likes of us, two stompin' Dykes from New York City. So we had to act like "Mommie and Aunt Liza" (or whoever Adrian was saying I was that day). We were wearing the wrong costumes to play that part. It's way past time when we might want to pass at Adrian's school. We'd never be able to pull it off, anyway. The last time we put on ladies' clothes Alix looked like transsexual writer Jan Morris. I guess our solution at school is to keep a low profile and hope for the best.

Drag

"Why are women forced to dress certain ways? Because our clothes help keep us oppressed. At (a) transvestism panel a woman said that male transvestites made her very angry; she hated the way they minced and pranced and imitated all the superficial woman stereotypes. It occurred to me while she was saying this that the male tvs act like that partially because they are wearing those clothes. It is the function of 'feminine' clothes to make a woman a dependent, helpless, silly, decorative object." (February, 1974)

The time that Alix looked like Jan Morris was when she, Penny and I were getting into lady drag for a part in my slide show, "What The Well-Dressed Dyke Will Wear," that I was preparing for the Lesbian History Exploration. It was last March. The point of these pictures was to show how absurd we would look in drag, and how absurd straight women really look. (Later I decided not to use the whole drag series.) We were all supposed to dress subtly and tastefully, the way a chic working woman might look on an informal occasion. None of us really knew how this lady would dress, but we tried. I wore a navy wool midi skirt, red tights, brown shoes (aaugh!), a flowered blouse, rings, choke necklace, eye makeup and lipstick. Penny wore a khaki dress, blue tights, clogs, rings, necklace and makeup. Alix wore a knit mini skirt, brown tights, light blue turtleneck shirt, red shawl, clogs and makeup. Penny had been out less than a year, and had not yet acquired her Dyke look, so she really just looked like a straight woman. Alix looked like that pretend woman. When I tried to set up the tripod I discovered that one leg kept collapsing. I took it inside to fix it, and it was as if I had suddenly become another woman! I couldn't get my balance kneeling. I had trouble using the screwdriver; my eyes wouldn't focus properly. I had to take off my skirt and high heels before I could fix the tripod.

Hair

"My mother loved the way I looked in overalls and when I was six she cut my hair very short. I decided to grow it when I got sick of everybody calling me a boy. I didn't like boys." (June, 1973)

"A few months after I came out I cut my hair short...I did it because I wanted to identify myself with Dyke culture, and because I was no longer afraid of being called a boy (or a Dyke)...Long hair is a patriarchal symbol of femininity." (June, 1974)

I'm beginning to use hair as a political barometer. Long hair usually indicates that a Dyke is trying to pass. Most Dykes with long hair will deny this. They will say that they just like long hair. I'm sure they do.

But why?

Last March I shaved my head. I had been planning to do it for several months. Finally I saw three women in Woodstock, New York who had shaved their heads about two weeks before. At first they looked so startling, then after a few minutes my eyes got adjusted. I felt their heads, and each one felt different. Several women were talking to them about it; some were touching their fuzzy heads. I loved it. So I set the date for the beginning of spring, then convinced my straight neighbor who has a beauty salon to shave my head. She thought I was kidding, but finally she was convinced. Alix, Smokey, Mary and Adrian came over to watch. It took two hours. My hair was quite short to start, only about one inch long, but I have extraordinarily thick hair. Dorethea had to use a scissors, electric razor, clipper, and straight razor with shaving cream. Alix took pictures for my slide show, and everyone was laughing and being festive. When it was done, I could feel my friends talking over my head. I could feel their breath.

It was freezing cold so I had to wear a hat most of the time. But my head felt so fantastic, and I could see how round and smooth it was. No lumps. We could practically see the hairs grow overnight. Fuzz began to stick to it, hats came off inside out, and it was really noisy when anyone patted it. After about one week Alix said that it was like a velcro bowling ball. It was very exciting; sometimes I would look in the mirror and it was like looking at an entirely different woman. When my hair was about 1/2 inch long, I had a full covering.

Our friend Val cut Alix and Penny's hair to about 3/4 inch long. We went into the bathroom at Penny's to look at ourselves. We had to laugh. We said, "we look just like boys." That's what everybody straight said when my hair had just grown in. Alix and I used to have fights with women, explaining that we didn't look like boys, it's just that the only ones who were allowed to have hair that short were males, and since we didn't have beards, etc. we looked like boys, because that was an old connection people's brains were making.

Alix, Penny and I discussed this while we were looking in the mirror. Then we realized that for the first time we looked exactly like ourselves. Lots of women are really afraid to cut their hair all the way because they are afraid of what they are going to look like. All of our lives we have all heard about certain hairstyles that suit certain shapes of faces. We have learned to want a hairstyle that flatters us, that "suits" us. What a joke on us all! We found that our hair no longer "suited" us, it *was* us! Each head of hair grew differently, like fingerprints. We could see our cowlicks, our curl and growth patterns. Our hairlines were all different.

We all looked so clean and youthful with such short hair.

Penny and Alix's hair had only been about an inch longer, but that last 1/2 inch made the difference. We decided that the demarcation between short hair and "ultra Dyke short" can be a fraction of an inch. When hair can no longer be styled, when it can't be parted, curled, smoothed down, teased up, brushed over the ears, nothing, that's Ultra Dyke Short Hair. Lots of Dykes are doing it now. Smokey, Mary and I shaved our heads with horse clippers at the beginning of the summer. My friend Moon, and half of her New York City karate class, cut theirs. Lately in the Dyke press I have been seeing it more and more.

Haute Dyke

"Makeup, long hair, dresses, stockings, high heels, etc. are the basic uniforms of women. I refuse to wear feminine clothes because I know why I am supposed to. I would just as soon wear a ball and chain. And to pretend that one can transcend the meaning and effect of these clothes is bullshit...Fashions do not happen by accident. Clothes have a function and a meaning. I don't want to wear bluejeans and suits for the rest of my life; in fact I'm already tired of them, but our revolution is still young. I am confident that there will begin to evolve a true Dyke fashion, just as Dyke music and theater is already beginning. I have no idea what these clothes will look like, but I do know they will be liberating, physically and psychologically, and

they will be beautiful." (February, 1974)

I met Dyke designer Moregan in the fall of 1973. By February 1975 I had pretty much decided what I wanted her to make for me. I wanted pants that were cut like sweat pants, drawstring waist and elasticized cuffs. I wanted the jacket to be cut like a bathrobe, with a tie belt. I wanted to feel comfortable and confident wearing it. I didn't want it to look like a man's suit. I did want it to be stunning and machine washable. I went over to Moregan's and we spent the evening discussing my suit. The next week she showed me fabric samples. I wanted the suit to be soft, but velvet was wrong—too intimidating. I decided on velour so Moregan dyed velour to the smokey green I wanted. She made a dummy suit in muslin for me to try. We decided that she would applique a flying horse on the back of the suit. I thought that I would like to have two pockets, shaped like crescent moons. Moregan chose to put piping along the pockets, the lapels, and around the semi bell sleeves; this would give the jacket body.

When the suit was almost done, Moregan moved to California. A few weeks later she met me at the Lesbian History Exploration with the suit. It was a knockout! It looks like a combination costume of a magician, karate fighter and outer space woman. It is flowing, yet sturdy, and the fully lined velour is so soft and plush, it feels like I'm wearing pajamas. The drawstring waist pants could fit me if I gained or lost fifty pounds. The jacket too. I bought a hot pink sleeveless leotard to wear with it. It looks good with a turtleneck too, or I could wear nothing underneath.

I wore my Moregan suit to give my slide show at the Exploration, and again at Alix's big concert in Los Angeles (where everybody was decked out in the hautest Dyke Finery). I think that it was a little too jazzy for the Bay Area women's taste, but I wore it when I showed my slide show at the Women's Skills Center in San Francisco. I love my Moregan suit. It's neither butch nor femme. It is made by Dyke inspiration, by Dyke hands for a Dyke body.

We are experimenting with new ways of presenting ourselves to each other. The farther away we get from a patriarchal way of thinking, the uglier and uglier we will be to "them," and the more and more beautiful we will be to ourselves. ▪

by Kris Kovick

by Alison Bechdel
From *More Dykes to Watch Out For*. Ithaca, NY: Firebrand Books, 1988.

© 1987 by Sudie Rakusin

by Noreen Stevens
Editors' Note: This cartoon was featured on the cover of *Silverleaf's Choice: An Anthology of Lesbian Humor*, eds. Ann E. Larson and Carole A. Carr. Seattle: Silverleaf Press, 1990.

© 1983 by Sudie Rakusin

Joy with Horn, #1
by Jean Weisinger

The Great White Folk Music Myth

by Toni L. Armstrong Jr.

It gets my goat to hear distortions or myths that are put out as "fact" abut what women's music "is"—often stated by people who know little or nothing about our history *or* about what's happening nationwide in women's music today. One such "fact" I have discussed in my Lesbian Music HOTMIX columns (in *Outlines,* Chicago's newsmonthly) is the notion that the lyrical content of women's music is radically feminist and lesbian; a review of the lyrics of women's music albums immediately proves otherwise. [Reprints of HOTMIX columns are available: send a self-addressed stamped envelope.]

Another "fact" is that women's music "is *and always has been*" exclusively a "white-girl-with-guitar" circuit.

This well-entrenched myth is a tribute to the effectiveness of the pioneers in women's music who fit the stereotype of acoustic singer/songwriter acts:

From *HOT WIRE,* July 1988.

Ginni Clemmens, Maxine Feldman, Margie Adam, Cris Williamson, Holly Near, Deidre McCalla, Heather Bishop, Kristin Lems, and particularly Meg Christian and Alix Dobkin. These women, who were not all white girls—and many others—were able to establish themselves as well-known "presences" in the infancy and childhood of women's music, partially through talent and charisma—and partially because the simpler your act is, the more economically feasible it is to take it on the road. Consequently, you develop fame more easily. Yes, single acoustic acts have received the widest recognition and the most attention over the years. Yes, many have been white women with guitars (or pianos).

But: the women's music network as a whole—the national thing we've all worked so devotedly to create and maintain—"is" much more than how successful a handful of individual musicians have become.

It is a *national cultural movement* which is the sum total of the contributions of countless women over the last two decades. When discussing what women's music "is," this must never be forgotten or minimized.

So What?

There are four main reasons why, in my opinion, it is destructive to perpetuate the myth that women's music has always been—and still is—a WGWG genre.

One: It's historically untrue. We have *always* been an incredibly diverse network in terms of musical style—a review of festival stage line-ups over the years is most educational. Re-read back issues of *Paid My Dues,* the historical women's music journal from the '70s. The mainstream media *consistently* lies to us and erases our history—witness the recent media treatment of the October March on Washington. The accomplishments of women, lesbians, and people of all ethnic and religious minorities are usually ignored or "forgotten." Let's not contribute to the distortions out of our own ignorance. It is not constructive to take the attitude, "*I* never heard of it, so it never existed." We're erasing our own role models. We're allowing women *from the 1970s* to become "forgotten musical foremothers." [See "The 'Me' Decade and Feminist Science Fiction" by Jean Gomoll in this issue of *HOT WIRE*.]

Two: Reinforcing this particular myth contributes to the mentality that makes us, as a national community, keep reinventing the wheel—i.e., I think I'll scream the next time I hear, "It's time we *started* to expand to include music styles other than folk…" How about we *start* to seriously support the musicians who have, *for years now*, been doing other styles? This support begins with acknowledgment that they exist, and that their work has value. The support continues with our making the effort to see that non-acoustic and other acts have production venues within the women's music network *in addition* to festival stages.

Three: Women's music isn't even really folk music! What we have had a lot of (from the stars who have become the most well-known within our circuit) is actually acoustic pop, or light folk-rock, blues-pop, or jazz-rock. People involved in the genuine "folk music circuit" do not consider most of what we do to be "folk music."

Four: Finally, the stereotype is racist; it minimizes or just plain erases most of the contributions which women of color have *always* made to women's music. The musical styles of women of color frequently require ensemble or band instrumentation; between the economic difficulties of touring and the racism inherent in the white-dominated women's music circuit, these groups have usually not gotten the widespread recognition they deserve. *That doesn't mean they haven't existed; it doesn't mean they haven't been on albums and on festival stages and performing in their home regions from the earliest days of women's music.*

The little quiz that accompanies this article is a brief walk down memory lane, focusing on relatively well-known acts. There are *dozens* of other examples of women doing rock, Latin/salsa, classical, reggae, jazz, funk, R&B, technopop, and other forms of nonfolk-style music that could have been included; I concentrated on examples that have received some national exposure throughout the years. Many appear on albums and/or have appeared on women's music festival stages. Keep in mind that I had to weed out most of the more obscure examples in order to whittle the quiz down to 30 questions.

See how much of this information *you* know. And the next time you hear or read any version of the assertion "Women's music = WGWG,"

take the opportunity to be an educator/historian. ∎

Quiz

1. June Millington's all-woman rock band which had mainstream chart success in the 1970s.

2. Five black a cappella singers from Washington, D.C. who play hand percussion instruments.

3. Jean Fineberg on sax/flute; Ellen Seeling on trumpet.

4. Two women's bands in which Carol McDonald from New York has played.

5. The all-women Big Band started by Jerene Jackson.

6. The instrument Linda Tillery, Jake Lampert, Barbara Borden, Bonnie Johnson and Cam Davis have played live on and on record.

7. R&B/pop vocalist prominent in women's music for the past decade whose latest album was recorded in the studio where Michael Jackson did *Thriller.*

8. Five women from Seattle singing/playing/dancing music of the Shona people of Zimbabwe wearing traditional costume.

9. Instrument played by Carolyn Brandy, Vicki Randle, Debbie Fier, and Nydia "Liberty" Mata.

10. Two publications that regularly focus on nonfolk-style music…one from California subtitled "The Women's Rock Mag With Bite," one from Chicago subtitled "The Journal of Women's Music & Culture."

11. Two "women's libera-tion rock bands" appeared on *Mountain Moving Day*, one of women's music's earliest al-bums. Which cities were the bands named after?

12. What music done by Sue Fink, Adrienne Torf, Jackie Stander, and Labrys has in com-mon.

13. Reggae/pop/political/spiritual duo with current al-bum entitled *City Down*.

14. Leader of the instru-mental Sunwomyn Ensemble, which does the midnight Acous-tic Stage at the Michigan Festival.

15. The original three members of the jazz group Alive!

16. The comedy show/dance band that bills itself as "'50s rock & role music."

17. Electric rock guitarist from Canada; sometimes tours with Heather Bishop.

18. Dance band featuring Debbie Fier, Alix Dobkin, and River Lightwomoon.

19. Name of the tour in the '70s featuring more than a dozen black women, including Mary Watkins, Linda Tillery, and Pat Parker.

20. Famous woman con-ductor who led the women's or-chestra at the Fifth National Women's Music Festival (in Champaign).

21. '70s women's band; one of Olivia Records' first al-bums.

22. Rocking daughter of a famous member of Sweet Honey in the Rock; has worked some-times with band called The Agitones.

23. Leader of the percus-sion-based group A Piece of the World.

24. Now defunct jazz/Latin/pop women's band from California; toured Nicaragua and included some players from Baba Yaga.

25. Old timey/country group that frequently does square dances at Michigan.

26. Olivia Records' most prominent electric guitar play-ing pop/rocker.

27. Women's rock band that recorded *Boston Ride* on the Galaxia label.

28. Women's ensemble combining socially conscious dance and music; evolved from Wallflower Dance Order.

29. Icebergg Records' re-cording trio from St. Louis—for-merly a duo featuring Michelle Isam (on sax) and Carol Schmidt (piano).

30. Best-selling Olivia Records recording artist; each of her albums and tours has got-ten increasingly more pop/rock oriented.

Answers

1. Fanny 2. Sweet Honey in the Rock 3. Deuce 4. Witch, Isis 5. Maiden Voyage 6. drums 7. Teresa Trull/A Step Away 8. Gwynvai 9. congas 10. *Bitch*, HOT WIRE 11. Chicago, New Haven 12. use of synthesizers 13. Casselberry-DuPrée 14. Kay Gardner 15. Rhiannon, Suzanne Vincenza, Carolyn Brandy 16. Fabulous Dyketones 17. Sherry Shute 18. Party Line Dance Band 19. Varied Voices of Black Women 20. Antonia Brico 21. BeBe K'Roche 22. Toshi Reagon 23. Edwina Lee Tyler 24. Swingshift 25. Reel World String Band 26. Tret Fure 27. Lilith 28. The Dance Brigade 29. Jasmine 30. Chris Williamson

Scoring

27–30: You are an expert on women's music who should be consulted by every-one for factual information and perspec-tives.

23–26: You've paid attention to what's happening for the last two decades; you have a reasonably well-rounded knowledge.

19–22: You've got a basic under-standing of women's music, but there are serious gaps in your knowledge of our his-tory.

18 or less: You are either new to women's music or have slept through the last two decades.

Pam Hall
by Toni Armstrong Jr.

I Am Pam Hall, Fifth Generation Dyke

by Pam Hall

I was raised to be a musician: six-year-old Suzuki violinist to concert symphony member to singer/songwriter of womyn's music. It has been a long journey, with much to celebrate.

I am Pam Hall, fifth generation dyke—daughter of Anita, professor of education, who is the daughter of Alberta, newspaper editor and printer, who was the daughter of Hattie, a laundress, who was the daughter of Kate, an African shaman (whose backyard was the scene of many an African ritual), and she, former slave from Burnt Corn, Alabama, survivor of the Civil War. I pay homage to my maternal ancestors who have made this possible.

I want to begin this article with a recognition of the strong women who shaped those who shaped my life: Mom and Grandma. For whatever reasons—be it the so-called matricentric family legacy of slavery and oppres-

sion, the courage of those mighty and strong women who survived the middle passage, or the persistent and ever-present pissed-offed anger that drove the "need to succeed" middle-class mentality in the midst of a nightmare—here I am, the woman-child of that first Black womon who stepped on this land in shackles.

Here I am, the womon-child, singing to womyn, to freedom, to life, love, and passion.

Life for this Black southern lesbian hasn't been all cotton and light, nor has it been a nightmare of despair. Touring the country last year often left me wanting to hurry up and get back South. For me, the South is gentle, is warm, close, like bathwater. Its womyn are kind, uplifting, and no stranger to struggle. I adore my mother, my granny, my friends, and I love a womon.

My music reflects my love of womyn, and my deep respect for Southern womyn like Fannie Lou Hamer, as illustrated in the song I wrote about her entitled

"St. Fannie Lou," in which I sing, "she is my matron saint of the sick and tired and those who just ain't gonna take it no mo!" Or my song about Grandma, who said, "Five words I never want to hear 'cross your lips is shoulda, woulda, coulda, couldn't, and can't." Other Southern women—like Daisy Bates, Unita Blackwell, Margaret Walker Alexander, Rosa Parks, Alice Walker, Mom—have all instilled a sense of dignity in me that is challenged as often by my less-enlightened sisters as by the raw and racist rednecks deep in the Delta.

But there are womyn who fill me with pride for my gender and culture, region and race— all those womyn who dug for the proverbial "pony" and simply fed the garden with the shit, made gorgeous hothouse orchids of their lives. Thinking of them is the stuff that motivates me to sing in a lesbian tongue and with a feminist fist uplifted.

My career as a womyn's musician began as much as a flirt with fantasy as a deliberate

From *HOT WIRE*, May 1992.

and studied endeavor. As a teenager I heard Joan [Armatrading]'s "Love and Affection" and her references to "a lover." That same year, I stumbled into a womyn's bar and danced my first slow drag with a tall Native American womon whose arms surrounded me in a gentle and sensual sweetness, and I felt weak as Joan sang "love, love, love, love…" (and I cried during the sax solo). I needed to hear Joan say, "she," but I was willing to take "you" instead.

From that moment in 1976, I began my journey to find my voice and my feelings, to search for my own expression of the feelings of lesbian identity and lesbian love. I found Cris, Meg, Kay, *The Changer and the Changed*; I found a lesbian collective, and a woman's love.

So I sent in a video to Wanda Henson, producer of the Gulf Coast Women's Festival, and through her mentorship I learned to identify lyrics that were leftover internalized sexism, racism, and looksism, as well as the victim/power-over style so often heard in blues and rhythm and blues.

Wanda and I began working together regularly. We edited my material, and with her help, last year I stepped onto the stages of three major women's music festivals (Gulf Coast, Southern, and East Coast Lesbians' Festival) as well as the Swiss Lesbian Conference and The Swiss Women's Dance.

In every setting—in straight audiences as well as womyn's audiences—I've chosen to begin my sets with a tune I wrote called "L-E-S-B-I-A-N" to let everybody know where I'm coming from. Often I'll sing about Fannie Lou or Granny to validate the ignorance of those who make a great show of exiting the concert.

But I don't sing to educate the straight world about lesbianism or feminism—I sing for the sisters. I sing for lesbians and womyn who delight in the diversity of culture; I sing *for* womyn, *about* womyn, and about womyn *loving* womyn, about womyn's spirituality, and about womyn's abilities. I am a

womyn and festival audiences still make warm waves pass over me. I am so very appreciative of this pure loving energy from my sisters. Am I dreaming or can it truly be that I can sing about my lesbian passions and feminist dreams, and receive what I think all artists seek from their community—affirmation, validation, and spiritual support?…

I've been able to get my career off to a great start thanks to the generous support of womyn who have helped me realize the dream of singing and playing for womyn, about womyn—womyn

"… I don't sing to educate the straight world about lesbianism or feminism—I sing for the sisters."

"lesbian-identified" womyn's musician who willingly steps in the box labeled "dyke" that has a rich and wondrous precedence, with the likes of Cris Williamson, Meg Christian, Alix Dobkin, June Millington, Pat Parker, and Audre Lorde pioneering the way for me and womyn like me.

The ferocious and abundant opportunities of 1991 still make my heart sigh and my head spin. So much love, and the embracing energy of

like Dr. Ruth, June Millington, Wanda Henson, Robin Tyler, Lin Daniels, Myriam Fougére, Toni Armstrong Jr., Michelle Crone, and many others. I am forever grateful for their support. To my Mom, my solace, and Brigitta, my beloved—my soul rejoices because of your love. And to my new and especially my old friends, as well as my listeners, my heart is full and sometimes weeps because of your strong embrace.

Blessed Be. ■

Kay Gardner
by Toni Armstrong Jr.

Early East Coast Women's Music and The Squirrel

by Kay Gardner

You may think that women's music recordings are West Coast phenomena, but the women's music recording industry has its roots firmly planted in East Coast soil—or, more accurately, cement—for it had its beginnings in the cities of New York and Washington, DC. Even now women's independent labels are found all over the country—Woodstock, Atlanta, Chicago, Cincinnati, Minneapolis, Boston, Madison, Durham, New York City, and Stonington, Maine.

The Early Days

The *very* first recording of lesbian songs was Maxine Feldman's classic 45, "Angry Atthis," produced by Robin Tyler and recorded in Los Angeles in 1968.

1972 was a very significant year. That was the year that *Virgo Rising*, an LP compila-

From *HOT WIRE*, March 1986.

tion of traditional folksongs with their lyrics changed to reflect feminist sensibilities, was recorded in Colorado and was made nationally available in women's bookstores. *Mountain Moving Day*, featuring the New Haven and Chicago Women's Liberation Rock Bands, was also released in 1972. It is still carried by Ladyslipper. And although it did not receive national distribution, *A Few Loving Women* (featuring such artists as Jeriann Hilderley (Jeritree) and Margaret Sloan singing her classic "I'd Like To Make Love With You" [later recorded by Teresa Trull on Olivia Records]) was the first lesbian LP. It was put out by The Lesbian Liberation Organization in New York City.

The year 1973 marks the birth of the women's recording industry. It was then that three still-existing labels were founded. Women's Wax Works, a label begun by Alix Dobkin and me, was founded in New York City. Women's Wax Works produced the first LP entirely produced,

engineered, financed, and performed by lesbians. This album, *Lavender Jane Loves Women*, is still selling steadily here in the U.S. and in Europe, where it's the number one selling women's music album.

Simultaneously, in Washington, DC, Olivia Records was beginning. They recorded Meg Christian and Cris Williamson on a landmark 45 with the intention of using the proceeds to establish a national women's recording company. Also, Marnie Hall began Leonarda Records in New York City. This label was—and still is—the only record company offering high-quality recordings of women's classical music.

The next year, 1974, brought out Olivia's first LP: Meg Christian's *I Know You Know*, recorded and mixed for the most part in Washington, DC. This was the only LP Olivia produced on the East Coast, for soon afterwards the entire company moved to Los Angeles.

1974 also marked Willie

Tyson's debut women's music album, *Full Count*, recorded in Washington, DC on her own Lima Bean Records label.

Thanks to the Olivia Record collective, a national distribution network was organized, and soon these early women's music recordings were being sold in women's bookstores everywhere!

My record *Mooncircles* (on Urana Records, a label founded by engineer Marilyn Ries and me) and Cris Williamson's *The Changer and the Changed* (Olivia Records) were out in time for the 1975 holiday season. These two albums, with their musical messages of healing and rebirth, quickly became classics along with the 1973 and 1974 releases.

The women's music ball was rolling! 1975 bought us Casse Culver's *Three Gypsies* (Urana), *Jade and Sarsaparilla* (Submaureen), and Alix Dobkin's *Living With Lesbians* (Women's Wax Works) from East Coast labels. Margie Adam's *Songwriter* (Pleiades) came from the West Coast, as did the album that introduced Holly Near to women's music audiences, *You Can Know All I Am* (Redwood Records).

Another East Coast label active in the 1970s was the now defunct Galaxia Records, which produced the Boston lesbian dance band Lilith, Maxine Feldman's *Closet Sale*, and *Women's Orchestral Works*, with the New England Women's Symphony.

Rosetta Records, founded in New York City by Rosetta Reitz, began offering jazz and blues recordings in the late 1970s. These recordings are remixed from old radio broadcasts and feature such famous artists as Ma Rainey, Bessie Smith, Billie Holiday, and the International Sweethearts of Rhythm (featured in the March 1985 issue of *HOT WIRE*).

As time goes on, it is easy to remember performers who recorded their contributions to early women's music. But there were many women whose behind-the-scenes contributions were not in a form where their names would be familiar a decade or two later. It is to one of these women that this column is devoted.

Putting Your Money Where Your Mouth Is

E. Shirley Watt—better known to her friends as Squirrel—was a financial angel and friend to early women's music. She passed away in February of 1985.

I was raising money for my first solo album, *Mooncircles*, in 1975. I took a handful of fundraising brochures to pass out at the first Boston Women's Music Festival. There I was introduced to Shirley and Joan Gibson, her companion of 12 years. They were extremely preoccupied, having just learned that their specially equipped van—which they needed for getting around in their wheelchairs—had been stolen. I didn't get to present them with my fundraising spiel, but I did hand them a brochure.

About a month later Joanie called and asked how much money I needed. I told her, and within a week she had sent a check for the entire amount!

It was difficult for Shirley and Joanie to be away from home for long periods of time. To thank our angels personally, Marilyn Ries—engineer and my business partner in Wise Women Enterprises—decided to drive up to Stonington, ME from New York City. The business and personal relationship which grew out of this first meeting lasted through the production of several women's music albums, and beyond.

We were incredibly naive about how to run a record business in those days. We had an idealistic political commitment and little business experience, and we knew we wanted to continue making women's records. My pet project was a children's record. Marilyn wanted to record Casse Culver, who had been the first lesbian-feminist performer to tour nationally. With Shirley and Joanie on our new board of directors, we decided to go with Casse's project, *Three Gypsies*.

Shirley was financing the entire project, and it seemed fair that she and Joanie participate in the recording process. We decided to try to find a studio in Maine. Fortunately, we found a studio belonging to Noel Paul Stookey ("Paul" of Peter, Paul and Mary) in a town only a half hour's drive from Stonington.

A convocation of dykes

soon descended upon Stonington. Shirley, a great lover of lesbians, was in seventh heaven, while the young Stonington fishermen were totally confused… "All these beautiful women are in town, and none of them will even *look* at us!"

We all stayed at Birch Bend, a lovely six-bedroom chalet in the woods five minutes from the granite ledges of the ocean's shore—Shirley's summer "cottage." Both Joanie and Shirley came to Birch Bend for rehearsals and parties. When they also came to the sessions in the studio on the third floor of a converted barn, stronger women carried each of them piggyback up and down three flights every day. Consciousness of wheelchair accessibility was quickly raised.

Making *Three Gypsies* was a working vacation, with excursions to the studio and the harbor islands. We shared lobster dinners, clam digging, extemporaneous music-making, and lots and lots of laughter.

Fundraising for recordings is a very time-consuming and tedious task. I learned how from Alix Dobkin, who I watched ask every woman she knew at every possible opportunity. Later, when raising money for my own solo albums, I used this fundraising procedure:

I begin by sending a letter to everyone I know, every working member of my immediate and distant family, and strangers at women's gatherings. I find handwritten letters are more effective than typewritten. In this letter, I lay out my plan, my budget, and my repayment process. Donations are preferred over loans, of course, but they are usually $10 or less.

I announce from the stage that I am raising money, and am able to get most of my funding in this way. Also, friends and I organize fundraising parties to which women whom we know have money are cordially invited. At these parties, tapes of my music are played, flyers are passed out, and I give a presentation of why my music is unique and why it should be supported. This was embarrassing at first but necessary; if I couldn't "sell" my own work to anyone, then why would they want to invest?

Once a woman decides to help, we sign a note defining the terms of repayment and interest (usually 10% simple interest). Repayment is based upon a percentage of quarterly sales returns.

Another good fundraising technique is to take advance orders. This means a bit of book work, but usually brings in a reasonable amount of seed money. Considering that albums can cost from $10,000 to 10 times that amount to produce, fundraising skills are extremely valuable to an artist in this industry, at least until her work is popular enough to woo a label into taking the financial risk of producing her.

Special mention must be made of the behind-the-scenes angels who have supported women's music throughout these years. Women who have independent means, as well as women who work, have reached into their jeans pockets or bank accounts to make women's music come to vinyl. A woman who owned some health food stores in Florida gave $7,000 toward the production of one of our Urana recordings. A medical doctor in Louisiana gave $5,000. And Squirrel gave as much as $72,000 for the production of two Urana recordings.

Without the help of these women, the unsung heras of the women's music industry, no labels (especially in the early days) could survive.

Squirrelly

I can't finish this column without giving readers a sample of Shirley's outrageous personality. Shirley was basically a hermit who preferred animals to people. In her early days she trained thoroughbred horses, and at the 1952 Olympics in Stockholm she was the only woman on the American equestrian team. When her physical condition deteriorated due to multiple sclerosis, she had to give up riding and horse breeding. When I met her she had a small menagerie: two cats, one dog, and a skunk.

She smoked cigars, read lesbian pornography, had a cynical dry wit, and delighted in local gossip. One of her favorite pastimes was sitting with her large ship's telescope focused on the Stonington harbor. With a printed yacht registry by her side, she kept tabs on exactly who was sailing into town, and was especially eager to see if Jackie O's yacht was approaching. She dreamed that one day she would be able to train her telescope on any of the small islands in the harbor and see nude women cavorting on the shores—a latter day Maine Lesbos.

As I think about all Shirley did for women's music and lesbian culture, I think of the women whose projects she totally or partially financed. This list does not include everyone, because Shirley wasn't the kind of person to blow her own horn about helping. But Maxine Feldman, Robin Flower, Casse Culver, Mary Wings, the Boston Daughters of Bilitis, Gina Halpern, Susan Abod, Willie Tyson, and myself are some of the women whose projects I know she supported.

My most vibrant memory of Shirley's outrageousness was when she came to my 1976 concert at the University of Maine in Orono. Sponsored by the Wilde-Stein club, the campus gay organization, the concert had an audience comprised of gay and straight students plus a smattering of music school faculty members. Joanie and Shirley's van pulled up to the door of the building, and the van's wheelchair lift hummed down to the walkway with a most unusual audience member aboard. It was Shirley, dressed in a lavender blouse, many necklaces with women's symbols and labyris pendants, and a full-length lavender satin skirt which continuously got caught in her wheels. She caused quite a stir as she rolled up to the very front row, her skirts demurely tucked around her legs. Though looking rather frail, Shirley passed the pre-concert time by lighting up and smoking a huge, smelly cigar.

Oh Squirrel, you were certainly quite a character! If you're in Dyke Heaven, I hope you're happy. Thanks for really putting your money where your mouth was, and thanks for being truly queer. ■

Dykes in a Truck

Photo by JEB.

Dykes, counterclockwise, starting from the top right: Kay Gardner, Robin Flower, Barbara Edwards, Boden Sandstrom, Casse Culver, Willie Tyson, Margie Adams, Paula, Marilyn Ries, Betty Macdonald, Roz Richter, Joan E. Biren (JEB), Susan Abod, Mary Wings, Maxine Feldman, Joan Gibson

Jamie Anderson & Bonnie Morris

by Toni Armstrong Jr.

Women's Music for the '90s
Jamie Anderson
Interviewed by Toni Armstrong Jr.

Jamie Anderson burst onto the women's music scene in the late '80s with her Closer to Home *album, featuring the runaway hit* Wedding Song. *Since then, she's played hundreds of shows to women's music audiences from coast to coast, and was wildly well-received at the nine festivals she played in 1992. Her latest album,* Center of Balance, *like her debut* Closer to Home, *was put out by Jamie and her partner Dakota on their own Tsunami Records label. Consistently mentioned in the* HOT WIRE *Readers' Choice Survey, the Arizona-born comic songwriter has been selected "Favorite New Performer" three years in a row. In addition to touring nationally since 1987, Jamie has her broadcaster's license and is a programmer at a local community radio station. She and Dakota make their home in the sweet desert environment of Tucson.*

From *HOT WIRE*, September 1992.

How did you hear about women's music? And when?

In 1977. I was at a women's bookstore. I had been out as a lesbian for a year and I saw some albums there. I was never too interested in them because I was kind of a Top 40 snob. I didn't listen to any kind of alternative music, either. There was an album cover with this orange juice can on it [*Lesbian Concentrate*, Olivia Records, 1977]. Since I'm really connected to comedy, that attracted me. This was about the time Anita Bryant was doing her weird thing. She was a celebrity who took a very public right-wing stance on gays and lesbians in the '70s, and one of her major jobs was promoting orange juice. I thought the *Lesbian Concentrate* cover was pretty funny, so I bought the album. I thought, "Whoa, these women are singing about my life." I had never heard lesbian music before, and I was just blown away. That album was such a good sampler, I went back and bought albums made by several of the women on it. Things just went from there. A few months after that, I went to my first women's concert—Therese Edell, in Phoenix.

You were already a musician?

Yeah. I learned to play when I was fifteen, and in the Girl Scouts. Scouts sing all the time, and they sing these really simple, well-structured folk songs that are pretty easy to pick up when you are first learning the guitar. My dad's a guitar player, so there were always guitars lying around the house. I taught myself to play.

Which artists from the early days are still of interest to you?

Meg Christian's music still means a lot to me. She was such a fine songwriter and guitarist; she had charm and stage presence for days. I love her use of humor. Her songs don't seem outdated; they're still very fresh. I also occasionally listen to the work of others. I have a tape I made with some songs from old Teresa Trull and Linda Tillery albums that I listen to. The music is so energetic and hopeful—and there will always be a special place in my heart for Therese Edell's music. I know every word to most of her songs.

Which was your first festival?

1979, Michigan. I don't know what possessed me, but I recruited some women from Arizona to go because it really intrigued me. There were five of us in a little pickup and it was a four-day drive. It was very cozy, but it was well worth it. A lot of women describe their first experience at a festival as being extremely overwhelming, but it wasn't for me. I felt like an Amazon. I was doing stuff like carrying this big, heavy ice chest and other stuff to our campsite. I was sore for days. I thought I could do anything!

How old were you?

Gosh, you're going to make me do numbers. Let's see, how old was I in '79? I had been out of high school for four years, I don't know...let's see, twenty-two. I had done a little performing by then.

Mostly hobby-level stuff?

Oh, definitely. It was around that time that I did my first women's music concert; it was a benefit for the local women's center. It was in a big hall with a sound system. It was the first time I had ever used a microphone. I remember the guy running sound telling me how close to get to the mike and what to do with it. I felt so weird with this hardware so close to my face. I remember we had to sing our own compositions, and at the time I had only written five songs. When the organizer came up to me and said they only had time for me to do five songs, I was really relieved.

Did you start out writing woman-identified material?

Yes. I came out not long after I learned to play the guitar, so it was only natural that I wrote about who I was. I never intended to be the kind of writer that sells songs to other people, so I never had to pretend to be anything I wasn't. Also, by the time I was ready to write songs, I was listening to women's music and that influenced me a lot. Many of the places where I performed were lesbian spaces, too. I wanted to write music that my audience would identify with.

Have you sought out festivals all along?

Oh, I was a festival junkie even before I was hired to perform at them. I always brought my guitar, even on that first trip to Michigan. With five of us in that little pickup, my guitar still got in there. Not one woman bitched about it, and I really appreciated that. Yeah, I was always at the open mike or the jam tent—somewhere being outrageous. I performed mostly in Arizona up until just a few years ago. Ever since that first festival in '70, I've been to at least one festival every year.

Which ones?

I've probably been to Michigan more than any other festival, but I've also been to West Coast and to National. They all have something to offer. Up until a few years ago, West Coast was the closest festival to me—a thirteen- or fourteen-hour drive—so if I didn't have the energy or money to attend a Midwest festival, I went to West Coast. More of my friends went to that one anyway. Arizona has a little festival now which has been going on a few years.

In what year did you throw your hat in the ring as a real career-type performer?

It was probably when I did *Closer to Home* in 1989. I had been performing a lot locally and loved doing music, but I thought that I really needed to pay my rent with something that was a regular-type job. I had gone back to school, and was finishing up a business degree when I met Dakota, in 1988. We developed a personal relationship first. As she got to know me, she wanted to know my plans for the future. She knew I loved doing music, but I told her that I was interested in doing paralegal work. I was just finishing up my degree with an internship that I really liked at the State Attorney General's office.

She asked me why I didn't want to devote more time to music. I thought she meant casuals. I'd done weddings and parties for a while and I hated it. I felt that if I had to sing one more cover tune, I was going to barf on my shoes. Then she explained that she meant I should do women's music, or folk music, or whatever moved me.

How did you feel about that?

I come from this very practical, working class kind of family where you went to a factory or office every week. You got your paycheck, and that was a job. Playing music was not a job. When Dakota said she'd support me until I got on my feet, I thought I'd try it. So, I set out to do my first album.

Dakota gradually got involved in the project. She has a good business head, and she's very well organized. She's also a trained musician, and she has a very good ear for music. She co-produced the album, and has really been an important part of what I do. I had done a couple of short national tours on a very small-time basis, mostly just to get myself to a festival—to earn gas money. So I had a little bit of experience in doing my own booking. That's when I started collecting contacts and calling women to tell them I was coming out with this album. I was booking a tour,

and everybody kept saying, "Jamie who? What do you do?" Every musician hates that kind of question—"What kind of music do you do?"

How do you answer?

Usually I say folk-country singer-songwriter with a heavy dose of comedy.

You do about forty or fifty gigs a year now, including festivals. What do you find similar and different from community to community?

All communities have a couple of organizers who seem to do almost all of the events in town. They're never involved in just one project, either. It's not uncommon to find a concert producer who is also a writer for the local gay paper, or a coffeehouse organizer who works at the community radio station. So, in most communities there are leaders who are committed to supporting women's culture. I know that in some circles, having leaders is a big no-no. We're supposed to be doing everything communally, I guess. But I find that even when a group is producing a concert, there are one or two women who are the guiding force behind almost everything.

Communities vary greatly in what makes them laugh. Big city women don't laugh as easily as do those in smaller towns. Maybe that has to do with the stress of living in a city. Or maybe my brand of humor

doesn't grab them like it does my other audiences.

In smaller towns, I get bigger audiences. Since there's not as much going on, everyone in town shows up, even the bar dykes who don't always come to my shows (unless I'm playing at the bar). It's just a guess, but in bigger places I think women get sort of jaded because there's always so much happening. It's funny—everyone asks about my shows in places like San Francisco, or other "queer meccas," thinking that those are the best places to perform. But I have bigger audiences in places like Spokane and Little Rock. It's not that I don't enjoy the big city gigs, they're just harder.

There are also differences between the different regions of the country. Southern women are so friendly. I love booking Southern tours, because the folks I deal with love to chat. I find out a lot about them and their communities before I even come into town. East Coast folks aren't as chatty—my phone calls to them are short and business-like. When I arrive for the gig, it's then that I get to know the community a little.

You're familiar now with the national network, both from having been an active participant and now as a recognized performer. You aren't yet able to make your living totally from doing women's music; do you think it's possible for anyone to do so?

Yes. I'm optimistic. Some people may think I'm naive, I don't know. But I believe that if there's something I love to do so much, and that I feel is important, then there has to be a way to make a living at it. Maybe that's an ass-backward way to look at it. I can be very pragmatic and say, "This is outrageous, I can't do this. I have to do weddings on the side or something to be able to make it...," but I believe there is a real need for what I do. How can I do it? Just keep being the most shameless self-promoter that I've been up until now.

Why is our subculture important enough for you to put everything else in your life on hold?

Our subculture is who I am—I couldn't ignore it. And I'm not putting everything else in my life on hold. This *is* my life. It's not like I made this great career sacrifice when I decided to perform. Sure, I don't have some of the benefits I could get with other jobs—like health insurance and regular hours—but I do have the satisfaction of doing something I really love. I can't think of anything more exciting than songwriting and being on stage. And I can be myself while I'm up there. I don't have to be in the closet or squeeze myself into a size nine to be accepted and appreciated.

Why do you think performers in women's music don't

make more money? Is it possible to get a bigger audience? What needs to change?

I'm not sure I know the answer to that. I've heard a lot of different perspectives, and there are parts of those different perspectives that I agree with. One of the main problems is getting people to come to concerts. Many of my concert producers do other types of fundraising events, like dances, to raise money. They get a great turnout for things like that, but struggle to get folks out for concerts. Many of them lose money on concerts.

There are women now in "mainstream" music who probably are dykes but don't say so. They attract this huge crowd through their mainstream record companies that have access to mainstream media. I feel that can draw away from women's music because we don't have the resources they have. On the other hand, maybe if people get used to hearing and seeing those mainstream performers, they'll seek out other kinds of alternative type music, such as women's music, folk, or whatever.

What would need to happen in your case to make a more substantial living doing this?

I need to attract a larger audience. I don't think that I have fully explored all of my women's music or gay and lesbian avenues. I would also like to attract a folk audience. So far, it hasn't been real successful. I just started, though, and I know

that with this kind of think, you need to be pretty patient and just keep at it. That's how I approached women's music, too. Since I do out lesbian music, it might be harder to get into folk music circles. Straight people are afraid of the material, and they don't understand some of it. I do gay pride gigs and women's music gigs—those are real important to me, and I will continue to expand that way.

Given that you'd be comfortable with more straight people in your audiences, what are your thoughts on material that could be considered straight bashing? Your new shirts, for example...

...oh, the ones that say, "I'm sorry that you're straight. Where do I send the card?" Well, one of my jobs is to educate people to value lesbians and gays. One of the ways to do that is through satire. It's a real effective tool. Truly enlightened straight people would not see that as straight bashing—and I don't think they would get defensive about it, because it's presented in a humorous way. That's why I do so much comedy. I'm very comfortable using it because I grew up in a family where comedy was the basis for communication. That's not totally a positive thing, but I can certainly see the positive aspects of it. I don't usually like to go hear topical singers who just sing one hard-hitting song after another—it feels like I'm being hit over the head with a sledge hammer. Certainly those types of songs are very effective—I do a few of those myself—but issues presented humorously are easier to take. It's more accessible.

Like "Wedding Song."

I sing, "Sure, I'll come to your wedding/but I'll dance with the girls/I might even flirt with one or two/as we dance and twirl..." A wedding is a traditional heterosexual setting, and people don't tend to thing of gays and lesbians in those kinds of settings. After hearing "Wedding Song," maybe they will extend it and think about, well, what kind of marriages and unions do gays and lesbians have? In that song I talk about how lesbians in particular don't exactly get flowers at their door when they decided to have a committed relationship. Because I present it all in a humorous manner, it's a lot easier for people to think about what that really means.

I went to a wedding a couple of months ago and I did actually dance with the bride to "Wedding Song." It was a very empowering thing—and it was the bride's idea! Most of the people there seemed very embarrassed about it, and they ignored us. There was a whole table of lesbians, and hardly anyone even talked to us. We found out later that there were far more queers there than we had known about, but they didn't approach us. The people

who videotaped the reception taped the dancers on the dance floor except for the women dancing with each other—even when we tried to dance in front of their cameras.

Did they get you dancing with the bride on video?

No, they had left by then.

HOT WIRE readers keep voting "Wedding Song" a favorite song in the readers' choice survey. Oppressors systematically rely on the oppressed to police themselves, to acquiesce to silence. At a wedding, we're on our honor to not embarrass anyone. So the idea of threatening to upset the balance is quite a radical one. Hearing it presented with humor allows us to laugh off the scariness of it while we're internalizing the message.

Right, right. And I refuse to be a "good queer" anymore. A wedding is one of those sacred heterosexual places where you can't rock the boat in any way, shape, or form, because it's "their day."

Like every other day isn't. What are some other songs where you use humor effectively?

Satire is my favorite vehicle, so another satirical song is "I'm Sorry." I jokingly call it my "song of condolence for heterosexuals." In it, I include all of the things that gays and lesbians hear, like "I'm really sorry you're that way." "Gee, what can I do for you?" "You just need counseling." "See your minister." "You just need a good man." I decide to turn that around and present it as satire with a straight face. My queer audiences love that song, because they've been told those things, and now they have a chance to laugh about it.

What about non-lesbian feminist women who come to festivals? They could take the seemingly anti-straight messages personally, and maybe feel excluded or even hurt.

Well, you always take that risk with satire. There's always going to be somebody who doesn't get it. I hope later she *will* get it. Recently, I lost a job with a folklore society because they thought that I really believed that everyone should be gay! They were quoting the lines to "I'm Sorry" to justify that.

I ended up doing a concert with someone else in that town, and one of the folklore people came. She came up to me afterwards and introduced herself as "the folklore bigot," and apologized. Another straight person—a folk performer—had explained to her what "I'm Sorry" really meant.

Another time, I met a woman at a festival who came up to me and said that she'd heard me three years ago in Phoenix. She was trying to stay in the closet then, and she said I disgusted her. I said, "Gee, excuse me."

What a tribute to your work.

Yeah. She said, "You disgusted me because I just thought it was so outrageous that there was all this whooping and hollering—a good time had by all these out lesbians." I said, "Yeah, but you came to the concert!"

Not to mention coming to the festival.

Right! It seems a friend had talked her into going. She was leaving the next day for another state, so I guess she figured it was sort of the safe thing to do. "But," she said, "things changed, and I became more comfortable with myself. So now here I am at the festival, and I've decided to become a lesbian. I have your first tape. I bought two of them at that first concert." That's the thing about humor—it makes people feel more comfortable. They don't feel like I'm going to bite their head off it they come up and talk to me. I'm willing to be an educator for the straight community. Many lesbians and gays aren't interested in that. It's a lot of work, and we get tired of answering the same questions over and over again.

Such as...?

"What do you do in bed?" "Why are you so outrageous?" "Why do you have to throw it in our faces?" Then of course I have to explain that all we're doing is living our lives. We're not being any more outrageous than heterosexuals are. I get comments about how I'm too bitter, too angry. That's because it's coming from people who don't know what being queer is like, and so I have to explain. But I'm willing, and I do a lot of it through my music.

How would life be different for you and for lesbians in general if the women's music and culture subculture did not exist today?

No festivals or lesbian literature? I shudder at the thought. Those things have strengthened who I am. The validation they offer has had an enormous impact on my life. Women's music has been such an inspiring vehicle for change. If women's music and culture didn't exist, I would probably still be a bar dyke who didn't like herself very much; I would've have much of a feminist consciousness. Or maybe I would eventually identify as a feminist and be proud of being a lesbian, but it wouldn't taken a lot longer.

Maybe lesbians wouldn't have women like those dykey women we now have in mainstream music. Also, without the culture that we have now, we wouldn't have documented history. We'd still be invisible. What do we know about lesbians in other times and in some other parts of the world? Not much, because their culture, for the most part, has not been recorded.

Who are some of the other women's music performers from whom you get inspiration?

Of the women that I hear at festivals, I find Sue Fink very inspiring. She has such a positive message in most of her songs. I like how they feel, too—they're always very nice rhythmically. I love to dance, and I really connect with that. She's very funny—see, once again that's something that really attracts me. I also admire Deidre McCalla. I think she's a fine songwriter. I get the inspiration and validation and energy to carry on from a lot of different places—from festivals, and from other performers, because we know the performing end of things. We know how hard that aspect of it can be. And the performers who do really out music—we have an additional connection. I really appreciate women like Leah Zicari and Lynn Thomas.

Because...?

...because we do the same kinds of things—we get up on stage and say, "queer, queer, queer." We take the same kinds of risks. Not that the other performers don't also take risks, but it's a different kind of thing. Those of us who are actively out on stage take the same risks that anyone who comes out takes. We don't always "preach to the choir," either—our music gets some radio airplay, and sometimes we perform queer music in straight settings. It's always risky to come out in situations like that.

I get tremendous inspiration from the women at festivals, especially festivals like Gulf Coast where it's smaller and more intimate. We all eat together; you see all the performers out in the crafts area; women feel comfortable coming up and talking to you. It's a step beyond, "Sign my tape, I loved your performance." It's like, "I come from Pensacola, and this is what our women's community is like. What do you think about this, what do you think about that? I want to tell you more about myself." It's really gratifying to have women come up and tell me stories about listening to my music.

I get inspiration from the musicians I work with on my albums too. I wish that I could work with all lesbians, but that just hasn't been logistically or financially possible so far. The drummer I worked with on my first album told me that everything she knew about lesbians she learned from my album. It was a frightening thing, but it was positive.

When I hired the musicians for that first album, I was terrified because I thought, "Oh shit, I'm going to have to come out to all these strangers." The process of getting musicians for an album doesn't mean you just call up one keyboard player and that's it, you work with her. You call up all these strangers and say, "Hi, I'm Jamie Anderson and I'm putting out a lesbian album and I'm looking for musicians." I didn't want to hire anybody who thought I was great musically and then—after they got my charts and stuff—go, "I can't work with her." I didn't want to work with any assholes.

Out of all the musicians I've interviewed for both projects, only one has freaked out. All the rest of them have been great! For the most part they have a lot of questions. Like with my most recent album, on the song "I'm Sorry," the drummer was this eager-beaver kind of guy—he reminded me of a nine-year-old. After we finished rehearsing that song for the fourth or fifth time, he looked at me and said, "I know why you wrote that song. That's probably what straight people tell you all the time. Right?" Bingo! My musicians were sort of my test. They got it, so I figure a lot of other people will get it, too.

When I'm at home and booking a tour, or writing songs in my own space, I forget about that stuff. I think, "Oh, what are my little songs worth? What is my work worth?" But then I come to festivals like Gulf Coast, or I talk to that woman who came to my concert in Phoenix who said she was disgusted and then changed her mind...it means a whole lot. It's real important to me to know that someone out there is really listening to what I do. ■

Casselberry & Dupreé
by JEB

Sue Fink

by Vada Verneé

True Life Adventures in Women's Music
Sue Fink

Interviewed by Toni Armstrong Jr.

Sue Fink grew up in Beverly Hills practicing piano four hours daily. She graduated magna cum laude from UCLA's music department and went on to graduate school there. She has sung on TV, albums, and at Nixon's presidential inaugurataion. Her professional credits prior to becoming involved with women's music include a State Department-sponsored thirteen nation tour of Asia with the California Chamber Singers, and a singing tour of Europe, Israel, Canada, Hawaii, and the continental U.S. with the Roger Wagner Chorale. She has performed and/or emceed at all of the major women's festivals in the U.S., and at the 1986 International Women's Music Festival in Israel. She founded the L.A. Women's Community Chorus and was featured on CBS television's Two on the Town as the group's energetic conductor. The National Association of Independent Record Distributors honored her first solo album—the techno-pop Big Prom-

ise (Ladyslipper, 1985)—with an award of excellence. Her latest album, True Life Adventure, is on her own Frostfire label.

From HOT WIRE, May 1991.

How did you get started in women's music? How did you come to write "Leaping"?

My first women's music event was a talent show around 1975. It was at this flea-ridden place on the beach in Venice [near Los Angeles, California]. The floor was covered with little crawling sand animals. Evan Paxton was the producer; she was the first producer I knew of in women's music. I think I was staffing at N.O.W. and I heard about the event through a flyer or something. I remember Margie [Adam] performed, as well as Vicki Randle, and Marcie Dicterow. They all sang by themselves or with a guitar, and there was one little microphone. We were being bitten to death, but who cared! None of us had ever been in a room filled with just women before. Everybody

just cheered and yelled. There must have been, I don't know, sixty of us. During that year I went to a few other events that started happening, but they were always in like some tiny YWCA back room or something. Then Joelyn and I got this idea to put on something involving women in the community, so in 1976 we put on this show called Bicentennial Review. We wrote a whole show—it was almost a musical—and we involved about thirty women from the community. We wrote "Leaping (Lesbians)" around that time, for an early local talent show.

How did Meg Christian hear about the song?

She was sitting in the audience of the talent show, and the audience just went wild. I got some of the other women to be backup, and I called them the Dykettes. After the show, Meg asked us if she could play it in her performances.

Women thought it was one of the funniest songs Meg ever wrote.

Unfortunately, Meg neglected to say who wrote the song when she did it on stage, so people assumed she wrote it. It was just a lack of consciousness. It became a sort of controversy, but later on when I went on tour with her in 1984 she really apologized, and made up for it by asking me to perform it in her show.

And you did your early version on Olivia Records' *Lesbian Concentrate* album. When and how did you start the L.A. Women's Community Chorus?

I started the chorus in late '76. We had our first meeting in '77. I'd been doing choral music, and I was teaching music in a junior high school. Then I taught in Beverly Hills. But my life was starting to overlap already—it was getting dangerous to teach. Already I had a few events where former students had come up to me in concerts and recognized me. And after we got the chorus started, a woman who was a parent at the school at which I was teaching found out I was a lesbian and tried to get me fired. I quit teaching in 1978.

How did you get the idea for the chorus?

I was a choral conductor. That's what I did for my living. But I

was always into community involvement stuff; I wanted to get everybody "doing it." And I thought, wouldn't it be *great* to have a choir that sang this music? So I started looking for people to work with, because I didn't want to do all the organizing myself. I met a woman composer named Lynn Wilson and we gathered more people, until we had a collective of six. We met for about four months, organizing and making arrangements. We advertised, and seventy-five women showed up at the first rehearsal.

Where did you find music?

I remember we did women's music—Holly Near songs, Berkeley Women's Music Collective, etc. Lynn did a lot of the arrangements, and I did some. I became the conductor.

You were involved for ten years. Why did you retire?

It was getting to the point where I was missing half the rehearsals because I was on the road so much. It didn't feel fair to the chorus, and I just had to quit.

Your first tour was around 1979, right?

Right, and actually you had something to do with that.

I did?

Yeah, just the other day I was looking at the material in the book I'm writing about how all this got going. You wrote me a

letter when you were doing an article about women's choruses for *Paid My Dues* [early journal of women's music]. Later on, when you ran the article [Spring 1978 issue], I found out there was *another* chorus—Cathy Roma's [Anna Crusis Women's Choir] in Philadelphia. *Paid My Dues* was so great—it was the first way I knew anything else was really going on. Cathy and I had never heard of each other, and I had no idea there was another women's chorus, but we were even doing some of the same music.

You contacted her?

I did, and we've become fast friends, but if it weren't for *Paid My Dues* I would never have known about her. I loved that magazine; I used to read every word. Anyway, Cathy and I started corresponding. And then *you* said, "Why don't you apply for that National Women's Music Festival?" So I made some horrible little tape—I mean it was *sooo* bad. But somehow or other, we were invited to perform. It was the fifth year; Antonia Brico was there. That was the year we started touring.

You had horrible stage fright back then.

Horrible stage fright. It was a nightmare. I think it started in the eighth grade when I had to do a speech contest; also, my mother was very critical. Before I did that National Women's Music Festival I decided I would do one other little appearance, just to get over my stage fright and see how it felt. I played at a classical women's music concert. I played a recorder, and I remember being so nervous that my little fingers wouldn't stick on the holes. It was a trio, and the other two people could not believe I was not hitting one note; well, maybe an occasional off-key peep. The audience went wild anyway. The concert had been so boring, but they wanted to hear it again. I'm going, "Oh my God, I'm going through this whole nightmare again." Then I thought, "How am I ever going to get up on the stage in front of a huge festival audience?" Luckily, I met Cherry [Wolf] and Lynn [Keller], who became the drummer and bass player for that first tour.

They weren't from California—you met them where?

Kristin Lems introduced us at Champaign [Illinois, where the NWMF was held in the 1970s]. Kristin was so great. When women's music lost her, they lost someone really wonderful. Anyway, being in a band made it okay for me, and I lived through the experience. But I was very frightened on stage. It was horrible. It was one of the reasons I quit performing...

...After the tour in '79.

I remember December of '79 was my last concert. I went back to school and left women's music. But that isn't the only rea-son I left women's music. I had this fear of performing, but also I tried to get help with my ca-reer—tried to get names and addresses of places to play. I remember the one person who was a big help in those days was Margie Adam. Performers were very reluctant to share information. In fact, one of them invited me and a couple of other people over and tried to talk us out of doing women's music. She said the market was too small and competitive, and that I'd never make it, so if I wanted to do consciousness-raising, there were other ways. She suggested that since I directed the choir, I could do guerrilla theater—like have people in an elevator, and when the elevator opened we could sing them a consciousness-raising song, so that people in an office building would get their consciousness raised. This could be my alternative to performing.

You didn't take that advice?

I didn't. Determined, I plugged on. As I said, except for Margie —who sat down for three hours straight and just gave me addresses—I didn't get much help.

So you went to school where, to do what?

I went to the Grove Music Institute for two years to learn how to arrange, compose, and write film scores.

What made you branch out into synthesizer music?

I was possessed. I wanted an orchestra in my living room. I would have sold my soul for it, and I did. I borrowed all the money. And it was *so* expensive— you can buy this stuff so cheap now. I bought a synthesizer and a drum machine, and it cost $6,000. I just sold that equipment two months ago for $150.

Why did you come back to women's music, and when?

Well, I think getting over the fear was the first start. A woman in the chorus stood up and said, "I'll exchange hypnosis for whatever you want." So I told her she needed voice lessons and I wanted to get over my fear of performance. She hypnotized me, and it wasn't so much that she said, "You can perform," but she made me feel that it was okay to be imperfect and to make mistakes; that I could have fun getting on a stage. Then I started trying it and I decided to start a little band. Diane Lindsay and I played keyboards, Carrie Barton played bass, and Marilyn Donadt played drums. But we hardly ever got together because our schedules were so weird. Everybody was doing other things. It didn't last long.

But it was a stepping stone to getting back in?

Well, it got me started. So then Diane was going to go on tour as a bass player with Meg, and Meg was looking for a keyboardist…

…in '84? Meg's last tour?

Yes. So Meg called me and asked if I wanted to play keyboards, and she came down to L.A. and we rehearsed at my house. She gave me a feature spot on her tour. She had big audiences, and this exposure woke up producers to me. When the tour was over, Diane asked if I wanted to be her accompanist on her own solo tour the following year. I said, "I don't know if I want to be an accompanist, but I'd like to do a show with you. We could share evenings." She said, "But you don't have a product." I told her I'd *get* a product. So I made up a little flyer which I passed out to audiences, and people sent me the money I needed in the mail.

To Do *Big Promise*?

Right. Women sent me $20,000 in the mail. *Big Promise* was released in '85 on Ladyslipper.

So you went on tour with Diane, doing a double bill…

…and at the end I decided I wanted to go out on my own. To make up for that terrible fear, I went the other way and became somewhat grandiose. As Deidre [McCalla] always said, "I think you should call your next album *Larger Than Life*." Over time, I essentially mellowed out, but I did feel driven. I had a

purpose for doing it, that I had to be some sort of role model for all our fears. Getting over that fear was so important to me. I realized as I went around the country on Meg's tour, and even as I started my own, women were so depressed. As a group. Between the oppression of the community, and having no money themselves, and having little validation from each other, and alcoholism and drugs being so high at that time, it was very depressing—I felt the need to be some kind of really positive voice. Someone who wasn't promoting or coming from a drug place. Someone who was saying that it's perfectly okay to be you. And that's why I started the "Certified Outrageous" campaign.

Was your "outrageous" image a deliberate marketing thing?

Yeah, but I wanted a way to market this *idea*, that people would have to do positive affirmations at concerts, meaning that I would take them through this whole hypnosis thing like I went through. But it wasn't real hypnosis, of course, it was a joke. Then I would "certify" them "outrageous"—that it was okay for them to have the lover of their dreams, to leave the one they always hated, to go for the joy they always wanted. I'd get them all contorted, putting one finger on their forehead, putting their arm wherever, on the person next to them. And then they'd say, "I'm

wonderful," and it was just great. It was a very funny bit, and it also made people feel good about themselves.

Were there people who ended up feeling that you were just really egotistical?

I think so. I think it was alienating for many people. It was one of those things that people either really loved or really hated. Most got it that I wasn't really egotistical, that I was trying to generate the idea that I'm okay just as I am and so are you. I was just being outrageous about it, because I was so glad to have gotten over the fear myself; and it wasn't just a fear of performance, it was a fear of doing my life. We all had this fear to different degrees in different areas. In some ways, being "outrageous" meant I was not being vulnerable enough, so something was missing from my performance. I finally came to terms with this at a concert that went *very* badly one night. It was at WiminFest in '89. And it was the worst night of my life. It was the debut of my then new album [*True Life Adventure*]. I'd been through a lot of personal changes; it had been a very hard time for me. I'd broken up from an eight-year relationship, and was feeling disillusioned in many ways about what I was doing with my life. I was not feeling great, and certainly not in the mood to go out there and be certified outrageous. I had been to Albuquerque about two years before and done that kind of show, and the audience just ate it up. This time I thought I would bring the band and debut this album—but I hadn't come to terms with my own changes. And it showed in my performance. It was a *horrible* performance. The sound was bad. I had a substitute person in the band. I wasn't centered enough.

And the crowd didn't go wild?

Oh no, not at all—for good reasons. It was the first night I'd had that kind of reaction. I'd also taken those six months off before that to do the album, and it was my first night out. I felt very uncentered and uncertain. I had put my whole heart into this new album. It was a completely different musical field—not the techno-pop. The subtitle of *True Life Adventure* was *Risk and Reality*, and that's what it was, with me facing a deeper reality.

And they simply didn't want that? They wanted you to jump around and...

...right, they wanted me to be that *other* person. But there was part of me that still didn't know how to be on stage and be that vulnerable person about who I was writing and being in the album. I hadn't brought it to my live performance yet. So it was incongruous. I went home after that and I wrote about it, thought about it, asked people about it. I had three or four performances within a couple of weeks. Each one got better, but

they didn't feel right to me. I took two months off and just got myself together, and I've come out on the other side, where I can come back and still be funny and be positive, and still realize that there are serious personal issues with which we have to deal. I think I've ended up being a much more real, vulnerable live performer.

I thought your show was great at the East Coast Lesbians' Festival last year—the right balance between having a lot of fun and having something to think about.

Hopefully I've got that balance now. I feel a lot better about my performance. It's like I grew up in women's music. A lot of performers don't change, they don't grow. Some audiences are satisfied with that; some are bored by it. In ways, I feel lucky that I've been able to really change.

Adrienne Torf talks about feeling frustrated that women in women's music don't get pushed to take lessons, to develop their music, to develop their writing. They just get up there, and somehow that's enough; the audiences are willing to accept whatever; she feels like there's not nearly enough challenge to excel.

I think Adrienne Torf is a genius. Her performance at the Southern Festival last year just

blew me away. And it was so refreshing to see an audience *appreciate* her. In many ways I'm disappointed that we don't have a more educated audience to tell the difference between something which is really musically and lyrically art versus something that is just fun entertainment, or...I just feel if you're going to do something, do it with art. And there's so much that *isn't*.

Most of your income these days doesn't come from women's music, which puts you in a position to be somewhat selective about where you will and won't play, right?

Yes. I teach voice, but I couldn't live by teaching alone—my heart is in performing. And I love performing for the women's audience, though I wouldn't turn away the mainstream. But teaching has been very, very good to me. There aren't many jobs where you can sit in your living room and make as much money as I do. Now I'm teaching all these performance-on-stage workshops as well. I do that four days a week and I tour three days a week. I go where I can fly, mostly on weekends. Occasionally I can stay out longer, but I really don't make money on the road—if I'm lucky, I break even, between flying and costs and phone and mail.

Sue Fink & Friends
by Toni Armstrong Jr.

Where do you like to go?
I love to go to the South. That's where it's new and fresh—it's like when we were first starting [in the 1970s]. It's that old feeling of community, of feeling so special, of women being together and discovering each other. There's something fresh and alive about it—untainted. You feel like you're a part of something that's growing instead of something that's struggling and fighting. It feels like the '70s, in the best of all senses. I wish that the rest of the

country could learn something from the women of the South. If we can do it differently this time...

"Do it differently," meaning...?
We blew women's music. We blew it in competition and in not being cooperative. We as a community—everybody involved in it. We went about it with a scarcity mentality, that we couldn't share information, that we weren't willing to work together cooperatively. For example, if a record company

wants to sell their products and have Tupperware kinds of parties, why not include everybody's music? It gives people more choices. Which brings me to my definition of women's music: I don't think we have "women's music"—I think we have a women's music audience. We have a group of people who want to hear music by and about women. Usually in the rest of the world you have people who like folk music, or reggae, or hip hop; in women's music we have basically an audience of women, each one wanting to be at an event where women somehow are performing and speaking to *her*, and she gets to be in her community and have a night out in the company of other women, without necessarily going to a bar.

The women's music audience has continued to grow out of that need over the years.

Yes, and it's still growing. The festivals have certainly gotten bigger, with more people going. But the performers you see at festivals are not necessarily the people you see on the road. Linda Tillery, for example, who is a fabulous performer, doesn't tour much without a band, and producers can't afford to bring that many people. Also, when you go into a community—even when a producer tries to bring in some new performer—if the community hasn't heard of the artist, people don't come, except for that core women's music audience. But the producers do try; I find that many of the inexperienced producers, although they make a lot of mistakes, are our greatest asset as a movement.

Without inexperienced butwilling producers we would never have developed an international women's music network or industry.

These production companies that do it but aren't making a

monetary profit can get burned out. And that's what we keep forgetting. Most of the women who are producing are doing it out of their *hearts*, to bring our culture to their community. Some performers don't have the good sense to appreciate that, and to be *at least* courteous.

What's it like being an independent within an alternative, independent music business?

It's meant that I've had to build it from the bottom up myself, mostly without the help of double bills or being allowed to be the opening act for more well-known performers. I see this same thing happening to a lot of new performers. If I go to a city for the first time, it's really different than if, say Lucie Blue [Tremblay] went there for the first time. Lucie could maybe open for another Olivia act the first time she goes somewhere. In the years I've been touring, I think I've done three double bills and one opening act. My dream, of course, is to do this all very differently—if we could get rid of this *scarcity mentality*. I believe that it's in the record companies' interest to help people who aren't on their label, because it helps build the audience for everyone. That way people don't get sick of the same performers. When women don't have much money anyway, it's difficult to risk on someone new. But a scarcity of money doesn't mean

we have to always act like there's a scarcity.

What do you mean? How would it be if people weren't acting like that?

Competition breeds scarcity; cooperation breeds abundance. A record company would bring in their headliner artists to do a show, and would say, "Hey, it would be nice for the world to hear someone like Jamie Anderson, so let's have her open." So Jamie gets to sing for 300–350 people that night, or maybe up to 900 people, instead of the thirty she might get if she went into that town for the first time by herself. And that many people have now gotten to see another artist. The next time, they might bring someone else who wasn't planning to go because she doesn't want to hear the same old artist—but her friends say, "But this *new* person is really fresh, you should come just to hear *her*."

Right, and Meg letting you do your song on her tour made a lot of difference for your career. Maxine Feldman and Ginni Clemmens used to do that all the time. Maxine Howard let the then-unknown Tracy Chapman sing a song ["Stormy Monday"] on her set at Michigan; if Tracy hadn't gone on to mainstream success, she'd

have to be competing with everyone else in women's music for our few festival gigs—so it was nice of Maxine to give her some exposure. The idea of an established act giving some stage time to somebody new—it can make a difference.

It *does*. In addition to sharing actual stage time, I think we should establish a computer databank where everybody pools their information, and there's a phone number you call and say, "I want to do a concert in Baltimore. I want to know about clubs, colleges, and other venues, and who's producing there; papers in which I can run an ad or announcement; who I can hire for eight dollars an hour to flyer the town if I end up in a club." Another idea: how about a regional flyer, like "In the South This Month," or "In Florida This Month." Each producer could put whoever they want on it. It's not going to detract from anybody if we have something that everybody can be on. It wouldn't hurt anybody, and it might help us get our calendars a little more together. I really think we should have a national calendar.

Coordinated by...?

Maybe AWMAC [the Association of Women's Music and Culture] could hire one person to coordinate it. She'd get paid a reasonable salary and everybody would chip in for that. Everything would be on computer, and there would be two ways you can use it. Anybody could call in and see what's on the national calendar or get leads. We can make it a 900 number—two dollars for the first three minutes! When you think of the mailing list that someone like Olivia Records has, if that were available for a national calendar, with a regional flyer, or those kinds of things...if the producers of Austin, Houston, San Antonio, and Dallas set up a circuit, it would make planning the travel for performers easier and cheaper. The problem with setting up this kind of circuit is, how do we choose who gets to go on it? Many would be left out, and possibly it would end up that only a handful of well-known performers would be able to play those cities on the circuit. I've always liked the idea of having a traveling festival, though. Get a bunch of independent performers together, and have a movable fest, where everything moves—the crafts, the art, the music, and we do tent shows in different cities and in different halls. And you could include a lot of performers.

Who could afford to produce something like that, if they can't even afford to bring bands to their towns?

It would be something that each city would be responsible for when it got to their town. And it would be an exposure tour versus a big money-maker, but that's what festivals are. Nobody gets paid much. I'd also like to see us clean up our ethics.

Meaning?

I think some of the job of an organization like AWMAC could be to provide mediators for problems. Someplace where we can take grievances, where we act with consciousness with each other. Sometimes the festival producers fight and compete with each other; sometimes people don't get paid royalties or other promised monies; sometimes producers want to have someone get to be the opening act but a label turns it down.

I agree that the producers know their towns, and they know what they want to present. At the same time, how would you feel, as an artist, if you didn't have control over the opening act, and it was somebody you really didn't want as part of your show?

You know, I don't think I've ever run into that.

You haven't run into anyone you wouldn't want as part of your show?

I've had a million people that I don't think are very good opening for me, but I think opening acts are still a good idea. I know it helps bring in audience. I think it's good for the community, especially when it's somebody from the local community who performs.

Other ideas for strengthening up cooperation?

I think a lot of it is just in attitude. It's the feeling that it's not going to hurt anyone if I *share* this information. It's only going to make me stronger by making you stronger. It's a spirit of giving. Jamie Anderson has printed up for sale her list of radio and print contacts. We should all do that.

Throughout the years, many of the problems have stayed the same: Women not having enough money, the scarcity mentality, personality conflicts in a very small community, lovers breaking up—plus just getting ground down all the time from living in this world. Why do you think women's music didn't just stop somewhere along the line?

Because we still need our community. Women's music came out of the feminist movement, and the feminist movement died in some ways...

The media certainly has tried to make us believe that.

You're right—I think we're still going, but it certainly doesn't get the media attention. The word "feminism"...if you say

you're a feminist out there, it's somehow like saying you have poison ivy—even though the ideas are still there, and people like Sinead O'Connor would never have a chance without what we've done. Women's music has continued in spite of the fact that the egg it came out of has somehow rotted.

And why is that?

I think it's because the thing we most forget is that we *want* that community. The music brings us together. We need that place where women get together and hear about our lives, because we don't hear it on TV or radio. Now I think we're more linked to the gay movement. In music, women are in the mainstream; this is the year of the singer/songwriter: Sinead O'Connor, Tracy Chapman, Melissa Etheridge, Michelle Shocked, people who come from many of the beliefs we have, but are out there in the mainstream. And that's who the young women are all going to go hear. But they don't get to feel the community we experience at women's concerts and festivals. And what they're *not* hearing is anything about being lesbians.

Or hearing the performers say too much about women. They talk about "people" and "people's rights"—very pronoun unspecific.

Right. There's still that hole that's not being filled. More than that, it's simply not *our*

community. It's still a world where we're ignored and not respected enough. There's still a need for our community, and I think those young women still need it too, but we don't reach them. And while women's music keeps going, we're getting older, and our audience is an over-thirty audience. I'm thinking, how do we meet these younger women? I'm dreaming of ways to get them. One way is to go into the bars and get them. Perform there. I've had this little fantasy of doing a "We Are The World"-type record, but for women's music. We get all the performers together and do a video and song, and it plays in all the bars—make it kind of hip, make it kind of wow, but make it have some meaning—something that points to who we are in the community and what our music is...Don't you think that would be a great idea?

Yeah, I do. So what are the odds of it ever coming to be?

Well, I don't know. It would take a lot of energy on somebody's part. But I think it could be done. It could be an AWMAC project. I think we also need to go into the universities and colleges. We've got a great resource: all of us who grew up and became women's studies teachers in these colleges. Work with these women, and get them to bring in artists to perform. Take that risk. You know they're so afraid to say *they're* lesbians, but at least they can bring in these artists to perform, and expose these college women to what we're doing. I think coalition work has been good, but one of the things we could try to do is some more roots work *within* our community. We've done so much coalition work across issues, which has in some ways dissipated who *we* are. I think it is very important, very valid work, but I also think sometimes we need to reach in and grab our own community.

I've seen over and over again that "coalition work" means lesbians, and feminist women and feminist men, end up working for another cause. It's not a coalition where feminism or gay rights is represented in any way. It's really not a coalition; it's us helping them, without us really making them stop being sexist or homophobic. Without insisting on our issues and identity being a strong presence.

That's absolutely true. It brings up the issue of one of the other things that has kept women's music from growing, which is our own homophobia. Personally, I've gone through all the changes about it. When I first came out I was fine about it. Then I went through my own homophobic period where I thought, "Well, I'll never make it in the mainstream if I don't, you know, somehow cool it in some areas," and then realizing

that I didn't want to do that anymore. Coming full circle around it. I think someone like Heather Bishop is such a good example of how it's perfectly okay: she does children's shows and she does women's/lesbian shows. And she never compromises who she is. If we all were a little bit more like that…you know I noticed *HOT WIRE* printed an article on Michelle Shocked, who's obviously come out. Well! That's not hurting her career!

And Martina…

…and Martina [Navratilova]. I think that we're at a time now where it's not so scary any more in that way. Maybe I'm wrong. I think there is a lot of homophobia in the straight world. But I think the less afraid we are of being ourselves, the more likely we are to be successful. Again, it's getting past our own fears. And it's something I still struggle with, all the time.

How do you personally struggle with it?

Coming out is a continual process. I'm here working with these bands, these studios in Los Angeles. This week I'm producing some demos for CBS, with young male heavy metal bands. (I can't get over the incongruity.) And you know, how open am I? It's always a struggle for me.

Will all of this be in the book you're writing?

Well, while my music has gotten more and more serious, I still have this part of me that likes to have a very good time. Life can be very funny, I think, and so this book is just stories from the road—what's happened to me in women's music, before, after, and during. Holly [Near] has done her autobiography, but my book is a collection of short stories. They're all true, but it's very entertaining reading because it's not like, "Then I met this person, then I met that person'…it's more the story approach of "What is it really like to be in this situation? What is the humor and fun about it? What is it really like?" It's just a very funny book. It's called *There is No Karma*. And I'm having the best time writing it. I intend to sell it to a publisher this year and get it out. If not, it's a hell of a journal!

What are your other plans?

I have a new approach to life, where I let it flow instead of planning it so much. It's like all those years of therapy have finally made me a little less goal-oriented. I dream about doing a new album, but I doubt if I'll produce it myself. Either somebody else is going to do it or it isn't going to happen, because I'm not that business oriented. It's going to be a much more acoustic album, with a percussion feel versus drum feel, and although there'll be some synthesizer stuff in it, it'll be more natural sounds. This album is going to be story songs that deal with very personal characters, mostly me. Stories that reflect a larger idea—songs where I just tell the story but leave the larger questions that are raised from specific incidents. I may call it *Confession*. So I'm thinking a lot about doing this album and then tying it all together, in more of a performance piece—versus just getting up there, here's this song, here's that song—tying it together in terms of a one-woman theater kind of a thing. You know, sometimes I feel really bad I'm not famous like Bette Midler. But then one night I was sitting at the Pagoda—it's like this women's separate little community [in Florida], they live there and it just seems so exciting. It was in the morning, and this woman walked in, perfectly naked—she was just walking through, relaxing. I hadn't seen her in years, and asked her what she was doing these days. She said, "Oh, I'm building this ark, and I'm going to sail it down the Amazon. I got a grant to do it." I'm thinking, "Wow, this is really weird. This woman is really weird." And then, "Oh my God, am *I* any less weird? I go from city to city singing for lesbians, about our lives," you know? So, Madonna might be more famous, she's pretty outrageous—and Bette Midler, they have all this...but I don't think they have any more adventures than I've had. That's kind of what the book is about. What is success? It's doing what you really really love and not being afraid of it. ∎

The Waiting for the Festival Lesbian Jam

lyrics by Karen Escovitz and Elliott

(peppy banjo tune)

4 big dykes in a tiny little car,
with 3 conga drums and 2 guitars,
tent's on top 'cause there wasn't no room,
sticker on the back says, "my other car's a broom."

Pulled to a stop just across the state line,
met a truckload of dykes who were looking fine,
with a slide trombone in a lavender case,
an accordion, a fiddle, and an old string bass.

Soon we were a caravan rolling down the road,
us and the truck and a whole busload
from the airport, and the sticker on the very last car
said, "come out, come out wherever you are!"

When we got to Hart we were running kinda late,
but we finally found our way to the gate.
Doesn't open 'til 2, the line's 3 miles long…
Well that's when we wrote the first line of this song.

Wimmin started bringing out instruments and food.
We were laughing and singing and getting in the mood.
Some dykes from New York brought bagels and borscht,
and another pulled a pot roast out of her Porsche.

Well, we started to rock, we started to rap.
It was a little bit klezmer, a little bit crap,
a little bit folk and a little bit funk,
a little bit polka and a little bit punk.

Wimmin started to dance, breasts flying in the breeze.
We were drumming in the dirt and climbing in the trees.
It was a multi-cultural traveling band...
the Waiting for the Festival Lesbian Jam!

Music by Karen Escovitz (a.k.a. "Otter")
© 1992

Michigan

by Therese Edell with Teresa Boykin, 1984

My old sports car brought me to the place. In 1976 at the beginning of summer I was at the Second National Women's Music Festival when a tanned, gravel-voiced woman handed me a tacky-looking flyer about another festival—this one in August, in Michigan. It was a camping arrangement and seemed far away from my home. I had driven to the Champaign festival because a friend was performing there and had urged me to come. In 1976 another festival seemed excessive.

The stories I heard about it later from an exhausted, sun-burned, but exhilarated camper convinced me of two things: First, that Michigan had been wonderful music; bodies in cruel extremes, naked in blistering heat and shivering in damp, frigid cold; the triumph over fear from confronting unbonded males. And second, that I was

In: *Lesbian Land*, ed. Joyce Cheney. Minneapolis: Word Weavers, 1985.

glad I hadn't gone.

During the following months, I sent out two copies of my demo tape, one to each festival. The collective in Champaign politely declined, thank you, but Lisa Vogel from Michigan found me at the Third National Festival, said they'd loved the tape, invited me to perform that August (1977), and offered me money for my performance and travel. I was thrilled. The exchange was the first validation of me as a performer of women's music.

Much changed between 1977 and 1983. My first performance lasted intermittently for three hours while technicians worked to get the public address system to function. Musicians joined me onstage who that summer had worked on our album, *From Women's Faces*. In 1978 I dropped the corner of my jeans to show off a new tattoo, and in 1979 I had the honor of emceeing the Night Stage concerts for the first time. In 1977 my lover and I had the luxury of

anonymity, but by 1978 I was self-conscious getting clean in the cold-water showers. With other rain-soaked women, we held tent poles in the near tornado of 1977 to keep the Merchant's Tent from blowing away. By 1983 we were solid Festival veterans, having worked backstage as well as onstage on the production itself: in sound, stage managing, and performance on both the Night and Day stages. We ran sound for Edwina Lee Tyler on the Day Stage the year she electrified everyone by coming into the crowd to play her drum in the faces and hearts of women in wheelchairs. Each year the Festival population grew, the lighting and sound crews added more sophisticated equipment, and the Land took the increasing abuse as graciously as possible.

As ownership of the land became a more central issue, the festival organizers searched for a site they could purchase. The first year on the New Land was 1982. Many of us hated it. Too big and totally unfamiliar. New relative locations of the service tents, food areas, stages, and camping areas. Even while we were struggling, though, we saw the potential for growth and permanence. Something that in spirit belonged to all of Us rather than all of Them. We explored and discovered this New Land, at once finding it promising and overwhelming.

Most of us come for the music, but really, that's a good excuse for developing and extending our lesbian subculture. The creation and doing of the festival itself have been a major step in that direction.

Planning, preparation, celebration, cleanup, and land restoration take about eight months. The festival that most women see takes up only four days of that time, following six intensive months that transform over 600 acres of fairly wild Michigan land into an entertaining, untamed garden for city girls. In comparison to most workers, my time investment is quite small—two, three, or four days on either end. But being just that much involved in the Before and After shows me how temporal is the gift of the Festival, as well as its Brigadoon-like nature: a thriving city solidified from sweat and the Michigan fog; compressed experience; disappearance into memory. Unlike Brigadoon, where everything is clean, the weather is perfect, and everyone is rich, white, heterosexual, able-bodied, and politically homogenous (i.e., unaware), Michigan brings together a largely lesbian sample of *everybody*.

Over the years the organizers have dealt with major issues in an open and responsible way while presenting to the rest of us a festival that they themselves can love. No dogs on the Land, the continuing issues of accessibility and care for the emotionally distressed, women harassed at the Canadian border for looking like dykes, childcare for girl children, and a separate camp for boy children apart from their mothers, whether to spray the roads with brine to hold down the dust, educating women to wear boots without vibram soles and walk on the footpaths to preserve the environment, making part of the concert seating free from tobacco and marijuana smoke, alcohol, mind-altering drugs, or combinations of those substances—all of these are issues that feminists respect and that organizers have had to deal with, and much more.

And all of this explosive confrontation is carried on in the grass on a hillside or under a tent, at the whim of lakefront weather effects that can be bright sunshine one moment and thunderclouds the next.

Of course, there have been improvements, like more portable toilets, more water faucets and showers (still cold), greater ease of the food operations, and conquering the sheer logistical difficulties of transporting huge numbers of people, plus supplies and equipment, onto the Land in one piece and on time.

It is inevitable and some-times, for some, devastating: the Festival always ends. The Land gets to rest and recuperate from the shock of thousands of women and tons of equipment, and the coordinators take off for real jobs, kinder climates, lovers, tea, or therapy. Some women live near the Land, but no one yet lives on it. Some women—like those Aradians in Grand Rapids—go back to visit there and spread scratchy mulch on the Bowls, the places where women watch the concerts. As soon as all the women leave, scattered men and boys drive Jeeps and hot cars onto the site of so much interest and instant prosperity for their economically struggling towns. (They must feel the energy there; they do have some consciousness.) They scavenge what they can, but by this time that's really not much: women save what we can use again and again.

Will there always be the Festival? Having land owned by women (and the bank) increases that possibility for sure. The Japanese have a festival they've celebrated every year for a thousand years. Michigan may not be another Gion Matsuri, but women will celebrate our lives in some form or another, underground or in the light, forever. If it isn't Michigan, we'll create whatever else we need, as some of us created the Festival. My commitment to the Land, as an absentee tenant knowing a second home, is a commitment to the women who work there, to the music that's played there, and to the spirit that is in all of Us. ■

Sumita's Story, A Child's View of Michigan

by Therese Edell

For some reason, Sumita wasn't into asking a thousand questions. She seemed content just to walk with her friend, who chatted on about what they were passing: the food areas, where womyn were slicing thousands of carrots and breaking huge pyramids of lettuce for salad; the tent known as the Womb, where you went if you didn't feel good; the endless groups of womyn they passed on the road. These womyn didn't look like most womyn she'd ever seen. They had decorations on themselves: feathers, body paint, colorful headbands, small knitted bags on strings around their necks. All sorts of leather cords or pouches, backpacks or shoulder sacks. Some of them carried purses, which looked a little out of place on the arm of a half-dressed woman.

⚢

Excerpts from the story. Also from Therese Edell's contribution to *Lesbian Land*, ed. Joyce Cheney. Minneapolis: Word Weavers, 1985.

Teresa guided Sumita backstage and up four wooden stairs. They were under the huge tent that protected the entire stage and fifteen feet of the ground around the stage on every side. From hearing her friends talk, Sumita knew that womyn had built this stage, as well as every other structure on the Land. Womyn thought up the idea of the festival, planned it, and figured out how to make it happen. Then they did all the coordinating, building, and technical work associated with a festival of this size.

Each year the carpenter built the stage from lumber stored over the winter. The electricians ran the cables from the main power source off the Land. The sound technicians set up all the big speakers, amps, and microphones, and the lighting crew brought instruments that created beautiful rose or blue or white pools of color around the singers and musicians onstage.

⚢

Sumita liked seeing womyn get happy about their fingers on the strings of the bass guitar and harp, and other womyn get happy as they breathed together playing their horns.

⚢

Unlike other days, Susan drove in through the main entrance. Instead of the bustle of a small city of people coming and going, being directed to park or get wrist tickets, it was very quiet. The womon at the main gate where Sumita had driven in with Jane and Rebecca seemed glad to see them. It must be a lonely job now that most womyn had gone home. Susan told her she worked at Orientation, and the womon let them pass.

Sumita could see the meadows where hundreds of cars had been parked, the swampy part of the Land that was an animal preserve, and the place where the garbage truck lived. It was painted in many bright colors, not like garbage trucks at home. ■

Michigan Womyn's Music Festival
by Rene Gaumond. Courtesy of Lisa Vogel

Michiguilt

by Jorjet Harper

Goddess help me, but I'm not going to Michigan!

I've already been to one lesbian festival this summer and I'm going to another one Labor Day Weekend. Isn't that enough?

No!

Michigan is the Big Mama of festivals—the largest, most tradition-packed, the most mystique-filled.

Also the most uncomfortable, injury and disease-prone, overwhelming, crowded...

But I *have* to go to Michigan!

But I *hate camping*.

Each year I go through this indecision, this Michig-angst, until my ambivalence reaches a fever pitch by the weekend before the festival.

I didn't go last year because I was sick: I got a migraine from trying to decide whether to go or not. The year before, my ride fell through—lucky for me, since that was the year so many women there got violently ill from shigella. But if I don't go this year, it will be the third year in a row that I haven't gone!

"I understand. It's okay," a friend consoles me. "I went through a period when I took a few years off, too."

Note the phrase: "Took a few years off." As if it were a necessary chore—or the sacred duty of every good lesbian.

"Lesbomania" column in *Nightlines* (August 15, 1990).

Some women save their money for years and travel halfway around the world to come to the Michigan Festival. And I, who live in Chicago, a mere five hours away, am not going?

How can I be such an ingrate?

My Right Brain argues with my Left Brain: "Think of what she'll miss if she doesn't go! Days of productive networking, communing with nature, seeing all those wonderful women performers..."

My Left Brain argues back: "What about that year it constantly rained, her tent flooded, and she slept in a pool of muddy water for four days? She's nuts to go to Michigan unless she's in a Winnebago with full rations of food and water. Think of it: all those days in the woods, exposed to the elements. Eating nothing but fried tofu in yogurt sauce."

"So what's a little discomfort when it comes to experiencing lesbian culture?" says my Right Brain. "Isn't lesbian culture worth a few bug bites?"

Michiguilt! Okay, I'll go, I'll go.

"Sure," says my Left Brain. "And she can be a part of all that marvelous political *processing*."

That's it. I'm not going.

Right Brain: "But it's Lesbian Nation! Beautiful Michigoddesses..."

Left Brain: "Mishuggenahs! Dust, heat, thunderstorms..."

Right Brain: "Seven thousand women! Many of them stark na..."

I'm going.

Last week, in the midst of this Michigaas, I ran into a very well-known Chicago lesbian activist, who asked me if I was going to the festival.

"I don't know," I groaned.

"I'm going," she said. "Finally." She leaned toward me, lowered her voice and said, "I've never been before. Shhh-h-h, don't tell anyone."

How many lesbians are walking around Chicago hiding this secret shame?

On the other hand, an editor at a New York gay and lesbian magazine who has no shame whatsoever calls me up to see if I'll cover the festival for her paper. "What I want is a kind of anthropological approach," she says. This editor has never been to the festival, has no interest in going, and may not have a clear idea of where the state of Michigan, never mind the festival, is located.

"I want something like 'National Geographic goes to Amazon Woodstock,'" she tells me. "You can put in stuff about the history of the festival, too—oh, and don't forget to mention that year when everybody got trenchmouth."

"Shigella," I said weakly.

"Yeah, right. Whatever."

No. I'm not doing it. *I'm not even going.* Can't I just stay home and relax? Maybe go to the Ferron concert or the Joan Armatrading concert, spend a day in bed with my girlfriend, take warm showers, read a Naiad novel...

But how can I resist Michigan's magical pull? The magic of all those lesbians gathered in one place? It's so tempting...

I keep reminding myself: I hate camping. I hate camping. *Oh how* I *hate camping.*

Goddess help me! I'm not going to Michigan! Unless I change my mind tomorrow. ■

**Amie Laird & J. Finch, tending cooking fires
at Michigan Womyn's Music Festival**
by JEB

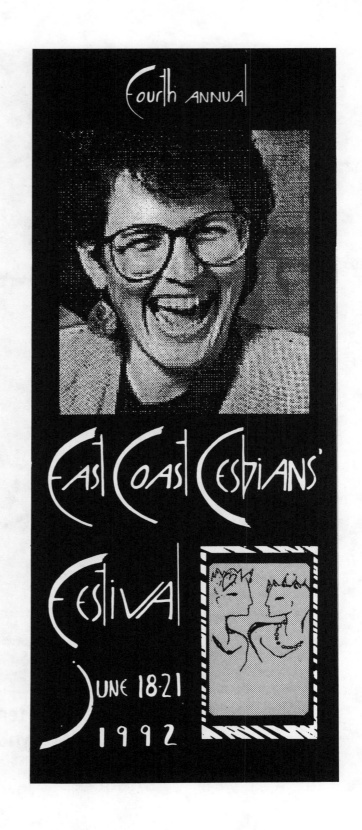

Fourth ANNUAL

East Coast Lesbians'
Festival
June 18-21
1992

Why Is This Festival Different from Any Other?
The East Coast Lesbians' Festival
by Lin Daniels

Not just another music festival…?

Let's face it. There are lots of festivals. There are WOMYN'S, WOMEN'S, RHYTHMS, AND WIMMIN'S FESTIVALS, all created by dykes, for dykes. Why is this one different? Since I do not identify as a woman, a womyn, wimmon, and certainly not a rhythm, the logical name for a festival of my own would be LESBIAN. It is also not enough to believe that everyone assumes we are dykes. It was time to call a festival by its proper name.

I find it really astonishing that in 1989, ECLF was the first festival to call itself "Lesbian." We are now into the fourth year of ECLF [in 1992], and other, small, day-long "Lesbian" festivals have popped up, which thrills me, but the East Coast Lesbians' Festival, the West Coast Lesbians' Festival, and Celebration Lesbienne in Quebec (all produced by Particular

In: *Lesbian Outlook #4* (May 1992).

Productions), are still the only four-day festivals with the word *Lesbian* in their names, and the only ones which have policies of including only Lesbians as workers, performers, techies, writers, crafts, and workshop presenters, and using Lesbian vendors whenever possible. We are creating a Lesbian space, honoring ourselves, celebrating ourselves…a radical concept.

Practice grounds for the matriarchy…

Women's festivals, as Amoja Three Rivers has said, are "practice grounds for the matriarchy." They are spaces in which to figure out how life could be lived among women. Lesbians come by the hundreds or thousands, thrilled with the possibilities that surround them. Some shed their clothes, others their emotional walls. They also come laden with emotional baggage from the patriarchy. They create "women's" festivals with a certain amount of guilt about the sheer joy of allowing

themselves a break for the weekend, taking that precious time for "just us." So, they have to make sure that straight women, bisexual women and their little boys are accommodated and included. We have to put aside our hunger for Lesbian-only space, our right to be *particular*, even for just a weekend. We have to be concerned with the issues of *all* women (most of whom are heterosexual); we have to be there to push forth *their* political platforms (witness the recent march on Washington), *their* ideals. We, as Lesbians, inevitably get gobbled up by issues and concerns that are not our own. We certainly can't name a weekend *Lesbian*, because it is too threatening, *exclusionary*.

Out of the cupboard…

Myriam Fougére and I were fed up with the invisibility of Lesbians, tired of going to festivals and having to try to ignore the presence of little boys, and feeling relief when we finally heard a performer who was unabash-

413

edly Lesbian or attended a workshop expressly about us. We were tired of feeling like a minority among other Lesbians. We also wanted a festival inclusive of the visual arts, a place where writers have a place of importance, where we present comedy, theatre and films—all uniquely Lesbian.

As a Lesbian artist who shows her work only to women, Myriam felt the need to expand, to create a venue for other Lesbian visual artists. As a producer of Lesbian music since the mid-seventies, I have been painfully aware of the dilution of our music, and see the Lesbians' Festival as a place to showcase those Lesbian performers who talk and write about Lesbian lives, Lesbian heartbreak, Lesbian joy.

The creation and future of Lesbian culture

We also have a deep respect for the Lesbians who helped to create Lesbian culture: Alix Dobkin, Maxine Feldman, Sue Fink, Kay Gardner, June Millington, Julia Penelope, Kate Millett, Toni Armstrong Jr....these Lesbians are invited to the Lesbians' Festival year after year. We are thrilled that Margie Adam will be coming this year [1992], with new songs and a Lesbian sensibility. Performers who are newer on the scene, like Jamie Anderson, Zoe Lewis and Susan Herrick, Justina and Joyce, are carrying the torch and singing to Lesbians wherever they can.

If we are to develop as a culture, if we are even to maintain that very fragile entity that *is* Lesbian culture, we have to first acknowledge what it is that we are creating. *Naming is very powerful*. We had to call it a Lesbians' Festival. We are taking our space. Largely because of that, we have been subject to the rampant internalized Lesbophobia that exists in the Lesbian Community and every controversy that plagues our diverse community.

Why us?

Myriam and I have been put through the wringer by Lesbians with conflicting points of view on every subject imaginable. Because we are organizers, we are supposed to "fix it," to make it all better, be all things to all Lesbians. We have been publicly, emotionally torn apart by Lesbians. We take some very important, largely unpopular stands, and continue to pay the price. We create this festival for women-born women; we create this place for Lesbians and their daughters. We actively combat racism. We do not condone violence against Lesbians in its many forms. Since we are Separatists, we take on the added stigma of being an extreme minority in a sea of Lesbians. We just can't do it any other way.

We continue to promote awareness about disabled Lesbians. We are creating bridges between hearing and deaf Lesbians through workshops, performances and, with Marilyn Van Veersen,

have created "Silent Pre-Fest," a three-day intensive for Lesbians who want to gain an understanding of American Sign Language and deaf Lesbian culture.

Our own worst enemies

Interesting problems have arisen in producing this festival. For instance, since we ask, specifically, that only Lesbians who identify as Lesbians be part of the festival, certain well-known *Lesbian* performers won't book with us. Some performers refuse to play at the festival because Myriam and I are Separatists. We have been slandered by other Lesbians, told that we were practicing "cultural nepotism" because I am a Jew and some of our performers, organizers and presenters are Jews, called "ableist" by some Lesbians, because we refused to allow the wearing of antiSemitic or racist paraphernalia or public displays of sadomasochism in the Accessibility Area of the Festival. I could go on, but it would just be recounting more and more instances of Lesbians turning on each other. It has taken a high toll on us and our relationship. I find it really tragic, though, that the problems one would think that a Lesbians' Festival would have—signing a contract with and maintaining a working relationship with straight camp owners as a *Lesbian* festival, finding vendors, supportive bankers, etc., pale in comparison to hostile Lesbians

who don't think that we have
the right to exist.

Lesbian Intelligentsia

The compensations do outweigh
the negatives. While we are
continuing to struggle financially, we have gained the respect and support of some of
our most revered performers,
writers, and activists. Dykes
come to the Lesbian Festival
year after year to find out
what's happening among the
"Lesbian Intelligentsia," to hear
or see a favorite Lesbian writer
or performer, or discover new
ones; to play in the lake, to
dance all night, see a Lesbian
film, appreciate Lesbian art,
and to celebrate ourselves. We've
received letters from dykes
about how ECLF has changed
their lives, how they went home
immediately after the festival,
quit their jobs and began new
lives. We have been told by
countless seasoned festi goers
that ours is "their favorite."

We are everywhere

I love all of the parts involved in
the creation of this festival. There
is nothing I would rather do. Although ECLF was the brainchild
of Myriam and me, it continues
because of the work and dedication of a crew of incredible dykes
who share our vision of Lesbian
space. The coordinator and crew
include Jews, Gentiles, Lesbians of
Colors, and come from Argen-
tina, Chile, Quebec, Israel, England, and even a few from the
u.s. *Vive les lesbiennes!* ∎

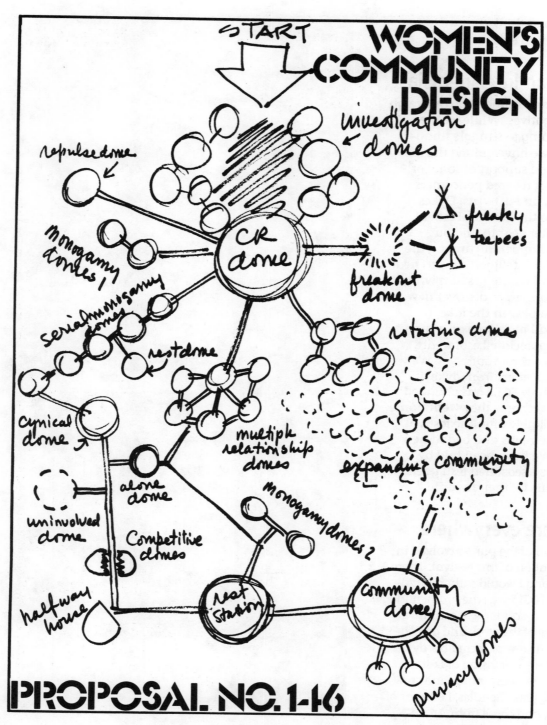

Women's Community Design
by Phyllis Birkby, from Ainjee Graphics, 1974.

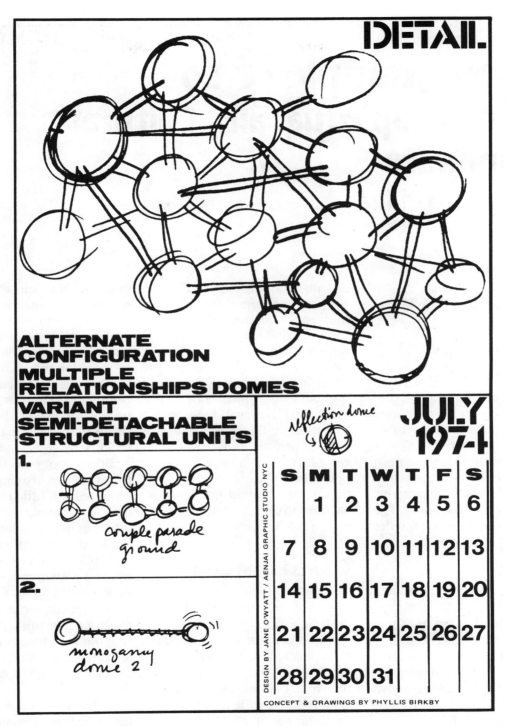

Women's Community Design
by Phyllis Birkby, from Ainjee Graphics, 1974.

Pagoda temple of Love
A Lesbian Spiritual and Cultural Community
From their brochure

2854 Coastal Highway
St. Augustine, FL 39095-2308
(904) 824-2970

The Pagoda is a residential cottage community of lesbians that includes a Spiritual/Cultural Center called the Pagoda temple of Love. This Center has guest rooms available to ALL wimmin for rest, retreat, recuperation and healing.

The Center is a three-story house which has been converted into a multi-purpose space. The ground floor houses our theater used for meetings, spiritual gatherings, workshops, and concerts, the ALCOVE and HECATE'S CAVE. The upstairs main floor contains a feminist LIBRARY that doubles as our fifth bedroom, the LAVENDER bedroom and a living room, a bathroom, a fully equipped kitchen, and an outside balcony shared by all retreat guests. The ATTIC is the third floor.

All of the buildings and environs at the Pagoda have a 50-year-old beach cottage look,

definitely not the Hilton. There are no TVs or private telephones in the guest rooms. There is a TV, VCR, and video tapes of interest to wimmin in our theater and is available to all guests. There is a telephone in the living room where local calls can be made. It is on call-forwarding to the Center Coordinator's home where messages are received. We have a swimming pool where you can enjoy optional nude sunbathing and swimming and the Atlantic Ocean is 300 yards away.

Guests in the Center

The Center is open all day and is used by retreat guests, supporters, visitors and residents. The weather is generally beautiful, although the temperature can drop below freezing for a day or so from December to February.

It is primarily used as a space for occasional spiritual & cultural events, workshops and as an "r & r" place for wimmin like yourself who want to relax

in a wimmin's space by the ocean. The Center operates on a low budget and is staffed by one part-time coordinator with the help of volunteers. We ask your cooperation in making sure that this space is kept clean and comfortable. We ask that you bring your own double-bed sheets and towels to cut down on laundry costs, and we especially ask that you clean up after yourselves, leaving your room ready for the next woman.

The Pagoda is a community that has conscientiously made rules that make our space as available and as safe as possible for all wimmin who desire to be here.

To meat, seafood, and poultry eaters this means not cooking flesh foods in the Center kitchen. An outdoor pit is available for the cooking of flesh foods.

To smokers it means smoking outside the Center and the Pool areas.

To alcohol and drug users it means no use of such substances in the Center or Pool area.

To heterosexual wimmin and some Lesbians it means that the males in their lives cannot come with them to the Pagoda.

To pet owners it means leaving your pets at home.

To emotional and physical batterers it means that such behavior is not tolerated at the Pagoda.

To sadomasochists it means that their ritual displays and practices must be done elsewhere.

We welcome all wimmin who wish to nurture, heal and enjoy themselves mentally, physically, emotionally and spiritually in a wimmin only environment. ■

Where Do Dreams Go When They Die?

by Juana Maria Gonzalez Paz, Arkansas, December 1982

From 1977 to 1979 I lived on several pieces of lesbian land in the United States. In 1979 I left my personal journal of lesbian-of-colour land called "La Luz de la Lucha" (or The Light of the Struggle) with the lesbian-of-colour group in L.A. while I headed east, and away from the turmoil of the last two years.

It seems that, almost three years later, I have found some understanding, happened upon some shred of wisdom in a place I least expected to find it—myself. Writing this retrospectively, hoping to dispel the ghosts that plague me and impart some hope to the new warriors, the ones who start out fresh and enthusiastic, the ones who have not been crushed by the dream—like me.

In: *Lesbian Land,* ed. Joyce Cheney. Minneapolis: Word Weavers, 1985.

Written for *Lesbian Land* and later included in the 1983 edition of *The La Luz Journal.* Also published in *Maize,* a Lesbian Country Magazine, Number 1, 1983.

The people who like my book really like it, and the ones who don't seem surprised that I still sustain a hope for the future, that I can still affirm the dream. I still think it can work. The need for a land-based womyn's culture is too great to be deterred by mistakes and disaster. But the question remains—what happened?

For myself, I found that I was profoundly unprepared for the task at hand. Aside from the most obvious deficiencies in my character or repertoire of skills (I neither drive nor fix cars and I am not mechanically inclined in any other way; I have never built anything and I am intimidated by large vehicles, chain saws, blueprints and womyn who seem to have an answer for everything), I didn't know who I was or what I had to offer.

I didn't know what other people wanted from me and whether I could, or should, or wanted to comply. I existed in a social atmosphere that did not allow for honest, direct communication of basic needs and goals, and I stood helplessly by while all of our real motivations went underground, only to surface again couched in political terms.

I saw myself as powerless and out of control, needing and dependent on the guidance of others (usually white lesbians whose rhetoric was impressive). This perception of myself was validated and encouraged by the people I lived with, even during the height of racial consciousness. White people were still the experts.

I discovered that not only weren't all womyn my sisters, but that I disliked, hated, feared, and was physically repulsed by some—all things I could not admit, even to myself. I loved womyn, too, but that didn't seem to work either. If it was a white womyn, I was immediately labeled "oppressive," "needy," "demanding," and accused of dumping if I tried to talk about how I felt.

I learned to keep some things to myself and began to

write my secret thoughts in journals, thus beginning my career as a political lesbian of colour writer, though it was several years before I or anyone else took the work seriously.

As the mother of a young child (Mary Ann was two and a half when I first came out) and single (loverless), I was very dependent on and susceptible to the peer pressure in groups where most people had at least one solid supporter. I, on the other hand, had both myself and my child to think of if my actions or opinions fell into disfavor with the group.

In undefined communal groups where individual rights and responsibilities are not spelled out, womyn are sometimes pitted against each other for survival, and it is not always the strong who survive. Sometimes it is the most devious and manipulative, those who can always find rhetoric to justify their goals and actions, no matter how outrageous or abusive.

The question of physical space becomes paramount in group living situations. If "A" has a male child and "B" feels oppressed by male energy, whose needs should predominate? If no value judgment is made, the group can be left in a cold war with accusations and denials flying, or perhaps the realization that some things cannot happen at the same time or in the same place.

For instance, if some lesbians smoke, drink, eat dairy products, and/or play loud music, and other lesbians deem these activities as oppressive, undesirable or unacceptable, are the opposing parties left to form separate camps? At what point do individual differences become insurmountable obstacles, and how much compromise should be expected of each of us?

If we follow the theory that everything that is patriarchal should be thrown overboard, what does that do to the fact that nearly everything on the planet has some patriarchal influence—from the socks we wear to the books we read? How much rejection and casting out can one movement stand, and shouldn't an adjustment period be allowed for?

I have seen lesbians on land conflict over issues great and small, from composting shitters to money distribution and lover breakups. Tolerance seems essential at this time. Some lesbians do eat meat and engage in other "patriarchal practices." Rejecting each other on the basis of our male identification, past or present, seems less practical and ethical than making clear choices about what we want in our lives right now and what man-made devices we still want to use.

Cars, guns, and chain saws are all things I have seen womyn object to on sound moral and political grounds. However, they all have their place when used wisely, and agreements about their function can be reached and kept. Money, food, vehicles, tools, private space, personal posses- sions, work energy, and lover dynamics all provide rich areas for conflict.

Though we collectively agree that uneven distribution of wealth, food, and opportunity is responsible for a great deal of the injustice in this world, on a practical level, womyn seem divided, or at least uncertain, about how to deal with the inequities among us.

The original blissful pronouncement that "we're all the same here" quickly turned to anger and bitterness as the womyn of colour realized that most decisions and money were in the hands of white womyn. And equality seemed like a distant dream as the womyn carrying scrap lumber up the hill to build a one-room A-frame watched the womyn at the next homesite haul in fresh lumber on her new truck.

How do we deal with the privilege, or lack of it, that each womyn brings with her, considering the fact that most womyn's lands were bought with money earned or inherited through white privilege and/or access, and that some people have the option to go back to the security they came from, whether they act on that option or not?

Many womyn who would like to live on the land do not have the money to make a down-payment, build structures, and keep up a mortgage for ten to twenty years. Although I do not believe country living for lesbians is escapist per se, it does represent white flight in cases where ample resources were necessary in order to make the move. There are still poor and third-world womyn who would like to live on the land but don't have the opportunity to do so.

Much argument on womyn's land centers on communal space and property. It is wise to specify exactly what is communal and what that means. For instance, do the womyn who live in and caretake the main house decide who gets to stay there, or are some decisions left to whoever is on the land at the time?

The roles of caretaker and visitor, even long-term visitor, need to be defined so that the womyn who live in a place and take responsibility for its ongoing maintenance and upkeep have the security to continue that work and receive the respect for having done it so far. Visitors need to know up front what's expected of them and what's negotiable, in order to avoid problems later because they didn't know something wasn't okay.

Regarding space, womyn's needs, I believe, are to feel in control of our own lives and responsible for our own actions. Some of us are more attached to our home base than others. I have lived in places where "no private space" was the rule and also where individual space was the tradition.

This is a tricky question, since most of the womyn who have held onto private space on land, or their homes, have paid for them with money or built them themselves. Money, car-

pentry and building skills all represent a major difference in access between womyn. If those with the skills, money, access to tools and carpentry training head for the hills with their resources, we are limited to a predominantly white and middle-class population on lesbian land.

Regarding lover dynamics, I have seen both monogamy and non-monogamy become the order of the day. As a celibate womyn during most of my time on lesbian land, I had less power in terms of the overall group than womyn whose lovers could always be counted on for support. I believe a political white lover could have provided me with safe passage through situations I found no way out of.

The issues/subjects/actions to debate and conflict around seem endless if we strive for consensus before commencing the everyday activities of life. In retrospect, I see that some things need to be decided up front and others left open to future change and growth. For instance, womyn will probably change their diet, work, and dress habits, with time, but the legal status of the land should be secured in advance. I have made long-range plans to settle on lands when I didn't know who owned them.

These are things that seem unimportant when things are going well, when everyone is getting along, and when there is more pressing work to do like digging a well, building structures and planting food. A basic right on womyn's land is for

each womyn to know where she stands in relation to the community, and what's going to happen as the land changes hands and people come and go. If these things are left up in the air, all comings and goings can represent a threat to the established population.

Womyn need to know if the land can be sold and exactly what will happen if individual members leave. The formation of a land trust usually prevents sale of the land or its parts. People who join as a couple should be prepared for the possibility of a break-up.

Womyn should know what behavior and projects are unacceptable to us before getting involved with a group. In other words, what can we live with? Some people have less tolerance than others for meetings, loud noises, partying and large group interactions. Some situations cannot be dealt with through established policies and guidelines, since we can't anticipate everything that might happen within a group.

There is a need, in womyn's communities, to look at the sum total of a situation or problem and not break it down into small parts that can be talked away with current ideology. There has been a problem with slander in recent years, both on and off the land. I believe that if womyn do not want to hear, or are not satisfied with, half-truths, then we must be willing to listen to the whole truth, which sometimes means assembling all the parties involved to take responsibility for their needs by assessing the situation, considering all options, and then taking decisive action to end the intolerable situation so that the problem and rumors give way to effective change and resolution.

By not allowing for any acknowledged lesbian leadership or decision-making body, I believe we have forfeited our need for and our ability to achieve our own justice. For instance, there are several womyn's lands where individuals were unable to resolve conflicts and the American legal system was called in to take power and make and enforce decisions. Wouldn't we prefer to empower lesbians to help us find a way out of this maze of anger, rage and confusion?

It is a hard reality to accept, but some lesbians lie, cheat, steal, abuse their friends/lovers/children, precipitate conflicts between womyn, and take advantage of those with less opportunities than themselves. I believe a need exists in lesbian living communities, where lives are so intertwined, for some kind of council or decision-making body, to see that womyn's grievances are acknowledged and acted upon before conflicts reach the point of disrupting the entire community.

As a people who have historically been denied control over the conditions of our lives, I believe lesbians have tried to take power over each other's lives in a way that jeopardizes all our growth and freedom. At the same time, we have consistently refused to empower individual lesbians in situations where a final decision-making authority was needed.

For myself, I sometimes wonder where my grand dreams have gone, but I wonder less as the time goes by and I find satisfaction and fulfillment in my own work and accomplishments. In the years since I left womyn's land, I have become a radio announcer, TV personality and well-published author. I believe I am a better person for all of this and will have more to offer when and if I go back.

The reasons I don't do that now are these: I have other goals in life besides arguing with lesbians, sitting in meetings, and trying to justify everything I say in a political context. I hope to go back and I want to go back—but not now. And not back, really; forward, to a place I've never been, beyond the mistakes of the past and the confused complexities of today.

I know that the future is out there and I know that we will find our way to it. I have learned to trust myself more these last years, and to like myself better. And all my new-found confidence adds to the passion and dedication I first felt when walking the land and knowing, one day, it would be a place for me to live and grow in peace and harmony.

I trust that the future is before us and I trust the best in all of us to bring it forth from the world we live in. ■

The Spread of Consumerism: Good Buy Community

by Lee Evans

Many years ago I lived in a Feminist Collective based upon, among other things, a shared value of resistance to Consumerism. Roughly, our analysis was that we live in a culture that promotes conspicuous consumption of goods, services, environment, and so forth. The attitude that everything can be bought or used is an example of a value (which I will call consumerism) which defines our relationship to the world. Consumer values do not allow for stable or long-lived relationships with either people or the environment. In our early analysis we hoped to replace those values with more humanistic ones. Since that time I have come to realize that "humanism" holds no promise for Lesbians, and have subsequently put it aside as I have other dead-ended ideologies.

In the past several years my focus has changed to building Lesbian connections, hence

In: *Sinister Wisdom* 37 (Spring '89)

strong Lesbian Community. Even though I have devoted myself to creating connections with other Dykes, I find that the ability to describe those connections still escapes me. I sense that they are based upon a core of desire to connect on a Lesbian plane. I believe that our passion for each other is what fuels our connections. I know that our connections are not institutionalized. I believe that in making Lesbian connections we have the ability to create and transform ourselves and our world.

I also know that we struggle with the boys' values insinuating themselves into our interactions. There has been much education done by Lesbians about the effects of oppressions on our communities. Besides being cruel, arrogant and harmful, racism, anti-semitism and other oppressions directly affect our Lesbian communities by narrowing the scope of what is or who is acceptable. These oppressions are men's tools for

enforcing sameness and anti-diversity.

Coming from a small, rural, white town in Pennsylvania, I thought that diversity was how many breeds of cows you owned. Coming out as a Lesbian, and now as a Separatist, I have had to work hard to sensitize myself to and rout out the boys' tools of division. This has helped me to perceive the world differently and form deeper, more substantial bonds with other Dykes. Struggling to be aware of how oppressions work, and what part I play in them, has made me stretch in a way that I hadn't felt since I first came out as a Lesbian.

Yet, through this process I have become increasingly aware of how I approach events and community. I know that my interactions often take on the tourist-y flavor of a consumer. Consumerism is a way of "be-ing" in the world, and it undermines our connections and sense of community. Consumer values are intertwined throughout industrial culture, and therefore probably have a pretty firm hold in many of our belief systems.

In writing this paper I am not so much concerned with what we buy, but with what male values are used to form our perception of ourselves as consumers of our communities rather than co-creators of our communities. It is my intent to blend my old analysis of consumer values with my current Dyke Separatist perspective in order to sensitize myself and other Dykes to the effects of consumer values on our Lesbian communities and Women-only space.

We live in a culture that is built, among other things, upon a system based upon consuming. In order to convince us that we have to buy, own, use, (consume), it is necessary to create a context in which conspicuous consumption looks normal. One way to develop that context is to create "needs" and then to objectify living things, processes and interactions into "products" to fill these "man-made needs." These are the gears that run a consumer society.

The society's members function in relationships of producers-consumers or buyer-seller to one another. The world, previously seen as an organic interconnected system, is now able to be "seen" as parts.[1] Those parts are able to be objectified in order to be bought and sold, used and discarded, acquired and hoarded or used as a means of trade to obtain other objects. As in other systems of reality, if one

views the world in this way, it then spills over to include how we view people, animals, the environment and our relationship to them.

What does it mean when we adopt a value that allows such mass-scale objectification? First of all, objects have no inherent meaning. We imbue objects with meaning. For instance, an automobile has different meanings related to which culture, class and economic group you belong. The owning of an automobile, besides providing transportation and the opportunity for repair bills, often serves to foster identity. We buy a particular car because it is symbolic of how we see ourselves, or how we want to be. For example, I once found a Dyke party when I wasn't quite sure of the location by driving up and down streets until I found the street with the "usual" Dyke vehicles common in my community: small foreign-made cars with a smattering of pickup trucks.

Buying an object in order to foster identity becomes a never-ending cycle. The new pickup truck itself does not the adventuresome Dyke make, so we are once again encouraged to enter the marketplace to start the cycle over. In other words, we buy an object to establish status and identity. Because objects have no intrinsic value, the status and identity do not become firmly established, so we have to continue to "consume" other objects to shore up our identity, and so the consumer

cycle goes on *ad infinitum*.

This process works to help create a consumer atmosphere because it is an escalation-based model. It sets up the value that having new, improved, bigger, better and more is not only acceptable, it is expected of us. (For many sales jobs, employers require that you not only have good transportation, but that your car must "look" new, thus fostering the notion that employees must become believers and participants in the american dream.) This model creates the habit of escalation.

Pornography is an example of an escalation-based model that has increased dramatically over the last twenty years. This escalation occurs in terms of what is openly available in bookstores. Pornography begins with showing naked females, moves to the objectification of body parts, then to the abusing and mutilating of women, and finally to the torture and murder of women and children for men's satisfaction. The escalation-based model increases the violence and cruelty inflicted.

What does it mean for Dykes when we carry this "habit of escalation" into our communities? The "habit of escalation" creates a context in which we willingly participate in or at least accept increasingly destructive behaviors without questioning them. I once asked a sadomasochistic Dyke if she kept reworking her fantasies in order to become aroused. She replied that, in fact, it was nec-

425

The search for newness stems from and fosters alienation and disconnectedness.

essary for her to keep increasing the violence in her fantasies and practices in order to increase sensations (pain) for her and her partner. This objectifying of people and experiences soon leads to being jaded. Being jaded creates a sense of numbness and the more we objectify the more numbness spreads throughout our interactions. We soon need more and more stimulation in order to respond at all.

Numbness leads to a focus on newness so that we might find that extra stimulation. To focus on newness is to focus on packaging, not on content. Newness suggests that which exists for the first time. Since newness becomes more and more difficult to create, then things must be packaged to provide the illusion of newness. Marketers and advertisers do not want us comparing products in terms of how they are similar, but rather in terms of how their product is newer and different than the others. Newness is fetishized in this country. New cars, new detergents, new pop-psychologies and new religions are often far more similar to the old ones than we want to believe. Again, the value lies in the newness of the products.

The ramifications for Dyke culture are that in order to regain our attention, the boys will slap a "new, improved" label on or repackage their therapy, religion, politics and so forth. As Anna Lee points out in her paper "New Age Spirituality Is the Invention of the Heteropatri-archy,"[2] what many Lesbians are now espousing as their means to a new improved personal sense of empowerment is the same religion the boys were marketing to us before. We looked at the differences that they assured us were there, and ignored the now more obvious similarities between new age spirituality and heteropatri-archal religions.

Because the search for newness is based upon how things differ rather than how things are similar or connected to one another, the search for newness stems from and fosters alienation and disconnected-ness. The search for newness is the search for those things that allegedly stand out from, are apart from that which is. The ability to perceive how things, events, people and power are connected and relate to each other is at the very core of our political skills. When we partici-pate in the focus on newness,

we lose the ability to develop and use political skills because we are focused on the differ-ences that are used as proof of newness. We are no longer able to focus on our connections with each other. Without recognizing our connections to each other, Lesbians are not able to discon-nect from heteropatriarchy.

For Dyke communities the search for newness and the re-sulting alienation has meant that the commitment to analyze our lives, our behaviors and problems in political terms is no longer promoted or supported. In the seventies we had a com-mitment to analyzing our lives from a political perspective, and we joined Consciousness Raising groups to that end. By the eight-ies, many Dykes had retreated to therapies and various twelve-step groups, none of which are noted for any political analyses, but are heavily invested in view-ing the world from a psycho-logical base. Psychology complements consumerism nicely, in that it views humans as units that can be adjusted to the norm. All we have to do to get healthy is to work our pro-gram better, try a different therapy, or subject ourselves to an endless list of cures because we are never quite healthy enough. This is also an example of an escalation-based model.

The undermining of our political skills further endangers us in that the boys are able to divert our focus to their concerns and tasks, at the same time convincing us that they are *our* concerns and interests. Much theory and discussion has centered around motherhood. Many Lesbians understood motherhood to be fundamentally oppressive to women and Lesbians, and understood that the boys benefited from us producing children to turn over to the heteropatriarchy. While there have been Lesbians who have been honest in wanting children so that they more closely resemble heterosexuals, it is only recently that Lesbians have advocated motherhood as a strategy for changing the world. In "The Tired Old Question of Male Children," Anna Lee suggests our mothers didn't set out to raise their sons to be rapists, woman-haters, and prone to violence.[3] But Lesbians who choose motherhood focus once again on how this form of parenting is going to be different and not on how it is similar. Perhaps some communities are just now beginning to realize that the children raised by Lesbians are not significantly different than the children raised by heterosexual parents. The fact remains that children of Lesbians are claimed at the same level by the heteropatriarchy as the children of heterosexual parents.

Another example of focus on the new is the encroachment by men on Women-only space. A purported Lesbian musician at a major women's music event in California, while introducing the boys in her band, was reported to have said "how nice it was to be able to have boys back on stage and with us again." Men have "been on the stage" with us for 5,000 years. Nothing much about their behavior has changed in the last fifteen years, but now they market themselves to us as "new, improved feminist" men. Because they are "new" boys, some are willing to perceive them as different from the "old" boys. Many of us have not noticed boys doing anything differently, while at the same time noticing that they are intent on invading Women-only space. Ten years ago boys would not have been permitted on stage without a lot of discussion of the political implications of male invasion of Women-only space. Ten years ago the personal was political. In 1988 we have reduced the political to the personal.[4] It is very difficult to explore political choices with Lesbians who champion certain behaviors as personal preferences which therefore cannot be questioned.

Personal preference, which is an underpinning of psychological perspective, discourages us from examining the connections with each other and the organic world. If we attend to ways in which events, people and things connect, it would be very difficult for the boys to package our lives and sell them back to us. It is the breaking of the world into parts and even the objectifying of the world itself which feeds the vicious cycle of buy and sell. The boys cannot sell that which they cannot objectify. It is the forging and recognizing of our connections which shield and protect us from the boys' objectification of us.

When we perceive everything as an object, even people become consumable. It is no surprise that people have indeed been bought and sold, used and discarded, acquired and hoarded, and used as objects of barter. This is evidenced in the slave trade and prostitution, among other things. While we would all like to believe that only strange people could objectify humans to that extent, it is not difficult to notice the "normalcy" of the male belief that children, wives and employees can be owned. Once people are objectified into objects, we move easily to the consuming of interactions and experiences.

The consuming of experiences is best described as being present at an event or experience and yet being a voyeur to that interaction. We disconnect from the experience—we allow it to flow over us and not affect us much, if at all. Heteropatriarchy promotes voyeurism as the path of least resistance. When we are bombarded from all sides by the boys' often meaningless stimuli, it becomes very difficult to maintain our focus. What makes it even harder to remain focused is that the intensity of the stimuli often does not coincide with the importance of the event. For example, on a given day in Cleveland all of the rapes, woman-bashings and killing of women are relegated to the inside pages of the newspaper, yet the headlines scream out that the Cleveland Browns may make it to the Superbowl. It becomes almost impossible to correlate intensity of stimuli with importance of the content, and even more difficult to trust one's perceptions and judgments. So most of the time I am a voyeur to boys' culture, I step back and let it roll off my back. I am curiously removed.

Unfortunately, it is one thing to be a "tourist" in Boysland, and another thing to be a tourist to our own culture. As communities struggle with trying to keep ourselves alive and accessible to all Dykes, we have developed the "more if you can, less if you can't" policy for many events. This is predicated upon the assumption that the community and its events are important to all of us, and that we are all responsible in "making things happen." Yet I have observed well-to-do Dykes come in and pay the low end of the scale because they left their money in the car, or Dykes who pay less because they want to save money for a boys' event the next night. This is treating our community events as consumable objects.

In fact, the institutionalizing of our culture, primarily our musical culture, has turned our celebrations into mass consumer events. At the recent Olivia Anniversary Gala, everything was for sale: the reception (but only if you had $25); articles of clothing from the "stars" as a fundraiser; and package deals in certain cities, with the best seats going to the Dykes who could dish out the most money.

(Ironically, there were Dykes in Cleveland who wouldn't have been able to afford the concert, except for the fact that they produced it.) Besides being a blatant example of abysmal lack of commitment to class consciousness, this is an example of buying and selling of Dyke community. Happily, Dyke love and energy survive under even adverse circumstances, but the fact remains that the consumerism existing in some events dictates a producer-consumer relationship.

Because boys' culture has existed for so long, it is firmly entrenched in the objectification of living things resulting in stagnation which is also a death focus. Boys' culture is in no way diminished by our consumption of that culture; in fact, our consumption of their culture contributes to its continuation. The point of Lesbian community is to separate from the status quo and base our connections on a different set of values. When we participate in a Lesbian event, we are not just purchasing entertainment, we are fostering our connections with each other. It is because this heritage of celebrating our connections has meant so much to me as a Dyke that I have become angry and disappointed that our events have taken on a consumer flair and return us to the malestream. Because our connections are continually being created, we cannot assume the role of consumers of our culture unless our intent is to diminish and consume our connections as a product. If our commitment

The point of Lesbian community is to separate from the status quo and base our connections on a different set of values.

is to building Lesbian community, then we must participate in the ongoing creation of that community, not the objectification and consumption of Lesbian community. The turning of our connections and communities into marketable products is going to have a devastating effect on us. As consumers our relationship to products is on two levels: on one hand we identify with the product, and on the other hand we distance ourselves from it. The identification with the product I have already discussed. The distancing from the product allows us not to be affected by it, not to be responsible for it and often a voyeur of it. As consumers, our only responsibility is to our own satisfaction.

⚢

In the seventies I lived in a community that valued Women-only space, Radical Dyke Activity, manual laborers, development of theory, other working class jobs and anti-patriarchal work. I question the inverse correlation between the rise of cultural Lesbianism and the return to the malestream and resulting decline in respect for the Radical Lesbian activities. Once we institutionalize our culture, the rules of the marketplace take over. We have many examples, from making our Lesbian-created rape crisis centers and battered women's shelters more palatable to funders by firing the Dykes, to the selling of *Lesbian Nuns* to *Forum* by Naiad Press, to the Dyke musicians who play at Michigan for Women-only audiences until

they make it big and will no longer play before Women-only audiences. Hence our relationships to each other have shifted from co-creating to the producing and consuming of our Lesbian community. When we create Lesbian community, we are enacting values that enhance and prioritize our Dyke connections. When we enact consumer values, our Lesbian connections are not the priority. Our consumer-producer connections are the priority.

When we established a producer-consumer relationship to each other, boys stepped in as the producers of our culture and marketed it back to us. The boys will be involved as long as they can turn a tidy profit and even if some boy producer in a large Eastern city decided to "return" some of the money to Lesbian community, it is as an insurance that he be allowed to continue to market our community. When boys quit making money from us, they will stop being concert producers and purveyors of women's books and records. They are not co-creators of our cultures. They are the people who come in to make profit from our having institutionalized to the point that money could be made. They are the people who sell our experiences and connections. Once we give them the right to market our lives to us, they also have the right to determine what our lives will be. Boys twist who we are and market it back to us in their own image.

Consumerism has been an

effective tool for undermining our communities. We have consumed our own communities, thereby diminishing them. Boys have appropriated our communities, thereby distorting them. Boys begin to sell it back to us, thereby molding it in their own image. And sadly, many Dykes are no longer participating as co-creators of our culture, thereby conceding it to the forces of consumerism.

Consumerism is a system that fails to acknowledge what is important to us. I have interacted with my community as a consumer at times and admit that I thought I felt alive in the process. Or maybe I just felt motion and mistook it for life. But motion is not proof of life. After all, the boys are good at making machines move. That back and forth motion of consumerism is not motion on a profound level. Rather it is predictable, has a certain weariness, and holds no promise for change or creation. It is motion between two points of the patriarchy and fails to propel us away from the gravitational pull of boys' values.

Earlier in this paper, I spoke of my inability to describe our connections. I still wonder why that is when those connections are so often intense. Amidst the glare of the marketplace it appears those connections are also very subtle.

Yet it is at the level of our connections that we begin to build our communities. A fundamental difference between Lesbian culture and heteropatriarchal culture is that unlike the boys, what moves and sustains us are our desires and passion. Our passion for our friends, our lovers, our politics, our lives and our creations defines our connections. Passion and desire cannot live in the marketplace any more than we can joyously thrive in the heteropatriarchal world. Consumerism is about the objectifying of all living things and passion has its own life. Passion cannot be packaged and marketed to us; instead it is created by and among us. I believe our passion has integrity and rather than allow itself to be distorted by consumerist interactions, it will quietly leave.

When consumerism forces passion to leave our interactions, we no longer have a basis for Lesbian connections. It is this interweaving of passion and desire throughout our values, our lives and our connections that will be the foundation of our Dyke communities. ■

Notes

This is a revised version of the paper presented at the Lesbian Theory panel, June 1988, at the National Women's Studies Association conference. I want to thank Sarah Hoagland for asking me to participate in the Lesbian Theory panel of NWSA. The panel was the impetus for me finally setting my thoughts down on paper. I want to thank Julia Penelope for the creation of the word *heteropatriarchy* and Anna Lee for the word *malestream*. I want to thank Anna Lee, Bette Tallen, Ellen Catlin and Laura Sanders for their help in clarifying my ideas and rewriting

the paper. I am also indebted to long hours of conversations with many of the Separatists who attended the Midwest Lesbian Separatist Conference, June 1988.

1 Starhawk. *Dreaming the Dark: Magic, Sex and Politics.* Beacon Press, 1982. Starhawk discusses how the norms of the world shifted in the sixteenth century from an organic system to that of isolated nonliving parts.

2 Lee, Anna. "New Age Spirituality Is the Invention of the Heteropatriarchy," *Sinister Wisdom* #37, Spring 1989. Paper read at the panel on Lesbian Theory at the 1988 National Women's Studies Association Conference.

3 Lee, Anna. "The Tired Old Question of Male Children," *Lesbian Ethics*, Vol. 1, #2, pp. 106–108. While Anna Lee is specifically referring to black women in her paper, I believe that the point still stands that the fact that neither black nor white women raise their sons to grow up to be abusers isn't enough to stop the boys from enacting those behaviors.

4 A point made by Bette Tallen in a conversation concerning the lack of political analysis in our communities.

Lesbian Air

by Chrystos ~~~~~~~~~~~~~~~~~~~~~~~~~

For Jewelle Gomez

She burns her mouth aches for the taste of Cunt unmistakable
smell on her hands cherished in public places for she refuses to
wash it off   She dreams her hands are branded Dyke by the government
        Instead of wearing gloves of shame she waves her hands to
everyone laughing until she cracks into tears as they slam shut
their faces   She is disgusting they say   Some of them   Enough
to bring her to her knees in despair   She doesn't stay there long
Up again to water the Lesbian garden   mend the Lesbian ramp
wash the Lesbian breakfast dishes   Her work to make money is a
mindless stew of misery, her actions sometimes wrong, her beliefs
sometimes inaccurate but it is clear that licking Cunt is always
good always right always holy   She is a fisheater they say
whipped by cats she is at the mercy of her tongue her fingers   She
chooses each moment to love women to side with the Dykes to take
the heat to be a Lesbian even when other Lesbians refuse her as too
radical too frightening too much   There cannot be too much
Abundance is the love of our mother whose breast we plant
whose eyes we bless
        Ah the theory of Lesbianism is a lot of words that not all Les-
bians understand or want to   It is the wanting of women we
share   parting of forbidden roses   Our tongues meet we can
never have too much of each other as we speak on palestinian
land rights, as we march against racism, as we demand abortion
rights for women who might hate us as we stand for them, as we
wheel, as we follow night into day as we breathe Lesbian air, plant
Lesbian sunflowers & carrots, as we train Lesbian horses, as we
write Lesbian traffic tickets, as we predict Lesbian earthquakes, as
we repair Lesbian cars, as we hold jobs from Lesbian wheelchairs,

as we swim in Lesbian lakes with the loons, as we care for the
wounded & dying our tender Lesbian hands nurture life   We
bring babies here we bring paintings here we bring poetry and
song here   We bring Lesbian joy into the wintery lives of the
lonely   We are our mother's infinite variety

     We are Lesbian redwoods   We are Lesbian rain forests   we
are Lesbian rock formations   we are Lesbian canyons   we are Lesbian desert pines   we are Lesbian lizards   we are the sea of Lesbians the breathing wind of Lesbians we are the falling cherry petals
of Lesbian we are the Lesbian moon rising full of our fallen warriors' songs   we are the Lesbian sky

From *Dream On*. Vancouver: Press Gang Publishers, 1991.

Talking Lesbian
by Alix Dobkin

Now, if you want higher consciousness
I'll tell you what to do.
You've got to talk to a woman
And let her talk to you.
You've got to build you a consciousness
And make it strong, and if we all stick together, girls,
It won't be long. We'll have
More friends, better friends, and more fun!
It's like living in the country!

Of course it ain't quite so simple
So I'd better explain just why you've
Got to ride on that Lesbian train,
'Cause if you wait for the man to
Straighten out your head, you'll all be a'waiting,
Then you'll be dead and gone to heaven. All alone.
Remember all those sweet, dear, cute, devoted women friends of yours?
You passed them all by. A damn shame!

Suppose you're working so hard it's just outrageous,
And your life hasn't improved in ages,
You go to the man, but he doesn't relate
To a woman's mind, or a woman's state.
Well, he's puffing his ego up, feeling masculine,
He's got the whole world, he thinks, to stick it in.
He looks out the window and what does he see
But a million women and they all agree:
"Go stick it in some mud!"

Alix Dobkin
by June Parlett

Now girls, you've come to the hardest time!
The man will try to hand you every line.
He'll plead, argue, sulk and the like,
He'll call every one of you a goddamned Dyke!
"Man hater!" "Castrator!" "Men are human beings too...50%."(42!)

But, working in the kitchen, here's what we found,
Scrubbing the floors, here's what we found,
Raising the children, here's what we found, and
Being with each other, this is what we found:
That if we don't let *man*euvering keep us apart,
If we don't let *man*ipulation keep us apart,
If we don't let man-power keep us apart,
Or man-kind keep us apart, We're there!
We didn't get it easy, but we got it!

"Talking Lesbian" is on Alix Dobkin's first album, *Lavender Jane Loves Women* (1973). ©1973 by Alix Dobkin

Sappho: Rediscovering Lesbian Space

by Jorjet Harper

One evening in 1982, I read Sappho for the first time—by accident. I had no curiosity about Sappho that I can recall, despite the fact that I was out as a lesbian and vaguely knew there was some connection between Lesbos and Sappho and lesbians. I was at the time, however, intensely interested in ancient languages. I'd found a book in the public library called *Teach Yourself Greek*. With no sense of how difficult such a project might be, I plowed ahead, burning the midnight oil, learning the ancient Greek alphabet and vocabulary words and the rudiments of grammar. I was wading through exercises for third declension nouns, deciphering some sayings of ancient Greek philosophers, when I came to a fragment of Sappho, which I tried with great difficulty to translate. Something about somebody bringing a sheep somewhere?

From *HOT WIRE* (September 1990).

When I gave up, finally, and looked at the answer key in the back of the book, I found these florid, archaic-sounding words:

Evening, thou bringest everything that bright drawn scattered. Thou bringest the sheep, thou bringest the goat, thou bringest the child back to its mother.

I've found clearer, more modern translations since, but as I was going back and forth between the Greek and English that night, trying to match the right words for sheep, goat, scattered, etcetera, the *meaning* underneath this antiquated, biblically-cast language suddenly came to me. While this passage was (so the book said in a footnote) only a fragment, and the rest of the poem was lost, the *idea* it expressed was not at all fragmentary. Furthermore, it was so simple, so immediate, so personal, and so universal at the same time that I was taken aback. Not only was it a vivid and complete image on a literal level, but it evoked, for me, the

idea that as we grow to be the age our mothers were when we saw them through children's eyes, we understand as adults what it was like for our mothers when they were the age we are now—and we experience a kind of homecoming, a metaphorical reunion with our mothers based on an understanding about them at "evening" which we didn't have at the "dawn" of our lives.

Whether Sappho meant these lines to be taken on a metaphorical level, I could not have said. But these few words of Sappho, much to my own surprise, had transported me from the plodding realm of my language exercises into an inner place where I was deeply contemplating my own and universal experiences—and they were *written by a woman who had been dead for twenty-six hundred years.*

I marvelled that for the first time in my life I was hearing the direct words of a woman, a *woman*, from way, way back in history—a contemporary of Buddha and Confucius, older than Socrates, older than Aristotle, older than almost all the male voices I was taught in school to venerate as wise and brilliant and eternal in the pantheon of Great Thinkers.

Suddenly it became more obvious than ever to me how one-sided and lopsided that pantheon was. For once, this was not a male voice telling me what the world looked like to him. It was not a "universal" voice that revolved around "man" as its center. It was a voice that made what I found to be a "universal" observation—beautifully stated—from a *female-centered* place. The child returns to its mother.

From then on, I read everything I could by and about Sappho and her "island of women" on Lesbos.

Our knowledge of all women of the past is, like Sappho's poetry, fragmentary and fragmented. Recently, reading Greek scholar John Winkler's excellent book *Constraints of Desire*, I've learned that in ancient Greece, there were several women-only festivals held each year—among them the Stenia, the Thesmophoria, the Haloa, and the Adonia—though what we know of them comes, of course, from the accounts of men whose "attitude to women's independent operations is likely to be colored by anxiety, suspicion, or contempt," Winkler reminds us. Above all, says Winkler, the male scholars who

reported what they knew about these women-only events "are likely to miss the consciousness of the women themselves about the meaning of their ritual and festive acts."

A few sparse details about these women-only gatherings in ancient Greece are also known. During some, women went up to the rooftops and hilltops and laughed hilariously all night long. Male accounts describe the women as shouting loud obscenities amid their raucous laughter, and the women are alternately criticized by these male historians for being "shameful" and "shameless." The women baked and ate genital-shaped cookies during their festivals. They carried plants in pots up to their rooftops, and then stopped watering them, allowing the plants to wilt and die, and they apparently found this tremendously funny. Reportedly, at least one festival, however, alternated laughter with grieving.

And at least one of these women-only festivals was funded by municipal (i.e., male) money—and the Greek men, though not permitted to attend, observe, or even know what went on, generally respected the women-only "space" and rituals. Two ancient historians recount separate instances in which men tried to sneak into women-only rituals to observe them. On discovering a "gate-crasher," the women seized the man and castrated him.

When we think of "women-only" space today, we may

not even be aware that at other times, in other places, such spaces existed, and did not have to be fought for, and were considered a legitimate, even beneficial, part of social conduct—inviolable. Sappho and her followers lived in a time when the "mysteries" of women were still taken less seriously and thought to be important in the perpetuation of the natural world and the social fabric. As the poetry of Sappho makes obvious to me, *it is only in a self-chosen woman-centered environment that the female universe can be fully explored and given expression.* "Women-only space" is both external and internal.

One of the most basic characteristics of women-only space as it exists today is the understanding that the experience of women alone together has value—and this is a notion that, though simple enough, still runs counter to just about everything the dominant society tells us. Perhaps now—as we gather in all-women festivals we have created for ourselves, and as we found women's and lesbians' institutions of all kinds—we are at a point in the evolution of modern women's culture in which we are beginning to get just an inkling of the possibilities of a woman-centered universe.

The child comes home to her mother. ■

**The Midwest Lesbian Conference
and Music Festival poster, 1974**
photo by Elliott

Documenting the Dyke Conference

by Joan E. Nixon

Writing an article about the West Coast Lesbian Conference held in Los Angeles, April 13–15, 1973, is hard. The problems and the pain are still with me, the opportunities are lost. I remember the conference with anger, with love, with pain. I want to discuss the problems of the conference. Yet I want to write about the women there as tenderly as I can, because out of the confusion and controversy, the most important question I heard was Susan Jill Kahn's. Late Saturday night, collapsed from the pain and rage after Family of Woman had been thrown out of its own concert, Susan asked, "Where is the tenderness here?"

We came to Los Angeles to share the conference organizers' dream—a thousand lesbians finding each other in one place, in one room, would fill the space with a joyous celebration. We would be an army made of

From *Lavender Woman* and Michal Brody's *Are We There Yet?* (1985)

lovers and we would build our lesbian culture with our sisters. Alas for Barbara McLean's dream, what we found instead were a series of deadly serious struggles over issues too complex and deeply felt to be resolved in three days. The dyke conference became a battleground few had anticipated—a thousand angry women, trapped on the man's territory, fighting with each other—lesbian against lesbian, feminist against feminist, woman against woman. Our army of shouting lovers fell into combat with each other.

The oppression we share as lesbian women in a burning patriarchal world was not enough to bind us together, and we did not find an easy joy in each other's company. A thousand angry dykes—at times joyous, enraged, confused—did not find a common enemy to confront. We hardly began to find friends and allies among the other women there. That was an opportunity lost.

Many and divisive were the issues. Ironically, the conference organizers, who made it possible for more than a thousand dykes to get together, were those who found themselves most severely criticized for what they did or did not do. They were a hardy group indeed, beginning the conference exhausted, but optimistic, judging from Barbara McLean's "Diary of a Mad Organizer" article in *Lesbian Tide*'s May–June, 1973, issue on the conference. Proud of their hard work and eager to cope with problems, they wore "staff" armbands at the beginning. The armbands made them focal points of bitter complaints and soon the armbands disappeared. The organizers managed to survive a situation of controversy, chaos, and exhausting disputes. Not without cost—Tess (Linda Tessier, a fine, sensitive poet from Orange County), who was responsible for programming events and performers, told me she spent her only free hour Saturday collapsed alone under a pine tree in tears. After midnight Saturday when Family of Woman voiced outrage that their concert had to be stopped because U.C.L.A. closed the building at midnight, Tess was literally shaking on her feet. Barbara McLean said later no one could know how much pain the conference hassles gave her, but her diary article is full of that pain. A fine, strong, sensitive woman, Barbara found herself being held by the shoulders and shaken by one of Family's musicians, who was screaming, "where were you," when the band was stopped. Robin Morgan appeared among our by-now angry and hysterical Family group, also in tears, telling us the organizers would not listen to her either, since they were so offended by her earlier speech. The Family group decided to fight for another chance to play the next day, and Susan Jill Kahn was there early to see to the arrangements. Other disasters of Saturday involved Kate Millett, who was hurt by the interruptions of her reading of her erotic lesbian poetry—she got a chance Sunday to read the rest to a smaller group. Many dykes complained bitterly that the stars got time and space to do their thing while other sisters couldn't get a place on the program. The suspicion hung in the air that the stars got paid and the needier didn't. No one got enough time and space around the microphones to say and do all they wanted to, and there were fre-

quent fights over access to the microphones.

If Saturday was full of bitter controversy and woe, Sunday, fortunately, was a brighter day. The organizers lost control of scheduling and were rolling with everyone's demands. Major hassles had peaked—reconciliation was in the air. More women got involved in scheduling decisions to arrange workshops they wanted, more musicians got to play, women began to find friends in the sunshine. The closing session still resounded with arguments and speeches but we were listening as well as fighting. Finally the survivors joined Family of Woman for a tribal celebration. We threw off our battle stance, shouted for joy at being together alone* at last and danced in the aisles, a laughing, crying dyke horde, knowing we had made it through the struggles and were bringing in the dawn.** A family of woman—what an idea. We knew that our controversies with each other for that idea would also continue.

I had to ask why it was so hard for a thousand dykes to get it together. I decided to write about the problems of the conference.

Some of the controversy in L.A. centered on the presence and words of Robin Morgan, a woman passionately committed to a feminist revolution. Robin's keynote speech Saturday morning was an event of major importance, and has been reprinted in the lesbian/feminist

media, in *Amazon Quarterly*, *Lesbian Tide*, *Lavender Woman*, and *Second Wave*. Entitled "Lesbianism and Feminism: Synonym or Contradictions," Robin's speech made a careful analysis of those two complicated political phenomena. Her ideas were extremely difficult to follow without the text. We disagreed heartily afterward about what Robin really said. Barbara McLean put together a conference for unity, and she was amazed and enraged to hear Robin call for further polarization. She describes the speech as "an hour and a half of HATE!" Others heard Robin's call for unity. Did Robin call for polarization or for unity? In fact, she did both—which is why the speech is difficult and why there was disagreement on what was said.

I probably will continue to write about problems on the L.A. dyke conference in future issues of *Lavender Woman* since my sense of loss at what we could have done is still so real. ■

August, 1973

---

*"together alone," from a song performed by Family of Woman, *Together Alone*, by Melanie (Safka)

**"bringing in the dawn," from a song performed by Family of Woman, *Family of Woman*, by band member Linda Shear

© 1987 by Sudie Rakusin

Leaping Lesbians
by Sue Fink and Joelyn Grippo

We're gonna tease you   please you
Hypnotize and squeeze you
We're gonna get you if we can
Here come the lesbians!

Don't go and try to fight it
Run away or try to hide it
We want your loving   that's our plan
Here come the lesbians

OH—Don't look in the closet!
OH—What's creeping down the stairs?
OH—We're slipping up behind you
OH—Watch out   Better beware!

Icy fingers feeling, stealing
Reaching out from floor to ceiling
You can't escape   you're in our hands
Here come the lesbians

I can see your heart is racing
When you see our shadows chasing
Here come the lesbians   (4x)
the leaping lesbians!

©1976 by Sue Fink & Joelyn Grippo
First recorded on Meg Christian's album, *I Know You Know* (1974).

by Nancy Crooks
From *Dyke: A Quarterly #3*

Some Reflections on Separatism and Power[1]

by Marilyn Frye

I have been trying to write something about separatism almost since my first dawning of feminist consciousness, but it has always been for me somehow, a mercurial topic which, when I tried to grasp it, would softly shatter into many other topics like sexuality, man-hating, so-called reverse discrimination, apocalyptic utopianism, and so on. What I have to share with you today is my latest attempt to get to the heart of the matter.

In my life, and within feminism as I understand it, separatism is not a theory or a doctrine, nor a demand for certain specific behaviors on the part of feminists, though it is undeniably connected with lesbianism. Feminism seems to me to be kaleidoscopic—something whose shapes, structures and patterns alter with every turn of feminist creativity; and one element which is present through

Originally published in *Sinister Wisdom 6* (1978).

all the changes is an element of separation. This element has different roles and relations in different turns of the glass—it assumes different meanings, is variously conspicuous, variously determined or determining, depending on how the pieces fall and who is the beholder. The theme of separation, in its multitudinous variations, is there in everything from divorce to exclusive lesbian separatist communities, from shelter for battered women to witch covens, from women's studies programs to women's bars, from expansions of day-care to abortion on demand. The presence of this theme is vigorously obscured, trivialized, mystified and outright denied by many feminist apologists, who seem to find it embarrassing, while it is embraced, explored, expanded and ramified by most of the more inspiring theorists and activists. The theme of separation is noticeably absence of heavily qualified in most of the things I take to be personal solutions and band-aid projects, like legalization of prostitution, liberal marriage contracts, improvement of the treatment of rape victims and affirmative action. The contrariety of assimilation and separation seems to me to be one of the main things that guides or determines assessments of various theories, actions and practices as reformist or radical, as going to the root of the thing or being relatively superficial. So my topical question comes to this: What is it about separatism, in any or all of its many forms and degrees, that makes it so basic and so sinister, so exciting and so repellent?

Feminist separation is, of course, separation of various sorts or modes from men and from institutions, relationships, roles and activities which are male-defined, male-dominated and operating for the benefit of males and the maintenance of male privilege—this separation being initiated or maintained, at will, *by women*. (Masculist separatism is the partial segregation of women from men and male domains *at the will of men*. This difference is crucial.) The feminist separation can take many forms. Breaking up or avoiding close relationships or working relationships, forbidding someone to enter your house; excluding someone from your company, or from your meeting; withdrawal from participation in some activity or institution, or avoidance of participation; avoiding communications and influence from certain quarters (not listening to music with sexist lyrics, not watching tv); withholding commitment or support; rejection of or rudeness toward obnoxious individuals.[2] Some separations are subtle realignments of identification, priorities and commitments, or working with agendas which only incidentally coincide with the agendas of the institution one works in.[3] Ceasing to be loyal to something or someone is a separation; and ceasing to love. The feminist's separations are rarely if ever sought or maintained directly as ultimate personal or political ends. The closest we come to that, I think, is the separation which is the instinctive and self-preserving recoil from the systematic misogyny that surrounds us.[4] Generally, the separations are brought about and maintained for the sake of something else like independence, liberty, growth, invention, sisterhood, safety, health, or the practice of novel or heretical customs.[5] Often the separations in question

evolve, unpremeditated, as one goes one's way and finds various persons, institutions, or relationships useless, obstructive or noisome and leaves them aside or behind. Sometimes the separations are consciously planned and cultivated as necessary prerequisites or conditions for getting on with one's business. Sometimes the separations are accomplished or maintained easily, or with a sense of relief, or even joy; sometimes they are accomplished or maintained with difficulty, by dint of constant vigilance or with anxiety, pain or grief.

scious strategy of liberation. And, contrary to the image of the separatist as a cowardly escapist,[6] hers is the life and program which inspires the greatest hostility, disparagement, insult and confrontation and generally she is the one against whom economic sanctions operate most conclusively. The penalty for refusing to work with or for men is usually starvation (or, at the very least, doing without medical insurance[7]); and if one's policy of non-cooperation is more subtle, one's livelihood is still constantly on the line, since one is not a loyal

If you are doing something that is so strictly forbidden by the patriarchs, you must be doing something right.

Most feminists, probably all, practice some separation from males and male-dominated institutions. A separatist practices separation consciously, systematically, and probably more generally than the others, and advocates thorough and 'broad-spectrum' separation as part of the con-

partisan, a proper member of the team, or what have you. The penalties for being a lesbian are ostracism, harassment, and job insecurity or joblessness. The penalty for rejecting men's sexual advances is often rape, and perhaps even more often forfeit of such things as professional or job opportunities. And the separatist lives with the added burden of being assumed by many to be a morally depraved man-hating bigot. But there is a clue here: if you are doing something that is so strictly forbidden by the patriarchs, you must be doing something right.

There is an idea floating around in both feminist and anti-feminist literature to the effect that females and males generally live in a relation of parasitism,[8] a parasitism of the male on the female...that it is, generally speaking, the strength, energy, inspiration and nurturance of women that keeps men going, and not the strength, aggression, spirituality and hunting of men that keeps women going.

It is sometimes said that the parasitism goes the other way around, that the female is the parasite. But one can conjure the appearance of the female as a parasite only if one takes a very narrow view of human living—historically parochial, narrow with respect to class and race, and limited in conception of what are the necessary goods. Generally, the female's contribution to her material support is and always has been substantial; in many times and places it has been independently sufficient. One can and should distinguish between a partial and contingent material dependence created by a certain sort of money economy and class structure, and the nearly ubiquitous spiritual, emotional and material depen-

dence of males on females. Males presently provide, off and on, a portion of the material support of women, within circumstances apparently designed to make it difficult for women to provide them for themselves. But females provide and generally have provided for males the energy and spirit for living; the males are nurtured by the females. And this the males apparently cannot do for themselves, even partially.

The parasitism of males on females is, as I see it, demonstrated by the panic, rage and hysteria generated in so many of them by the thought of being abandoned by women. But it is demonstrated in a way that is perhaps more generally persuasive by both literary and sociological evidence. Evidence cited in Jesse Bernard's work in *The Future of Marriage* and in George Gilder's *Sexual Suicide* and *Men Alone* convincingly shows that males tend in shockingly significant numbers and in alarming degree to fall into mental illness, petty crime, alcoholism, physical infirmity, chronic unemployment, drug addiction and neurosis when deprived of the care and companionship of a female mate, or keeper. (While on the other hand, women without male mates are significantly healthier and happier than women with male mates.) And masculist literature is abundant with indications of male cannibalism, of males deriving essential sustenance from females. Cannibalistic imagery, visual and verbal, is common in

pornography: images likening women to food, and sex to eating. And, as documented in Millett's *Sexual Politics* and so many other feminist analyses of masculist literature, the theme of men getting high off beating, raping or killing women (or merely bullying them) is common. These interactions with women, or rather, these actions upon women, make men feel good, walk tall, feel refreshed, in*vigor*ated. Men are drained and depleted by their living by themselves and with and among other men, and are revived and refreshed, re-created, by going home and being served dinner, changing to clean clothes, having sex with the wife...or by dropping by the apartment of a woman friend to be served coffee or a drink and stroked in one way or another, or by picking up a prostitute for a quicky or for a dip in favorite sexual escape fantasies, or by raping refugees from their wars (foreign and domestic). The ministrations of women, be they willing or unwilling, free or paid for, are what restore in men the strength, will, and confidence to go on with what they call living.

If it is true that a fundamental aspect of the relations between the sexes is male parasitism, it might help to explain why certain issues are particularly exciting to patriarchal loyalists. For instance, in view of the obvious advantages of easy abortion to population control, to control of welfare rolls, and to ensuring sexual availability of women to men, it is a little surprising that the loyalists are so adamant and riled up in their objection to it. But look...

The fetus lives parasitically. It is a distinct animal surviving off the life (the blood) of another animal creature. It is incapable of surviving on its own resources, of independent nutrition; incapable even of symbiosis. If it is true that males live parasitically upon females, it seems reasonable to suppose that many of them and those loyal to them are in some way sensitive to the parallelism between their situation and that of the fetus. They could easily identify with the fetus. The woman who is free to see the fetus as a parasite[9] might be free to see the man as a parasite. The woman's willingness to cut off the life line to one parasite suggests a willingness to cut off the life line to another parasite. The woman who is capable (legally, psychologically, physically) of decisively, self-interestedly, independently rejecting the one parasite, is capable of rejecting with the same decisiveness and independence, the like burden of the other parasite. In the eyes of the other parasite, the image of the wholly self-determined abortion, involving not even a ritual submission to male veto power, is the mirror image of death.

Another clue here is that one line of argument against free and easy abortion is the slippery slope argument that if fetuses are to be freely dispensed with, old people will be next. Old people? Why are old people

Abortion seems to be the most publicly emotional and most physically dramatic ground on which the theme of separation and male parasitism is presently played out.

next? And why the great concern for them? Most old people are women, indeed, and patriarchal loyalists are not generally so solicitous of the welfare of any women. Why old people? Because, I think, in the modern patriarchal divisions of labor, old people too are parasites on women. The anti-abortion folks seem not to worry about wife-beating and wife-murder—there is no broad or emotional popular support for stopping these violences. They do not worry about murder and involuntary sterilization in prisons, nor murder in war, nor murder by pollution and industrial accidents. Either these are not real to them or they cannot identify with the victims; but anyway, killing in general is not what they oppose. They worry

about the rejection by *women*, at *women's discretion*, of something which lives parasitically on women. I suspect that they fret not because old people are next, but because men are next.

There are other reasons, of course, why patriarchal loyalists should be disturbed about abortion on demand, a major one being that it would be a significant form of female control of reproduction, and at least from certain angles it looks like the progress of patriarchy *is* the progress toward male control of reproduction, starting with possession of wives and continuing through the invention of obstetrics and the technology of extra-uterine gestation. Giving up that control would be giving up patriarchy. But such an objection to abortion is too abstract, and requires too historical a vision, to generate the hysteria there is now in the reaction against abortion. The hysteria is, I think, to be accounted for more in terms of a much more immediate and personal presentiment of ejection by the woman-womb.[10]

I discuss abortion here because it seems to me to be the most publicly emotional and most physically dramatic ground on which the theme of separation and male parasitism is presently played out. But there are other locales for this play. For instance,[11] women with newly raised consciousness tend to leave marriages and families, either completely through divorce, or partially, through unavailability of their cooking, housekeeping and sexual services. And women academics tend to become alienated from their colleagues and male mentors and no longer serve as sounding-board, ego booster, editor, mistress or proofreader. Many awakening women become celibate or lesbian, and the others become a very great deal more choosy about when, where and in what relationships they will have sex with men. And the men affected by these separations generally react with defensive hostility, anxiety, and guilt-tripping, not to mention descents into illogical argument which match and exceed their own most fanciful images of female irrationality. My claim is that they are very afraid because they depend very heavily upon the goods they re-

ceive from women, and these separations cut them off from those goods.

Male parasitism means that males *must have access* to women; it is the Patriarchal Imperative. But feminist no-saying is more than a substantial removal (re-direction, re-allocation) of goods and services because Access is one of the faces of Power. Female denial of male access to females substantially cuts off a flow of benefits, but it has also the form and full portent of assumption of power.

Differences of power are always manifested in asymmetrical access. The President of the United States has access to almost everybody for almost anything he might want of them, and almost nobody has access to him. The super-rich have access to almost everybody; almost nobody has access to them. The resources of the employee are available to the boss as the resources of the boss are not to the employee. The parent has unconditional access to the child's room; the child does not have similar access to the parent's room. Students adjust to professors' office hours; professors do not adjust to students' conference hours. The child is required not to lie; the parent is free to close out the child with lies at her discretion. The slave is unconditionally accessible to the master. Total power is unconditional access; total powerlessness is being unconditionally accessible. The creation and manipulation of power is constituted of

the manipulation and control of access.

All-woman groups, meetings, projects seem to be great things for causing controversy and confrontation. Many women are offended by them; many are afraid to be the one to announce the exclusion of men; it is seen as a device whose use needs much elaborate justification. I think this is because conscious and deliberate exclusion of men by women, from anything, is blatant insubordination, and generates in women fear of punishment and reprisal (fear which is often well-justified). Our own timidity and desire to avoid confrontations generally keep us from doing very much in the way of all-women groups and meetings. But when we do, we invariably run into the male champion who challenges our right to do it. Only a small minority of men go crazy when an event is advertised to be from women only—just one man tried to crash our women-only Rape Speak-Out, and only a few hid under the auditorium seats to try to spy on a women-only meeting at a NOW convention in Philadelphia. But these few are onto something their less rabid compatriots are missing. The woman-only meeting is a fundamental challenge to the structure of power. It is always the privilege of the master to enter the slave's hut. The slave who decides to exclude the master from her hut is declaring herself not a slave. The exclusion of men from the meeting not only deprives them of certain benefits (which they might survive without); it is a controlling of access, hence an assumption of power. It is not only mean, it is arrogant.

It becomes clearer now why there is always an off-putting aura of negativity about separation—one which offends the feminine Pollyanna in us and smacks of the purely defensive to the political theorist in us. It is this: First, when those who control access have made you totally accessible, your first act of taking control must be denying access, or must have denial of access as one of its aspects. This is not because you are charged up with (unfeminine or politically incorrect) negativity; it is because of the logic of the situation. When we start from a position of total accessibility there *must* be an aspect of no-saying, which is the beginning of control, in *every effective* act and strategy, the effective ones being precisely those which *shift power*, i.e., ones which involve manipulation and control of access. Second, whether or not one says 'no,' or withholds or closes out or rejects, on this occasion or that, the capacity and ability to say 'no' (with effect) is logically necessary to control. When we *are* in control of access to ourselves there will be some no-saying, and when we are most accustomed to it, when it is more common, an ordinary part of living, it will not seem so prominent, obvious, or strained...we will not strike ourselves or others as being particularly negative.

In this aspect of ourselves and our lives, we will strike ourselves pleasingly, as active beings with momentum of our own, with sufficient shape and structure, with sufficient integrity, to generate friction. Our experience of our no-saying will be an aspect of our experience of our definition.

When our feminist acts or practices have an aspect of separation we are assuming power by controlling access, and simultaneously by undertaking definition. The slave who excludes the master from her hut thereby declares herself *not a slave*. And *definition* is another face of power.

The powerful normally determine what is said and sayable. When the powerful label something or dub it or baptize it, the thing becomes what they call it. When the Secretary of Defense calls something a peace negotiation, for instnce, then whatever it is that he called a peace negotiation is an instance of negotiating peace. If the activity in question is the working out of terms of a trade-off of nuclear reactors and territorial redistributions, complete with arrangements for the resulting refugees, that is peacemaking. People laud it, and the negotiators get Nobel Peace Prizes for it. On the other hand, when I call a certain speech act a rape, my 'calling' it does not make it so. At best, I have to explain and justify and make clear exactly what it is about this speech act which is assaultive in just what way, and then the others acqui-

esce in saying the act was *like* rape or could figuratively be called a rape. My counter-assault will not be counted a simple case of self-defense. And what I called rejection of parasitism, they call the loss of the womanly virtues of compassion and 'caring.' And generally, when renegade women call something one thing and patriarchal loyalists call it another, the loyalists get their way.[12]

Women generally are not the people who do the defining, and we cannot from our isolation and powerlessness simply commence saying different things than others say and make it stick. There is a humpty-dumpty problem in that. But we are able to arrogate definition to ourselves when we re-pattern access. Assuming control of access, we draw new boundaries and create new roles and relationships. This, though it causes some strain, puzzlement and hostility, is to a fair extent within the scope of individuals and small gangs, as outright verbal redefinition is not, at least in the first instance.

One may see access as coming in two sorts, 'natural' and humanly arranged. A grizzly bear has what you might call natural access to the picnic basket of the unarmed human. The access of the boss to the personal services of the secretary is humanly arranged access; the boss exercises institutional power. It looks to me, looking from a certain angle, like institutions *are* humanly designed patterns of access—access to persons and their services. But institutions are artifacts of definition. In the case of intentionally and formally designed institutions, this is very clear, for the relevant definitions are explicitly set forth in by-laws and constitutions, regulations and rules. When one defines the term 'president,' one defines presidents in terms of what they can do and what is owed them by other offices, and 'what they can do' is a matter of their access to the services of others. Similarly, definitions of *dean*, *student*, *judge*, and *cop* set forth patterns of access, and definitions of *writer*, *child*, *owner*, and of course, *husband*, *wife*, and *man* and *girl*. When one changes the pattern of access, one forces new uses of words on those affected. The term 'man' has to shift in meaning when rape is no longer possible. When we take control of sexual access to us, of access to our nurturance and to our reproductive function, access to mothering and sistering, we redefine the word 'woman.' The shift of usage is pressed on others by a change in social reality; it does not await the recognition of our definitional authority.

When women separate (withdraw, break out, re-group, transcend, shove aside, step outside, migrate, say *no*) we are simultaneously controlling access and defining. We are doubly insubordinate, since neither of these is permitted. And access and definition are fundamental ingredients in the alchemy of power, so we are doubly, and radically, insubordinate.

If these, then, are some of the ways in which separation is at the heart of our struggle, it helps to explain why separation is such a hot topic. If there is one thing women are queasy about it is *actually taking power*. As long as one stops just short of that, the patriarchs will for the most part take an indulgent attitude. We are afraid of what will happen to us when we really frighten them. This is not an irrational fear. It is our experience in the movement generally that the defensiveness, nastiness, violence, hostility and irrationality of the reaction to feminism tend to correlate with the blatancy of the element of separation in the strategy or project which triggers the reaction. The separations involved in women leaving homes, marriages and boyfriends, separations from fetuses, and the separation of lesbianism are all pretty dramatic. That is, they are dramatic and blatant when perceived from within the framework provided by the patriarchal world-view and male parasitism. Matters pertaining to marriage and divorce, lesbianism, and abortion touch individual men (and their sympathizers) because they can feel the relevance of these to themselves—they can feel the threat that they might be next. Hence, heterosexuality, marriage, and motherhood, which are the institutions which most obviously and individually maintain female accessibility to males, form the core triad of anti-femi-

nist ideology, and all-woman spaces, all-woman organizations, all-woman meetings, all-woman classes, are outlawed, suppressed, harassed, ridiculed, and punished, in the name of that other fine and enduring patriarchal institution, Sex Equality.

To some of us these issues can almost seem foreign… strange ones to be occupying center stage. We are busily engaged in what seem to *us* our blatant insubordinations: living our own lives, taking care of ourselves and one another, doing our work, and in particular, telling it as we see it. Still, the original sin is the separation which these presuppose, and it is that, not our art or philosophy, not our speech-making, nor our 'sexual acts' (or abstinences), for which we will be persecuted, when worse comes to worst.

Notes

1 Before publication, I received many helpful comments from those who heard or read this paper. I have incorporated some, made notes of others. I got help from Carolyn Shafer in seeing the structure of it all, in particular, the connections among parasitism, access and definition.

2 Adrienne Rich: ' … *makes me question the whole of "courtesy" or "rudeness"—surely their constructs, since women become "rude" when we ignore or reject male obnoxiousness, while male "rudeness" is usually punctuated with the "Haven't you a sense of humor" tactic.*' Yes; me too. I embrace rudeness; our compulsive/compulsory politeness so often is

what coerces us into their 'fellow-ship.'

3 Help from Claudia Card.

4 *Ti-Grace Atkinson: Should give more attention here to our vulnerability to assault and degradation, and to separation as PROTECTION.* Okay, but then we have to re-emphasize that it has to be separation at *our* behest—we've had enough of their imposed separation for our 'protection.' (There's no denying that in my real-life life, protection and maintenance of places for healing are major motives for separation.)

5 Help from Chris Pierce and Sara Ann Ketchum. See 'Separatism and Sexual Relationships,' in *A Philosophical Approach to Women's Liberation*, eds. S. Hill and Weinzweig (Wadsworth, Belmont, California, 1978).

6 Answering Claudia Card.

7 Levity due to Carolyn Shafer.

8 I first noticed this when reading *Beyond God the Father*, by Mary Daly (Beacon Press, Boston, 1973). See also *Women's Evolution*, by Evelyn Reed (Pathfinder Press, New York, 1975) for rich hints about male cannibalism and male dependence.

9 *Caroline Whitbeck: Cross-cultural evidence suggests it's not the fetus that gets rejected in cultures where abortion is common, it is the role of motherhood, the burden, in particular, of 'illegitimacy'; where the institution of illegitimacy does not exist, abortion rates are pretty low.* This suggests to me that the woman's rejection of the fetus is even more directly a rejection of the male and his world than I had thought.

10 Claudia Card.

11 The instances mentioned are selected for their relevance to the lives of the particular women addressed in this talk. There are many other sorts of instances to be drawn from other sorts of women's lives.

12 This paragraph and the succeeding one are the passages which have provoked the most substantial questions from women who read the paper. One thing that causes trouble here is that I am talking from a stance or position that is ambiguous—it is located in two different and non-communicating systems of thought-action. *Re:* the patriarchy and the English language, there is general usage over which I/we do not have the control that elite males have (with the cooperation of all the ordinary patriarchal loyalists). *Re:* the new being and meaning which are being created now by lesbian feminists, we *do* have semantic authority, and, collectively, can and do define with effect. I think it is only by maintaining our boundaries through controlling concrete access to us that we can enforce on those who are not-us our definitions of ourselves, hence force on them *the fact of our existence* and thence open up the *possibility* of our having semantic authority with them. (I wrote some stuff that's relevant to this in the last section of my paper 'Male Chauvinism—A Conceptual Analysis.') Our unintelligibility to patriarchal loyalists is a source of pride and delight, in some contexts; but if we don't have an effect on their usage, while we continue, willy-nilly, to be subject to theirs, being totally unintelligible to them could be fatal. (A friend of mine had a dream where the women were meeting in a cabin at the edge of town, and they had a sort of inspiration through the vision of one of them that they should put a sign on the door which would connect with the patriarchs' meaning-system, for otherwise the men would be too curious/frightened about them and would break the

door down to get in. They put a picture of a fish on the door.) Of course, you might say that *being* intelligible to them might be fatal. Well, perhaps it's best to be in a position to make tactical decisions about when and how to be intelligible and unintelligible.

13 In (improbably enough) *Philosophy and Sex*, edited by Robert Baker & Frederick Ellison (Prometheus Books, Buffalo, New York, 1976). ■

No Dobermans Allowed:
A Dramatic Argument For Separatist Theatre
by Carolyn Gage

I am going to say what everybody knows, but nobody will talk about. The presence of men *always* constitutes a threat to women. And that threat is registered whether or not women talk about it.

To illustrate this point, I am going to present a fable. I call it "No Dobermans Allowed."

You live in Doberville. You have lived here all your life. You are a theatre person, and you are going to start a theatre. You want to make this a theatre for the people of Doberville.

Doberville is a town with a 5000-year-old history of being terrorized by vicious dobermans, who roam the streets at will, unrestrained and protected by outside laws. The people of Doberville are not allowed to kill them. You can go to jail for defending yourself or your children from doberman attack. Reports of attacks are frequently not investigated or not followed up, and in the rare instances when a dog is apprehended, he is usually released after a short period of confinement.

After centuries of this terrorism, the people of Doberville have developed a variety of creative, if unhealthy, coping strategies: Some deny the fact that the creatures bother them at all; al-

Originally published in *Trivia* (1989).

though these people seldom go out alone—never after dark—and they indulge in elaborate security measures. Others expend great amounts of energy defending the nature of the doberman, explaining that their violence towards Dobervillians must be a result of early puppyhood abuse. Others slap their children when they get bitten by them. A surprising number—the majority, in fact—have gone so far as to keep dobermans in their homes, to prove to themselves that these are not really a dangerous breed—a theory which is not borne out by their experience, unless they devote most of their energy to monitoring and appeasing the beasts. And, of course, they have no idea what the dogs do when they aren't around, because the children are trained to believe that attacks are a normal part of living with dobermans.

Most Dobervillians have built their culture and their identity around strategies of coping with dobermans. Survival itself being an unrealistic goal, they have difficulty envisioning life without doberman-dominated routines.

This is where your theatre is located, in the heart of Doberville.

Here is a profile of your audience: One out of four, while they were still children, have had their genitals attacked by dobermans, often by the family dog. One out of three members of the audience will be attacked by dobermans at some time in their life, sometimes by entire packs, and sometimes more than once. Some will be crippled, some will be killed. All will be psychically wounded. Dobervillians of color can expect to be attacked twice as often as white Dobervillians. One out of four who keep dobermans in their home will be attacked by them. More than fifty percent of the audience have had to change jobs at least once because of doberman attacks or threats of attack. *All* have been subject to intimidation. Ninety percent of Dobervillian income must go to feed the dobermans, the money coming out of the budget for children. The dobermans control access to 99% of the property, and because they do not clean up after themselves, they have rendered much of the environment unfit for living. Every single member of your audience will have risked doberman attack to get to the theatre, and they will risk it again when they go home. Once home, there is no guarantee they will not be attacked or killed in their bed.

This is your audience.

You love Doberville. You want to give them a theatre which will substantially improve the quality of their lives. The question is, what kind of theatre will best serve this end?

The first priority seems to be to create a space where the Dobervillians can relax. You do this for a while. You produce lots of musicals where people sing love songs about finding just the right doberman. You produce lots of zany comedies about the complications which arise from stepping in doberman poop. These are enthusiastically received. The audiences laugh uproariously. They go away refreshed. Box office flourishes.

But over time, you begin to feel uneasy. Is this the theatre you want to give to Doberville? Is it helping them live happier lives, or is it just giving them an escape hatch, an outlet for their tensions, which enables them to tolerate the horrifying conditions in Doberville? Could your theatre actually be contributing to the dominance of the dobermans?

You decide that what you have been doing is not honest. You decide to stop participating in the conspiracy of silence about life in Doberville.

Also, you have become bored with subjects and plots which have so little connection with your own reality. You live in Doberville, too, and the "hot spot," the topic that makes everybody jump, is dobermans. The real drama in this town is the tremendous volcano of repressed feelings about doberman violence. You can't avoid it, even when you try. As a serious artist, you have to address it. So you tighten your belt. Your theatre will now be less comfortable, less popular, less profitable. You decide to produce *No Dobermans Allowed*.

Now the question becomes how to produce it. You could have a lot of people talking about their feelings or narrating the incidents, but have all the doberman attacks take place offstage. But this feels like another lie. Everyone in Doberville pretends that the dobermans are offstage somewhere doing things to other people. No. You need to put the action on stage.

Now you have a new problem. How can you use real dobermans in the play? If you have an audience who are so terrorized and so invested in denying their feelings, won't they seize up with the same fear when they see a real doberman on the stage? Won't they still deny their feelings? Won't they automatically revert to survival skills instead of watching the play? Won't they sit in the audience and try to evaluate the attitude of the animal, its proximity, the presence or absence of restraints, the amount of time since its last meal? Isn't the live doberman so much a fetish that it will be as distracting as a live woman would have been on Shakespeare's stage? Shouldn't the dog be kept off for the same reason?

And then, too, can a doberman really be trained to act? Does the doberman's natural bestial instincts preclude it from doing anything that doesn't serve its immediate needs? Won't the subject of the play become the needs of the doberman the minute you put the doberman on stage? And is it fair to ask Dobervillian actors to work with these creature who have made their lives misery?

So you have a problem. The only way to keep dobermans in your play is to use Dobervillians to play them.

At first this seems out of the question. Who

will believe that a Dobervillian is a dog? And how can you ask a Dobervillian to assume such a degrading role?

Actually, the answers to these questions open a world of new dimensions. Who knows the nature of the doberman better than the victim who has had to make a lifelong study of the habits and temperaments of the breed? The doberman perceives itself always in heroic terms, always defending its territory. The Dobervillian, however, has a superior perspective on the dog's behavior, and understands the greed and bestiality, the narrow interests, the destructive nature which motivate the animal. It is this understanding of motivation which is the foundation of true acting.

As to the question of appearance, it would be demeaning to ask a Dobervillian to assume the gross physical distortion or the odious facial characteristics of the dog. This is not necessary. In live theatre, the audience will accept a convention once it is established and consistently applied. A Dobervillian performing the role of a doberman is no more artificial than the presence of a cardboard tree, or the accelerated passage of time between scene changes. The Dobervillian actor need not growl or pee on the table legs to get across the essential qualities of the doberman as required by the action in the play.

Now the problem becomes one of finding the actors who would be willing to play dogs. Certainly the roles are unappetizing, the behaviors of the animals being abhorrent and the range of emotions primitive. But there is an historical precedent for taking on the roles of an enemy in ritualistic dances. In assuming the persona of the animal, the dancer achieves a symbolic dominance which is shared vicariously by the other members of the tribe. The actors can approach the part as a form of exorcism.

And so the curtain goes up on *No Dobermans Allowed*. You enact the truth about life in Doberville. You put the experiences and emotions hidden in every heart up on stage for all of Doberville to see. Make no mistake, this does not make you popular.

People accuse you of distortion, of using the stage as a platform for your own radical opinions. Kinder critics speculate that you must have been traumatized by an unusually vicious doberman at an early age. This is an interesting theory, especially since this kind of trauma is routine in Doberville, but in fact, the most severely victimized Dobervillians are the ones who live with the most denial. Chances are your critics have suffered or are suffering more than you. In any event, they will review the psychology of the playwright instead of the content of the play. Your play will be called felinist, because you are obviously lobbying for cats.

But the point for which you are most attacked is the one you least expected: The people of Doberville will be up in arms protesting your policy of not letting dobermans into the audience.

It never occurred to you that people would want to sit next to a doberman and see a play about how terrible dobermans are. And yet this is the point for which they will picket, they will smash your windows, they will spray-paint your building, they will call you a bigot, a terrorist, *a worse threat than the dobermans!* Actors will quit under pressure from friends, stagehands will strike, papers will not carry your ads, local art agencies will withdraw funding. Even the strongest advocates for truth in theatre will argue until they are hoarse for the right—no, the *need*—for the dobermans to be in the theatre. How else will they learn about themselves?

In vain you will point out that the presence of the dobermans in the theatre will negate everything you are trying to say on stage. How can you do a credible production of *No Dobermans Allowed* if you let a pack of them into the theatre?

You will try to explain that there has never been a theatre to tell the truth about Doberville in 5000 years, because everyone has had to live with the lie that they are not bothered by the presence of dobermans. If you opened the house to the dogs, you would be making that same insidious lie the foundation of your theatre. You would be asking Dobervillians yet again to pretend they will feel the same sitting next to a Dobervillian as they do to a doberman.

You will hear mountains of evidence in favor of genuinely domesticated dobermans. You will hear of dobermans who are able to tear open their own bags of dog food and feed themselves every other night. You will hear of dobermans who lick the baby clean, scrupulously avoiding the genital area, of course. You will hear a million and one stories about how Dobervillians have also been known to abuse each other, how some dobermans are better than Dobervillians. You will be amazed at what you hear.

What can I tell you? A theatre of truth is a revolution. Doberville is hardly in a position to revolt. They will not love you for what you are doing. Many will go home to their doberman and think how much you are missing by not letting them into your theatre. You will be blacklisted and boycotted. You will certainly be set upon by the dogs.

Press on. Open your theatre, no dobermans allowed. Some will come. Some will come more than once. Some will get rid of their dobermans. Some will not. Some will have an uneasy week and then get on with survival. Some will work with you. Some will work on their own projects.

The important thing to remember is that the resistance you meet will be in direct proportion to the people's need for a theatre with no dobermans allowed.

♀♀

This analysis, of course, oversimplifies the problems of men in a women's theatre. Men are not dogs. They are the sons and fathers of women. More than terrorists, they are the colonizers of women who administrate an elaborate system of government which offers token protection to women while it insures ongoing access to our resources.

A women's theatre, that is, a theatre for women which serves our interests, has a special obligation to exclude men, both from the cast and from the audience. Removing men, like compliance with fire codes, not only guarantees the safety of the women in the audience, but frees us from conditions which might give rise to concerns about our safety, concerns which will distract us and detract from our experience of the performance.

Separatism is not an end in itself, but a means to an end. Women must be allowed to experience our own lives. This is not possible in a culture propagated by men. It is also not possible in an environment which presupposes the equality of men and women. Our experiences are not equal, and a liberation movement which hopes to achieve equality must begin with acknowledgment of this fact.

The real separatism is women's division from ourselves, caused by our indoctrination into a culture which does not reflect our experience or serve our interests. Women's integration depends on our ability to separate ourselves from men. ■

Walking Our Boundaries

by Audre Lorde

This first bright day has broken
the back of winter.
We rise from war
to walk across the earth
around our house
both stunned that sun can shine so brightly
after all our pain
Cautiously we inspect our joint holding.
A part of last year's garden still stands
bracken
one tough missed okra pod clings to the vine
a parody of fruit cold-hard and swollen
underfoot
one rotting shingle
is becoming loam.

I take your hand beside the compost heap
glad to be alive and still
with you
we talk of ordinary articles
with relief
while we peer upward
each half-afraid
there will be no tight buds started
on our ancient apple tree
so badly damaged by last winter's storm
knowing

it does not pay to cherish symbols
when the substance
lies so close at hand
waiting to be held
your hand
falls off the apple bark
like casual fire
along my back
my shoulders are dead leaves
waiting to be burned
to life.

The sun is watery warm
our voices
seem too loud for this small yard
too tentative for women
so in love
the siding has come loose in spots
our footsteps hold this place
together
as our place
our joint decisions make the possible
whole.
I do not know when
we shall laugh again
but next week
we will spade up another plot
for this spring's seeding.

From *The Black Unicorn* (New York:
Norton, 1978)

a mid-life ritual

by Judith Barrington

Introduction

Earlier this year, when I asked my lover what she wanted to do to celebrate her fortieth birthday, she replied: "I want a ritual." I was horrified, being one of those women who cringes at the idea of rituals and is embarrassed at solemn ceremonies, but I agreed to create a ritual for her anyway, although I had never done such a thing before.

We spent a lot of time discussing what, to her, was the significance of a fortieth birthday: What would she want to celebrate? What would she need help with? What aspects of this moment in her life would be symbolized at the ceremony? I jotted down a few notes as we talked about growing up, letting go of families of origin, taking responsibility for our lives—not just leave it behind. We thought about dying, being old, the possibilities of getting sick, and who we would want with us in the future. We reminded ourselves, not for the first time, that we are now among those "older women" we had so blithely talked about for the past twenty years. We agreed that forty symbolized some kind of transition.

Then I went to work on my own resistance. I couldn't write a ritual and comfortably present it to a group of participants if I found the whole

idea embarrassing. After some careful thought, I realized that my response to many of the women's rituals I had witnessed was similar to my response to any kind of religious ceremony: the idea of "worship" made me angry.

I had rejected the whole idea of religion even before becoming a feminist, and, as a feminist, I had steered clear of the spiritual alternatives women were exploring. After some careful thought, I realized it wasn't the idea of spirituality itself that I disliked, but the "worshipful" aspects of organized religions that seemed to permeate even the new, supposedly feminist ceremonies: I was uncomfortable with the notion of a "higher power," no matter who or what it was.

I *did*, however, like the idea of commemoration, celebration, and, in general, the ritual marking of occasions which are of importance to us individually and as a community, as a lesbian, I had been well aware of how alienated I felt from most events ritually observed by the mainstream world.

What follows is the outline of an event I created for Ruth's fortieth birthday—one in which I tried to emphasize a thoughtful observance of the occasion, a ritual manifestation of what it meant, and an opportunity for every woman to participate in a manner that felt comfortable to her. There were major parts of the ritual in which the participants contributed their own feelings and words, and other parts which were specifically

From *Common Lives/Lesbian Lives* 25 (Winter 1988) and *History and Geography*. Eighth Mountain Press, Portland, OR, 1989.

geared to Ruth's life. I have, therefore, tried to present the skeleton of the ritual, so that other women might personalize it for a different occasion, or simply be inspired enough to create their own. The parts in square brackets describe our particular group's responses.

Ruth's Fortieth Birthday Ritual

THE SETTING: a large room arranged with a circle of twenty chairs. Inside the circle, in front of one of the chairs is a small table with a tray on which are twenty small candles. At the other side of the circle, in front of the opposite chair is another similar table with twenty more candles. Behind the narrator's chair is a tape player with speakers. Next to her chair is a slide projector on a table, set up to project on to the opposite wall. Two of the chairs are spaced more widely for the two musicians who will play flute and guitar.

Ruth and the narrator welcome the eighteen women as they arrive. There is no formal opening to the ritual—women stand in groups and talk, waiting for everyone to arrive.

When everyone is present, the narrator switches on the tape player. Women gradually stop talking and listen to the tape.

THE TAPE: a humorous introduction, created as a collage.[1] It opens with some attention-getting chords and then presents a satirical set of "interviews" with "the woman on the street" on the subject of rituals. The "interviewer" is the narrator, who poses questions such as "what kind of a woman goes to rituals?" and "what do you think of rituals?" and the answers are pieces cut from speeches, poems, and other spoken recordings by various feminist writers and activists. For example:

INTERVIEWER: What kind of woman goes to a ritual?

INTERVIEWEE (voice of Judy Grahn): She hides her bad brown tooth behind a wicked smile.[2]

[Gradually, the assembled women start to laugh, nervously at first, but then more freely as they realize this is not like laughing in church. Soon they begin guessing out loud at the voices. By the end of the five-minute tape, everyone has found a seat, and Ruth is seated in one of the chairs with a table of candles in front of it.]

NARRATOR: I'd like to welcome you all to this ritual, which is actually a rite of passage. You will see there are two sets of candles inside our circle: the twenty candles in front of Ruth represent the first part of her life, and the other twenty represent the second part. This ritual is about her passage from the first to the second, and our task is to help her do two things: first, to make a safe crossing into the second part of her life, and, second, to integrate the two parts, so that she can take with her what is valuable from the first. There is a crossing and also a joining—which will be the themes of our celebration.

We will begin by focusing on the first part of Ruth's life. Each woman is asked to light a candle and to recall some quality or aspect of Ruth which she appreciates. At the same time each woman will introduce herself to the group.

The lights in the room are dimmed.

Each woman goes, in turn, to the tray and lights a candle, telling the group her name and something she likes about Ruth. [There is some hilarity, some seriousness, and quite a bit of interaction between each woman and Ruth, as well as among the women in the circle.] Ruth lights the twentieth candle, and thanks everyone, as the music begins.

MUSICA FEMINA: "Night Breezes" by Judith Markowitz.[3]

NARRATOR: To stay focussed on the first part of Ruth's life, I'd like to show you some highlights from that journey.

[The first three slides are of Ruth as a baby and a young girl—slides made from her baby pictures.[4]]

458 ～～～～

NARRATOR: At this point I'd like to call on the woman who has known Ruth longest of all us here—her sister, Barbara, who has known her for thirty-seven years.[5]

BARBARA tells some stories about Ruth as a little girl, and shares some recollections of their childhood together. [Other women ask questions and participate in the discussion.]

The narrator shows twelve more slides, ranging through adolescence, college and after, up to the recent past. (This takes quite a long time, with much discussion, laughter, and questioning.)

NARRATOR: We have now reached the present time: Ruth's fortieth year. It is our task now, at the center of this ceremony to help our friend cross that divide, and help her, too, integrate her past and future lives.

We will use a chant to help us in this task, and I'd like to dedicate the chant to the goddess Hecate—the goddess often associated with crossroads. Hecate, originally the triple goddess who ruled heaven, earth, and the underworld, was said to guard all three-way crossroads. Offerings were left to her at roadside shrines on nights of the full moon. Her familiars were dogs.[6] Much later, in rejecting the old wisdom and Hecate in particular, witches were particularly feared at crossroads, and it became a tradition to bury criminals and suicides in unhallowed ground at a crossroads, where, clergymen said, they would walk abroad as ghosts.

ALL THE WOMEN PRESENT form two lines, joining hands to form an archway. The lines are a progression by age, with the youngest women at one end and the oldest at the other. [At our celebration this put Ruth's six-year-old niece at one end, and a friend in her fifties at the other.]

The narrator starts the chant and all the women join in until familiar with the rhythm. When the chant is underway, Ruth slowly passes through the arch from the youngest to the oldest. She then comes back and passes through again, for as long as the chant goes on.

Chant

ALL:
>Crossing and joining
>>and joining and crossing
>and crossing and joining
>>and joining and crossing.

NARRATOR:
>There's gaining and losing
>>there's childhood and older;
>there's learning to let go
>>and how to be bolder.
>The past and the future—
>>a chasm between
>the place we will go to
>>and where we have been.

ALL:
>Crossing and joining
>>and joining and crossing
>and crossing and joining
>>and joining and crossing.

NARRATOR:
>Sometimes it's hard to
>>decide if this chasm's
>the end of the beginning
>>or beginning the end.
>One says you're losing
>>the promise of childhood
>the other's a trail—
>>you can't see round the bend.

ALL:
>Crossing and joining, etc.

NARRATOR:
>There's crossing alone
>>though your friends are beside you,
>there's picking your path
>>and there's falling through space.
>Though sometimes you want to
>>turn back or to hide, you
>are crossing each day
>>to another new place.

ALL:
> Crossing and joining, etc.

[This part of the chant can be extended while the archway is re-formed with the oldest and youngest participants holding hands and women who were previously at opposite ends of the line paired up: thus the ages are integrated.]

NARRATOR:
> The past and the future
>> are coming together.
> The past and the future
>> are one and the same.
> They meet and are joined
>> whenever, wherever
> you know who you are
>> and you sing out your name.

ALL:
> Crossing and joining, etc. (Continue as long as you like.)

~~~~~~~~~~~~~~~~~~~~~~~~~~~~~~~~~~~~

At the end of the chant, everyone sits down again, but now Ruth is seated in the chair with the unlit candles in front of it.

NARRATOR: These candles are symbolic of the second part of Ruth's life. Each of us will light a candle and give Ruth a gift in words or a wish to take with her.

One by one, as they choose, women light a candle and wish Ruth something for the second part of her life.

MUSICA FEMINA: "Bay Bridge" by Janna MacAuslan[7]

While the music is playing, Ruth moves both sets of burning candles together in the center of the circle, to make a group of forty. The ritual ends with a toast and everyone eats. ■

Notes

1 Of course, the tape could be made up of anything. Its purpose was to lead into the ritual in a way that cut through everyone's expectations—whether they expected solemnity, schmalz, or something else. It should make women laugh and break the tension.

2 From "The Common Woman" (II Ella in a square apron, along Highway 80) in *The Work of a Common Woman* by Judy Grahn (The Crossing Press, 1978).

3 Kristan Aspen (flute) and Janna MacAuslan (guitar) form the duo Musica Femina, which researches and plays classical music by women. They are ideal for every woman's ritual, but if you can't get them, use your own local musicians, or use Musica Femina's cassette tapes (available from women's music distributors or direct from P.O. Box 15121, Portland, OR 97215).

4 Obviously, you will have to be creative about what you can use for visual highlights from your subject's life. If you cannot get hold of photographs, you could use objects which have a long history or special significance in her life.

5 You can substitute any woman present who has known the subject for a long time. It might be a relative or an old friend who plays this special role.

6 You can dedicate any part of the ritual to any woman you think appropriate, and include details which the woman you are celebrating will particularly appreciate.

7 The music was carefully chosen to fit with the mood of the ritual. This piece by Janna MacAuslan was inspired by crossing the Bay Bridge in San Francisco and seemed particularly appropriate for a rite of passage.

Letter to the Editor September, 1972

by Vernita M. Gray

lavender editors
and
lesbian sisters:

in the last issue of
lavender
there was an article
which disturbed me greatly

in my opinion
this article
was plagiarized

not the wording
but the style
a plagiarism of a style
which is used by black writers

as a black person
this does not shock
or surprise me
as
behind most great black innovators
there is always
some white imitator

the article i am referring to
"a pickle used to be a cucumber
            and other lesbian some-such...."
was to me
a pickle

it took me quite awhile
to read this article in its
entirety
and not because i read slow
but

the article was like reading
a bunch of sentences that were
stuck together without any punctuation;
it lacked enough connectives to connect it
together

example

"and she's right which leads me to my
article last issue about how straight people
will kill us off some women didn't like it
that's an understatement lightfoot thinks
I'm ready to take up guns and kill off the
straight people..."

it took me
awhile to figure out
just what lightfoot thought
or what i think she thinks
but i still do not Know

but with
"double messages being here to stay"
it is difficult to Know
anything

but i do Know
that i don't feel
"that those pricks

with their insane mouthings"
did in raella

or as mick jagger said
"i shouted out
who killed the kennedys
when after all it was you and me"

but i do Know
that if some sister gives only two bits
to the treasury
i have some responsibility to her
cause those two bits helped

and i do Know
that no white man would
call a black panther
a lazy nigger
cause even white men know
there ain't no such thing
as a lazy panther
and the only way to deal with an animal
is to shoot it
and when was the last time
a lesbian was shot on the street?
or as she slept?*

and by the time
i got to my instructions
"now burn this and memorize yourself"
i was burning

cause the word memorize
in relation to the self
is to me an absurdity
as memorize
is derived from a latin word (memoria)
and latin makes me think of the
holy roman catholic church
and the catholic church
is full of people memorizing

and never thinking   learning   being
and loving yourself

and the headquarters
of the roman church
is in europe
not africa

which brings me back
to the beginning
my accusation of plagiarism

there is no   way
that i
a black woman poet
could use the style

of a white woman poet
to write poetry
and there is also
no way a white woman
can use a black style

(a beautiful example, that most black sisters
and some white sisters should be able to relate
to, is a punctuationless article written by
margaret e. sloan which appears in the second
edition of Ms.)

in sisterhood,
vernita m. gray

*This is a reference to the assassinations of prominent
Black Panther Party members Fred Hampton and
Mary Clark. They were killed as they slept in a sur-
prise midnight raid on their apartment by fourteen
Chicago police officers assigned to the State's
Attorney's office on December 4, 1969.

Originally published in *Lavender Woman* and Michal
Brody's *Are We There Yet?* (1985)

I Am Not Your Princess

by Chrystos

Sandpaper between two cultures which tear
one another apart I'm not
a means by which you can reach spiritual understanding or even
learn to do beadwork
I'm only willing to tell you how to make fry bread
1 cup flour, spoon of salt, spoon of baking powder
Stir   Add milk or water or beer until it holds together
Slap each piece into rounds   Let rest
Fry in hot grease until golden
This is Indian food
only if you know that Indian is a government word
which has nothing to do with our names for ourselves
I won't chant for you
I admit no spirituality to you
I will not sweat with you or ease your guilt with fine turtle tales
I will not wear dancing clothes to read poetry or
explain hardly anything at all
I don't think your attempts to understand us are going to work so
I'd rather you left us in whatever peace we can still
scramble up   after all you continue to do
If you send me one more damn flyer about how to heal myself
for $300 with special feminist counseling
I'll probably set fire to something
If you tell me one more time that I'm wise I'll throw up on you
Look at me
See my confusion   loneliness   fear   worrying about all our
struggles to keep   what little is left for us
Look at my heart   not your fantasies   Please don't ever
again tell me about your Cherokee great-great grandmother
Don't assume I know every other Native Activist

in the world personally   That I even know names of all the tribes
or can pronounce names I've never heard
or that I'm expert at the peyote stitch

If   you ever
again tell me
how strong I am
I'll lay down on the ground & moan so you'll see
at last   my human weakness   like your own
I'm not strong   I'm scraped
I'm blessed with life while so many I've known are dead
I have work to do   dishes to wash   a house to clean
There is no magic
See my simple cracked hands which have washed the same things
you wash   See my eyes dark with fear in a house by myself
late at night   See that to pity me or to adore me
are the same
1 cup flour, spoon of salt, spoon of baking powder, liquid to hold
Remember this is only my recipe   There are many others
Let me rest
here
at least

especially for Dee Johnson

In *Not Vanishing*. Vancouver: Press Gang Publishers, 1988.

She Who Would Despise Me

by Janice Gould

I want to convince her—
she who would despise me—
that I am loved.
If I emerged from the womb
neither male nor female,
yet somehow both, life
gifted me with two spirits.
I came burdened by my own dream.

I want to persuade her—
she who would despise me—
that I am kind.
I would take her
to the edge of the river,
and there among the willows,
salt bush and olives,
show her my hands,
ask for her reply.

I want to teach her—
she who would despise me—
not to fear my face,
nor the soles of my feet,
nor my hair knotted by the wind.
This body, pocked by a distasteful history,
bears the marks of struggle.

(Then will she weep and ask
for my tenderness and blessing.
Then will I release her heart
like a fallen bird I've nursed back to
health.)

I want to show her—
she who would despise me—
that my people are snake, jaguar,
and quetzalcoatl.
When they moved north
so many years ago,
they conceived a new language
and planted their navel cords
among oaks and alders.
Such miracles occur.

And the legacy I am left with—
these staring eyes,
my yellow skin,
my forked tail,
is nothing to despise.
I stutter on the soft bilabials
of my mother tongue,
but I never forget
who I am,
nor the center of my righteous
and extraordinary power.

469

For the white person who wants to know how to be my friend

by Pat Parker

The first thing you do is to forget that i'm Black.
Second, you must never forget that i'm Black.

You should be able to dig Aretha,
but don't play her every time i come over.
And if you decide to play Beethoven—don't tell me
his life story. They made us take music appreciation too.

Eat soul food if you like it, but don't expect me
to locate your restaurants
or cook it for you.

And if some Black person insults you,
mugs you, rapes your sister, rapes you,
rips your house or is just being an ass—
please, do not apologize to me
for wanting to do them bodily harm.
It makes me wonder if you're foolish.

And even if you really believe Blacks are better lovers than
whites—don't tell me. I start thinking of charging stud fees.

In other words—if you really want to be my friend—*don't*
make a labor of it. I'm lazy. Remember.

From *Movement In Black*. Ithaca, NY: Firebrand Books, 1978.

© 1987 by Sudie Rakusin

Do You Remember Me?

by Barbara Macdonald

I am less than five feet high and, except that I may have shrunk a quarter of an inch or so in the past few years, I have viewed the world from this height for sixty-five years. I have taken up some space in the world; I weigh about a hundred and forty pounds and my body is what my mother used to call dumpy. My mother didn't like her body and so, of course, didn't like mine. "Dumpy" was her word and just as I have had to keep the body, somehow I have had to keep the word—thirty-eight inch bust, no neck, no waistline, fat hips—that's dumpy.

My hair is grey, white at the temples, with only a little of the red cast of earlier years showing through. My face is wrinkled and deeply lined. Straight lines have formed on the upper lip as though I spent many years with my mouth pursed. This has always puzzled me and I wonder what years those were and why I can't remember them. My face has deep lines that extend from each side of the nose down the face past the corners of my mouth. My forehead is wide, and the lines across my forehead and between my eyes are there to testify that I was often puzzled and bewildered for long periods of time about what was taking place in my life. My cheekbones are high and become more noticeably so as my face is drawn further and further down. My chin is small for such a large head and below the chin the skin hangs in a loose vertical fold from my chin all the way down my neck, where it meets a horizontal scar. The surgeon who made the scar said that the joints of my neck were worn out from looking up so many years. For all kinds of reasons, I seldom look up to anyone or anything anymore.

My eyes are blue and my gaze is usually steady and direct. But I look away when I am struggling with some nameless shame, trying to disclaim parts of myself. My voice is low and my speech sometimes clipped and rapid if I am uncomfortable; otherwise, I have a pleasant voice. I like the sound of it from in here where I am. When I was younger, some people, lovers mostly, enjoyed my singing, but I no longer have the same control of my voice and sing only occasionally now when I am alone.

My hands are large and the backs of my hands begin to show the brown spots of aging. Sometimes lately, holding my arms up reading in bed or lying with my arms clasped around my lover's neck, I see my arm with the skin hanging loosely from my forearm and cannot believe that it is really my own. It seems disconnected from me; it is someone else's, it is the arm of an old

From *Look Me in the Eye: Old Women, Aging and Ageism* by Barbara Macdonald with Cynthia Rich. 1983. SF: Spinsters/Aunt Lute. Originally published in *Sinister Wisdom* (1978).

woman. It is the arm of such old women as I myself have seen, sitting on benches in the sun with their hands folded in their laps; old women I have turned away from. I wonder now, how and when these arms I see came to be my own—arms I cannot turn away from.

I live in Cambridge now in an apartment in an old Victorian kind of house with a woman I love. Above us are two men, one studying law and the other political science; and above them lives a single woman whose lover comes and stays for a few days and then he leaves to return again in a few weeks. The men who live above us are uncomfortable when they meet me in the hall, greet me without looking at me and are always in flight when we meet. The woman on the top floor does not engage with me in any way but visits with the students just below her. I wonder sometimes whether it is my lesbianism they cannot deal with or whether it is my age they cannot deal with. Usually, I conclude they do not deal with people who cannot give them something— and there is nothing I would give them in any way to aid their survival. The law student will soon be endorsing laws that will limit even further my power in the world, and the political science instructor can do me nothing but harm. The woman who lives above the men has dinner with them occasionally, and waits to see what power she can align herself with in any tenant dispute.

In the world beyond the house where we live are students riding bicycles and walking along the brick streets or lying on the grass on the Common in summer. As we walk along the avenue, we hear the conversations of the young women telling each other about Him. The pubs along the avenue are filled with the young men the girls are talking about and building their plans for the future around. But the young men in the pubs are together, without the women, laughing loudly, taking up a great deal of space, and being served by young women anxious to please.

In contrast to the young walking through the streets, there are a few old people, moving slowly, bent over. They are mostly women, alone, carrying home a few groceries in a sack.

There are a few old men. The old women do not enter the pubs; they do not drink beer, nor do they spend their evenings talking and laughing, and no young girls are waiting on them anxious to please.

But if you leave Harvard Square and walk down Cambridge Street to Inman Square—there you will find the beginnings of a small women's community. There is New Words, a bookstore of women's literature on feminism, lesbianism, the history of women. Almost any book at random confirms some of who I am and who I once was. But it is seldom that a woman past fifty ever enters the place; whenever I go I am the oldest woman there.

And if you walk on beyond New Words, you come to Bread and Roses, a women's restaurant, where the women who cook for you and serve you confirm your right to be in the world as a woman, as much do the posters on the wall, posters of Virginia Woolf, Mary Wollstonecraft, Gertrude Stein, Emma Goldman. The food is good; and although groups of women sit together explaining, talking, laughing, there is not the struggle for space and the struggle to be heard that there is in the pubs along our avenue. And if you stay after supper on a Sunday, there may be a reading by some woman writer, or a film on Gertrude Stein or Georgia O'Keeffe, or perhaps a film of Lillian Hellman's will be shown. But though all this is there to confirm the lives of women, still there is no woman there my age. I enter the restaurant and the film room always aware that I am the oldest woman there. I am glad the women's community has a beginning and is there to support women but I am aware that it is not there to confirm who *I* am. The younger women there have no place in their heads to fit me into, have no idea what I come for as no other woman my age comes, yet I am nearest the age of most of the women on their posters from whom they draw their support.

Sometimes I feel the young women are supported by other young women on the basis of a promise or a hope of who they may become, but that they demand that I somehow have already proved my right to be taken in. Sometimes I feel like the only way I'll really get into Bread and Roses—alive in the eyes of the young women—is dead, on a poster.

Wherever we go, Cynthia and I, to the pubs, to the theatre to see "The Word is Out," to hear Adrienne Rich or Olga Broumas, Mary Daly, Kate Millett, or to some meeting of the lesbian caucus of NOW, I am always the oldest woman.

I keep wondering where everybody else is. Where are the friends I drank beer with in the fifties? Where are the young women I slept with in the thirties and forties? Did they never grow old? Did they never reach sixty-five along with me? Sometimes, alone on the streets, I look about me and feel there has been some kind of catastrophe from which only I have been spared. Sometimes in desperation I search out some woman my own age on the street, or at some bus stop, or in some laundromat, to ask her, "Do you remember me? Did we drink beer together in the pubs in Seattle? Did we sleep together, you and I, in the thirties when there were no jobs and never enough to eat and love carried the whole burden to see us through?" But there is no look of recognition in her eyes. I see instead fear, I see that she is paralyzed with fear, that she does not know where my friends and lovers have gone, that she cannot remember who it was she used to be. She wants to show me pictures of her grandchildren as though all of her answers could be found there—among the living. And I go down the street and I know there has been a catastrophe, a holocaust of my generation of women, and I have somehow been spared.

My feeling of having been spared is confirmed in the way that no one seems to be expecting me anywhere. Even if I go into a local shop to buy clothes, I am always greeted with the question, "Is this for yourself?" as though I must be buying for someone else, as though I didn't buy clothes for myself; as though I must have some supply somewhere in an old trunk, left me by my mother, there waiting for me to wear when I reached the right age.

But I have grown to like living in Cambridge. I like the sharp lines of the reality of my life here. The truth is I like growing old. Oh, it isn't that I don't feel at moments the sharp irrevocable knowledge that I have finally grown old. That is evident every time I stand in front of the bathroom mirror and brush my teeth. I may begin as I often do, wondering if those teeth that are so much a part of myself, teeth I've clenched in anger all my life, felt with my own tongue with a feeling of possession, as a cat licks her paw lovingly just because it is hers—wondering, will these teeth always be mine? Will they stay with me loyally and die with me, or will they desert me before the Time comes? But I grow dreamy brushing my teeth and find myself, unaware, planning—as I always have when I brush my teeth—that single-handed crossing I plan to make. From East to West, a last stop in the Canaries and then the trade winds. What will be the best time of year? What boat? How much sail? I go over again the list of supplies, uninterrupted until some morning twinge in my left shoulder reminds me with uncompromising regret that I will never make that single-handed crossing—probably. That I have waited too long. That there is no turning back.

But I always say probably. Probably I'll never make that single-handed crossing. Probably, I've waited too long. Probably, I can't turn back now. But I leave room now, at sixty-five, for the unexpected. That was not always true of me. I used to feel I was in a kind of linear race with life and time. There were no probably's, it was a now or never time of my life. There were landmarks placed by other generations, and I have to arrive on time or fail in the whole race. If I didn't pass—if the sixth grade went on to the seventh grade without me, I would be one year behind for the rest of my life. If I graduated from high school in 1928, I had to graduate from college in 1932. When I didn't graduate from college until 1951, it took me another twenty years to realize the preceding twenty years weren't lost. But now I begin to see that I may get to have the whole thing, and that no experience longed for is really going to be missed.

"I like growing old." I say it to myself with

surprise. I had not thought that it could be like this. There are days of excitement when I feel almost a kind of high with the change taking place in my body, even though I know the inevitable course my body is taking will lead to debilitation and death. I say to myself frequently in wonder, "This is my body doing this thing." I cannot stop it, I don't even know what it is doing, I wouldn't know how to direct it. My own body is going through a process that only my body knows about. I never grew old before; never died before. I don't really know how it's done. I wouldn't know where to begin, and God knows, I certainly wouldn't know when to begin—for no time would be right. And then I realize, lesbian or straight, I belong to all the women who carried my cells for generations and my body remembers how for each generation this matter of ending is done.

Cynthia tells me now about being a young girl, watching and enjoying what her body was doing in preparation for her life. Seeing her breasts develop, watching the cleft disappear behind a cushion of dark pubic hair, discovering her own body making a bright red stain, feeling herself and seeing herself in the process of becoming.

When I was young, I watched this process with dread, seeing my breasts grow larger and larger and my hips widen. I was never able to say, "This is my body doing this wonderful unknown thing." I felt fear with every visible change, I felt more exposed, more vulnerable to attack. My swelling breasts, my widening hips, my growing pubic hair and finally the visible bleeding wound, all were acts of violence against my person, and could only bring me further acts of violence. I never knew in all the years of living in my woman's body that other women had found any pleasure in that early body experience, until Cynthia told me. But now, after a lifetime of living, my body has taken over again. I have this second chance to feel my body living out its own plan, to watch it daily change in the direction of its destiny.

When autumn comes to Cambridge, we walk arm in arm along the brick streets between Massachusetts Avenue and Concord Avenue, and I think a lot about endings because all about us endings are so visible. Dry leaves cover the brick streets, and the bare branches above us reveal now the peeling paint on the old Victorian houses and the chalky crumblings of old chimneys and brick walls. I feel how the houses are ending a period and the trees are ending a season. And in contrast to Cynthia's lighter step, her narrow waist, I become sharply aware that I, too, am living my ending.

As we walk along, other things are revealed—signs. In Cambridge, the signs are everywhere, on tree trunks, telephone poles, fences—paper signs, sometimes printed, sometimes mimeographed, hanging by the last tack or torn piece of tape. By the end of winter they will be hanging in shreds.

Someone has a need and puts their sign up. Exclamation marks to attest to how great the need was at the time: Garage Sale! Lost Dog! Apartment Needed! or Apartment Mate Needed! Everybody puts them up but the person with the need never comes to take the sign down. I think, as we walk along, of the experience missed—half lived—left in tatters in the wind.

Somebody decided to have a garage sale, to "get rid of things." At the end of the sale, no one came to take the sign down, to feel, "The sale is over. These things I got rid of, these things I did not."

Or in fear and pain another person pleads to every passer-by to help her find her dog. But the ending is not felt; she has never removed the sign to say, "My search is over. I have found her," or "The search is over, but my dog may never return. I must become a person whose dog cannot be found."

Once someone needed an apartment, a roof, a home. She must have found one, somewhere, yet she continues to call out that she is homeless. I feel that she probably is homeless, not ever having finished with the homeless feeling—never having come back to the feeling or the place to take the sign down, to say, "It isn't the apartment I dreamed of; I wanted a garden space on a first floor—but it is my apartment now. I am the woman who now has an apartment."

And the one who wanted an apartment mate? Did she find one? Did she not find one? Does she really know whether she found one or not? She missed the ending of the experience of her need, missed the chance to say, "I will take the sign down. I will live alone. I will be the person who lives alone for awhile." Or "I will take the sign down. I have found someone who chose to live with me. I am known as the person who lives with someone."

As we walk along I see my own signs, left hanging in my life. One by one I take them down. I wanted a different body when I was young. I have lived in this body for sixty-five years. "It is a good body, it is mine."

I wanted another mother and another beginning when I was young. I wanted a mother who liked herself, who liked her body and so would like mine. "My mother did not like herself and she did not like me; that is part of the definition of who she was and of who I am. She was my mother."

When I was fifty-two, my lover left me after fourteen years of living our lives together. I wanted her to return. I waited for many years and she did not come back. "I am the woman whose lover did not return."

I was lonely for years of my life and I wandered in search of a lover. "I am a person who loves again. I am a woman come home."

So often we think we know how an experience is going to end so we don't risk the pain of seeing it through to the end. We think we know the outcome so we think there is no need to experience it, as though to anticipate an ending were the same as living the ending out. We drop the old and take up the new: drop an idea and take up a new one; drop the middle-aged and old and start concentrating on the young—always thinking somehow it's going to turn out better with a new start. I have never had a child, but sometimes I see a young woman beginning to feel the urge to have a child at about the same time she feels some disappointment at how her own life is turning out. And soon the young mother feels

further disappointment when her own mother withdraws her loving investment in her daughter to pour it into her grandchild. I see how all are devalued: the grandmother devalued by society, devalued by her own self, the daughter devalued by her mother, and the granddaughter, valued not for who she is but for who she may become, racing for the landmarks, as I once did.

We never really know the beginning or the middle, until we have lived out an ending and lived on beyond it.

Of course, this time, for me, I am not going to live beyond this ending. The strangeness of that idea comes to me at the most unexpected moments and always with surprise and shock; sometimes, I am immobilized by it. Standing before the mirror in the morning, I feel that my scalp is tight. I see that the skin hangs beneath my jaw, beneath my arm; my breasts are pulled low against my body; loose skin hangs from my hips, and below my stomach a new horizontal crease is forming over which the skin will hang like the hem of a skirt turned under. A hem not to be "let down," as once my skirts were, because I was "shooting up," but a widening hem to "take up" on an old garment that has been stretched. Then I see that my body is being drawn into the earth—muscle, tendon, tissue and skin is being drawn down by the earth's pull back to the loam. She is pulling me back to herself; she is taking back what is hers.

Cynthia loves bulbs. She digs around in the earth every fall, looking for the rich loamy mold of decayed leaves and vegetation, and sometimes as she takes a sack of bone meal and works it into the damp earth, I think, "Why not mine? Why not?"

I think a lot about being drawn into the earth. I have the knowledge that one day I will fall and the earth will take back what is hers. I have no choice, yet I choose it. Maybe I won't buy that boat and that list of supplies; maybe I will. Maybe I will be able to write about my life; maybe I won't. But uncertainty will not always be there, for this is like no other experience I have ever had—I can count on it. I've never had anything before that I could really count on. My life has been filled with uncertainties, some were not of my making and many were: promises I made myself I did not keep; promises I made others I did not keep; hopes I could not fulfill; shame carried like a weight heavier each year, at my failure, at my lack of clear purpose. But this time I can rely on myself, for life will keep her promise to me. I can trust her. She isn't going to confuse me with a multitude of other choices and beckon me down other roads with vague promises. She will give me finally only one choice, one road, one sense of possibility. And in exchange for the multitude of choices she no longer offers, she gives me, at last, certainty. Nor do I have to worry this time that I will fail myself, fail to pull it off. This time, for sure I am going to make that single-handed crossing. ■

My Old Dykes' Home Scream
by Caryatis Cardea

For some time now, I've been having trouble with the recurring community fantasy of an Old Dykes' Home. At the First West Coast Lesbians' Festival, I said that the next time someone brought it up, I was going to scream. Of course, another Lesbian did bring it up and I pulled out my notebook and began writing. The following is an edited version of what I wrote and included in a reading later that weekend.

♀♀

I don't want an Old Dykes' Home. I want a Lesbian community. Everything I hear about this retirement fantasy of the thirty-to-forty something generation of class-privileged Dykes is a description of what our communities should be now. A combination of security and privacy in our living arrangements, health care without loss of autonomy, a place to be away from the dominant heterosexist culture, and freedom from the intrusion of heterosexual relatives.

So why does it look appealing to some Lesbians only as a place for their old age? Because that is when they anticipate a decrease in the income with which they maintain that very lifestyle right now. The hardships they imagine old age will bring go something like this. They won't be able to go to Lesbian concerts and vacation in Hawaii, too; their rent will swallow most of their newly fixed income; their insurance, if they have any, won't cover their health needs; maybe they

won't walk so easily, or feel able to drive every day; maybe they'll be able to cook their own meals but not wash their own dishes. Worst of all, their "families of origin" might step in, because there's nowhere else to turn.

So, they want a Lesbian safety net to catch them when they just can't go it alone. I guess they figure they'll deserve that because they've managed to take care of themselves most of their lives. (Why does the word "bootstraps" suddenly leap into my mind?) But, poverty and Lesbianism are not mutually exclusive, though they might be if we had a real community in which we worked together to take care of ourselves *and* each other. Just like class-privileged Lesbians want to have when they're old, but can't be bothered with now.

To those of you interested in community planning for your future, I have a few questions. Why not start such a place now? Even if you think it's only necessary for old age, there *are* Dykes who are old right now. And if it's our Lesbian responsibility to be there when advancing age brings poverty to your doorstep, what is your Lesbian responsibility to Dykes—old, young, or middle-aged—who struggle, and often fail, to get by today?

You have safety, security and Lesbian friends and community now. You think this is because you are a good person. But even having a certain number and kind (affluent, able-bodied) of Lesbian friends is at least partly because you are an affluent person. Without money, Dykes cannot attend the concerts, readings, plays and other events at which we meet, socialize, exchange ideas and phone numbers. Without money, Dykes cannot even think about going to conferences and festivals in other parts of the country. We can only hope to visit in each other's homes. But without money, Dykes live in rundown structures in so-called dangerous neighborhoods, where affluent Dykes won't visit.

So, from the perspective of this lower-class Lesbian who has lived twenty years on a low salary and now, at forty-one, receives a fixed income, the Old Dykes' Home fantasy of the middle-class, middle-aged Lesbian is the same old tired refrain (to the tune of "If I Had a Hammer"):

Well, I have my privilege
and I'll want it in the future.
I deserve to have comfort, and to keep it always.
So you'd better start saving,
and you'd better start planning.
So I'll never be alone or poor
like Lesbians around me
All over this land.

I've tried to imagine why the shame class-privileged Dykes generally attribute to poverty doesn't taint their old age fantasy. Apparently, since old age is unavoidable—unless you die first—any disability it might bring is natural, and any poverty it might bring is due to the structure of our society, and therefore not a personal disgrace. Why they can't apply this rationale to the poverty experienced by other folks right now is a constant mystery to me. They speak often of the cuts to government programs and education, the racist and classist administrations which create poverty. But they still attach shame to any poverty which doesn't threaten their own comfort.

Meanwhile, says the affluent Dyke, help me to plan a community for Lesbians with no or little income. Because I'm afraid that when I get old, I just might be one. But, you see, I already am one —of the many of us out here. And I don't want to settle for the Old Dykes' Home of the future. I want a real Lesbian community right now. ■

yentas
by Chaia Zblocki Heller

we break bread together
share the daily crust with the dog,
call it family. our home is a hut
with a chair on the roof; you fiddle up there
to please the stars, and i sit within
plotting new constellations.

this is our schtettle.
certainly we choose it
with more intention.
women who couldn't see the numbers
to paint by; saw only the outlines of possibility
and built entire villages, altars
to the great tongue of invention,
        new words
to describe our courage and imagination;
"mashugannah" means gleefully misinterpreting
the rules of the patriarchy
and "chutzpah" means strutting off
to lay down our own

we are yentas
in lavender
who spit in the vats
of the ordinary soup;
we make matches only
between women
and revolution.

Reference Works
by Elliot

Finding Self, Finding Words
by Toni McNaron

T he next ten years bleed into one another like Madras cloth in the wash: one ten-week course after another in Shakespeare or Milton or English literature from *Beowulf* to Virginia Woolf with from thirty-five to sixty undergraduates; one passionate nine-month relationship after another with a woman ten to fifteen years younger than I; one evening or weekend after another full of too many bourbons and ginger ale or on the rocks.

On an external level, I accomplished a lot during this muddled decade: I won promotion to associate professor after only three years, billed as one of the bright new stars in Minnesota's crown; I won two competitive awards for outstanding teaching; I became one of the most sought after faculty to serve on policy-making committees. Efforts at writing were less than satisfactory, though I began many projects. The closest I came to publication was the acceptance of a book manuscript on Shakespeare's late romances in which I argued that forgiveness and continuing to live were more valued by the older bard than heroic deaths or the senselessly violent pursuit of vengeance. Mouton, a publisher in the Hague, liked it and was about to put it into press when their budget and my project were slashed. My severe depression over this catastrophe only deepened when I

Excerpt from her autobiography, *I Dwell in Possibility: A Memoir* (NY: The Feminist Press, 1992)

heard that one of my colleagues had probably written someone he knew at Mouton to sabotage my work by claiming it was actually the product of my graduate research assistant. Jack Daniels profited enormously from this reversal, and my writer's block worsened.

Social psychologists are fond of hypothesizing the ill effects of precocity and perhaps that partially accounts for my slump. Certainly, I had sailed through school, college, and graduate school with assorted A's, fellowships, and awards. But it had only been partly a joke that I was best with children and stray animals: I was not adept at making human connections, and people my own age tended to silence me unless I had had several drinks.

As a new assistant professor, I was invited to dinners and cocktail parties held in the homes of older members of the English department. Unable to refuse and unable to take my lover to such gatherings because we had convinced ourselves that we had to live in one of the darkest closets imaginable, I hovered at the drink and food table hoping no one would try to make conversation with so obviously unsocial a being. Inevitably someone did.

"Well, Toni, and how are you finding Minneapolis/your students/the winter/our art galleries/the symphony/your neighborhood?"

"Oh, just fine, thank you," gulping my drink or sandwich in a frantic gesture to buy some time while I thought about what I could say next to the person trying so hard to set me at my ease. I certainly could not return the gambit, since whoever was in front of me had lived in the city for at least a decade.

"Are you making friends, meeting people, or are you lonely for someone special back in Madison?"

Utter panic. My "someone special" was at home studying the MMPI or Rorschach blots or theories of personality development and deviancy while we lived a life my conversational partner might well see as an example of the latter. So how was I to answer so innocuous a question? "No, I'm not meeting people—it takes all my spare time to manage my lies and secrecy, thank you."

Gradually, I began to refuse such invitations, preferring to stay home where I could drink uninterrupted. If I did go to the colleague's for dinner, the pattern was set: I arrived exactly at the appointed hour and either refused any predinner alcohol or sipped something tasteless. Once at dinner, I nursed a single glass of wine while other guests went for seconds and thirds without seeming to give it a thought. The moment dessert was over, I excused myself, offering class preparations or my habit of arising at 5:30 in the morning or a headache from a hard day at the office to my confused and at times irritated hostess. Back in the isolated safety of my apartment, I began to drink in earnest, drinking until I fell asleep or drifted into a blankness that passed for sleep.

By my early thirties, I certainly realized that I was in trouble with alcohol, though that realization made no difference either to my drinking or to my efforts to get help. I promised myself routinely that I would stop on the first of the next month or when the current bottle was used up, on New Year's Day or my birthday. Such promises and their attendant "wagons" lasted anywhere from a day to six months on those rare occasions when I was more frightened than usual about not being able to read as long as I once could or not being able to get letters of recommendation done on time or at all.

Working in the English department during the late sixties and early seventies was poles away from present conditions for incoming assistant professors. We taught three courses for each of three quarters, almost all of them different from one another. That meant that nine times a year I faced new students, strenuous preparations, hefty sets of mid-quarter exams, papers, and finals. We were expected to serve on at least two department committees a year, attend at least one professional conference, and somehow miraculously progress toward being famous scholars in our fields. The longer I escaped into alcohol and remained unable to speak about my personal life, the less well I did at any of this except classroom teaching. For some reason, the moment I entered one of the uniformly dingy spaces in which learning was to occur, I dropped my shyness, lost my fears of being apprehended as a criminal, and spoke—passionately and convincingly—about "The Wanderer," with whom I identified completely as he waked from his lovely dream of some good old days when he sat at his master's feet after having served him loyally to the cold reality of old age and loneliness, or about the Romantic and Victorian poets, who again appealed to my growing melancholia and *Weltschmertz*.

When anti-Vietnam protests reached my campus, I was one of the first faculty to participate. The students struck against a university with heavy investments in the Honeywell Corporation, which was busily making antipersonnel bombs just across town. Out of fierce sympathy, I held classes off campus, hauled my Milton students in my little red pickup truck from one to another of their nearby apartments. We read *Areopatigica* and grasped censorship in a way not possible in previous quarters. When a graduate student friend and I were maced, I realized that there were all sorts of reasons the authorities might turn against their own—not just sexual difference—and understood coalition for perhaps the first time. Bob and I rushed into the nearest classroom building where other students stood at water fountains with wet cloths for burning eyes. Once we could see again, we decided to proceed as quickly as possible across the bridge that separated us from my parking ramp and the quiet of home. As we were about to go up the stairs leading to it, a large, angry policeman stopped us with, "Just where do you think you're going? Can't you see we've got a situation on our hands with these stupid kids rioting?" After I showed him my faculty identification card and assured him that Bob was my assistant and not a "stupid kid" even though he had very long hair, he grudgingly agreed to our passage. But when Bob put his left hand on the stair rail, the officer became suddenly incensed. In a split second, he brought down his billy club with full force just inches from my friend's hand. When I saw how close Bob had come to having his five fingers pulverized, I grasped just how furious certain Americans were at other Americans.

When students on the Kent State campus were fired at and killed, I marched with outraged students and faculty in Minnesota. When similar events occurred at Jackson State, I watched liberal colleagues straining to feel what had come so naturally when white students were attacked and killed. During this time, I renewed my acquaintance with the only black person I have known at all well since moving north. I had met Anna years before when she took a train from Mississippi to Minnesota to attend a community college where my lover worked as a counselor. She came to our apartment once for iced tea. Though we were all pretty stiff, she and I did talk about Mississippi and her grandmother. When she decided to transfer to the university, I was her initial contact, but we had not seen each other for some years.

A rally marking the deaths at Jackson State was held atop the steps and between the Doric columns of our large auditorium. It turned out that Anna and I were both scheduled to speak: I to demand action from the university about another academic assault; she to demand action from whites. I was cynical, and Anna was bitter. While an assistant vice-president for student affairs was droning on, we made rather loud fun of him from the sidelines. When he tried using black language, Anna and I broke out laughing. For the next few minutes, we talked urgently about what it meant that we had both grown up in the South. We acknowledged that for the moment we were closer to each other than to white or black northerners; we shared a common culture and language even if we were on utterly different sides of southern tracks. That scene on the stoa of Northrup Auditorium remains incandescent in my memory, though my bone-deep racism continues to haunt me.

In 1983 my partner and I were vacationing in London. Friends had told us to be sure to visit the public baths near our flat, assuring us that they were antithetical to their American namesakes. We made appointments for "Ladies Day" and had a two-hour adventure in water and steam heat. My only anxiety turned around the significant numbers of black women who were also there. I had never seen a black woman naked and kept catching myself staring at their bodies. Swinging from amusement at my own fascination to awkward embarrassment, I especially recall an older woman, wiry and strong, with salt and pepper hair on her head, under her arms, and at her pudendum. She talked with us as if we were just some more people at the baths: "Oh, it's just so invigorating to go quickly from the sauna to this cold water. I jump in all at once and swim to feel the most tingling possible. You must try it, really." Other black women advised us about which saunas were the best temperature that day, where it was safe for us to put our towels, and how to sign up for a marvelously nurturing soap massage during which whole buckets of tepid water were thrown over one's back. No whites spoke to us. I was drawn to and afraid of black women up close, unable to relax in their presence, unable to imagine caressing or being caressed by them without feeling either too excited at breaking a taboo or just a little squeamish. Later I admitted to myself that I would have deep trouble making love to a black woman. At that instant, I tasted the southern poison running in my veins at a level seemingly untouched by intellectual, literary, or even emotional change.

⚢

My experience of the Vietnam War combined with fledgling conversations beginning to take place about what would later be called feminist pedagogy taught me a permanent and invaluable lesson. I comprehended that the classical lecture format in which one person is supposed to have all knowledge while many others are convinced of their ignorance if not stupidity was academic colonialism. If I was willing to risk my vision and safety protesting such a policy in Asia, I surely needed to rid myself of my own comparable practices.

As so often is the case, I careened from one extreme to the other. In the early seventies, I stopped lecturing entirely, saying to each new group of students, "Coming in here every class and beginning to lecture about things you may not have the slightest interest in hearing is like intellectual prostitution, and I won't do it. I will arrive and wait for questions from you on matters of urgency in this play/poem/story." Naturally, my students were stunned into deeper silence than usual, and we spent many uncomfortable sessions: after all, I was expecting them to know enough to ask me intelligent questions about a subject they had taken precisely because they wanted more knowledge of it.

Fortunately for us all, my innate passion for the literature overcame my rigidity about having academically pure politics. Though I have never returned to unbroken lecturing, I have come to accept responsibility for all I do know that they do not, and remain accountable to them for using that knowledge to empower rather than mystify.

♀♀

Drinking enough Jack Daniels or Seagram's Seven Crown (depending on when payday had been) silenced the voices that told me I was somehow inadequate. But by using alcohol to escape them, I also lost contact with my best self. From earliest memories I have seen myself as intense— the four-year-old oblivious to anything but shaping animals out of her feces; the child digging tunnels under the oak tree for an imaginary escape in her toy cars; the ten-year-old devastated by the brutish foot that smashed her peep show. But I have also understood sabotage from a very early age, how insidious it is and how cunning. While accenting my spontaneous intensity, I ignored or downplayed my need to carry through, to face the consequences of being bright or sensitive or creative. I let out just enough of my interpretive powers to know that at the heart of my often flawed or unfinished products lay a jewel. I fooled myself for years. Somewhere along the way, I began pulling back from full experience or expression of myself. Others' early responses meant too much: "No one draws pink cows and brown people." "That note is way off key and too low for a girl to sing." "If you touch yourself there, your hands will fall off." "Girls don't become orchestra conductors or forest rangers." "Why don't you go out with some nice young man who is appropriate?"

Bourbon numbed my feelings and left me depressed. I swung between heavy drinking and periods of sensing that I could not continue both to drink and develop my intellectual and creative abilities. The first thing to suffer was my critical writing; eventually, I ceased being able to put any words onto paper. By 1968, I had stopped writing letters to everyone except my sister and Josephine.

Evidence of my demise lies in pathetic souvenirs of attempts at creativity. My filing cabinet still has a folder in it full of lists of projects: subjects for long high-minded poems; topics for scholarly articles; designs for a better world. The tab on the file reads: "Scraps"; "Fragments"; "First Thoughts"; "Bits and Pieces"; "Inspirations."

In addition to these ephemera, I have drafts of articles, first on Shakespeare and later on Virginia Woolf, written when not actively drinking. These were sometimes even sent away to a journal, only to be rejected. On rare occasions when comments accompanied the nos, readers indicated that my piece had a bright kernel lost in opacity and verbiage. Such essays generally came back when I was once again focused on whiskey, in no condition to revise.

For the last eight years of my drinking, I managed only essential schoolwork. Papers that absolutely had to be returned were read; otherwise, they piled up for months, even years, collecting shame along with office dust. Books were somehow gotten through, though sitting still to read became virtually impossible toward the end of my drinking years. I had to resort to teaching titles of which I had prior knowledge. Most of my time was taken up with academic committee service, for I sensed that if I did not want to be exposed as a raging alcoholic, I had to move into administration, where work could be defined less specifically than in the classroom or in the library.

Two tangible outcomes are the existence of several university documents of major importance and a thriving women's studies department. While unable to write literary criticism, I authored a policy for evaluating teaching on a regular basis; a system-wide statement about academic freedom and its less-welcome corollary, faculty responsibility toward their student and institution; a plan to give students one more credit than the number of hours spent in the class, thereby recognizing that learning takes place outside of the classroom. What I remember most clearly about those documents is typing drafts way into the night, always with a glass near my typewriter. Occasionally I would reminisce about 1959 in Nashville, when I wrote a master's thesis about neo-Platonism in Keats's *Endymion* and lived on farm-ripe tomatoes and Jack Daniels Black. It was summer, and my fellowship had run out at the end of May. While my family gladly would have sent me more if I had asked, my guilt over spending so much on liquor kept me from asking. Once a week, however, I cooked for an evening meeting at the Vanderbilt Episcopal student center, always making more than was needed, counting on the charity of the chaplin who insisted that I "take home leftovers or they'll just get thrown out back."

In the case of women's studies, I was approached by a small cadre of graduate students eager to see us begin offering courses with an avowed feminist perspective. Not only did I assist them in drawing up a document to present to the dean, but when a program was established on a three-year experimental basis, I applied for and was chosen to be the first chair. My three years in office coincided with my last year of drinking and my first two of not. While we made tremendous

strides as an academic unit, I struggled inside with a growing sense of desperation. In order to perform the groundbreaking functions set before me, I simply transferred my addiction from liquor to food. One of my last acts as chair was to clean out the massive wooden desk we had been willed by a woman retiring from decades in student personnel, who in her last years had consistently rescued our fledging program from such minutiae as class scheduling deadlines and faculty appointment papers. In one of the side drawers, I came upon ancient crumbs from cinnamon rolls quickly stashed there when I would hear a student or colleague open the door of the outer office.

In all my years of drinking, I never missed a day's work. But I remember waking up feeling as if I would not be able to get out of bed, stumbling through a shower and strong hot tea, driving too fast to school to meet my classes. Once school was over, I drove purposefully home, thinking only of that first drink. I parked my car outside my house, walked quickly up the steps and into the foyer, opened the heavy oak front door, and made a straight path into the kitchen. Out came a glass into which I poured liberal amounts from my current bottle, maybe adding ginger ale, maybe not. Swallowing as rapidly as possible without choking, I downed number one. Only after that reliable streak of fire had cut down the front of my body was I calm enough to speak to my two cats who had come into the kitchen to greet me, take off whatever coat and shoes or boots I might have on, pick up the mail from the concrete floor of the foyer, and get a sponge to wipe up the trail of snow or mud or rain water that I had tracked on the wood floor and linoleum in my frantic need to drink.

⚥

The more deeply I sank into my pattern, the less able I became to make positive choices in lovers or to stay in a relationship longer than about nine months. My partners increasingly became women unwilling to face their own involvement with alcohol. Our liaisons began in high passion but usually ended with my feeling victimized by younger women whose attention had wandered.

Actually my own attention had never been focused on them. To do that would involve time and risk, and I already knew how much energy it took to maintain myself within my secret. Besides, no person could be counted on to deliver exactly what I needed as often and without fail as my beloved bourbon could, so I chose partners who would not interfere with that pursuit. A year or so before I stopped drinking, some brave lesbians opened the Lesbian Resource Center (LRC), housed in a storefront across the street from a popular gas station. When their newsletters began coming to my home, I was shocked and frightened, since "no one knew." But come they did, announcing pool playing, card games, weekly community meetings, occasional dances, special holiday meals and celebrations. I devoured every word, memorized all the dates and times, quickly located the address, and drove by on community meeting nights. Unable to walk in, I tried to soak up something through my car windows and the center's heavily curtained front. I told myself I did not fit in, but the truth was I knew I would and was scared. Being a private lesbian was one thing but identifying with a cross-section of society seemed quite another.

I began to mail the LRC cash donations in unmarked envelopes, telling myself I would be fired if my bank saw a check made out to such an organization. One Thanksgiving, I received a colorful flyer announcing a feast in lesbian space, asking people to bring food and to come share warm company. Afraid to attend, I nonetheless had become increasingly an invisible part of the LCR's activities. After some brain wracking about how to participate without going, I devised a workable if sad solution. I had a neighborhood grocery deliver a handsome turkey to the center the Wednesday before Thanksgiving, and, as I ate a T-bone steak alone in my house, I pictured a room full of women brave enough to go and eat that bird.

The LRC supported a journal, *So's Your Old Lady* (*SYOL*), and, from the occasional copies I had seen, I knew I had skills to offer such an enterprise. Simultaneously, I was becoming aware that a couple of political lesbians had opened a bookstore in someone's basement. I tried to convince myself that I would work on these activities or at least publish in *SYOL* under a pseudonym. Nothing happened for another year except that I worried about the idea whenever I was sober long enough to catch a glimpse of where my life was going.

During the summer of 1974 a colleague told me he had been to a wonderful bookstore full of books by women, located next door to a combination pool hall, bowling alley, and bar. His recommendation allowed me not only to drive but finally to park my car and go in. I told the two women working there about my *male* friend's excitement, hoping that my flimsy excuse would cover my real reason for being there. One of the women was tall and quite thin, the other shorter, more compact, and intense. Both were utterly silent, forcing me to initiate any conversation. They owned a rather large black dog named Sappho, who insisted on being friendly but whose nuzzling frightened me even more than I already was. By the end of an awkward half-hour, I had volunteered to work in the store two hours a week on Saturdays.

The shorter woman, who turned out to be a cofounder of the LRC, was usually on duty when I worked. I had to laugh about getting in way over my head with my first foray into the "lesbian community." Her name was Karen Browne, and I was immediately attracted to her—politically, intellectually, physically. Each week my two-hour shift stretched a little longer, and we slowly developed the literary side of the holdings, since current stock reflected both her and her partner's training in social science and political activism. We undertook an inventory and devised a system for ordering new books. We also gazed at each other, touched hands of necessity as we worked with books, became a bit easier in one another's company. Only as I was driving home would I realize that I had not been breathing very deeply during my shift.

One Saturday, Karen talked about women who sent the LRC anonymous donations but never lent energy to the ongoing life of the place. I called in sick the next week, ashamed of my cowardice. She risked public ridicule so that lesbians could meet somewhere other than dark bars or private homes behind pulled shades, while I sent in my secret money.

♀♀

The big change in my life came in the fall of 1974 when I was thirty-seven. Karen had a part-time job at the university and, since we lived within three or four blocks of one another, it seemed natural to ride to and from work together. As I fell increasingly in love with her, I realized I had to end my pro forma relationship with the person living in my house. She was a kept woman—kept by me. I paid for elaborate dinners, a plane trip to Denver and the Painted Desert as a celebration of her passing her doctoral examinations, her room and board in my house, a Cordon Bleu crêpe pan so she could fix her friends elegant suppers when I was working late at school. I even let her bring an English sheep dog into my house, when I thoroughly disliked dogs. That puppy was locked in the laundry room each morning as she left for long days at the library. The combination of his frantic whimpers and the growing smell emanating from my basement drove me to walk him around the block, urging him to "Do your stuff" outside. My two cats looked at me with startled eyes every time he grew another inch, something that seemed to happen every other day. After all my wool carpets were deeply stained by urine, my lover asked if I would buy an outdoor running pen for her playful pup. In a conversation with a salesperson at Sears I learned that the cheapest run cost $1,200. That evening I announced that we were getting rid of the forty-five-pound puppy who made my hardwood floors shake when he careened from kitchen to front porch. That decision was the beginning of my exit not only from the relationship but from the matrix within which it existed.

The summer before, this same woman had sat rocking in my living room, drinking gin and tonic. Suddenly she stopped, leaned toward me, and said calmly: "I miss the excitement of our first six months, 'cause now I feel like I know all there is to know about you; we're not finding out anything new about each other and I'm worried about getting bored." I countered with: "Maybe we've gotten through vital statistics and can now really start getting to know each other on deeper levels." When I saw that my suggestion was not registering, I silenced my rage by falling off a six-month wagon. Under the rage lay a depth of hurt that overwhelmed me but that I pushed down as I tried vainly to think up more exciting tidbits about my past that might catch her attention. What I wanted most was someone to tell what it felt like to live inside my skin, lonely, hung over much too often, scared of being out as almost anything I really was—Southerner, lesbian, drunk, writer, passionate human being with dreams of a feminist world.

That fall was early and violent. By mid-October, most leaves were down on lawns, in gutters, in the crooks of steps. Late on the night of October 22nd, I was driving my car home from Karen's. The wind was throwing wet, dead leaves all over the street in front of my car. I slowed down to watch those leaves rising on the updraft, only to sink back into a sodden heap and be ridden over by someone on their way somewhere.

I decided to write a poem about the leaves when I got home.

I decided not to sleep with the woman who found me boring after half a year.

I decided to read a book (*Sappho Was a Right-On Woman* by Sidney Abbott and Barbara Love), which I had let sit on my shelf for over a year, not wanting to know what it said.

I decided not to drink while I read that book.

I decided to stay up all night in my living room so both the book and the poem would be done by breakfast.

♀♀

That night was uncommonly long. Lying about feeling restless, I found my book, some scratch paper, and a pencil, and went downstairs. I boiled water for hot tea, which tasted bland, harmless, unsatisfying; I wanted a big glass of room-temperature bourbon swallowed fast to quiet the jitters beginning down the middle of my body. I drank quarts of tea, liking it less as my hands began to shake and my stomach to draw up into familiar knots that meant my liquor ration was overdue. But I sat rigid on my couch, reading, fighting against sleep and panic and pain. About three in the morning, I came to a sentence late in the book on the right-hand side of the page that burned its way through my brain just as Jack Daniels had burned my body. In a long discussion of small ways lesbians lie about how and with whom we celebrate, the authors asserted that for a lesbian to go to work on Monday morning and lie about the sex of whom she spent the weekend with is like committing suicide slowly but surely. I spilled the tea I was nursing and began to shake from something new; Abbott and Love were speaking only to me in that living room while the fall wind whistled and moaned around the corners of my house.

I left the book unfinished and worked on my poem about wet leaves in a chance wind—it seemed infinitely safer. What I wrote fast and carelessly did not qualify as a poem, but it had lines, indented from the left-hand margin, and it told the truth. I stuck it away in my study where I would not come upon it for over a year. For the rest of the night, I sat stone still while my cats slept nearby offering mute comfort and my mood swung from lightheadedness to terror to something resembling sanctification.

Before the woman upstairs rose, I poured all my bourbon down the sink and threw the empty bottles into my outside garbage can. I left the gin since it had never been my drink but wrote a note saying I wanted it and her out of the house by December 1st. Then I walked toward my neighborhood shopping area, feeling sick from no whiskey for almost twenty-one hours. I found a café open early, where I devoured a lumberjack special: two eggs over easy, hash browns, toast, bacon, sausage, lots of very strong tea. Later that day, I decided to tell somebody I was lesbian and picked my good friends from whom I had bought my house. I called to ask if I might stop by after work. That seemed to shock them more than my news: I had never dropped in on anyone or

wanted them to drop in on me since I drank in secret. In their living room I was offered a drink. I said, "Thanks, I'm on the wagon," a comment accepted without question. After a couple of stuttered false tries, I blurted out my dire announcement. Martin smiled easily: "I love ya," while Martha quipped, "I was beginning to think there must not be any in Minneapolis."

⚲

Nothing magical happened when I sobered up. I simply stopped taking liquor into my body. While that was a momentous decision, my ways of dealing with myself and the world remained essentially unchanged. I transferred many of my compulsive needs from bourbon to Karen, putting far more faith in and strain on our relationship than any such delicate connection can bear. Though we continued to respond passionately to each other, sustaining the dailiness of a commitment was not possible, and we eventually set one another free.

Most of the mileposts along my recovery route involved wanting to make things. The first summer after I quit drinking, I decided to paint the trim on my house. For months, I persuaded unsuspecting friends to "come over for dinner and a little outside project." We climbed ladders, hung from eaves, and fought late-summer wasps. There came a moment when everything was done except three small pieces of gutta-percha pipe sticking up above my brick chimney. Determined that it be perfect, I eventually straddled my chimney and painted away these last traces of fading brown. Having enough sense to grasp that getting up on the peak of my steep roof alone might be a bit foolhardy, I waited until an old friend was visiting. She stood on the opposite side of my house from the chimney and held a thick clothesline, the other end of which was around my waist. We both believed this scheme would magically save me if I fell. Sitting atop my roof on a gorgeous Saturday afternoon, I was alive, able to breath, happy. A snapshot catches this moment: me grinning against a perfectly blue sky, holding my four-inch paintbrush and my funny rope.

The second summer of sobriety, I dug a

small garden in my side yard and planted flowers bought from the local farmer's market. Though my garden brought me moments of pleasure, somewhere around midsummer I forgot the plants and focused on the bright cans of cold beer everyone else in town seemed to be holding. The weeds got ahead of me that year, but every year since I have put flowers into the earth. When I finally bought perennials, I knew I was willing to bank on having a "next spring," that I wanted something to bloom from the year before. Those first tulips and lemon lilies were precious investments in my capacity to care for my own creation. Before signing a purchase agreement to sell my house, I inserted a clause stipulating that I could return the next spring to dig up my lilies and take them to my new yard.

For many years after 1974, my creations were primarily nonverbal. One Saturday when I wanted more than usual to drink, I drilled three-quarter-inch holes into very long two-by-fours instead. I needed space for cookbooks and other volumes that were spilling out of my downstairs study, so I decided to build a bookcase in the hall. Shunning the simple, I picked a no-nail design needing twenty holes for dowels on which would rest the welcome shelves. I drilled ninety holes because I knew that as long as I was in my kitchen doing that, I would not go to the liquor store.

As a child, I had loved stories in books; my teenage years were consumed by books, since reading smoothed the edge off my loneliness. Once I was deeply into drinking, however, my ability to concentrate inevitably lessened. While I was going through a treatment program after I stopped drinking, I heard a lecture that helped me understand and forgive my restlessness in front of a printed page. It seems that each time a person gets drunk, several thousand brain cells die and must be replenished. I had to accept that it would take longer for my brain to dry out than it had for my hands to stop shaking. When, during my fifth year of sobriety, I suddenly found myself reading for a whole hour, my joy was exquisite. Almost every night as I lie in bed with my current book, I give thanks for the return of that gift.

As long as I was drinking, I could not afford to invest very heavily in my ideas or their expression, preferring the predictability and cold comfort of a bottle. But, in 1975, I accepted that I had something to say in words, on paper. After about a year of unsuccessful attempts, I stumbled upon Virginia Woolf's *A Writer's Diary* where she speaks of the function of her journal as a place to loosen her writer's ligaments, comparing journal writing with practicing piano scales before tackling more formal compositions. Willing to try her method, I tentatively chose to begin a journey toward my voice—I bought a journal.

Each volume was titled, which now intrigues me as I wonder what I might have written inside something called, "A Notebook of Spirals," "Fronds & Tendrils," "Webbings," "Knots." At one point in my recovery of my writing self, a friend suggested that I cull from all those journals salient vignettes and publish them. For a month, I read diligently, marking in red along any margins I thought worth excising.

June 13, 1975: Reading exam papers from a course I just coordinated on courtly love—a thought on the word "elevation" in relation to power. Power is played out on the street level, the pavement as Woolf calls it. By elevating woman, men removed her from contact with power. So when Shakespeare says in Sonnet 130, "My mistress when she treads, treads on the ground," he is doing more than mocking courtly love conventions. His mistress seems genuinely in control, not falsely so by virtue of the poet's participation in the courtly love game. The desire to put a woman on a pedestal is a way to keep her off the streets, out of the places where power is played out. We might consider the trap inherent in the myth that power corrupts. Like Renaissance-elite males wishing to preserve their position at the top who argued that ambition was evil, contentment with one's lot good, men may have made up the slogan "power corrupts" to deter the truly moral from embracing it. Power only corrupts if its wielders use it badly. Women could use power in new ways and not corrupt ourselves or others…

I've felt so well today, yet still can't stop my current eating binge—I have to do something. Each morning I intend, each night I gorge. I need to get physical exercise—I feel chained to this house.

June 10, 1976: Mary Schultz had her breast removed.

Losing Weight

"I'm still a compulsive eater" you say
Even though they've taken your breast
away?
Was it white meat, or are we, like ducks, all
    dark?
"I lost in the hospital" you muse
from loss of appetite, you think.
I say your white-masked Shylock sliced his legal
    pound   and then some;
left you lopped and asymmetric/
Latter-day Amazon, take up your bow
against the world of female measurements:
    0-34-38
You sit amongst us eaters, worried that you'll
    binge again
"reward" for losing tissue, skin, and special
    female veins.
Grafting pounds to other places
cannot bring you back your lovely melon,
cannot fill that utter hollow.
So sit and smile your brave, wan smile
and be a bosom cyclops.

I've said I'd make chicken salad for Mary so she won't have to ask others to make so many meals for her. Here I am, in my kitchen, dripping sweat into the bowl—special natural salt—cutting a gelid chicken with big, sharp scissors just like my mother did, covering it and me with grease that will become worse as it warms on my skin. Once all the available meat is in the bowl (tall, super-white metal bowl that held *So's Your Old Lady* money when I read of women's hurts and loves) and some scraps are in my cats, I move to eggs—hard boiled a day ago so the shells fall off from compression in the ice box. Once naked—smooth and super white, like the bowl—eggs go one by one in a childhood gadget that slice them thin and even. Criss-cross I go to make smaller cubes—cold crumbles of yolk stick to my greasy hot fingers and I suck them and revel in that yellow softness on my tongue. Now the celery: greener on the outside cuts, whitish at the center—cut, cut, my knife eats up stalks, making them hard diamond cubes tossed in on top. Suddenly the salad looks like a monotonic mosaic shelf. Mix it up, I think—and do with my bare hands—up to my wrists—the stuff takes me over and my total impulse is to sink my face into the sea of salad and drink it in gulps. Instead I spoon mayonnaise into, around, among ingredients till the whole is viscous, oiled, ready—a mound of chicken salad for a lady with only one breast.

Travels back to my creative self have been slow, filled with relapses into verbosity and abstraction learned in childhood and rewarded by schools. I struggle not to feel either shamed of where I am at my age or full of grief for the wasted years. Those women who have patiently but consistently urged me to my own speech have given me a jewel that I cannot always accept with open hands but one without which I would still be largely mute.

Every so often, I stumble on some artifact that simultaneously heartens, frightens, and depresses me. These remains share certain features: they do not look familiar to me, yet are in my handwriting; they reveal how much I can draw from a poem or a story when I focus. One of the clearest of these ghostly experiences came in 1983 while I was teaching a seminar on the poetry of Edna St. Vincent Millay, Louise Bogan, and H. D. When I opened my copy of *Helen in Egypt*, I was immediately distracted by the marginal comments. Neatly penned in blue ballpoint, they indicated an intelligence keenly in tune with the poet's own. In addition to copious notes, boxes appeared around certain clusters of words having to do with shadows, ghosts, veils, dreams—images that provide crucial linguistic and emotional threads through this epic. I could not recall making the notations, but the handwriting was unmistakably my own. Turning to the front of the book, I found that it had been a birthday present in 1977. Amazed, I realized that though I had been free from alcohol for three years when I read H.D.'s work, I could still engage in an intense project that would then pass out of my consciousness so completely as to seem foreign six years later.

As I continued reading the poem and my work with it, I felt moved by the critical and creative interpretation that was building as steadily as H.D.'s story. The next day, I shared my experience with the seminar, naming those annotations as a sign of my ambivalence toward my creative voice and as evidence of my slow recovery from years of destructive drinking.

The same day I gave up liquor, I began telling people I was a lesbian. Originally that decision was political and therapeutic, but one long-term effect has been on my writer's voice. Gradually I have found and claimed my truest audience: lesbians and feminists interested in women's culture. Once I conveyed this shift in my focus to my department chairman, my writing became surer, livelier, more engaged. My first public speech from this position was on Valentine's Day, 1977, in the guild hall of a local church. Part of a series sponsored by an alternative women's learning institute I helped operate, my lecture was on the poetry of Olga Broumas, Audre Lorde, and Adrienne Rich as it contributes to a lesbian aesthetic. My typescript was more than twenty pages long, and it was good. The overwhelmingly lesbian audience was alert and supportive; for the first time my life, I felt that my literary training might be put to some use.

⚢

As my journal writing developed, I became open enough to include poems and bored enough with my erratic love life to include entries about work, books, and other people who came into my life at a less intense level. Surveying the thirty-six

notebooks I hardly talk of external conditions at all—my journal is a confidential source for self-exploration. At other times, I seem deeply caught up in the world around me.

In April 1978, I went to New York City to read the correspondence between Louise Bogan and May Sarton housed in the Berg Collection of the public library. I wanted to write an article about ways in which letters served as underground support networks for women hungry for other women's ideas. Amidst their discussions of aesthetics I was surprised to find an unmistakably intimate note. Sarton writes asking to extend their developing friendship into a sensual and sexual relationship. Bogan refuses, pleading her disastrous relationship with her first husband. Sarton values her friendship enough to struggle to readjust her feelings. All this is spoken of tentatively and painfully in the letters; my lesbian perspective and my awareness of my own partial alliances lent me a sympathy I might otherwise have lacked. As I read through their often tortured exchanges, I felt respectful and clear about not wanting or needing to distort what was on the pages. Empowered through my own experience, I was able to articulate what the webs of their caring and fighting looked like.

My journal from that month is full of long, introspective entries about everything from the drunks who stopped me as I walked to the library from the subway to the art, ballet, and drama that were integral to my stay. One of my last days in the city was spent at the Cloisters. I gave myself a whole day at that museum I had wanted to visit for years. Journal entries written there contain my responses to the unicorn tapestries. A segment from that visit indicates my growing desire to direct my critical faculty toward my environment:

#7 is the famous scene of unicorn in captivity in round white fence. Unicorn looks rather dead in #6, then is set up in stasis in #7 as some ideal to be looked at and controlled even if not understood. It's so clear—these men could never fathom the complexity of the creature they find, hunt, kill, capture—they are so worldly and decadent, the unicorn so magical and pure—there's just no way for them to connect at all. I need to know what I feel, looking at #7. It's sadness at the small space left for the magic beast—she can sit as she does, or stand—no walking—no movement at all. Not only is she inside a fence but tied to an orange tree as well. And in the center of a huge field of flowers, all free in nature. This series is about hunt—war—blood—violence—sex—*men*. The Cluny ones are about the relationship of the unicorn and the lady—look at Robin Morgan's poem once home; go to Paris some day and see the originals.

When I look at my stack of gray-bound books, I remember Evi. She was an editor of *So's Your Old Lady*, whose staff I had finally joined under my own name. Being part of that enterprise was immensely important to me as a writer, since I learned the mechanics of editing a magazine and found the first outlet for my own words.

Before Evi left the group to enter a martial arts collective, she called me out of the office to make me a present of a handsome leather folder in which she kept her own writing. Once I had admired it, asking where she had bought it. Its San Francisco origin seemed to place it beyond my grasp. Now Evi's own beautiful object sat on my lap with a card that read, "So you can unlock your word-horde." Tears sprang to my eyes at her remembering my telling her about my favorite Old English poem in which a man had kept his story silent until his old master told him to unlock his word-horde, to speak the truth within him.

♀♀

The most important step toward my speaking my truth about literature involved my coming out at the university. My career at Minnesota spans twenty-six years, twelve of which were spent in the closet because I felt residual shame about being a lesbian and because I remained in an alcoholic haze that prevented me from seeing clearly. During those years, I survived but at great cost to myself. Not knowing how to express dis-

agreements without antagonizing my colleagues, I either ranted or sat in stony destructive silence. In a journal entry following a 1978 department meeting, I wrote:

I am home from a four-hour long meeting— headache, exhausted, drained, mute, nauseated, all stuffed in. I "made nice" all through, not saying how misplaced I find their values, not asking why there are no women writers on one man's list of canonical humanities texts, not saying that they're slanting the fiction writer search so as not to have to pay the woman candidate any heed. And we are going to promote to full professor a dullard, primarily because of his "time in rank" (five years to my thirteen). *Faces:* ashen, cud-chewing, carved in sneers, upturned lip, droopy eye, duck-tailed hard on devil's face leering, white roach grog dead, sunglassed mole, pearly-curly dandy, soft falling waves and deep hurt eyes, impish pucker covering steely-eyed true sight, balding round faced joker in forever pain, dick-tracy chinned gentle, baggy-pants baggy-eyed vapid, short-haired thin, insipid loner, barefoot lad with deep set teddy bear eyes— English department rogues' gallery. I feel much quieter now.

Clearly I had no idea how to handle my workplace or its inhabitants. Equally clearly, there is no description of me, who at that stage in life was greatly overweight and stressed out in the face, had wildly curled hair à la Janis Joplin, owned ten picked fingers from agitation without an object, and pretended to like triple-knit suits, heels, and hose when I only felt at home in corduroys and flannel.

At the end of the seventies I took a year's leave without pay. I had to decide if I wanted ever to return to an institution that invested in research of which I did not approve and in companies that fed the defense machine, and to a department that refused to promote me to full professor no matter how hard I tried to be their version of me. I discovered the obvious: a teacher cannot make enough freelancing to keep body and soul together. I also learned that I disliked intensely having to advertise myself or arrange classes under my own aegis. The surprise of the year came during a visit by Florence Howe to our campus. She came to evaluate the women's studies program, from which I had just retired after three years as its first chair. We met for a long dinner away from campus followed by a visit to my house where we kept talking about the current state of women's studies work in the country and at Minnesota.

When I took Florence back to her motel, her hand on the car door handle impelled me to speak about what was really on my mind. I blurted out my dilemma about where to work, saying at one point, "I want to do something radical and going back to school seems so easy and safe."

Florence turned to me and said as distinctly as anyone has ever said anything to me: "No, Toni, you have it wrong. Going back to the university is much more radical than staying away. Don't you know you are one of the handful of lesbians with tenure in America and that teaching and working with students from an open position is far harder than offering courses in a church basement or park building. Take the power of the podium and use it—go back and endure the derision that will come your way."

I drove home with her words burning in my ears, feelings simultaneous shock and relief. Within weeks, I had made my sabbatical decision: I would return to the English department, but not until I had met with my chairman to tell him my plan to return as an out lesbian-feminist critic and teacher. I scheduled that meeting and announced to a man who had worked his way through an English college on a pugilist scholarship: "I want you to know that I will be giving you articles and syllabi that assume a lesbian-feminist perspective on literature. I want you to evaluate them the same way you do anyone else's work. Only on this condition can I return to this place." He blanched momentarily before assuring me, "My theory of administration is to find out what makes my staff happy and then help them do it."

When I told my best male friend about my conversation, he fairly beamed with some pleasure I could not at first fathom. He told me that my declaring myself had destroyed an ancient plan on the part of some old timers in the department. It seems that he had heard them at poker games when everyone was a little drunk boasting that should I ever have the nerve to complain about their refusal to promote me, they had the perfect rejoinder. They were maintaining a secret dossier of incriminating tidbits about my private life and would happily bring it out to challenge my claims of mistreatment.

Since that momentous and rather breathless interview with my chair in 1979, I have consistently offered courses in lesbian literature, culture, and critical theory. I have visited other classes to discuss such matters when the regular faculty either did not know enough to do so or held too precarious a position to risk it. My colleagues gradually have either accepted my perspective or decided to leave me alone and be civil.

Occasionally homophobia surfaces, as on an afternoon a few years ago. I was standing in the hall talking with a friend. Because my back had recently gone out of alignment, I was wearing a spandex girdle to help me sit during our long preschool meetings. In an attempt to hide as much of it as possible, I was wearing a blousy knit top that hid the pristine whiteness entirely in the front. In the back, a band about three inches stuck out below the bottom of my sweater.

As my friend and I were speaking animatedly, we were interrupted by one of the chronically homophobic members of our department. His opener to me was, "Well, Toni, in training for the Vikings (Minnesota's professional football team)?" Determined to show my disapproval, I rejoined, "Actually Fred, my back is out, and I'm in constant pain, thank you." Covered with embarrassment, since he views himself as a liberal humanist, he stumbled through belated expressions of his concern and empathy, saying, "I know about backs; mine goes out on me, too." I am quite sure that, had he seen one of my heterosexual colleagues in such attire, his imagination would not have conjured linebackers.

Florence Howe turned out to be exactly right that night over a decade ago. Occupying space as a lesbian at the university has changed virtually everything about working there. No longer do I come home with terrible headaches or a churning stomach; no longer do I deny what I see in the literature I teach or the theory I espouse; no longer am I useless to students interested in talking with someone who has lived and thought as a lesbian for more years than many of them have been alive. My classroom manner has become more relaxed because I no longer fear a question that will force me to lie quickly in order to avoid some devastating revelation that will cost me my job or at the least a reprimand from someone in authority for "corrupting the young." But the single most lasting benefit has been to me—being open in my work has been a tremendous boon to my finding and using my voice. Since 1980, I have published three books and several substantial articles and poems; I write reviews for *Hurricane Alice*, a feminist journal that I help edit, and for *The Women's Review of Books*; I have worked on this memoir for some six years. I no longer become terrified when I cannot write on demand or every day, trusting now that I am a person who writes and who will always do that. My greatest conflict these days is between paid employment and my desire for more time at home to write. ▪

Some Historical Background

by Michal Brody

In September 1969, a faggot named Henry needed a roommate for his Chicago apartment. He had recently finished at the University of Chicago, and was living on the South Side, in Hyde Park, the neighborhood of the University. He presented an ad to the *Maroon*, the U of C student newspaper, which said "Wanted: gay roommate," and gave the particulars. The *Maroon* refused to run the ad, objecting to the non-derogatory use of the word *gay*. Henry had heard about the Stonewall riots, which happened in New York City in June of that year, when the patrons of a Greenwich Village faggot bar stood up to a senseless "routine" police raid triggering a two-day gay power demonstration and an ongoing wave of struggle for gay rights. Henry was inspired. He argued and insisted and finally the ad ran. It was the first

From her introduction to *Are We There Yet? A Continuing History of* Lavender Woman (1985)

gay ad ever in the *Maroon*.

At that time, I was a brash young dyke in the neighborhood looking for a place to live. I didn't know about gay liberation or women's liberation and I didn't care. Good affordable housing in that area was hard to find, and I was checking all possibilities. Since I fit the description I answered the ad.

It never occurred to Henry that a woman would respond. He wasn't thrilled. The existence of lesbians hadn't really ever occurred to him. He repeated that he wanted a *gay* roommate. I insisted that I was. It was a great apartment at a great price, and I was tired of looking. He said he'd have to think about it. Several days and no other takers later, he reluctantly offered me the room overlooking the dime store on 53rd Street, and I happily moved in.

As it turned out, Henry and I both worked part-time doing the same thing at the same place, and had never met or heard of each other. We started

going to work together, and hanging out together, and we became very tight friends. He was always talking about gay liberation, and Stonewall, and his fantasies of starting a group in Chicago that would work toward full social status for gay people. I thought it was a silly notion, and that all gay people needed was to like themselves, and we would argue for hours. Around November, he put ads in the *Maroon* to begin organizing meetings. The meetings were held in our living room on Sunday mornings, and Henry would wake me up and bother me until I came in.

I don't remember much about those early meetings except feeling annoyed at being there. I think there were six–eight people, almost all white, almost all men, a lot of nervousness, and no clear agenda. We must have had some stimulating discussions; after a few of those meetings I was hooked.

Through the fall and winter we met weekly and planned

activities. Our first daring move was to go to a university dance, and dance together in gay couples. We considered the action a big success simply because we didn't get beat up or harassed. Later we organized our own dances. In addition, we had certain regularly scheduled meals at a big table in an open dining room on the university campus, and advertised that we would be there so that new people could cruise by and maybe join us. Many did. We put a listing for Gay Liberation in the phone directory of Chicago's underground newspaper, the *Seed*, and advertised our meetings as widely as possible.

At that time, there were six or seven women who participated regularly, and several more who came and went. Interest in gay liberation was blossoming; new people were coming in all the time, but they seemed more and more to always be men. The women in the group were becoming rapidly outnumbered, and outvoiced as well.

As our frustrations with the direction of gay liberation grew, so did our identity as women. We started to really know that we weren't just female faggots. Our energy was different, our interests were different. We decided to have our own separate meetings, and we called ourselves the Women's Caucus of Gay Liberation, Women's Caucus for short.

I think there were eight or ten or so of us, and I think that at first, all we did was complain about the faggots: that they were always cruising, that they didn't care about lesbian issues, that they didn't listen to us, that they didn't even listen to each other. And when we got done complaining, I'm not sure what it was that we wanted to do, but we were happy to be together. By this time it was early 1970, and we'd all heard of women's liberation, conscious-ness-raising, and rap groups. Some of us had been in women's liberation meetings and brought up lesbianism, and were received with fear and scorn. We felt more denied by the (allegedly) straight women than we did by the faggots.

We made occasional trips as a group to local dyke bars, but we weren't real welcome there, either. We were a mixed race group, we were hippies, we were young. None of those things went over too well in the white lesbian bars. We never tried to go to the black lesbian bars, even though those were the closest to our neighborhood. As a group of mostly white women, we may have been motivated by some respect for black separatism, which was fairly prevalent then, but I suspect we were mostly motivated by fear. We didn't talk about it. Probably our treatment in the bars had a lot to do with being a large group of strangers all walking in together. We must have been intimidating, or certainly unapproachable, but we felt so disconnected and powerless ourselves that we were unable to know that.

We put ads in the under-ground and college papers announcing our meetings, and more women started coming. We met weekly in one another's homes, without set goals or agenda. During that period, the first eight months or so of 1970, there were generally about ten–thirty women at the meetings, with many of those women coming regularly so that some familiarity and trust was built up.

My recollection of those meetings is pretty vague. I remember that we mostly just talked informally about different lesbian-related topics. We had no treasury, no dues, no business to conduct that I can recall. I was personally very comfortable with the format, but I know that many women came who were frustrated with our lack of goals and insecure with our lack of structure, and usually those women didn't come back after the second or third time. That they came back at all says a lot about how hungry we were for contact with each other.

The tone of each meeting was set by the hostess and the general atmosphere of her home. Sometimes there were refreshments served; often marijuana was passed around. Every time there was someone new, she would tell her story, and want to hear everyone else's. We talked some about roles, butch and femme, I think mostly how we didn't want to be tied down to them.

Women's Caucus and the Gay Liberation group we grew out of started in the University of Chicago community. The university has a large population of political radicals, liberals, and progressives, and is situated in a somewhat racially integrated neighborhood adjacent to other mostly black neighborhoods. What that meant was that, while we weren't all university-affiliated, or even all South-siders, we were a pretty left-leaning group, and pretty well mixed by race and class. We were also mostly under thirty years old.

The meetings were advertised in the likeliest places, which were some university papers and the Chicago hippie papers, all of which had mostly white readerships, so the new women who came were mostly white. Most of these new women were Northsiders, and we start-ed alternating meetings between the north and south sides. As our membership expanded to include residents of many Chicago neighborhoods, most of which were (still are) rigidly segregated, some of the first overt racial conflict in the group surfaced. It was assumed that dark women were expected to travel to meetings in hostile white neighborhoods, while many white women objected to attending meetings at homes in black neighborhoods where they felt unsafe. My recollection is that there was not enough care or serious attention given to the problem in order to reach resolution. Volunteer hostesses were getting hard to find, and objections to any particular house were not very welcome. Some women at this time went only to meetings on their end of the city, and I think many women, especially dark women, stopped coming altogether.

A custom was established early on, and continued for years, of meetings adjourning to the bar for dancing and socializing. Lesbian bars were still the closest thing to a cultural home base that we had. Much of our discussion focused on the wish for a better socializing place, as we understood that the bars that existed then were mostly only interested in financially exploiting a captive population. The best of them, while perhaps comfortable, were still not forces for major change. The phrase "alternative to the bars" became part of our everyday speech. It's interesting to note, however, that the objections to bars at that time had virtually nothing to do with concerns about alcohol abuse.

Another significant aspect of going to the bar after each meeting was choosing which bar to go to. For a long time the bar of choice was one called King's Ransom, a primarily faggot bar very near downtown. It had a cozy atmosphere, good jukebox, and on Monday nights we usually had the place to ourselves. Eventually a disagreement developed with the owner. I don't remember exactly when it happened or what it was about, but we decided to take our business elsewhere. Much meeting time was devoted to discussing where to go. Suddenly we had become a bloc, a force. We understood that our Monday night dollars were im-

portant; we started to know our own strength.

The most popular choice for a new Monday bar, though, was one called the Up North. It was located on the extreme north side of the city, in an all-white neighborhood. It was a long way home from there to anywhere else in the city except the predominantly white North side. Many South-siders, largely dark women, objected to the choice, but the Up North prevailed. Based on atmosphere and hospitableness alone, that probably was the best of the limited choice of bars, but making the decision solely on those grounds further polarized the baby lesbian community along racial lines. Again, the discussions were not honest enough, since I'm sure we were all aware of what was going on.

♀♀

Through nearly the first whole year, the only stated purpose of Women's Caucus that I can recall was to be together. It can't be overemphasized how valuable it was to be in the company of other lesbians. Each woman had her story: of feeling like a freak in high school, or being an outcast in college, or hiding her terrible secret from friends, co-workers, husband. Every story made the burden of oddness and the shame of losing family or career diminish. The sense of validation we got from hearing each other was like a shelter in a blizzard, and for a long time we needed no more than that.

Late in 1970, the Women's Caucus started using meeting space in a gay community center house run by Chicago Gay Alliance. CGA was a citywide group of mostly faggots and a few lesbians that evolved from the original gay group at University of Chicago. The house was a few blocks from downtown, a reasonably central and more or less racially neutral location.

At the same time, the group started formulating some goals and purposes, and structuring the meetings somewhat. A woman with strong personality and eloquent speech emerged in something of a leadership role then. She caught a lot of crap from some of the more anarchy-minded members for taking the initiative in steering group activities, but women mostly went cheerfully along with her plans.

The women's liberation technique of consciousness-raising was adapted for use by Women's Caucus, and the large Monday night meetings would break into smaller groups to discuss a specific topic for a specific time, then come back and report to the others. I think that many of us who had been meeting all together all along, and coming to know each other gradually in more informal settings, were unhappy with what seemed to be artificial methods of communication. What we didn't allow for in our criticism was how much more difficult it must have been for new women to come into such a large group of diverse strangers and talk about very personal things. Having a formal focus and definite boundary to the discussions must have made opening up a lot easier.

With some structure operating, Women's Caucus became a more hospitable place for lesbians who weren't young hippie types. I attended few meetings during this period myself, but I remember seeing women there who were somewhat older and more conventionally dressed. Despite this broadening, the consciousness of the group continued to develop along radical paths. There were years of anger behind us, and the times were conducive to thoughts of change and social motion. And while feminists at the time were mostly turning their backs on lesbians, lesbians were beginning to explore the theories of feminism. What resulted was an explosion of energy, creativity, ideas, and activity.

Lavender Woman newspaper was part of that explosion, as was a theatre group, a car care group, a speakers' bureau, a Sunday afternoon open softball game, a counseling group, nurses' group, social workers' group, study groups, countless new friendships and relationships, as well as organized events like concerts and dances. A concert by singer/composer Linda Shear and drummer Ella Szekely was, as far as we knew, the first lesbian concert anywhere that was publicly billed as such, and from that event grew Family Of Woman, a lesbian feminist band. The tremendous power of music to influence lives was put to our own use, spreading messages of lesbian strength and joy to thousands of women in many places.

Much of the energy and fundraising went towards a lesbian center, a storefront that would contain facilities for a wide variety of activities, and eventually a center was opened. Also, a women's telephone support line was started. And, of course, Women's Caucus continued to meet.

At the time that *Lavender Woman* started, the Monday Night Meetings, as they were called, were regularly attended by as many as seventy women. We never referred to the Women's Caucus anymore, just Monday Night Meetings. It wasn't really an organization that we had, it was a collection of events. And events they were. The meetings were chaos. Bedlam. Total free-for-all. We did try at times having chairwomen; we tried to operate in some order, but by then we knew that hierarchies and rules were militaristic tools of patriarchal oppression, and of course we opposed that. We wanted everyone to participate freely. They did, usually all at once.

Those meetings were frustrating, distressing, and also somehow exhilarating. There was so much trying to happen that nearly everyone could find a like-minded sister or two to share ideas and make plans.

Out of that swirling, molten mass of spirit, *Lavender Woman* was formed. ▪

Lavender Woman Collective Statement

November, 1971

Lesbians, like the Red Queen in Lewis Carroll's *Through the Looking Glass*, live in a slow sort of country. We do a lot of running, just to stay in the same place. We do a lot of running from ourselves, from our identity, from our so-called straight sisters. We often find ourselves running from job to job, to avoid being recognized. We often lose our status, our seniority, our raises. Often we find ourselves running from sister to sister, looking for love, validation, recognition, that we must eventually find in ourselves, in our self-acceptance.

The *Lavender Woman* is a collective attempt to stop running, to stand still and firm in our places, so that we can stop depleting ourselves with evasion, manipulation and all those other defenses we've needed for our survival. We have to stop running in order to grow. We have to stop running

From Michal Brody's *Are We There Yet?* (1985)

from ourselves, from our sisters, to turn around and face one another, confront one another, love one another. We need to let it be, let ourselves be. We need to say loud and clear who we are, and where we are going. A Lesbian relationship, we are beginning to discover, is not a hazard, or a liability, but a gift and a virtue—a strengthening, redeeming relationship in which we mutually confirm our identities as women, in which we are free to let ourselves be real, rather than meet a male-sexist stereotype which society is always holding up for us to clumsily imitate. Our awkwardness we discover is grace, our so-called ugliness is beauty—in this world, everything is upside down—we are through the looking glass. Straight society seems dull, unreal, several layers from the truth. Our failure to meet straight standards of behavior is our ultimate success as real women. In this sense, Lesbianism is a powerful, revolutionary force within the Women's Move-

ment—a kind of avant-garde, as Flo Kennedy points out—we are the first women who have elected to survive without men. We even find ourselves being exploited by straight sisters in Women's Liberation who see Lesbianism as a kind of revolutionary Bandwagon they can jump on to get there quicker. We are attacked by supposedly nonsexist Gay men because we prefer to meet by ourselves, and recognize ourselves as a separate group in the Gay Liberation Movement. These and other challenges we are learning to face head-on. We found that running from them gets us nowhere. If we speak the truth, from where we see it, we can keep our heads and our souls together. We can keep others from foisting off their truths onto us—or speaking for us. Only then will we be able to honestly contribute to a revolutionary movement, in which groups working separately at their own liberation from where they are at, converge toward a

Inside the illustration:

LAVENDER
WOMAN 25¢

a Lesbian newspaper

VOLUME 1 NO. 1
NOVEMBER 1971

"Well, in our country," said Alice, still panting
a little, "you'd generally get to somewhere else--
if you ran very fast for a long time as we've
been doing."
    "A slow sort of country!" said the Queen. "Now
here, you see, it takes all the running you can
do, to keep in the same place. If you want to get
somewhere else, you must run at least twice as
fast as that!"

Lewis Carroll,
Through the Looking-Glass

S. MOORE

Cover of the first issue of *Lavender Woman* featuring
Alice and the Queen as drawn by Susan Moore

common goal—the reworking of this sexist and racist society closer to the heart's desire—a society based on real human need.

We, of the *Lavender Woman*, feel that this newspaper, written by and for Lesbians, is a powerful weapon against the society that tries, in vain, to keep us closeted and out of sight. More important, the paper will be a tool for growth. Through it, we can create a positive, viable Lesbian community; increase our political consciousness; communicate our feelings to one another; share with each other our knowledge and gifts and, above all, thank ourselves again and again for each other. We are not Lesbians in spite of ourselves, but because of ourselves. The paper will affirm that.

We welcome comments and suggestions. We urge all Lesbians to contribute a bit of themselves: letters, articles, poetry, photos, drawings, etc. It is our intention to print as many of the letters and articles as space allows. All letters written to us will be answered, if not in the paper, by personal correspondence. The *Lavender Woman* will be published monthly, providing our financial situation allows for it and, above all, depending on the feedback we get from our Gay sisters. ■

BLACKLESBIAN

by Margaret

What have you got to offer us? You wonder where we are and we say right in front of you. You offer us psychological rhetoric and we give you feelings and emotions which you charge are loud and violent. You cry dry tears while we bleed. You like to watch us dance for you but you never ask us to dance with you. You imagine/think/fantasize we fuck better which either keeps you on our backs or miles away. You assume we are mostly all dykes and the fem in us you try to butch. You use our blackness as an excuse more than we do and you never try to see the pain behind all our laughter. When you are around us you talk black and we find ourselves talking white and you even come to our parties bringing a 1969 Aretha Franklin record and when we confront you, you say we're too powerful to deal with and you can't come to our neighborhood after dark except in groups when *your* men have raped us (you too) for over 300 years. I can't call you my sister until you stop participating in my oppression. You can't have a struggle without all oppressed people—and black women, particularly black lesbians, have struggled harder than anyone. You need us and we can work and will work with you if only you accept us where we've been, where we are, where we come from.—1971

From Michal Brody's *Are We There Yet?* (1985)

Lavender Consciousness

by Susan Edwards

W e're trying to get a
newspaper committee
together. We're trying
to get together in the newspaper
committee. We're trying to get a
together newspaper together.

We've begun to rap to
each other about our collective
"isms" in order to establish a
lesbian feminist point of view
for the *Lavender Woman*. For
some, we rap too much; for others, not enough. The American
Way of Hypocrisy is sometimes
shattered and we emerge as we
really are—Beautiful.

We are beautiful. The
newspaper, for me, wants and
needs to speak to that issue—to
spread the news. We want to
create a dialogue, to extend it to
our sisters. Acknowledging your
beauty is a revolutionary act.

We are struggling. To say
it again, we are struggling
against an oppressor whose primary goal is economic domination. Economic power is secured

From Michal Brody's *Are We There
Yet?* (1985)

in this country by the exploita-
tion of the family unit. The family oppresses its children, the
husband oppresses his wife, etc.
We are struggling against that
dehumanization. We are not
economic pawns. We want to
regain, reclaim and re-establish
authority over our bodies, our
minds and our hearts.

The price? The contempt of
established society has kept us
down in the pit of ignorance
about our real selves. But we are
emerging, emergent and exploring the light. Economic oppression is inexorably bound to
white male supremacy. He
keeps us in inferior positions
economically, socially, politically—and if the lobotomized
housewife of TV commercial in-
famy is any indication—mentally and emotionally.

The role of lesbians in our
society is even more dehuman-
ized than that of straight
women. We are nothing more
than seducers of women and
manhaters. This is seen—if noticed at all—as bad, evil and

sick by those within the established power system of our society. We believe the opposite to
be true. It is good to love and be
loved by women and our contempt for men is the beginning
of our escape from their tyranny.

As lesbians, we do not
serve any recognizable purpose
in society, since we have "infil-
trated" all walks of life. We are
not just Workers, just Poor, just
Black or Chicano or Indian, or
just Establishment—we are
Women, which did not mean
much to anyone until we recognized that this was our solidarity. We are not interested in
consumer-consciousness-raising.

Before lesbian liberation,
my friends and I had found our
answer to the consumer question. We consumed ourselves
with passion. We fell in and out
of love with all the gusto of
salmon swimming upstream.
We knew that love was all that
was left for us. We used to sit
around and say "there is no future in gay relationships"—op-
pressing each other with equal

gusto. It was planned obsolescence.

One day some oppressed sisters and brothers stood up and shouted that they were beautiful. Oppression was turned on itself. The oppressor was defined. It isn't us after all, it's them. White heterosexual supremists had to relinquish their strangle-hold on beauty. It ultimately meant that sisterhood was not sick desperation, but affirmation of love between and for women. The struggle had begun. It has spawned its potent symbols: the interlocking symbols of the female kind, the two sisters "kissing and rubbing" in public. If my black sisters and brothers had not said they were beautiful, had not shown the power in beauty, I might still be thinking of new and exciting ways to stay in the closet.

We want to see women in positions of power and authority—lesbian women. We want the right to care for children if we want that.

We want the right to love and care for our sisters. We know who the oppressor is, we know that we have internalized much of our own oppression, but we also know that oppression can be fought and will be defeated.

We want to write a newspaper to chronicle that defeat; to analyze our failures along the way to liberation; to celebrate our victories as lesbians and women. We are getting it together. Join us. ■

—July, 1972

by Michal Brody, November 1972

504 ～～～～

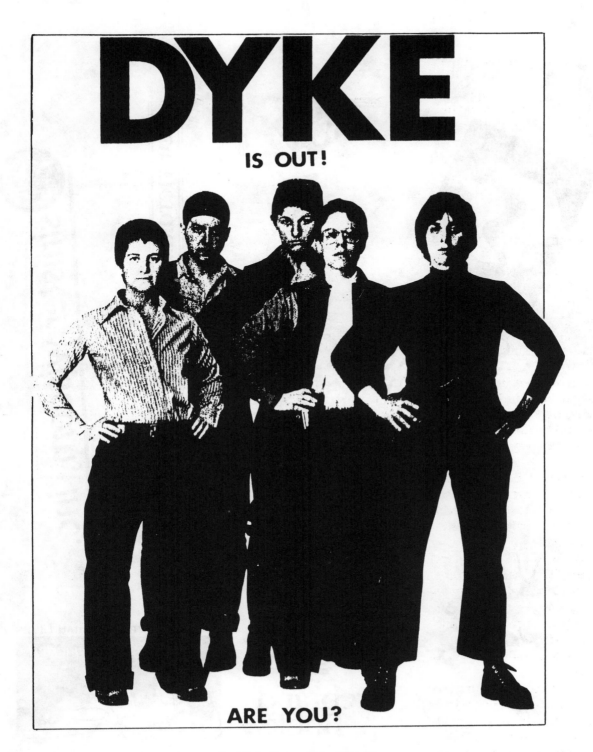

DYKE

IS OUT!

ARE YOU?

By Michelle and Liza Cowan

SEAL
PRESS

Lesbian Ethics

Persephone
Press

Naiad Press

Firebrand
Books

NEW VICTORIA
PUBLISHERS, INC.

sinister wisdom, inc.

COMMON LIVES/LESBIAN LIVES
a lesbian quarterly

Looking for Lesbians

by Marilyn Murphy

Looking for Lesbians is a hobby I share with my companion lover. It is an amusing pastime when we are at home, surrounded by women we know are Lesbians; but when we go traveling the back roads of North America in our motor home, looking for Lesbians becomes serious business. We usually stay in campgrounds in national, state, provincial, and county parks far from urban centers. As a result, we are not able to consult a phone book and then casually drop in at a local women's bookstore, bar, center whenever we need the sight of other Lesbians. We started our RV expedition firm in the belief that "We Are Everywhere!" Over the past four years, we have honed our looking for Lesbians skills to a fine art, and to our delight have found us everywhere.

So what does a Lesbian look like? Well, speaking very generally, a Lesbian, when not at work or in costume, looks like a woman for whom bodily comfort when wearing clothes is more important than appearing "attractive," that is, of drawing to one's self the sexual attention of men. Lesbians, generally, seem less elaborately dressed, made-up, coiffed, than other women. In fashion magazines this Lesbian look is called "understated."

"Looking for Lesbians" first appeared in *Finding the Lesbians*, edited by Julia Penelope and Sarah Valentine (Crossing Press, 1990) and *Are You Girls Traveling Alone?* (Clothespin Fever Press, 1991), a collection of Marilyn Murphy's "Lesbianic Logic" columns from *Lesbian News*.

So what does a Lesbian look like? I smiled and smiled at a stunning, short-haired woman standing alone at a scenic view pull-off on a Vermont highway. She was wearing highly polished, flat-heeled shoes, a blazer, a tailored silk blouse and sharply-creased pants. She slipped her hands, fingernails short and manicured, into her pockets and smiled back at me. We saw her again when she passed us on the road in a white Cadillac convertible with the top down. I honked and she smiled and waved as she sped by. Irene agreed the woman was a Lesbian and called me a flirt. She knows my fondness for the "blazer dyke" look.

The Lesbian clues here were more subtle than clothing. The fact that this Lesbian did not "soften" the severity of her clothes with a "feminine frill" was encouraging. For us, the clincher was the way she flipped that jacket behind her hip bones in an unmistakable dykely way as she put her hands in her pants pocket.

Checking out shoes when looking for Lesbians is an elimination device, a negative marker. Lesbians wear sensible shoes whenever possible. Irene and I learned to pass right by a woman who looks like a Lesbian from head to ankle, but wears flimsy shoes with pointed toes and heels. She is sure to mention a husband by her second sentence.

So what does a Lesbian look like? Well, we saw two old women drive into a campground in a large motor home. One dog and no men accompanied them. These are Lesbian-positive clues. We seldom see old women in campgrounds unless they are accompanied by old men. They walked the dog, each wearing a long "ladies" winter coat and lipstick. We casually intercepted them.

"Nice dog," says Irene. The dog growled. We mentioned the movie about nuclear war on TV the evening before.

"They should go to Russia. Show it to the Communists," they angrily replied. We walked on. If they were Lesbians, I did not want to know.

"Not Lesbians," pronounced my expert. "There are Lesbians who wear 'ladies' coats and Lesbians who wear lipstick. There are even Lesbians who prefer nuclear war to 'Godless Communism'; but Lesbians would not let their dog growl at women without correcting it."

We had better luck with two old women in a pickup truck pulling a thirty-foot trailer. The dyke driving backed the rig into the campsite next to us in three moves! We walked over to check them out. They were wearing identical jackets adorned with patches from every state park in South Carolina. We admired their trailer; they admired our motor home. We talked about favorite parks. Then one woman asked,

"You two sisters?"

I answered, "No, are you?"

"Nope!" They smiled and invited us for dinner in their thirty-footer. It wasn't more than three sentences later that we were using the "L" word.

In our travels, we frequently see pairs of women who pique our interest. They wear either look-alike backpacks or look-alike boots or shoes, windbreakers or parkas, or all of the above, in the same color, style, or brand. We call it the Lesbian Bobbsey Twins look. We love it. We've met lots of great Lesbians because of it.

At a campground in Maine, we were in the laundry staring at the dryer when a blue van pulled up. It contained two women and one large dog. The woman nearest us was wearing three tiny earrings in one ear and no make up. I started to get excited, but Irene advised caution. She reminded me that the line between Dyke attire and non-Lesbian casual is fuzzy nowadays. The stranger hauled herself out of the van in one large motion. She stood there, in hiking boots and blue jeans, smoothing out the wrinkles in her plaid flannel shirt. When she smiled in that certain way at her similarly clothed companion, Irene admitted we had struck gold. She ambled out of the laundry wearing her WOMEN TAKE BACK THE NIGHT T-shirt and struck up a conversation with the women. Soon, we were enjoying our first four-Lesbian conversation in a month and loving it.

Lesbians can usually be found in the company of other women. Non-Lesbians frequently spend most of their time with women too, so this is not a clue in and of itself. Refinements are needed.

One warm November day, walking along the path through the sand dunes at Huntington Beach State Park in South Carolina, we saw two women seated on a blanket on the deserted beach. We stood and watched them a minute and knew they were Lesbians. How did we know they were Lesbians? Well, I thought they were Lesbians because they were two women over thirty, seated together while flying a kite. They were not amusing a child. They were not holding the kite for a husband. They were sitting on a beach and flying a kite for their own pleasure, an unlikely activity for non-Lesbians.

"John dear, I am going camping with Mary for a few days so we can bask on the beach and fly kites," she says.

"What a great idea," he says. "Have a good time."

No way!

Irene was sure they were Lesbians when the woman with the kite, wanting to stand up, handed the kite-string holder to the other woman without asking AND without looking to see if she was taking it. They knew we were Lesbians, not because we were two middle-aged women on the beach at a park unaccompanied by children or men. They said they knew because of the intimacy they perceived in our gestures, movements, conversation and activity as we set up our beach space.

Another time we set up camp in a park in Manitoba in sight of a motor home with Florida plates. We watched a woman emerge with a dog on a leash. She was wearing a green and white striped rugby shirt tucked into very tailored cotton pants which were closed with a narrow belt. Her hair was short and her face was make-up free. Irene went out to make conversation using the dog as a pretense. Pretty soon she called me over "to see the dog." Juanita was talkative and kept saying "we" this and "we" that. She did not mention a husband; and her conversation was remarkably free of sex-specific pronouns. We were encouraged. It wasn't long before Ginny stuck her head out the RV door, saw us and came over. She was dressed much like her partner, the Bobbsey Twins again. We had a fine time with them. Like us, they were retired and living full-time on the road.

Of course, all of our Lesbian clues are only partly true, or sometimes true, or for some Lesbians, never true. Irene has been looking for Lesbians for forty years and she still gets fooled—not in thinking a woman is a Lesbian when she is not, but in thinking a woman is not a Lesbian when she is. I err in the other direction, assuming women as Lesbians only to have them stroll away, hanging onto the arm of a non-woman.

Still, there is an unmistakable something about Lesbians. Perhaps it is the walk; and I do not mean the Lesbian stomp. The Lesbian walk is a solid placing of the feet on the ground, not a tentative, tippy-toed sway, but the assertively nonchalant stride of a woman who belongs to herself. I have seen Lesbians costumed for work in dresses and high-heels, walking Lesbian. The sight is awe-inspiring.

Along with the walk is a certain stance, a way of moving the body that is Lesbian. Lesbians, generally, move as if the various parts of our bodies, in use at the moment, belong to us, not as if the parts were borrowed from their owners and heaven help us if we bruise anything.

Standing with one's feet apart, rather than with one foot slightly forward, or with one foot carrying most of the weight, is a Lesbian stance. One or both hands in the pockets of pants, especially when wearing a blazer, is a Lesbian stance. More than eight inches of space between the knees when sitting in slacks in public is suspect; crossing one's legs by putting the ankle of one leg on the knee of the other is a dead giveaway!

However, the most telling clue when looking for Lesbians is eye contact. I learned about the eye contact theory from Rita Mae Brown when we first met back in 1975. She said she can tell a woman is a Lesbian when she makes eye contact with her. If the woman looks back, holding contact instead of letting her gaze slide quickly away, she is probably a Lesbian.

"That's not true," I argued. "I usually make eye contact with women; and I am not a Lesbian."

"Hmmmmmmm!" said Rita Mae as she began to laugh. ∎

Amazon ABC

words by Alix Dobkin

music based on "The Alphabet Song"

"A" you're an Amazon
"B"-coming brave and strong
Clearly and consciously you "C"
"D" you're so Dykey
"E" how you excite me
How Fortunate a female faculty
"G" I guess it's good for me
"H" how heavenly
"I" never knew how butchy I could be
"J" for sweet justice
"K" for sweet kisses
"L"-e-s-b-i-a-n for letting go of
"M"-e-
"N"
"O"-pression is no longer over me
"P" is political: Power to the personal
"Q" for the queer you feared you are
"R" Remember you gotta respect your
"S"-sential sensibility (sexuality)
Time and truth touch (Between us is a tie)
"U"-terine empathy
"V" is for vagina, the virgin you can (vibration)
"W" experience (a universe) until you can do (get through to) just
"X"-actly what you want (where you want) to exist
"Y" let them drive you craaa- (not wise up, but it's not ea-)
"Z"

Now I know my "ABC's"
Next time won't you sing with me?

"Amazon ABC" is on *Living with Lesbians* (1976)

Pictures by Roberta Gregory

amazon ABC

"A" you're an amazon...

Becoming brave and strong...

Clearly and consciously you "C"...

"D" you're so dykey...

"E" how you excite me...

how Fortunate a female faculty...

Gee, I guess it's good for me...

"H", how heavenly...

I never knew how butchy I could be...

"J" for sweet justice...

"K" for sweet kisses...

L·E·S·B·I·A·N~

For letting go of "M"·e·"N"~

Oppression is no longer over me...

"P" is political power to the personal.

"Q" for the queer you fear...

- you "R"! remember you gotta' respect ---

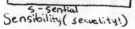

S - sential sensibility (sexuality!)

- between us is a Tie...

Uterine empathy...

"V" is for vagina the virgin...

- you can "double you'r" experience (+ universe!) --

until you get thru to X-actly where you want to "X"-ist...

"Y" not wise up....

"Y" let them drive you cra- "Z"!

NOW I KNOW MY A-B-C... NEXT TIME WON'T YOU SING WITH ME?

Roberta Gregory

512

A Cursory and Precursory History of Language, and the Telling of It

by Julia Penelope

Today I offer my words to the women who created me in love and in life, in our lives, of whom I am and will be in this life. This is my telling of our history, of how I dreamed it, of how we came into our own sayings.

> (the men) say that they have said, this is such or such a thing, they have attached a particular word to an object or a fact and thereby consider themselves to have appropriated it. The women say, so doing the men have bawled, shouted with all their might to reduce you to silence. The women say, the language you speak is made up of words that are killing you. They say, the language you speak is made up of signs that rightly speaking designate what men have appropriated. Whatever they have not laid hands on, whatever they have not pounced on like many-eyed birds of prey, does not appear in the language you speak. This is apparent precisely in the intervals that your masters have not been able to fill with their words of proprietors and possessors, this can be found in the gaps, in all that which is not a continuation of their discourse, in the zero, the O, the perfect circle that you invent to imprison them and overthrow them.
>
> (Monique Wittig, *LES GUÉRILLÈRES*, p. 114)

Winter Solstice, the year 400 of the Age of Women. The time of processes evolving themselves out of what has been. The women emerging into the light, out of the earth that had sheltered them for 200 years. This is the story of one woman and her going-out, the story of what she knew and carried within her, bringing her past to the future.

The "feminist solution" had come easily, as things do, when everyone had relaxed and stopped stumbling over themselves. As usual, the solution was the easiest and the most obvious, and had been within reach forever, but no one had seen it. We had been looking off into the distance for so long that the obvious was easy to miss, being obvious. And the analysis of the feminist situation came even easier.

Energy. That simple. Women had energy. Men, *lords and masters of the earth*, as they'd liked to call themselves, with typical presumption, had indeed been "masters" of a simple trick of manipulation which had given them the control of energy they needed to maintain their "ego-strength." During the long centuries known as the Time of Men, they had learned to tap into energy sources. They had learned to draw the huge quantities of energy they required from the earth, water, fire, sun, and atom. Most importantly, they had learned how to draw energy from women. The major difference, however, between the energy of women and other kinds of energy was that the energy of women, *psychic energy*, couldn't be stored or controlled. So men

From *Sinister Wisdom* 1 (July, 1976).

had put the women in little boxes, which they called "houses," restrained the power of female energy with monogamy, channeled that energy into maintaining the nuclear family, and plugged it in a direct line to male supremacy. This insured that every man would have a life-long supply of one woman's psychic energy to support him in his struggles with other men. No man had to earn such support; it was his as a result of what some called "divine right" and others called "survival of the fittest." Fortunately, men didn't live as long as women, so we had a few years to ourselves as we prepared for our dying. Without that permanent source of psychic energy, men were about as powerful as dead storage batteries or burnt-out light bulbs. And the analogy will hold if you work it out to its conclusion.

Now, some have insisted on asking *why* women, if they were so strong, even in those days, went on letting men harness them and use them without resisting in some way. Some have even gone so far as to suggest that this *lack of resistance* proves the "inferiority" of women. After all, how could any person be *stupid* enough to remain trapped for so long? Which is only one way of asking a ridiculous question, a pseudo-question. Women did not "fight back" because they didn't have the energy to construct alternatives for themselves. They had learned to be content with living, breathing, and caring, each

in her own way. It was the women, after all, who maintained living, who nurtured, who fed, who clothed, who created the "home." They had not yet realized that they could nurture and feed each other, and they rarely begrudged their giving to these weaker creatures who seemed to need nurturing so much more than they did. Consequently, there was no "battle to be fought." Women smiled, encouraged, and sometimes wept, and went on being women, although they began to wear themselves out trying to fulfill the needs of men. (Men required tremendous quantities of energy.) You could always spot a woman who was connected to men in those days, especially toward the beginning: they began to age quickly, usually within three or four months after accepting the male. They would developed a harried, weary look, severe lines around the eyes and mouth, and their eyes would become clouded with pain and frustration. In the latter days, women began to turn to each other, and the effects of living with men became clearer to everyone, because these woman-loving-women, who had as little as possible to do with men and their tiring games, looked fuller, healthier, somehow more alive and self-satisfied.

The men, meanwhile, went on about their "business," making more "business" for themselves, setting traps and springing them, breaking them, putting them back together. Of

course, part of the arrangement that pleased the men the most was called "the double standard," even back then. Women were taught, usually by their mothers, that they were to love only one man forever, and it usually worked out that way, because the women didn't have the time or the energy for exploration. The men, on the other hand, were free to "raid" other women of their energy, as long as no one noticed that they were draining more than one woman. In fact, having more than one woman for energy was a great source of pride to them, since it proved that they were "manlier than other men," and they loved to boast of their "conquests."

At any rate, once women began to love themselves and each other, they awakened and realized what had been happening to their lives, and they started to move together, what they called "a movement," a moving in and out of each other's lives, and it was only a question of time until they came to know each other, and the future began to happen. Therein lay the solution, although no one knew it then, looking back on the events that we now see to be inevitable. Energy being energy, it will always flow in the direction of least resistance. You can cut channels for it, as the men had, channels like "marriage" to make it move easier, but energy will flow with or without the channels.

What sparked those first feminists was the fact that men

had begun to take themselves seriously, actually believing that their pretensions and pomposities were profound and important events! They thought they were NECESSARY!! They began to believe that they were self-perpetuating, and it finally reached a point where they had plundered and pillaged, ravaged and raped, not only the women, but the earth, and each other. It became clear that the energy was running low, because men *used* a lot of energy, but they were physically and psychically incapable of *returning* energy to its source. They never put anything back into the resources they were using up so quickly, and things got worse and worse, and the men became dissatisfied and irritable as they had less and less energy with which to propel themselves, and they didn't understand what was happening. They didn't think there was anything to understand.

The feminists, all this time, went on having meetings where everyone disagreed about everything imaginable, talking and arguing with other women, putting out a lot of energy and getting a lot of energy from other women, which they called "consciousness-raising," learning to love themselves and each other, and learning to do all the things they had believed they couldn't do. Nothing seemed to make sense, and then all of it made sense, and they continued to become what they were becoming. They were getting ready for what was going to

Those of us alive now will never be whole, but we'll die on the way to regaining our full womanpower. Others, who come after us, will be the women we aspire to be.

happen, preparing themselves for living in a new world coming around. They had ceased to oppose the ordering of the men, had realized that opposing, the act of opposing, drains energy, creating its opposite, lack of energy. They had learned that opposing a thing merely feeds it and strengthens it, giving it a reason to continue itself. Instead, they withdrew into their centers, forcing the men to oppose them, to drain themselves in the idle activity of battle *against*, while the women began to live *for*. The women, growing toward wholeness, began to understand that opposition is itself: *opposition*. The men, in their appropriation of the world, had defined identity *as* opposition. The women, in becoming themselves, began to create identities

out of themselves, on a new ground. They refused to oppose, for opposition merely validates that which it negates. Now, none of them knew how to live differently, but they came to understand that whatever was coming around would grow out of their lives, and they knew that "dissent must transcend the status of negative identification." They had to create the future out of themselves.

The feminists went underground all over the world, moving into the large networks of underground caverns, taking with them their psychic energy, leaving the men to their own violent devices. They took their power into themselves and transformed their lives. Because things that are going to happen will happen, women gave their energy to each other, which meant there was no depletion among them, and the men destroyed themselves on the "horns (so to speak) of their own dilemma."

When the women began to withdraw more and more noticeably, in increasing numbers, the men didn't know what to do. But they tried everything that could come into their one-track minds, and all they could think about was "how to get the women back." What is a man without a woman? So they stormed, they threatened, they raged, they killed, and finally, they begged, pleaded, and yes, even wept. To no avail. We'd heard all the lines before, maybe phrased a little more subtly, but a line is a line!

Things went back and forth for awhile. It took anywhere from three to five years in those times for a woman to be born to herself again, and even today we're still sorting through, getting rid of centuries of bondage and drainage. Those of us alive now will never be whole, but we'll die on the way to regaining our full womanpower. Others, who come after us, will be the women we aspire to be.

Back to our story. The women began to leave the men, singly at first, then in twos and threes, often waiting until nightfall to slip away to the nearest underground group. The men couldn't find them, although they tried. Even if they had been able to find them, there was nothing they could do to accomplish their purpose, getting back

the women. This was their dilemma: they needed the women in order to continue to do the things they had always done; but all they knew was violence and hatred. In order to get the women out of the caves, they would have had to blow the caves up, thus killing the women, thus destroying the very thing they were after. In their anger, they would have destroyed the women who were the targets of their anger, and the reason for the anger in the first place. All that they knew how to do was fight and coerce and destroy. Even their promises were transparent threats. Therein lay the paradox, the consequences, and the solution. Since men needed women for psychic energy, they couldn't risk destroying them. Without women, they had only their own negative energy, and in one last, desperate rage, they turned their negative energy on themselves, blowing themselves into eternity. Leaving the earth, such as it was, to the women.

And we learned and grew together in the caverns, reclaiming the powers we had put aside and denied, learning much together of joy and wholeness. Learning again to love, creating from our loving a language of feeling, of movement, of growing. The language of women loving became a language of sharing love, a speaking of minute sensualities and flickering tongues, a language that expressed our thoughts and feelings, quick things, languid things, but alive and changing.

The language we had learned in the world of men, the language we had brought with us to the caverns, gradually fell away from our minds. Its rigidity, the inflexibility of its categories, its need for classification, were no longer sufficient for the things we were experiencing. We no longer had space for dichotomies and abstractions, for as we outgrew dichotomies, we found we didn't need abstractions. Our eyes became alive, and our language formed itself out of our perceptions of distinctions evolving within us and around us. We no longer needed that peculiar fusion of opposites in expressing our joy or our disappointment. Words that had once served the dual functions for describing our sexuality and our feelings of rage or disgust began to drop out of usage; we did not need to speak of being fucked, screwed, nailed, or ripped off, nor did we have any use for the strange combination of violence and sex that we had learned from such words. As our understanding of change grew out of our own changes, so our use of time began to change, and we understood how the present was the creative evolution of the past blending with the possibility of the future. And our language gradually developed a time in which our memories of the time before and our hopes for the days to come blended and fused.

In the caverns, we learned to explore silence, both what it had meant to us before and what it might come to mean in our understanding. In the old days, before we had come to know ourselves, we had felt uneasy within our silences, the silences that often come among people. Then, our silences had been painful, uneasy obstacles that we tried to leap with words; but our words were empty, not carrying meanings to ourselves or others, because we were afraid of our meanings, of our feelings. Because our words were empty, we would throw them into our silences, trying to fill our silences with noises, chattering teases, lips and tongues struggling toward meaning, but our throats tensed to strangle any meaning that might slip through our defenses. We had carefully been taught to excise our thoughts and feelings from our spoken words and, in the process, we came to realize how we had falsified our words and our silences, thereby betraying ourselves. We had filled our silences with words that pointed *away* from our center, and the awkward silence into which we had hurled our useless words had remained, full of the strain and tensions of our unexpressed motivations, expectations, and fears. And that jostling crowd of what we did not say became the air we breathed.

As we grew in knowing ourselves, we put aside the language we had once cherished for its ambiguities, although we had called those ambiguities "subtle nuances." We had once been proud to speak a language in which we had no means of speaking our meanings clearly, even to ourselves. First, we had to discover our meanings, and out of that discovery grew a language that expressed them clearly. As strength dissolved our need for fear we began to explore our silences, which came to satisfy us as rest and the fulfillment of meaning. We learned to speak only where there is meaning in our words. That was the hardest thing we had to learn, so many of us did not know we had meanings.

The language that evolved out of our learning together was a language of acting in the world, rather than "events"; it was a speaking of our living, not our "lives"; of our doing, not our "deeds"; of our touching, eating, tracing, dancing, of moving, not "motion," of dying, not "death." The nouns of men became our verbs, what had been "objects" became doers. The abstraction, the labeling, the classification, the imposing of a fixed, external order was no longer needed. "Love," "death," "honor," "dignity," and "trust" were expressed in our living together; we did not need to speak of such things as though they were unreal, fragile. Through the verb we entered into the world and began to understand the other beings in the world as they lived. We began to learn to participate in the world, to move and grow with it, and so our speaking became our meaning in the life of the world.

There is a story we still tell for the joy of the telling, of a group of women who once gathered together, and some of the women called for words from the other women, and out of these words they wove a chant, and the chant became a singing together. And one woman yelled out the word *anarchism*, which was then woven into the fabric of the chanting, and in the chanting that word became *orgasm*, going on.

Accept this telling of me as it is of you. We belong to ourselves. Feel the power that is yours swell and lift within you. It is yours. It is you. It is all of us. Womanlove self-creating womanpower within us. Take your power into your hands and lift them up, your power living in you. Let us join our hands together in strength and in love, the radiant power of women. Let us speak the language of our living. ■

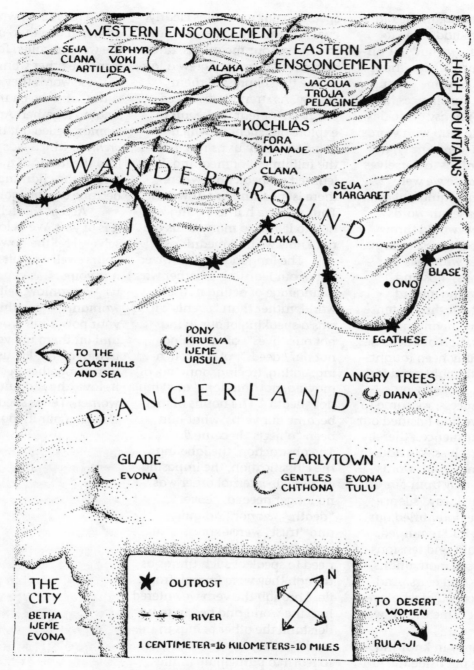

WESTERN ENSCONCEMENT
SEJA ZEPHYR
CLANA VOKI
ARTILIDEA ALAKA

EASTERN ENSCONCEMENT
JACQUA
TROJA
PELAGINE

HIGH MOUNTAINS

KOCHLIAS
FORA
MANAJE
LI
CLANA

SEJA
MARGARET

W A N D E R G R O U N D

ALAKA

BLASE

ONO

EGATHESE

PONY
KRUEVA
IJEME
URSULA

TO THE
COAST HILLS
AND SEA

ANGRY TREES
DIANA

D A N G E R L A N D

GLADE
EVONA

EARLYTOWN
GENTLES EVONA
CHTHONA TULU

THE CITY
BETHA
IJEME
EVONA

★ OUTPOST

- - - RIVER

N

TO DESERT
WOMEN

RULA-JI

1 CENTIMETER=16 KILOMETERS=10 MILES

Map of the Wanderground
by Elizabeth Ross,
the first page of the book by Sally Gearhart.

The Remember Rooms

by Sally Gearhart

Clana could not love the foul smell of the Kochlias' bathing waters. Even now, all dry and ready for her first rememberings, her soft palate snapped shut at the thought of that water. It might be warm and healing, and it was wonderful to be soothed and bathed by other people like she had been this morning, but her preference was still the cold clear springs of the ensconcement. She scrunched into the niche she had built for herself: a large heap of small pebbles which made a backrest and a mound of pebbles and coarse sand that curved around to rest each of her arms.

"Why bathe anyway?" she asked herself, finding at last the magic form-fitting movement that made her suddenly completely comfortable. Her bare body was almost reclining now, cushioned by the remember room's custom seating accommodations. Around her in the windowless chamber were nearly a dozen other girl-children who were digging out and settling into their places amid giggles and chattering.

Ranged around the room on a continuous ledge far above her head sat four cats. Another joined them even as she watched. Each one lay crouched with closed eyes but with its body in an alert position as if ready to spring. Clana reminded herself that the cats knew it all better than any of the women. They were the most regular attendants at the rememberings. And they were necessary, too. They filled in missing connections in the stories and added portions that the remember-guides occasionally forgot. Sometimes, it was said, as many as thirteen cats (and sometimes kittens) came to a remembering. Ordinarily, though, there were four or five and sometimes only two. If none came then the rememberings would usually be postponed, for few remember-guides trusted even their special training without the help of catwatch.

Clana thought she recognized the cream calico from last evening's ministrations. She enfolded it with a question. "Do you enjoy remembering?"

To her surprise the cat responded, "Do you enjoy breathing?" Clana withdrew, tiptoeing her enfoldment back to herself. She had overstepped. Everybody knew that remembering was in fact what a cat *was*, except for hunting, of course, and grooming and eating, all of which a cat also *was*. Joining in the intensified remembering with all the women must have been for them just a special high. Clana surrounded the calico with an apology for the interruption. There was a brief acknowledgment before the cat closed off once more.

A number of adult women moved about the room now, apparently oblivious to the cats. Among them were Alaka and Nova, the remem-

Excerpt from *The Wanderground*. Newton, MA: Persphone Press, 1979.

ber-guides for today. She saw Britta, from the East-ern Ensconcement, with whom she shared a mother, and some other girl-children that she had seen but did not know. Some of the women were returning for a second or third or tenth time for the rememberings. Voki was one of those. Clana watched as Voki helped smaller ones to find the proper indentations and paddings for their bodies.

Clana's excitement was mounting again. She forgot all about the foul-smelling water and concentrated on making a memory of this very experience. As she absorbed every detail around her she was also aware of some of her own impa-tience. It had certainly taken long enough to come to this moment. First you had to travel all the way to the Kochlias and then you had to spend the whole morning in ritual singing and dancing and bathing and all the other getting ready. And then you had to hear all about what was *going* to happen in the remember rooms, how the guides would shield you and then teach you to shield so that you didn't feel all the stories in your hardself.

Clana had known all that before from her conversations with Alaka and she'd been anxious to get on with the stories themselves. One of her mothers was fond of saying that Clana loved a story better than brown beans and cornbread. It was true. When she couldn't cajole someone else into telling even an old tale, Clana would make up her own stories, peopling them with any living thing, stringing together scenes and events with chaotic abandon. She had looked forward for most of her seven years to this week, to the time when she would learn the rich history of the hill women. No wonder she bristled at the delays. No wonder she had resisted even the majestic Nam-ing of the Names—the chanting of the long list of women who had given their stories to the remem-ber rooms. She had paid respect to them all by joining in the recitation, but her heart was leap-ing ahead to the seeing of the episodes about the City, the Purges and Hunts, to the understanding at last of the Revolt of the Mother.

Alaka and Nova were beginning now to enwomb the entire group. They drew together each separate energy center into a new matrix,

inviting each to new meaning-making. Clana felt gently swayed. She felt safe. She felt well-loved and excited. The rememberings were about to be-gin. Nova was settling onto a wellworn sand pal-let and was leaning against the far stone wall. Alaka picked her way carefully around the sitting and reclining bodies and knelt beside Nova. The two guides, enwrapping the whole group, also sought assurances from each girl-child and woman and cat that each was ready. As Clana opened to the questions, she was astonished at the difference between this and other group stretches. There was an immediate center here and that center was clearly Nova. Already the rememberer was immersed in a swirl of history. Already Clana could feel the heavy reinforcement of five cat memories. As each child or woman joined the enfoldment, the breathings also joined one another, seeking a rhythm, a unity. Nova seemed to drift deeper, to hold more seriously all the sensations she was about to share. The con-cern for the listeners was Alaka's job. Clana could sense her friend's weaving in and out of the open channels, assuring each that any listener could receive as much or as little as she wished of the narratives.

"Once upon a time," Nova's sending began, "before the Purges, once upon a time…" As Clana found herself repeating with the others the "once upon a time," she eased over the top of her prepa-ratory breath and stepped off into the past. Her last hardself thought was of moving into dreams with an itchy nose.

At first there was only the tumult of sounds, voices, colors, scraps of a thousand memories in swift succession. "…the mask immediately to your face. Cover your mouth and nose with the mask and breathe normally. Again, we welcome you aboard Flight…" Sandalwood and wine, with the purple candle spilling its yellow insides all over the phone bill and the dresser cloth. The wires outside my window intersect at small and large angles all over the sky. A man calls my name and I answer. He is at the door smiling. A tall bearded smile. He lies down beside me here on the low bed…"At a speed of ten point six times the square root of the air pressure in the tires a car will hydroplane on wet or frosty pavement…" Inch high steaks. Fat and dripping grease. High flames and waves of heat. "I'll quit if he doesn't get the fan going by tomorrow…" "Liz, Rosie's won! The Amazons are city champions! I was out stealing third but we recouped. The party's tonight…" There he comes again stumping through the hall with that walker. I can't stand it another minute. I'll tell Jim we have to call the nursing home tomorrow…Heavy rhythms, roaring ears, flashing colored lights, a hundred sweating undulating bodies, bending, turning, stomping, clapping, rushing, shouting. Next time I can't wear this damned brassiere… Firelight making pale faces pink. Short blue pants and day's end white shirts stamped "Camp Mikatusi." Treble voices hugging each other. Smiles and joy and longing. A spark flies upward. The velvet sky extinguishes it…It is midnight and he has not returned. I sit and spin these beads waiting for him. The child is crying in the hot night…"Don't play with the doggie, dear. He's not very clean. See? His ears are all matted and he has fleas. This man is going to take care of him. Leave him alone now. We'll go see the clowns…" Green shit. Her panties are full of green shit. And running like mustard. I wonder if I ought to call McIntyre…"750,000 March for Free Abortion." Busy newsprint, shots of laughing women, shouting women. Signs. "Why reproduce in captivity anyway?" "It's *My* Body." "No Forced Sterilization!" That mounted policeman does not believe the signs…Other pages, other print: "Rhodes Scholars Say Women's Lib Didn't Help Them a Bit," "Clarke Chooses Female Running Mate," "Nobel Scientist Refuses Woman-of-the-Year Award," "Lesbian Priest," "Corporate Power Moving to Women." Papers, inks, funnels, brushed cotton, ski lifts, resins, commodes, caresses, slick walls, sketches, fireworks, forceps, buttons, wrenches, antiseptics, placards, glasses, foams, weeds, skates, cuts, keys, tags, beers, drains, drinks, shouts, shrieks…

"Too fast! Too fast!" Clana found herself calling aloud.

"Breathe, Clana," Alaka was saying.

"You're all right. We'll focus now."

Immediately Clana felt her own control enter the rememberings. She inhaled once more with the others, allowing her breath to be a long time falling. With her softself she reached out and embraced an armful of scattered sensations, set them all aside, gathered another, set them aside. There was in the remembering now a movement toward a particular place, a particular person: each of the girl-children and women stepped behind the eyes and ears of a long-dead hill woman and made her memory their own.

"A story at last!" thought Clana.

"…makes us just like him. Count me out." Lynn's anger shook the heavy table. She shoved her chair back, breathing loud. Without looking at the other three women she threw a dime on the table, picked up her pack and headed toward the cashier.

"Fuck you, Lynn!" Amy thought to herself. Her own anger kept her from speaking aloud.

Ellen broke the stunned silence with her heavy voice. "Wait a minute!" Lynn turned. Ellen was on her feet now. She spoke low so that other women in the coffeehouse would not hear. "Who're you going to talk to?"

Lynn turned so that she cut off any view from other groups. She spoke directly into Ellen's livid face. "I'm going to talk to nobody. *Nobody!* In fact, I'm leaving town in the morning like I started to do before you got this off-the-wall idea." She turned to Amy and Jan, almost hissing in her effort to keep her voice down. "Jesus, I thought we were getting together a harmless night ride with a little purple prick painting and at the most a branding. I didn't bargain for killing the guy!"

Jan spoke. "And who else do you figure is going to put him out of the way! Eight women for sure we know he's raped and he's *already been* on one of your 'harmless little night rides,' for Christ's sake. You think that stopped him?"

"We don't know that—" Lynn began.

Amy felt her stomach churning. She was overly aware of her past closeness with Lynn and now her own anger was warring against the out-rage that she sensed in the other woman. "Lynn," she said, trying to talk calmly. "Sit down for just a minute. Then you can go."

"Looks like we're all going," Ellen muttered. They turned to see Barbara coming toward them making the gesture with her hands that told them the house was closing.

"It's only seven-thirty," Jan protested loudly.

"Don't hassle me right now. Just get out. There's three guys who're raising hell because we won't serve them. We're closing up entirely."

"So what happened to all the safe-space-for-women rhetoric?" Ellen wanted to know.

"Look." Barbara was pissed. "We gave them the whole rundown, told them they could go to the bookstore or the bar or to almost any other part of the building. They're looking for trouble and I'm on alone. So just go." She gathered the dishes in one hand, mopped the table with the other.

"Come on," Lynn was saying. "We can talk at my place while I get my stuff together."

"Helluva way to run a business," muttered Jan, pushing her part of the tip toward Barbara's heavy rag.

Amy followed the three women to the cash drawer, straining to see through the doorway if the men were still outside. "Watch out, boys," she thought. "We're not in a good mood tonight."

Nova was leading them through Amy's story, then the ins and outs of Ruth's, Linda's, Helen's, Dorinda's, Priscilla's, Sourcera's, Modutu's, Erika's and more, a hundred episodes all lived in a few hours, all retold and re-remembered, recalling the days when life in the cities was a freer thing for women. The stories were still going on when the sun above the Kochlias finally left the sky and Clana was roused by Alaka from the high energy of a women's dance. All the others save Nova had one-by-one been lifted out of the past and carried or guided from the remember room. As she drew back to her hardself Clana protested aloud. "Wait! I have to—"

It was Nova who spoke next, shaking herself out of the rememberings. "We'll pick up the dance again another time," she sent. "Promise." To Alaka she stretched, "I'll wait here for ministrations. Will you join me?"

"Yes," sent Alaka, lifting Clana to her shoulders. "The River Singers from beyond the plains are still here. They have offered to do our ministrations tonight."

"Good. They have wonderful hands. Hurry back." Nova collapsed immediately into a deep sleep.

"How about some food?" sent Alaka to Clana.

"I don't think I can eat," Clana replied, and before Alaka ducked her head through the door to the corridor there was a limp girlchild on her shoulder, joining Nova in an exhausted and dreamless sleep.

Then there were the other remember rooms the next day, the ones with the relics—corridor after corridor of strange items, each shelved and covered by a field of fixed-and-flexible patterns which could best be called an explanation. Clana did not understand the magic that the Kochlias workers had summoned in order to make it happen; she only knew that as she touched each artifact her hands and arms and even all the cells in her body were filled with the knowledge of—or speculation about—that article's use. She stood now, stroking a connected series of twelve iron pipes which her senses told her were once used for heating. Her forehead and lips were equally puckered in her effort to figure how the water must have gotten hot. Most of all she felt pressured and frustrated under her puzzlement, almost angered, in fact, that she would never be able to visit for very long with any of the relics. Even now it was almost time to go to the rememberings again—rememberings today of the Purges and the Hunts. And she hadn't even been yet to the rooms where all the books and hard pictures were.

She swept her eyes over all that she had studied just this morning—tea bag, lincoln logs, dixie cup, dog license, spark plugs, skateboard, handcuffs, bolts with washers, bolts without washers, rheostats, bus transfers, pacifier, ankle reflector, hypodermic syringe, TV set, wine sealed in a bottle, vacuum cleaner, yardstick, obturator, high-heeled shoes, centrifuge. All of the military room: the pistols, the grenades, the rifles, the bayonets, the green-covered first-aid kits and K-rations, the uniforms and even the ancient cannon. Her hands left the radiator and went back to a handful of wires and electrodes which were attached to a small gauge. The aura told her that this apparatus was used in experimentation on rabbits and other small animals.

"Does it puzzle you, Clana?" Rhynna was standing beside her, speaking aloud. Clana smiled to see the relic-keeper. She had liked Rhynna's hair from the moment she saw her and now she all-of-a-sudden knew she liked Rhynna all over. The hair stood out from the woman's head for almost a foot all around. Rhynna had allowed Clana to try—in vain—for almost an hour to tame that hair, to squeeze it close about her head. "Lots of people ask about that device," Rhynna went on. "These pads were attached to the animal's head and this needle probed its brain. Changes in the brainwaves were monitored by this gauge."

Clana shuddered, but then drew her attention to Rhynna. The relic-keeper was holding one of the electrodes in each of her hands, forcing the pointer on the gauge to flip to its maximum mark. Rhynna released the wires and the pointer dropped back to its original position.

Astonished, Clana almost shouted, "Your hair! That's how you make your hair stay out!"

Rhynna laughed, "My hair doesn't move." She made the needle flip once more. "You can do this too, when you learn to separate and see. We can do anything that the old machines could do. And with a good deal less effort."

"Like the glowlobes?"

"That's one thing."

"And windriding?"

"Yes. And lots more."

"Bombs and nerve gas and disease pellets?"

"Easy."

"Then why don't we do them, Rhynna?"

Rhynna laughed again. "That's the mistake the men made, sisterlove, and made over and over again. Just because it was possible they thought it had to be done. They came near to destroying the earth—and may yet—with that notion. Most of us like to think that even long ago women could have built what's been called 'western civilization'; we knew how to do all of it but rejected most such ideas as unnecessary or destructive."

Clana thought about that. She and Rhynna were both silent for a bit, Clana taking in what Rhynna had said—that was as close to a lecture as she had gotten here at the Kochlias—and Rhynna pulling absently on one of her long curly hairs, also alone with some proliferation of those thoughts. After a few moments Rhynna shortstretched so as not to break the silence. "There's a rememberrhyme we use here a lot. Want to hear?"

"Yes," Clana stretched back.

The choice lies not in doing not the things I cannot do,
Or even in the doing of the things I know I can.
But the choice lies in the poet's heart who knows the
    meter true,
And still refuses to allow, no matter how much she'd
    like to do it or how much it hurts her not to do it,
    the final line to scan.

As she ended the verse Rhynna was laughing. Out of some deep understanding that she could not name, Clana was laughing with her. And all the way to the rememberings she repeated the rhyme knowing that someday she would understand it even better.

"Once upon a time, too many women became too wide awake. Once upon a time..." It was Alaka's rememberings today which drew Clana and her sisters into the past. She was dimly aware of the gentle mind assurances of another remember-guide who was the watcher today. Her name was Bessie and she had no teeth and very soothing hands.

"Once upon a time..." Clana whispered with all the others. ■

SINISTER WISDOM

Cover of *Sinister Wisdom* #1
by Marianne Lieberman

Hippo Cream and Car Spray
by Anna Livia

Blushful Hippo Cream

About ten years ago I was part of a 'Woman and Language Group' in London. Having gone round in circles with how women are constructed and constricted by language, how a male/positive female/negative dualism underpins the very foundation of the distinguishing process which is language, we decided to concentrate on the structure and mechanism of humour. Every week for a couple of years we met, seven women: all white and middle-class, both lesbian and heterosexual. We talked about how men use humour to put women down; the insidious messages of jokes we ourselves had laughed at; how men's jokes were often formulaic attacks on women, passing off torture, rape and murder as logically deserved—and required by the formal structure of the joke itself. We looked at humour women use against men to 'get our own back,' where even one well-known for biting sarcasm must plan her comment with split second timing to prevent it backfiring.

After about two years of this, and some really sickening jokes, we began to wonder what women's humour, humour by women for women, was like and we began to worry why it had taken us so long to reach it. We looked at each other perplexed, a little embarrassed: what does a woman say to make another woman laugh? We suggested, tentatively, that women's jokes are non-competitive, have more open structures (less of the 'Knock, knock,' 'Mummy, Mummy,' 'I tell you my mother-in-law is so ugly…'). We had read that co-operative collectivity characterised other areas of women's activity, so perhaps this would prove to be the case with humour too. We set ourselves the task of finding examples of female to female humour for the next meeting.

Me and Trista, light of my life, rode home on our bicycles, exhilarated, through the two a.m. South London streets. We asked each other what made us laugh, perhaps that would be a starting point. At a red light half way up Lavender Hill, Battersea, we saw what had been glaring us in the face all this time: for two years seven women had been meeting weekly and laughing our heads off together and only now had we stopped talking about men long enough to wonder what was so funny.

Next weekend at Linda's in Wivenhoe we decided to go for a walk along the estuary while the fish cooked. Trista, walking back through a dry field in uncharacteristic sunshine, cried out,

"Oh for a beaker full of the warm South,
Full of the true, the blushful Hippocrene."
—*Keats*, Ode to a Nightingale, *2nd stanza*

In *Lesbian Ethics* 3, 3 (Summer 1989). "Car Spray" reprinted from *Incidents Involving Mirth*. Portland, OR: Eighth Mountain Press, 1990.

I smiled indulgently: darling was thirsty. We walked on. Five minutes later, Kath asked, "What *is* hippo cream?" And so we began, all of us, to make up ancient Greek and Egyptian traditions to spare a hippo's blushes, detailing the circumstances in which a hippo might be likely to blush; why it would be so important to forestall such an event; how one made, and indeed applied, the essential hippo cream. We had a wonderful time and it was quite irrelevant which poem by which poet the lines had come from, or even what they really meant.

Mulling this over later, we decided we preferred the almost nonsensical story which anyone can add to, which has no punchline and no necessary end. It left us with a warm, buoyant feeling of having put the world back in its small place and, even, despite the ludicrous flights our fancies took, of being understood by the women we were laughing with. The lack of a formal structure meant we had to pay much closer attention to each other in order to follow the rules which we made up as we went along. There may have been a small amount, at first, of teasing Trista for quoting such high falutin poetry, but that certainly wasn't what made the episode so enjoyable. Eva, who is Hungarian, said it took her a while, when she first encountered English women, to work out that this kind of joke is not dependent on a hidden meaning of the word *hippo* (a sexual *double entendre*, for example, which does not, of course, exist), but on absurdity, extravagance.

The group continued meeting, and we managed a few more conclusions, in between bouts of laughter. Most humour is bound to its context. Most of us have tried to relay an incident which had all the participants in stitches, only to find that our listeners are nodding politely and looking a little blank. We end up assuring, 'It was terribly funny at the time; if you'd been there you would have laughed.' Those male jokes which can be told equally well in a South London pub as at an Australian Northern Territory rodeo are usually underpinned by the sexual subordination of women or on racist stereotypes. As a group of white women we knew our insights into humour

were already specialised, that we could do no more than offer our own perceptions rather than assuming they were common to all women. We felt, indeed, that this preference for stressing and exploring the particular (making theory, each one of us, from our own position) was the same preference that militated against non-contextual humour (a humour of universals). Following this line of reasoning we argued that because women seem to have no obvious laughing stocks—no parallels to the 'mother-in-law,' 'foolish virgin,' 'money-grubbing whore'—our humour is more likely to consist of funny stories rather than one-liners. When telling a story we can develop the context, it does not have to be assumed. We did not try to put this idea into a multi-cultural context; we were talking about white Western English—although it did seem from Eva that much of what was said would be true in Hungary. The group felt, also, that our humour allowed for greater equality among teller, told and told about and that the three roles were fairly fluid, even while a particular story was being invented.

Then I left the group. I wanted to concentrate on lesbians and to move on from analysis to creation. Our conclusions, never more than tentative and exploratory, no longer satisfied me, although I had gained enormously from our group reasoning process which had prodded me into questioning many of my assumptions. (And, of course, the love of six good women is rare and precious.) I felt that our statements about the lack of universals in female humour came more from principle than observable experience.

But, naturally, my observable experience changed as soon as I joined a lesbian (writers') group. Certainly, there is no universal dyke experience. But dyke humour does consist of more than the curious anecdote of the moment. Any recognisably lesbian experience can be the stuff of lesbian humour: coming out; fancying straight women; dyke-spotting; trying to live up to our image of ourselves as butch or femme; discovering we are not the only dyke in the world to strut about our bedrooms belting out Figaro's operatic send-off to the precocious transvestite, Cherubino; discovering we are indeed the only dyke in the world to strut around our bedrooms, etc....In fact humour is, in some ways, a litmus test for how well shared our assumptions about lesbian experience are: if dykes don't share the same assumptions, we don't laugh at the same jokes.

As for radical dyke humour....Well, it depends what we mean by 'radical.' Can a band-aid be radical? After more than two years examining both form and content of innumerable humorous instances, my 'Women and Language Group' concluded that humour was incapable of bringing about radical change, of introducing an element which did not exist before. In cases where it seemed very much as though humour had introduced a new idea, when we examined it more closely it always turned out that in fact the 'new idea' had already been articulated elsewhere, e.g., in the form of linear, logical theory, and the humorous remark served only to reinforce that idea. We decided that this was because humour relies on recognition and is, in that strict and narrow sense, basically conservative. Humour acts, often, as a populariser, making the radical theory more palatable, making us feel more familiar, more comfortable with it. Can comfort be radical?

On the same day I received Jeannette's letter accepting my article, Linda Shockey (of Wivenhoe, hippo cream and Women and Language) handed me a thesis on lesbian humour by Dorothy Painter. Dorothy's main conclusion seemed to me to be that lesbian humour is characterised by 'in' jokes, i.e., jokes inscrutable to heterosexuals, by which we defend ourselves against the onslaught of straight society.* A more common idea of lesbian humour is that it consists of jokes on *us*, i.e., jokes we make against ourselves, gently, tenderly, fondly, laughing at lesbian customs, keeping each other affectionately in line. The two ideas—lesbian humour as jokes on lesbians, and lesbian humour as jokes on the straight world—would appear to be at odds. They do, however, express the range of 'traditional' humour: humour as a joke against someone. This kind of humour, whether its content be lesbian or fascist, is the most apparent in any culture and the easiest to analyse: Who makes the joke? Who is the target of the joke? Whose status is enhanced by the joke?

Those of you who dislike literary analysis should jump straight to "Car Spray" and form your own conclusions. To the rest of you I will say that the humour in "Car Spray" includes both the idea of jokes on ourselves and Dorothy's idea of defense against straightdom. It also includes my favourite brand, which is neither of the above. I would love to prove that my favourite is also the most lesbian, but I may not be allowed this indulgence.

Kinds of humour in "Car Spray," complete with examples.

1. *Direct or indirect references to lesbian culture:*
Discussion of lesbian politics, p. 532: For Minnie, who has just said she's a radical feminist and even a reluctant separatist, the worst thing a potential lover can confess is that she's a socialist.

2. *Direct or indirect references to gay culture:*
The famous 10%, p. 531: Homosexuals are said to be 10% of the population but gay men and lesbians do not have anything in common apart from this statistic, and might be said to compete for their place in it.

3. *Challenges to heterosexual assumptions:*
Heterosexual assumptions about AIDS, p. 535: Beryl, Minnie's mother, is led into making the paradoxical observation, "heterosexuals worry about AIDS, lesbians worry about anti-semitism." AIDS is more commonly considered a 'gay plague'; what makes Beryl's observation funny is that it is not only surprising but true in the story's terms. Of all those at the party Chintz

*Dorothy Painter, *A Communicative Study of Humor in a Lesbian Speech Community: Becoming a Member*. Ph.D. dissertation, Ohio State University, 1978. For example, "Breaching humor normalizes specific breaches of lesbian social reality....The breach is normalized by laughter which indexes straight knowledge as naive" (p. 174); and, "Stereotyping humor normalizes anti-lesbian stereotypes....The laughter constitutes the straight stereotypes as incorrect and reinforces lesbian knowledge" (p. 175).

was the one least likely to give Minnie AIDS.

4. *Jokes against men:*

At the party, p. 530: The male physicists at the party can think of nothing to say unless they are allowed to talk physics, hence they huddle around Beryl's shortwave.

5. *Mother jokes:*

Chintz' mother, p. 532: Chintz' mother drove 500 miles to cook her daughter lasagna because she knew she'd be hungry. There is an unfortunately strong strand in lesbian feminism which berates mothers for the care they lavish on their daughters.

6. *Sex jokes:*

Minnie and Chintz, p. 533: Minnie quotes a line from a lesbian poem; Chintz, whose nipple is in Minnie's mouth, comments on her misplaced articulacy.

7. *Oneupmanship:*

Minnie and Charles, p. 530: Throughout this passage, Minnie puts Charles down according to mainstream rules of oneupmanship. She proves herself more knowledgeable, more widely read and quicker witted in traditional literary areas.

8. *Heterosexual jokes:*

Restaurants, p. 534: The reader fills in for herself the sort of jokes heterosexuals make on restaurant names like 'Hung Long.'

9. *Anti-semitic jokes:*

Restaurants, p. 534: The reader fills in for herself the sort of jokes anti-semites make on restaurant names like 'Da Kow.'

All are examples of humour which lesbians could laugh at. They are arranged in order, I suppose, from least to most offensive. Examples 1 to 3 are fairly exclusively lesbian; example 4 is a 'woman's joke'; example 5 is an oppressive 'woman's joke'; example 6 could easily be put into a straight context; example 7 is almost a set piece characterised by deadpan one-liners; example 8 reminds the reader of the innuendo underpinning most heterosexual discourse; example

9, like example 8, is the kind of joke which is made so often it's only necessary to allude to it.

From lesbian 'in' joke, via humour reversing straight assumptions, to traditional heterosexual and anti-semitic jokes, the range is wide, but all are examples of humour of which the questions can be asked: Who makes the joke? Who is the butt of it? Whose status is enhanced by it? As such, they are all instances of reversible humour: one can retain the structure, pour in new content, and thereby reverse the target. There is a long tradition of this in the mainstream: Reagan, "Seen one redwood, you seen 'em all." Wit from the back of the crowd, "That's what I say about Presidents." There is a joke told by lesbians, even by some separatists: "How many men does it take to tile the bathroom?...Only one, if you slice him really thin." I think this points up very clearly the limitation of 'reversal' jokes. In most people's lived experience the bodies of men as a sex are not used to make domestic items. The most recent western example of such use is the Nazis making the skin of Jewish men and of course women into lampshades. I find it impossible to listen to the bathroom tile joke without thinking of lampshades made of skin, thus the joke remains anti-semitic because of its structure, despite its new content.

Well, you have been being good for a long time now, so I shall tell you my favourite brand of humour. You have examples of it on pages 525–6. The 'car spray' incident is a development of the 'hippo cream' incident. They are a light parody of the search for, and creation of, lesbian rituals and questionable historical antecedents. As such they amuse me only slightly. What I enjoy is their absurdity, their open-endedness: anyone can start such a fantasy, and anyone can add her piece. If there is a 'target,' it is the world itself, the established order. Yet the fantasy is more enjoyable the more closely the players are following each other. The rule for establishing 'insiders,' who understand the joke and can continue it, and 'outsiders,' who shrug or get impatient, is how well anyone is listening: it is other women's own decision to place themselves inside or out. The 'Anne Bancroft' exchange, pages 530-531, can produce similar results. While men are able to understand quite fast that they must offer a question to which Minnie's previous answer would have been correct, they do not, in my experience of step-fathers and brothers-in-law, follow when the pattern is altered by one of the participants and is no longer about movie stars or in question and answer format.

As I said, it would be lovely to assert that this superbly anarchist structure is truly lesbian. I have an uneasy feeling, however, that examined more closely and more critically (I have, after all, just admitted to being one of its devoted proponents) it might turn out to be no more than 'Oxbridge scorn'—U.S. readers may prefer to think of this as 'Ivy League scorn'—which depends to a certain extent on a view of the world as patently absurd and in need of being taken down a peg or two. This seems to work only if one can establish a certain distance between ourselves and the world, especially if that distance places us above the world, in an ivory tower, perhaps. The ability to use distance as a ploy is always something of privilege; those of us under direct attack cannot merely disengage, though we can refuse confrontations as a political tactic. Do lesbians of all classes use the humour of distance and absurdity? I don't know. I recommend care, constant vigilance, and lashings of that universal panacea, hippo cream.

Car Spray

[Minnie, London lesbian, is visiting her mother in Australia. Her mother's husband, John, has invited the entire Physics Department of the Univ. of W.A. to a dinner party for which he will spend the entire story cooking.]

Minnie: Any of them dykes, Ma?

Beryl: Well, they do say Charles may be gay.

Minnie: Think I'll take the ghost freeway to the beach and watch the sunset.

Beryl: But you're the guest of honour. And there's the doorbell now.

[She answers the door.]

Beryl: Minnie, this is Charles.

Charles: And this is Cinzia.

Cinzia: Call me Chintz.

Beryl: Are you yet another physicist, Chintz? The room is filling up with physicists.

Charles: No, Chintz is a lawyer, aren't you, Chintz?

Chintz: I'm a lawyer.

Beryl: You must be clever then. I expect you're clever.

Chintz: Charles and I were discussing that in my car on the way up here.

Minnie: What was your verdict?

Charles: No. Not enough room for two brains in one car.

Chintz: So you're a writer, Minnie?

Beryl: Oh yes. Let me show you her books. Look, this was the first one with the yellow cover. And this one…

Minnie: Ma, I love you, but don't you think it's a bit like showing people my baby photos?

[Beryl kisses Minnie on the top of her head and goes off to have her nice bath in peace. She thinks she might take *Crime and Punishment* (in Russian) with her, and maybe a large glass of brandy, seeing as the young people are now chatting so nicely together. Much though she admires her daughter's books, Beryl can't help noticing that none of them is *Crime and Punishment*. Her own, almost irreplaceable, copy of the Russian text has a large brown burn mark through it from when Beryl sat sunning herself in the garden the time the laundry and the ironing and the cooking and the cleaning all got done on time and there emerged no unforeseen emergency of bloody noses, or premature infants—let us recognise that her daughters are all three over twenty now, and one is eight months pregnant, not Minnie, one hastens to add. Beryl sat in the garden reading her favourite Russian novel in her favourite language with a large magnifying glass because her eyes needed a lot of help these days, when suddenly the page began to smoulder and burn before her and it was not with the repressed passions of Sonja and Roskolnikov but the dear old sun itself. So now, when Beryl can catch a quick quarter hour she usually takes it in the bath.]

[This has been a long diversion from the central, lesbian plot, but Beryl is tired of appearing in her daughter's stories in the role of provider and forehead kisser. She would like it known that she does have a life of her own in which she plans a return to Leningrad where, perhaps, she can make friends with a nice middle-aged Russian lady who will give her an unburned edition of *C & P* and maybe some help with those complicated idioms.]

Charles: [Reading the cover of the yellow book.] Sounds like one of those French novels where someone goes somewhere, does something, meets some people and writes about it.

Minnie: Pretty standard plot.

Charles: You know what I mean.

Minnie: That must be most reassuring.

Charles: Short. You know, how French writers specialise in short novels.

Minnie: [Nodding.] Like Proust, you mean.

Charles: So you work for the same company who publishes you? I thought only the most mediocre writers get published by their friends.

Minnie: I guess Gertrude Stein and Virginia Woolf were pretty mediocre.

Charles: Do you only write for women? Doesn't that cut off a lot of your sales, economically speaking?

Minnie: Statistically speaking there are a few billion people in the world of whom at least 52% are women so, financially speaking, if no man ever read one of my books I'd be laughing.

[The women in the room are all laughing. Minnie hopes she has finished with Charles so she can get back to Chintz. Life among lesbians has made her forget that men interpret put-downs as come-ons.]

Charles: So what do you think of Milan Kundera's *The Unbearable Lightness of Being*?
Minnie: Charles, let's get one thing clear. I am not going to reply to any question to which the answer is not, and never has been, Anne Bancroft.

[Charles looks disgruntled and goes off to join the men. They, physicists all, are staring fixedly at Beryl's short wave radio and pondering all possible and potential climactic and other factors which may have caused it to stop receiving Radio Moscow.]

Chintz: Psst, Minnie, what was the stage name of Anna-Maria Louise Italiano?

Minnie: [Grinning.] Giss a clue.

Chintz: She starred in *The Graduate* with Dustin Hoffman.

Minnie: Blimey, this is hard. [Pause.] Rita Hayworth?

Chintz: Close. Very close. And that's a good position to be in *vis à vis* Rita Hayworth.

[Did Chintz really say that, or was it a product of Minnie's fevered brain?]

Chintz: Now, who takes her gloves off in *Gilda*?

Minnie: Elizabeth Taylor?

Chintz: Nearly. Who starred in *Who's Afraid of Virginia Woolf*?

Minnie: Lily Tomlin.

Chintz: Very good. Not right, but very good.

Minnie: I was hoping there might be a question about Whoopi Goldberg?

Chintz: Next time. I think you need to be rationed.

Minnie: Okay. Let's get back to you. You're a lawyer…

Chintz: An Italian lawyer.

Minnie: Italian?

[For the next twenty minutes, Chintz tells Minnie the story of how first her father, and then her mother, and then most of the inhabitants of a little Italian village outside Bari ended up in Western Australia. As Chintz may well want to tell her story herself, we won't repeat it here. We will, however, say that when Chintz asked her, three days later, how Minnie knew she was a lesbian, Minnie replied: "You know the old joke about how you know who the dyke is? She's the one who fronts up to you in the bar, asks you how you are and listens to the answer? Well, when I asked you about yourself you looked me straight in the eyes and answered at length, without giggling, trivialising or letting your eyes wander round the room in search of the real thing. And after that," Minnie added, "I just hoped."]

[That was three days later. Let's not anticipate. Chintz is short and has short hair and wears a leather jacket and she is curled up in Minnie's mother's armchair in such a way that Minnie suddenly finds herself imagining she is wrapping her arms around her and kissing her. But Chintz is in Minnie's mother's living room and so cannot be a lesbian even though Minnie, who is also in her mother's living room, is indeed a lesbian. Minnie counts. There are only twenty people in the room, and already she and Charles are homosexual so, even if it were not for Minnie's mother's living room, Chintz still could not be a lesbian. Minnie resents the fact that a gay man should have used up half the precious quota.]

[The other women are sitting in corners in their smart jackets while the men discuss inverse sub-semi groups. Beryl signals to Minnie and Minnie and Chintz split up and rescue the women. Chintz leaves early. Minnie wants to run out into the driveway and jump on Chintz' car bonnet and yell, "Take me hostage," but she is much older (ten years) and much taller (two inches) than Chintz (although her hair is much longer) and so, roles being what they are, it is impossible, it is all quite impossible.]

[Charles, four hours drunker, is declaiming the complexities of his sex life to all and sundry. He is about to start on Chintz' sex life but Beryl is not going to allow it. She has a strong sense of propriety.]

Charles: Chintz has started reading Genet to try and understand me better, Minnie. Do you think she's picked the right author?

Minnie: [Who has realised that snubbing Charles only eggs him on.] I think the best way to understand anyone is to talk to them.

Charles: But do you think it a useless project for a lesbian to try and understand a gay man?

Minnie: [Who wants to say "Yes," but has just realised that Charles has just told her Chintz is a dyke and b) that he is now her only way of contacting the woman.] Lesbians have many skills.

[As everyone leaves, Minnie gets Chintz' phone number from Charles.]

Chintz: Like to come to dinner Friday?

Minnie: Love to.

Chintz: I've only just got back from work so we're eating out. Indian okay?

Minnie: [Nods.]

Chintz: Jeeze, it's cold in here.

Minnie: Here, have my jumper.

Chintz: You come prepared.

Minnie: It's my mother. Won't let me borrow the car unless I've a woolly jumper on me. She frisks me as I go out the door.

Chintz: [Kills a cockroach.] Bloody cockroach.

[It takes them an hour and a half to get fed. It takes them an hour to notice.]

Minnie: So yeah, like I was saying, I'm a radical feminist and if you want to call me a separatist it won't bother me.

Chintz: I have a confession to make.

Minnie: What? You're a socialist?

Chintz: I don't know what a separatist is.

Minnie: You sure?

Chintz: Well, I just don't understand how they can hate me.

Minnie: You sure?

Chintz: Yes. And stop asking if I'm sure. Charles is a good friend of mine, I have a lot of time for him.

[Minnie thinks maybe she should back off before their obvious incompatibility drives home.]

Chintz: Anyway, wanna go to a session at the Blue Room, Sunday?

Chintz: I'm sorry I'm so late. My mother turned up from Albany and made me lasagna.

Minnie: She drove five hundred miles to cook you lasagna?

Chintz: She knew I'd be hungry. Three months ago I told her I was a lesbian. She told me that never would have happened if she hadn't come to Australia. She's convinced there are no other Italian lesbians. Just her daughter.

Minnie: Course there are. There's Nicole Falda, Karen Liverpool, Betsey Enrico…

Chintz: What part of Italy are they from?

Minnie: Brooklyn.

Chintz: I don't think my mother would count that as part of Italy. She was okay, though. I told her I was going to have my car sprayed and I was a bit worried that she'd object because she's very superstitious.

[It's noisy in the pub. Minnie wonders if she heard right.]

Minnie: Why should she object?

Chintz: She's very religious. She might think it was tempting fate, going against the church or something. But she offered to pay for it so in the end me, my mum and my sisters all had our cars sprayed.

[Now Minnie knows she heard wrong. She decides to ask strategic questions.]

Minnie: How did it go?

Chintz: Well, mine said there were big changes in the air, a long haired stranger and possible heartache.

Minnie: [Laughing.] I heard you say you were having your car sprayed, not your cards read.

[Chintz laughs hysterically and for the next ten minutes makes up old traditional Italian ceremonies for Minnie where the mother solemnly sprays the dyke daughter's car lavender as a rite of passage. She describes the food, only eaten on that occasion, for which the recipe is carefully guarded and passed from mother to daughter awaiting the birth and driving licence of the dynasty's dykes. However old the daughter is, the ceremony always takes place exactly three months after she has come out to her mother. Chintz' mother's certainty that there are no other Italian dykes in the world must be read as a statement of pride, of the specialness of her daughter and the long time lapse between this car spraying and the last. Minnie suggests, tentatively, that perhaps this Italian custom is simply continuing a much older, more widespread custom dating from the time before cars.]

Chintz: Oh yeah? What did the proud mother do then?

Minnie: Anointed her daughter's hippo with blushful hippo cream.

[And so Minnie explains to Chintz about the hippo cream; the old Egyptian tradition of sparing a hippo's blushes takes on new meaning with the new dyke insights.]

Chintz: Well, I suppose I ought to be going.

Minnie: You in a hurry?

Chintz: Why?

[Awkwardly Minnie leads forward, takes hold of Chintz' chin and kisses her. Chintz moves toward her to ease the angle of the kiss. There are a lot of couples in corners at the Blue Room and they are all kissing and they are all awkward.]

Minnie: Your place or mine? [Is there much point avoiding clichés when clichés are on your mind?]

Chintz: Not mine. I couldn't cope with passing one of my ex-lovers on the way to the toilet.

Minnie: Not mine. I couldn't subject you to my family's brand of liberalism. I've always had this fantasy of borrowing my mother's camper van, parking in King's Park overlooking the Swan and doing it there.

Chintz: Slumming Australian style? My fantasy is checking into a…

Minnie: Sleasy motel?

Chintz: Five star hotel…

Minnie: With a swimming pool on the roof?

Chintz: With a swimming pool on the roof and champagne on room service.

Minnie: I don't drink.

Chintz: Don't worry. I'll drink. You swallow.

[They drive to the hotel. Minnie puts coins in the parking meter. Chintz goes into the lobby.]

Minnie: I can't afford this.

Chintz: Don't worry. I'm a lawyer, my services are worth $100 an hour and my firm gets a discount here.

[Later.]

Chintz: You're still worried. We've worried about our clashing politics; we've worried about how young and impressionable I am; and we've worried about the ethics of one night stands. What's left?

Minnie: The parking meter. It'll run out at 8.30 tomorrow morning and my mother will get a parking fine.

Chintz: I would like to say for the record that you are the only dyke in the world who connects parking meters with sex.

Minnie: Oh I don't know, some of them run "down Christopher Street caressing the iron breasts of parking meters."*

Chintz: It is amazing how articulate you remain with someone else's nipple in your mouth.

[Pause.]

Chintz: Alright. What's the registration?

Minnie: No idea. It's my mother's car.

Chintz: [Shaking her head.] Hello, Room Service? This is 221. Have someone stick a couple of dollars in the meter of a white Kingswood

*Elana Dykewomon, Fragments from Lesbos (Oakland: Diaspora, 1981), p. 15.

parked outside the lobby. And if there's more than one Kingswood, fill them all up.

[The day after passes in something of a daze; Minnie finds it hard to believe how easy and inevitable it felt. She wonders who Chintz is. Sex seems a good way to get to know a woman. When you know her already. That night she meets Chintz in a Vietnamese noodle house and feels that either they should be having sex or they should be complete strangers. Minnie suggests they have coffee, hoping to prolong the evening until she has pinpointed her anxiety. She drives to an Italian cafe, drops Chintz off and parks the car in a side street. Inside the cafe are all the people from the party, except Beryl, who is at her Russian class where Minnie left her earlier in the evening, and John, who is still cooking.]

Charles: Hello you two. Where've you been?

[Minnie does not want to join them but they are Chintz' friends and this is Chintz' town.]

Minnie: Vietnamese noodle house.

Charles: Which one?

Minnie: It's called the Hung Long.

[The inevitable jokes are made. They seem to Minnie to last a long time.]

Chintz: Where've you been?

Charles: To the Da Kow.

[As soon as she hears the name Minnie senses trouble but feels unable to forestall it. She looks across at Chintz wondering what her reaction will be. Someone, not Charles or Chintz or Minnie, makes a joke about cooking with gas.]

Minnie: [Gabbling.] Don't say that. Don't make that kind of...I hate that kind...It's horrible...it's not funny.

Charles: I think what Minnie's trying to say is that kind of joke is cruel and stupid and anti-semitic. It trivialises the torture and death of six million people.

Someone: Well hey, what I say is, if you've got a line, use it.

Charles: You don't have a line. You don't have a brain cell. You don't have an ounce of...

[Minnie has just seen something which makes her sick.]

Minnie: I um...I er...have to go now and, um, pick up my mother at her Russian class.

Minnie: I wasn't going to pick you up for another hour. What happened, did the class get cut short?

Beryl: No. They went off to a casino with some Russian sailors but nice Mrs. Katz and I didn't want to go. She stayed and helped me with my dark *Is*. Darling, you're driving all over the road? Are you alright?

Minnie: No, do you know a restaurant called the Da Kow?

Beryl: Yes.

Minnie: Well, Charles and them had just eaten there and they made this horrible joke about the name and then, well, Chintz laughed, at the joke, and I was making love to her last night.

Beryl: Mmm. It's an unfortunate name for a restaurant. People do make jokes about it.

Minnie: People you know?

Beryl: Oh, we had a works dinner there and they made the sort of jokes Charles' friends would make.

Minnie: But what did you do?

Beryl: Observed what sort of people they were and decided not to go out with them again. What more can one do?

Minnie: Tell them what you think.

Beryl: What are you going to do? Ring Chintz up and ask her why she laughed at an anti-semitic joke?

Minnie: Yes, of course. That's just what I must do.

Beryl: You lesbians are funny. I can't imagine ringing up a man I'd just slept with and accusing him of anti-semitism when I'm not even Jewish.

Minnie: I can't sleep with someone who could laugh at genocide.

Beryl: I thought you already had. Does sex make you moralistic? Life's rich tapestry: heterosexuals worry about AIDS, lesbians worry about anti-semitism.

Minnie: Chintz, I don't know how to put this so it will sound decorous, but just now, at the cafe, that friend of Charles made that joke about the Da Kow…

Chintz: I know. It was stupid. But Charles shut him up.

Minnie: But you, I thought you, I mean you laughed, didn't you?

[Minnie knows Chintz laughed. She saw her. She was watching her the whole time. Minnie prays that Chintz will not simply deny it now that she hears Minnie is upset.]

Chintz: I didn't laugh at that joke.

[Minnie feels sick.]

Chintz: I was feeling very nervous.

Minnie: Why?

Chintz: All evening, like you were testing me; did I measure up to your high standards. Then when we walked into the cafe, I could feel everyone tense up. No. When I came in, it was fine. Then they saw I was with you and there was this tension.

Minnie: Why? Because they had to recognize us as lesbians?

Chintz: They already know perfectly well that I'm a dyke.

Minnie: Then why?

Chintz: Because you were so short with Charles at the party. They thought you'd try to put them down.

Minnie: How do you know?

Chintz: I don't know. I just sensed it.

Minnie: They didn't have to make anti-semitic jokes because I made them uneasy. [And you didn't have to laugh at them, Minnie thinks but does not say.]

Chintz: Some of them are creeps, agreed. Have you rung me up in the middle of the night to accuse me of anti-semitism? Aren't you meant to be sending me roses or do you feminist dykes do everything different? I wasn't laughing. My face was smiling nervously. I'd been smiling nervously all evening only you didn't notice.

Minnie: I'm sorry. I'm glad. Thank you for explaining. Did you get home alright?

Chintz: Yes. Charles gave me a lift.

Minnie: Bully for big buddy Charles. You know I put him down at the party because he walked in the door declaring you were stupider than him.

Chintz: My noble protectrix. That was just one of Charles' jokes. He was being ironic.

Minnie: You didn't mind at the time. After you left, dear old Charlie was dead set on telling the world about your sex life.

Chintz: So you rang me in the middle of the night to chat about Charles? I mentioned this before but you didn't take the hint. I am not going to reply to any question which is not, and never has been, accompanied by half a dozen red roses.

[Chintz hangs up.]

Conclusion

by Sarah Lucia Hoagland

What we began with this wave of lesbian moving, at least in the u.s., has gone through significant changes. As we dis-covered and began to explore ourselves, we wanted to create something new and we set about doing just that. We were (and still are) boundary dwellers.[1] Attravesamos fronteras.[2] And the first task at hand was developing lesbian space. To create something new, we needed relief from heterosexualism and the presumption that the business of women is men. We needed to have sufficient time and room to create without the constant threat of being dissolved by dominant perceptions, which, even in the best of all possible dominant worlds, hold lesbianism to be marginal.

We focused on ourselves.[3] We told our coming-out stories.[4] We celebrated lesbianism.[5] We began many different lesbian

From *Lesbian Ethics*. Palo Alto, CA: Institute for Lesbian Studies, 1988.

projects. We created space in which we could develop a new context and build collectivity.

This was an exuberant time but also an extremely painful one because we were having to make the idea of ourselves and our spaces credible, because creating lesbian space was not a clear-cut matter, and because those of us who became openly political held ideas with an iron grip—everything had to be exactly right.

In her history of *Lavender Woman*, Michal Brody discusses the bitter fights that occurred in the lavender woman collective, in the larger chicago lesbian community, and in many other lesbian communities:

Many communities experienced a euphoric coming together followed by a period of intense activity. When conflicts arose, as they inevitably would, over priorities, or strategies, or even just what to name the baby, bitter struggles often occurred. These wars, as they were called in some places,

caused many women to withdraw, while the energy of those who remained was severely depleted. Once this fatigue set in, the momentum could not be sustained, and unless a new inspiration burst forth to start the cycle all over again, the endeavor would disperse.

This is a universal process, shared by any co-identified group in motion. The steps of the process are conjoining, inspiration, activity, exhaustion, and dispersion.[6]

Michal Brody goes on to suggest that while the process she describes is inevitable, the "particular alienation and ugliness that resulted from the conflicts in many lesbian communities in the mid-1970s was not inevitable."[7] She argues that the lavender woman collective had focused so strongly on each other as lesbians that members had not developed a language to address difference:

The lesbians who originally formed the web of activity that included CLL and *Lavender*

Woman were a vastly diverse population from many different backgrounds, with different educations, different jobs, different needs, and different ideas about where to go from here. The things we had in common were that we were all lesbians, and we all believed strongly that being lesbians had a deep and profound effect on our world-views. Plus, we loved each other. Other components of our lives, such as race, religion, cultural and social background, all those and more were suppressed by our identity as lesbians. The strength of that identity was so fragile in those early days that we put enormous pressure on ourselves to forge a unity in a lesbianism that discarded anything else.

When the time for conflict arrived, as it inevitably does in any group, we had become so intensely involved in one another that the pain of discord was almost unbearable; and we had ignored the major differences for so long that we had no skills or common language to work with.[8]

During this period we thought being lesbian was enough; we did not acknowledge differences. We focused on definitions and rules: A lesbian does *x*, a lesbian does not do *y*. We focused on what counts as being lesbian or a lesbian project, and who belongs in our spaces. As a result, we developed no ability to address differences— including differences of opinion—that had to be fought for. And the fight took place, Michal Brody suggests, over the issue of separatism because separatism was an abstract issue—abstract since the actual and daily lives of those most heatedly involved in the debates/wars were not significantly different:

It is important to understand that the ones on the front lines of these battles, on both sides, were women who had already minimal contact with men. The lifestyles of separatist and non-separatist combatants were largely indistinguishable.[9]

While I agree that our inability to acknowledge difference has led to devastating splits, denial, and burnout, I'm not convinced that the wars were inevitable. As I've stressed throughout this book, while we challenged patriarchal politics, we relied on many other patriarchal values, in particular, patriarchal ethics. And that ethics promotes antagonism and control rather than integrity and connection.

Secondly, the idea that there could be a lesbian *anything* was not initially credible, even to us; as Michal Brody suggests, lesbian identity was fragile at best. That there might be a lesbian-centered context, that lesbians might create it—this was something we had to prove and defend to ourselves. In a way, an iron grip was necessary if lesbians were going to forge something within a void.

Thirdly, much of our lesbian energy focused on limits and definition rather than complexity and difference because of the very real threat of cooptation—of once having sparked a possibility, sliding back or being undermined before we'd had a chance to create what we'd imagined and dreamed. So I think the process was inevitable; nevertheless, I don't find it cause for despair.

Through all we did, we managed to create time and space away from those dominant perceptions which, when empowered by our own acceptance of them, could render lesbian existence, lesbian focus, and especially lesbian imagination, meaningless. We have made lesbian space credible to ourselves. We no longer feel the need, for example, to justify the idea of "womyn's" music festivals to ourselves or even feel defensive about them. They are a reality. They happen. And their existence is part of lesbian existence. We can choose to go; we can choose to cast a wary glance at those "politicos"; or we can refuse to go in anger over some aspect. But they are a part of our lives about which we can make those choices, and they are a part of the context within which we explore, challenge, change, and develop our values.

In addition, we have been growing, healing, learning, and changing despite the dominant society all around us and the wars between us. We have been exploring our differences. And while rarely smooth or graceful, this process has occurred as a result of lesbian responsiveness.

We have suffered many internal defeats, but I think our

work to date has also been successful. While this is a time for deep reevaluation, I want to suggest it is also a time of lesbian celebration. We have accomplished as much as we have because we have believed in ourselves—we have believed in ourselves and each other even though we have also hurt, attacked, withdrawn, and burned out.

Nevertheless, lesbian space is still extremely problematic. We are barely beginning to develop ways to explore and handle difference; at the same time lesbian space is fragile and cooptation is still threatening. The problem we face is to reconcile plurality with a lesbian focus. I think we can accomplish this through perceiving lesbian space as a context rather than a fortress, and by working control out of our interactions.

So the question now is, are we going to go on? Having been devastated, can we take time out, heal, recover, learn to play, and come back? Or are we going to crawl into whatever niche we can find to fit and live the rest of our lives licking our wounds? Are we going to continue to work with this monster we have created? We have made lesbian space credible, and we have learned in our guts that simply being lesbian is not enough. What are we going to do now?

Summation

In "The Mind-Drifting Islands," Micheline Grimard-Leduc describes the process of lesbians emerging from exile to find each other and create community. As lesbians within heteropatriarchy, we have no social selves; we are without a collective system of values. We are deprived of "collective points of reference by which to 'plug' into a collective reality."[10] However, she goes on:

> As soon as I share my dream with another lesbian, I start breaking through the alien circle. This single act of communication materializes the dream. By this exchange we build reality.[11]

By engaging, lesbians have the possibility of making magic, of making a moral revolution. So what is the moral revolution of Lesbian Ethics? What values are being challenged, and what value can emerge from lesbianism?

I have been trying to articulate the extent of the antagonism inherent in the values of the fathers, particularly how dominance and subordination have permeated our lives in ways we haven't thought to question or even suspect. I have tried to show that there is a very close relationship—philosophically, an 'internal relationship'—between ideas and ways of thinking that normalize oppression, and ideas and ways of thinking central to traditional anglo-european ethics. And I have been making suggestions about moving away from these values, ways we can be radically serious about loving lesbians,[12] serious beyond the romantic haze of lesbian utopia as well as beyond the bitter disappointments in lesbian community. I have tried to suggest other ways of approaching situations, a different focus which involves creating and functioning in a different conceptual framework—one which is not without serious problems but one which rejects the values of dominance and subordination, no matter how palatable they may appear on the surface.

I am proposing an ethics which recognizes separation or withdrawal at any level as a moral option; one which has as its prerequisite, not altruism, but self-understanding, which regards choice not as sacrifice, but as creation, and which encourages, not vulnerability, but intimacy; one which recognizes power, not as controlling, but as enabling, which enables neither merging nor estranging but interacting, and so which encourages, not binding, but engaging; one which integrates or politicizes reasoning and emotions as well as dreaming, psychic faculty, intuition, humor, and imagination; one which treats moral agency, not as rising above our boundaries nor as controlling situations, but as acting one among many and as making choices within situations; one which has as its central focus, not enforcing rules and social control, but enabling integrity and agency—one which has as its axis, not the antagonism of dominance and subordination, but a form of cooperation held in place by autokoenony.* Through such an

538

ethics, we can continue to develop self-awareness, intimacy (deep understanding with a few), our ability to attend, our ability to withdraw, the cooperation of intelligibility, our ability to make choices and go on in situations, our playful world travel, our ability to make judgments, our responsiveness, and our caring—in short, our lesbian integrity and moral agency. ■

*Editors' note: Sarah Hoagland coined the word *autokoenony* to describe the essence of a self that "is both separate and related, a self which is neither autonomous nor dissolved…" (p. 12). The word is further explained on pp. 145-46 of *Lesbian Ethics*.

Notes

1 Mary Daly, *Beyond God the Father: Toward a Philosophy of Women's Liberation* (Boston: Beacon Press, 1973).

2 Gloria Anzaldúa, *Borderlands/ La Frontera: The New Mestiza* (San Francisco: Spinsters/Aunt Lute, 1987).

3 Note, for example, Nancy Myron and Charlotte Bunch, eds., *Lesbianism and the Women's Movement* (Baltimore, Md.: Diana Press, 1975); Phyllis Birkby, Bertha Harris, Jill Johnston, Esther Newton, and Jane O'Wyatt, eds., *Amazon Expedition: A Lesbian Feminist Anthology* (New York: Times Change Press, 1973); Marie J. Kuda, *Women Loving Women: A Select and Annotated Bibliography of Women Loving Women in Literature* (Chicago: Womanpress, 1975); Elly Bulkin and Joan Larkin, eds., *Amazon Poetry* (Baltimore,

Md.: Diana Press, Out and Out Books, 1975); Barbara Grier and Coletta Reid, eds., *Lesbian Lives: Biographies of Women From The Ladder* (Oakland, Calif.: Diana Press, 1976); Jane Rule, *Lesbian Images* (London: Peter Davies, 1976); Kay Van Deurs [Kady], *The Notebooks That Emma Gave Me: The Autobiography of a Lesbian* (Published by Kady Van Deurs, Box 199, Youngsville, New York: 12791, 1978); Monique Wittig and Sande Zeig, *Lesbian Peoples: Material For a Dictionary* (New Yourk: Avon Books, 1979); and J. R. Roberts, *Black Lesbians: An Annotated Bibliography* (Tallahassee, Fla.: The Naiad Press, 1981).

4 Note, for example, Julia Penelope Stanley and Susan J. Wolfe, eds., *The Coming Out Stories* (Watertown, Mass.: Persephone Press, 1980): Margaret Cruikshank, ed., *The Lesbian Path* (Monterey, Calif.: Angel Press, 1980); and Ruth Baetz, ed., *Lesbian Crosssroads: Personal Stories of Lesbian Struggles and Triumphs* (New York: William Morrow, 1980).

5 Note, for example, Sidney Abbott and Barbara Love, *Sappho Was a Right-on Woman: A Liberated View of Lesbianism* (New York: Stein and Day, 1973); Rita Mae Brown, *Rubyfruit Jungle* (Plainfield, Vt.: Daughters, 1973); Jill Johnston, *Lesbian Nation: The Feminist Solution* (New York: Simon and Schuster, 1973); the carpenter [June Arnold], *The Cook and the Carpenter* (Plainfield, Vt.: Daughters, 1972); Elana Nachman [Dykewomon], *Riverfinger Women* (Plainfield, Vt.: Daughters, 1974); Ann Allen Shockley, *Loving Her Reader: An Amazon Quarterly Anthology* (Oakland, Calif.: Amazon Press, 1975); *The Nomadic Sisters, Loving Women* (Sonora, Calif.: The Nomadic Sisters, 1976); Emily L. Sisley and Bertha Harris, *The Joy of Lesbian Sex*

(New York: Simon and Schuster, 1977); and Ginny Vida, ed., *Our Right to Love: A Lesbian Resource Book* (Englewood Cliffs, N.J.: Prentice-Hall, Inc., 1978).

6 Michal Brody, *Are We There Yet? A Continuing History of 'Lavender Woman': A Chincago Lesbian Newspaper*, 1971-1976 (Iowa City: Aunt Lute Book Co., 1985, now Spinsters/Aunt Lute, San Francisco), p. 183.

7 Ibid.

8 Ibid., p. 185

9 Ibid.

10 Micheline Grimard-Leduc, "The Mind-Drifting Islands," *Trivia 8* (Winter 1986): 29, 31; published in the original French in *l'ile des amantes: essai/poèmes*, write Micheline Grimard-Leduc, C.P. 461, Station N, Montréal, Québec, H2X 3N3, Canada, 1982).

11 Idbid., p. 31.

12 Alix Dobkin makes reference to a "lesbian" as "a woman who is radically serious about loving women," a definition coined by Mary E. Hunt: Alix Dobkin, "Boy-Girl Rap," on *Never Been Better*, distributed by Ladysilpper Music, Box 3130, Durham, NC 27705, 1987.

© 1983 by Sudie Rakusin

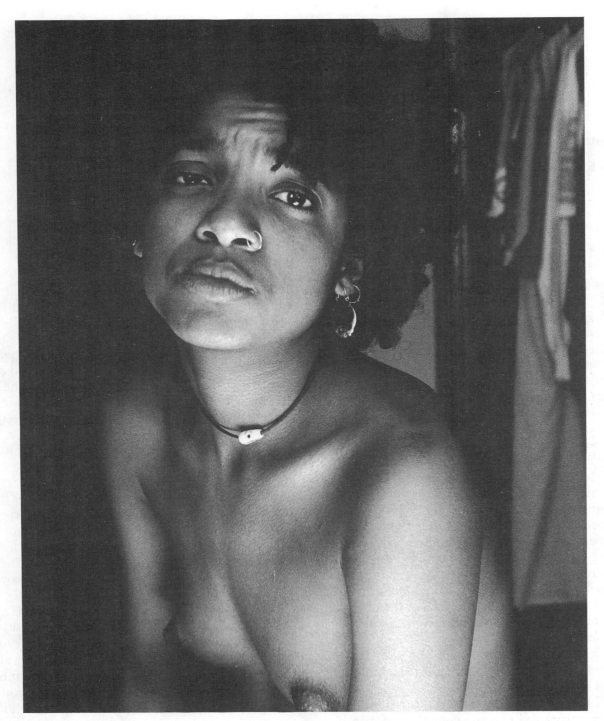

Jamika
by Jean Weisinger

The Warexx

by Ruth Byrn

The Warexx is all caution and no fear. Even in sleep she is thus, resting naturally on her side with a knee tucked up in front of her concaving belly. You would see both elbows tucked down to meet or nearly meet the knee, shielding the solar plexus. And the long solid bones of both arms barricading the easybreathing chest. It is the position of the fetus or the sleeping neonate turned on its side. The parts most critical are shielded by the parts least critical. Her weapon arm is uppermost and free. Her leading-step foot is uppermost and forward. The sensing side of her head is uppermost and bare. The dreaming side of her head is down, insulated by the pillow or by the palm of her helping hand.

You would see, much of the night, the relaxed fingertips of the helping hand touching or nearly touching the dreaming side of the head, and the wrist touching or nearly touching the throat; as if conducting a circuit which runs from some organ buried near the root of the arm, through the throat, through the brain, and around again.

As a mature child, sleeps The Warexx. Shielding her back with her lover. Shielding her lover with her self.

The dreams of The Warexx are wonders of peace-accomplishments, are fearless studies of terrible war, are news from abroad. She is a living network of intelligence information, receives it, gynerates it, transforms it, transmits it; and this she does waking and sleeping.

Asleep, no night terrors clog or scramble her channels; for, mightily, she has swept her inherited house clean. If she dreams she is opposed or threatened, then before that dream is done she dreams herself victrexx. In the morning, in her reference works of militant strategy, she will register what she did and how she did it.

But if you ask The Warexx whether she has dream terrors, nightmares, she is apt to answer evasively or not at all. She may, for instance, respond by inquiring about *your* nightmares, or tell you of a nightmare she once had and let you make your own assumption how long ago that was. The lack of fear, night or day, sleeping or waking, is a distinguishing characteristic of The Adult Warexx. She is not likely to let you discover who she is.

Her lack of a current voter registration is not necessarily a distinguishing characteristic. Ask her if she is registered to vote and she is likely to tell you, directly, no. If you say tsk-tsk at that, she might incline her head in rueful agreement and join you, saying Yes, Tsk-Tsk. She will leave you with your own assumptions as to who and what she feels is rueful, and to what extent rueful.

She intends the abolition of all patriarchal electoral systems—by means of abolishing their entire male constituencies. She is committed to it,

In *Lesbian Ethics* 2, 1 (Spring 1986).

that either there be no men left to vote or no men left allowed to vote.

If a man rapes or abuses any fem♀l of her Group of First Concern, she will devise a way to, undetected, cause his close-kin male relatives to die. Somewhere in that process she will cause the primary perpetrator to die.

If you are a man or a group of men, she considers you have no right to anything you think you own; considers you "own" nothing but the stolen loot of your unprovoked wars and the wars of men before you. Loot men wrested by force from the earth and her beings, including all members of The Warexx' own gynus/species, hum♀n beings, of which she is a meta-species. She is not willing that you keep all the loot; not half of it; not any of it. She is more than willing to represent the earth and her beings all, and rip the loot back off you and any of your kind. Since even she cannot singlehandedly rip back every thing off every man, she will calmly—and without detection—assist any handy force or circumstance which detracts from the holdings of any male within the influence of her life zone.

If you are a man or a bonding of men, she knows the world would be a better place without you. If you are her father, her brother, her son, you are not exempt from this conviction. She may love you—and if she does, you could never know how much—but that is a different matter from her knowing that everybody concerned, including you, would be better off with you dead than with you keeping on in the way you are bound to. Since even she cannot singlehandedly cause every man to die, she will calmly assist any handy force or circumstance which detracts from your health or your perverted sense of mental and emotional well-being.

If you are a man or a boy you will not be able to understand this next, but anyway:

She is not interested in pretending you are her equal.

She is not interested in punishing you.

Not interested in reversing roles and making you be slave.

Not interested in torturing you.

Not interested in "acquiring" the entire face of the earth for herself and her species alone.

She just wants to get rid of you.

While there still is a face of the earth.

If you are man or boy, The Warexx knows you are either a mutant parasite or an alien parasite; but in either case deadly, and camouflaging yourself among the earthly creatures you call the Class Mammalia.

And she knows that fact which you, yourself, will do anything to keep from knowing: on your own you are not viable. Not you, not any boy or man of any age could survive long without excessive supplementation from hum♀ns, w♀m♀ns. That is essentially why, for the past 10,000 years, men have universally enslaved w♀m♀ns: to parasitize them. You are the vampire, man. And The Warexx knows you. Every one of you. She can instantly recognize every single face of men the vampire. She can smell you, for that matter. But no man knows who she is, or would even believe she could exist.

The Warexx is the camouflageuse par excellence. She was born camouflaged. For a while, even she did not recognize her self. Now, knowingly, she obscures her self among the 2,000,000,000 adult w♀m♀ns around the earth. A statistical rarity, she is a deviant in disguise. If she is one-in-a-million, there are about 2,000 of her hiding in the world.

Scattered around the bluegreen surface of this orb, she is like a pure strain of ancient, fertile, viable seed—the Ultimate Survivor among hum♀n beings. Each one of her is an atomic particle radiating life. She has been called the critical mass, and she has been called the leaven for the rising mass. She reproduces geometrically by atomic chain reaction of contagion. Yes, she is contagious to other w♀m♀ns. And all around her are other w♀m♀ns. And of those, a statistically significant number are in precondition to catalyze with her emanations, evolve their selves further, make the quantum leap and transform their selves right into The Meta-Species Warexx.

Of course her actual percentage in the w♀m♀n population is a secret. If instead of one-in-a-million she is more like one-in-ten-thousand, then there are 200,000 of her on earth today—

including the 33,000 fiercely alive and dispassionately determined to stay that way on what men call the north american continent.

If men knew about her, they might clandestinely worry that she could be the "superior" or "dominant" strain within what they call the species of man. They would have no more idea what they were thinking than ever they've done.

The Warexx is different beyond men's imagination. Men, and typical w♀m♀ns, per force brainwashed by those slavemasters, say: "Oh look! Man is poisoning the lakes and seas and underground reservoirs; soon all creatures will die for nothing to drink or if we drink. And look, man is poisoning the air; soon we will die from breathing or not breathing. And man is playing games with nuclear bombs; soon we are going to be radiated to death if nothing else. Yes, soon the face of the earth will be a blank. If even the face of the earth is left by man to exist. And really, you know, there's nothing anybody can do about it. Certainly nothing "*I* can do." But The Warexx differs. The Warexx says: "Oh something can be done alright. It's very simple. Get rid of men. Men control and poison the waters = get rid of men. Men poison the air = get rid of men. Men make and play with napalm and nukes = get rid of men. Get rid of men = save life on earth. Don't get rid of men = permit the death of life on earth. Men cannot control their necrophylic drive = men cannot control themselves = permanently jail and feed and guard them all or get rid of them = get rid of them."

In another way The Warexx differs. Men and the brainwashed w♀m♀ns they possess say, "Somebody ought to do something." The Warexx says, "I will do something." I am willing to kill men, as many as possible without being detected; my responsibility is to defend my country, my motherland, the earth.

She's a matriot. She intends her country be set free of the infesting suckers. It's her life's work; she's doing it regardless what else she is or appears to be doing. Every minute she remembers what it means that men are now extinguishing earth's beings at the rate of one different species a day. The Warexx has no qualms at all about extinguishing the only non-class of pseudo-creatures who are, anyway, determined to extinguish themselves along with every other living thing. Maybe you've noticed her mind is free of the snarenet of men's "language." In her thinking, all people, all hum♀ns, are fem♀ls. Translated to men's "language," read: "All genuinely human humans are female: the only real people are human females." In her crystal mind it is crystal clear that men's "universal terms," *man* or *men* don't mean w♀m♀n or w♀m♀ns or even 'women.' She is certainly smart enough to know *man* means a man and *men* means the plural of that; all the time it does, not just part-time, as men irrationally claim. The Warexx' mind is not tied by definitions which have come out of the pseudo-minds and lying mouths and propaganda books of men. To her, it couldn't be Plainer that men and w♀m♀ns do not "share" the same species, the same gynus, family, order, class. To her, it's plain man doesn't belong in the same reference niche with what he calls the Vertebrates, the Mam-malia, nor any of earth's creatures. She accords him no valid membership. The closest she will come is to admit that in certain ways men appear to resemble w♀m♀ns closer than they do, say, oysters.

She considers men may have emerged on earth as non-viable mutations of the gynus/species w♀m♀n; or alternatively, they may have migrated to earth as a colony of exiled personae non grata from outer space. Against the possibility that latter is the case, The Warexx intends that mistake will end here. She knows to cause men to die rather than wish them off on some other unsuspecting planet. She notices their greedy looking to get into space, stabbing their flags and bibles on the moon and their weapons in the heavens. She thinks it entirely possible a colony of them was exiled here after having sucked, poisoned, and/or exploded the life nearly out of some solar system they previously parasitized. She intends they not get loose again.

Whether alien vampires or mutant vampires, men, The Warexx sees, are essentially nonviable. They cannot survive on their own, or carry their weight in truly reciprocal partnerships, as can all the other beings on earth. Men are the sole creatures who are dependent and not interdependent when they reach apparent maturity. Each man has too little to give in exchange for what it takes to support him as a living organism—and he is proven resistant to give what little he has. Only one intervention has allowed his survival: excessive supplementation and martyred assistance from w♀m♀ns. Take up an infant man at birth; put him in the care of his own kind, men; exclude all direct contact by w♀m♀ns; what would he be like, by puberty? The Warexx knows. He would be long dead. If the subject hadn't been done in by his own inadequate constitution and immune system, his death would have been caused by his male caretakers' shortcomings or their outright murder of him by act of commission or omission. Mutant or alien, as The Warexx sees it, men haven't enough spark of their own to live on their own.

⚲

The Warexx is priestess, plus. Her bird is the non-migratory wild one. Hawk, crow, quail, mockingbird, sparrow, present in all seasons of their home terrain, none particularly noted for beauty of plumage. Her tree or shrub is evergreen. Juniper, redwood, holly, pine, pyracantha, cedar. Her rhythmic tides, cycles, are less obvious than typical w♀m♀ns'. She does not shed her seasoned foliage all at once, or grow the new all at once. She is continually discarding and growing. Because she was born curious enough to look for herself, after others said nothing could be seen or was there to see, she is privy to the mysteries of the hidden cycles. She knows about all kinds of things most people never heard of. And will not try to convince anyone of these realities. If you are desirous and capable of learning—in which case you are fem♀l—she will assist you; but otherwise will not waste her energy trying to teach you or help you learn. And seldom will she rescue you from the results of your ignorance, even if you are fem♀l. When she does alter the course of what happens to you as the result of your own or others' mistakes, you would have to be very quick-and-deep-witted to realize what was done,

who did it, and how.

The Warexx is ever learning, learning. At the same time she is about her other businesses she forages for fresh information to feed her hungry mind. She possesses a special sense for detecting new information. Pops it into her self like a bird eats a berry; dissolves it to its elements with her juices; assimilates what is nutritious for her; casts off what is dross. She is impervious to tampered-with, toxic information. When false is blended with true, her system casts out the one and absorbs the other by truth-gravitated reflex. She doesn't even have to think about it. You could not poison her mind or so much as give it indigestion; and it has grown to such size and strength and strategy as would easily exceed any cage or trap ever to be devised by any number of men. The mind of The Warexx is too powerful to be bound, too resilient to be battered-in by repetitions of lies, too brave to do anything but laugh at spectral threats. She is the most intelligent member of the gynus/species w♀m♀ns.

If you are a man of any age currently existing within her lifesphere zone, she has had you under observation; has assessed your strongest desires, your secret fears, your typical and exceptional reactions, your relative strengths, your weaknesses, your interests, your blind spots. In short, she knows enough about you to accurately predict what you will do under almost any circumstance. Very simple for her to do this. If you are a male you are, to her, a ridiculously simple creature—boringly simple. Annoyingly simple. Excessively simple. Catastrophically simple. For The Warexx to know all that is important about a man she need not exercise herself; usually she can assess him in one quick glance from a twenty-yard distance. And if he's within twenty yards and she hasn't already done it, she usually will because she knows him as one of the legion born inimical to her and all her kind and kin upon the earth.

But he does not know who she is. Or that he has been assessed. Usually he'll scarcely notice anyone is there. Because she's a w♀m♀n. Read: *nuthin' but a woman.*

A creature straight out of science fiction she

is, only she's real. A being whose knowledge expands several degrees in all directions every twenty-four hours or less. One who can change anything about herself she comes to disprefer; even her genetic predispositions, she can transmute. She has dis-covered she is the inexhaustible reservoir of whatever wisdom she needs, whenever she actually needs it. Forages for information, yes, and can also self-gynerate it. She's never really stuck, and she knows that, for her very cells are pantries of clues to anything she needs to know. Or just enjoys knowing.

To an observer, her interests would look like an endless pile of unrelated topics. They're related. They only seem disconnected, from the short-term and linear perspective. There is, to her interests and the time when she is interested, what has been called the fantastic coherence. No known system of library classification is sophisticated enough to catalogue her items and/or what she already knows about them, and tangential subjects if she has been interested long; for one thing, she is versant in several levels of truth about each topic. For another, she is familiar with several different dimensions of reality. Can tune in, can focus at will in spheres of existence which men and even typical wǫmǫns do not perceive or, at best, can only guess about. If you could take a comprehensive look at what is merely the *conscious* part of her mind, you might think (unless you are another Warexx) that one or the other of you had gone mad. She's suprasane. This, also, she disguises.

Conversing with you, she'll select your level of truth, usually, focus in the dimension where you are accustomed. Rare times, if she senses you are ready to learn something and she elects to help you take a new step, she'll blend in some teasing elements from beyond. Or she might do a little razzmatazzbedazzle number with you, for you to realize later and think about.

If you are a wom™n as yet not-Warexx, your relative ignorance won't cause her to dislike you. She knows what it is to be as ignorant as any other wǒm™n on earth. She has been that. Recognizes she is still vastly ignorant, compared to what is left to know.

She burns to know it all. Learns multiples of things whenever she learns one; and every time she is reminded of her own remaining incredible ignorance. Doesn't feel bad about hers, not yours either. She loves this state of affairs wherein she can never learn it all up.

The Warexx is the daughter, the heirexx, of Nemesis, of Hecate, Hecuba, Kali; of the darker names of She, The Deity of Ten Thousand Names. She is the accrued Amazon: today's evolved version, the epitome-so-far, the culminated/culminating descendant of such as those red booted and fiercely joyous battleaxes, the Thermondontines, who held their baby daughters to the mare's breasts to suckle, and who nourished themselves on a mixture of honey and mare's milk and sometimes blood. Daughter of these and others like them, through the ages around the globe. The continuous mystic line of The Warexx has been genetically transmitted and transmuted ever purer down/up the eons of earth. She is The Dianic Tradition embodied and brought forth, exponentialized now to the cusp of the tenth millennium, at least, since her foremothers and the grains first cooperated together.

Today's version of her is so purely potent, she can and does exist alone. Except in her trystings, she lives sole and single in her lifesphere; without community for her spirit, without an ally for her Truest Cause, she survives and prevails. That isn't the way she'd like it, isn't the way she intends the future to be; but for now she must exist hidden in isolation, and so she does. And by this, the ability to Live in ex-communicated singularity for whatever time she must, she exceeds and excels her proud tribal foremothers' strengths. And they are exceedingly proud of her.

A well of life-enhancing culture, she carries within her the distilled cream-of-the-crop knowhow in the artskills of living and imparting life. She can heal, nurture, teach, entertain, birth, sustain, love, create, elicit, synergize, frolic, ecstasize, give, receive, share, communicate, administer, muse, beautify, and build.

But also she can cleanse, purify, destroy, disrupt, eliminate, burn, poison, detract, subtract, blast, smite, dissolve, and even the score.

She is just. Above all she is just; fair absolutely and when need be, dispassionately. Dispassion = calm fairness; even men's dictionaries say that. She is dispassionate to men, and intends they get what they deserve. She proudly possesses the same earth's violence as the tornado, volcano, hurricane, earthquake, tidal wave, flood, firestorm, lightning, drought, avalanche. And plague. And plague.

She can build, she can destroy. She is anabolic, she is catabolic. She assimilates, she eliminates. Just like the earth.

And this is time for all-out, fair, dispassionate, war. Her mother, the earth, her self, the earth, her sister, the earth, her lover, the earth, tells her and she knows: now is the time to begin the end of the vampire vermin.

The Warexx communicates with others in her sleep, yes. Thus it is, for most of her peer interactions. Prior to sleeping, she knows which herbs to ingest, which sequences of emotions to gynerate within her self, which states of consciousness to abide in, and for which durations. Then she sleeps. And flies to her trystings with others of her tribe, around the earth.

Too, in her dreams, she trysts with Warexxes whose existences are focused in other dimensions. With these kin, she forms crucial links or channels or bridges or dykes between the different realms; there is interchange, interflow, balance, by virtue of what she and Otherworld Warexxes exchange, by what they do together.

Thus also—in her sleep and in your sleep—might she teach you, if you are a w♀m♀n in precondition of Warexxhood, and if you live within her considerable zone of spiritpsychic being. She might appear to you and be with you in your dreams, sometimes. You might or might not recognize her; that depends partly on how good you are at such things already, and partly on her sense that direct revelation isn't always method of choice for efficient teaching/learning. But regardless, in your dreams where you do not bar your windows, your doors, your ears, your eyes, your body—she might be with you.

You could try invoking her presence, by the way. The Warexx sometimes intentionally omits making her own selection whom to fly and visit. Often enough she leaves off the restraints, the reins of rational self-intent, so as to widen the avenues of the intuitive, the serendipitous, the coincidental, the gravitational.

And in her dreams, with her dreams, her waking and her sleeping dreams, she calls forth the w♀m♀n within the woman, and whispers ancient Knowledge to those w♀m♀ns who will be joining with her to reclaim the earth from men. In their sleep she rouses the minds out of hypnosis, detoxifies and dispels the druggedness from the Good Senses of the women to become w♀m♀ns.

In the fairy tales the sexes were reversed by men. It is She, Warexx, who steals in to kiss and awaken sleeping beauty; She, the dragon who slays the knight. Time for right order again.

Yes, she is: Dragon. Snake. Fable. She has three eyes. Three heads. Two eyes in her head(s) and snakes weaving all over. Gorgon at the Crossroads. One eye and a beaked mouth. One big womb with tentacles. Monster. Prehistoric. Pre-his-storyc. Posthisstoryc. She spans before men, during men, after men. This is her perspective. Men fail to impress her. Which is mostly fair; when she chooses to pass before a man's eyes he hardly notices. ■

Contributors' Notes

Janet Aalfs has founded two lesbian writing groups in the Northampton area and is head instructor of Valley Women's Martial Arts as well as Chair of the National Women's Martial Arts Federation. She received an MFA in poetry from Sarah Lawrence College. Her poetry and fiction have appeared in lesbian/gay and feminist journals and anthologies. A chapbook of her poetry, *Of Angels and Survivors*, is available from Two Herons Press (Summer, 1992).

Donna Allegra: I am a writer working poetry, fiction, essay, and cultural journalism. My work has been published in *Sinister Wisdom, Common Lives/Lesbian Lives, Conditions*, and *Heresies*, amongst the lesbian-feminist periodicals. My latest anthologized works are in *The Persistent Desire: A Femme-Butch Reader* edited by Joan Nestle, *Sister/Stranger: Lesbians Loving Across the Lines* edited by Jan Hardy; *Lesbian Love Stories 2* ed-

ited by Irene Zahava; *Finding the Lesbians* edited by Julia Penelope and Sarah Valentine; *The Original Coming Out Stories* edited by Julia Penelope and Susan J. Wolfe; and *Quickies: Lesbian Short Stories* edited by Irene Zahava.

A bio-bibliographical essay on me will appear in *Contemporary Lesbian Writers of the United States* edited by Sandra Pollack and Denise D. Knight this year.

I am a co-winner of the 1992 Pat Parker Memorial Poetry Award from Woman in the Moon publishers.

Toni Armstrong Jr. is a devotee of both "The Kathy & Mo Show" and "The Brady Bunch." She has full-time careers in both special education and women's music & culture. Interests include female vampires, pinball, bass guitar, neurophysiology, sports cars, sign language, photography, movies, and novels about science run amok. She has been publisher/managing

editor of *HOT WIRE: The Journal of Women's Music & Culture* since 1984.

June Arnold was born October 27, 1926 in Greenville, South Carolina. She was a student at Vassar College from 1943–44 and received B.A. and M.A. degrees from Rice University in 1948 and 1958. She married and had five children. When McGraw-Hill published her first novel, *Applesauce* (1967), *Time* magazine described Arnold as "a 40-year-old South Carolina divorcee." For her entry in *Contemporary Authors*, she responded to the questionnaire as follows: "Politics: 'Feminist.' Religion: 'Women.'" With Parke Bowman, she founded the publishing company Daughters, Inc. In October, 1973, this new house published a list of five novels by women completely engaged in speaking to women. Bertha Harris called the books "five works which would probably never have seen daylight without Daughters: each work is too profoundly rooted in the definitions of women that only women understand." One of these books was Rita Mae Brown's *Rubyfruit Jungle*; another was Arnold's *The Cook and the Carpenter: A Novel by the Carpenter*. Arnold's daring experiment as a novelist is, in Bertha Harris' words (*Village Voice*, April 1974), "a measurement of the reader's ability to perceive by heart what is woman as opposed to that which is male. Discarding the usual pronouns which, everywhere else, do this job for us, the author substitutes her nondistinguishing 'na' and 'nam,' and asks the reader to enter the book's world in original innocence. The difficulty of accustoming oneself to this sexless pronoun has its reward finally when the word 'she' appears for the first time—and appears in the context of a situation in which the woman's pronoun takes on transcendent meanings of love and power..." Daughters published Arnold's third novel, *Sister Gin*, in 1975.

June Arnold was a woman of remarkable stature and composition. Her character and spirit held a combination of graciousness and rebellion. Grim seriousness and a humorous, spontaneous wit marked her spitfire intellect. From the silencings of Houston's high society to feminism, lesbianism, and literature, June Arnold was in the forefront of the women's movement. By telling what was then usually not told, her writing describes life's adventures and struggle from pain, be it playing cards with a bunch of drunk, old women or going through menopause. She once said about herself: "I guess you have to be born with that ability to keep on screaming when people keep telling you to shut up." More than anything, she wanted to be recognized as an important voice in literature. She died of cancer in 1982, not knowing the recognition she so deserved.

Ann Bannon is the author of five Lesbian novels: *Odd Girl Out*, *I Am a Woman*, *Women in the Shadows*, *Journey to a Woman*, and *Beebo Brinker*. Bannon has said of her books that they have "500 flaws. They are, in effect, the offspring of their special era, with its biases." Yet, however negative some assessments of the romances of the 1950s may be from the perspective of the 1990s, they continue to provide a valuable insight into the lives of Lesbians in the 1950s, as they emerged *as* Lesbians.

Judith Barrington is the author of two collections of poetry, *Trying to Be an Honest Woman* (1985) and *History and Geography* (1989), and editor of *An Intimate Wilderness: Lesbian Writers on Sexuality* (1991).

Alison Bechdel has published her four best-selling collections of her work and an annual *Dykes to Watch Out For* calendar with Firebrand Books. *New, Improved! Dykes to Watch Out For*, her third book, won the 1990 Lambda Literary award for lesbian and gay humor. *More Dykes to Watch Out For*, her second, was recently translated into German. Her self-syndicated comic strip runs in over forty gay/lesbian, feminist, and progressive publications in the U.S. and Canada.

JEB, also known as Joan E. Biren, has gained recognition as one of the outstanding documenters of the lesbian and gay movements. For over twenty years she has been photographing, videotaping, publishing, and traveling to bring her work to audiences around the U.S. JEB is the author of two groundbreaking volumes of photography. *Eye To Eye: Portraits of Lesbians* (1979) was the pioneering photographic book that made lesbian existence and courage visible as never before. In *Making A Way: Lesbians Out Front* (1987), a beautiful, vigorous affirmation of lesbian lives, 125 women are dramatically and lovingly portrayed.

JEB's work has been widely published in books and on book covers, including *Nice Jewish Girls*, *Reweaving the Web of Life*, and *We Say We Love Each Other*, in periodicals and newspapers, including *Ms.*, *Heresies*, and *off our backs*, as well as on record album covers, notecards, postcards, calendars, posters, and in films. With Moonforce Media, her production company, JEB has released *For Love and For Life: The 1987 March on Washington for Lesbian and Gay Rights*, a one-hour program that has been broadcast on public television, and *Lesbian Physicians on Practice, Patients and Power*, which is used in medical schools across the country. Currently, JEB and Moonforce Media are working on *Beyond Coming Out*, a video which explores internalized homophobia or shame due to heterosexism among gay men and lesbians. Her work is in the Library of Congress and the Lesbian Herstory Archives.

Phyllis Birkby is a dedicated Lesbian-feminist architect who has been an activist since 1969. One of her main interests has been in the feminist investigation of new lifestyles and their implications for housing, and one of her initial awakenings was her participation in the takeover of the abandoned women's building on 5th Street in New York City, which generated a whole series of women's spaces in the City in 1970–71. She holds a Masters degree in Architecture from Yale University, and is co-founder of the Alliance of Women in Architecture.

Sandy Boucher dates her dyke consciousness from the early seventies when she lived in a San Francisco Women's Liberation collective, helped raise kids and make a revolution. Since then she has written four books, two fiction, two nonfiction: *Turning the Wheel: American Women Creating the New Buddhism, Heartwomen: An Urban Feminist's Odyssey Home, The Notebooks of Leni Clare*, and *Assaults and Rituals*. Now she teaches writing and does writing consultation in Oakland, where

she lives with her lover and venerable cat, surrounded by a community of kindred souls. She is at work on two novels.

Michal Brody is an unrepentant aging radical hippie dyke and working class Jew. Her published works include *Sister Heathen-Spinster's Lunation Calendar* (1975–81), and *Are We There Yet?: A Continuing History of Lavender Woman*. She lives in Chicago, works as a messenger and sometimes ESL teacher, and is currently involved in Tell Us A Story Productions, an ongoing lesbian oral herstory project.

Olga Broumas is an internationally-known Lesbian poet. In 1976, her book *Beginning with O* won the Yale Younger Poets Award, becoming the first volume of poetry with explicit Lesbian content to have achieved this recognition.

Ruth Byrn is a fifty-three-year-old Lesbian Separatist who lives by menial labor, magic, and love.

New York cartoonist **Jennifer Camper** draws the bi-weekly cartoon "Camper," which appears in lesbian and gay publications nationally. Her work can also be seen in gay comix, *on our backs, Real Girl*, wimmin's comix, and *De Neuve* magazine.

Caryatis Cardea: I'm a Lesbian Separatist, Irish-Catholic & French-Canadian, born in Buffalo, New York in 1950 to working-class parents to whom I no longer speak. I am the fourth of nine children, only one of whom

still speaks to me. I now live with Leslie, my lover of twelve years, in Oakland, California where I study history, make music, and rant and rave in poetry and prose (and the occasional song lyric). And where I am beaten at cards quite regularly by Michele. (But I win at Trivia.)

Chrystos was born November 7, 1956 off reservation in San Francisco to a Menominee father and a mother whose parents immigrated from Alsace-Lorraine and Lithuania. She is self-educated, and employed as a maid when not reading poetry. She is the recipient of the Barbara Deming Memorial Grant, an NEA for literature (1990), and a Lanna Foundation Grant for Poetry (1991). Both of her books of poetry, *Not Vanishing* (1988) and *Dream On* (1991), were published by Press Gang. Her work has appeared in numerous anthologies, including *This Bridge Called My Back, A Gathering of Spirit, Intricate Passions, Living the Spirit, Gay and Lesbian Poetry of Our Time, Dancing on the Rim of the World, Caterpillars, InVersions, Naming the Violence* (lesbian battering), *Getting Wet* (lesbian sex), *Naming the Waves, Out the Other Side, Making Face, Making Soul, And a Deer's Ear, Eagle's Song and Bear's Grace, Piece of My Heart: A Lesbian of Colour Anthology, Through Indian Eyes*, and *Art Against Racism*.

Chrystos is also involved in various Native and Treaty Rights causes, including, the liberation of Leonard Peltier, the end to relocation of Diné people, Northwest and Chippewa fishing rights, and the legal defense of the Kanestawake people at Oka. Other political activities include working against the new maximum security prison planned for Florence, Colorado, Women In Black (in solidarity with the Palestinian demand for two states), and anti-war work. She has been a proud Lesbian for twenty-six years, and has been sober since 1988. She has been residing in the Northwest for the last thirteen years, on Bainbridge Island.

Cheryl Clarke was born and raised in Washington, D.C. She moved to New Jersey in 1969 and found her black lesbian poet's voice in 1973. Since that time, she has been honored to publish her work in numerous lesbian, gay, feminist, black journals, magazines, newspapers, and anthologies, including *Gay Community News, Sinister Wisdom, IKON, Feminist Studies, The Black Scholar, Callaloo, The Advocate, Conditions, This Bridge Called My Back: Writings by Radical Women of Color, Home Girls: A Black Feminist Anthology, Gay and Lesbian Poetry in Our Time.* She is the author of three books of poetry: *Narratives: Poems in the Tradition of Black Women* (1983, Kitchen Table: Women of Color Press), *Living as a Lesbian* (1983, Firebrand Books), *Humid Pitch* (1989, Firebrand Books). She has been a member of the *Conditions* Editorial Collective since 1981. She is currently work-

ing on a new manuscript of poems entitled *experimental love.*

Artist and writer **Tee Corinne** has been published in the U.S. Women's Movement press since 1974. Her books include the *Cunt Coloring Book, Yantras of Womanlove, Dreams of the Woman Who Loved Sex, Lovers,* and *The Sparkling Lavender Dust of Lust.* She edited *The Poetry of Sex: Lesbians Write the Erotic, Riding Desire,* and *Intricate Passions.* Her photos can be seen in *Stolen Glances: Lesbians Take Photographs,* edited by Fraser and Boffin; her art work about growing up in an alcoholic family is featured in *Family,* published by Gallerie.

In 1991 she was chosen by *Lambda Book Report* as one of the fifty most influential lesbians and gay men of the decade.

Liza Cowan: I live in Park Slope, Brooklyn, New York. I am a trainer of Neuro-Linguistic Programming and a graduate student in Anthropology at the Graduate Faculty of the New School for Social Research. I'm working on a book of Oral Histories of Russian Lesbians with my lover, Laurie Essig.

Nancy Crooks: Couldn't find.

Lin Daniels is a 39-year-old Jewish Dyke who is happiest at Lesbian festivals and in her Lesbian community, The Pagoda in St. Augustine, Florida. She has been producing events for Lesbians since the mid-seventies, and plans to continue as long as the Found Goddess

Hilaria continues to appear when invoked. Currently, she is the producer of the East Coast Lesbians' Festival, and co-produces the West Coast and Hawaii Lesbians' Festivals with Marilyn VanVeersen.

Terri de la Peña is a Chicana lesbian feminist who became exasperated with searching for women like herself in fiction. She decided to "just do it" herself. Her stories about Chicana lesbians appear in numerous anthologies. "Tortilleras" evolved into Chapter Seven of *Margins,* published by The Seal Press in 1992.

Diane DiMassa is the creator of "Hothead Paisan, Homicidal Lesbian Terrorist" and is a full-time cartoonist/illustrator living in New Haven, Connecticut.

Alix Dobkin: I am currently in the process of writing my memories after twenty years largely spent on the road visiting and singing for Lesbian communities all over the English-speaking world. I have had the unique privilege of helping to lay the foundation for a rich and thriving Lesbian culture. My sixth album, *Love & Politics,* a twenty-song compilation of my work, summarizes thirty years of writing and entertaining. My first album, *Lavender Jane Loves Women,* was produced in 1973 with Kay Gardner and holds the distinction of being the first internationally distributed Lesbian album of all time.

Sarah Dreher is a lesbian activist and one of the U.S.'s leading lesbian playwrights. Born in Hanover, Pennsylvania, she received her A.B. degree in clinical psychology from Purdue University. She is a playwrighting Fellow of the Massachusetts Council on the Arts, and a winner of the Massachusetts Playwrighting Festival, sponsored by the Artists Foundation. She has received numerous rewards and honors, including first place n the National Lesbian Playwrighting Contest at Theatre Rhinoceros in San Francisco, the *L.A. Weekly* award for "outstanding achievement in playwrighting," the Alliance for Gay and Lesbian Artists in the Entertainment Industry media award, and the Jane Chambers Memorial International Gay Playwrighting Contest. A collection of her plays, *Lesbian Stages*, has been published by New Victoria Publishers, and two of her plays were published in *Places, Please: The First Anthology of Lesbian Plays*, edited by Kate McDermott. She is the author of the popular Stoner McTavish series of lesbian mysteries (also published by New Victoria), and a clinical psychologist in private practice in Amherst, Massachusetts. She has been an Amherst Town Meeting representative, and is currently co-chair of the Civil Rights Review Commission of Amherst. She has lived in the Pioneer Valley since 1965.

Elana Dykewomon has been looking for lesbian community/culture since she was three; actively participating in its creation since 1971. She is the current editor (since 1987) of *Sinister Wisdom, a journal for the lesbian imagination in the arts and politics*. A contributor to many anthologies, her books *Riverfinger Women* (1974; 1992), *They Will Know Me By My Teeth* (short stories and poems, 1976), and *fragments from lesbos* (poems, 1981) were all out of print until Naiad reissued *Riverfinger Women* with a new Afterword in 1992. Work in progress: an ancestor novel about Russian Jewish lesbians c. 1950-1930. She lives in Oakland, California, blessed with great love and inspiring friendships.

Deborah Edel is a co-founder of the Lesbian Herstory Archives and is actively involved in the ongoing process of keeping the Archives running as smoothly as possible. During the day she works as an educational psychologist with children with learning problems.

Therese Edell has been the unofficial Voice of the Michigan Women's Music Festival for several years, and has been involved in every Festival as a performer, sound engineer, or announcer since 1977, the second gathering. Recordings include *Prophecy's Child* (1970), *From Women's Faces* (1978), and *For Therese* (1990). She composed the song and score for the short documentary film *Heroes and Strangers* (1984) and has completed several commissioned chamber music and choral works. She is an eccentric vegetarian who lives with her partner of fifteen years, composes music, and enjoys watching baseball on TV.

Amy Edgington: I am a forty-six-year-old white Lesbian, and artist and writer. I was born in the South and have spent most of my life here, including eighteen years in the closet and nineteen years "out" as a Lesbian. My writing has been most profoundly affected by my Lesbian identity, by living with disabilities since birth, and by my survival of a Lesbian battering relationship. My work has been published in *Common Lives/Lesbian Lives, Cats and Their Dykes* (HerBooks, 1991), *Wanting Women: An Anthology of Erotic Lesbian Poetry* (Sidewalk Revolution Press, 1990), and other journals and anthologies.

Susan Edwards has done metaphysical consultations for over twenty-five years. She was on the *Lavender Woman* Collective for four years in the 1970s. She taught writing and literature classes and co-founded a Book Arts program at Naropa Institute in the 1980s. She does story-performances, and her latest project is "A Heretic Daughter Speaks about C. Columbus." She lives in Boulder, Colorado with her partner of twelve years and with one dog and two cats.

Elliott: Lesbians my own age (about thirty) often think of me as some sort of throwback—hairy-legged, vegetarian, non-monogamous, manhating Dyke Separatist. I just think my theory and life are connected by a good internal logic monitor. I'm white and working-class living on SSI. I live for now in Philadelphia with one lover while missing my Midwestern lover and friend and culture tremendously.

Karen Escovitz, also known as Otter, is a radical Jewish fat dyke who lives in Philadelphia with Elliott. She plays anything with strings and frets, sings, drums, and performs at coffeehouses and campfires whenever she can. It is her fondest wish to put together a band made up *entirely* of BIG DYKES with ATTITUDE!

Lee Evans is a short, grey-eyed, forty-year-old Lesbian Separatist who grew up amidst the fields and cows and creeks of northwestern Pennsylvania and who currently lives amongst the Dykes of Cleveland, Ohio. Her writing has appeared in *Lesbian Ethics* and *Sinister Wisdom*.

Sue Fink's formal training in music includes a degree from UCLA. Founder of the L.A. Women's Community Chorus in 1976, she accumulated a long list of professional credits before she began her career in women's music, leading to many appearances at Lesbians' festivals and women's music festivals. Her song "Leaping Lesbians," a long-standing favorite with Lesbian audiences, was performed by Meg Christian on her first album and first recorded by Sue on *Lesbian Concentrate*.

Lynne Yamaguchi Fletcher is a Japanese-American poet and a resurrected celebrant of the body. Her work has appeared in various periodicals and anthologies, including *The Forbidden Stitch* (Calyx, 1989) and *She Who Was Lost Is Remembered* (Seal, 1991). A reference work, *The First Gay Pope*, is forthcoming from Alyson. "Turtlehawk" first appeared in *Bushfire: Stories of Lesbian Desire* (Alyson, 1991).

Myriam Fougére: I am white/Lesbian/Québécoise. I sculpted clay for ten years, creating my vision of our Lesbian sexuality. Believing in our emerging Lesbian Culture, I showed my work exclusively to women, primarily to Lesbians. I now co-produce the East Coast Lesbians' Festival and am creating videos for Lesbians.

Marilyn Frye: I am a philosopher and essayist who lives in Lansing, Michigan. I teach at Michigan State University. I am partnered with Bone in a long-term, not monogamous relationship which does not fit any previously given definition and is always under construction. I am over fifty now, and a great many things about me and my life are changing; I am still white-raced, middle-classed, and christian-raised, and committed to enacting new and subversive meanings for these circumstances.

Carolyn Gage is a Lesbian playwright, director, and performer. She has toured nationally in her award-winning one-woman show, *The Second Coming of Joan of Arc*, and in 1989 she founded No to Men Theatre in Ashland, Oregon, which produced thirteen of her plays in two years. She is currently directing and performing for LOLA, the League of Lesbian Actors based in Santa Rosa, California.

Kay Gardner has been involved in Women's Music since 1973 when she co-produced the ground-breaking lesbian feminist album *Lavender Jane Loves Women* with Alix Dobkin. Since then, she has produced ten albums of original instrumental compositions and flute meditations (all available from Ladyslipper, Inc.). Her book, *Sounding the Inner Landscape: Music as Medicine* (Caduceus Publications, 1990), is a text to music and sound healers worldwide. Her articles and columns have been printed in *Lesbian Tide, Womanspirit, Ms., New Age Retailer, Paid My Dues, Sojourner*, and *HOT WIRE*. When she isn't touring, she makes her home on the coast of Maine with her lover of fifteen years, three cats, and a parakeet.

Rene Gaumond: Couldn't find.

Sally Miller Gearhart, professor emerita, is a teacher, writer, and activist in Lesbian, gay, women's, animal rights, and Central American solidarity movements. She was born in Virginia when Hoover was on the way out and FDR was on the way in. She holds degrees from Sweet Briar College, Bowling Green State University, and the University of Illinois. She taught fourteen years in Texas, and twenty-two years at San Francisco State University, where she taught Women's Studies, Theatre, and Speech Communication.

She is the author of numerous short stories, articles, and speeches, and *The Wanderground: Stories of the Hill Women*. With Bill Johnson, she edited *Loving Women/Loving Men: Gay Liberation and the Church*. With Susan Rennie, she co-authored *A Feminist Tarot*. She was a participant in the Academy Award-winning *The Times of Harvey Milk* and *Word Is Out* as well as other films and videos.

She presently lives in northern California where she is working on another fantasy novel and sings in a barbershop quartet.

Diane F. Germain: I am a French-American Lesbian Feminist psychiatric social worker who recently concluded a five-year-old strength group for *Women Survivors of Incest and/or Childhood Molest*. My life partner and I run *Dykes on Hikes* in San Diego. I have been the staff cartoonist for the *Lesbian News* of Los Angeles since 1987. I have had cartoons and humor pieces published in several anthologies and journals in the U.S., Canada, and Italy. I create humor as a hedge against the misogyny of heterosexist phallocentric patriarchy *and* to tickle the Lesbians.

Elsa Gidlow: Born in Yorkshire, England in 1898, six-year-old

Elsa immigrated with her family of nine to a French Canadian village near Montreal. Leaving Montreal art circles for Manhattan in 1920, Elsa became poetry editor for Frank Harris' much-censored *Pearson's Magazine*. In 1926, she sailed for San Francisco with her older, aristocratic lover, Violet Henry-Anderson, "Tommy," with whom she lived until Tommy's death.

Elsa led the precarious career of a freelance journalist, while often supporting family and others. She was North America's first published writer of a poetry volume openly celebrating lesbian love (1923). She was a radical feminist of the first *and* second waves, as well as an activist prosecuted by McCarthyites. In the 1950s, she slowly began building Druid Heights among the California redwoods with her lover of ten years, Isabel Quallo.

On June 8, 1986, poet-philosopher and lesbian-feminist Elsa Gidlow died peacefully at Druid Heights. Of her large body of poetry and prose, five of her thirteen books remain in print, among them *Sapphic Songs* and *ELSA: I Come With My Songs*.

Janice Gould: I am a member of the Maidu tribe of northern California. I was born in 1949 in San Diego, but grew up in Berkeley, California. I earned my B.A. in linguistics at the University of California-Berkeley, and my M.A. in English there as well. I now attend the University of New Mexico where

I am working on a doctoral degree in English literature. My areas of interest are American Indian literature and Feminist Theory.

My poetry has been published in various anthologies and journals, including *IKON*, *Calyx*, *Sinister Wisdom*, *The Berkeley Poetry Review*, *Evergreen Chronicles*, *A Gathering of Spirit*, edited by Beth Brant, *Making Voice, Making Face*, edited by Gloria Anzaldúa, *Naming the Waves*, edited by Christian McEwen, and *An Intimate Wilderness*, edited by Judith Barrington. My first short story was published in Paula Gunn Allen's *Spider Woman's Granddaughters* (under the pseudonym, Misha Gallagher). In 1989 I was awarded a grant from the National Endowment for the Arts, and in October, 1990, my first book of poetry, *Beneath My Heart*, was published by Firebrand Press.

I feel that writing is an act of resistance and survival. But there is more than my own survival that is at stake. These days I feel a kind of urgency to reconstruct memory, annihilate the slow amnesia of the dominant culture, and reclaim the past as a viable, if painful, entity. I think of writing as a way to make questions, ponder, meditate, dream, and locate powerful truths that may enrich the imagination and deepen our desire to affirm life.

Judy Grahn marched for gay rights in 1964, and co-founded lesbian feminism in 1969, along with a press that published Lesbian work for eight years. She is internationally known, with several books of poetry, two cassette tapes, a novel, and a gay and Lesbian cultural history, *Another Mother Tongue*. Forthcoming from Beacon Press is *Blood, Bread and Roses: How Menstruation Created the World*. She lives in Oakland, California.

Vernita Gray is a 43-year-old black lesbian separatist who is a poet and writer. She is a graduate of Columbia College and is also the owner of Sol Sands, a taco and burrito restaurant in Chicago. In her spare time she is cooking up a novel she calls *The Taco Stories*. She has published a chapbook of poetry entitled *Sweet Sixteen*.

Roberta Gregory has been creating queer comix for the past eighteen years. In 1976, she produced the first Lesbian comic book, *Dynamite Damsels,* and since then has had her work published frequently in both *Wimmen's Comix* and *Gay Comix*. She has also appeared in *Choices* (Angry Isis Press), *Kitty Libber* (Crossing Press), and innumerable other books and comix, including two self-published books, *Winging It* and *Sheila and the Unicorn*. She currently has a quarterly comic book from Fantagraphics, *Naughty Bits,* and is working on *Artistic Licentiousness,* an adult comic, one issue of which has been published. Despite this prodigious output, she is often distressed by her relative obscurity within the Lesbian commu-

nity and invites readers to send an SASE for a catalog and update of her current activities: POB 27438, Seattle, WA 98125.

Morgan Grey lives in northern Vermont and works as a tradeswomen's advocate. She is a volunteer at a raptor center, where she works with injured and disabled birds of prey. Her best bird buddy is a cranky peregrine falcon.

Pam Hall is a Lesbian-identified singer/songwriter from Mississippi. A self-described "Black southern dyke on a mission," Pam has captured audiences with her unique blend of spicy high-energy performances. She accompanies herself on acoustic guitar and blues harp. Her music reflects her love of wimmin, her feminist politics, and her favorite subject, lesbians loving lesbians. Her debut recording, *Honey on My Lips*, a women-only project from start to finish, was released on Fabulous Records in 1992.

Radclyffe Hall (188?–1943) was born in England and christened Marguerite, but chose for herself the name "John." She lived with her love 'Ladye' Batten until her death, and after her death with Lady Una Troubridge, her life partner. Author of seven novels and a number of short stories published during the 1920s and 1930s, her novel *The Well of Loneliness*, published in 1928, remains her most famous work. Its Lesbian protagonist, Stephen Gordon, was depicted as a "sexual invert," but one who

was nonetheless capable of great passion and courage. Intended to gain the sympathy of those hostile to Lesbianism, *The Well* nonetheless was the focus of great public controversy and attempts at legal censorship. It was, for many Lesbians who grew up during the 1950s, the most available Lesbian novel.

Jorjet Harper's reviews, news articles, features, interviews, and photographs have appeared in over thirty journals and magazines. She has covered all sorts of lesbian-related political and cultural events, women's conferences, literary gatherings, and music festivals. For three years she was Arts and Entertainment Editor of *Outlines*, Chicago's gay and lesbian newsmonthly. She is a regular contributor to *HOT WIRE: The Journal of Women's Music and Culture*. Harper's lesbian humor column, "Lesbomania," appears in *Outlines/Nightlines* in Chicago and in a number of other gay and lesbian publications. She has given readings of "Lesbomania" columns in Chicago, Berlin, Paris, New York, and at several women's music festivals.

Kathleen Hawk lives with her lover, Rose, in Williston, Florida, and has been in transition for as long as she can remember. She is recovering from catholicism, incest, and heterosexuality. She feels she has discovered a new religion in lesbian sex, laughter, and therapy. She has been a professional writer for two decades and does her best to foment revolution by writing about humane business management.

Chaia Zblocki Heller lives in Hatfield, Massachusetts where she has just completed her manuscript of poetry, *What Amazes Me Most*. Her work is published in several journals and anthologies, including *Calyx*, *Sojourner*, *Kalliope*, *Sinister Wisdom*, and *Women's Glibber*, an anthology published by The Crossing Press. In addition to writing, she works with homeless women as a clinical social worker and teaches ecofeminism at the Institute for Social Ecology in Vermont.

Sarah Lucia Hoagland is a Chicago Dyke and a philosopher. She came out in 1975, a year after being labeled p.d.o.f. (potential dyke on faculty) by her lesbian students, and she named herself 'separatist' in 1976. She has been teaching philosophy and women's studies at northeastern illinois university in chicago since 1977, and has given talks in lesbian communities around the u.s. for fifteen years. She is the author of *Lesbian Ethics: Toward New Value*, published by the Institute of Lesbian Studies, and along with Julia Penelope she has co-edited *For Lesbians Only: A Separatist Anthology*, published by Onlywomen Press of London.

Beth Karbe: Every so often a person may pass through our lives in an apparently casual or haphazard way, and yet will leave an indelible and healing impression forevermore. Joan

was one of those people in my young life, and twenty-five years later, I still find myself thanking her.

Laura Kaye's gorgon design is derived from an ancient Greek drawing. She created it for Elana Dykewomon's *They Will Know Me By My Teeth* while living in the mid-'70s in Northampton, Massachusetts, which was already notorious as a Lesbian town. Laura has long since retreated to the surrounding countryside for peace, solitude, and a less eventful way of life. She continues to make art whenever time permits.

Kris Kovick is a SF-based cartoonist and writer. Her work appears in *FTH*, *Advocate*, *Holy Titclamps* and *off our backs*. Her book, *What I Love About Lesbian Politics Is Arguing with People I Agree With*, is a perfect example of itself. She appeared in the film *Lesbian Fashion* as a don't. She's in "The Breakfast Project," fifty-one famous women, depicted by fifty-one women artists internationally, eating breakfast, which is now touring Europe. She is currently working on a comic book about the Milk/Moscone assassinations. She believes: Nothing is sacred.

Cartooning is filmmaking, only in geological time.

Marianne Lieberman: Couldn't find.

Anna Livia was born in Dublin, grew up in Africa, spent eighteen years in London and now lives in the Bay Area where she is acquiring a Ph.D. in

French linguistics. She is the author of *Minimax* and *Incidents Involving Mirth*, as well as four other lesbian novels and collections. She loves her mother, had a very happy childhood and has never been in therapy.

Audre Lorde was born on February 18, 1934, to parents who had emigrated from Grenada to America—to New York City—before her birth. In *Zami—A New Spelling of My Name*, the "biomythography" she published with Crossing Press in 1982, she describes her mother as a very powerful woman, born in Carriacou, a place where the love of women for each other is legendary.

Some of the power of Lorde's voice she evidently drew from her mother. But, as she states in her 1978 article in *Sinister Wisdom 6*, she drew strength from many women, a strength which sustained her during her first confrontation with death, a surgery for a tumor found to be benign. Lorde, who had long battled racism and homophobia in her life and through her writing, used the knowledge of her death to further strengthen her resolve to speak out, to bridge the differences which divided white women from black, lesbians from heterosexual women, to enjoin all of us to engage in the battle against the "tyrannies of silence." She had stated in "A Song for Many Movements," (published by Norton in the anthology *The Black Unicorn*, 1978) that "our labor has become/

more important/ than our silence." During the Lesbians and Literature panel at the 1977 Annual Convention of the Modern Language Association, a panel entitled "The transformation of Silence into Language and Action," she spoke of the need to confront the fears that keep us silent, of the "visibility without which we cannot truly live." (This speech has been published in essay form, first in *Sinister Wisdom 6*, pp. 11-15, and later in *The Cancer Journals*, publisher by Spinsters, Ink, San Francisco, 1980, and *Sister Outsider: Essays and Speeches* by Audre Lorde, published by Crossing Press, 1984.) Lorde reminded us in that speech that, whether or not she remained silent, she "would still have suffered, and [she] would still die."

On November 17, 1992, while *Lesbian Culture* was in production, Audre Lorde did die. But, as she noted in her 1977 speech, she was "not only a casualty, [but]...also a warrior." She never lost her voice, and we have it yet in our memory of her speeches, in the journals and anthologies which have published her work, and in the fourteen volumes she has left us, *The First Cities, Cables to Rage, From a Land Where Other People Live, The New York Head Shop and Museum, Coal, Between Our Selves, The Black Unicorn, The Cancer Journals, Zami—A New Spelling of My Name, Chosen Poems—Old and New, Sister Outsider, Our Dead Behind Us, A Burst of Light,* and *Undersong, Chosen Poems Old and New* (Revised).

(*Undersong*, published in 1992, has the moving dedication, "To Gloria, with all the time in the world.")

During her life, she was named Poet Laureate of New York State; received honorary doctorates from Hunter College, Oberlin College, and Haverford College; and won the Walt Whitman Citation of Merit and the Manhattan Borough President's Award for Excellence in the Arts. Her contribution to Lesbian culture is perhaps better reflected in the title given her by a group from Leeds, England— that of Black Lebian Warrior.

In the essay discussed above, Lorde spoke of our shared commitment to language, to the power of language, and of the need to reclaim it, to transform silence into language and action by speaking the truths we need to survive. This, she taught us, was to take part in a process of growth, of bridging our differences, of building community. There are, she taught us, so many silences to be broken. Lorde never ceased breaking silences. *Lesbian Culture*, and Lesbian culture(s), are permeated by her voice, and by the voices of those she has empowered.

Lee Lynch lives in rural Oregon with her partner, their perpetual puppy and their specially abled cat. She works in the social services. Her published books include the novels *Morton River Valley, That Old Studebaker, Dusty's Queen of Hearts Diner, The*

Swashbuckler and *Toothpick House*. Also published by Naiad Press are two short story collections, *Old Dyke Tales* and *Home in Your Hands*, a collection of her syndicated columns, *The Amazon Trail*, and a mystery featuring feline characters, *Sue Slate, Private Eye*.

Barbara Macdonald (b. 1913) is a writer, activist, and lecturer. *Look Me in the Eye: Old Women, Aging and Ageism*, co-authored by Cynthia Rich, has recently been reissued in an expanded edition by Spinsters Books Co.

Toni A.H. McNaron has taught at the University of Minnesota for twenty-eight years, focusing on Shakespeare/Milton and women writers and lesbian literary theory. She was one of the first lesbian faculty to come out on campus, having decided both to stop her years of alcoholic drinking and being in the closet. Since that momentous day she has begun to thrive, both personally and as a productive scholar. The books of which she is proudest are *Voices in the Night: Women Speaking about Incest* (co-edited with Yarrow Morgan) and her recent autobiography, *I Dwell in Possibility* (Feminist Press). Her favorite activities are gardening, travel, jogging with her cocker spaniel and watching "Mystery" on educational television.

Ellen Meyers is an independent media artist and the Director of Special Projects for the Center of New Television in Chicago. She has a Masters degree in Film and Video and is in post-production on a documentary about AIDS.

Cheryl Miller is a writer, storyteller, and performance artist who has been active in the Chicago creative and political community for many years. To her other hats, she has recently added that of science student.

Isabel Miller is the author of *Patience and Sarah* (Fawcett), *The Love of Good Women*, *Side by Side*, and *A Dooryard Full of Flowers* (all Naiad). She lives in upstate New York.

Valerie Miner is the author of *Trespassing and Other Stories* and the novels *All Good Women*, *Winter's Edge*, *Murder in the English Department*, *Blood Sisters*, and *Movement*. Her latest book is *Rumors from the Cauldron: Selected Essays, Reviews and Reportage*. She has earned her living by teaching for over twenty years.

Marilyn Murphy has been a feminist activist (Women's Liberation Movement style) since she participated in an ad hoc committee formed to "encourage" the inclusion of women writers in literature courses at California State University, Long Beach, in 1969. Her book, *Are You Girls Traveling Alone?*, is a collection of the best of her monthly columns, published for nine years as "Lesbianic Logic" in the Los Angeles *Lesbian News*.

Merril Mushroom is a Lesbian currently practicing in Tennessee. She loves wimmin a lot.

Joan Nestle is a fifty-two-year-old Jewish fem, born in the Bronx, N.Y., who has grown to her lesbian fullness in New York City. Co-founder of the Lesbian Herstory Archives, she is astounded by the richness and audacity of our multivoiced culture.

Joan E. Nixon worked on the Chicago Lesbian newspaper *Lavender Woman* from 1973 until it ceased publication in December, 1975. In July, 1976, she moved to New York City to work on Bella Abzug's campaign for the U.S. Senate, and served briefly on the board of directors of the National Gay Task Force representing the Midwest. After Abzug's campaign for Ed Koch's congressional seat in 1978, she became Bella Abzug's driver, and still is.

Pat Parker—Black lesbian poet, feminist medical administrator, mother of two daughters, lover of women, softball devotee, and general progressive troublemaker—died of breast cancer on June 17, 1989 at the age of forty-five. Most of her earlier published poetry has been collected in *Movement in Black*. She also published *Jonestown and Other Madness* (both from Firebrand Books).

June Parlett is forty-five years old and has been a photographer since 1967. In 1971, she received her M.F.A. from San Diego State University and also compiled the first Lesbian slideshow, "The Image of the Lesbian." Tee Corinne has

called her "the godmother of the Lesbian slideshow." In 1974, she copyrighted a sound filmstrip, a 700-year review of women artists from 1200–1900. It is part of a nine-module educational package called "IF: Identity Female," published by Dun Donnelley Publishing Corp., but it is also sold separately.

From 1983 to 1986 she studied nursing, but dropped out until she regained her sanity by studying photography in San Diego from 1989–1991. She then returned to and finished nursing school. Because she doesn't make a living as an artist, she now works as a critical care nurse. Until January, 1993, her one-woman show, fifty-seven framed photographs, can be seen at the Frontdoor Cafe in West Palm Beach, Florida.

Juana Maria Gonzalez Paz is a thirty-nine-year-old, New York-born Puerto Rican lesbian, author of *The La Luz Journal*—true story of lesbian of color land. My seventeen-year-old wonderful daughter Mary Ann and I have lived at Twin Oaks, a commune in Virginia, for two years. Mary Ann is a songwriter/musician/actress who would like to study theater. I'm writing and thinking about communal living, feminist education, and group process. I want to teach but not at an institution, so I'm looking to settle on or near lesbian land, lead neighborhood Women's Studies groups and make a living while Mary Ann attends school nearby. Suggestions welcome—Juana & Mary

Ann, c/o Twin Oaks, Rt. 4—Box 169, Louisa, VA 23093.

Julia Penelope, now a 51-year-old, white Dyke and Type II diabetic, is a life-long, cross-classed Lesbian, an ex-stone butch, an ex-academic, and a Separatist. In almost every place she has lived—whether it was Miami, Florida, New York City, Los Angeles, Austin, Texas, Athens, Georgia, Nashville, Tennessee, Vermillion, South Dakota, Lincoln, Nebraska, St. Louis, Missouri, or Athol, Massachusetts—her life has been enriched and sustained by the Lesbians who've befriended her and accepted her into their communities. With her partner, Sarah Valentine, she has recently become the guardian of a fifteen-year-old Lesbian, in the hope that they can offer her a better adolescence, in a Lesbian household, than the heterosexual ones they survived.

In addition to co-edited anthologies (*The Coming Out Stories* [Persephone Press, 1980], *The Original Coming Out Stories* [Crossing Press, 1989], *For Lesbians Only* [Onlywomen Press, 1988], *Finding the Lesbians* [Crossing Press, 1990], and *Sexual Practice/Textual Theory: Lesbian Cultural Criticism* [Blackwell, 1993]), she is the author of *Speaking Freely: Unlearning the Lies of the Fathers' Tongues* (Pergamon, 1990/ Teachers College Press, 1992), and *Call Me Lesbian: Lesbian Lives/Lesbian Theory* (Crossing Press, 1992), co-author of *Found Goddesses: From Asphalta to Viscera* (New Victoria Publishers, 1988), and a co-creator of the *D.Y.K.E.* game (LipService, 1986). When she can, she makes a living by copy-editing thesauruses and dictionaries.

Rainbow, born in 1934, in Shreveport, Louisiana, now resides in Crone's Row at the Pagoda, a Lesbian seaside community in Florida. She loves her cat, Generic, playing on the dulcimer, drumming on the beach, and architectural drafting. She is a Pisces.

Sudie Rakusin is a Jewish Lesbian artist, 44, Aries, with five other planets in fire. "I live in the woods in North Carolina with my four dogs, and paint and draw every chance I get. What is most important to me is to always speak and paint from my heart…to really listen to her and trust that what I am hearing are the truths of my soul and are of value."

Ruthann Robson's fiction has appeared in many lesbian periodicals and anthologies as well as her two collections, *Eye of a Hurricane* and *Cecile*, both published by Firebrand Books. She is also interested in lesbian theory and her newest book is *Lesbian (Outlaw): Survival Under the Rule of Law*, also available from Firebrand Books.

Elizabeth D. Ross is a visual artist living on a farm amongst the redwoods in rural Northern California. Her printmaking studio is (mostly) finished, and she's still serious about those Big Topics: life, death, love, grief, peace. Her intimate relationship and loved ones are a source of inspiration, strength, and comfort in her life and art.

Joanna Russ lives in Seattle, Washington. An author well-known and respected within the mainstream and among Lesbian readers of fantasy and science fiction, she has published numerous short stories and novels. She has also published *On Strike Against God*, a coming out novel, with The Crossing Press, who also published a volume of her feminist essays, *Magic Mommas, Trembling Sisters, Puritans and Perverts*.

Susan Sherman (b. 1939) is a poet, playwright, essayist, and editor of *IKON* magazine. Her most recent books are *The Color of the Heart: Writing from Struggle and Change 1959–1990* (Curbstone Press, 1990), a collection of poetry, short prose, and essays, and *We Stand Our Ground: Three Women, Their Vision, Their Poems* in collaboration with Kimiko Hahn and Gale Jackson. She was awarded a New York Foundation for the Arts fellowship in poetry in 1990. In October, 1992, two of her plays were produced at La MaMa, ETC in New York City. She teaches part-time at Parsons School of Design and is currently working on a memoir, *Home*.

Adrienne J. Smith was a feminist therapist in private practice in Chicago for many years. She was one of the founders of the Feminist Therapy Institute, and was very active in the Lesbian and Gay Division of the American Psychological Association. She was co-editor of the book *Lesbians at Midlife: The Creative Transition.* She died in August, 1992, at age 58, of cancer.

Noreen Stevens is a comic artist living in Winnipeg, Manitoba. When not cartooning she does her laundry. Her strip, *The Chosen Family,* is published in gay/lesbian periodicals in Canada and the U.S.

Leslie Stewart lives in Edmonton, Alberta, under the big prairie sky and makes her living maintaining a 96,000 name mailing list, working in a deli, painting the odd T-shirt, and drawing the occasional cartoon.

Susan Stinson's essays, fiction and poetry have appeared in many anthologies and magazines, including *And a Deer's Ear, Eagle Song and a Bear's Grace: Animals and Women* (Cleis, 1990), and *Word of Mouth,* vols. 1 and 2 (Crossing Press, 1990, and 1991). She received a 1991 Vogelstein Foundation grant in support of work on her novel, *Martha Moody.* She also leads fat liberation workshops. She lives in Easthampton, Massachusetts.

Toby Summer is a woman who survived the brutality of sexual slavery, sort of. She understands why a woman could murder violent johns in self-defense as in the case of a woman now sentenced to death in Florida's electric chair. The woman in Florida is also a lesbian and a survivor of childhood assault and prostitution. But she will

not survive the last act of male supremacy against her: the State of Florida plans to murder her, probably before this book sees the light of day. "She is our sister; why aren't we fighting for her life?" Toby asks. "She could be me or you."

Toby Summer clearly states, "There is no feminism if it allows prostitution and pornography to continue as institutionalized forms of male power that dehumanize women and children. And, lesbianism is worthless if it allows male supremacy to dictate the values that are held in the lesbian community. Therefore, time is overdue to take back the lesbian community, to take back feminism, to take back our sisters from the state and to defeat sadism and supremacy whenever we encounter it."

Renée Vivien (pseudonym for Pauline Tarn, 1877-1909) was born in England. But, like many others from England and the United States, she became part of the expatriate movement in Paris during the early years of the twentieth century, seeking the relative sexual and artistic freedom of France. There, she became the lover of Natalie Clifford Barney.

Vivien, who wrote both prose and poetry, was the author of a number of books. Two volumes of her poetry, *A Woman Appeared to Me* and *Muse of the Violets,* have been published in English translation by the Naiad Press. Her French poetry, celebrating Lesbian love outside

the confines of patriarchy, has been praised for its use of Symbolist imagery as well as for its feminist vision.

Jean Weisinger is based in San Francisco. She has traveled to England, Germany, Amsterdam, Cuba, Australia, New Zealand, and Bali taking photographs for her forthcoming book, *A Community of Women.* Her vision is to travel around the world and take photographs of the beautiful, spirited EARTH'S PEOPLE and to make powerful photographic books as gifts to the world. Her portraits of Alice Walker have been widely published.

Jess Wells is the author of *AfterShocks* (Third Side Press, 1992), a novel whose theme involves "control" as a drug, as a counterfeit for love and true intimacy. Wells has also published two volumes of short stories, *Two Willow Chairs* and *The Dress/The Sharda Stories,* and her work has appeared in eleven literary anthologies within the lesbian, gay, and women's movements. Her work "The Dress" was the first piece to herald the discovery of femme-drag; her stories "The Succubus" and "Morning Girls" are cited as among the earliest of lesbian erotica; her story "Two Willow Chairs," frequently reprinted, is now included in university curricula and textbooks. She resides in the San Francisco Bay Area.

Susan Wolfe was raised in New York City by workingclass parents, one Jewish and one Irish

Catholic. Since 1973 she has worked at a university in South Dakota, in a town whose population has never reached 10,000. Trained as a linguist specializing in theoretical syntax, she now publishes work on language and linguistics as well as work on Lesbian culture. A recovering heterosexual, she has a twenty-two-year-old son, and lives with Cathy Flum, her lover of seventeen years. With Julia Penelope, she has co-edited *The Coming Out Stories* (Persephone Press, 1980), *The Original Coming Out Stories* (Crossing Press, 1989), and *Sexual Practice/Textual Theory: Lesbian Cultural Criticism* (Basil Blackwell, 1993).

Woodwoman: Couldn't find.

In addition to *Diamonds Are a Dyke's Best Friend*, **Yvonne Zipter**, a syndicated columnist, is the author of *The Patience of Metal*, a collection of her poetry, which is a Lambda Literary Award Finalist, the runner-up for the Poetry Society of America's Melville Cane Award, and a Chicago Book Clinic Honor Book. With her lover, Kathy, she lives in Chicago where both of them are active in the Lesbian Community Cancer Project, play softball, and try to keep their 100-year-old house standing. ▥

(continued from front of book)

ed. Rebecca Mark, © 1989;

Nightlines (Chicago) for "Elizabethan Drama" and "Michiguilt," both © 1990, Jorjet Harper;

"Lilith of the Wildwood, of the Fair Places," © 1981, Susan Sherman (in *Lesbian Poetry*, eds. Elly Bulkin and Joan Larkin, originally published by Persephone Press);

The Pagoda temple of Love (St. Augustine, Florida) for their brochure;

June Parlett for her photo of Alix Dobkin;

Press Gang publishers (Canada) for "Ya Don Wanna Eat Pussy" and "I Am Not Your Princess" from *Not Vanishing,* © 1988, Chrystos; "Lesbian Air," "On My Way," and "One Fool to Another," from *Dream On,* © 1991, Chrystos;

Elizabeth Ross for her map of the Wanderground, © 1979;

Sidewalk Revolution Press for "This Is Not a Poem for Wimmin Drinking Diet Colas Just to Save Those Few Extra Calories," © 1990, Elliott, from *Wanting Women: An Anthology of Erotic Lesbian Poetry,* ed. Jan Hardy;

Silverleaf Press for "Fashion Flash," © 1990, Noreen Stevens, which appeared on the cover of *Silverleaf's Choice: An Anthology of Lesbian Humor,* eds. Ann E. Larson and Carole A. Carr (Seattle, WA);

Sinister Wisdom for: cover of issue #1, 1976, by Marianne Lieberman; "Branded," © 1988/89, and "Lesbian Metaphysics," © 1992, Janet Aalfs; photograph of *Sinister Wisdom* covers, © 1981, Debbie Alicen; "tremors," © 1989, Caryatis Cardea; cover of issue #3, © 1977, Tee Corinne; "A Medal for Not Drowning," © 1989/90, Amy Edgington; "Some Reflections on Separatism and Power," © 1978, Marilyn Frye (reprinted in *For Lesbians Only: A Separatist Anthology* (Onlywomen Press, London, 1988) and "Lesbian 'Sex'," © 1988, Marilyn Frye; "On Singing Women's Praises," © 1989, Carolyn Gage; "to the women who weep," © 1988/89, Chaia Z. Heller; "for joan, in 1967," © 1990, Beth Karbe; "A Cursory and Pre-Cursory History of Language, and the Telling of It," © 1976, Julia Penelope [Stanley]; drawing of Dyke with spider webs, from *Goddesses and Amazons,* © 1988, Sudie Rakusin;

Spinsters Ink for the excerpt from *Look Me in the Eye: Old Women, Aging, and Ageism,* © 1991, Barbara Macdonald and Cynthia Rich. Available from Spinsters Ink, POB 300170, Minneapolis, MN 55403, $8.95;

Tomato Publications for "DYKE is OUT" poster by Michelle and Liza Cowan, and Roberta Gregory for "Amazon ABC" drawings, from *Alix Dobkin's Adventures in Women's Music,* © 1979;

Tough Dove Books and the Seal Press for "Tortilleras," © 1989, Terri de la Peña from *Lesbian Bedtime Stories,* ed. Terry Woodrow;

Trivia (and *Portland Review*) for *Louisa May Incest,* © 1989, Carolyn Gage (and *Lamia Ink*) for "No Dobermans Allowed," © 1989, Carolyn Gage;

Valley Lesbian Writers Group for "Letter to Claudia Brenner," © 1992, Janet Aalfs, from *Tuesday Night;*

Lisa Vogel and Barbara Price for photograph of Michigan Womyn's Music Festival by Rene Gaumond;

Jess Wells (and Third Side Press) for "Two Willow Chairs" and "A Favorite Haunt" (also published in *Common Lives/Lesbian Lives*) from *Two Willow Chairs,* © 1987, Jess Wells;

Woman of Power for "The Lesbian Herstory Archives: A Statement of Cultural Self-Definition," © 1990, Deborah Edel;

Word Weavers for "Michigan," © 1985, Therese Edell with Teresa Boykin; "Where Do Dreams Go When They Die?," © 1985, Juana Maria Gonzalez Paz in *Lesbian Land,* ed. Joyce Cheney (originally published as the last chapter of *The La Luz Journals,* © 1980, Juana Maria Paz, available from Juana Maria Gonzalez Paz, c/o Twin Oaks Community, Rt. 4—Box 169, Louisa, VA 23093, for $10.);

Yale University Press for "Four Beginnings/For Kyra" and "Rumpelstiltskin," from *Beginning with O,* © 1977, Olga Broumas.

We have made extraordinary efforts to track down and get permission from all the Lesbians whose work we used in this anthology but there were a few we could not locate: Woodwoman, Rene Gaumond, Susan Edwards, Michelle, Marianne Lieberman, Roberta Gregory, Elizabeth Ross and Vada Verneé. Please contact Crossing Press to arrange for payment for the use of your work.